T0137423

Transactions on Computer Systems and Networks

Series Editor

Amlan Chakrabarti, Director and Professor, A. K. Choudhury School of
Information Technology, Kolkata, West Bengal, India

Transactions on Computer Systems and Networks is a unique series that aims to capture advances in evolution of computer hardware and software systems and progress in computer networks. Computing Systems in present world span from miniature IoT nodes and embedded computing systems to large-scale cloud infrastructures, which necessitates developing systems architecture, storage infrastructure and process management to work at various scales. Present day networking technologies provide pervasive global coverage on a scale and enable multitude of transformative technologies. The new landscape of computing comprises of self-aware autonomous systems, which are built upon a software-hardware collaborative framework. These systems are designed to execute critical and non-critical tasks involving a variety of processing resources like multi-core CPUs, reconfigurable hardware, GPUs and TPUs which are managed through virtualisation, real-time process management and fault-tolerance. While AI, Machine Learning and Deep Learning tasks are predominantly increasing in the application space the computing system research aim towards efficient means of data processing, memory management, real-time task scheduling, scalable, secured and energy aware computing. The paradigm of computer networks also extends it support to this evolving application scenario through various advanced protocols, architectures and services. This series aims to present leading works on advances in theory, design, behaviour and applications in computing systems and networks. The Series accepts research monographs, introductory and advanced textbooks, professional books, reference works, and select conference proceedings.

Samira Hosseini · Diego Hernan Peluffo ·
Julius Nganji · Arturo Arrona-Palacios
Editors

Technology-Enabled Innovations in Education

Select Proceedings of CIIE 2020

 Springer

Editors
Samira Hosseini
Tecnologico de Monterrey
Monterrey, Mexico

Julius Nganji
University of Toronto
Toronto, ON, Canada

Diego Hernan Peluffo
Yachay Tech University
Urcuquí, Ecuador

Mohammed VI Polytechnic University
Ben Guerir, Morocco

Arturo Arrona-Palacios
Harvard University
Boston, MA, USA

ISSN 2730-7484   ISSN 2730-7492   (electronic)
Transactions on Computer Systems and Networks
ISBN 978-981-19-3385-1   ISBN 978-981-19-3383-7   (eBook)
https://doi.org/10.1007/978-981-19-3383-7

This Springer imprint is published by the registered company Springer Nature Singapore Pte Ltd.
The registered company address is: 152 Beach Road, #21-01/04 Gateway East, Singapore 189721,
Singapore

Las memorias del Congreso Internacional de Innovación Educativa están dedicadas al fundador del Tecnológico de Monterrey, Don Eugenio Garza Sada.

Preface

Across disciplines, from engineering to medicine, from social sciences and humanities to architecture and design or even law and business, Education penetrates every aspect of our daily life. This marks continuous improvement of the teaching models as a major task for everyone involved in Education at all academic levels. The all-encompassing nature of Education reaches research and innovation, entrepreneurship, management, and public policy which, in turn, requires a strong alliance between stakeholders across the Educational ecosystem. As the world tackles international crises such as poverty, limited access to technological means, and global pandemics, Innovation in Education, today, finds essentiality more than ever before. The growing complexities of the world we live in are evidenced by the need for more novel approaches to delivering the Educational contents. The transition from in-person to online classrooms requires a new set of skills and an improved level of flexibility and adaptability. New Educational trends and emerging technologies address some of the main challenges we face globally, while pedagogy-informed applications of technology present a window to understanding how Education will be shaped as a result of the drastic changes the world is undertaking.

The 7th International Conference on Educational Innovation (CIIE 2020) presents an excellent forum for introducing Educational practices and technologies complemented by various innovative approaches that enhance the Educational outcomes. In line with the Sustainable Development Goal 4 (Quality Education) of the United Nations in the Agenda 2030, CIIE 2020 has attempted to "ensure inclusive and equitable quality education and promote lifelong learning opportunities for all." The CIIE 2020 book of proceedings offers a diverse dissemination of innovations, knowledge, and lessons learned to familiarize readership with new pedagogical-oriented, technology-driven Educational strategies along with their applications to emphasize their impact on a large spectrum of stakeholders including students, teachers and professors, administrators, policy makers, entrepreneurs, governments, international organizations, and NGOs.

Monterrey, Mexico	Samira Hosseini
Urcuquí, Ecuador/Ben Guerir, Morocco	Diego Hernan Peluffo
Toronto, Canada	Julius Nganji
Boston, USA	Arturo Arrona-Palacios

Acknowledgments The editors would like to acknowledge the financial and technical support of Writing Lab, Institute for the Future of Education (IFE), Tecnologico de Monterrey, Mexico. Additionally, the editors would like to express their ample gratitude for the relentless work and support of Dr. Ivan Acebo, the national coordinator of Writing Lab, Sofia Reveles, the internal coordinator of Writing Lab, Dalia Lopez, the assistant of Writing Lab, Ana E. Sosa-Flores, the assistant of Writing Lab, and the team of translation and editing under the leadership of Daniel Wetta.

Contents

Editors and Contributors

About the Editors

Prof. Samira Hosseini obtained her B.Sc. degree in Applied Physics from the University of North Tehran, Iran, and her M.Sc. degree in Polymer Chemistry and a Ph.D. degree in Biomedical Engineering from the University of Malaya, Kuala Lumpur, Malaysia. She served as a Postdoctoral Associate at Tecnologico de Monterrey, Mexico, and as a postdoctoral fellow at the Massachusetts Institute of Technology, Cambridge, USA. Currently, she is the Director of the Writing Lab at the Institute for the Future of Education at Tecnologico de Monterrey, Mexico. She also holds the position of research professor at the School of Engineering and Sciences, Tecnologico de Monterrey, Mexico. She is the author/co-author of more than 60 scientific publications and the inventor/co-inventor of 5 intellectual properties in addition to holding editorial position in multiple international journals. She is a member of the Mexican National Academy of Researchers (level one). e-mail: samira.hosseini@tec.mx

Prof. Diego Hernan Peluffo received his degree in Electronic Engineering, M.Eng. and Ph.D. from the Universidad Nacional de Colombia—Manizales, Colombia, in 2008, 2010, and 2013, respectively. In 2012, he undertook his doctoral internship at KU Leuven—Leuven, Belgium. From 2013 to 2014, he worked as Postdoctoral Researcher at Université Catholique de Louvain—Louvain la-Neuve, Belgium. Currently, he is working as an Assistant Professor in the Modeling, Simulation and Data Analysis (MSDA) Research Program at Mohammed VI Polytechnic University, Morocco. He is also working as a consultant/curriculum author at deeplearning.ai. He is the Founder and Head of the SDAS Research Group. He is an external collaborator at Writing Lab from Tecnológico de Monterrey—Mexico. e-mail: diego.peluffo@sdas-group.com

Prof. Julius Nganji received his M.Sc. in Website Design and Development, a Postgraduate Diploma in Research Training, and a Ph.D. in Computer Science from the University of Hull, UK. His research interests are in e-learning personalization, digital accessibility, usability, human-computer interaction, and special education technology. He collaborates with other researchers worldwide on various research projects and publishes findings in journals, conference proceedings, and chapters. Currently, he is an Adjunct Lecturer at the University of Toronto. e-mail: j.nganji@ utoronto.ca

Dr. Arturo Arrona-Palacios obtained his B.Sc. and M.Sc. degree in Criminology and Forensic Sciences from the Autonomous University of Tamaulipas in Reynosa, Tamaulipas, Mexico. He received his Ph.D. in Psychology from the Autonomous University of Nuevo Leon, Monterrey, Mexico. Currently, he is a part of the Brigham and Women's Hospital and Harvard University, the United States. He is the author/co-author of various scientific articles, conference proceedings, and chapters. He is a member of the National Academy of Researchers in the National Council of Science and Technology in Mexico and is part of the editorial board of the journal *Sleep Advances from the Sleep Research Society*. e-mail: aarronapalacios@bwh.harvard. edu

Contributors

Abbas Asad Writing Lab, Institute for the Future of Education, Tecnológico de Monterrey, Monterrey, NL, Mexico;
School of Government and Public Transformation, Tecnológico de Monterrey, San Pedro Garza García, Mexico

Acosta Vicente Román Brain Training Institute, Mexico, Mexico

Acosta-Medina Julieth Katherin Escuela de Estudios Industriales y Empresariales, Universidad Industrial de Santander, Bucaramanga, Colombia

Aguilar-Mejía José Rafael Escuela de Ingeniería y Ciencias, Tecnologico de Monterrey, Monterrey, Mexico

Alvarez Juan Pablo Nigenda Tecnologico de Monterrey, School of Medicine and Health Sciences, Monterrey, Mexico

Alvarez-Delgado Alvaro School of Humanities Sciences, Tecnologico de Monterrey, Ciudad de Mexico, Mexico

Amarilla Jessica Universidad Nacional de Asunción, San Lorenzo, Paraguay

Amiri Mohammadreza KITE Research Institute, Toronto Rehabilitation Institute – University Health Network, Toronto, Canada;
School of Pharmacy, Taylor's University, Subang Jaya, Malaysia

Aparicio Ponce Marcelino Sociedad Interactiva de Capacitación y Educación Para El Desarrollo Sustentable, Estado de México, México

Molina Arturo School of Engineering and Sciences, Tecnologico de Monterrey, Mexico City, Mexico

Astudillo Gabriel Santiago, Chile

Ayala Carlos Aguirre Escuela de Informática, Universidad Tecnologica de El Salvador, San Salvador, El Salvador

Baltazar Reyes Germán E. Tecnologico de Monterrey, Mexico City, Mexico

Barahona Camila Intituto de Éticas Aplicadas, Pontificia Universidad Católica, Santiago, Chile

Batres Rafael Tecnologico de Monterrey, Queretaro, Mexico

Bazán-Perkins Blanca School of Medicine and Health Sciences, Tecnologico de Monterrey, Mexico City, Mexico;
Immunopharmacology Laboratory, Instituto Nacional de Enfermedades Respiratorias, Mexico City, Mexico

Bermeo-Giraldo Maria Camila Centro de Investigaciones Escolme, Institución Universitaria Escolme, Medellin, Colombia

Cabezas Verónica School of Education, CEPPE UC, Pontificia Universidad Católica de Chile, Santiago, Chile

Cameron Deb Department of Occupational Science and Occupational Therapy, University of Toronto, Toronto, Canada

Canese Valentina Universidad Nacional de Asunción, San Lorenzo, Paraguay

Caratozzolo Patricia Institute for the Future of Education, School of Engineering and Sciences, Tecnologico de Monterrey, Ciudad de Mexico, Mexico

Cárdenas Lizette Susana Hernández Tecnologico de Monterrey, School of Medicine and Health Sciences, Monterrey, Mexico

Carvallo Cristian Academy of Aeronautical Sciences, Universidad Técnica Federico Santa María, Santiago, Chile

Cervantes Bárbara School of Engineering and Sciences, Tecnologico de Monterrey, Estado de México, Mexico

Chamizo Juan Manuel García Departamento de Tecnología Informática Y Computación, Universidad de Alicante, Alicante, España

Chowdhury Anika Master of Public Service, University of Waterloo, Waterloo, Canada

Cockburn Lynn Department of Occupational Science and Occupational Therapy, University of Toronto, Toronto, Canada

Cruz Yamile Peña Master of Science in Higher Education, University of Havana, Havana, Cuba

Cruz-Cruz Eduardo Instituto Tecnológico del Valle de Etla, Santiago Suchilquitongo, Etla, México

Cruz-Ramírez Sergio Rolando Escuela de Ingeniería y Ciencias, Tecnologico de Monterrey, San Luis Potosí, SLP, Mexico

Daniel Cortés School of Engineering and Sciences, Tecnologico de Monterrey, Mexico City, Mexico

Davis Jane A. Department of Occupational Science and Occupational Therapy, University of Toronto, Toronto, Canada

de J. Lozoya-Santos Jorge School of Engineering and Sciences, Tecnologico de Monterrey, Monterrey, México

de León Enrique Díaz School of Engineering and Sciences, Tecnologico de Monterrey, Monterrey, México

de la Garza Lorena Alemán Tecnologico de Monterrey, Monterrey, México

de la O José Francisco Enriquez Academic Vice-Presidency, Tecnologico de Monterrey, Monterrey, México

De la Peña Consuegra Geilert Ph.D. in Pedagogical Sciences, Technical University of Manabí, Portoviejo, Ecuador

del Carmen Mungarro Robles Gloria Benemérita y Centenaria Escuela Normal del Estado de Sonora, Hermosillo, Sonora, Mexico

Delgado-Cepeda Francisco Javier School of Engineering and Science, Tecnologico de Monterrey, Mexico City, Mexico

Enríquez-Flores Marco Benjamín School of Engineering and Science, Tecnologico de Monterrey, Santa Fe, Mexico

Farías Martínez Gabriela María Tecnologico de Monterrey, Monterrey, Mexico

Ferreira Arturo Corona Universidad Juárez Autónoma de Tabasco, Cunduacán Tabasco, Mexico

Figueroa Iglesias Catalina CEPPE UC, Pontificia Universidad Católica de Chile, Santiago, Chile

Flora Rodríguez Fabiola Tecnologico de Monterrey, Monterrey, Mexico; CESER, Centro de Estudios Superiores de Educación Rural "Luis Hidalgo Monroy", Tantoyuca, Mexico

Flores-Bueno Daniel Department of Humanities, Universidad Peruana de Ciencias Aplicadas, Lima, Peru

Flores-Cortez Omar Otoniel Escuela de Ciencias Aplicadas, Universidad Tecnologica de El Salvador, San Salvador, El Salvador

Flores-Palacios María Leticia Media and Digital Culture, Tecnologico de Monterrey, Monterrey, Mexico

Garay-Rondero Claudia Lizette Escuela de Ingeniería y Ciencias, Tecnologico de Monterrey, Institute for the Future of Education, Monterrey, Mexico

García Rosa Estela Russi Instituto Politecnico Nacional, Centro de Estudios Científicos y Tecnológicos No 1, Ciudad de México, México;
Center of Scientific and Technological Studies, No 1 Instituto Politécnico Nacional, Mexico City, Mexico

García García Andrés David Escuela de Ingeniería y Ciencias, Instituto Tecnológico y de Estudios Superiores de Monterrey, Estado de México, México

García-Martínez Moisés Escuela de Ingeniería y Ciencias, Tecnologico de Monterrey, San Luis Potosí, SLP, Mexico

Godoy Manuel A. Information Technology, NIC México, Nuevo Leon, Mexico

Gómez Patricia Sofía Madrazo Brain Training Institute, Mexico, Mexico

Goñi Julian "Iñaki" DILAB School of Engineering, Pontificia Universidad Católica de Chile, Santiago, Chile

González Marcos Cabezas Department Didáctica, Organización y Métodos de Investigación, Universidad de Salamanca, Salamanca, España

González Mauricio Martínez Tecnologico de Monterrey, Educational Innovation and Production and Creative Design, Monterrey, Mexico

Guzmán-Segura José Guillermo PrepaTec Cumbres, Tec de Monterrey, Monterrey, Mexico

Guzmán-Segura Juan Pablo Economics, School of Social Sciences and Government, Tec de Monterrey, Monterrey, Mexico

Guzmán-Segura Nancy María Chemical Engineering, School of Engineering, Tec de Monterrey, Monterrey, Mexico

Hernández Emilio Garduño Tecnologico de Monterrey, Queretaro, Mexico

Hernández Rosa María Navarrete Instituto Politecnico Nacional, Centro de Estudios Científicos y Tecnológicos No 1, Ciudad de México, México;
Center of Scientific and Technological Studies, No 1 Instituto Politécnico Nacional, Mexico City, Mexico

Hilliger Isabel School of Engineering, Pontificia Universidad Católica, Santiago, Chile

Hosseini Samira Writing Lab, Institute for the Future of Education, Vicerrectoria de Investigacion y Transferencia de Tecnologia, Monterrey, Mexico;
Writing Lab, Institute for the Future of Education Escuela de Ingenieria y Ciencias, Tecnologico de Monterrey, Monterrey, Mexico

Huidobro Alicia School of Engineering and Sciences, Tecnologico de Monterrey, Estado de México, Mexico

Jaimes-Nájera Alfonso Isaac School of Engineering and Science, Tecnologico de Monterrey, Monterrey, Mexico

Jianhong Wang School of Electronic Engineering, Jiangxi University of Science and Technology, Ganzhou City, P.R. China

Jiménez Brenda Tecnologico de Monterrey, Mexico City, Mexico

José Ramírez School of Engineering and Sciences, Tecnologico de Monterrey, Mexico City, Mexico

Julián Rebeca Román Brain Training Institute, Mexico, Mexico

Lee Soomin Department of Occupational Science and Occupational Therapy, University of Toronto, Toronto, Canada

Lerma-Noriega Claudia Alicia Media and Digital Culture, Tecnologico de Monterrey, Monterrey, Mexico

Limaymanta Cesar H. Department of Library and Information Sciences, Universidad Mayor de San Marcos, Lima, Peru

Lippi Luis Santiago, Chile

Lopez Edgar Omar Tecnologico de Monterrey, Mexico City, Mexico

Lopez Juan R. Tecnologico de Monterrey School of Engineering and Sciences, Mexico City, Tlalpan, Mexico

Lopez-Cruz Claudia S. Center for Teacher Development and Education Innovation, Tecnologico de Monterrey, Monterrey, México

López-Guajardo Enrique A. School of Engineering and Sciences, Tecnologico de Monterrey, Monterrey, México

Luna Mireya López Universidad de la Sierra Juárez, Ixtlán de Juárez, México

Mannan Abdul Faculty of Health and Medicine, School of Biomedical Sciences and Pharmacy, University of Newcastle, Callaghan, NSW, Australia

María Díaz-López Mónica Departamento de Educación Médica, Universidad de la Sabana, Chía, Colombia

Martín Sonia Casillas Department Didáctica, Organización y Métodos de Investigación, Universidad de Salamanca, Salamanca, España

Martín-Núñez José Luis Instituto de Ciencias de la Educación, Universidad Politécnica de Madrid, Madrid, Spain

Mateo Erika Yunuen Morales Universidad Juárez Autónoma de Tabasco, Cunduacán Tabasco, Mexico

Mazon Nancy Universidad Autónoma de México, Mexico City, Mexico

Mbibeh Louis University of Bamenda, Bamenda, Cameroon

Medina-Labrador Manuel Industrial Engineering, Pontificia Universidad Javeriana, Bogota, Colombia

Mendoza Ana Gabriela Rodríguez Tecnologico de Monterrey, Educational Innovation and Production and Creative Design, Monterrey, Mexico

Miranda-Palma Carlos Universidad Autónoma de Yucatán, Unidad Multidisciplinaria Tizimín, Tizimín, México

Molina Arturo Tecnologico de Monterrey School of Engineering and Sciences, Mexico City, Tlalpan, Mexico

Monroy Raúl School of Engineering and Sciences, Tecnologico de Monterrey, Estado de México, Mexico

Morales Jimena López Universidad de la Sierra Juárez, Ixtlán de Juárez, México

Morales-Menéndez Rubén School of Engineering and Sciences, Tecnologico de Monterrey, Monterrey, México

Mora-Rivera Jorge Tecnologico de Monterrey, School of Social Sciences and Government, Mexico City, Mexico;
Tecnologico de Monterrey, Business School, Department of Accounting and Finance, Mexico City, Mexico;
Tecnologico de Monterrey, Escuela de Ciencias Sociales y Gobierno, Departamento de Economía, Ciudad de México, México

Moreno José Manuel Valencia School of Administrative and Social Sciences of the Autonomous University of Baja California, Tijuana, Mexico

Muñoz-Repiso Ana García-Valcárcel Department Didáctica, Organización y Métodos de Investigación, Universidad de Salamanca, Salamanca, España

Murray Ellen E Murray Consulting, Toronto, Canada

Nganji Julius Department of Occupational Science and Occupational Therapy, University of Toronto, Toronto, Canada

Nsangong Kfukfu Department of Educational Administration and Leadership, St. Cloud State University, St. Cloud, USA

Núñez-del-Río María Cristina Instituto de Ciencias de la Educación, Universidad Politécnica de Madrid, Madrid, Spain

Olais-Govea José Manuel Escuela de Ingeniería y Ciencias, Tecnologico de Monterrey, San Luis Potosí, SLP, Mexico;
Tecnologico de Monterrey, Writing Lab, TecLab, Vicerrectoría de Investigación y Transferencia de Tecnología, Monterrey, Nuevo León, Mexico

Osorio Hugo Postgraduate Director, Universidad San Sebastián, Santiago, Chile

Oyarzún Gómez Denise Universidad Central de Chile, Santiago, Chile

Paba-Medina Maira Camila Escuela de Estudios Industriales y Empresariales, Universidad Industrial de Santander, Bucaramanga, Colombia

Paez Roberto Universidad Nacional de Asunción, San Lorenzo, Paraguay

Paola De Jesús Rodríguez Luisa Instituto Politecnico Nacional, Centro de Estudios Científicos y Tecnológicos No 1, Ciudad de México, México

Pereira Mardones Sebastián CEPPE UC, Pontificia Universidad Católica de Chile, Santiago, Chile

Pérez Adriana Departamento de Español, Universidad del Norte, Barranquilla, Colombia

Pérez Diana Angélica Parra Escuela de Idiomas, Universidad de Antioquia, Medellín, Colombia

Ponce Pedro Tecnologico de Monterrey School of Engineering and Sciences, Mexico City, Tlalpan, Mexico

Quintana María Guadalupe Siqueiros Benemérita y Centenaria Escuela Normal del Estado de Sonora, Hermosillo, Sonora, Mexico

Quintero Sebastian Martinez Industrial Engineering, Pontificia Universidad Javeriana, Bogota, Colombia

Ramirez-Lopez Carla Victoria Vicerrectoría Académica y de Innovación Educativa, Tecnologico de Monterrey, Monterrey, Mexico

Ramirez-Mendoza Ricardo A. School of Engineering and Sciences, Tecnologico de Monterrey, Monterrey, México

Rebolledo-Méndez Genaro Writing Lab, Institute for the Future of Education, Tecnologico de Monterrey, Monterrey, Mexico

Rincón Alejandra Sarmiento Industrial Engineering, Pontificia Universidad Javeriana, Bogota, Colombia

Rivera Lorenza Illanes Díaz Intelligent System Center, Tecnologico de Monterrey, Monterrey, México

Roa Alana F. Departamento de Español, Universidad del Norte, Barranquilla, Colombia

Rodríguez María Fernanda Facultad de Educación, Psicología y Familia, Universidad Finis Terrae, Santiago, Chile

Rodriguez Pamela Universidad Nacional de Asunción, San Lorenzo, Paraguay

Rodríguez Patricio Institute of Education and Center for Advanced Research in Education, University of Chile, Santiago, Chile

Rodríguez Roberto Retes Department International Degrees, Universidad Peruana de Ciencias Aplicadas, Lima, Perú

Rodríguez Rodolfo Alan Martínez School of Administrative and Social Sciences of the Autonomous University of Baja California, Tijuana, Mexico

Rojas-López Miguel D. Departamento de Ingenieria de las Organización, Universidad Nacional de Colombia, Medellin, Colombia

Romero González Rosa María Universidad Autónoma de Querétaro, Juriquilla, México

Rosa Verónica Idalia Escuela de Informática, Universidad Tecnologica de El Salvador, San Salvador, El Salvador

Rosado-Mendinueta Nayibe Departamento de Español, Universidad del Norte, Barranquilla, Colombia

Rosado-Tamariz Erik Tecnologico de Monterrey, Queretaro, Mexico

Sahu Sonal Finance and Accounting, Tecnologico de Monterrey, Zapopan, Mexico

Sastre-Merino Susana Instituto de Ciencias de la Educación, Universidad Politécnica de Madrid, Madrid, Spain

Segura-Azuara Nancy de los Ángeles Basic Medical Sciences, School of Medicine and Health Sciences, Tec de Monterrey, Monterrey, Mexico

Serrano Alma Alejandra Soberano School of Administrative and Social Sciences of the Autonomous University of Baja California, Tijuana, Mexico

Sikapa Lesley Lepawa Faculty of Arts and Science, University of Toronto, Toronto, Canada

Sosa-Flores Ana E. Writing Lab, Institute for the Future of Education, Tecnologico de Monterrey, Monterrey, Mexico;
UAS Technikum Wien, Vienna, Austria

Straub Barrientos Camila CEPPE UC, Pontificia Universidad Católica de Chile, Santiago, Chile

Suarez David Escobar Industrial Engineering, Pontificia Universidad Javeriana, Bogota, Colombia

Sukhai Mahadeo Research and IDEA Teams, Canadian National Institute for the Blind, Department of Ophthalmology, Faculty of Health Sciences, Queens University, Kingston, Canada

Tarazón Heidi Sacnicté Robles Benemérita y Centenaria Escuela Normal del Estado de Sonora, Hermosillo, Sonora, Mexico

Tejeda Santa Escuela de Ingeniería y Ciencias, Tecnologico de Monterrey, Institute for the Future of Education, Monterrey, Mexico

Tlalpan Patricia Tecnologico de Monterrey, Mexico City, Mexico

Toriz García Elizabeth Griselda Escuela de Ingeniería y Ciencias, Instituto Tecnológico y de Estudios Superiores de Monterrey, Estado de México, México

Torres María Catalina Caro International Center of Foreign Languages and Cultures, Universidad de La Sabana, Chía, Colombia

Torres-Barreto Martha Liliana Escuela de Estudios Industriales y Empresariales, Universidad Industrial de Santander, Bucaramanga, Colombia

Valencia-Rodríguez Susana María Departamento de Ingenieria de las Organización, Universidad Nacional de Colombia, Medellin, Colombia

Vásquez-Quevedo Noemí Tecnologico de Monterrey, Business School, Department of Accounting and Finance, Mexico City, Mexico;
Tecnologico de Monterrey, Escuela de Negocios, Departamento de Contabilidad y Finanzas, Ciudad de México, México

Victoria Oliva Denisse Mejía School of Administrative and Social Sciences of the Autonomous University of Baja California, Tijuana, Mexico

Villalobos Juan Manuel López Instituto Politecnico Nacional, Centro de Estudios Científicos y Tecnológicos No 1, Ciudad de México, México

Villanueva Alexis Center for Advanced Research in Education, University of Chile, Santiago, Chile

Villaseñor Martha Guadalupe Escoto Instituto Politecnico Nacional, Centro de Estudios Científicos y Tecnológicos No 1, Ciudad de México, México;
Center of Scientific and Technological Studies, No 1 Instituto Politécnico Nacional, Mexico City, Mexico

Wang Liya Center of Microbes, Development and Health, Institut Pasteur of Shanghai Chinese Academy of Sciences, Shanghai, China

Xavier Pimienta Rodríguez Samuel M Sc Informática Educativa, Universidad de la Sabana, Chia, Colombia

Zermeño Marcela Georgina Gómez Tecnologico de Monterrey, Monterrey, México

Chapter 1
Natural Language Processing for Video Essays and Podcasts in Engineering

Patricia Caratozzolo, Alvaro Alvarez-Delgado, and Samira Hosseini

1.1 Introduction

The Organization for Economic Cooperation and Development (OECD), in its document "Future of Education and Skills 2030" (Howells 2030), and the World Economic Forum (WEF), in its report "Towards a Reskilling Revolution" (World Economic Forum Boston Consulting Group 2018), emphasize the need for new cognitive tools to develop and assess the transversal skills that Generation Z students must have. The reports highlight the following skills as fundamental: analytical thinking, innovation, creativity, originality, critical thinking, reasoning, problem-solving, and ideation. Today, with unpredictable global risks, such as the COVID-19 crisis, the educational models of Higher Education Institutions (HEI) must be flexible, adapting and implementing the necessary tools within viable models of quality education to avert the obsolescence of future engineers' skills.

With the support of NOVUS Grant, 2021–2022, Institute for the Future of Education, Tecnologico de Monterrey, Mexico.

P. Caratozzolo (✉)
Institute for the Future of Education, School of Engineering and Sciences, Tecnologico de Monterrey, Campus Santa Fe, Ciudad de Mexico, Mexico
e-mail: pcaratozzolo@tec.mx

A. Alvarez-Delgado
School of Humanities Sciences, Tecnologico de Monterrey, Campus Santa Fe, Ciudad de Mexico, Mexico
e-mail: alvarez.delgado@tec.mx

S. Hosseini
Writing Lab, Institute for the Future of Education, Tecnologico de Monterrey, Monterrey, Mexico
e-mail: samira.hosseini@tec.mx

Current HEI students are considered Generation Z (born after January 1, 1995) and have different communication skills and storytelling habits. In terms of their written communication outside of academia, Generation Z students prefer to communicate with short, quick text messages on social media platforms. For oral communications, they prefer to record short videos without much discussion and with improvised content. (Smith and Cawthon 2017; Cilliers 2017). These "narrative practices" of young people in their daily lives harm their academic and professional roles, weakening the strength of their scientific arguments, making it difficult to acquire technical vocabulary, and interfering with their critical inference and deduction skills (Caratozzolo et al. 2020). This problem triggered the present study, which framed the research question: How to effectively assess and improve Generation Z students' critical and creative thinking, overcoming their difficulties expressing orally and in writing their opinions, arguments, and logical deductions?

The answer to this question may lie in the possibility of using natural language processing (NLP) techniques to perform modular analyses of their written presentations (executive reports, questionnaires, and case analyses) and oral presentations (speech and transcription in video essays and podcasts) and subsequently using the data for agile, timely feedback sessions. This project does not intend to create an automated essay scoring (AES) or a platform for automatically grading student essays written by students. Instead, we intend the project to support HEI instructors with better review and feedback sessions to students, providing personalized reports of their oral and written communication skills, language fluency, vocabulary level, structural complexity of arguments, and organized speech content.

The study's objective was to leverage the functionalities and advantages of NLP to complement the evaluation of soft skills of engineering students (critical thinking and creativity), which is usually done manually by the instructor of each subject (Gunawansyah et al. 2020).

This study is a continuation of previous work, "Creativity in Criticality: Tools for Generation Z Students in STEM," presented in April 2021 at the IEEE EDUCON Conference (Caratozzolo et al. 2021).

1.2   Theoretical Framework

Jerome Bruner points out two modalities of cognitive functioning. Each offers distinct ways of constructing reality and ordering experience (Bruner 2009). The *logical-scientific modality (critical thinking)* tries to fulfill the ideal of a formal mathematical system of description and explanation; and the *artistic-narrative modality (creative thinking)* deals with students' ability to develop new technological products by converting imagined concepts into a dependable reality (Spuzic et al. 2016).

While the strategies for evaluating critical thinking are well known and used in engineering, the same is not the case with evaluating creativity since the options are limited to the well-known TTCT-style creativity tests (Caratozzolo et al. 2019). When choosing methods for assessing creativity, it was essential to understand the qualities that students need to express it, that is, to unravel their cognitive process (Walia 2019). To build a flexible NLP model in this project, we considered the following characteristics of creative thinking:

Fluency, understood as the number of relevant ideas.

Originality, the amount of statistically uncommon, unusual, and unique ideas.

Elaboration, combining and adapting ideas of others, giving them "another twist," showing a conviction to be creative.

Abstractness of titles (also known as abstract articulation or verbal intelligence), the ability to reason. It involves synthesis and organization and distinguishing the essence of information and recognizing what is essential.

Additionally, specific *serious storytelling* tools were used in the present study to improve the ability to analyze and combine existing ideas, texts, and images through new disruptive and alternative solutions. Serious storytelling enables opinions and perspectives to be developed contextually in scientific and technical applications, using narratives for a purpose beyond entertainment (Caratozzolo et al. 2020). The essential components of the storytelling approach considered to develop critical thinking and creativity were as follows:

Perspective: the subjective point of view that involves story characteristics that evoke cognition and emotion.

Narrative: the actual content of the story that includes mimesis and diegesis.

Interactivity: the essential interaction between the speaker and the audience that features engagement and decision.

Medium: the message that includes features such as content and forms.

Storytelling was an ideal cognitive tool to include in our competency-based learning approach in engineering because it involves active and collaborative learning and originates from students' knowledge and previous experiences (Caratozzolo et al. 2019a).

1.3 Methodology

1.3.1 Research Design

A total of 323 undergraduate Generation Z engineering students voluntarily participated in our study. One hundred seventy-three of them underwent metacognitive instruction (experimental group), while 150 students did not receive the intervention (control group). A total of fifteen groups were involved over ten semesters, from January 2016 to November 2020. The project design was experimental, using the four-group Solomon type methodology: (1) experimental group with Pre-Test and treatment (EG-PreT-T); (2) experimental group without Pre-Test, only treatment (EG-T); (3) control group with Pre-Test (CG-PreT), and (4) control group without Pre-Test (CG) (Dawson 2019).

In this study, tests were designed to identify the following biases in the communication skills of Generation Z students: Inability to make intrinsically motivated, cognitive efforts; comfortable only reading predigested texts; lack of concentration when writing; and almost all written expression in texting language. The simultaneous combination of these characteristics presented an additional challenge to design an NLP approach to critical thinking—knowing that thinking is done in language—because students create their own language in their academic works and shortcut it by copying and pasting documents, relying on automatic word processors to correct spelling, and using Web sources of dubious academic quality for their reports.

1.3.2   Instrumentation (Pre-Tests and Post-Tests)

Different types of instruments were considered for the study. Some validating tests for data collection and research were questionnaires, interviews, surveys, observation lists, VALUE Rubrics, and other tools to handle parametric data statistically.

Pre-Tests: Vocabulary tests, designed to establish the approximate lexicon level of each student, were compared to the Corpus of Contemporary American English, COCA, that contains 60,000 ranked words (Davies 2010); creativity scale self-reports and lateral thinking-ability checklists.

Post-Test: Fluency and originality tests, and rubrics *based on* the Valid Assessment of Learning in Undergraduate Education Rubric (VALUE Rubric) of the Association of American Colleges and Universities (AAC&U) (Rhodes 2010).

1.3.3   Experimental Settings (Treatment)

One of the best strategic didactic interventions incorporating the activities based on the cognitive understanding level of the students was training in the shifting mode of thinking experiences (Caratozzolo et al. 2019b). Our study considered the stiffness of the shifting mode among thinking modalities per the magnitude of two cognitive biases (Lu et al. 2017). *Premature closure* is the cognitive bias causing the student not to consider reasonable alternatives after an initial diagnosis of a problem. *Cognitive fixation* is the cognitive bias that causes the student to evaluate the functionality of an object only in the way it is traditionally used. Three types of activities were developed with students: dialogue seminars, supervised questioning sessions, and video essays and podcast recordings.

Dialogue Seminars. The dialogue seminar consisted of a meeting between a small group of students and a mentor during which students read their essays and the whole group shared their experiences. The inclusion of online sessions represented an additional advantage because it facilitated recording the sessions and the subsequent transcription of the participants' interventions. The texts obtained from transcribing the sessions were analyzed with the Python NLP algorithms. (We obtained the students' prior consent and ensured personal data protection to preserve the participants' anonymity).

Supervised Questioning Sessions. The supervised questioning method stimulated the recall of knowledge acquired in previous sessions, sharpened understanding of concepts, and taught students to self-construct critical thinking skills. The method had the additional advantage of promoting peer interaction in a psychologically safe environment for discussion and argumentation (Duran-Novoa et al. 2019).

Table 1.1 shows an example of the application of the supervised questioning method.

Video Essays and Podcast Recordings (including transcriptions). The video essay is the audiovisual equivalent of the written essay, in which the "message" uses visual elements (and not just words) to enhance the point the interlocutor is making. Because Generation Z engineering students have trouble writing texts of more than several pages coherently, we considered the video essay an attractive tool due to its two main characteristics (Hernández-de-Menéndez et al. 2019): (a) its length, since most video essays do not last more than a few minutes, which allows the script to be relatively short in length, (b) the video essay is free-form; its format and rhetorical strategies can differ enormously from one video essay to another. From the point of view of the teaching–learning process in engineering, video essays show the audience things that could not be easily described in a traditional essay. Additionally, because the script was written following a serious storytelling technique, the visuals significantly enhanced the story and the plot.

The technological tools chosen for the present study were video essays and second-generation podcasts (podcasts with video), created from screencasts, with scripts prepared by the students on topics selected from the official syllabus of each course. They were recorded at the radio station facilities or with portable recording equipment (Myers and Visosevic 2017). The scripts were carefully prepared to offer a certain proportion of words belonging to the higher rank of the Corpus of Contemporary American English (COCA) (Davies 2010). The script also had a structure that facilitated shifting modes so that the student reached a higher cognitive stage to reflect on the nature of the subjects with a higher level of abstraction.

The following subsection includes some of the functionalities and experiences modeled in NLTK for different subjects in the sustainability development department. The experiment performed by the students was the analysis of the responses in the argumentative tests based on technical IEEE articles and a specialized dictionary on the subjects' syllabus topics, selected from updated IEEE databases (*Electrification* magazine and *Power and Energy* magazine) (Agüero and Khodaei 2018).

Table 1.1 Example of interference analysis (with NTLK/inference module) to determine the cognition level of students during Post-Tests

Dimensions and taxonomies	Question type (all in the high cognitive level)	Sample questions
Nonhierarchical questions	Brainstorm	If you could design a *transactive energy* research strategy, based on the IEEE's suggestions, what characteristics would it have?
	Divergent	Mexico was not ready in 2018 for the modernization of the Power Network. Why?
	Focal	Does the relationship between costs in the corresponding figure seem reasonable to you? Justify your answer
Questions based on cognitive dimension	Analyzing	Given the participation of *investor-owned utilities (IOUs)*, what would be the most favorable agreement among the parties to achieve the objectives of the *renewable portfolio*?
	Evaluating	Based on the surveys in the IEEE text, what do you think was the biggest obstacle to the evolution of *utilities business models*? Could it be extrapolated to Mexico?
	Creating	Given the challenge of incorporating emerging and advanced technologies to modernize the network, how would you mitigate the associated risks?
Questions based on knowledge dimension	Factual	According to the IEEE article, in 2018, some states in the USA were highly committed to modernizing the network. In what way and under what conditions could equivalent participation be considered in Mexico?
	Conceptual	There are different business models for the alternative utility. What similarities and differences do you find between them?
	Procedural	Considering the structure of the *distribution system operator (DSO)* shown in the corresponding figure Y, what are the strengths and weaknesses of a system with these attributions?
	Metacognitive	Considering the level of satisfaction you have when delivering this work, what do you think could help you in the future to produce a better deliverable?

1.3.4 Use of NLTK with Python

Natural language processing is a practical approach to understand the effectiveness of learning processes in engineering programs. Additionally, NLP provides solutions in a variety of fields and social and cultural contexts of competency-based learning.

It assists in writing, analyzing, and evaluating critical thinking and creativity in advanced engineering subjects (Berdanier et al. 2020).

We chose NLTK with Python from the different specialized software platforms (which also included GeSim, SapCy, or Stanford Core NLP) because it is focused on research and education, and there are a lot of free open resources associated with it (http://www.nltk.org) (Natural Language Toolkit 2021). NLTK with Python includes a large number of libraries, data, and downloadable documentation in its platform. It also has a modular structure that allows quick familiarization with most of the tasks required in our study: tokenization, tagging, stemming, parsing, chunking, classification, semantic reasoning, using *Corpora*, and structure analysis.

To implement the dynamic NLP model, we had to understand the pipeline of language-understanding components. These components map from speech input (in our study, we did not use speech recognition software; instead, we transcribe the audios with an external platform) through syntactic parsing to a representation of meaning (the application, reasoning, and execution based on the proficiency level). With that representation, we were then able to turn the concept into a morphological realization in NLP. The architecture included some data repository libraries related to the language required for its operation: *corpora*, with morphological rules; *syntax*, lexical and grammar rules; and *semantics*, with the discourse content. In this project, to make a flexible model in NLP, we proposed an instructional method to develop creative thinking with three personality traits:

- Storytelling articulation (verbally expressive)
- Richness of imagery (passionate)
- Colorfulness of imagery (perceptive).

Table 1.1 shows an example of an inference process to evaluate the application of the supervised questioning method explained in the previous subsection. This module was especially useful to avoid the situation, relatively frequent, in which instructors ask lower-level cognitive questions that do not effectively stimulate critical thinking. The generation of questions with this NLTK module improved the assessment and the generation of test items (questions). The external platform "Word and Phrase" (https://www.wordandphrase.info/), taking data from the COCA, was used as a design model for the NLTK modules in this study. Table 1.2 shows the analysis of a 459-word text extracted from the transcription of a video essay. The document had 34% of the highest-ranking words in the comparison corpus, which means that the student could be considered within the "Capstone" level of the group (Table 1.5 of the next section).

Some of the most common tasks that students had to perform on their tests and assignments included remembering previous knowledge, demonstrating understanding of abstract concepts, solving ill-defined problems, arguing and supporting their hypotheses, judging and criticizing results, and designing innovative solutions. The last stage of this process was the most difficult for the instructor to evaluate: The students' cognitive efforts behind oral or written answers must show the different levels they unequivocally attained in Anderson & Krathwohl's taxonomy (Urgo et al. 2019). The process of demonstrating a proficiency level, that is, "translating" their

Table 1.2 Word analysis example (with NLTK /corpus Module)

459-word text parsing with NLTK

LOW freq words Range 1–500 34%	MID freq words Range 500–3000 14%	HIGH freq words Range > 3000 36%
7: grid **5:** distribution **3:** automation, efficient substation **2:** behind-the-meter, **deployment**, implementation, improvement, mechanisms, reliability, reliable, utilization **1:** accurately, actively, adoption, allocated, bulk, calculate, cross-subsidies, defection, dispatch, diversification, grid-connected…	**6:** benefits **4:** technologies **3:** available, **2:** aims, associated, capacity, concepts, consumer, consumers, demands, industry, instance, investments, operation, solutions **1:** activities, address, aimed, charging, communications, competition, concept, conducted, currently, customer, developing, due, energy, ensure, estimating…	**22:** and **18:** of 17: the 15: to 7: in, new, that 6: at 5: is, this 4: also, which 3: are, as, level 2: all, but, by, costs, for, help, include, interest, models, not, on, or, provide, provided, service, services, when 1: a, among, an, area, be, being, better, both, business…

[a][Numbers in bold type means # of word repetition]

Table 1.3 Example of chunking process (with module NLTK/chunk) for commonly used acronyms in the energy distribution and electricity markets Pre-Tests

AMI	Advanced metering infrastructure
DER	Distributed energy resources
DLMP	Distribution locational marginal pricing
DRP	Distribution resources plan
DSO	Distribution system operator
DSP	Distribution system platform
FLISR	Fault location, isolation and service restoration
IOU	Investor-owned utility
ISO	Independent system operator
NEM	Net energy metering
OMS	Outage management systems
PUC	Public utilities commission
TE	Transactive energy
VOST	Value of solar tariff
ZNE	Zero net energy

thoughts into language, involved understanding words and forming sentences that were grammatically and structurally correct. In NLP, some of these tasks involved tokenization, fragmentation, part speech tagging, analytics, machine translation, and speech recognition. Table 1.3 shows an example of a chunking process to create the most common acronym repository in Energy Distribution and Electricity Markets obtained from analyzing the samples collected from the experimental group.

1.4   Results

Results related to vocabulary corpus. To verify that the students in the experimental and control groups had similar initial lexicons, we compared the results of the vocabulary Pre-Test in both groups. The initial comparison between 182 students (101 students of the EG-PreT-T and 72 of the CG-PreT) where the Pre-Tests were applied revealed no significant differences in their vocabulary backgrounds. However, the Post-Test comparison of the vocabulary scores revealed that the EG-PreTest-T group showed significant improvement over the CG-PreTest. The improvement in vocabulary obtained in the EG sample (+4.96%, $N = 173$) is very notable compared to that obtained by the CG sample ($N = 150$, +1.15%,) as shown in Table 1.4.

Results related to cognition maturity. The Post-Tests using AAC&U rubrics showed that the experimental group attained 37% improvement over the students in the control group in the upper "Capstone" level and a 35% decrease in the number of students remaining at the lowest "Benchmark" level of the rubric. These results are shown in Table 1.5.

Table 1.4   Vocabulary enrichment comparison between EG and CG

	Year	Pre-Test	Post-Test	Average difference (%)
		Vocabulary tests scores	Vocabulary tests scores	
EG-PreT-T	2017	72.55	76.10	+4.89
	2018	75.78	79.57	+5.00
	2019	74.14	77.23	+4.17
	2020	72.17	76.34	+5.78
		73.66	**77.31**	**+4.96**
CG-PreT	2017 2020	73.12	73.96	+1.15
		73.12	**73.96**	**+1.15**

Table 1.5   AAC&U Rubrics distribution for EG and CG

	Value rubrics			
Groups	Capstone 4 (%)	Milestones		Benchmark 1 (%)
		3 (%)	2 (%)	
EG	22	35	23	20
CG	16	18	35	31
	+37	**+94**	**−34**	**−35**

Fig. 1.1 AAC&U
distributions for
experimental and control
groups

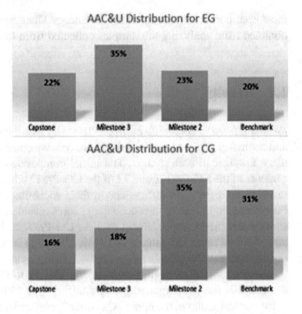

AAC&U Distribution for EG

Capstone	Milestone 3	Milestone 2	Benchmark
22%	35%	23%	20%

AAC&U Distribution for CG

Capstone	Milestone 3	Milestone 2	Benchmark
16%	18%	35%	31%

The analysis of the students' Post-Test results distributions revealed that the Gaussian bell shapes of the experimental group (EG) displayed a left skewness and, in the case of the control group (CG), a right skewness, as shown in the graphs of Fig. 1.1.

Results related to Post-Tests. To determine the correlations of active learning instruction, the ability to use technological tools, and the development of digital skills, we computed the Pearson coefficient to ensure knowing the possible correlations between results obtained in Post-Tests with VALUE Rubrics. In all cases, considering that the present study uses social data, the strength of the correlation according to Evans' criteria ($0.6 < r < 0.79$, $36\% < R2 < 64\%$) can be considered strongly positive (Ingleby 2012). Figure 1.2a shows the impact of creativity on critical thinking in the experimental group. It can be seen that there is a strong correlation between the students' final grades in the Post-Tests and assessment scores for perspective, narrative, interactivity, articulateness, fluency, originality, and elaboration. Figure 1.2b shows that the control groups obtained significantly lower final grades per almost all skill assessments, except in "Elaboration," a skill developed by all Generation Z students regardless of their treatment.

In the exit interviews and opinion polls, 87% of the students stated that *active reading* activities were among the most successful strategies for understanding abstract concepts and describing processes in detail. Likewise, 83% of the students stated that *reading comprehension* exercises helped them find the main idea and supporting details in technical texts; determining the author's intent or purpose; and thinking about the relationships within sentences, paragraphs, and longer passages.

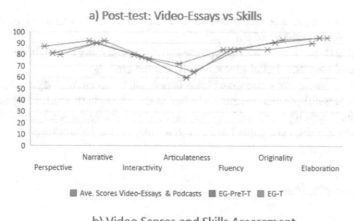

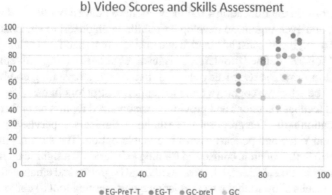

Fig. 1.2 a Correlation between final scores and Post-Test assessment. **b** Final scores and skills assessment in each group

1.5   Discussions

During 2016–2018, preliminary studies were conducted to determine with greater accuracy which were the instruments that best determined students' levels of cognitive development in the dimensions of knowledge and cognitive process. In 2019 and 2020, studies were repeated to improve the design of the treatment (experiences and activities). The method to assess the development of creativity and critical thinking through the indirect measurement of natural language processing had to include *fact questions* (asking about specific information mentioned in the academic texts) and *inference questions* (asking about information not explicitly stated but only implied or suggested).

Python was an advantageous programming language, ideal for handling essential language processing functions, such as word spelling and morphological checking. Also, it was a versatile NLP software to evaluate higher-order functions, such as sentence syntax parsing, interpretation inference, and the determination of levels of cognitive understanding of concepts.

VALUE Rubrics were used to evaluate and discuss learning related to the students' interdisciplinary and digital literacy skills, not the grading.

The small group activities were highly beneficial. Our methodology can be considered a successful practice because it included the concepts of scaffolding and zone of proximal development, which were especially suitable for students to face the challenges of mixed cognitive levels, even in fully online environments.

1.6   Conclusions

Recent reports on the Education 4.0 framework have pointed out that it is absolutely necessary, and even urgent, to develop soft skills in engineering students. Twenty-first-century engineers must be creative and critical enough to form values and judgments and solve ill-defined problems. This involves understanding and remembering conceptual information. Our study showed that serious storytelling combined with NLP could be effective cognitive tools to support instructors in carrying out better review and feedback sessions and providing personalized reports on oral and written communication skills. Our proposal to use dialogue seminars, supervised questioning sessions, and video and podcast essays is a viable option. The students themselves recognize (in both academic course and training exit surveys) a significant increase in their communication abilities, language skills, and cognitive and emotional empathy. The study results showed that a natural language processing toolkit could indirectly evaluate the understanding of scientific concepts and help develop the soft skills of creativity and criticality.

Acknowledgements The authors acknowledge the financial and technical support of Writing Lab, Institute for the Future of Education, Tecnologico de Monterrey, Mexico, in the production of this work. The authors also acknowledge the financial support of the Novus Grant with PEP no. PHHT085-21ZZNV016, Institute for the Future of Education, Tecnologico de Monterrey, in the production of this work.

References

Agüero JR, Khodaei A (2018) Grid Modernization, der integration & utility business models—trends & challenges. IEEE Power Energy Mag 16(2):112–121. https://doi.org/10.1109/MPE.2018.2811817
Berdanier CGP, McComb CM, Zhu W (2020) Natural language processing for theoretical framework selection in engineering education research. In: Proceedings—frontiers in education conference, FIE, Oct 2020. https://doi.org/10.1109/FIE44824.2020.9274115
Bruner J (2009) Actual minds, possible worlds

Caratozzolo P, Alvarez-Delgado A, Hosseini S (2019) Strengthening critical thinking in engineering students. Int J Interact Des Manuf 13(3):995–1012. https://doi.org/10.1007/s12008-019-00559-6

Caratozzolo P, Alvarez-Delgado A, Gonzalez-Pineda Z, Hosseini S (2019a) Enhancing interdisciplinary skills in engineering with the cognitive tools of storytelling. In: Proceedings of the SEFI 47th annual conference, pp 206–215 (Online). Available: https://www.researchgate.net/publication/336441003

Caratozzolo P, Alvarez-Delgado A, Hosseini S (2019b) Fostering specific dispositions of critical thinking for student engagement in engineering. In: IEEE global engineering education conference, EDUCON, April 2019b. https://doi.org/10.1109/EDUCON.2019.8725094

Caratozzolo P, Alvarez-Delgado A, Hosseini S (2020) Perspectives on the use of serious-storytelling for creative thinking awareness in engineering. In: Proceedings—frontiers in education conference, FIE, Oct 2020. https://doi.org/10.1109/FIE44824.2020.9273994

Cilliers EJ (2017) The challenge of teaching Generation Z. PEOPLE. Int J Soc Sci 3:188–198

Davies M. The corpus of contemporary American English as the first reliable monitor corpus of English. academic.oup.com. https://doi.org/10.1093/llc/fqq018

Dawson C (2019) Introduction to research methods, 5th edn. A practical guide for anyone undertaking a research project

Duran-Novoa R, Lozoya-Santos J, Ramírez-Mendoza R, Torres-Benoni F, Vargas-Martínez A (2019) Influence of the method used in the generation of valid engineering concepts. Int J Interact Des Manuf 13(3):1073–1088. https://doi.org/10.1007/s12008-019-00577-4

Caratozzolo P, Alvarez-Delgado A, Hosseini S (2021) Creativity in criticality: tools for generation Z students in STEM. In: 2021 IEEE global engineering education conference (EDUCON), pp 591–598. https://doi.org/10.1109/EDUCON46332.2021.9454110

Gunawansyah, Rahayu R, Nurwathi, Sugiarto B, Gunawan (2020) Automated essay scoring using natural language processing and text mining method. https://doi.org/10.1109/TSSA51342.2020.9310845

Hernández-de-Menéndez M, Vallejo Guevara A, Tudón Martínez JC, Hernández Alcántara D, Morales-Menendez R (2019) Active learning in engineering education. A review of fundamentals, best practices and experiences. Int J Interact Des Manuf 13(3):909–922. https://doi.org/10.1007/s12008-019-00557-8

Howells K (2018) The future of education and skills: education 2030: the future we want. Accessed: 25 Aug 2020 (Online). Available: http://create.canterbury.ac.uk/17331/1/E2030PositionPaper (05.04.2018).pdf

Ingleby E (2012) Research methods in education, vol 38, no 3

Lu JG, Akinola M, Mason MF (2017) 'Switching On' creativity: task switching can increase creativity by reducing cognitive fixation. Organ Behav Hum Decis Process 139:63–75. https://doi.org/10.1016/j.obhdp.2017.01.005

Myers A, Visosevic T (2017) Video essay: the multimodal assignment of now (Online). Available: https://www.researchgate.net/publication/318672031

Natural Language Toolkit—NLTK 3.5 documentation. http://www.nltk.org/. Accessed 15 Mar 2021

Rhodes T (2010) Assessing outcomes and improving achievement: tips and tools for using rubrics. Association of American Colleges & Universities

Smith T, Cawthon TW (2017) Generation Z goes to college. Coll Student Aff J 35(1):101–102. https://doi.org/10.1353/csj.2017.0008

Spuzic S et al (2016) The synergy of creativity and critical thinking in engineering design: the role of interdisciplinary augmentation and the fine arts. Technol Soc 45:1–7. https://doi.org/10.1016/j.techsoc.2015.11.005

Urgo K, Arguello J, Capra R (2019) Anderson and Krathwohl's two-dimensional taxonomy applied to task creation and learning assessment. In: ICTIR 2019—Proceedings of the 2019 ACM SIGIR international conference on theory of information retrieval, pp 117–124. https://doi.org/10.1145/3341981.3344226

Walia C (2019) A dynamic definition of creativity. Creat Res J. https://doi.org/10.1080/10400419.2019.1641787

World Economic Forum Boston Consulting Group (2018) Towards a reskilling revolution: a future of jobs for all. Accessed: 25 Aug 2020 (Online). Available: https://www.voced.edu.au/content/ngv:78746

Chapter 2
Action Research as a Way to Guide Research Projects in Engineering

Rafael Batres, Erik Rosado-Tamariz, and Emilio Garduño Hernández

2.1 Introduction

Graduate research education has gained attention in recent years. The success of graduate training has been associated with supervision pedagogy and models of supervision (McCallin and Nayar 2012). As a result, the literature on graduate research education has emphasized these two aspects. Much research has been done regarding the supervisor–student relationship. For example, Mainhard et al. (2009) discuss the need to match the interpersonal style of the supervisor to a particular student. Gatfield (2005) discusses the different supervisory styles at different phases of the doctoral process. Moreover, Bastliach (2015) suggests a need to focus on innovation and disciplinary contexts rather than the abilities of individual researchers.

The processes of collaborative creativity are essential in graduate research supervision. Specifically, creativity can be enhanced through interactions between the graduate student and the supervisor and other students in sessions where ideas are flexibly explored, modified, or adapted (Whitelock et al. 2008). However, the literature on graduate research education seems to lack methodologies that support collaborative creativity.

Action research can guide the progression of several graduate theses through the years. Action research can be conceived as a series of interconnected cycles of planning, acting, observing, and reflecting, where one cycle informs the successive cycles (Kemmis and Mctaggart 1981). The steps are to identify or define the problem,

R. Batres (✉) · E. Rosado-Tamariz · E. Garduño Hernández
Tecnologico de Monterrey, Queretaro, Mexico
e-mail: rafael.batres@tec.mx

E. Rosado-Tamariz
e-mail: erik.rosado@tec.mx

E. Garduño Hernández
e-mail: emilio.gh@tec.mx

© The Author(s), under exclusive license to Springer Nature Singapore Pte Ltd. 2022   15
S. Hosseini et al. (eds.), *Technology-Enabled Innovations in Education*,
Transactions on Computer Systems and Networks,
https://doi.org/10.1007/978-981-19-3383-7_2

plan alternative courses of action to solve the problem, select and implement one, evaluate the results, and identify general findings.

This process is suitable for tackling ill-defined problems, which often fall in the domain of "wicked problems." Wicked problems are challenging because they lack definitive information for understanding, formulating, and solving the problem. Rourke and Sweller (2009) suggest that an effective teaching method for some wicked problems is to provide novice learners with worked examples during the solution process. Tawfik (2017) concluded that a library of case studies could be an excellent resource to foster the ability of students to solve wicked problems. Learners use cases similar to the problem they are trying to solve; thus, the case library aids the research process.

Middleton (2002) proposes a problem-space model where understanding the nature of the problem is the first step in the problem-solving process while at the same time realizing the possibility that there may be multiple ways to conceive and address the problem.

This paper reports the results of an approach to foster collaborative creativity, applying the concept of Weltanschauung and reusing previous research outcomes for operating procedure synthesis. The remainder of this research article is organized as follows: Sect. 2.2 presents a brief review of operating procedure synthesis. Section 2.3 describes the concept of Weltanschauung. Section 2.4 describes the evolution of a Weltanschauung for the operating procedure synthesis of a mixing tank and a drum boiler. Finally, Sect. 2.5 provides discussion and conclusions.

2.2   Operating Procedure Synthesis

The synthesis of operating procedures requires finding an ordered sequence of operations to take an industrial plant process from an initial state to a goal state. The sequence of actions must be carried out in the shortest time possible in a way that meets safety and other constraints. Operating procedures contain the tasks for startup and shutdown, the data to be recorded, and the operating conditions to be maintained.

Startup and shutdown are similar to the take-off and landing of an airplane because those processes are complicated and involve high risk. More than 20% of incidents in the industry processes occur during startups and shutdowns (IChemE 2006). Similarly, millions of dollars per year are wasted in a single site because of incidents related to inadequate operating procedures (Kucharyson 2006). A startup is defined as the sequence of actions (operations) that bring the plant from a non-operational state to stable operations. Shutdown brings the plant from the operational to a non-operational state. There are three categories of shutdown:

- Normal shutdown: for example, shutdowns for maintenance, retrofitting, or ending a batch.
- Emergency shutdown: an unexpected shutdown caused by events such as a process variable exceeding its safety limits, equipment failures, and utility supply failures.

- Partial shutdown: a routine or emergency shutdown to bring a part of the plant to a non-operational state.

The automatic operating procedure synthesis is challenging because exploring all the possible operation combinations is prohibitive. Besides, such problems do not align with multiple local optima.

2.3 Modeling with an Explicit Worldview

2.3.1 Weltanschauung

According to systems theory, Weltanschauung (1998) describes the view through which the real world is perceived (Fig. 2.1). Weltanschauung is what makes a particular model meaningful and limits or enhances the ability to develop new research. Sometimes this worldview exists in our minds, but it is not explicitly stated. For example, most chemical engineering courses teach that in order to heat a fluid, the necessary heating is achieved by heat exchangers that use a thermal source such as high-temperature steam. Thus, unconsciously, heat exchangers become the students' device of choice for heating a fluid. However, with a worldview that separates the phenomenon from the device, one can consider other heating technologies such as ultraviolet light, microwaves, or radio-frequency technologies. Without this worldview, innovative heating alternatives are likely to be left out when students face a design problem that requires heating. The reason is that heating, cooling, and distillation are typically seen as part of a physical device rather than phenomena that take place in that physical device (Batres 2021).

As illustrated in Fig. 2.1, Weltanschauung influences how we identify and represent a problem. Once the problem has been identified and presented, models are created for developing solutions. Each time a solution is obtained, it must be translated into real-world representation. If the Weltanschauung changes, new models are developed and new solutions found.

Fig. 2.1 Illustration of the Weltanschauung concept

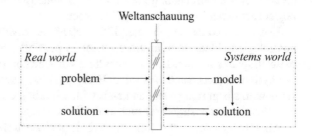

2.3.2   Three Dimensional (3D) Weltanschauung

Batres et al. (1999) proposed a formalism for artifacts in three dimensions: behavioral, physical, and operational. The behavioral dimension refers to physicochemical phenomena. The physical dimension is related to the connectivity and geometry of the device (e.g. plant equipment), and the operational dimension refers to the management and operational aspects of the artifact.

For example, consider a tank connected to a liquid-feed line in which the feed flow rate is regulated using a control valve. Using the 3-dimension Weltanschauung, one comes up with multiple models. First, a model can be developed in the physical dimension that describes the connectivity between the valve, the feed line, and the tank. A model in the behavioral dimension could describe the changes in the tank's liquid level as the flow rate changes.[1] A model can be developed in the operational dimension that dictates how the valve actuator's position should be manipulated.

Activities appear in the operational dimension as well as in the behavioral dimension. Activity is never found in isolation but linked to physical objects that participate (Akmal and Batres 2013). The activity can change some physical objects, some can be produced by the activity, some others can execute the activity, and there are physical objects not affected by the activity (Batres et al. 2014). Let us assume a pressure controller opens a control valve from fully closed to a fully open position, resulting in a liquid flowing through the valve. In this example, opening the valve is an activity. The controller, the control valve, and the liquid are physical objects.

The operation of the plant can go well beyond a single task, such as a plant-wide startup or shutdown. In this sense, operations change some properties of some physical dimension elements to achieve the expected or desired state of the behavior.

2.3.3   The ISO 15926 Weltanschauung

The standard ISO 15926 Part 2 specifies an upper ontology for long-term information sharing and exchange (ISO-TC184, 2003) (Batres et al. 2007). The ontology is based on another Weltanschauung known as "four dimensionalism." In four dimensions, objects are extended in time as well as space.

Every classification in the ISO 15926 is divided into two classes: a possible_individual or an abstract_object. A possible_individual is something that exists in space and time. This includes things that are non-physical such as an activity, or physical objects, such as a valve. Every possible_individual has a life cycle that starts with a beginning event and ends with an ending event. An abstract object is a classification for abstractions such as numbers or sets.

An activity occurs at a time interval. It is characterized by its ability to bring about change by causing an event. A *participation relation* is used to specify that a

---

[1] Notice, that undesired behavior can also be modeled. For instance, a model about the mechanical stress can be linked to the rest of the models.

Fig. 2.2 The action research spiral

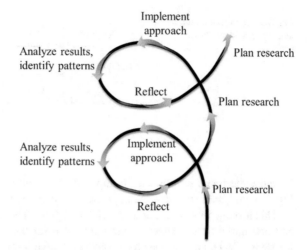

physical_object is involved in an activity. Since the ISO 15926 ontology commits to an explicit representation of what exists, it is the Weltanschauung of choice for the ultimate translation of the solution in the systems world to the solution in the real world.

2.4 The Action Research Spiral

This action research is the product of supervising four research projects over 20 years that came to illustrate the research spiral cycle we describe below. Action research was chosen because of its iterative and collaborative nature. In our work, we adapted the cycles of planning, acting, observing, and reflecting to planning the research project, implementing the approach, analyzing the results, and reflecting upon those results. As shown in Fig. 2.2, these cycles continue in a spiral; each spiral level corresponds to a postdoctoral or graduate research project.

In the planning phase, the models and algorithms were proposed based on the 3-dimensional Weltanschauung. The implementation phase focused on the computer implementation of the algorithms. The analysis was made based on the performance measures defined in the planning phase. The problem was sometimes redefined in the reflection phase, and ideas for the following research project were organized.

2.5 Operations Models

Here, we focused on different models in the operations dimension and their impact on the operational and computational performance during the startup and shutdown.

Fig. 2.3 The mixing tank in
an acrylic-acid synthesis
process

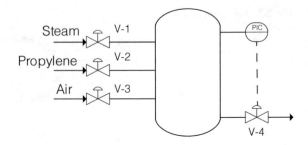

Initially, the focus was on the startup and shutdown of the mixing tank shown in Fig. 2.3, and, subsequently, the approach was extended to a more complex system.

This mixing tank is part of an acrylic acid plant. The vessel has three inlet valves and one outlet valve. There is one inlet valve for the admission of air (V-3), one for steam (V-1), and another for propylene (valve V-2). The outlet valve is for the discharge of the mixture. The outlet flow is regulated with a local controller that keeps the pressure constant at any time.

The objective was to determine the optimum startup and shutdown operating procedures that minimize the risk of producing a flammable mixture. Entering the flammability envelope poses a fire and explosion hazard, so any concentration within the flammability envelope should be avoided.

In the startup case, the vessel is initially filled with air. The goal state is determined by a specified mass composition of the steam–air-propylene mixture outside the flammable envelope. On the other hand, shutdown transfers the system to a state that is 100% air.

These operation models were developed by students and researchers supervised by the same professor. In all the operation models, the inlet valves were operated in a bang-bang fashion or with multiple valve positions.

Since the possible positions of the valves are proposed in advance, and it is a question of determining which operations are conducted and the best sequence, the optimization problem is combinatorial. In other words, the set of solutions to the optimization problem is finite but too large to search for the optimal solution exhaustively. Therefore, in all the research projects, metaheuristic optimization was used.

The changes in concentration and pressure were calculated in the behavioral dimension with a dynamic simulator containing a differential–algebraic equation model. Dynamic simulation is necessary because, after changing valve positions, the effects on the behavior variables (concentration and pressure) are not instantaneous but felt over time. This is similar to controlling the shower water temperature by regulating the hot-water and the cold-water valves. We realize that there is a delay between opening or closing the valves and the change in water temperature.

Fig. 2.4 An illustration of
the shortest-path problem

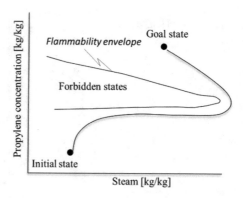

2.5.1 The Weltanschauung Robot Analogy

The first approach to the startup of the mixing tank was proposed in 1999 (Asprey et al. 1999). It consisted of a two-layer method for startup sequences. The upper layer used a Simulated Annealing (SA) algorithm to optimize the overall operations time. This algorithm adjusted a parameter called action duration and passed it to the lower layer. The A* pathfinding method was implemented in the lower layer to generate the operating procedure (the sequence of valve operations) to minimize the difference between the current mixture composition and the goal state. The action duration denotes the time duration for which a combination of valve positions is maintained. This approach prevented actions such as opening a valve 0.05% for 0.3 s, which is not physically realizable.

The role of the A^* method was to find the shortest path in a behavior-state graph, as Fig. 2.4 illustrates. Each state represented a specific concentration of air, steam, and propylene mass. The pathfinding process can be imagined as a robot that is located at one corner of the room (initial state), finding its way to another location in the room (goal state) while avoiding obstacles (forbidden states in the flammability envelope). The objective is to attain a final state as close as possible to the goal state in a minimum time. Although the two-layer method can generate an optimal global solution, it does so at the expense of a high number of simulations. Moreover, keeping the same operator-time constant for all the operations misses solutions that would otherwise be obtained with heterogeneous values for this parameter (Fig. 2.4).

2.5.2 The Local Search Approach

We implemented a Tabu search algorithm in the subsequent study to reduce the computational effort and increase the diversity of solutions. We allowed neighboring solutions to include heterogeneous values for the operator-time constant (Suzuki et al. 2009). The operator time durations were defined as 15, 20, 25, 30, 35, 40, and 45 s.

Fig. 2.5 Local search
approach

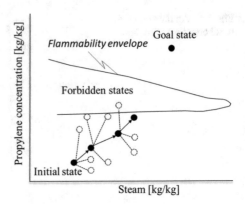

The valve positions were set as 10% open, completely open, or completely closed. This resulted in an overall operations time of 531 s and an average computation time of 1.7 s using a Pentium 266 MHz computer processor, compared to 730 s with the Simulated-Annealing-A* approach on the same computer. However, being a pure local search, this approach was prone to get trapped in an optimal local solution, so global optimization was not guaranteed. Figure 2.5 illustrates the local-search approach. The white circles denote the states resulting from neighboring solutions, and the black circles indicate the states that result from the selected solution.

2.5.3 The Variable-Length Representation

The subsequent approach for global optimization consisted of performing optimization on a search-space composed of complete operating procedures (Batres 2013). The model in the operation dimension was transformed from a model of a single operation to a model that represented the whole sequence of operations (the operating procedure). In this approach, each solution was represented as a variable-length sequence. Each element in the list represented an operation defined per the three valves' positions and a value corresponding to the action duration (Fig. 2.6). Therefore, each solution was a sequence of operations that took the system from the initial to the final state. Under this scheme, infeasible solutions[2] could appear during the optimization process and add diversity to the solutions. However, an optimal global solution could be obtained.

The near-optimal solution is obtained by developing a micro-genetic algorithm (μGA), which is characterized by small populations (between 5 and 10 individuals). A μGA has an inner loop and an outer loop (Fig. 2.7). Within the inner loop, selection and genetic operations are applied. In each iteration in the inner loop, the best-fit individual of each generation is stored. Once convergence is achieved, a new population

---

[2] An infeasible solution is either one passing through forbidden intermediate states or a solution with a final state that is far from the goal state.

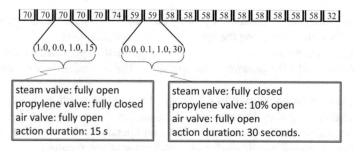

Fig. 2.6   An example of the variable-length list used to represent an operating procedure

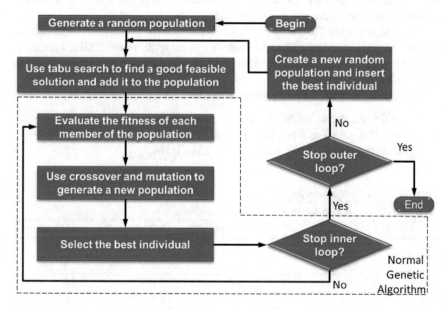

Fig. 2.7   The micro genetic algorithm

is generated, and the best-fit individual from the converged inner-loop is added to the population. In other words, the best-fit individual is inserted into an initial population of randomly generated individuals. Thanks to the small populations, convergence can be achieved faster and less memory is required to store the population.

Before starting the μGA algorithm, a feasible solution was to generate the local search and then insert it into the initial population of randomly generated solutions. Then we performed the μGA until the stopping criteria were achieved. A maximum number of generations of the inner loop and a maximum number of epochs of the outer loop were fixed and set as stopping criteria.

Traditional genetic algorithms implement two types of operators: crossover and mutation. In addition, the shrink, growth, swap, and parameter-change mutation operators (Brie and Morignot 2005) were implemented, as described below.

The shrink mutation consists of picking one random point in the chromosome of the parent and then removing the operation at that specific point.

The growth mutation is carried out by selecting a random point in the chromosome of the parent and then inserting one operation. The operation is also selected at random.

The swap mutation consists of randomly selecting two positions in the chromosome and then swapping their respective elements.

The parameter-change mutation replaces an operation with another having the same valve positions but with different values in the action duration.

Despite the advantage of less memory and faster convergence, this approach requires many parameters to be adjusted, namely, the probabilities for mutation, crossover, growth, swap, and parameter change.

The best sequence (70 70 70 70 18 13 59 58 59 6 6 58 58 58 58 58 58 58) had a total operations time of 450 s and took 76 s to compute on a 3.2 GHz Intel Xeon computer with 8 GB RAM r. The corresponding sequence of valve actions is shown in Table 2.1.

This can be translated to a representation based on a point in time:

At $t = 0$ s, set V-1 to 100%, V-2 to 10%, V-3 to 0%.
At $t = 135$ s, set v1 to 10%, V-2 to 100%, v3 to 10%.
At $t = 150$ s, set v1 to 0%, V-2 to 100%, v3 to 100%.

Table 2.1 Example of a valve sequence

Operation ID	Action duration (s)	Valve positions		
		V-1 (steam)	V-2 (propylene)	V-3 (air)
70	30	1	0.1	0
70	30	1	0.1	0
70	30	1	0.1	0
70	30	1	0.1	0
18	15	1	0.1	0
13	15	0.1	1	0.1
59	30	0	1	1
58	30	0	0.1	1
59	30	0	1	1
6	15	0	0.1	1
6	15	0	0.1	1
58	30	0	0.1	1
58	30	0	0.1	1
58	30	0	0.1	1
58	30	0	0.1	1
58	30	0	0.1	1
58	30	0	0.1	1

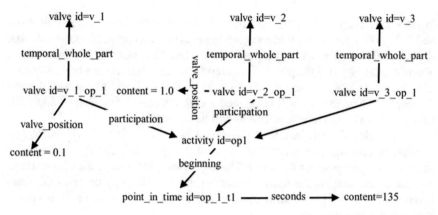

Fig. 2.8 Graphical representation of the second operation in the operating procedure based on the classes and relationships defined in ISO 15926

At $t = 180$ s, set v1 to 0%, V-2 to 10%, v3 to 100%.
At $t = 210$ s, set v1 to 0%, V-2 to 100%, v3 to 100%.
At $t = 240$ s, set v1 to 0%, V-2 to 10%, v3 to 100%.

This sequence information implies that valves V-1, V-2, and V-3 participate in each operation. Using the classes and relationships defined in the ISO 15926 standard, such information becomes explicit. Figure 2.8 depicts a graphical representation of the second operation of the operating procedure.

As the tank concentrations change dynamically, it is also possible to express the operating procedure in terms of the behavior state, thus:

When ysteam = 0% and ypropylene = 0% and yair = 100%, set V-1 to 100%, V-2 to 10%, and V-3 to 0%.
When ysteam = 33.947% and ypropylene = 3.4003% and yair = 62.6652%, set V-1 to 10%, V-2 to 100%,and V-3 to 10%.
When ysteam = 32.4253% and ypropylene = 8.1492% and yair = 59.4374%, set V-1 to 0%, V-2 to 100%, and V-3 to 100%.
When ysteam = 26.6368% and ypropylene = 15.6202% and yair = 57.7526%, set V-1 to 0%, V-2 to 10%, and V-3 to 100%.
When ysteam = 23.9827% and ypropylene = 14.9696% and yair = 61.0564%, set V-1 to 0%, V-2 to 100%, and V-3 to 100%.
When ysteam = 19.9235% and ypropylene = 20.8987% and yair = 59.185%, set V-1 to 0%, V-2 to 10%, and V-3 to 100%.

2.5.4 The Finite Sequence Model

During the observation phase of the previous approach, we discovered that every final solution had one or more operations repeated n times consecutively. For example, in Table 2.1, it can be seen that operation 70 (V-1 $= 100\%$ open, V-2 $= 10\%$ open, and V-3 $= 0\%$ open, with an action duration of 30 s) is repeated consecutively four times. Similarly, operation 6 is repeated twice, and 58 is repeated six times. These observations suggested the possibility of representing a solution as a finite sequence $(A_1, A_2, A_3, \ldots, A_m)$ where $A_i = (< O_i, T_i >, R_i)$. O_i is an operation, T_i denotes the length in time that O_i will be applied and R_i denotes the number of times that the operation O_i with length in time T_i will be repeated.

An operation O_i is defined as an element of the set $O = \{(I_j, P_{jkl})\}$ where I_j is a unique integer that serves as an identifier of the operation, and P_{jkl} is a numeric value of the valve-position of valve l. The implementation is done with three arrays: the first array contains the operation indices, the second array contains the time-length values, and the third array contains the number of times that each operation is repeated consecutively.

This finite sequence model of operations was used to start up a drum boiler, illustrated in Fig. 2.9. The drum boiler is a core piece of equipment involved in the startup process of a steam generator. In the behavior dimension, we developed a simulation model based on a well-known and widely studied differential–algebraic equation.

To implement the model, we used the OpenModelica environment, which allows the development of dynamic simulators (Fritzson et al. 2018). OpenModelica has algorithms for solving systems of differential equations, making it possible to predict changes in the behavior variables over time. The model was developed to produce a simulation for a given sequence of valve operations.

The optimization problem for the drum boiler consists of finding the sequence of valve operations that brings the temperatures and pressures from the initial state to a goal state while avoiding the excessive formation of thermal stresses.

Fig. 2.9 An illustration of a drum boiler

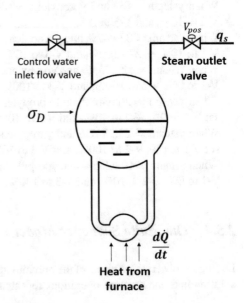

The experiments used three values for the action duration (60, 120, and 180 s) and three valve positions (0% open, 60% open, and 100% open). The heat inlet valve was adjusted for the heat flow rate (8 MW/min, 16 MW/min, and 24 MW/min). As a result, eight different actions were obtained from the combination of three valve positions for the two valves (the case of both valves closed was not considered). The repetition parameter was set to take integer values from 0 to 10. The length of the sequence was fixed to 9 elements.

The mGA probabilities used in the numerical experiments were 10% for mutation and 20% for crossover. The population of the mGA consisted of 5 individuals, and the termination criteria were set to a maximum of 40 generations and 20 epochs, respectively.

The proposed approach was compared against that reported by Belkhir et al. (2015). With the proposed approach, the goal was reached in 1600 s, compared to the startup time of 3000 s reported by Belkhir.

Based on the independence of the three dimensions, a student working on the drum-boiler startup proposed to replace the mGA with a modified Tabu search algorithm that kept the mutation operations for neighbor generation. Both algorithms are iterative methods based on a heuristic that guides them to explore the search space without evaluating each solution of the search space. After that, a simulated annealing algorithm was also tested.

The modified Tabu search approach resulted in a similar performance, reaching the goal state in 1560 s. The following was the best result:

Operation ID	8	3	9	9	7	2	8	1	3
Time	60	120	180	120	120	60	120	120	60
Repetition	1	7	8	3	8	5	1	9	5

The point-in-time-based operating procedure is as follows:

At $t = 0$ s, set the heat inlet valve to 24 MW/min and the steam outlet valve to 60%.

At $t = 840$ s, set the heat inlet valve to 8 MW/min and the steam outlet valve to 100%.

At $t = 660$ s, set the heat inlet valve to 24 MW/min and the steam outlet valve to 100%.

2.6   Conclusions

This paper illustrated how action research provides a convenient and effective way to guide research projects. It helped identify patterns that were useful for successive research projects, redefine the problem, and adjust the Weltanschauungs to enhance the effectiveness of the research contributions. The example on operating procedure synthesis showed the evolution of operations models and their relationship to the optimization approach.

We showed that the insights and improvements of the operating procedure synthesis approaches align with the operations models' evolution. An explicit world view led to increased engagement, facilitated observation, ignited student curiosity, and enabled the students and researchers to acquire new skills and knowledge, expanding their creativity and innovation. The transfer of knowledge also gave students the confidence to continue the research and motivated them to try more challenging research.

Regarding the time-to-degree of graduate students, the average time for Masters students was two years and four years for Ph.D. students. The completion rate was 100%. Furthermore, all students produced conference and journal papers.

Acknowledgements The authors would like to acknowledge the financial and technical support of the National Council of Science and Technology (CONACYT). The authors also acknowledge the technical support of the Writing Lab, Institute for the Future of Education, Tecnologico de Monterrey, Mexico, in the production of this work.

References

Akmal S, Batres R (2013) A methodology for developing manufacturing process ontologies. J Jpn Ind Manage Assoc 64(2):303–316

Asprey SP, Batres R, Fuchino T, Naka Y (1999) Optimal simulation-based operations planning with quantitative safety constraints. Ind Eng Chem Res 36(6):2364–2374

Bastalich W (2015) Content and context in knowledge production: a critical review of doctoral supervision literature. Stud High Educ 42:1–13

Batres R (2013) Generation of operating procedures for a mixing tank with a micro genetic algorithm. Comput Chem Eng 57:112–121

Batres R, Naka Y, Lu ML (1999) A multidimensional design framework and its implementation in an engineering design environment. Concurr Eng 7(1):43–54

Batres R, West M, Leal D, Price D, Katsube M, Shimada Y, Fuchino T (2007) An upper ontology based on ISO 15926. Comput Chem Eng 31(5–6):519–534

Batres R, Fujihara S, Shimada Y, Fuchino T (2014) The use of ontologies for enhancing the use of accident information. Process Saf Environ Prot 92(2):119–130

Belkhir F, Cabo DK, Feigner F, Frey G (2015) Optimal startup control of a steam power plant using the Jmodelica platform. IFAC-PapersOnLine 48:204–209

Brie AH, Morignot P (2005) Genetic planning using variable-length chromosomes. ICAPS 2005:320–329

Batres R (2021) Teaching ill-defined problems in engineering. Int J Interactive Des Manuf

Fritzson P, Pop A, Asghar A, Bachmann AB, Braun W, Braun R, Buffoni L, Casella F, Castro R, Danós RA et al (2019) The OpenModelica integrated modeling, simulation, and optimization environment. In: Proceedings of the American Modelica conference 2018, Cambridge MA, USA, 9–10 October 2019, Linköping University Electronic Press, Linköping, Sweden, pp 206–219

Gatfield T (2005) An investigation into PhD supervisory management styles: development of a dynamic conceptual model and its managerial implications. J High Educ Policy Manag 27(3):311–325

IChemE (2006) BP process safety series: safe ups and downs for process units, 6th edn. IChemE.

Kemmis S, Mctaggart R (1981) The action research planner. Deakin University, Geelong, Australia

Kucharyson R (2006) Optimized procedural operations. Pet Technol Q Q3:93–101

Lamp J (1998) Using petri nets to model weltanschauung alternatives. In: Soft systems methodology Australian conference on requirements engineering, pp 91–100

Mainhard T, van der Rijst R, van Tartwijk J (2009) A model for the supervisor–doctoral student relationship. High Educ 58:359–373

McCallin A, Nayar S (2012) Postgraduate research supervision: a critical review of current practice. Teach High Educ 17(1):63–74

Middleton H (2002) Complex problem-solving in a workplace setting. Int J Educ Res 37:67–84

Rourke A, Sweller J (2009) The worked-example effect using ill-defined problems: learning to recognize designers' styles. Learn Instr 19:185–199

Suzuki M, Batres R (2009) A tabu-search approach for generating safer operations sequences. In: 2009 ICCAS-SICE, Fukuoka, Japan, pp 5199–5202

Tawfik A (2017) Do cases teach themselves? A comparison of case library prompts in supporting problem-solving during argumentation. J Comput High Educ 29(2):267–285

Whitelock D, Faulkner D, Miell D (2008) Promoting creativity in PhD supervision: tensions and dilemmas. Thinking Skills Creativity 3:143–153

Chapter 3
A Contrast-Pattern Characterization of Web Site Visitors in Terms of Conversions

Alicia Huidobro, Raúl Monroy, Manuel A. Godoy, and Bárbara Cervantes

3.1 Introduction

Companies constantly look for strategies to increase traffic to their Web sites (Rocha et al. 2019), especially those that enable visitor actions with an underlying business goal, like increasing sales, raising profits, attracting new clients, improving brand image, etc. (Charlesworth 2014; Deiss and Henneberry 2017; Palmatier et al. 2017; Stieler 2016). In marketing, such visitor actions are called *conversions* (Kotler and Gary 2007; Armstrong et al. 2017; Kotler et al. 2017). Example conversions include paying for a product, filling in a form with contact details, posting a product review, or rating a product. To design a strategy for increasing the conversion rate in a Web site, marketing experts benefit from knowing the characteristics of the visitors who perform each kind of conversion.

Web analytics solutions (WAS) (Velkumar and Thendral 2020; Wang et al. 2020; Google Analytics 2021; Matomo 2021; OMNITURE 2021; Leadfeeder 2021; VMO 2021; PAVEAI 2021; WOOPRA 2021) present visitor traffic via spread tables and

---

The research reported here was supported by CONACYT studentship 957,562 to the first author. The authors would like to acknowledge the financial and technical support of the Writing Lab, Institute for the Future of Education, Tecnologico de Monterrey, Mexico, in producing this work.

A. Huidobro (✉) · R. Monroy · B. Cervantes
School of Engineering and Sciences, Tecnologico de Monterrey, Estado de México, Mexico
e-mail: a01749803@itesm.mx

R. Monroy
e-mail: raulm@tec.mx

B. Cervantes
e-mail: bcervantesg@tec.mx

M. A. Godoy
Information Technology, NIC México, Nuevo Leon, Mexico
e-mail: mgodoy@nic.mx

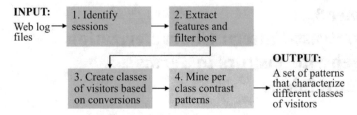

Fig. 3.1 Methodology to characterize Web site visitors in terms of conversions

charts, considering one characteristic at a time (e.g., gender). However, whether commercial or academic, they do not attempt to group visitors in terms of a business goal, let alone identify the characteristics that members of each group have in common and how groups contrast one another. Some WAS use machine learning to find clusters of visitors (Serin and Lawrance 2018), but such clusters are not necessarily related to a conversion; moreover, these WAS do not provide a characterization of each cluster of visitors.

In this paper, we take a few steps towards filling this gap: We introduce a means of characterizing Web site visitors (see Fig. 3.1). Roughly, we first group the activities performed by each unique visitor during a period into a *visitor session* (Cooley et al. 1999; Mehrotra et al. 2017; Neelima and Rodda 2016; Mughal 2018; Soonu Aravindan and Vivekanandan 2017). Then, for each visitor session, we identify what conversions were achieved, if any. Next, we associate each conversion to a sales funnel, which consists of sequence steps that can be used to characterize the level of engagement shown by a visitor to a Web site, from *visitor awareness* to *visitor loyalty* (Charlesworth 2014; Deiss and Henneberry 2017; Palmatier et al. 2017; Stieler 2016). This way, we can now associate every visitor session with a particular step in the sales funnel, forming as many classes as the steps in the funnel. Then, we use a data-miner for each class to obtain a set of expressions, called *contrast patterns*, which describe (characterize) each visitor class. These patterns describe the properties of the class members so that such properties are not shared with members of other classes (they are contrasted) (Loyola-González et al. 2017; Dong 2019).

Our results show that a few patterns are enough to characterize a visitor class. Although a pattern miner usually yields thousands of patterns, lots of redundant patterns can be filtered. One can easily order the remaining patterns using the pattern support (which amounts to the percentage of a target population the corresponding pattern covers (Loyola-González et al. 2020). Since each class is associated with a sales-funnel step, and hence with a conversion, an expert can easily use the class patterns to draw conclusions to account for the class and identify what makes it different from other classes.

The remainder of this paper is organized as follows. In Sect. 3.2, we present the limitations of existing Web analytics solutions. In Sect. 3.3, the core of this paper, we explain how we characterize Web site visitors. In Sect. 3.4, we summarize our results. Finally, in Sect. 3.5, we describe the conclusions drawn from this study and discuss further work.

3.2   Previous Work

In this section, we present existing solutions related to the characterization of visitors. In Sect. 3.2.1, we describe existing commercial software. Then, in Sect. 3.2.2, we present previous literature approaches. Finally, in Sect. 3.2.3, we present our conclusions about the previous work.

From the wide variety of commercial software, we center our analysis on Google Analytics and Matomo. Google Analytics is the most popular Web Analytics software (Kumar and Ogunmola 2020; https://w3techs.com; https://www.g2.com/). Matomo, on the other hand, is an alternative that overcomes some limitations of Google Analytics (Matomo 2021), and it was used in previous approaches (Cervantes et al. 2019; Gómez 2018). Both provide similar functionality.

3.2.1   Commercial Software

Google Analytics and Matomo have similar Web analytics reports, but none of them characterizes visitors. Instead, they show scattered tables and charts to analyze the characteristics of visitors. These are grouped in different categories, for example, demographics, interests, and geographical. In Fig. 3.2, we show an example of the charts in the "demographics" category in Google Analytics. Characteristics can be used to create segments, and different segments can be compared (Google Analytics 2021; Matomo 2021). A segment is a portion of visitors with specific characteristics, for example, "male visitors from Mexico who are between 25 and 54 years old." However, the main disadvantage is that the characteristics of segments are shown

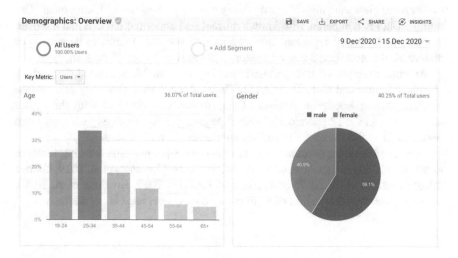

Fig. 3.2 Example of charts in the category "demographics" in google analytics

separately. There is not a report that sums up the distinguishing characteristics for a segment of visitors.

To characterize Web site visitors, we use conversions associated with a five-step sales funnel. Sales funnels can be built with Google Analytics or Matomo (Google Analytics 2021; Matomo 2021). However, they do not characterize visitors using standard sales-funnel steps (e.g., awareness, consideration, intent, purchase, and loyalty). Instead, a sales funnel built with Google Analytics or Matomo shows the sequence of pages to reach a given goal (conversion), for example, making a purchase (Google Analytics 2021; Matomo 2021). These sales funnels provide information about the visited pages but do not show the characteristics of visitors at each step.

3.2.2 Literature Research

There exist weblog mining approaches in which the characteristics of visitors are analyzed. However, they are centered around identifying clusters of visitors for different purposes, not on characterizing visitors. For example, Prabhu et al. (2020) propose grouping Web site visitors to prioritize live, human-assisted support. They use different features to group visitors online, such as browser, country, current page, campaign source, and landing page. They prioritize live support based on the group to which the visitor belongs.

Another example is from Maxwell et al. (2020). They use Web site data to group visitors and determine malicious sources. They use variables like country, browser, hardware identifier, and the presence of cookies. They determine possible combinations of variables in pairs, for example, "Country-URL" and "Browser-URL". They create vectors to capture the distribution of each pair of variables. Then, they execute one or more clustering algorithms on the vectors (e.g., k-means or hierarchical clustering). Data is compared with known normal and abnormal data. When a cluster contains a significant representation of a pair of variables known to be normal or abnormal, it is considered that all visitors from the cluster are of the same type.

Another example of unsupervised learning is from M. Santhanakumar et al. (Santhanakumar and Columbus 2015). They calculate user similarity and session similarity using Euclidean distance. User similarity is obtained with the visitor attributes (e.g., the IP address and visited pages). Session similarity compares two sessions. They use the user and session similarities to find clusters.

Besides previous approaches, there is also extensive machine learning research to use the characteristics of visitors for filtering bots (Cervantes et al. 2019; Gómez 2018; González et al. 2017; Suchacka and Iwa'nski 2020; Rovettaa et al. 2020). However, the characterization of visitors based on conversions is not addressed.

3.2.3   Conclusions from Previous Work

Commercial software shows Web site metrics in multiple tables and charts (Google Analytics 2021; Matomo 2021). It hinders finding multiple-feature patterns or grouping visitors into classes that are not previously configured. Besides, configuration changes do not apply retroactively (Google Analytics 2021; Matomo 2021). Machine learning algorithms have been used for classifying visitors with different purposes (Anand et al. 2018; Devageorge et al. 2020; Maxwell et al. 2020; Santhanakumar and Columbus 2015; Cervantes et al. 2019; Loyola-González et al. 2017; Aissaoui et al. 2018). However, the characterization of visitors for marketing purposes and using conversions as classes have not been previously addressed. From the above, our contribution is to characterize different classes of visitors based on business goals. We achieved it by obtaining a set of contrast patterns for the visitors who perform each type of conversion.

3.3   Characterization of Web Site Visitors Based on Conversions

This section describes how we characterize visitors in terms of the conversions they make and how we contrast types of visitors. This is valuable to develop a strategy for encouraging certain visitors to make a conversion that they otherwise would not make.

To achieve this goal, one needs to set apart what counts as a visitor to a Web site in the first place. A "visitor" explicitly references a unique "user" browsing the Web site during a specific time. Then, a visitor is represented by the collection of sessions occurring during a period.

Given a weblog recording activity in a Web site during a period, one can identify the set of all visitors to the site. Then, for a correct analysis of the Web site's performance, one has to extract the features (raw or composed) that best describe visitors and remove any activity that suspiciously comes from a non-genuine visitor. To extract relevant features, we conducted feature engineering and obtained a feature space that describes sessions. To identify non-genuine visitors, we first used those descriptive features to identify what counts as actual behavior and not. Building upon previous research, we then apply different classification mechanisms, which help us separate many bots even on supposedly clean weblogs, according to our partner security experts.

Each session in our dataset would now be allegedly genuine and easily associated with one or more conversions.

Turning a prospect into a loyal buyer requires multiple steps, known in the marketing field as the sales funnel. To improve conversions, marketing experts have to understand the characteristics of visitors at each step of the sales funnel. Therefore, besides associating each session with conversions, we have partitioned all conversion types into a five-layer sales funnel.

Having sessions associated with conversions, we consider each type of conversion as a class of visitor to characterize. To this aim, we use a miner based on contrast patterns. So, each pattern is such that it characterizes what elements of a class have in common and how one class differs from the others. With this process, we successfully identified a set of patterns for each class. We also interpreted these patterns and obtained relevant insights for each step of the sales funnel.

To validate the interpretability and interestingness of our results, we presented them to a partner company. Experts from both information technology and marketing departments confirmed that our results were easy to interpret and provided information not obtained from standard web analytics reports.

3.3.1   Identify Sessions

We now introduce a method using a weblog as input that returns a collection of sessions, each associated with a user.

Our input data were weblogs that contained 3 million requests. Those logs corresponded to two weeks of Web traffic. Each **request** represents a web page petitioned to the server. Logs have an extended version of the NSCA Common Log Format (CLF). Figure 3.3 shows an example of the CLF.

We transformed each weblog request into an object describing the request but with information oriented for human consumption. For example, we extracted the Web browser, operating system, and device instead of recording the visitor user-agent. Table 3.1 indicates the features that we obtained from the Combined Log Format (CLF). Whenever we mention **request features**, we refer to the features listed in the second column of Table 3.1.

The process of identifying the sessions of each visitor is two-step. In the first step, we identify the requests that belong to the same visitor using a **fingerprint** (Suchacka 2014; Stevanovic et al. 2012; Tan and Vipin Kumar 2002). In the second step, we group the requests of each visitor into sessions.

(1)   Identification of requests per visitor: We compose a fingerprint with *IP address + device name + OS name*. We omit the browser and OS versions to avoid

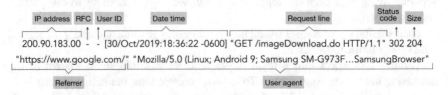

Fig. 3.3 Structure of the combined log format

Table 3.1 Request features

Part of the CFL	Request features (Features extracted from the CLF)
IP address	IP address, city, country, subdivision, organization
RFC	Not applicable [a]
User ID	Not applicable [a]
Date time	Date time, day of the week, hour
Request line	Method, requested URL, URL type, depth
Status code	Status
Size	Bytes downloaded
Referrer	Referrer URL
User-agent	Web browser, operating system, device

[a] No feature was extracted from this part of the CLF

identifying a visitor as different upon a system update. This fingerprint does not allow us to identify multiple devices of the same user. Due to privacy reasons, we reject the use of other tracking tools (like cookies, web beacons, or script codes). Using this fingerprint, we identified 24,000 different visitors.

(2)   Grouping of requests as sessions: Using the fingerprint, we extracted: (1) a list of visitors that, in later steps, is used to identify if a visitor is new or recurrent and (2) the list of requests executed by a visitor, chronologically ordered. The list of requests describes visitor actions from one or more sessions. Having identified the first visitor action (request) on a session, we mark the end of that session upon the occurrence of a visitor action that leads to a 25-min interval of visitor silence (no activity). Then, the following visitor action, if any, becomes the first entry of a new session. The 25-min interval has been commonly applied in previous Web traffic analyses (Suchacka 2014; Stevanovic et al. 2012), similar to the interval used by Web Analytics software (Google Analytics 2021; Matomo 2021).

We obtained a list of 66,000 sessions. The next step was to obtain the features that summarize each session.

3.3.2   Extract Features

To characterize visitors, one needs to extract features that describe sessions and to remove sessions suspiciously performed by a non-genuine visitor. Next, we describe these steps.

(1)   Extract session features: We analyzed the feature space of previous weblog mining research (Cooley et al. 1999; Suchacka 2014; Stevanovic et al. 2012;

Tan and Vipin Kumar 2002; Guerbas et al. 2013; Pabarskaite and Raudys 2007; Michael 2013; Andrea 2016) and features generally used by Web Analytics software (Google Analytics 2021; Matomo 2021). As a result, we propose the feature space for describing the sessions of any Web site. We group that feature space into seven categories (see Fig. 3.4). We extract them, obtaining a dataset that describes sessions as feature vectors. In Sect. 3.3, we explain in detail how we obtain features of the category "Conversion".

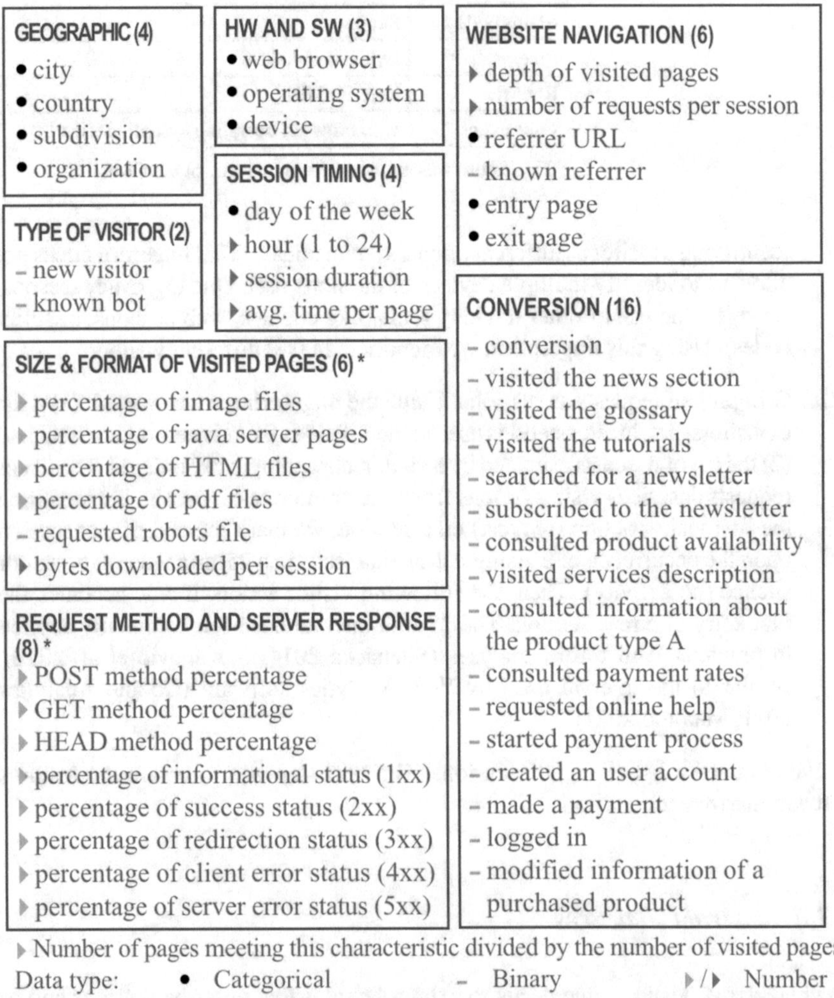

GEOGRAPHIC (4)
- city
- country
- subdivision
- organization

TYPE OF VISITOR (2)
– new visitor
– known bot

HW AND SW (3)
- web browser
- operating system
- device

SESSION TIMING (4)
- day of the week
▶ hour (1 to 24)
▶ session duration
▶ avg. time per page

WEBSITE NAVIGATION (6)
▶ depth of visited pages
▶ number of requests per session
- referrer URL
– known referrer
- entry page
- exit page

SIZE & FORMAT OF VISITED PAGES (6) *
▶ percentage of image files
▶ percentage of java server pages
▶ percentage of HTML files
▶ percentage of pdf files
– requested robots file
▶ bytes downloaded per session

REQUEST METHOD AND SERVER RESPONSE (8) *
▶ POST method percentage
▶ GET method percentage
▶ HEAD method percentage
▶ percentage of informational status (1xx)
▶ percentage of success status (2xx)
▶ percentage of redirection status (3xx)
▶ percentage of client error status (4xx)
▶ percentage of server error status (5xx)

CONVERSION (16)
– conversion
– visited the news section
– visited the glossary
– visited the tutorials
– searched for a newsletter
– subscribed to the newsletter
– consulted product availability
– visited services description
– consulted information about the product type A
– consulted payment rates
– requested online help
– started payment process
– created an user account
– made a payment
– logged in
– modified information of a purchased product

▶ Number of pages meeting this characteristic divided by the number of visited pages.
Data type: • Categorical   – Binary   ▶ / ▶ Number

Fig. 3.4 Summary of features extracted from sessions. The 16 "CONVERSION" features are used as binary labels. We did not use features from the categories marked with an asterisk (*) because their values were not suspiciously high or low. However, it could be different for another dataset

(2)   *Remove bots:* can be up to 37.9% of Web site traffic (Global dots 2019). It is
       necessary to filter them to make correct conclusions based on the characteristics
       of human visitors. We filter bots with two methods: (1) a fast filter and (2) a
       machine learning model. The fast filter is based on the binary features "Known
       bot" and "Requested robots file." The first feature allows identifying sessions
       that come from known-bots sources. The second feature indicates if the robots
       file was requested. We eliminated sessions with the value "True" in at least
       one of these two features. In the machine learning model, we used Bagging-
       RandomMiner as an anomaly detection algorithm. It allows identifying atypical
       values in the dataset. Bagging-RandomMiner has shown good results in data
       mining tasks (Bagging-RandomMiner 2018), and it has been previously tested
       for filtering bots (Cervantes et al. 2019). We found 23% of bot traffic in the
       dataset. According to our partner security experts, that percentage is high,
       considering that the input data was supposedly clean of bots.

   After removing bots, data is ready to be partitioned into different classes of visitors.
We explain this process next.

3.3.3   Create Classes of Visitors Based on Conversions

One contribution of our approach is the use of conversions associated with the sales
funnel as classes of visitors. To this aim, we follow two steps:

(1)   *Identify conversions that can be performed on the Web* site: We identify web
       pages that correspond to different types of conversions, obtaining at least one
       URL per conversion. Then, we manually associate each conversion with the
       corresponding step of the sales funnel. We used a five-step sales funnel whose
       steps are: (1) Awareness, (2) Consideration, (3) Intent, (4) Purchase, and (5)
       Loyalty. Figure 3.5 shows the identified conversions associated with the sales-
       funnel steps.

(2)   Data labeling: We use each conversion listed in Fig. 3.5 as a binary feature.
       We identify the conversions performed in each **session**, if any. We also use a
       binary feature called a *conversion*. It is set to "True" if at least one of the 15
       possible conversions was performed in the session.

   The 16 features are used as a label. This way, we classify sessions according
to conversions associated with the sales funnel. The labeled dataset is the input
data for mining contrast patterns. Before mining contrast patterns, it is essential
to know which classes are of interest to marketing experts. For example, the class
"Conversion" is linearly dependent on the other 15 classes. It is only useful to contrast
visitors who had any engagement on the site with those who did not.

Fig. 3.5 Available conversions on the analyzed Web site. Each conversion listed on the right corresponds to one or more Web site pages (URL), and it is associated with the sales-funnel step shown on the left. The leaky funnel represents the dynamic of gradually losing clients (or potential clients)

3.3.4 Mine Per Class Contrast Patterns

To characterize visitors, we are interested in finding out the characteristics of the visitors who made each conversion and the visitors who did not. Therefore, we apply data mining techniques based on contrast patterns. Next, we explain our four-step pattern mining process.

(1) Dataset exploration: We explore the percentage of visitors that performed each conversion. In Fig. 3.6, we can see that the percentage of visitors who perform each conversion type in our dataset is low. It means that we are dealing with imbalanced classes. We also explore features from the categories "request and server response" and "size and format of visited pages." They are relevant only if they are suspiciously high or low. For example, the "GET" method indicates that the visitor requested all the page's content. Most traffic is expected to

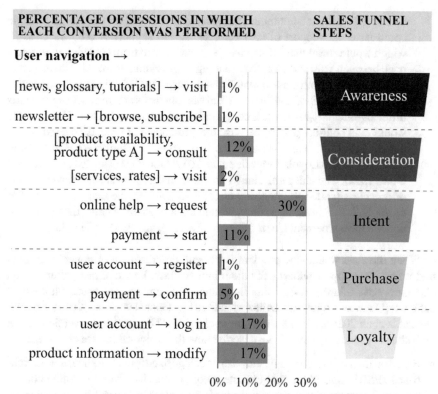

| PERCENTAGE OF SESSIONS IN WHICH EACH CONVERSION WAS PERFORMED | SALES FUNNEL STEPS |

User navigation →

[news, glossary, tutorials] → visit	1%	Awareness
newsletter → [browse, subscribe]	1%	
[product availability, product type A] → consult	12%	Consideration
[services, rates] → visit	2%	
online help → request	30%	Intent
payment → start	11%	
user account → register	1%	Purchase
payment → confirm	5%	
user account → log in	17%	Loyalty
product information → modify	17%	

0% 10% 20% 30%

■ The percentage corresponds to sessions labeled as *True* in each type of conversion.

Fig. 3.6 Summary of features extracted from sessions. The 16 conversion features were used as binary labels

use this method. Hence, it is not relevant if it is found in 90% of visitors. We eliminated features of the two mentioned categories because they were not suspiciously high or low. However, those features could be helpful for a dataset with different values.

(2) Selection of the contrast pattern algorithm: A **pattern** is a characteristic or a set of characteristics that describe a group of objects (Loyola-González et al. 2020; Canete-Sifuentes et al. 2019). That set of characteristics is usually represented by a conjunction of relational statements. For example, the pattern [country = Canada] [hour \in Velkumar and Thendral (2020); OMNITURE 2021)] $\wedge$ [conversion = true] refers to visitors from Canada that requested a page between 7:00 and 11:00 and made a conversion. Each pattern has correspondent **support** (Loyola-González et al. 2020). The support indicates the proportion of objects that meet the description of the pattern in a class (Loyola-González et al. 2020). Consider d the number of objects in the dataset D that meet the description of the pattern p. The support of the pattern p is calculated

dividing d by the total number of objects in D. The pattern used as an example could have the support of 0.07 for class A and support of 0.85 for class B, which would mean that 7% of visitors in class A are from Canada requesting a page between 7:00 and 11:00 and making a conversion. It would also mean that 85% of visitors from class B match that description (Octavio Loyola-González et al. 2017; González et al. 2017). **Contrast patterns** are those whose supports differ significantly in one class compared to the remaining classes. Our example would be a contrast pattern because the percentage of objects covered by the pattern is very different between the two classes: 85% in class B and 7% in class A (Octavio Loyola-González et al. 2017; González et al. 2017; Zhang and Dong 2012). The **class imbalance problem** means significantly fewer objects of one class (called the minority class) than another (the majority class). For example, for contrasting visitors who made a payment against those who did not, we have a percentage of 5% and 95%, respectively (See Fig. 3.6).

When the class imbalance problem is present, contrast pattern miners may only find a few low-support patterns for the minority class. Few contrast pattern-based classifiers have addressed the class imbalance problem and are based on contrast patterns (Octavio Loyola-González et al. 2017; González et al. 2017; Loyola-González et al. 2020). We use one of those classifiers because the conversion rate in Web sites is usually low. Next, we describe how these algorithms are classified:

- Based on their mining strategy, they can be categorized into (1) Exhaustive-search-based (ESB): algorithms that execute a comprehensive search of value combinations for features that are significant in one class compared to other classes. (2) Decision tree-based (DTB): algorithms that extract contrasts patterns using decision trees (Loyola-González et al. 2020).
- Per their pattern filtering strategy, algorithms are based on set theory or quality measures for patterns. The first reduces redundancy (Loyola-González et al. 2020).

We use a DTB algorithm because ESB algorithms usually transform numerical features into nominal by creating disjoint intervals (bins) using an initial discretization. Since that discretization does not consider the values of other features, it could hide relations between objects. Also, contrasts patterns obtained with ESB algorithms have the symbol $=$ as the only relational operator. The initial discretization produces information loss and reduced interpretability. Another disadvantage of some ESB algorithms is that they modify the original dataset using resampling methods, creating a bias toward the majority class, extracting patterns that are not representative of the problem. DTB algorithms for mining contrast patterns avoid those drawbacks and also reduce computational costs. Defiance when mining patterns is the exponential number of possible patterns. Therefore, we selected an algorithm that helps us reduce the redundancy of patterns (Octavio Loyola-González et al. 2017; González et al. 2017; Loyola-González et al. 2020; Loyola-González et al. 2016; García-Borroto et al. 2017).

Based on the mining and filtering strategy of algorithms, we selected PBC4cip. It is a contrast pattern-based classifier that tackles the class imbalance problem. Its mining strategy is decision tree-based, and its filtering method is based on set theory. PBC4cip avoids resampling methods and extracts patterns that are easy to interpret (Octavio Loyola-González et al. 2017; Loyola-González et al. 2020).

(3) Experimental setup: We use the Weka implementation of PBC4cip. Below we describe our experimental setup:

- PBC4cip has two variants: univariate (Octavio Loyola-González et al. 2017) and multivariate (Canete-Sifuentes et al. 2019) decision trees. The multivariate version finds multivariate relations and has reported better classification results (Canete-Sifuentes et al. 2019). However, we use the univariate decision tree builder because multivariate patterns may be difficult to interpret for marketing experts. Below we show an example of both types of relation:

  - Univariate relation: number Of Visited Pages < 17
  - Multivariate relation: 0.01 * number Of Visited Pages + 0.01 * depth > 0.0403

- We use the One-versus-Rest strategy to obtain contrast patterns for each conversion type (class of visitors). We have 16 conversion features (classes). We use each one as a binary class at a time (we run PBC4cip 16 times). We contrast visitors who performed each conversion against its complement. For example, using the feature *requestOnlineHelp* as the binary class, we contrasted the 70% of visitors who did not request online help against the 30% of visitors who did.

  We use the One-versus-Rest strategy to obtain contrast patterns for each conversion type (class of visitors). We have 16 conversion features (classes). We use each one as a binary class at a time (we run PBC4cip 16 times). We contrast visitors who performed each conversion against its complement. For example, using the feature *requestOnlineHelp* as the binary class, we contrasted the 70% of visitors who did not request online help against the 30% of visitors who did.

- We use random forest miner and Hellinger distance as distribution evaluators. This configuration has provided good AUC results in previous research (Octavio Loyola-González et al. 2017; Cervantes et al. 2019).
- We obtained contrast patterns for both classes using 50, 100, or 150 trees. As a rule of thumb, one can use 150 trees because it has provided good classification results (Canete-Sifuentes et al. 2019).
- Usually, there are duplicated patterns because they are obtained from numerous decision trees generated from the same dataset (Canete-Sifuentes et al. 2019; Loyola-González 2017). To remove duplicated patterns, we use the filtering option available in the Weka implementation of PBC4cip.

We obtained thousands of patterns for each conversion. Therefore, it was necessary to select the best contrast patterns.

(4) Pattern selection: We follow five steps to select the best patterns:

- **Selecting representative patterns**: To select contrast patterns in a representative proportion of sessions, we use a minimum of 0.10 support as the threshold. This criterion drastically reduces the number of patterns. We are not interested in patterns in less than 10% of the sessions, but a different threshold can be used. This support threshold has been used to select contrast patterns in previous research (Cervantes et al. 2019; Gómez 2018).
- **Removing redundant items**: We eliminate pattern items that are contained in a more specific item. For example, in the pattern *sessionDuration* $\leq$ *1.5 (s)* $\wedge$ *sessionDuration* $\leq$ *5 (seconds)* $\wedge$ *userIsNew = True*, we can eliminate the item *sessionDuration* $\leq$ *5 (seconds)* because all sessions with a duration $\leq$ 1.5 have also a duration $\leq$ 5. Then, the pattern would be simplified as *sessionDuration* $\leq$ *1.5 (s)* $\wedge$ *userIsNew = True*. This criterion has been used in previous contrast patterns research (Canete-Sifuentes et al. 2019; Loyola-González 2017; Loyola-González et al. 2019).
- **Removing specific contrast patterns**: We remove contrast patterns that are more specific than other contrast patterns. A pattern P1 is more specific than a pattern P2 if P2 is contained in P1 and P1 has at least one more item. Consider P1 $=$ *sessionDuration* $\leq$ *1.5 (seconds)* $\wedge$ *userIsNew = True* $\wedge$ *madePayment = True* and P2 $=$ *sessionDuration* $\leq$ *1.5 (seconds)* $\wedge$ *userIsNew = True*. We remove P1 because it is more specific than P2. This criterion has been used in previous contrast pattern research (Michael 2013; Canete-Sifuentes et al. 2019; Loyola-González 2017; Loyola-González et al. 2019).
- **Selecting patterns with a smaller number of items**: The adequate number of items in a pattern is subjective, but, in general, patterns with fewer items are easier to interpret. We kept only patterns with three or fewer items, which we consider easier to transform into actionable information.
- **Interestingness**: It is a subjective selection usually made by a domain expert. It allows identifying the most relevant patterns according to business objectives. For example, the pattern *initialPage* $\neq$ *.../newsletters/* $\wedge$ *requestedHelp = False* could be not interesting for the expert because knowing that the initial page was not ".../newsletters" leaves hundreds of possible initial pages. Nevertheless, the feature "initial page" is informative when it refers to a relevant page such as "Home" or when it comes with the relational operator " $=$ ".

The previous criteria allow for a representative and informative set of contrast patterns. Assessing different quality metrics is not in the scope of this research. However, other objective and subjective quality measures can be used for selecting contrast patterns (García-Borroto et al. 2017; Guillet and Hamilton 2007; Loyola-González et al. 2016; Loyola-González et al. 2014). A comparison of objective

Table 3.2 Example of selected contrast patterns

Pattern	Support Class F[a]	Support Class T[b]
country = Mexico ∧ requestOnlineHelp = True	[0.00	0.53]
consultProductAvailability = False ∧ requestOnlineHelp = True ∧ numberOfVisitedPages > 25	[0.00	0.53]
userIsNew = False ∧ numberOfVisitedPages > 37	[0.00	0.68]
sessionDuration > 1.5 (seconds) ∧ requestOnlineHelp = True	[0.00	0.68]
knownReferrer = False ∧ numberOfVisitedPages ≤ 3	[0.72	0.00]
sessionDuration ≤ 1.5 (seconds)	[0.76	0.00]
averageSecPerRequest = 0.00	[0.81	0.00]
numberOfVisitedPages ≤ 10	[0.92	0.00]

[a]Class F refers to sessions in which no conversion was performed
[b]Class T refers to sessions in which at least one conversion was performed. For example, the last pattern refers to visitors who visited at most ten pages. This pattern was found in 92% of visitors who did not perform any conversion, and it was not found in visitors who performed at least one conversion

quality measures for selecting contrast patterns is in the research of García-Borroto et al. (2017). There is also research, from Loyola-González et al., regarding the class imbalance in quality measures (Loyola-González et al. 2016; Loyola-González et al. 2014).

In Table 3.2, we show, as an example, some patterns obtained using the feature conversion as the class. This feature indicates whether at least one conversion was performed in the session or not. The support is in the form *[Class F Class T]*:

- *Class F* indicates the proportion of sessions in which no conversion was performed (objects labeled "False").
- *Class T* indicates the proportion of sessions in which at least one conversion was performed (objects labeled "True").

(5) *Pattern interpretation:* The last step of our methodology is the interpretation of patterns by a marketing expert. We interpreted selected patterns for each conversion and validated them with a marketing expert. Table 3.2 shows an example of the interpretation of patterns.

The scope of this group of patterns is to find what distinguishes visitors who made at least one conversion (42%) from those who did not (58%).

From the visitors who did not make a conversion (Class F):

- 92% visited at most ten pages.
- 81% left each page almost immediately, on average.
- 76% were on the Web site at most 1.5 s.
- 72% came from an unknown referrer (were organic traffic) and visited at most three pages.

From the visitors who made a conversion (Class T):

- 68% were on the Web site for more than 1.5 s and requested online help.
- 68% were recurrent visitors and visited more than 37 pages.
- 53% did not consult product availability, requested help, and visited more than 25 pages.
- 53% were from Mexico and requested online help.

For each conversion type, we replicate the interpretation method exemplified in the previous paragraph.

3.4 Results

We present an approach for characterizing visitors using conversions associated with the sales funnel as classes. We propose a methodology that can be replicated using weblogs from any Web site as input data. The result is a characterization of different classes of visitors that is easy to interpret and could be meaningful for marketing experts.

To evaluate the quality of the output (the set of contrast patterns), we use objective and subjective quality measures. As an objective measure, we can highlight the minimum of 0.10 support as a threshold to select representative patterns for each class. This ensures that relevant patterns have been obtained for both the majority and minority classes. As a subjective measure, we use interestingness to confirm that results are relevant per the business objectives.

One contribution is the use of conversions associated with the sales funnel as classes of visitors. We propose this approach because *conversions* and *sales funnel* are relevant for measuring and improving the effectiveness of a Web site. Besides, marketing experts are familiar with both concepts. Using conversions as classes of visitors allows us to obtain specific characteristics for visitors who performed, or did not perform, each type of conversion. By associating conversions with steps of the sales funnel, results could improve the effectiveness of conversions at a given sales-funnel step. That is useful because no company can serve all customers with the same level of satisfaction (Kotler and Gary 2007; Armstrong et al. 2017).

We propose a pattern mining approach to determine the visitors' distinguishing characteristics who performed each conversion. We consider each type of conversion as a class. Then, we obtain a set of contrast patterns for each type of conversion. This approach allows us to obtain results that are easy to interpret and meaningful for marketing experts.

We obtain a set of contrast patterns for each step of the sales funnel and each type of conversion. This result is more informative than having a single aggregated metric. For example, we found that 42% of the visitors performed at least one conversion. Nevertheless, the percentage of visitors who performed each conversion ranged from 0 to 30%. Aggregated metrics may hide relevant information. Knowing the conversion rate for each type of conversion and the characteristics of visitors who performed them could help identify strengths and weaknesses in each conversion. That is relevant because the methods to motivate a client to move from one point to another are different at each sales-funnel step. For example, based on the conversion rate, we found that the Web site effectively gets visitors with purchase intention, but most of them are lost before closing the purchase.

Three aspects allow us to obtain contrast patterns for the visitors who performed or did not perform each conversion:

(1)   The descriptive feature space for representing sessions. It allows us to obtain patterns that are informative and easy to interpret.
(2)   The use of a contrast pattern-based classifier that tackles the problem of imbalanced classes. PBC4cip allows us to obtain patterns in the majority and the minority classes (Octavio Loyola-González et al. 2017). It also avoids using resampling methods and an initial discretization of numerical features (Octavio Loyola-González et al. 2017).
(3)   The use of conversions as classes of visitors associated with the steps of the sales funnel. It allows us to characterize the visitors who performed each conversion type instead of obtaining a generalized characterization.

There are two main differences between our approach and previous work: (1) the use of conversions as classes of visitors and (2) the characterization of classes of Web site visitors. Previous work is mainly oriented to identify classes of visitors using supervised or unsupervised learning, not to provide a characterization of those classes. Commercial software tracks Web site metrics in multiple tables and charts, making it challenging to find multiple-feature patterns or group visitors into classes based on business goals. The characterization of visitors using conversions as classes was not previously addressed.

3.5   Conclusions and Future Work

It is becoming easier to create campaigns for attracting visitors to a Web site. However, not all visitors provide an immediate business benefit. Some visitors are ready to buy a particular product. Others need more information to decide. Some visitors will never purchase the product. Attracting more visitors might be easy, but attracting the right visitors requires in-depth knowledge of them. For this knowledge, in this research, we propose determining the characteristics of visitors who perform each conversion. The above is the main contribution of this research and the basis for further work. We use each conversion as a binary attribute to create two classes: visitors who performed the conversion and visitors who did not. It allows us to find contrast patterns for both classes.

The PBC4cip algorithm provides contrast patterns that are easy to interpret and are ordered based on their support. Nevertheless, it requires additional filtering, e.g., according to the interestingness of patterns. This task could be automated, for example, by using a measure of feature relevance. A disadvantage of this approach is that criteria may be specific for one industry or even for each Web site. A method could be developed for automating pattern filtering without using specific business rules.

There are objective quality measures that might work better than support (García-Borroto et al. 2017; Loyola-González et al. 2016; Loyola-González et al. 2014). In-depth research would be useful to compare different objective metrics in weblog mining, using data from different Web sites. There is also a wide variety of subjective measures that could be used to select contrast patterns. It would be valuable to test a subjective metric to measure how well a pattern describes visitors at each sales-funnel stage.

Regardless of the quality measures used, it would be essential to incorporate a formal method to validate the interpretability of patterns. There are proven methods that could be used, such as the Delphi method, which experts use to reach a consensus. This method is robust because, besides requiring the opinion of three experts, it also considers their grade of expertise (Linstone and Turoff 2002; Sekayi and Kennedy 2017). We were limited to one marketing expert, but the consensus with more experts who validate the results would be beneficial.

The offline processing that we use allows analyzing historical data. Usually, it is not possible in Web Analytics software because changes in tracking configuration apply to future traffic. Nevertheless, the possibility of performing online analysis would also be helpful. Knowing the characteristics of visitors on the Web site at a given moment would allow marketing experts to make more timely decisions.

The development of a software tool where marketing experts can replicate and personalize the process could be useful. For example, they might be interested in analyzing a specific sales-funnel step or characterizing visitors based on specific features. There is a latent need to bridge the gap between machine learning and domain experts.

The sales funnel, which is different for each company, usually includes information about all the company's channels in each step. The Web site is one such channel, but it is part of a broader strategy. For example, the Web site could aim to attract new clients, and the closing of sales may be performed in different channels such as e-mail or telephone. Therefore, an improvement opportunity is to incorporate data from different sales channels.

Acknowledgements We thank the members of the GIEE-ML group at Tecnologico de Monterrey. We also thank NIC Mexico for providing data used in this research.

References

Attaur-Rahman, Dash S, Luhach AK, Chilamkurti N, Baek S, Nam Y (2019) A Neuro-fuzzy approach for user behavior classification and prediction. J Cloud Comput: Adv Syst Appl (8, 17). https://doi.org/10.1186/s13677-019-0144-9

Armstrong G, Kotler PT, Trifts V, Buchwitz LA (2017) Marketing: an introduction. Pearson, 6th edn. ISBN-13: 9780134470528

Andrea I (2016) Machine learning for the web. Packt Publishing. ISBN: 9781785886607

Anand SS, Mamodia AK, Acharya A, Padam KS, Bhingarkar S (2018) A Study of Classification Algorithms for categorizing website users using machine learning. Int J Pure Appl Math 118(16):333–348. ISSN: 1314-3395

Berman R, Israeli A (2020) The value of descriptive analytics: evidence from online retailers. Harvard Business School. Working paper 21-067

Bondarenko S, Laburtseva O, Sadchenko O, Lebedieva V, Haidukova O, Kharchenko T (2019) Modern lead generation in internet marketing for the development of enterprise potential. Int J Innov Technol Exploring Eng (IJITEE). ISSN: 2278-3075, vol 8, issue 12

Benito Camiña J, Medina-Pérez MA, Monroy-Borja R, Loyola-González O, Villanueva LAP, Gurrola LCG (2018) Bagging-RandomMiner: a one-class classifier for file access-based masquerade detection. In: Machine vision and applications

Charlesworth A (2014) Digital marketing: a practical approach, 2nd edn. Taylor and Francis Group. ISBN: 978-0-203-49371-1

Cervantes B, Gómez F, Loyola-González O, Medina-Pérez MA, Monroy R, Ramírez J (2019) Pattern-based and visual analytics for visitor analysis on websites. Appl Sci—Open Access J

Canete-Sifuentes L, Monroy R, Medina-Perez MA, Loyola-González O, Voronisky FV (2019) Classification based on multivariate contrast patterns. IEEE Access

Cooley R, Mobasher B, Srivastava J (1999) Data preparation for mining world wide web browsing patterns. Knowl Information Syst 1(1):5–32

Deiss R, Henneberry R (2017) Digital marketing for dummies, 2nd edn. John Wiley & Sons, Inc. ISBN: 978-1-119-66049

Dhamnani S, Vinay V, Kumari L, Sinha R (2020) Classification of website sessions using one-class labeling techniques. U. S. Patent US10,785,318B2, Adobe Inc

Devageorge JJP, Vembu M, Grandhi SA (2020) Methods and systems for grouping and prioritization of website visitors for live support. U. S. Patent US2020/074519A1, Zoho Corporation Private Limited

Dong G (2019) Exploiting the power of group differences: using patterns to solve data analysis problems. Synthesis Lect Data Mining Knowl Discovery 11(1):1–146

El Aissaoui O, El Madani Y, El Alami, Oughdir L, El Allioui Y (2018) Integrating web usage mining for an automatic learner profile detection: a learning styles-based approach. In: International conference on intelligent systems and computer vision (ISCV), Fez, pp 1–6. https://doi.org/10.1109/ISACV.2018.8354021

Guerbas A, Addam O, Zaarour O, Nagi M, Elhajj A, Ridley M, Alhajj R (2013) Effective weblog mining and online navigational pattern prediction. Knowl-Based Syst 49:50–62

Global dots (2019) 2019 Bad bot report

Google Analytics—Knowledgebase. https://developers.google.com/analytics, March 2021

García-Borroto M, Loyola-González O, Martínez-Trinidad JF, Carrasco-Ochoa JA (2017) Evaluation of quality measures for contrast patterns by using unseen objects. Expert Syst Appl 83:104–113

Guillet F, Hamilton HJ (2007) Quality measures in data mining. Springer, ISSN electronic edition: 1860-9503

Gómez F (2018) Visualization and machine learning techniques to support web traffic analysis. Thesis of the Master Program in Computer Science at Tecnológico de Monterrey

G2. https://www.g2.com/

HEAP website. https://heap.io/blog/product/google-analytics-limits, March 2021

Hassan S, Nadzim SZA, Shiratuddin N (2012) Strategic use of social media for small business based on the AIDA model. ScienceDirect, Global Conference on Business & Social Science-2014, GCBSS-2014, December, Kuala Lumpur

Hun TK, Yazdanifard R (2014) The impact of proper marketing communication channels on consumer's behavior and segmentation consumers. Asian J Bus Manage 02(02) (ISSN: 2321 - 2802)

Kumar V, Ogunmola GA (2020) Web analytics for knowledge creation: a systematic review of tools, techniques, and practices. Int J Cyber Behav Psychol Learn

Kotler P, Kartajaya H, Setiawan I (2017) Marketing 4.0. moving from traditional to digital. John Wiley & Sons, Inc. ISBN: 978-1-119-34106-2

Kotler P, Gary A (2007) Principles of marketing. Pearson Education, 12th edn, ISBN-13: 9780132390026

Loyola-González O, Medina-Pérez MA, Choo KKR (2020) A review of supervised classification based on contrast patterns: applications, trends, and challenges. J Grid Comput. https://doi.org/10.1007/s10723-020-09526-y

Linstone HA, Turoff M (2002) The delphi method, techniques and applications

Leadfeeder website. https://www.leadfeeder.com, March 2021

Log Files. http://httpd.apache.org/docs/2.2/logs.html\#combined

Loyola-González O, Medina-Pérez MA, Martínez J, Carrasco J, Monroy R, García M (2016) PBC4cip: a new contrast pattern-based classifier for class imbalance problems. Knowl Based Syst 115:100–109

Loyola-González O (2017) Supervised classifiers based on emerging patterns for class imbalance problems. Thesis for the degree of PhD in Computer Science at INAOE

Loyola-González O, Monroy R, Medina-Perez MA, Cervantes B, Grimaldo-Tijerina JE (2017) An approach based on contrast patterns for bot detection on weblog files. Wireless Pers Commun 97:2229–2247

Loyola-González O, García-Borroto M, Martínez-Trinidad JF, Carrasco-Ochoa JA (2014) An empirical comparison among quality measures for pattern based classifier. Intelli Data Anal 18:S5–S17. https://doi.org/10.3233/IDA-140705

Loyola-González O, Monroy R, Rodríguez J, López-Cuevas A, Mata-Sánchez JI (2019) Contrast pattern-based classification for bot detection on Twitter. IEEE Access. https://doi.org/10.1109/ACCESS.2019.2904220

Loyola-González O, Martínez-Trinidad JF, Carrasco-Ochoa JA, García-Borroto M (2016) Effect of class imbalance on quality measures for contrast patterns: an experimental study. Information Sci 374:179–192

Loyola-González O, Martínez-Trinidad JF, Carrasco-Ochoa JA, García-Borroto M (2016) Study of the impact of resampling methods for contrast pattern based classifiers in imbalanced databases. Neurocomputing 175(Part B):935–947

Mehrotra R, El Kholy A, Zitouni I, Shokouhi M, Hassan A (2017) Identifying user sessions in interactions with intelligent digital assistants. In: Proceedings of the 26th international conference on world wide web companion, pp 821–822. https://doi.org/10.1145/3041021.3054254

Mughal MJH (2018) Data mining: web data mining techniques, tools and algorithms: an overview. (IJACSA) Int J Adv Comput Sci Appl 9(6)

Mumtaz R (2019) Awareness and perspectives social media as new strategic marketing approach in minor industries; Notion grounded on AIDA model. J Content Community Commun 10, Dec 2019, ISSN: 2456-9011

Michael B (2013) Practical web analytics for user experience. Elsevier Inc. ISBN: 978-0-12-404619-1. ISBN: 978-0-12-404619-1

Matomo—Open analytics platform. https://developer.matomo.org, March 2021

Maxwell LA, McQueen DJ (2020) Systems and methods for network traffic analysis. U. S. Patent US2020/0382542A1, Oath Inc

Neelima G, Rodda S (2016) Predicting user behavior through sessions using the weblog mining. In: 2016 international conference on advances in human-machine interaction (HMI), Doddaballapur, pp 1–5. https://doi.org/10.1109/HMI.2016.7449167

OMNITURE website. https://marketing.adobe.com/resources/help, March 2021

PAVEAI website. https://www.paveai.com/referrer-spam-remover, March 2021

Palmatier RW, Kumar V, Harmeling CM (2017) Customer engagement marketing, 2nd edn. Springer Nature. https://doi.org/10.1007/987-3-319-61985-9_1

Pabarskaite Z, Raudys A (2007) A process of knowledge discovery from weblog data: systematization and critical review. J Intell Inf Syst 2007(28):79–104. https://doi.org/10.1007/s10844-006-0004-1

Rovettaa S, Suchackab G, Masulli F (2020) Bot recognition in a web store: an approach based on unsupervised learning. J Netw Comput Appl 157:102577

Rocha Á, Reis JL, Peter MK, Bogdanovic Z (2019) Marketing and smart technologies: proceedings of ICMarkTech 2019. In: Smart innovation, systems and technologies. Springer Nature. ISSN: 2190-3026

Suchacka G, Iwa\'nski J (2020) Identifying legitimate Web users and bots with different traffic profiles—an information Bottleneck approach. Knowl-Based Syst 197:105875

Suchacka G (2014) Analysis of aggregated bot and human traffic on e-commerce site. In: Proceedings of the 2014 federated conference on computer science and information systems, ACSIS, vol 2, pp 1123–1130. https://doi.org/10.15439/2014F346

Stieler M (2017) Creating marketing magic and innovative future marketing trends. In: Proceedings of the 2016 Academy of Marketing Science (AMS) annual conference. Springer Nature. ISBN: 978-3-319-45596-9

Stevanovic D, An A, Vlajic N (2012) Feature evaluation for web crawler detection with data mining techniques. Expert Syst Appl 39(2012):8707–8717

Soonu Aravindan J, Vivekanandan K (2017) An overview of pre-processing techniques in web usage mining. Int J Comput Trends Technol (IJCTT) 48(1)

Serin J, Lawrance R (2018) Clustering based association rule mining to discover user behavioral pattern in weblog mining. Int J Pure Appl Math 119(17):1937–1947, ISSN: 1314-3395

Sekayi D, Kennedy A (2017) Qualitative Delphi method: a four round process with a worked example. In: The qualitative report; Fort Lauderdale Tomo 22, N.° 10, Oct 2017, pp 2755–2763

Santhanakumar M, Columbus CC (2015) Web usage based analysis of web pages using RapidMiner. WSEAS Trans Comput

Search Engine Journal website. https://www.searchenginejournal.com/google-analytics-cant-tell/187131/\#close, March 2021

Tan P-N, Kumar V (2002) Discovery of web robot sessions based on their navigational patterns. Article in Data Mining and Knowledge Discovery

The Hypertext Transfer Protocol (HTTP). https://www.w3.org/Protocols/rfc2616/rfc2616.txt

Velkumar K, Thendral P (2020) A survey on web mining techniques. In: 2nd international conference on new scientific creations in engineering and technology (ICNSCET-20) International Journal of Recent Trends in Engineering & Research (IJRTER). Special Issue, March 2020. ISSN: 2455-1457

VMO website. https://vwo.com, March 2021

We Need To Talk About Conversion. https://hoteltechreport.com

Web Technology Surveys. https://w3techs.com

WOOPRA website. https://www.woopra.com, March 2021

Wang Y, Liu H, Liu Q (2020) Application research of weblog mining in the E-commerce. In: 2020 Chinese Control And Decision Conference (CCDC), IEEE, CCDC49329.2020.9164022, https://doi.org/10.1109/CCDC49329.2020.9164022

Zhang X, Dong G (2012) Overview and analysis of contrast pattern based classification. In: Contrast data mining: concepts, algorithms, and applications

Chapter 4
Massive-Flexible Digital Courses During COVID-19 Pandemic: From Course Structure to Enabling Tools

**Ricardo A. Ramirez-Mendoza, Enrique Díaz de León,
Jorge de J. Lozoya-Santos, Enrique A. López-Guajardo,
Claudia S. Lopez-Cruz, José Francisco Enríquez de la O,
Rubén Morales-Menéndez, and Wang Jianhong**

4.1 Introduction

In 2020, the COVID19 pandemic forced universities to migrate their classes from in-person modalities to remote, digital platforms. Initially, the professors, researchers,

R. A. Ramirez-Mendoza (✉) · E. Díaz de León · J. de J. Lozoya-Santos · E. A. López-Guajardo · R. Morales-Menéndez
School of Engineering and Sciences, Tecnologico de Monterrey, Monterrey, México
e-mail: ricardo.ramirez@tec.mx

E. Díaz de León
e-mail: ediazdeleon@tec.mx

J. de J. Lozoya-Santos
e-mail: jorge.lozoya@tec.mx

E. A. López-Guajardo
e-mail: enrique.alopezg@tec.mx

R. Morales-Menéndez
e-mail: rmm@tec.mx

C. S. Lopez-Cruz
Center for Teacher Development and Education Innovation, Tecnologico de Monterrey, Monterrey, México
e-mail: lopezclau@tec.mx

J. F. Enríquez de la O
Academic Vice-Presidency, Tecnologico de Monterrey, Monterrey, México
e-mail: enriquez@tec.mx

W. Jianhong
School of Electronic Engineering, Jiangxi University of Science and Technology, Ganzhou City, P.R. China
e-mail: 9120180002@jxust.edu.cn

53

S. Hosseini et al. (eds.), *Technology-Enabled Innovations in Education*,
Transactions on Computer Systems and Networks,
https://doi.org/10.1007/978-981-19-3383-7_4

and staff found it challenging to maintain students' engagement in their digital platform courses (Hodges et al. 2020), mainly due to common misconceptions about how to create a practical digital course, relying on digitalizing course material "as is" and improvisation (Hodges et al. 2020; Crawford et al. 2020). In a remote learning experience, different technological, and virtual tools must catalyze the teacher-student interactions and facilitate the students' learning process (Tudon-Martinez et al. 2020; Sangrà 2020). Moreover, socioeconomic and emotional factors must be considered external disturbances, which affect the student's engagement and comprehension (Grubic et al. 2020) in the learning process. Therefore, universities should improve their remote teaching pedagogy while leveraging the various digital tools and frameworks available (Mohmmed et al. 2020).

The challenges mentioned above could be overcome with the best educational techniques and digital practices. Rigorous course planning, session-time planning, and active learning activities decrease improvisation (Pardo and Cobo 2020). On the other hand, interest-driven and student-centered educational techniques such as *Flipped Classrooms* (*FC*) (Al-Hammouri et al. 2020; Al-Maroof and Al-Emran 2021), *Challenge-Based Learning* (*CBL*) (Khambari 2019; Membrillo-Hernández et al. 2019), and *Research-Based Learning (RBL)* (Brew and Saunders 2020) utilize active learning, which continuously engages and motivates the students. These techniques are versatile, flexible, and easily adaptable in an online environment; however, their success relies on the course design's synchronous and asynchronous synergy and appropriate digital tools.

Such student-centered methodologies comprise the core of Tecnologico de Monterrey's innovative Tec21 Educational Model. This model promotes the development of competencies by challenging the students to solve real-world engineering problems. The model is a hybrid that leverages digital media's flexibility, capabilities, and capacities in a digital framework. Thus, a massive online course with a masterclass approach can be offered to bolster students' overall motivation and learning experience with interactivity among students and professors using digital technologies. This model is called a *Massive Flexible Digital Masterclass* (*MFDM*). It allows the nation's best professors and experts on a specialized subject to improve the students' academic quality and learning experience through a masterclass. Leveraging digital tools and technologies, an educator or expert can teach approximately 300 students per class nationwide without physical limitations and positively impact their academic performance (Goodwin and Miller 2013).

This work presents a general description of the *MFDM* model and the enabling tools and techniques used. The paper discusses the implementation and quality assessment of the model, which was used for the 2019–2020 Mechanical Vibrations class.

4.2   State of the Art

The main objective of *Flipped Classroom* (*FC*) and *Challenge-Based Learning* (*CBL*) is to foster the development of competencies and sub-competencies such as innovation, creativity, teamwork, problem-solving, and other related hard and soft skills (Al-Maroof and Al-Emran 2021; Membrillo-Hernández et al. 2019; Usmeldi et al. 2017) required to solve real-world problems. Initially, the students learn at their own pace asynchronously in a flexible learning environment (Gaskins et al. 2015; Ozdamli and Asiksoy 2016), followed by a discussion of the concepts with the teacher synchronously to deepen their learning process. This process prepares the students to tackle real-world problems using all the concepts learned, and the competencies and transversal skills developed. During the first nine weeks of the course, the professor actively provides the students with concepts, competencies, tools, and information needed as described in the course syllabus. However, this type of interaction gradually decreases, and the teacher assumes a more passive role in weeks 10–16, mentoring the students as they address a real-world challenge presented to them. The challenge begins with nano- and micro-challenges (short-term problems) that progressively increase in complexity during these weeks, preparing the students for a smooth transition to the real-world challenge. Different student teams tackle these real industrial problems. They receive support from the professor regarding theory, and a partner from industry provides practical (applied) and empirical support (Membrillo-Hernández et al. 2019; Nichols et al. 2016; Morales-Avalos and Heredia-Escorza 2019).

Figure 4.1 presents the steps for implementing *FC* and the overall *CBL* course structure.

The *MFDM* model faces at least two significant challenges because of its massive nature (300+ students). The first relates to capturing the students' attention and interacting with them. The second one is the significant amount of course materials, deliverables (homework), project assignments, and examinations that require grading and feedback from the professor. If not handled carefully, these drawbacks can lead to lower student perception of the course quality.

Using existing technological and digital tools with active learning techniques can increase the students' motivation and engagement while being interactive, autonomous, and challenging. The synergy of various teaching–learning activities and technological tools helps the students deepen their comprehension of the concepts developed during the course while fostering transversal skills necessary for a collaborative solution to the challenge (real-world problem). Specialized tools can provide helpful monitoring and assessment information to the professor, decrease the grading workload through automated grading, and deliver timely feedback. (Savery and Duffy 1995; Savery 2006).

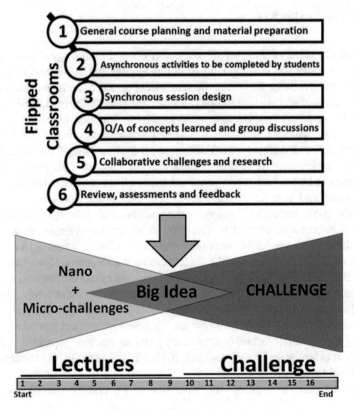

Fig. 4.1 Course structure steps for implementing FC and CBL

4.2.1 Examples of Available Digital Tools

Various technological tools are available to professors, requiring a minimum mastery to make the course practical and attractive. Professors can understand that a digital course requires digitalized material. New platforms and services are developed daily, making it challenging to be up to date, but general knowledge of some of the more popular tools could help master newer ones.

For instance, *Edpuzzle* (https://edpuzzle.com/) is a digital platform that provides a free forum for interactive video sharing. In this case, the professor can create a short video about a specific subject while adding notes, interactive questions (open-ended and multiple-choice) with instant feedback, audio clips (voiceovers), and other options. The video could expand and clarify the concepts reviewed in the synchronous session and show how some nano- and micro-challenges could be solved. Additionally, *Edpuzzle* is flexible. One could use existing videos from other video-sharing sites such as Youtube, TED talks, and Crash course, focusing on editing such media and decreasing the time required to design the activity. It is highly recommended that the duration of the interactive videos does not exceed 10 min, as the students' attention will decrease (Guo et al. 2014). In this platform, the student can instantly know their grade at the end of the activity. At the same time, *Edpuzzle* provides the professor with the necessary statistics to adapt or reinforce a specific concept based on students' answers.

Moreover, active learning techniques, such as simulation and gamification, frequently engage the students in synchronous and asynchronous sessions (Hernández-de-Menéndez et al. 2019). Simulation tools such as PhET Interactive Simulations (the University of Colorado Boulder, https://phet.colorado.edu/) help students infer concepts and laws before the synchronous sessions. Moreover, these tools aid the students in visualizing complex and abstract phenomena and interactions of different components. The students can play with different scenarios in the simulation, deepening their understanding.

Incorporating games into the synchronous sessions engages the students and motivates them to demonstrate their course knowledge. We recommend that the professors provide the students with incentives (extra credits) sometimes to foster the competitiveness of the activity. *Kahoot* (https://kahoot.com/schools-u/) is an attractive and partially free option. The professor creates visually appealing questions (multiple-choice) that the learners must answer before a pre-set time. The scoring system depends on the students' assertiveness and the timing of answers. High scores win the game and the extra credits.

4.2.2 Smart Tools: Chatbots

One of the critical features and advantages of digital tools under the *MFDM* model is that they continuously store and provide data. Armed with artificial intelligence tools, the academic team can monitor, analyze, and provide timely student feedback. In such an intelligent learning environment, the users leverage technology to mediate and adapt the learning process experienced by the students while interacting and providing guidance (hints, tips for assessments) and feedback (Iqbal et al. 2020). An example of this is the use of AI tools as conversational assistants (Chatbots). This technological tool provides an interactive medium to connect with the students through a language-based interface (Villegas-Ch et al. 2020). Chatbots replicate a human conversation and respond to the students' queries. Moreover, this conversational assistant captures and stores all the input and output information and data resulting from that interaction. A Chatbot's key component is the conversational AI engine required for the administration and understanding (processing) of natural language, pattern recognition, and output (answer to the student).

Moreover, the Chatbot AI could detect areas of opportunity such as a gap in the contents or the system's competencies and capabilities. With those opportunities known and the learning metrics, professors could train Chatbots or implement a machine learning or deep learning algorithm to increase its knowledge database and provide better answers and interactions (Rahman et al. 2017). Finally, the Chatbot instantly solves the students' queries, providing them with the information needed to

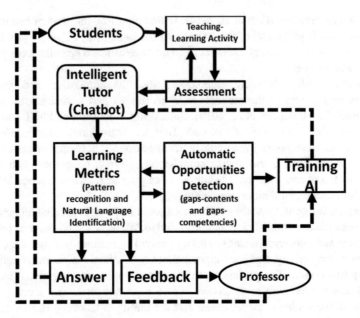

Fig. 4.2 Schematic of virtual conversation assistants utilization

solve the teaching–learning activity. Simultaneously, the professor could use a data report to adapt the course, reinforcing specific concepts or competencies, and further train the AI. Figure 4.2 presents a schematic of this process.

MFDM course design promotes the development of teaching–learning activities that encourage the use of this valuable tool. For instance, the professor can introduce the Chatbot during the synchronous session and recommend its use in a teaching–learning activity. Then, the students must complete an assessment asynchronously where some of the concepts are missing or deliberately were not introduced in the synchronous session, thus encouraging them to search for information with the tools provided (Chatbot, journal search engines, etc.). During the assessment and onwards, the Chatbot will answer the students' queries, from basic concepts that need reinforcement to the assessment-specific questions, while storing all the data and information from that interaction. From an analytical report of this data, the professors (or the AI if programmed to do so) could identify students' gaps in knowledge or predict their performance.

4.3 Methodology

The *MFDM* elements discussed above were considered to design and implement the Mechanical Vibrations course at Tecnologico de Monterrey, Campus Monterrey, during the August-December 2019, February-June 2020, and August–December

2020 semesters (approximately one year of the COVID-19 pandemic). A total of 140 engineering students were enrolled in the course, with 40 and 100 students in the 2019 and 2020 periods.

During the *Flipped Classroom* weeks (the first ten weeks), the class session structure was the following: (1) Recap, (2) Activity Concept Introduction, (3) Activity, (4) 5–10 min Break, (5) New Concept, (6) Closing Activity (Final Recap). Special care was taken to reduce the amount of time of theoretical learning without any activity. The main reason for this was to avoid student burnout. Weekly announcements were sent to the students detailing the activities and homework required for the following week. The activities introduced during the *FC* scheme rely on different technological tools such as simulations, interactive videos, and games using the platforms discussed above. Moreover, a Chatbot was designed and introduced as an early prototype for this course. The Chatbot was programmed in the Microsoft Assure platform and then incorporated into the Telegram app. Before programming the Chatbot, a previous assessment was conducted to obtain the most frequent topics and keywords the students sought and used. This database was enriched with complementary data and visual aids to help the students solve different activities and assessments.

During the *Challenge* (weeks 10–16), the students formed approximately eight five-person teams to work in several industries and institutions (John Deere, METALSA QUIMMCO, and MIT University). These institutions and companies and their respective assigned mentors defined and co-designed different real-life challenges to be solved by each team. Other mentoring sessions were carried out weekly and on-demand to solve the students' methodological and empirical questions during the challenge. The main objective was to reduce the various mechanical vibrations in the systems, equipment, and products designed by the companies/institutions.

The course quality was assessed at the end of the challenge by using and comparing: (1) a survey that evaluates the students' perception of different engineering competencies developed throughout the *MFDM* course, based on the "Engineering Criteria 2020–2021" (Table 4.1) from the Accreditation Board for Engineering and Technology (ABET) (ABET 2021); and (2) the students' challenge academic achievement.

The students' perception survey is available on-demand in Google forms. The scale used for the evaluation of each competency was: 1 = completely disagree; 2 = disagree; 3 = undefined; 4 = agree; and 5 = totally agree. A total of 140 students evaluated the course under the *MFDM* model.

For the academic achievement evaluation, ABET competencies A, B, and C were assessed during the final presentation of the challenge (the final challenge report and presentation) by an evaluating committee comprised of one academic mentor, four industrial mentors, and two teaching assistants. These competencies were chosen because they represent the students' methodological approach and understanding of a complex problem and their ability to properly communicate the solution. Table 4.2 presents the different mastery levels of the chosen ABET competencies. The survey and the achievement evaluation were compared to determine if the students' perception/satisfaction with the *MFDM* model matched their actual performance in

Table 4.1 ABET criteria used for the *MFDM* evaluation

Competency	ABET criteria 2020–2021
A	An ability to identify, formulate, and solve complex engineering problems by applying engineering, science, and mathematics principles
B	An ability to apply engineering design to produce solutions that meet specified needs with consideration of public health, safety, and welfare and global, cultural, social, environmental, and economic factors
C	An ability to communicate effectively with a range of audiences
D	An ability to recognize ethical and professional responsibilities in engineering situations and make informed judgments, which must consider the impact of engineering solutions in global, economic, environmental, and societal contexts
E	An ability to function effectively on a team whose members provide leadership, create a collaborative and inclusive environment, establish goals, plan tasks, and meet objectives
F	An ability to develop and conduct appropriate experimentation, analyze and interpret data, and use engineering judgment to draw conclusions
G	An ability to acquire and apply new knowledge as needed, using appropriate learning strategies

Table 4.2 Mastery levels for competencies a–b–c

Level of mastery	Description
1	No evidence of competency development
2	Elements are shown without argumentation and discussion (without analysis). The solution does not meet the requirements of the challenge
3	Some design methodology (backed) is shown. The solution is discussed in terms of the challenge requirements. Some calculations are backed by evidence without showing their purpose
4	Methodology and calculations are backed by evidence and purpose and are appropriately discussed. The analysis of the solution needs improvement
5	All variables, calculations, and solutions are discussed, well presented, and backed by evidence. The solution meets the specified requirements

developing competencies to solve real-world problems as presented in the Mechanical Vibrations course. Finally, the coefficient of variation was obtained for each evaluation instrument.

4.4 Evaluation of the *MFDM* Model—Results and Discussion

The implementation of the *MFDM* model highlights the different technological tools that increase the course's dynamism and the students' interactions with their peers and professor. Figure 4.3 shows the interaction between the students (questions and keywords) and the Chatbot (answers). This technology could increase students' incidence of asking questions and solving specific queries about the concepts reviewed during the synchronous sessions (especially if the use of the Chatbot is linked to an activity or an assessment). This is extremely valuable since one of the most frequent problems of any course is the psychological barriers that prevent some students from asking questions, such as shyness or fear of appearing dumb before their peers and professor, among others).

With the information collected, the professor adapted some of the courses and provided timely feedback to the students while expanding the Chatbot database. These adaptations resulted in several feedback and reinforcement sessions carried out throughout the course. These took shape as webinars and "virtual coffee talks." The students conversed with the professor to clarify their questions, solve extra problems, and learn more about applying the class theoretical concepts to real-world situations.

Fig. 4.3 Chatbot used in the mechanical vibrations course

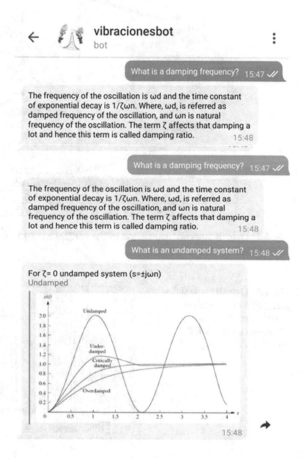

Figure 4.4 shows the average score and variability of the students' perception for each ABET criterion. Overall, the students had a good-to-excellent perception of the *MFDM* course, having a minimum score of 4.17/5. The students perceived that they had highly developed the ability to identify, formulate, and solve complex problems (competency A) and develop and conduct numerical experiments and interpret the results (competency F). Both competencies had lower variabilities than competencies C and E (effective communication and teamwork). The high variability of competencies C and E could be related to (1) scheduling problems between team members and industrial mentors, (2) misunderstandings within the team, and (3) lack of organization, integration, and interaction as a consequence of the digital medium used during the challenge.

Moreover, the above results were compared with the students' academic achievement during the real-world challenge evaluation (Fig. 4.5) for competencies A, B,

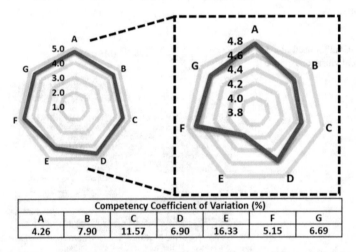

Competency Coefficient of Variation (%)						
A	B	C	D	E	F	G
4.26	7.90	11.57	6.90	16.33	5.15	6.69

Fig. 4.4 Overall students' perception of the *MFDM* model in the mechanical vibrations course using ABET criteria

Fig. 4.5 Overall students' perception of the *MFDM* model in mechanical vibrations using ABET criteria

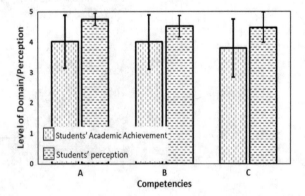

and C. The results showed that the students' academic achievement was relatively lower than their perception of competency development by 14.7%, 9.8%, and 14.5%, respectively. However, competencies A and B obtained an average mastery level above 4, while competency C represented an area of opportunity for the *MFDM* model (mastery level of 3.78).

Even though the students' academic achievement during the challenge represents relatively good results, the high variability obtained (20.4%, 21.4%, and 24% for competencies A, B, and C, respectively) could be related to different factors experienced by some teams. These factors include misinterpretation of the challenge and the industrial mentor requirements, lack of communication between the team members, academic mentor and industrial mentor, and poor presentation of the challenge results. These results highlight the importance of communication and presentation as an opportunity for the *MFDM* model, which could be solved by introducing in-person interactions when possible and increasing the number of activities in which the students are required to present their progress and results to a broader audience.

The obtained results (see Fig. 4.4) showed that involving different institutions and challenges increases the students' interest and motivates them throughout the course. Mainly, the students feel a sense of purpose: satisfaction with all the acquired knowledge and dominance of transversal skills that could be applied in different real-world engineering problems. These results were reinforced by the positive comments obtained from the students at the end of the course. Theory and knowledge without purpose will result in unmotivated and burned-out students. Another common positive comment praised the class dynamics, organization, and virtual tools used. As mentioned above, planning is key to the successful implementation of an *MFDM* course. Planning considers the activities, time distribution in synchronous sessions, and the dynamics between mentors and learners.

The *MFDM* model in the 2019–2020 Mechanical Vibrations course successfully complied with ABET's quality criteria. The students were motivated throughout the course and engaged in different activities that required various technological tools, which fostered their creativity while developing the necessary competencies to solve a real-world challenge.

The designed *MFDM* course offered the students (1) continuous, effective, and timely feedback (personal and virtual interactions); (2) attention to their emotional needs while decreasing some psychological barriers related to professor-student interactions and fostering discussions with their peers; and (3) engagement in different active learning activities and meaningful challenges. However, future work is needed regarding the impact of integrating a hybrid scheme in which part of the group receives face-to-face interactions while the other receives digital interaction only. Another future work could be incorporating multicultural and multidisciplinary teams to provide a broader point of view and enrich the proposed solutions for a real-world challenge.

4.5 Conclusions

This study developed and presented a massive Flexible Digital Masterclass (*MFDM*) model enabled by technological tools. This educational model synergistically incorporated elements of *Flipped Classrooms* (*FC*) and *Challenge-Based Learning* (*CBL*) to encourage the development of engineering competencies proscribed by *ABET* (problem-solving, critical thinking, teamwork, innovation-creativity, etc.). Course planning (including course organization, class dynamics, and active learning activities) is crucial to the model's success. The use of technological tools such as interactive videos, games, simulations, and Chatbots engages and motivates the students throughout their learning process and provides timely feedback to the student while giving the professor helpful information on how to better adapt the course. Thus, self-learning tools that provide instant feedback, such as Chatbots, can provide a medium for student interactions while diminishing some of the psychological barriers to asking questions (fear of peers, peer pressure, shyness, or introversion, for example).

The Mechanical Vibrations course was selected as a pilot study for the implementation of the *MFDM* model. This course was carried out during the COVID19 pandemic (therefore, it was tested in a 100% digital environment). The obtained results complied with the ABET criteria for a high-quality engineering course, with average scores above 4.5 out of 5 in each criterion. Specifically, the *MFDM* model promoted the competencies and transversal skills needed to solve a real-world industrial challenge. The students perceived that the knowledge acquired in the class had a meaningful purpose, thus increasing their motivation and engagement to solve a real-world challenge. Similarly, the model helped students understand the value of engineering criteria and judgment to make informed decisions during the challenge resolution.

Acknowledgements The authors acknowledge the technical support of Writing Lab, Institute for the Future of Education, Tecnologico de Monterrey, Mexico, in the production of this work.

The authors acknowledge the financial and technical support from the office of the Academic and Educational Innovation Rector at Tecnologico de Monterrey in the production of this work. The current project was funded by Tecnologico de Monterrey and Fundación FEMSA (Grant No. 0020206BB3, CAMPUSCITY Project).

References

ABET (2021) Criteria for accrediting engineering programs 2020–2021. ABET, Inc., Baltimore, MD 21201

Al-Hammouri MM, Rababah JA, Rowland ML, Tetreault AS, Aldalaykeh M (2020) Does a novel teaching approach work? A students' perspective. Nurse Educ Today 85:104229

Al-Maroof RA, Al-Emran M (2021) Research trends in flipped classroom: a systematic review. In: Studies in systems, decision and control, pp 253–275

Brew A, Saunders C (2020) Making sense of research-based learning in teacher education. Teach Teach Educ 87:102935

Crawford J et al (2020) COVID-19: 20 countries' higher education intra-period digital pedagogy responses. J Appl Learn Teach 3(1)

Gaskins WB, Johnson J, Maltbie C, Kukreti A (2015) Changing the learning environment in the college of engineering and applied science using challenge based learning. Int J Eng Pedagog 5(1):33

Goodwin B, Miller K (2013) Evidence on flipped classrooms is still coming in. Educ Leadersh 70(6):78–80

Grubic N, Badovinac S, Johri AM (2020) Student mental health in the midst of the COVID-19 pandemic: a call for further research and immediate solutions. Int J Soc Psychiatry

Guo PJ, Kim J, Rubin R (2014) How video production affects student engagement. In: Proceedings of the first ACM conference on learning @ scale conference, pp 41–50

Hernández-de-Menéndez M, Vallejo Guevara A, Tudón Martínez JC, Hernández Alcántara D, Morales-Menendez R (2019) Active learning in engineering education. A review of fundamentals, best practices and experiences. Int J Interact Des Manuf 13(3):909–922

Hodges C, Moore S, Lockee B, Trust T, Bond M (2020) The difference between emergency remote teaching and online learning. EDUCAUSE Review (Online). Available: https://er.educause.edu/articles/2020/3/the-difference-between-emergency-remote-teaching-and-online-learning

Iqbal HMN, Parra-Saldivar R, Zavala-Yoe R, Ramirez-Mendoza RA (2020) Smart educational tools and learning management systems: supportive framework. Int J Interact Des Manuf 14(4):1179–1193

Md Khambari MN (2019) Instilling innovativeness, building character, and enforcing camaraderie through interest-driven challenge-based learning approach. Res Pract Technol Enhanc Learn 14(1):19

Membrillo-Hernández J, Ramírez-Cadena MJ, Martínez-Acosta M, Cruz-Gómez E, Muñoz-Díaz E, Elizalde H (2019) Challenge based learning: the importance of world-leading companies as training partners. Int J Interact Des Manuf 13(3):1103–1113

Mohmmed AO, Khidhir BA, Nazeer A, Vijayan VJ (2020) Emergency remote teaching during Coronavirus pandemic: the current trend and future directive at Middle East College Oman. Innov Infrastruct Solut

Morales-Avalos JR, Heredia-Escorza Y (2019) The academia-industry relationship: igniting innovation in engineering schools. Int J Interact Des Manuf 13(4):1297–1312

Nichols M, Cator K, Torres M (2016) Challenge based learning guide. Digital Promise, Redwood City, CA

Ozdamli F, Asiksoy G (2016) Flipped classroom approach. World J Educ Technol 8(2):98

Pardo H, Cobo C (2020) Expandir la universidad más allá de la enseñanza remota de emergencia

Rahman AM, Al Mamun A, Islam A (2017) Programming challenges of chatbot: current and future prospective. In: 2017 IEEE region 10 humanitarian technology conference (R10-HTC), pp 75–78

Sangrà A (2020) Enseñar y aprender online: superando la distancia social. Universidad Oberta de Catalunya (Online). Available: https://www.uoc.edu/portal/es/coronavirus/docencia-emergencia/lista-webinars.html. Accessed: 17 Apr 2020

Savery JR (2006) Overview of problem-based learning: definitions and distinctions. Interdiscip J Probl Learn 1(1)

Savery JR, Duffy TM (1995) Problem-based learning: an instructional model and its constructivist framework. Educ Technol 35(5):31–38

Tudon-Martinez JC, Hernandez-Alcantara D, Rodriguez-Villalobos M, Aquines-Gutierrez O, Vivas-Lopez CA, Morales-Menendez R (2020) The effectiveness of computer-based simulations for numerical methods in engineering. Int J Interact Des Manuf 14(3):833–846

Usmeldi U, Amini R, Trisna S (2017) The development of research-based learning model with science, environment, technology, and society approaches to improve critical thinking of students. J Pendidik. IPA Indones 6(2):318

Villegas-Ch W, Arias-Navarrete A, Palacios-Pacheco X (2020) Proposal of an architecture for the integration of a chatbot with artificial intelligence in a smart campus for the improvement of learning. Sustainability 12(4):1500

Chapter 5
Design of a Novel High School Mathematics Class Through the Usability Analysis of a Robot Implementation

Germán E. Baltazar Reyes, Brenda Jiménez, Edgar Omar Lopez, Nancy Mazon, Patricia Tlalpan, and Pedro Ponce

5.1 Introduction

In Mexico, high-school-level teaching must be immediately applicable to everyday life to significantly impact society. This immediacy is facilitated by Information and Communication Technologies (ICTs) that improve teaching–learning processes in engineering education (Hernandez-de-Menendez and Morales-Menendez 2019). New technologies promote inclusiveness among students who must participate interactively in classes without being propped up by the teacher or their companions (Fang et al. 2014; Conti et al. 2020).

In most classes at the national level, teachers do not use suitable teaching materials due to a lack of creativity, time, proper training, or planning (Cituk Vela 2010).

It is essential to know how mathematics classes are developed in Mexico in the social and environmental contexts. Bazán et al. (2012) showed that students need better learning activities and assessment experiences in Mexico. The study found that the index of socio-economic and cultural status significantly and positively predicted achievement in mathematics. However, it did not change the negative correlations of

G. E. Baltazar Reyes (✉) · B. Jiménez · E. O. Lopez · P. Tlalpan · P. Ponce
Tecnologico de Monterrey, Mexico City, Mexico
e-mail: a01331329@itesm.mx

E. O. Lopez
e-mail: edlopez@tec.mx

P. Tlalpan
e-mail: prt@tec.mx

P. Ponce
e-mail: pedro.ponce@tec.mx

N. Mazon
Universidad Autónoma de México, Mexico City, Mexico
e-mail: nancymaz01@yahoo.com.mx

© The Author(s), under exclusive license to Springer Nature Singapore Pte Ltd. 2022
S. Hosseini et al. (eds.), *Technology-Enabled Innovations in Education*,
Transactions on Computer Systems and Networks,
https://doi.org/10.1007/978-981-19-3383-7_5

learning opportunities with learning mathematics. It was found that the anxiety of Mexican students toward mathematics can be reduced with adequate motivation, so the tool developed to improve learning outcomes also aimed to address the issue of motivation (Escalera-Chávez et al. 2016; Alemi et al. 2015; Ponce et al. 2019).

It is interesting to consider that technological tools help students achieve more efficient learning skills from different perspectives (Hernandez-de-Menendez and Morales-Menendez 2019). Acquiring meaningful learning, collaborative skills, and empathy within their social environments bestows students with desirable characteristics in their long-term training process. All technological tools could be of great help, but not all are effective if not used timely and moderately. Some educational scenarios that include ICT have better results than others. However, as seen in this work, it is not always possible to observe the effects of the most disruptive technologies (robotics or virtual laboratories, for example).

Educational robotics is a new teaching methodology that develops creativity, organizational skills, and collaborative work. This methodology is based on pedagogical constructivism that promotes creativity, innovation, and self-design (Coll 2000). Besides strengthening knowledge, this methodology enables students to adapt to current production processes. Incorporating robotics into the class design helps the teacher solve ponderous problems of competency development in students. The use of robotics in education sets out new activities for students to develop both disciplinary and transversal competencies.

However, it is not enough to implement the ICTs alone. It is required to evaluate and question which aspects of the class model are best implemented by the professor and the platform (Baltazar Reyes et al. 2020). According to Goodrich et al., it is essential to measure the robot's level of autonomy, its ability to exchange information, adapt, learn, and train and assess the structure of the model where the platform is being used (Goodrich et al. 2008). At the same time, it is necessary to observe the students' perception and attention as they interact with the robot (Yan et al. 2014) to evaluate the two sides of the class methodology.

This paper presents a case study of different high school math classes that offered students interactions with both the professor and an NAO robotic platform. The aim was to evaluate the students' attention span and performance and the usability of the robotic platform as a supportive educational tool for both the students and the professors.

5.2   Attention and Motivation in the Classroom

This work's main contribution was establishing a virtuous circle for the students, the robot, and teachers to create a new collaborative class environment. To improve learning, one must emphasize attention and motivation. Attention is how we actively process a fraction of enormous amounts of information that we access through the senses, our stored memories, and other cognitive processes (Sternberg et al. 2010). These processes are both conscious and unconscious.

The benefits of attention stand out, primarily when referring to conscious health processes. In addition to the overall value of attention, conscious attention serves three purposes in playing a causal role in cognition. First, it helps monitor our interactions with the environment, which allows us to be aware that we are adapting to our situation. Second, it helps to connect our past (memories) and our present (sensations) to give us a sense of continuity of experience. Such continuity may even be the basis of personal identity. Third, it makes it easier for us to monitor and plan our future actions. We can do this based on information from monitoring and connections between memories and present feelings. So, both attention and concentration are fundamental elements of all learning. The analysis of five indicators (concentration, habituation, dishabituation, distraction, and motivation) also contributes to understanding attention and the challenge of measuring it. Scientific knowledge allows us to study observable behaviors in a way that makes it possible to register and quantify them (Arnaiz Sanchez 2000) adequately. Certain conditions are desirable to obtain efficient observations (Kawulich 2005).

5.3   Use of the Nao Robot in Education

NAO robots as teaching assistants have become a popular choice in the world. The NAO robot's performance as an assistant to a language teacher at the National Central Taiwan University was evaluated during an English class (Shih et al. 2007). During the lesson, the robot and the teacher told a story to the students. The presence of the robot in the class held the students' attention for a longer time. Using the NAO as the narrator allowed the story to retain its structure with few content deviations.

Because the robot could quickly switch among its 21 programmed languages, the storytelling had fewer pronunciation, fluency, and diction errors than a Taiwanese teacher speaking English. The students were more comfortable and less shy about questioning the robot in English. In a traditional lesson, they often avoided asking questions for fear of being ridiculed for a mistake (Shih et al. 2007).

In a programming course at Nazarbayev University, Kazakhstan, the interactions with an NAO robot were evaluated during an activity that sought to teach computational logic through block programming (Diyas et al. 2016). The experiment was conducted in the presence of the teachers. During the interaction, the NAO robot provided clues and pointed out students' errors in solving a predefined challenge. The effectiveness of the robot in maintaining the interest of the students was observed. The average time they solved the presented challenge was less when the robot acted as a teacher (Diyas et al. 2016).

An analysis of the interaction with NAO during a pedagogical session was developed at the University of Sao Paulo (Tozadore et al. 2016). The investigation was a Wizard-of-Oz study to assess the level of interaction effects in a math lesson that used the NAO robot. The robot operates autonomously in the Wizard of Oz model, but the programmers control it where the test subjects cannot see them. In this way, it is possible to make the robot react to the test subjects' stimuli, and the routine can be adapted in real-time.

The students' attention is tenuous when the robot only delivers the lesson without interacting with them. While the robot's novelty and visual appeal attract the student's attention, the effect wears off after a while. This is not true when the robot interacts directly with the subjects, answers their questions, and gives them feedback. This interaction is possible thanks to the Wizard of Oz method. The students participating in the study concluded that the robot could not completely replace the human teacher's role. However, when the robot gives an interactive class, it can be a great tool to keep students' attention (Tozadore et al. 2016).

A brief review of the NAO robot's use in childcare reveals that the NAO robot repeatedly has been used in therapies for children with autism (Zheng et al. 2014; Kaboski et al. 2015; Bekele et al. 2014).

For this reason, Aldebaran Robotics launched the "ASK NAO: Autism Solution for Kids" initiative. The aim is to make the NAO robot a support tool in the special education classroom. The project offers unique applications for the NAO robot that promote social and learning skills in children with special needs. The applications are based on gaming. Through different activities, the application instills skills such as understanding emotions, communication, following directions, and others (Miskam et al. 2013; Ismail et al. 2012).

A teacher support network is also provided, allowing them to design a teaching program for each student, record individual progress, and manage learning sessions. The platform facilitates contact among teachers, parents, and specialists. It incorporates an interactive forum where users worldwide can exchange information and experiences to enhance learning.

Experiments with this platform have been conducted at the University of Notre Dame, Vanderbilt University, and the University of Connecticut (Villano et al. 2011; Shamsuddin et al. 2012).

5.4   Evaluation of Class Perception

According to Kember and Wong, it is possible to classify how students feel about their professors' class methodology and performance on four different scales (Kember and Wong 2000). As seen in Fig. 5.1, this classification compares the teaching process of the professors and the student's learning qualities. Depending on the situation, the professor needs to adjust the class model to gain more student attention. Nevertheless, it is still challenging to customize a class that meets all needs of each student. It was opted to construct the class model to attend to the larger group of students as a whole because of this problem.

Since every class group is different, it is not easy to establish a proper assessment to determine if the applied class methodology was the best option. It is then necessary to evaluate the class and professor's performance through a questionnaire that measures

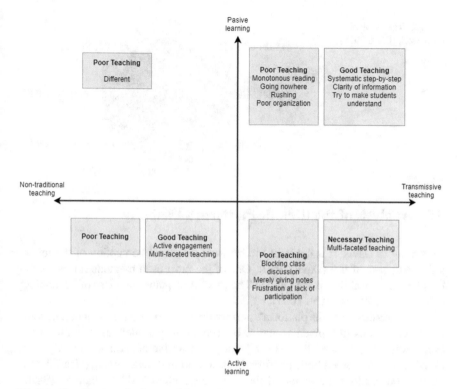

Fig. 5.1 Classification of a class model according to the students' and professors' profiles (Kember and Wong 2000)

the student's perception of the class. One of the most novel ways of assessing such performances is through a gamified evaluation (Baltazar Reyes et al. 2020).

5.5   The Octalysis Framework

"Gamification" refers to using design elements and characteristics of games in non-game contexts (Deterding et al. 2011). This methodology aims to increase users' activity, interaction, and quality of work (Hamari 2013) through the accumulation of points, leaderships, and badges (Hamari and Eranti 2011). Following this proposal, Chou developed a framework with eight different aspects to evaluate the implementation of a gamified experience in a given project. This framework is known as the "Octalysis framework" (Chou 2015). Figure 5.2 shows the eight areas of gamification assessed in this framework, assigning a positive or negative value to each experience. A better description of each area and how it is measured is shown in Chou (2015). Combining the two conceptions of Figs. 5.1 and 5.2 makes it possible to evaluate the implementation of a robotic platform as a novel, gamified student experience.

Fig. 5.2 The octalysis
framework (Chou 2015)

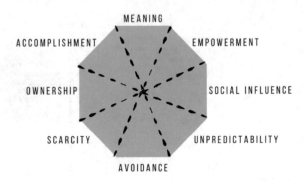

5.6 Analysis of the Robotic Platform's Usability

According to Davis, it is necessary to measure the users' perception of the robot's utility and ease of use (Davis 1989). One of the most used methods for evaluating the platform's usability is the Unified Theory of Acceptance and Use of Technology (UTAUT) (Venkatesh et al. 2003).

This study evaluates the platform's performance, effort, social influence, and facilitating conditions in a given scenario. Heerink et al. provided an example of this evaluation. They divided the UTAUT study into twelve constructs to analyze the users' acceptance of a robotic platform in an educational environment (Heerink et al. 2009). The results were validated through the Cronbach's Alpha method (Santos 1999; Serholt 2018) to measure the reproductivity of the experiment. This measurement is shown in Eq. (5.1), where K represents the number of items per construct, $\sigma^2 y_i$ the variance of item i for the sample, and $\sigma^2 x$ the variance of the whole test. For this study case, an acceptable Cronbach's Alpha value will be the same or greater than 0.7.

$$\alpha = \frac{K}{K-1}\left(1 - \frac{\sum_{i=1}^{K}\sigma^2 y_i}{\sigma^2 x}\right) \tag{5.1}$$

5.7 Methodology

This proposal consisted of a class conducted by an NAO robot and a mathematics teacher, following a script written by the high school teaching team. The robotic platform's explanations and topics followed the same thematic guide used in the junior high school session plan (Lopez Caudana et al. 2019).

The teachers who taught the subject were involved in the entire investigation process, working in their classrooms. They participated in designing the research and implementing the proposed methodology of this project. The study indicators selected for both classes were the students' attention span (analyzed through a behavioral observation scale), their attitudes toward mathematics, their learning capabilities, the usability of the robotic platform, and the general class perception (Baltazar Reyes et al. 2020). See reference (Baltazar Reyes et al. 2020) to know the complete details of every questionnaire.

The participating teachers designed the classes to be observed; they discussed with the research team how the robotic platform could support the teaching of topics during the classes.

Two professors collaborated during the experimental sessions, with a total of five different groups (classes). Two experimental learning blocks were designed based on the classes each professor had. The first professor had three classes, one for high-performance students (GARA) and two for regular students. The GARA group and a regular class were used as control (not interacting with the robot). Only two regular classes participated with the second professor; one interacted with the robot (experimental group), and the other did not (control group).

The student population characteristics were representative of all students of this grade level. Although the school type was particular, the population adequately represented the universe for these types of students. Attention to the control and experimental groups was as equivalent as possible. Both were given a first test (pre-test) on the topics to be reviewed. The same test was applied at the end of the intervention (post-test) to compare the students' learning under both conditions.

Psychology students observed the classes following the observation protocols used in Baltazar Reyes et al. (2020). The observers were familiar with the professors' information about each student's tough subjects and performance to annotate these in their corresponding protocols.

At the end of the intervention, the examination (post-test) and instrument to measure attitude toward mathematics were applied to find differences in both groups.

The robotic sessions occupied two of the sixteen weeks of the course's semester, having one class of 50 min every day in each group. Six sessions occurred during this time. Each group had the same syllabus, explanations, exercises, and evaluations during the semester, regardless of using the robotic platform or not. Depending on the session's day, each group had to answer a pre-test of the topic, theoretical explanations, and a final exercise.

After every topic was explained, the students were challenged with real-life situations and collaborative dynamics in each activity. In addition to the pre and post-surveys given to the students to quantitatively measure their perceptions of the class and robotic platform, a qualitative analysis was conducted each session on the students' psychological and corporal behavior. Figure 5.3 shows the class methodology's general structure based on the three days of interactions when the robot went to classes; this model was equal in all the classes. Since this proposal was an experimental one during a regular class semester, the school's directors only allowed three testing sessions to prevent an undesired learning rate and platform implementation throughout the whole semester.

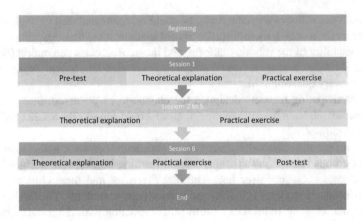

Fig. 5.3 Experimental sessions planning

5.8 Analysis of Results

Figures 5.4 and 5.5 show the relative percentages of the different behaviors of the observation scale dimensions during a class session (concentration, habituation, dishabituation, distraction, and motivation). The percentage was used because the groups were not equivalent in the number of students and total frequency of behaviors. The percentages equalized the analysis.

The most concurrent dimensions among all groups were concentration and motivation. However, there was also some increase in these dimensions comparing the teachers' control and experimental classes. Table 5.1 compares the exam grades obtained in both experimental and control groups.

A one-factor ANOVA was performed (experimental condition) to determine if there were differences between the groups. It was found that the experimental group

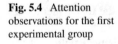

Fig. 5.4 Attention observations for the first experimental group

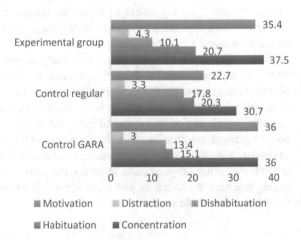

Fig. 5.5 Attention observations for the second experimental group

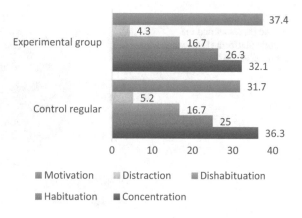

Table 5.1 Mean exam grades

	1st partial	2nd partial	Final exam
Control GARA	80.88	87.61	84.25
Control Prof. 1	80.61	83.80	81.89
Experimental Prof. 1	81.15	90.04	85.59
Control Prof. 2	83.12	75.25	79.19
Experimental Prof. 2	86.00	81.57	83.79

of Teacher 1 had significantly higher average grades in mathematics than the control group of Teacher 2 ($F = 2283$), $p = 0.063$; post hoc DMS $= 0.039$). The interpretation of the difference between the groups is complicated.

Although the Anova was just a specific factor (a group of participants who already included the condition and teacher), we cannot correctly speak of a combination of factors (such as the experimental condition and the teacher). There is the possibility that both the use of the robotic platform and Teacher 1's style resulted in more benefits in mathematics than Teacher 2's class without the platform.

After combining the usability and gamification questionnaires results, a general diagram was developed to determine the best areas of the class methodology planning where the robotic platform could perform better while leaving the social interactions and guidance to the professor. This partition is seen in Fig. 5.6, while the complete description of each test is given in Baltazar Reyes et al. (2020).

When comparing the general results of the traditional groups with the experimental ones, it can be seen that the robotic platform is helpful for the improvement of interactions with the students. Furthermore, when comparing the test results and the students' opinions, we conclude that it is preferable to use the platform in fewer and more specific sessions. The roles of the teacher and the robotic platform are relevant. Each dimension must be explored to generate a better class methodology that could help improve the perception of the class by other groups, considering the same dimensions as above.

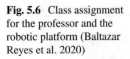

Fig. 5.6 Class assignment for the professor and the robotic platform (Baltazar Reyes et al. 2020)

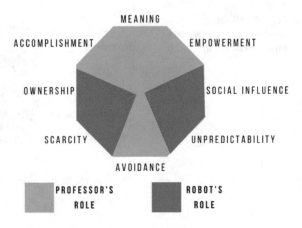

Several relevant considerations guide the development and use of this tool in different scenarios.

As already mentioned, mathematics was chosen because it is a subject with a high failure rate. However, a review of the robots' routines and interactions shows that it is relatively easy to employ them in other disciplines, such as physics or chemistry. Even the students mentioned that the robot could support language topics or subjects dissimilar to engineering and make them more engaging.

On the other hand, taking this platform to a more significant number of students highlights the need to have students who can help with the robots' programming. Precisely, in our project, the support of senior-year students turned out to be beneficial in two ways: (a) the students who programmed the robot benefited by developing programming skills in their engineering training, (b) the students who had the robot in their classes found it stimulated their learning. We recommend creating a team of students, coordinated by a lead teacher who is influential in various subjects to increase the intervention's impact.

5.9 Conclusions

Even though the numerical results were not highly significant when comparing the control and experimental groups, there was an improvement in the robot's classes, but we cannot claim the robot was the main trigger. However, the qualitative results were very relevant, mainly because the professors (in their own words) found the robot to be significant support in giving the class, a result that we did not anticipate.

We observed that students are the protagonists in their learning. The technological platform allows a constructive dialogue between student and teacher, promoting reflection on the contents reviewed in each session and the robot's visit. Similarly, in each class design, the teachers included activities making the student responsible for their learning. In future scenarios, we intend that the robots and their interactions with students will develop competencies in innovation and efficient collaboration through challenging and creative activities. We emphasize that this robotic platform's use is justified as long as a group of teachers commits to using this disruptive and supportive tool. It is useless to have an expensive robotic tool if the teacher is not convinced that meaningful and efficient learning will be achieved with greater involvement on their part.

References

Alemi M, Meghdari A, Ghazisaedy M (2015) The impact of social robotics on L2 learners anxiety and attitude in english vocabulary acquisition. Int J Soc Robot 7(4):523–535

Arnaiz Sanchez P (2000) Guia para la observacion de los parametros psicomotores. Rev Interuniv Form Del Profr 37:6385

Baltazar Reyes GE, López E, Ponce P, Mazón N (2020) Role assignment analysis of an assistive robotic platform in a high school mathematics class, through a gamification and usability evaluation. Int J Soc Robot 1–16

Bazán A, Backhoff E, Turullols R (2017) Oportunidades, experiencias y aprendizajes de las matemáticas: México en PISA 2012. REICE. Revista Electrónica Iberoamericana sobre Calidad, Eficacia y Cambio en Educación

Bekele E, Crittendon JA, Swanson A, Sarkar N, Warren ZE (2014) Pilot clinical application of an adaptive robotic system for young children with autism. Autism 18(5):598–608

Chou YK (2015) Actionable gamification. Beyond points, badges, and leaderboards

Cituk Vela DM (2010) Mexico y las TIC en la educación Basica Red Escolar, Rev. e-formadores, p 110

Coll C (2000) Constructivismo e intervención educativa. Barbera, Elena. El constructivismo en la práctica. Caracas: Laboratorio educativo, 157p, 11–32

Conti D, Cirasa C, Di Nuovo S, Di Nuovo A (2020) "Robot, tell me a tale!": a social robot as a tool for teachers in kindergarten. Interact Stud 21(2):220–242

Davis FD (1989) Perceived usefulness, perceived ease of use, and user acceptance of information technology. MIS Quarterly 319–340

Deterding S, Dixon D, Khaled R, Nacke L (2011) From game design elements to gamefulness: defining gamification. In: Proceedings of the 15th international academic MindTrek conference: envisioning future media environments. ACM, pp 9–15

Diyas Y, Brakk D, Aimambetov Y, Sandygulova A (2016) Evaluating peer versus teacher robot within an educational scenario of programming learning. In: 11th ACM/IEEE international conference on human-robot interaction (HRI), Christchurch, pp 425–426

Escalera-Chávez ME, Moreno-García E, García-Santillán A, Rojas-Kramer CA (2016) Factors that promote anxiety toward math in high school students. Eurasia J Math Sci Technol Educ 13(1):189–199

Fang HC, Ong SK, Nee AYC (2014) A novel augmented reality-based interface for robot path planning. Int J Interact Des Manuf 8:33–42. https://doi.org/10.1007/s12008-013-0191-2

Goodrich MA, Schultz AC et al (2008) Human-robot interaction: a survey. Foundations Trends® in Human-Comput Interaction 1(3):203–275

Hamari J (2013) Transforming homo economicus into homo ludens: a field experiment on gamification in a utilitarian peer-to-peer trading service. Electron Commer Res Appl 12(4):236–245

Hamari J, Eranti V (2011) Framework for designing and evaluating game achievements. In: Digra conference. Citeseer

Heerink M, Krose B, Evers V, Wielinga B (2009) Measuring acceptance of an assistive social robot: a suggested toolkit. In: RO-MAN 2009—the 18th IEEE international symposium on robot and human interactive communication. IEEE, pp 528–533

Hernandez-de-Menendez M, Morales-Menendez R (2019) Technological innovations and practices in engineering education: a review. Int J Interact Des Manuf 13:713–728. https://doi.org/10.1007/s12008-019-00550-1

Ismail LI, Shamsudin S, Yussof H, Hanapiah FA, Zahari NI (2012) A robot-based intervention program for autistic children with humanoid robot NAO: initial response in stereotyped behavior. Proc Eng 41:1441–1447

Kaboski JR, Diehl JJ, Beriont J, Crowell CR, Villano M, Wier K, Tang K (2015) Brief report: a pilot summer robotics camp to reduce social anxiety and improve social/vocational skills in adolescents with ASD. J Autism Dev Disord 45(12):3862–3869

Kawulich BB (2005) Participant observation as a data collection method. Forum Qual Sozialforsch/Forum Qual Soc Res 6(2) Qual Inq Res Arch Reuse

Kember D, Wong A (2000) Implications for evaluation from a study of students' perceptions of good and poor teaching. High Educ 40(1):69–97

Lopez Caudana EO, Baltazar Reyes GE, Acevedo RG, Ponce P, Mazon N, Hernandez JM (2019) Robotics: implementation of a robotic assistive platform in a mathematics high school class. In: IEEE 28th international symposium on industrial electronics (ISIE), Vancouver, BC, Canada, pp 1589–1594. https://doi.org/10.1109/ISIE.2019.8781520

Miskam MA, Hamid MAC, Yussof H, Shamsuddin S, Malik NA, Basir SN (2013) Study on social interaction between children with autism and humanoid robot NAO. In: Applied mechanics and materials, vol 393. Trans Tech Publications Ltd, pp 573–578

Ponce P, Molina A, Caudana EOL, Baltazar Reyes GE (2019) Improving education in developing countries using robotic platforms. Int J Interact Des Manuf 13:1401–1422. https://doi.org/10.1007/s12008-019-00576-5

Santos JRA (1999) Cronbach's alpha: a tool for assessing the reliability of scales. J Ext 37(2):1–5

Serholt S (2018) Breakdowns in children's interactions with a robotic tutor: a longitudinal study. Comput Hum Behav 81:250–264

Shamsuddin S, Yussof H, Ismail LI, Mohamed S, Hanapiah FA, Zahari NI (2012) Initial response in HRI-a case study on evaluation of a child with autism spectrum disorders interacting with a humanoid robot Nao. Proc Eng 41:1448–1455

Shih CF, Chang CW, Chen GD (2007) Robot as a storytelling partner in the english classroom—preliminary discussion. In: Seventh IEEE international conference on advanced learning technologies (ICALT 2007), Niigata, pp 678–682

Sternberg RJ, Salinas MEO, Julio ER, Ponce LR (2010) Psicologia cognoscitiva 5edicion. Cengage Learning

Tozadore DC, Pinto AH, Romero RA (2016) Variation in a humanoid robot behavior to analyze interaction quality in pedagogical sessions with children. In: Robotics symposium and IV Brazilian robotics symposium (LARS/SBR), 2016 XIII Latin American. IEEE, pp 133–138

Venkatesh V, Morris MG, Davis GB, Davis FD (2003) User acceptance of information technology: toward a unified view. MIS Quarterly 425–478

Villano M, Crowell CR, Wier K, Tang K, Thomas B, Shea N, Diehl JJ (2011) DOMER: a wizard of Oz interface for using interactive robots to scaffold social skills for children with autism spectrum disorders. In: 2011 6th ACM/IEEE international conference on human-robot interaction (HRI). IEEE, pp 279–280

Yan H, Ang MH, Poo AN (2014) A survey on perception methods for human-robot interaction in social robots. Int J Soc Robot 6(1):85–119

Zheng Z, Das S, Young EM, Swanson A, Warren Z, Sarkar N (2014) Autonomous robot-mediated imitation learning for children with autism. In: 2014 IEEE international conference on robotics and automation (ICRA). IEEE, pp 2707–2712

Chapter 6
Future Education for Harnessing Electrical Energy Resources Using Real-Time Simulation

Juan R. Lopez, Pedro Ponce, and Arturo Molina

6.1 Introduction

The energy and the electrical sector is currently dealing with the technical and environmental challenges of increasing electrical generation efficiency, minimizing the overall greenhouse gases produced in this sector, diversifying electrical power generation, and optimizing the distribution of costly assets. Moreover, due to the subordinate topology of grid components, one of the principal issues of the grid is domino-effect failures. These challenges cannot be resolved effectively within the current electrical grid model (Farhangi 2010). Thus, they have motivated the energy and electrical sector to implement the new grid model known as the smart grid. This new grid is characterized by enabling the user to control a two-way flow of energy, information, and communication, a characteristic of an automated, advanced distributed energy delivery network.

In the conventional electrical network, the power only flows in a single direction from the central or distributed generators to many customers or users. However, smart grids rely on implementing new information technologies to create communication strategies that enhance power transmission efficiency and resolve failures or grid disruptive events agilely. In other words, they connect the main stages in the power distribution plan using information technologies to improve the corrective action

J. R. Lopez (✉) · P. Ponce · A. Molina
School of Engineering and Sciences, Tecnologico de Monterrey , 14380 Mexico City, Tlalpan, Mexico
e-mail: robertolo@tec.mx

P. Ponce
e-mail: pedro.ponce@tec.mx

A. Molina
e-mail: armolina@tec.mx

© The Author(s), under exclusive license to Springer Nature Singapore Pte Ltd. 2022   79
S. Hosseini et al. (eds.), *Technology-Enabled Innovations in Education*,
Transactions on Computer Systems and Networks,
https://doi.org/10.1007/978-981-19-3383-7_6

responses to failures on any grid stage, such as the power generation, transmission, distribution, and consumption stages of the current electrical grid (Fang et al. 2012).

To take full advantage of the benefits provided by the Smart grid, designers must equip the new grids to reduce the impact of particular threats. These are classified as technological and socioeconomic. The socioeconomic challenges encompass high capital investment, end-user acceptance, maintenance costs, end-user privacy, cyber-security, and regulatory aspects (Bigerna et al. 2015). The technical aspects include the lack of an adequate communication infrastructure, the need to strengthen network security, reliable data management, efficient energy storage systems, stability of the distribution systems, and communication enhancements (Bari et al. 2014). Moreover, a pressing issue is the lack of an expert workforce trained explicitly for the Smart Grid. It is known that the majority of the electrical power industry workforce will be retiring in the next years (Collaborative 2009), thus, spawning the urgent need to develop and train future engineers in the interdisciplinary technical fields involved in the Smart Grid paradigm.

Figure 6.1 is a diagram of the technical fields proposed by Kezunovic (2010) that must be covered and comprehended by students in a smart grid engineering course. Sauer (2010) also remarks on the changes in traditional coursework that need to be made for Smart Grid construction. According to Sauer, electromagnetics, circuits, electronic devices, signal systems, transmission lines, and senior capstone design are core courses needed in the power engineering curricula.

Also, incorporating computer engineering topics is crucial for the power engineering coursework. These topics include communications, data management, control, optimization, signal processing, and numerical methods. Given the complexity of the smart grid paradigm and its challenges, the need for an integrative

Fig. 6.1 Integrative approach to smart grid engineering

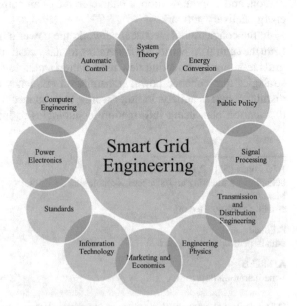

strategy for its correct design and operation is critical. Therefore, universities must consider combining several topics and technologies to teach the smart grid model successfully. Smart grid education benefits greatly from adopting simulation technologies that allow the student to understand the actual behavior of a smart grid system's response to any technical challenges, especially in control and communication. Commonly, traditional simulation technologies are conducted in a finite time frame with specific stimulation parameters that perform differently from each other. These simulation techniques are a good approximation of a real system; however, they do not guarantee the resultant behavior in a real-life scenario. Therefore, the student may have an atomistic understanding of a given topic.

Real-time simulation tools (RTST) can improve students' learning experience in a complex system such as the Smart Grid, providing a holistic understanding of a simulated system's behavior against any disturbances. RTST operate in a specific time frame in which all computational tasks must be performed so that the real-life behavior of the system can be guaranteed. Since the smart grid is a complex system with multiple inputs and outputs that may depend on each other, it is crucial to validate that the system operates within the required computational time frame to avoid any failures caused by incomplete computational tasks. Commonly, RTST is the last step in validating a designed controller or monitoring system, shortening the time gap between a conceptual idea and a product. Overall, the incorporation of RTST can redefine how smart grid courses are taught.

6.2   How Has the Smart Grid Been Taught?

As described before, there is a growing need for a qualified workforce with the technical capabilities, attributes, and educational background to confront the new grid paradigm topology (Collaborative 2009). However, the number of fields involved in the Smart Grid concept is too high to cover a single profile. Thus, educational institutions that offer Smart Grid courses require pinpointing the most relevant areas in the various engineering fields, understanding the challenges, and addressing them with correct teaching methodologies and courses. In the last ten years, several educational institutions have instituted or restructured electrical and computer engineering courses to counteract the lack of specialized engineers in smart grid infrastructures (Yardley et al. 2014). For instance, Srivastava et al. (2017) present their experience designing and teaching a smart grid cyber-infrastructure course. That course did not intend that the students become experts in the field. Instead, it was structured so that the student could understand the cyber-physical structure of the smart grid and its constraints to be able to arrive at reliable technical solutions.

Moreover, Bayram (2018) shows his experience by teaching a smart grid power course to a class comprised of graduates from different educational backgrounds like electrical, mechanical, chemical, petroleum, and materials engineering. The course tries to show the different disciplines that support the power grids and pulls together various perspectives within sustainability. On the other hand, Bell et al.

(2012) show the importance of the collaboration between industry and universities to attract, hire, and properly train students in electrical power engineering. This has led to the establishment of the Power Academy, which aims to draw future college students into electrical engineering programs and graduates into the electrical power industry. The program has had a positive response from students because they receive industrial work experience with the sponsor companies supporting and contributing to the Power Academy.

The importance of industry interaction in smart grid courses has also been noticed by Ahmed El- tom et al. (2018), who implemented a Smart Distribution System course lectured by industry professionals, with research projects endorsed by the industry, allowing the students to obtain real-world learning. The same study highlights the relevance of having some degree of flexibility in the course content topics.

Another case by Srinivasan (2016) is a course focused on introducing the concept of modern electrical energy systems and sustainable energy sources and presenting the smart grid concept. Within the course, different strategies are implemented to motivate students' interest and facilitate comprehension. Those strategies involve laboratory experiments, case studies, group projects, and industry lectures. These methods have proven to successfully engage the students in active learning by aligning the course content with the real world.

Finally, Soriano and Molina (2019) presents a virtual laboratory designed on the principles of co-simulation, co-modeling, and co-designing to specialized engineers in various smart grid fields. The work introduces a new framework including the previously mentioned strategies to provide an instrument that accelerates the design of solutions. Overall, and according to Molina et al. (2019), Smart Grid education can be achieved by developing different course methodologies, each with a different level of specialization according to the interest of the student: (i) basic level: general concepts related to energy and power are introduced; (ii) application level: practical skills are taught; and (iii) advanced level: specialization in Smart Grid technology. The latter should motivate universities to review and upgrade their laboratories to accommodate modern grid concepts introduced by the Smart Grid paradigms.

6.2.1 Physical Laboratories

Developing laboratories or testbeds to study smart grid technology focusing on power systems has had different approaches. For example, the College of New Jersey (Deese 2015) developed a reconfigurable six-bus, three-phase power system. The system was formed by induction motors, synchronous generators, transmission lines, transformers, constant loads, renewable-source energy emulators, energy storage devices, converters, power inverters, and remote measurement and control hardware. All those devices were arranged to simulate different stages of a power distribution system. Other laboratories have approached and focused on microgrids for further research in smart grid technologies. An example of this was developed in Washington State

University (Lu et al. 2010), where its testbed consisted basically of an intelligent power switch, power supply for conventional and renewable sources, loads, and a power meter. The information flow occurred through a wireless mesh network.

Since cybersecurity is a major topic in smart grid engineering, other institutions have developed Smart grid testbeds to conduct research and studies of possible cyber-attacks on the grid infrastructure. One example is presented by Annor-Asante and Pranggono (2018), in which a low-cost testbed was developed to study basic cyber-attacks like a denial-of-service attack. This same work mentions the high investment necessary to acquire a smart grid laboratory and the importance of developing low-cost laboratories. Likewise, Navarro et al. (2014) points out the benefit of studying cybersecurity as an educational topic in smart grid systems, primarily concerning the protection of the Supervisory Control and Data Acquisition (SCADA) interfaces.

While the literature covers a great variety of physical smart grid laboratories, the complexity of the paradigm has provoked various ways to conduct experiments and research about power systems. A clear example is the case of Drexel University (Deese et al. 2015), where simulation modules are used to analyze power distribution systems; Drexel seeks to enable a remote physical laboratory for experimentation. These alternatives are known as co-simulation and remote laboratories.

6.2.2   Co-simulation Laboratories

A coupled simulation (or co-simulation) is an approach where more than one simulation tool is used to model a system and design it for later coupling. The main reason for applying the co-simulation of a complex system is to study each of its elements in an adequate simulation package. Co-simulation might be preferred because there is no laboratory or one too expensive. The University of Applied Sciences of Technikum Wien (Vienna) expounded on a co-simulation platform comprised of various simulation tools and software to depict the behavior of the power distribution network, grid components, communication network, automation, and control system of a smart grid system (Strasser et al. 1997).

6.2.3   Real-Time Simulation Laboratory

A Smart Grid laboratory equipped with real-time simulation capabilities is a significant upgrade from a traditional laboratory facility. It focuses on developing engineers for the future workforce of Microgrids and Smart Grids. These areas benefit tremendously from this particular simulation technology. Using real-time simulation to attain microgrid and smart grid technologies is extensively reviewed in the literature (Strasser et al. 1997; Hannan et al. 2015). The main advantages of a real-time simulation include reducing the risks of actual implementations and diminishing the costs of extensive testing (Ibarra et al. 2017). Thus, this simulation technology becomes ideal for educational purposes and research-oriented studies.

The real-time technology is suitable for tackling the technical issues surrounding application areas such as control techniques, communication, distributed generation integration, grid-state estimation, grid automation, protection, and high-level field-oriented applications for microgrids and smart grid technologies (Dufour and Be´langer 2013). This would indicate that a well-equipped real-time laboratory can significantly impact research and academic projects that resolve the aforementioned challenges while accelerating the timeline between a laboratory operation and a field-oriented installation.

Merabet et al. (2017), for instance, presents the design and development of a stand-alone microgrid that uses renewable sources of energy such as wind and photovoltaic energy and storage energy systems. The energy from these resources is managed with a real-time control environment that uses control algorithms and reconfigurable power electronic converters to analyze the microgrid performance.

Aside from these benefits, RTST open the possibilities for other simulation strategies that can benefit the learning process of hardware manipulation and power applications. RTST can take the co-simulation concept and apply it so that a controller or communication protocol is verified in both systems, i.e., the plant and the control unit, and the Distributed Generation Units (DGUs) and Microgrid Central Controller (MGCC), respectively. Other simulation strategies derived from RTST are discussed in a following section of this work.

6.2.4 Remote Laboratories

Lately, universities worldwide have been developing remote laboratories to be shared among research institutions and other universities. Remote laboratories allow on-campus and off-campus students and teaching staff to use these resources at their convenience. Remote laboratories facilitate experimentation. The students can access them at any time to conduct exercises and analyze the systems' behaviors when they need to thoroughly understand the topic they have been studying. For instance, the University of South Australia has designed and constructed a smart grid laboratory with characteristics required for power storage of both conventional and renewable energy sources, including direct and alternate current loads. Those physical elements are integrated into a SCADA Server and then into a Web Server to enable remote access to the system (Nedic and Nafalski 2015).

Another example of a remote laboratory is the one developed by the Indian Institute of Technology, where an Eolic Generation System and a Photovoltaic System are controlled through a remote server and an interface developed in LabVIEW for use in three different modes. The first one allows the energy generated by the Eolic and photovoltaic system to be used directly on the grid; the second allows the energy generated to be stored in batteries for later use; and the third emulates the behavior

Table 6.1 Advantages and disadvantages of teaching platforms

Teaching platform	Advantages	Disadvantages
Physical laboratory	"Realistic" data Work with actual equipment (limited) Collaborative work	High investment Requires supervision Limited flexibility
Co-simulation laboratory	"Realistic" data High simulation flexibility	No supervision Not ideal for complex systems Limited to software
Real-time laboratory	Real-behavior data Collaborative work High simulation flexibility	High investment Requires supervision Steep learning curve
Remote laboratories	"Realistic" data Easy access Location convenient	No supervision Depends on a stable, good connection Pre-defined systems

of the generation systems through software (Ram et al. 2018). Finally, South West-phalia University in Soest, Germany, proposes the idea of using a remote laboratory set-up for an integrated hybrid power system and a cloud computing platform for data and computation. The system is comprised of a wind turbine, solar panel, data tracking, and control components (Kolhe and Bitzer 2015).

From this review of the literature, it can be seen that universities have focused more on developing students' skills through smart grid studies and engaging them with industry activities, multidisciplinary teams, and case studies. Moreover, various laboratory technologies and approaches have been created or developed to research the smart grid paradigm. Some of the advantages and disadvantages of each laboratory approach are found in Table 6.1.

6.3   Education on Real-Time Simulation Tools

Commonly, computer-based simulation is one of the first simulation methods an engineering student faces during their college years. Computer-based simulation depends on the computational power at hand and the accuracy and complexity of the simulated model. Although this simulation technology has been used efficiently, new simulation technologies have arisen in the past decades, featuring enhanced simulation capabilities and more reliable results that can be easily translated to a real-field operation. This simulation technology is commonly referred to as real-time simulation. Universities are starting to include this technology as part of their engineering curricula, recognizing the advantages this technology brings to the institution from an academic perspective to prepare the future workforce for the Smart Grid industry (Molina et al. 2019).

Real-time simulations are fixed-step, executed precisely at certain times; their accuracy depends on the time length of each step to obtain the desired result. To

Fig. 6.2 Real-time
simulation principle

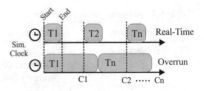

achieve Real-time simulation, the obtained outputs of a given number of tasks must occur before the next time step. If a specific task takes longer to compute its results than the established simulation time step, the simulation is considered erroneous; generally, this is denominated as an overrun fault. Figure 6.2 illustrates how a real-time execution is carried out as the overrun fault at a step time C_n.

A real-time simulation is a tool that can be used in many engineering fields. As already mentioned, Smart Grid laboratories benefit from this type of simulation technology since it can be used to simulate communication, control, and high-power level systems without compromising the integrity of actual equipment. RTST can be categorized according to their configuration in four main simulation strategies: (i) Rapid Control Prototyping (RCP): This strategy allows the student to tune a controller on the fly, appreciating the controller effect over the simulated plant; it is a quick iterative test of a given control strategy; (ii) Hardware-in-the-Loop (HIL): this strategy employs an external device to test and validate the proposed solutions. Here, the student can appreciate the real-life behavior of the proposed solution; (iii) Power Hardware-in-the-Loop (P-HIL): this strategy requires the use of a power interface and real hardware, familiarizing the future engineer with a field-oriented application; (iv) Real-time Co-simulation: in this case, more than two simulation tools can be connected to exchange data through compatible I/O ports, facilitating the validation of a more complex system (Soriano and Molina 2019).

Although some of the strategies mentioned above are directed to localized challenges in specific areas, there is no doubt that the evolution of simulation systems highly depends on the availability of more capable computing technologies. It is essential to comprehend that Smart Grid challenges can be localized or enclose a wide variety of systems. Therefore, one must clarify the limits and user preference for each simulation strategy derived from RTST, especially since the initial investment cost of RTST can be significant. This means that universities need to verify how the equipment going to be used and the preferred simulation strategy for a given topic or laboratory lecture.

One approach that can be used as a guideline in real-time laboratories is the V-diagram employed in project management-related areas (see Fig. 6.3). This diagram helps build specialized courses on smart grid applications such as control and communication from the design stage, passing through the prototyping process, and arriving at the technology transfer stage. The different marks in the V diagram are the following: (i) Conceptual Proposal: in this stage, t the course should focus on delimiting the problem at hand to determine whether the proposed ideas can be supported with the available resources; (ii) Design: here, flow diagrams can be used to sketch the connection from the problem to the solution in an organized fashion; (iii) Offline

Fig. 6.3 V-Diagram of RTST process

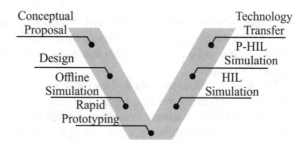

Simulation: this stage requires classical simulation methods to achieve the proof-of-concept and make early modifications; (iv) Rapid Prototyping: real-time simulation computers begin a quick proof and timing of the proposed solution in a "real" scenario; (v) HIL Simulation: here, a dynamic consistency is achieved between the proposed solution and the problem at hand; (vi) P-HIL: real-time simulation involving actual power transfer between the simulated system and the hardware being tested; and (vii) Technology transfer: at these stage, the proposed solution presents dynamic consistency under real-life operating conditions.

The above schematic shows how a Smart Grid course can be structured to enhance the learning process behind the application of RTST in the Smart Grid paradigm. However, this raises how educators can develop materials or tools that fulfill and follow the V-diagram path to provide the skills that would enable the students to transform the Smart Grid idea into a reality. In 1956, Benjamin Bloom conceived a taxonomy to explain how learning occurs in the cognitive domain. This taxonomy can be represented through a schematic, as illustrated in Fig. 6.4. Later in 2001, a revision of Bloom's Taxonomy was published under A Taxonomy for Teaching, Learning, and Assessment (Krathwohl 2002).

The revised taxonomy proposes using action words or verbs instead of nouns to tag the categories to describe the different taxonomy levels more clearly. Aside from the label change in each level, the most notable change is that the top levels were swapped concerning the first version. The evaluation stage is moved lower in the synthesis level, and the highest element becomes "creating." The hierarchical

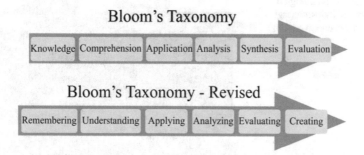

Fig. 6.4 Bloom's taxonomy

taxonomy structure outlines the levels of awareness from the most basic at the beginning of the schematic to the deepest at the end (Fig. 6.4). These attributes allow the schematic to be used as a reference for creating assessments, lesson plans, or curriculum maps.

Heydt et al. (2009) remarks that for the design and implementation of alternative solutions required by the smart grid, the student needs to have, at minimum, the studies that lead to a master's degree. Considering this, one sees the importance of analyzing how the V-diagram, supported by the taxonomy of Bloom, could help the student in the learning process and which types of activities would incite the highest levels of the taxonomy in the students.

6.4   Real-Time Simulation Tools

As mentioned previously, a real-time simulation can be performed diffidently, mainly depending on the available resources. Each challenge should be confronted differently for skills diversification, which the engineering student can acquire by studying this type of simulation. Consider this: a real-time laboratory focused mainly on simulating communication between the electrical agents in a smart grid would only endorse the competencies and skills of real-time co-simulation and HIL strategies. It would miss the possible competencies and technical skills developed by manipulating a real power system through a laboratory capable of P-HIL designed to control power interfaces.

The following subsections delve deeper into the various ramifications of real-time simulations. A description and possible applications of each RTST are detailed using the equipment located in the "Bi-national Laboratory" at the Tecnologico de Monterrey. The equipment consists of three real-time targets, configurable hardware, and a power interface to amplify P-HIL applications. Figure 6.5 shows the facilities with multiple RTST.

Fig. 6.5   Bi-national Laboratory" at Tecnologico de Monterrey (https://energi alab.tec.mx/es/energyopenin novationlab)

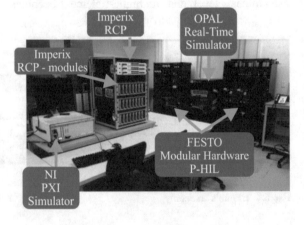

Fig. 6.6 RCP simulation
example

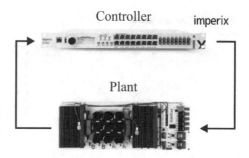

Controller   imperix

Plant

6.4.1   Rapid Control Prototyping

As previously described, RCP is an agile way to test control strategies on a real-time computer with a direct connection to the actual plant under test. This strategy is suitable for challenges regarding the control of low-level components in smart grid systems. Lectures designed mainly for entry-level education on RTST should be reconsidered with this simulation strategy because it is a fundamental building block for more specialized strategies.

In this particular stage, the students can learn to identify and correct errors at the start of the project, falling directly on the first two levels of the revised Bloom's taxonomy, remembering previous scenarios where the fault was first seen, and understanding the leading causes of the given error. With the correct understanding of the RCP process, the student can become more time-efficient in the debugging process, reducing simulation costs, and improving quality in a smart grid oriented job.

This simulation strategy allows quickly testing and adapting the parameter of a given controller in the functioning plant. Figure 6.6 shows the primary loop between a real-time target and the hardware to be tested. This particular example consisted of an Imperix RCP system for power electronic applications and PEH full-bridge modules. The latter consist of modules that can be reconfigured and assembled to create any down-scaled power converters, while the former is programmed to function as the hardware controller. This particular equipment configuration allows the students to quickly test and debug any control proposal for the configured plant safely.

6.4.2   Real-Time Co-simulation

As a strategy to simulate complex and large power systems, co-simulation separates the problem from different and distributed modules. When the separated modules are co-opted, the concept of co-simulation is created (Strasser et al. 1997). This strategy simulates each module in different platforms with direct data exchanges. In this manner, each simulator can solve a particular task independently, leading to a

Fig. 6.7 Co-simulation example

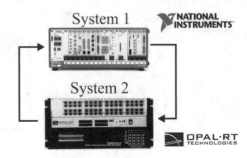

more realistic behavior between modules and facilitating the simulation of complex systems that can be infeasible to attain, such as smart grids.

A study conducted by Strasser (1997) shows the development of a co-simulation training platform for smart grid applications, addressing the issue of training professionals by familiarizing engineering students with power systems to cover the technical grid operation of active power distribution networks. The educational aspect covers the behavior of smart grids in different control scenarios. Nonetheless, the platform is not bound to only cover the control topic but also the communication network, monitoring of the power grid, and the automation of the grid.

A configuration example is illustrated in Fig. 6.7, where two real-time targets are interconnected. In some cases, this interconnection requires a translation module to properly couple the I/O ports and accurately synchronize both domains. The simulation targets can be programmed with complex systems that are unattainable in real-life or too expensive to have. Microgrids, smart grids, energy storage systems, diesel generators, and substations are possible systems that can be simulated. Thanks to this simulation strategy and its high flexibility, the dynamic interactions in complex systems can be analyzed.

6.4.3 *Hardware-In-The-Loop*

Laboratory courses in engineering education can include the use of specialized software and hardware. The correct manipulation and understating of hardware play a vital role in an engineer's formation. HIL simulation strategy is a safe practice for validating hardware and software (Soriano and Molina 2019). HIL can delve further into the revised Bloom's taxonomy chart simply by applying, analyzing, and evaluating the performance of the proposed solution in an external device to conclude its effectiveness per the stipulated objectives.

In Smart Grid studies, HIL is a powerful tool to test and validate embedded controllers. HIL simulation replicates a system's dynamics in natural circumstances in an embedded platform, leading to a more complete analysis of the simulated system ahead of the actual implementation. In this manner, the system and controller faults that previously could not be detected are identified in the early project stages. HIL

Fig. 6.8 HIL simulation example

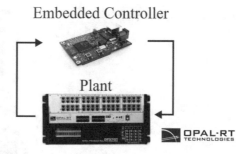

is the next stage in validating controller performance. The main difference between HIL and the co-simulation strategy is how the controller is implemented. In the latter, the controller is simulated in a secondary simulator. In contrast, in the former, the controller is into an embedded system that reads the simulator outputs and computes the controller signals in an external process.

Figure 6.8 shows an example of how this simulation strategy can be implemented. As mentioned, the designed controller is brought down to an embedded system by connecting its corresponding I/O ports to the real-time simulation target. The simulation target is programmed for the plant for which the controller was designed. In this manner, the controller can be tested in a safe environment without risking actual equipment. Typical applications for this simulation strategy are used in high power systems, where the controller is in charge of the interaction between DGUs and the simulated grid. An example is presented by Ivanović et al. (2012), where HIL is used to test the power flow control between energy storage systems and a simulated smart grid.

6.4.4 Power Hardware-In-The-Loop

Finally, P-HIL is the last level in the V-diagram before the technology transfer stage. At this point in the test and validation phase of the proposed solution, there is an actual power transfer between the real-time simulator and the interfaced hardware. Although this stage can be skipped by applications that do not require the evaluations of the power transfer for their operational validity, students must familiarize themselves with the actual hardware found in the smart grid applications. Similarly, as in the HIL strategy, P-HIL directly considers the applying, analyzing, and evaluating stages of the Revised Bloom's taxonomy.

According to Katsampopoulos (2017), HIL and P-HIL simulation strategies offer beneficial features in educational courses. These features include: (i) the flexibility to create models and tests that can be monitored under realistic operating conditions; (ii) real hardware immersion with actual inverters, relays, and microgrids to gain experience in operating actual equipment; (iii) testing "unattainable" systems such as smart Grids and monitoring the real-time interactions with actual equipment; (iv)

Fig. 6.9 P-HIL simulation
example

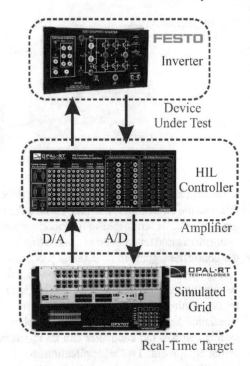

programmable faults to validate the performance of controllers without any adverse effects on the actual equipment.

Figure 6.9 shows an arrangement between the required interfaces to achieve P-HIL simulation. In this example, a smart grid can be simulated in the real-time target, and the connection to the hardware is achieved thanks to an amplifier module. P-HIL includes the hardware to be tested in the device under the test module. Here, power devices such as inverters, photovoltaic panels, and scaled wind turbines can be tested and their interactions with the simulated grid. A fundamental part of P-HIL is the amplification module. This element aims to transform the power produced by the interfaced hardware to signals that can be easily understood by the simulation hardware.

6.5 Expected Outcomes of RTST in Smart Grid Engineering

The implementation of RTST in electrical engineering courses has led to the expectation of improved learning outcomes in resolving the technical challenges of the future power grid. Including the real-time simulation strategies mentioned previously should aim to modernize electrical network courses and enrich engineering curricula by creating structured courses that fully leverage RTST in practical courses to develop various competencies in engineering students.

Real-time simulation produces an accurate model that can be turned into a physical one. For instance, designing a controller for renewable energies defines the dynamics of the electric grids. Thus, the simulation provides details about the real implementation of this controller. Also, using hardware in the loop is an alternative step in real-time simulations that increase engineering students' soft and technical skills. They develop new competencies such as teamwork, self-study, and oral and writing communication skills. Since the real-time simulation can be accessed remotely, it is possible to have international teams.

It could be a mistake to assume that specific skills can be cultivated only in theoretical courses during the educational phase. On the contrary, these skills first introduced to the students in conventional education can be strengthened in practical and analytical lectures, finally maturing during their professional life through experience in the industry. Meanwhile, in a real-time laboratory, the dominant competency group comprises technical skills (theory and experiments). In the case of engineering students, developing these skills is crucial for their development as professionals, especially in field-oriented works.

Consequently, the proper identification of these technical competencies is important for their assessment in courses that use RTST for a better understanding of a real-life system. According to work presented by Najwa et al. (2018), some critical technical competencies required in different industries are (i) application and practice of knowledge; (ii) problem-solving and decision-making; (iii) apply science and engineering principles; (iv) specific engineering discipline domination; (v) design and development of experiments; (vi) independent and autonomous learning; and (vii) quality and safety operation of equipment. In agreement with the studies presented by Osen (2019) and Strasser et al. (1997), where co-simulation and HIL simulation are used for educational purposes, these real-time simulation strategies develop independent and autonomous learning and problem-solving and decision-making in future engineers. All are defined as essential job competencies (Lim et al. 2020).

For that matter, structured courses should focus on mastering the fundamental RTST areas, modeling, simulation, and control of power systems (Strasser et al. 1997). This would allow a more fluid learning process to scale up the different stages in the V-diagram behind RTSD. Experimental and theoretical aspects should be covered to provide a holistic understanding of the subject. Students become engaged to learn and reflect on the abstract concepts by directly manipulating equipment; this increases knowledge retention and develops field-oriented skills that lead to active contributions to the Smart Grid industry; in other words, "learn by studying, retain by doing."

Courses should be designed based on Bloom's taxonomy. A clear example is a work reported by Martinez (2021), where a smart grid course educational platform was implemented comprising massive open online courses, a power system fundamentals textbook, and a remote smart grid laboratory. It achieved a satisfactory response by the majority of the students that finished the course.

Overall, the inclusion of RTST should provide the students with the necessary tools in a competent curriculum, training them to provide innovative solutions to the technical problems of Smart Grids. They can develop practical experience with real-time simulation technologies to improve their work and business opportunities as they become the future workforce prepared for the new grid paradigm.

The learning and teaching tool based on real-time is necessary because the cities must implement new energy topologies such as microgrids and smart grids. These topologies allow the integration of renewable energies such as wind or solar energy into the grid. Consequently, the environmental conditions also improve, and the CO_2 reduces. Real-time simulation is the answer for designing and validating the required technology because it is "low-cost" and can deal with complex systems.

Thus, the students can innovate and create technical solutions. Besides, these solutions can become products in the energy market swiftly. A real-time laboratory is also advantageous for studying low-level elements like power converters or digital controllers. Therefore, students can learn several layers of the energy grid. They will be able to propose novel solutions. In the future, when these technologies become standard in engineering education, undergraduate and graduate students will be able to solve more complex problems. Hence, RTST will be a driving factor in the energy systems training of the future workforce.

6.6 Conclusion

The evolution of the power grid has led to the development of new paradigms such as microgrids and smart Grids, forcing the adoption of new technologies by the energy sector and the modernization of education and training of the future electrical energy sector workforce. Real-time simulations enhance the learning process using different simulation strategies that help develop technical skills. This work presents the main simulation strategies derived from RTST, linking them to the product development process in a V-diagram structure. It also integrates Bloom's taxonomy in the learning process of the different real-time simulation strategies. This work can serve as a guide to implement a holistic educational platform based on RTST to develop the future Smart Grid workforce.

Acknowledgements The authors acknowledge the technical support of Writing Lab, Institute for the Future of Education, Tecnologico de Monterrey, Mexico, in the production of this work.

References

Annor-Asante M, Pranggono B (2018) Development of smart grid testbed with low-cost hardware and software for cybersecurity research and education. Wireless Personal Commun 101(3):1357–1377. [Online]. Available: https://doi.org/10.1007/s11277-018-5766-6

Bari JJ, Saad W, Arunita J (2014) Challenges in the smart grid applications: An overview. Int J Distri Sens Netw 2014:1–11

Bayram S (2018) Teaching smart power grids: a sustainability perspective. In: 2018 IEEE 12th international conference on compatibility, power electronics and power engineering (CPE-POWERENG 2018), pp 1–6

Bell RW, Fenton B, Griffiths H, Pal BC, McDonald JR (2012) Attracting graduates to power engineering in the U.K.: Successful university and industry collaboration. IEEE Trans Power Syst 27(1):450–457

Bigerna S, Bollino CA, Micheli S (2015) Overview of socioeconomic issues for smart grids development. In: 2015 International conference on smart cities and green ICT systems (SMARTGREENS), pp 1–6

Collaborative W (2009) PES, Preparing the U.S. foundation for future electricenergy systems: a strong power and energy engineering workforce, p 14

Deese S (2015) Development of smart electric power system (SEPS) laboratory for advanced research and undergraduate education. IEEE Trans Power Syst 30(3):1279–1287

Deese S, Cecchi V, Poudel B (2015) Introduction of emerging technologies to distribution system laboratory modules via simulation. In: 2015 IEEE power energy society general meeting, pp 1–5

Dufour, Be 'langer J (2013) On the use of real-time simulation technology in smart grid research and development. In: 2013 IEEE energy conversion congress and exposition, pp 2982–2989

Eltom WE, Sisworahardjo N, Hay R, Kobet G (2018) Smart distribution course for 21st-century power sector workforce. IEEE Trans Power Syst 33(5):5639–5647

Fang X, Misra S, Xue G, Yang D (2012) Smart grid the new and improved power grid: A survey. IEEE Communications Surveys Tutorials 14(4):944–980

Farhangi H (2010) The path of the smart grid. IEEE Power Energ Mag 8(1):18–28

Hannan MA, Ghani ZA, Mohamed A, Uddin MN (2015) Real-time testing of a fuzzy-logic-controller- based grid-connected photovoltaic inverter system. IEEE Trans Ind Appl 51(6):4775–4784

Heydt GT, Kezunovic M, Sauer PW, Bose A, McCalley JD, Singh C, Jewell WT, Ray DJ, Vittal V (2009) Professional resources to implement the "smart grid". In: 41st North American power symposium, pp 1–8

Ibarra AR, Ponce P, Molina A, Ayyanar R (2017) Overview of real-time simulation as a supporting effort to smart-grid attainment. Energies 10(6):817

Ivanović ZR, Adžić EM, Vekić MS, Grabić SU, Celanović NL, Katić VA (2012) HIL evaluation of power flow control strategies for energy storage connected to the smart grid under unbalanced conditions. IEEE Trans Power Electron 27(11), 4699–4710

Kezunovic M (2010) Teaching the smart grid fundamentals using modeling, simulation, and hands-on laboratory experiments. In: IEEE PES general meeting, pp 1–6

Kolhe P, Bitzer B (2015) Telelab with cloud computing for smart grid education. Springer 01:55–63

Kotsampopoulos PC, Kleftakis VA, Hatziargyriou ND (2017) Laboratory education of modern power systems using P-HIL simulation. IEEE Trans Power Syst 32(5):3992–4001

Krathwohl R (2002) A revision of bloom's taxonomy: an overview. Theory into Practice 41(4):212–218

Lim J, Yoon J, Kim M (2020) Analysis of the educational needs related to, and perceptions of the importance of, essential job competencies among science and engineering graduates. Educat Sci 10(4):85. [Online]. Available: https://www.mdpi.com/2227102/10/4/85

Lu G, De D, Song W (2010) SmartGridLab: a laboratory-based smart grid testbed. In: 2010 First IEEE international conference on smart grid communications, pp 143–148

Martinez A, Cruz PP, Gutierrez AM (2021) A holistic educational platform for the study of the smart grid. Int J Interact Des Manuf

Merabet KTA, Ibrahim H, Beguenane R, Ghias AMYM (2017) Energy management and control system for laboratory scale microgrid based wind-pv-battery. IEEE Trans Susta Energy 8(1):145–154

Molina A, Ponce P, Baltazar Reyes GE, Soriano LA (2019) Learning perceptions of Smart Grid class with a laboratory for undergraduate students. Int J Interact Des Manuf (IJIDeM) **13**(4), 1423–1439. [Online]. Available: https://doi.org/10.1007/s12008-019-006035

Najwa A, Yusri K, Khair NM (2018) Competencies of engineering graduates: what are the employer's expectations?. Int J Eng Technol 7:519

Navarro JC, Méndez KB, Ortiz-Rivera E, Arzuaga E (2014) Using cybersecurity as an engineering education approach on computer engineering to learn about smart grid technologies and the next generation of electric power systems. In: 2014 IEEE frontiers in education conference (FIE) proceedings, pp 1– 8

Nedic Z, Nafalski A (2015) Online smart grid laboratory. In: 2015 3rd Experiment international conference (exp.at'15), pp 272–275

Osen OL (2019) On the use of hardware-in-the-loop for teaching automation engineering. In: 2019 IEEE global engineering education conference (EDUCON), pp 1308–1315

Ram KB, Kumar SA, Ahlawat M, Parida SK, Prathap S, Biradar PS, Das V (2018) Smart grid remote laboratory. Smart Ind Smart Educ 47

Sauer P (2010) Educational needs for the "smart grid" workforce,". In: IEEE PES general meeting, pp 1–3

Soriano PP, Molina A (2019) A novel design of virtual laboratory. In: 2019 20th international conference on research and education in mechatronics (REM). IEEE, Wels, Austria, pp 1–6

Srinivasan D (2016) Teaching sustainable energy course through real-world case studies, projects and simulations. In: 2016 IEEE international conference on teaching, assessment, and learning for engineering (TALE), pp 436–440

Srivastava K, Hahn AL, Adesope OO, Hauser CH, Bakken DE (2017) Experience with a multidisciplinary, team-taught smart grid cyber infrastructure course. IEEE Trans Power Syst 32(3):2267–2275

Strasser T, Stifter M, Andre´n F, Palensky P (2014) Co-simulation training platform for smart grids. IEEE Trans Power Syst 29(4):1989–1997

Tecnologico de Monterrey, Energy open- innovation lab. [Online]. Available: https://energialab.tec.mx/es/energyopeninnovationlab

Yardley T, Uludag S, Nahrstedt K, Sauer P (2014) Developing a smart grid cybersecurity education platform and a preliminary assessment of its first application. In: 2014 IEEE frontiers in education conference (FIE) proceedings, pp 1–9

Chapter 7
An Early Introduction to Cryptography with Engineering Students

Moisés García-Martínez, Sergio Rolando Cruz-Ramírez, and José Manuel Olais-Govea

7.1 Introduction

Nowadays, *Cyber-Physical Systems* (CPS) pervade our cultural landscape. CPS is an ensemble of physical pieces whose functioning is controlled by computational algorithms (Baheti and Gill 2011). These systems are the basis of *artificial intelligence* (González García et al. 2019), one of the critical elements of *Industry 4.0* (Oztemel and Gursev 2020). This industrial revolution establishes the modern social context of a growing demand for new engineering profiles.

According to the Accreditation Board for Engineering and Technology criteria (Shuman et al. 2005), the general recommendations in STEM education (Bybee 2010), and the twenty-first-century skills cited in studies (Fisher et al. 2014), the challenges confronting present-and-future society necessitate improvements in the engineering educational programs offered by Higher Education (HE) Institutions.

The new engineering comprises people with various technical and professional skills, including creativity and design, oral and written communication, interdisciplinary thinking, teamwork, leadership, entrepreneurship, and global vision. In short, engineering education presents challenges for HE Institutions, notably, profound

M. García-Martínez (✉) · S. R. Cruz-Ramírez · J. M. Olais-Govea
Escuela de Ingeniería y Ciencias, Tecnologico de Monterrey, 78211 San Luis Potosí, SLP, Mexico
e-mail: moises.garcia@tec.mx

S. R. Cruz-Ramírez
e-mail: rolando.cruz@tec.mx

J. M. Olais-Govea
e-mail: olais@tec.mx

J. M. Olais-Govea
Writing Lab, Institute for the Future of Education, Tecnologico de Monterrey, 64849 Monterrey, Nuevo León, Mexico

© The Author(s), under exclusive license to Springer Nature Singapore Pte Ltd. 2022
S. Hosseini et al. (eds.), *Technology-Enabled Innovations in Education*,
Transactions on Computer Systems and Networks,
https://doi.org/10.1007/978-981-19-3383-7_7

continuous transformations of academic programs with technological innovations and various knowledge applications (Chatterton and Goddard 2000).

However, we cannot overlook that the rapid changes brought about by globalization, the knowledge society, and emerging technologies continuously define a new social order. In HE Institutions, mark a turning point characterized by new models of learning and teaching. In particular, the new educational models employ Competency-Based Education (CBE) (Williams 2019). Hence, engineering class models use problems from real contexts to help students apply knowledge and develop the right attitudes, values, and specific skills for the field of study in which the problem is located.

School environments that link practice with knowledge are a hallmark of engineering schools worldwide (Regis-Hernández et al. 2020). In this sense, *design-based research* is practical and relevant. By carefully studying the progressive approaches of ideal interventions in targeted environments, teachers can construct increasingly feasible and effective interventions, better articulating the principles that sustain its impact. As a research methodology in educative innovation, *action research* aims to develop empirically grounded theories through the combined study of the learning process and the means that support that process. Thus, *research-based design through action research* (Sim 2004) must be permanently reflective and iterative, incorporating design, evaluation, and revision cycles that continuously improve successive interventions. This methodology is based on theoretical assumptions accepted or rejected during the iteration process; the purpose is to provide guidelines for a theory that describes the educational reality addressed. Besides, the merit of a design is measured, in part, by its practicality for users in authentic contexts.

This chapter shows a learning experience design for mechatronics engineering students replicating the ENIGMA cipher machine (Hamer 1997) using LabVIEW as a technological and didactic tool. On the one hand, this machine is relevant because it was the first of its kind, and it is partly responsible for the encryption systems currently used. On the other hand, LabVIEW's primary advantage is offering students the possibility of increasing their level of abstraction to produce complex programming codes while simultaneously developing their autoregulation skills through problem-solving activities.

This manuscript has five sections. Section 2 describes some background and fundamentals of the ENIGMA machine, its electromechanical operation, and the digital version that we identify as the replica in this document. Sections 3 and 4 discuss teaching–learning aspects of implementing this replication with mechatronics engineering students in the first third of their professional careers. Finally, some conclusions and perspectives of this proposal's potential as an introduction to contemporary science issues are expounded in Section 5.

7.2   The ENIGMA Machine

7.2.1   Prelude. The Imitation Game

Since the Germans never doubted their encryption methods' reliability, the best way to analyze ENIGMAs development is not from the perspective of those who made it but those who defeated it. History is then read through the eyes of a brilliant historical personality and ponders the rotating drums of a pioneering machine of modern computing and Artificial Intelligence: Alan Turing and his Bombe machine, the one that beat the ENIGMA.

Turing was in the British spy service in the early 1940s in a secret location known as Bletchley Park, where the brightest minds in the UK fought the battles with just pencil and paper. The young mathematician had the idea of defeating ENIGMA, not with the human mind, but with a mind constructed of wires and metal. The remarkable construction of what became known as the Bombe machine haunted the King's College mathematician (Turing 1937); its birth and development must be conceived in the mathematical context of those days.

Ultimately what led to the development of Bombe was one of Turing's most significant works, the *Imitation Game* (Turing 1950), which follows a series of rules stemming from the answer to the question "Can machines think?" Preparing the world for what is known today as artificial intelligence, the game sets three persons A, B, and C, where C serves as the interrogator. C's task is to determine the sex of both individuals (A and B). Since the male sex corresponds to X and female to Y, A's task is to make C establish false statements, and, in turn, B must make C establish true statements. The fundamental assumption in the game is to ask the result of exchanging subject A for a machine. Hence, Bombe's main idea is a machine capable of evaluating all the ENIGMA machine's statements concerning its possible states until a logical result is determined, deducing the ENIGMA machine's initial state, thus, deciphering its codes.

This development at the hands of Alan Turing allowed the war to be won and shaped the world we know today. Unfortunately, the story of Alan Turing does not have an equally happy ending. He was condemned for his sexual orientation and sentenced to chemical castration on charges of "indecency." He took his life at the age of 41, leaving behind the dream of developing a "U" machine, a machine today known as a digital computer.

7.2.2   ENIGMA's Machine Hardware Description

The ENIGMA machine is perhaps the most famous encryption machine in history due to its impact during WWII. The machine was ahead of its time as it was the first electromechanical machine to efficiently automate replacement encryption processes.

The machine's physical structure consisted of various parts for its operation: input keyboard, light panel, connection panel, rotors, and reflector. Figure 7.1 shows a schematic diagram of the ENIGMA machine.

Figure 7.1 shows the keyboard for inputting the plain text for the data entry and a lighting keyboard for reading the encrypted text. The front panel could also be used to simultaneously carry out an extra replacement process for up to 10 letter substitutions. Each rotor contained 26 electrical contacts on each of its two sides, connected randomly in the interior. When a letter in the keyboard was pressed, first, the right rotor advanced one state; this resulted in a wiring change that led to a new cipher letter. Second, if the pressed letter had a patch panel substitution process, the values were exchanged differently, skipping this part and starting the rotors process, which behaved similarly to clock hands (seconds, minutes, and hours). When the

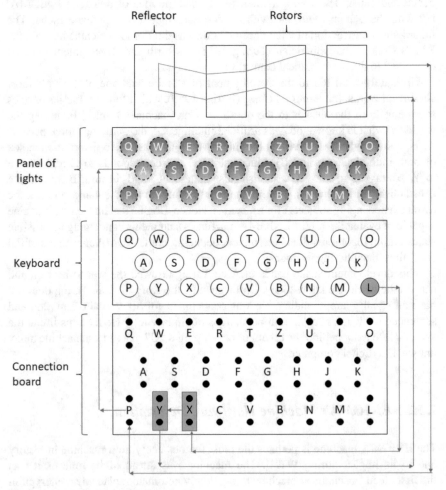

Fig. 7.1 Diagram of the ENIGMA machine

right rotor completed a cycle, the central rotor advanced to another state, and when that central rotor completed a cycle, the left rotor advanced to the next state. It is essential to mention that the internal wiring was different for each rotor, which was interchangeable. When the ENIGMA machine was created, the reflector was indispensable and unique in its class because it allowed the electrical signal to return through the rotors in a different trajectory. It was rechecked in the connection panel at the end of the way back, so the encrypted letter contained an extra substitution process. In the case it did not exist, this step was omitted.

The signal gave power to the illuminated keyboard that showed the encrypted letter. It is important to note that there were two types of reflectors; their unique difference was the internal wiring. Table 7.1 shows the substitution tables used in the work of the rotors (I–V); the reflectors (B and C) represent these elements' internal wiring. Recall that when a rotor completes a cycle, it sends a signal to the next rotor to advance. These cycles are defined and different in each of the rotors. Table 7.2 shows where these signals are located.

Finally, to decrypt messages, it was necessary to know the key. That required familiarity with the used rotors, their order, knowing their initial positions when the text was encrypted, the type of reflector, and the connections that could exist on the connection panel. Because of this complexity, it was believed that the ENIGMA machine was indecipherable.

Table 7.1 Rotor and reflector substitution tables define the internal wiring of these elements

Rotor	A	B	C	D	E	F	G	H	I	J	K	L	M	N	O	P	Q	R	S	T	U	V	W	X	Y	Z
I	E	K	M	F	L	G	D	Q	V	Z	N	T	O	W	Y	H	X	U	S	P	A	I	B	R	C	J
II	A	J	D	K	S	I	R	U	X	B	L	H	W	T	M	C	Q	G	Z	N	P	Y	F	V	O	E
III	B	D	F	H	J	L	C	P	R	T	X	V	Z	N	Y	E	I	W	G	A	K	M	U	S	Q	O
IV	E	S	O	V	P	Z	J	A	Y	Q	U	I	R	H	X	L	N	F	T	G	K	D	C	M	W	B
V	V	Z	B	R	G	I	T	Y	U	P	S	D	N	H	L	X	A	W	M	J	Q	O	F	E	C	K

Reflector	A	B	C	D	E	F	G	H	I	J	K	L	M	N	O	P	Q	R	S	T	U	V	W	X	Y	Z
B	Y	R	U	H	Q	S	L	D	P	X	N	G	O	K	M	I	E	B	F	Z	C	W	V	J	A	T
C	F	V	P	J	I	A	O	Y	E	D	R	Z	X	W	G	C	T	K	U	Q	S	B	N	M	H	L

Table 7.2 Shows in which letters lies the corresponding signal of advance in each of the five rotors

Rotor	
I	Q-R
II	E-F
III	V-W
IV	J-K
V	Z-A

7.2.3 ENIGMA's Machine Software Description

The implementation of the code was done with the LabVIEW platform, which allowed us to develop a user interface as similar as possible to the original ENIGMA machine, in such a way that, to encrypt some text, we used the input keyboard, which consists of a set of binary elements. The goal is, for each element, to represent a letter. There are several forms of implementation, which are shown in Fig. 7.2.

The input hinges on a conditional "if" element for each key. Its output has two possible numerical values: 0 or the numerical value equivalent to its letter position from 1 to 26 in the English alphabet. Another possible conversion form can be multiplication and a Boolean to numeric conversion element (*bool* to 0, 1). Another would be through an arrangement of Boolean elements where each position represents a bit such that there are 2^{26} possible combinations. However, the option used in this work is the one that requires the fewest operations.

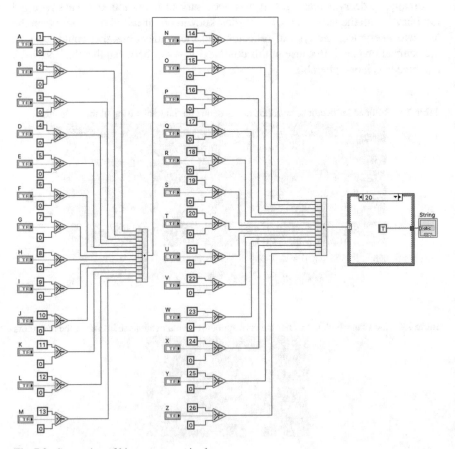

Fig. 7.2 Conversion of binary to numeric elements

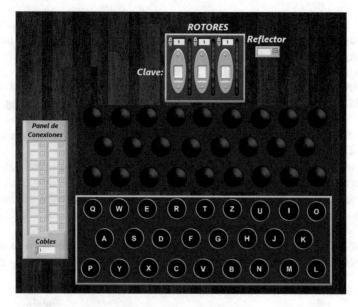

Fig. 7.3 ENIGMA machine user interface made in LabVIEW

Once a key has been pressed and is identified as the one pressed, the encryption process begins. The first instance is to check if the pressed key has a replacement through the connection panel. In Fig. 7.3, we can see the user interface configuring all the ENIGMA machine elements and even using the front panel to exchange letters. In this part, we used the encryption by substitution method.

It is must be noted that the entire software implementation is carried out employing arithmetic operations, so we need to manipulate the letters A–Z in their numerical equivalent; however, for better compression, both numbers and letters are always available. The code is shown in Fig. 7.4.

After this letter substitution, the rotors' position is updated by increasing the rotor on the right by one position. The other two rotors can be updated according to the current positions, shown in Table 7.2.

Then the encryption process begins, divided into two parts. The first path of the signal is directed by the right rotor, the central rotor, the left rotor, and the reflector.

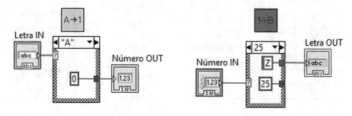

Fig. 7.4 Conversion of letters to numbers and numbers to letters

The second path of the signal is directed by the left rotor, the central rotor, the right rotor, the connection panel, and the illuminated keyboard. It is important to note that, in the original ENIGMA machine design, the letter substitution process was carried out through the internal wiring of the rotors using hardware.

However, in our implementation, we must replicate this process through software. This said, we can consider an arrangement of two columns, as shown in Fig. 7.5. In the first column are the letters arranged in ascending order (*C1*), and in the second column are the letters that will replace each (*C2*), according to the assignments in Table 7.1.

On the other hand, we need to know the rotors' order and the initial value each rotor has to encrypt and decrypt information. In our case, the rotor on the left will be *RLeft* and *KLeft* (the actual value of the Left Rotor); the central rotor will be *RCen*, and *KCen* (the actual value of the Central Rotor), and the right rotor will be *RRight* and *KRight* (the actual value of the Right Rotor).

We focus on the first part of the signal path for the software implementation, from right to left, and the reflector. The input letter *IL* is identified, coming directly

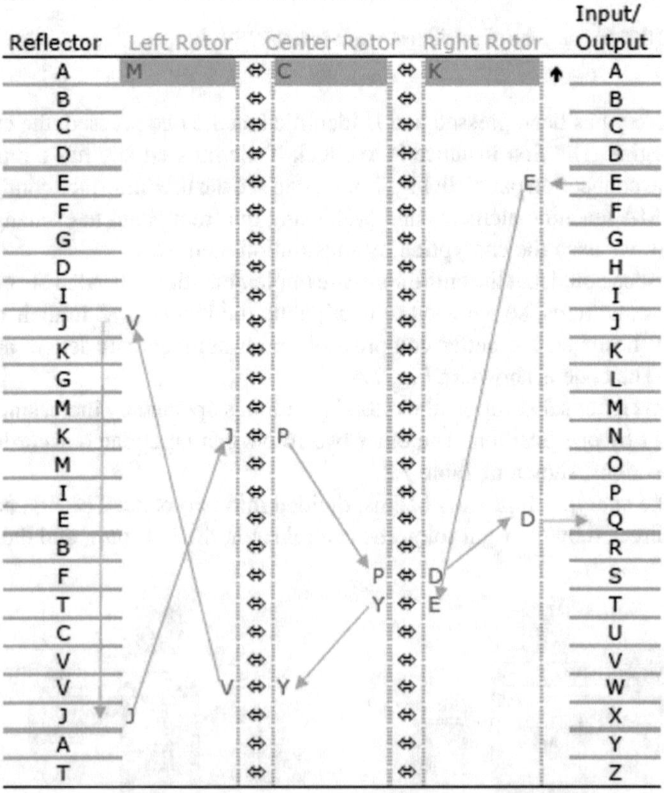

Fig. 7.5 Dynamic print that illustrates the step-by-step process of text encryption-decryption

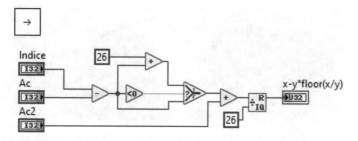

Fig. 7.6 The modular shift for letter representation

from the keyboard or the front panel. In this step, the letter (A–Z) is converted into a number (0–25) using the code in Fig. 7.4. The replacement by each rotor is carried out in two parts:

1. We must find the value placed in Column 2 (*C2*) of the right rotor *RRight* at the position of the input letter *IL*

$$C2RRG = KRight + IL \bmod 26.$$

   where *mod* 26 is a modular operation. All equations follow the notation: Column, Rotor (right, center, left), and way (Go, Back). This gives a numerical value that represents a letter.

2. For the letter that represents *C2RRG*, we must find its position in Column 1 (*C1*) of the current rotor *RRight*

$$C1RRG = C2RRG - KRight \bmod 26.$$

Thus, we guarantee that we always have numerical values representing letters from A to Z. The above can be implemented in programming, as shown in Fig. 7.6.

Repeating the previous steps for the central rotor *RCen* and taking *C1RRG* as the input letter:

1. We must find the value placed in column 2 of the central rotor *RCen* at the position of the input letter *C1RRG*

$$C2RCG = KCen + C1RRG \bmod 26.$$

2. For the letter that represents *C2RCG*, we must find its position in C1 of the current rotor *RCen*

$$C1RCG = C2RCG - KCen \bmod 26.$$

We repeat the previous steps for the left rotor *RLeft* and take *C1RCG* as the input letter:

Fig. 7.7 The reflector's internal wiring is shown on the left; a rotor's internal wiring is shown on the right

1. We must find the value placed in column 2 of the left rotor *RLeft* at the position of the input letter *C1RCG*

$$C2RLG = KLeft + C1RCG \bmod 26.$$

2. For the letter that represents *C2RLeftG*, we must find its position in *C1* of the current rotor *RLeft*

$$C1RLG = C2RLG - KLeft \bmod 26.$$

The next step is when the signal passes through the reflector. Remember that this element's function allows the signal to return through the three rotors using a different path. For this reason, the reflector, unlike the rotors, does not have random wiring. Figure 7.7 shows the internal wiring of the reflector.

For the reflector input, we take the last value we obtained from the rotor, in this case, *C1RLG*:

1. We must find what value is in *C2* of the Reflector *C2Ref* at the position of the input letter *C1RLG*

$$C2\mathrm{Ref} = C1RRG - KLeft \bmod 26$$

2. For the letter that represents *C2Ref*, we must find its position in *C1* of the reflector

$$C1Ref = C2Ref.$$

At this point, the signal's return starts a different path, and for its implementation in software, the previous process must be mirrored, which is explained below:

We take the last value *C1Ref* as an initial value, and the substitution in each rotor is carried out in two parts:

1. We must find the value placed in *C1* of the left rotor *RLeft* at the position of the input letter *C1Ref*

$$C1RLB = C1Ref + KLef \bmod 26.$$

This will give us a numerical value that represents a letter.
2.   For the letter that represents $C1RLB$, we must find its position in $C2$ of the current rotor $RLeft$

$$C2RLB = C1RLB - KLeft \bmod 26.$$

We repeat the previous steps for the central rotor $RCen$ and take $C2RLB$ as the input letter:
1.   We must find which letter is in column 1 of the central rotor $RCen$ in the position of the input letter $C2RLB$

$$C1RCB = C2RLB + KCen \bmod 26.$$

2.   For the letter that represents $C1RCB$, we must find its position in $C2$ of the current rotor $RCen$

$$C2RCB = C1RCB - KCen \bmod 26.$$

We repeat the previous steps for the rotor on the right $RRight$ and take $C2RCB$ as the input letter:
1.   We repeat the previous steps for the rotor on the right ($RRight$) and take $C2RCB$ as the input letter

$$C1RRB = C2RCB + KRight \bmod 26.$$

2.   For the letter that represents $C1RRB$, we must find its position in $C2$ of the current rotor $RRight$

$$C2RRB = C1RRB - KRight \bmod 26.$$

The value of $C2RRB$ represents the letter that replaces the input letter IL. If there is an extra process from the front panel, it should be carried out or omitted. After this, the corresponding letter is sent to the illuminated keyboard. The above process can be visualized in the coding in Fig. 7.8.

One ENIGMA machine characteristic is due to its intrinsic mechanical features. When a cycle of the rotor located in the central position completes, this rotor should advance one position, and a cycle is completed in the rotor on the right. However, when the central rotor reaches the corresponding letter to advance the left rotor and one cycle of the right rotor is completed, the central rotor advances two steps. This phenomenon is known as double stepping (Hamer 1997).

Currently, an alternative to manipulating the ENIGMA machine in a way closer to the original is through *virtual reality*. Using the ENIGMA Lite (Cortés 2019)

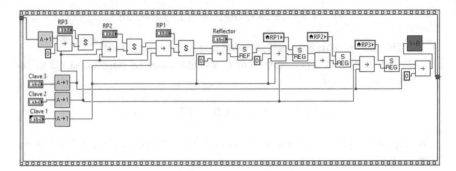

Fig. 7.8 Substitution process through rotors

Fig. 7.9 Enigma VR

application (see Fig. 7.9), it is possible to view a virtual model at 360° and manipulate it, that is, to configure its rotors, open and close its covers, and encrypt and decrypt messages. This certainly gives a better understanding of how the original ENIGMA machine was equipped.

7.3 Methodological Approach

This school project was framed within the paradigm of research based on design through teacher action research. Likewise, it was developed in the context of competency-based education (CBE) to promote computational thinking in students (Lewis and Smith 1993). This educational approach leaves open two methodological questions, namely, (i) *How to favorably influence, from the teaching practice, the formation of the student under CBE?* and (ii) *How to engage engineering students in their learning process within the CBE?* One possible answer lies in designing appropriate learning sequences to develop the students' transversal and disciplinary competencies. The designed experiments (or the design of the teaching intervention) aim to generate local theories that interpret educational reality based on iterative interventions (Christensen and West 2018). Each intervention has a structure chosen by the teacher and modified by a continuous, deep reflection on educational practice. This helps to describe and understand the learning process so that it can be modified later.

The learning sequence presented in this report is the product of three iterations with students from various engineering programs in a 40-hour immersive work modality completed in a single week. The solution of contextualized problems in the real world (Gore and Rosser 2020) was the intervention's methodological vehicle. The implemented iterations were carried out in 2017 with nine students, in 2018 with six, and in 2019. This iterative process led to creating a theoretical sample for this study, which covered the broadest range of opinions and points of view within the targeted social group. Therefore, this theoretical-qualitative sample was not statistically representative; instead, it tried to engage the different interests and discourses relevant to a given problem. Although there were no rigid criteria on how many people to select in this type of study, the saturation principle was followed (Altrichter et al. 1993), a theoretical tool that allows approaching the social composition of the real environment.

This section describes the implementation of the ENIGMA (Hamer 1997) machine using LabVIEW software as a technological and educational tool. The central objective of the learning sequence was to promote the student's disciplinary skills related to her computational thinking (Aho 2012). This proposal is an attractive way to engage students in a sequence of activities that promote essential cognitive skills for highly complex projects. The main finding in the implementation of this design was that using LabVIEW improves students' abstraction capacity, allowing them to produce sophisticated programming code while developing self-regulation skills during problem-solving.

7.3.1 Didactic Design

We planned the programming of the ENIGMA machine in 20 activities in the didactic sequence shown in Table 7.3 of Annex A. We show a possible relationship between each activity and the cognitive process students try to promote when they perform the activity. The implementation of this sequence was carried out under the methodological approach of *action research*. In this work, we employed this methodology in three phases, namely, the identification of the problem (F1), data collection (F2), and analysis (F3). Between phases F2 and F3, we implemented an action plan that emanated from systematic observations of the teaching–learning process. For this reason, it was repeated iteratively between these phases until a particular structure was identified in the observed social interactions. The appendix shows an outline of the methodology described below.

Table 7.3 Activities of the action plan

Activity	Objective	Evidence	Cognitive processes
[2]Creating user interface 1	Use controls of different types of variables	Code in LabVIEW with personalized controls Audio recording	Abstraction
[2]Keyboard programming	Use custom controls and interconnect different types of variables	Code in LabVIEW with personalized controls Audio recording	Logic
[2]Illuminated board programming	Use custom controls and interconnect different types of variables	Code in LabVIEW with personalized controls Audio recording	Logic
[3]Rotor programming	Be able to create replacement tables. There are different ways to do it	Code in LabVIEW in SubVI Audio recording	Abstraction
[3]Reflectors programming	Be able to create tables in pairs that only indicate a different path in the process. There are different ways to do it	Code in LabVIEW in SubVI Audio recording	Patterns and regularities
[3]Letter-number conversion program	How to interconnect different types of variables	Code in LabVIEW in SubVI Audio recording	Logic
[3]Number-letter conversion program	How to interconnect different types of variables	Code in LabVIEW in SubVI Audio recording	Logic
[3]Programming rotor advance	Create a programming logic based on modular operations and advance signals that depend on specific conditions	Code in LabVIEW in SubVI Audio recording	Algorithms
[3]Programming to calculate letters distance	Create a programming logic that can measure the distance between letters. This distance depends on the substitution tables of the others and the reflectors	Code in LabVIEW in SubVI Audio recording	Recursion Parallel thinking Algorithms
[4]First-stage process programming	Create a programming logic for the substitution in the specific order of the rotors: right, center, left	Code in LabVIEW Audio recording	Algorithms
[4]Reflector process programming	Create a programming logic for specific pair substitution for reflectors	Code in LabVIEW in SubVI Audio recording	Algorithms

(continued)

Table 7.3 (continued)

Activity	Objective	Evidence	Cognitive processes
[4]Second-stage process programming	Create a programming logic for the substitution in the specific order of the rotors: left, center, right	Code in LabVIEW Audio recording	Algorithms
[4]Front-panel programming	Add, sort, and group the elements used so far in the front panel	Code in LabVIEW with personalized elements in the front panel Audio recording	Abstraction
[4]Programming the entire process	Use all SubVI together to create the complete program	Code in LabVIEW Audio recording	Algorithms
[5]Creating user interface 2	Add, sort, and group the extra custom items that are required on the front panel	Code in LabVIEW with the Front panel Audio recording	Patterns and regularities
[5]Message encryption part I	Encrypt messages with specific parameters that will test critical elements in the program	Text file Audio recording	Abstraction Logic
[5]Message encryption part II	Encrypt messages with specific parameters that will test critical elements in the program	Text file Audio recording	Abstraction Logic
[5]Message encryption part III	Encrypt messages with specific parameters that will test critical elements in the program	Text file Audio recording	Abstraction Logic
[5]Message encryption part IV	Encrypt messages with specific parameters that will test critical elements in the program	Text file Audio recording	Abstraction Logic
[5]Message encryption part V	Encrypt messages with specific parameters that will test critical elements in the program	Text file Audio recording	Abstraction Logic

The super index to the left side of the name of each activity indicates the iteration number of teaching intervention. The second column of the table indicates the cognitive processes present during the development of the activity

7.3.2   Problem Identification

(F1) involved the learning objectives, initial conditions, and general educational and research intentions. From previous programming experiences (iteration 0), we had noted student deficiency in understanding the syntax inherent in programming languages, the conceptualization and use of programming commands, and, above all, the abstraction of the meaning of the information flow and instructions that comprise a particular code. We determined the form and means to carry out the analysis in the learning environment at this stage. Therefore, the starting point of this research was to answer the question: *How to improve students' code programming skills through LabVIEW's visualizations?* This question was the root of the action plan obtained after four iterations (teaching interventions), as indicated by the superscript on the left side of the name of each activity in Table 7.3.

The data collection (F2) phase consisted of adjusting the instructional design after reflection of the educational practice underlying the application of the ENIGMA project. To monitor the students' performance, we first broke down the general objective of the activity into tasks that, being linked to the development of code in programming, had only two values: true or false (depending on how the program works). This is a straightforward indicator closely linked to disciplinary work. At the end of each teaching intervention, the students were asked to record their achievements of the pre-established objectives in the activity, reducing their perceptions to answer *Did I achieve it?* (Carless et al. 2011). As we went through all the project activities, it was possible to describe each student's learning.

The data analysis (F3) examined the proportion of students achieving the objective of each of the activities shown in Table 7.3 versus those who did not achieve it. We also analyzed if the students' perception of achievement aligned with the correct operation of the code they had developed progressively during the 20 proposed activities.

7.4   Results and Discussion

As the first finding of this research, we highlight that the students could not recognize the basic programming commands and had difficulty understanding the flow of information in a given program. Therefore, we had the students review historical and classical encryption methods, such as substitution, modular sums (Vigenère), and statistical analyses of texts and ciphertexts. The students demonstrated a low level of programming skills and logical-mathematical thinking. Only 33% solved the introductory activities involving algorithms and programming. These initial activities formed the first iteration of the reflective cycles of the action research.

After the introductory activities, we divided the project into two stages: the recreation of the user interface (S1) and the programming step (S2). The left side of Fig. 7.10 shows the internal components of the ENIGMA machine. The right side shows the corresponding software implemented by the students after the first five activities of the sequence (see Table 7.3).

Students implemented the input keyboard in the next stage of the sequence (activities 6 and 7), establishing a set of Boolean buttons for numerical representations and later letter representations. This programming segment is shown in Fig. 7.11. The process is reversed to implement the illuminated exit keypad, i.e., it begins with

Fig. 7.10 The left side shows the original ENIGMA Machine. On the right is the digital version of the ENIGMA Machine implemented in LabVIEW

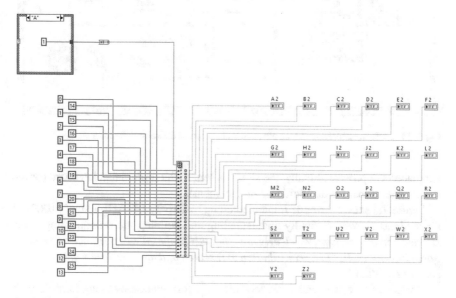

Fig. 7.11 Code in LabVIEW for the lighting keyboard

a letter. After this, it is converted to its numerical equivalent. Finally, we recover its Boolean representation.

The next stage of the project consisted of programming the rotors and reflectors that are the main components of the machine (activity 12 onwards in the sequence). At this programming stage, the challenge is that each rotor has a different advance signal, which is interchangeable, as we can see in the code segment shown in Fig. 7.12. After that, the activities of the sequence help the students understand: (i) the signal passes through the three rotors in a specific order (right, center, and left); (ii) where each performs a process of substituting one letter for another after going through the three rotors (iii) before going through the reflector, which allows (iv) returning the signal to the rotors (but in reverse order). This is a complex instruction due to the order and flow of instructions within the algorithm. Again, each rotor goes through

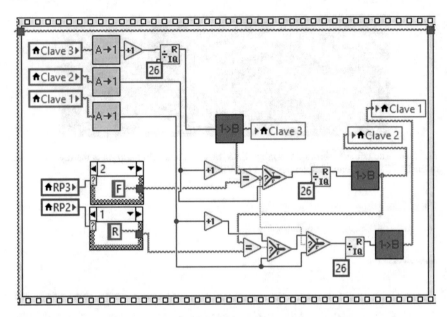

Fig. 7.12 Code in LabVIEW for the advance and update of the rotors' position

a replacement process. Finally, the signal is sent to the illuminated keyboard (or the patch panel if there is an additional replacement).

Figure 7.8 shows the code implemented up to activity 14. At this stage, 100% of the students showed difficulty understanding and building the programming code. *However, in this process, we clearly note that this proposal's importance and educational innovation lies in its contribution to research and the need to use the graphical code of LabVIEW.*

It was easier for students to understand code formulation by being familiar with data visualization and graphical modeling of processes and tasks, such as block diagrams and flowcharts. This becomes a fundamental factor when expressing an idea and implementing it because the graphic representation and the rules that govern the execution of the code combine to offer a programming experience that expresses the computational thinking of the students more directly than other programming languages.

On the other hand, the debugging process is more intuitive because the tool used by LabVIEW consists of the interactive flow of data through the cables. In this way, it is easier to find programming errors and correct them; moreover, the compilation of the program is automatic, so if there is an error in the code, the program does not run. In traditional languages, the compilation and debugging processes are independent. Thus, the LabVIEW tool has added value because it allows students to develop self-regulation skills when creating their code, become independent from the teacher, and develop more complex tasks independently. These last characteristics are typical of people who have acquired a certain degree of intellectual independence when

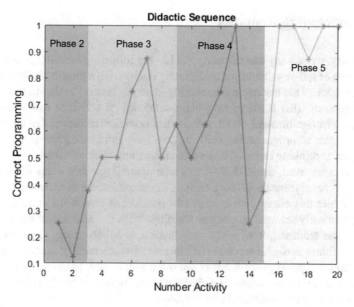

Fig. 7.13 The proportion of students who produced the correct programming code in each of the activities of the didactic sequence

resolving challenges and problems. In the end, 100% of the students were able to finish this project, and only 10% showed problems encrypting and decrypting messages (activities 17 to 20 of the sequence).

Figure 7.13 shows the proportion of students who perceived that they had achieved the objective of each proposed activity as long as the obtained programming code was executed correctly. As can be seen, during the first three activities (phase 2 of the sequence, per the super index shown in the activity name in Table 7.3), approximately 40% of the students managed to implement the code correctly. This is because students were exposed for the first time to using variables within the programming environment and understanding the flow of actions in it. However, in phase 3, it was observed that around 90% of students created and executed the code correctly, having already mastered the modular and displacement functions, among others.

On the other hand, activities 14 and 15 presented the highest level of difficulty in the project because they required the complete programming of the encryption and the front panel of the machine. Consequently, this phase of the activity registered the least number of successful students, with only 30% of students implementing it correctly. Once the rest of the students received feedback from the teacher and could complete the programming code, phase 5 was completed, and 100% of students executed the code correctly. This phase was much less complex because only the messages were transmitted and decrypted using the previously programmed code.

7.5   Concluding Remarks

In summary, we can say that this proposal has the following benefits: (i) it increases the learning of self-regulation and disciplinary content, (ii) it progressively eliminates the supervision of the teacher in the teaching–learning process as the student acquires work autonomy, (iii) it offers students a sequence of activities that activate and promote metacognition and, (iv) it includes technological resources that significantly improve students' programming skills by positively influencing the development of their superior thinking order within a critical learning environment.

On the other hand, the ENIGMA machine made it possible to lay the necessary foundations for cryptanalysis (for example, the attack known as a Chosen Ciphertext attack). While this encryption is currently considered unsafe for commercial use, it is academically relevant to student learning. With the analysis of the ENIGMA machine, the student got an early introduction to cybersecurity. This area has a promising future as digital services have increased exponentially, making it essential to develop encryption processes that are more secure and, at the same time, more efficient. This includes various branches with non-linear systems based on elliptical curves, which even constitute chaotic systems.

The authors consider that the value and contribution of the work presented here can be useful in understanding basic cryptography concepts and providing students with an introductory course in LabVIEW programming. According to the information gathered throughout the iterations of the proposed method, this visual resource suggests that the visualization of the graphical interface relaxes the abstract apprehension that the students carry during the didactic sequence. However, since this study emanates from a qualitative paradigm of socio-empirical research, statistical tests could not be carried out to verify this assumption with statistically significant student populations. In the present study, the work sample is only theoretical-qualitative in nature. Future work could entail submitting each of the activities comprising the sequence to quantitative validation with a large population of engineering students with characteristics similar to our original sample.

Acknowledgements The authors would like to acknowledge the financial and technical support of Writing Lab, Institute for the Future of Education, Tecnologico de Monterrey, Mexico, and the GIEE-Optimization and Data Science in the production of this work.

Appendix

See Table 7.3 and Fig. 7.14.

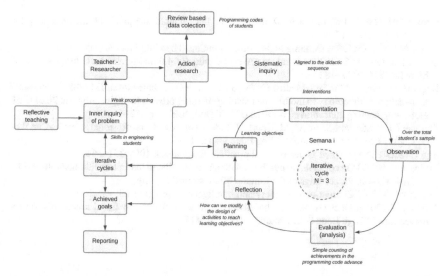

Fig. 7.14 The design of the reported didactic sequence is the product of the cycles of continuous reflection that emanate from the educational practice of the teacher. These iterative cycles give rise to the action plan that the teacher implements during each cycle until an optimal design of the didactic sequence is saturated. This final design responds to the research questions that the teacher initially posed as a central part of his/her reflection and experience process, thus achieving the research goals that emerge within this methodological process of analyzing social reality

References

Aho AV (2012) Computation and computational thinking. Comput J 55(7):832–835

Altrichter H, Posch P, Somekh B (1993) Teachers Investigate their work. An introduction to the methods of action research routledge, London

Baheti R, Gill H (2011) Cyber-physical systems. The Impact of Control Technol 12(1):161–166

Bybee RW (2010) Advancing STEM education: a 2020 vision. Technol Eng Teach 70(1):30

Carless D, Salter D, Yang M, Lam J (2011) Developing sustainable feedback practices. Stud High Educ 36(4):395–407

Chatterton P, Goddard J (2000) The response of higher education institutions to regional needs. Eur J Educ 35(4):475–496

Christensen K, West RE (2018) The development of design-based research. Foundations of learning and instructional design technology

Cortés A (2019) EnigmaAR Lite (v1.2) [mobile app]. Recovered from: https://play.google.com/store/apps/details?id=com.Cinvestav.EnigmaARLite&hl=en&gl=US

Fisher DR, Bagiati A, Sarma SE (2014) Fostering 21st-century skills in engineering undergraduates through co-curricular involvement. In: 2014 ASEE annual conference and Exposition, pp 24–623

García-Martínez M, Cruz-Ramírez SR, Olais-Govea JM (2021) Encryption activity to improve higher-order thinking in engineering students. Int J Interact Des Manufact (IJIDeM) 1–18.

González García C, Núñez Valdéz ER, García Díaz V, Pelayo García-Bustelo BC, Cueva Lovelle JM (2019) A review of artificial intelligence in the internet of things. Int J Interact Multimedia Artif Intell 5

Gore J, Rosser B (2020) Beyond content-focused professional development: powerful professional learning through genuine learning communities across grades and subjects. In: Professional development in education, pp 1–15

Hamer DH (1997) Enigma: actions involved in the "double stepping" of the middle rotor. Cryptologia 21(1):47–50

Lewis A, Smith D (1993) Defining higher-order thinking. Theo into Pract 32(3):131–137

Oztemel E, Gursev S (2020) Literature review of industry 4.0 and related technologies. J Intell Manufact 31(1):127–182

Regis-Hernández F, Martínez-Medina G, Borjas-Vázquez HC, Olais-Govea JM (2020) Semestre i as an active methodology to modify the teaching-learning process in engineering. In: 2020 IEEE global engineering education conference (EDUCON), IEEE, pp 652–666

Shuman LJ, Besterfield-Sacre M, McGourty J (2005) The ABET "professional skills"—Can they be taught? Can they be assessed? J Eng Educ 94(1):41–55

Sim C (2004) The personal as pedagogical practice. Teach Teach 10(4):351–364

Turing AM (1937) On computable numbers, with an application to the Entscheidungsproblem (1.a ed., vols s2–42). Proceedings of the London Mathematical Society.

Turing AM (1950) Computing machinery and intelligence. Springer Link

Williams P (2019) Does competency-based education with blockchain signal a new mission for universities? J High Educ Policy Manag 41(1):104–117

Chapter 8
Transforming Teaching in the Digital Age: Simulation in Virtual Laboratories

Lizette Susana Hernández Cárdenas, Juan Pablo Nigenda Alvarez, Ana Gabriela Rodríguez Mendoza, and Mauricio Martínez González

8.1 Introduction and Theoretical Framework

Our complex world requires motivational and challenging teaching that engages the students, who should be continuously assessed while they learn. Their evaluation goes beyond a written test; feedback is essential for their learning. We currently face a world in constant change, challenging us, as teachers, to seek innovative means for our students to acquire knowledge in practical, attractive, and flexible ways. Teaching methodologies must be adapted to a changing world where students absorbed in technology require new ways to learn. Nowadays, simulation and video games are commonly used, and gamification and storytelling have become innovative tools to support education. Therefore, teaching must be conducted not only with lectures, videos, capsules, articles, or books but also implemented with didactic strategies that attract students' attention, stimulate research, and lead to their dynamic, creative, and active participation (Vialart 2020).

In this experimental project, we simulated virtual laboratories for students in their first semester of Medicine and Health Sciences at Tecnologico de Monterrey, Campus Monterrey, and sixth-semester high school students at PrepaTec Garza Sada.

L. S. Hernández Cárdenas (✉) · J. P. Nigenda Alvarez
School of Medicine and Health Sciences, Tecnologico de Monterrey, Monterrey, Mexico
e-mail: lizette@tec.mx

J. P. Nigenda Alvarez
e-mail: jnigenda@tec.mx

A. G. Rodríguez Mendoza · M. Martínez González
Educational Innovation and Production and Creative Design, Tecnologico de Monterrey, Monterrey, Mexico
e-mail: anagaby.rodriguez@tec.mx

M. Martínez González
e-mail: mauriciomartinez@tec.mx

© The Author(s), under exclusive license to Springer Nature Singapore Pte Ltd. 2022   119
S. Hosseini et al. (eds.), *Technology-Enabled Innovations in Education*,
Transactions on Computer Systems and Networks,
https://doi.org/10.1007/978-981-19-3383-7_8

We worked with the Educational Innovation and Production and Creative Design team to develop a virtual laboratory to simulate experiments. In this first stage, the Virtual Laboratory was used in the "Water and pH" course during the August–December 2019 semester for the university students and the January–May 2020 semester for the sixth-semester high school students.

Urbina and Fuentes (Urbina 2003; Fuentes and García 2007) both point out that the term "educational software" describes the following characteristics: (1) It is developed for an educational purpose. (2) It uses computers or electronic devices as the technological means to perform assigned activities. (3) It is interactive. (4) It personalizes the students' work, tracking each student's progress. (5) It can adapt its activities to the student's performance. (6) It is user-friendly (Urbina 2003; Fuentes and García 2007).

Simulations are educational tools used to support medical education (Palés and Gomar 2010). In a broad sense, "simulations" can refer to any teaching activity that uses simulators to foster and facilitate learning while emulating, as much as possible, simple to complex clinical scenarios (Ziv 2009). Increasing the use of simulations in the education of healthcare professionals is an effective response to the rising focus on training for patient safety. New training models and standardized educational protocols enable practicing and honing skills in a controlled environment (Pawłowicz et al. 2020). Recently, the advancement of new simulation technologies in health sciences has given rise to the creation of simulation centers (Urra et al. 2017). Thus, simulation-based medical education includes educational techniques defined as any teaching activity that uses simulators to stimulate learning (Moya et al. 2017).

A clinical simulation creates an experience representing "a real event to practice, learn, assess, test or acquire knowledge of human systems or performances" (Horra 2010). "Simulation techniques have been used in academic medical education for more than 40 years" (Galindo and Visbal 2007). Simulation allows students to become acquainted with situations that are accurately extracted from actual healthcare events. These situations are staged in a room where learners interact and acquire intended knowledge, skills, and behaviors (Juguera et al. 2014). Vidal Ledo affirms the importance of using simulators in the medical education process during teaching and learning and the students' assessment (Vidal et al. 2019).

Using simulators in educational processes is an effective teaching method to develop sets of students' skills and abilities to achieve superior modes of action. The simulations offer the opportunity to perform a practice similar to what they will face in the reality of health care (Juguera et al. 2014). They also offer students a safe space to make mistakes, learn from them, and try again. Another advantage is that the student receives immediate and continuous feedback, so they improve and learn (Fernández 2015). Vázquez-Mata states that this type of training is always accompanied by a feedback session in which students and teachers analyze the performed activity, its strengths, and aspects to be improved. This analysis should be followed by reflection and critical thinking, which deepens the students' knowledge and leads them to make appropriate clinical applications (Vázquez-Mata and Guillamet-Lloveras 2009).

The term "virtual laboratory" refers to a simulated experimental laboratory where different activities of the "learning game" are carried out. This motivating technique strengthens learning through unlimited repetitions and allows observing the students' mastery with a completely objective evaluation tool (Trueba 2012). This simulation culture has grown over the years. Simulated objects on the computer screen are increasingly similar to real-life objects (Carbero-Almenara and Costas 2016).

8.2 Methodology

In this experimental project, we complemented our teaching of first-semester under-graduate students in the School of Medicine and Health Sciences on the Monterrey campus of Tecnologico de Monterrey and sixth-semester high school students at PrepaTec Garza Sada with virtual simulation laboratories.

The first stage, the development of the virtual laboratory, required collaborating for about a year with the Educational Innovation and Production and Creative Design team. With their help, we were able to create the laboratory simulation. Through face-to-face and online sessions, we established the design of the laboratory. We also visited the physical laboratories to take photos and images to ensure that the virtual laboratory resembled a real one as much as possible.

The experimental stage begins with setting the problem that the student must solve in the laboratory. We used the storytelling technique, which tells a story about the problem situation and what the student must do to solve it. The students then prepare the necessary safety items for laboratory work: lab coat, safety glasses, and gloves. When the students are ready, they can enter the laboratory and follow the step-by-step instructions to perform the practice, which, in our project, consists of measuring and titrating the pH of a test solution to decide how to neutralize the sample and dispose of it properly.

The procedure was the following:

Step 1: Pre-class reading of the topic—students read individually outside the classroom.
Step 2: Teacher's explanation of the topic—a lecture in the classroom, using supports such as a presentation, videos, and images.
Step 3: Quiz on the topic before the simulation.
Step 4: Simulation session.
Step 5: Quiz on the topic after the simulation.

8.3 Results

The graph in Fig. 8.1 shows the quiz results before the simulation session (*previo*) and after (*posterior*). The x-axis shows the total number of students, and the y-axis

Fig. 8.1 Results of the pre-quiz and post-quiz scores

shows the quiz scores based on a 100-point scale. The quiz questions were designed to assess the students' mastery of the topic.

The results showed that most of the students improved their scores in the rapid post-quiz. Some remained unchanged, and a few scores fell. We believe that the drop in scores was due to the short time to answer the quiz because of the simulators' rotation. When graphing the results, we saw that the pre-quiz scores were lower than the post-test scores. The latter scores were more consistent and showed improvement.

The overall averages of the quiz scores and the graphs show that the post-quiz average improved significantly compared to the pre-quiz. This indicates that the students acquired a better knowledge of the subject after the simulation (Fig. 8.2).

All the necessary materials and physical spaces were simulated to create the virtual laboratory. Figure 8.3 shows a photo of how the student visualizes the virtual laboratory in the simulator. Figure 8.4 shows a photo of the simulation session where students use virtual reality visors to carry out the classroom activity.

The use of virtual laboratory simulation has many advantages, including:

- Promoting learning through positive reinforcement: the simulator allows the student to actively participate in the practice. The student can make mistakes and try again as many times as necessary without consequences or risks. Also, it

Fig. 8.2 Comparison of
pre-quiz and post-quiz
averages

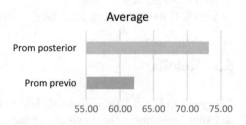

Fig. 8.3 Virtual laboratory

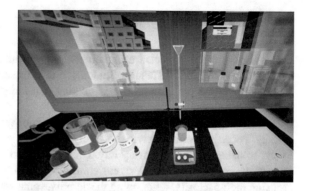

Fig. 8.4 Simulation session

avoids wasting substances that would have to be discarded, avoiding the cost of acquiring and discarding them.

- Capturing the student's attention by using gamification and storytelling with animated images, sounds, and texts.
- Preparing students to acquire job skills, such as problem-solving, bringing them closer to real-life practices.
- Simulators as a versatile teaching tool can be extended to any discipline.
- Using simulators is a practical alternative for schools and universities that do not have the resources to build a real laboratory. Through simulation, they can offer their students the possibility to acquire the necessary competencies, skills, and knowledge for their professional practices.

During the simulation practice, we had to consider that the teacher needed support from the Educational Innovation and Creative Design and Production team to help the students use the simulator and solve any problems that might arise. Also, to accommodate the times available for the simulators, we had to provide the students with the theoretical background before the simulation session.

8.4 Conclusions

In this experimental project, we implemented the simulation of virtual laboratories for teaching with excellent results. Students' post-quiz scores improved by more than 10 points over the pre-quiz scores, indicating that the students had better learning using the simulator.

The students accepted the challenge and were motivated to take on the challenge activity. These innovative activities are very well accepted by students who are accustomed to using technology every day. Doing the practice either on their computer or with the 3D viewers was very enriching for their learning, motivating them and arousing their curiosity. After doing the activity, some students even repeated it after class.

8.5 Limitations and Future Work

The limitations we faced were (1) the speed of the internet, (2) the different types of devices that students had and their accessibility to the internet, (3) the class duration, and (4) technical problems accessing the simulator. We resolved some of these during the activity, especially those related to accessibility and technology; however, we recommend that you consider the class schedule for at least 2 h.

We are currently developing a second virtual practice for the Comet Assay theme to observe DNA damage in cells.

This activity has a high capitalization potential. Simulation can be used as a teaching tool in any semester and discipline by finding the appropriate simulators.

Acknowledgements This simulation was possible thanks to the Educational Innovation and Production and Creative Design team's collaboration, the Department of Basic Sciences, and the School of Medicine and Health Sciences of Tecnologico de Monterrey, Campus Monterrey.

The authors wish to acknowledge the technical support of Writing Lab, Institute for the Future of Education, Tecnologico de Monterrey, Mexico, in the production of this paper.

References

Carbero-Almenara J, Costas J (2016) La utilización de simuladores para la formación de los alumnos. Prisma Social, núm. 17. España, pp 343–372

De la Horra I (2010) La simulación clínica como herramienta de evaluación de competencias en la formación de enfermería. Reduca (Enfermería, Fisioterapia y Podología) Serie Trabajos Fin de Máster, pp 549–580

Fernández I (2015) Juego serio: gamificación y aprendizaje", Centro de comunicación y pedagogía, España

Fuentes JA, García FA (2007) Nuevas tecnologías para la educación en la era digital. Pirámide, Madrid, pp 251–259

Galindo J, Visbal L (2007) Simulación, herramienta para la educación médica. Salud Uninorte, Barranquilla, Colombia, pp 79–95

Juguera L, Díaz JL, Pérez ML, Leal C, Rojo A, Echevarría P (2014) La simulación clínica como herramienta pedagógica: percepción de los alumnos de Grado en Enfermería en la UCAM (Universidad Católica San Antonio de Murcia. Enfermería Global 13(33):175–190. Accessed: 01 Mar 2021. [Online]. Available: http://scielo.isciii.es/scielo.php?script=sci_arttext&pid=S1695-61412014000100008&lng=es&tlng=es

Moya R, Ruz M, Parraguez E, Carreño V, Rodríguez A, Froes P (2017) Efectividad de la simulación en la educación médica desde la perspectiva de seguridad de pacientes. Revista médica de Chile 145(4):514–526. https://doi.org/10.4067/S0034-98872017000400012 [Online]. Available: https://scielo.conicyt.cl/scielo.php?pid=S0034-98872017000400012&script=sci_arttext&tlng=en

Palés JL, Gomar C (2021) El uso de las simulaciones en Educación Médica. Educat Knowl Soc 11(2):147–170, June, 2010. Accessed: 10 Apr 2021. https://doi.org/10.14201/eks.7075 [Online]. Available: https://revistas.usal.es/index.php/eks/article/view/7075

Pawłowicz E, Kulesza M, Szymańska A, Masajtis Zagajewska A, Bartczak M, Nowicki M (2020) I hear and I forget. I see and I remember. I do and I understand-incorporating high-fidelity medical simulation into the undergraduate nephrology course. Renal Fail 42(1):1184–91, December 2020. Accessed: 10 Sept 2021. [Online]. Available: https://doi.org/10.1080/0886022X.2020.1847722

Trueba A (2012) "El simulador como herramienta de aprendizaje en las enseñanzas naúticas", Departamento de Ciencias y Técnicas de la Navegación y de la Construcción Naval. Universidad de Cantabria, España

Urbina S (2003) Medios y herramientas de comunicación para la educación universitaria. Edutec, Panamá, pp 101–114

Urra E, Sandoval S, Irribarren F (2017) El desafío y futuro de la simulación como estrategia de enseñanza en enfermería. Investigación en educación médica 6(22):119–125. https://doi.org/10.1016/j.riem.2017.01.147. [Online]. Available: http://riem.facmed.unam.mx/node/632

Vázquez-Mata G, Guillamet-Lloveras A (2021) El entrenamiento basado en la simulación como innovación imprescindible en la formación médica. Educación Médica 12(3):149–155. Accessed 04 Mar 2021. [Online]. Available: http://scielo.isciii.es/scielo.php?script=sci_arttext&pid=S1575-18132009000400004&lng=es&tlng=pt

Vialart MN (2020) Estrategias didácticas para la virtualización del proceso enseñanza aprendizaje en tiempos de COVID-19. Educ Med Super. Accessed: 10 Sept 2021. [Online]. Available: http://www.ems.sld.cu/index.php/ems/article/view/2594/1057

Vidal MJ, Avello R, Rodríguez MA, Menéndez JA (2021) Simuladores como medios de enseñanza. Educación Médica Superior 33(4). Accessed 05 Mar 2021. [Online]. Available: http://scielo.sld.cu/scielo.php?script=sci_arttext&pid=S0864-21412019000400008&lng=es&tlng=es

Ziv A (2009) Simulators and simulation-based medical education. In: Dent J, Harden RM (eds) A practical guide for medical teachers, Elsevier, Edinburgh

Chapter 9
Quantum Information Education and Research Through a Digital Approach During the COVID-19 Lockdown: A Case Study

Francisco Javier Delgado-Cepeda, Marco Benjamín Enríquez-Flores, and Alfonso Isaac Jaimes-Nájera

9.1 Introduction

Quantum technologies have emerged recently as a rich field of knowledge contributing to healthy economies, as developed countries recognize (NSF 1999; nIU 2016). The number of disciplines touched by developments involving quantum mechanics knowledge and applications increase daily; thus, skilled multidisciplinary professionals are in high demand. Despite the technological developments, quantum knowledge is still poorly disseminated and accessible for non-specialized professionals in other disciplines who require this knowledge. Several specialized research groups worldwide have made committed efforts to diminish this shortage of knowledge in cutting-edge science, transferring technical approaches and attracting the attention of professionals to collaborate. Such effort includes undergraduate and graduate students (Delgado-Cepeda 2018).

Nevertheless, notwithstanding such efforts, quantum knowledge has a mathematical and abstract basis that commonly requires guidance mainly in the first

Research supported by the initiative NOVUS for the innovation in Education and the School of Engineering and Science of Tecnologico de Monterrey.

F. J. Delgado-Cepeda (✉)
School of Engineering and Science, Tecnologico de Monterrey, Mexico City, Mexico
e-mail: fdelgado@tec.mx

M. B. Enríquez-Flores
School of Engineering and Science, Tecnologico de Monterrey, Santa Fe, Mexico
e-mail: menriquezf@tec.mx

A. I. Jaimes-Nájera
School of Engineering and Science, Tecnologico de Monterrey, Monterrey, Mexico
e-mail: ajaimes@tec.mx

stages of learning, e.g., through seminars, conferences, assessments, and collaboration. The COVID-19 confinements changed the direction of strategists and many
researchers engaged in collaborative activities, bringing some collaborations to a halt.
To this effect, this work examines the challenges of adaptation made by a quantum
information research group trying to maintain students' interest and involvement
in learning and research in the field. Practically, it considered undergraduate and
graduate students coming into the research group. Together, those students already
involved in a research project or learning process teach their new partners. The
second contribution of this paper (addressed in section II) presents the context of
quantum information and education in terms of the strategies established, the social
background during the recent pandemic, and the new strategies adopted by the educational institutions. The precedents and changes to adapt the group strategy, e.g., by our
research group (Quantum Information Processing Group) (ITESM 2021), together
with the description of our research community, are also presented in the third section
of this paper. Empirical discussion of the outcomes and analysis in terms of productivity is considered in the fourth section. Finally, the conclusions and the future work
are provided in the last section.

9.2 Comparative Social and Educative Context

The COVID-19 pandemic has impulsed education worldwide in new directions by
revealing the gaps and opportunity differences for students in different grades, types
of schools, and countries (Balkhi et al. 2020). Published reports from many countries
about research in different educative levels and areas have described educational
experiences in teaching during the pandemic (Code et al. 2020; Delgado 2021a).
Despite this, few of them have depicted the efforts in research education and the new
technologies involved during this restrictive historical period of humankind.

   The persistence in research education and the scaffolding of efforts to maintain
interest in science have suffered fierce resistance. Together, distance and blended
learning and research and advanced studies must overcome challenges and obstacles
to reach and sustain their goals, embracing complexity, diversity, and adaptation. For
these reasons, authors have selected this topic to report experiences and sustained
efforts at the university level, which has motivated a higher level of discipline and
the adaptation of resources and technology commonly used in the regular courses
during confinement. This work succinctly describes the experience and measured
outcomes in the research group to which the authors belong. This section presents
a contextual preamble about the resources and organization of the research group's
work.

9.2.1   Quantum Information Education Before COVID-19

The COVID-19 lockdown in Mexico evolved differently for the various educational levels and sectors of schools (public and private) for over sixteen months. In general, the educative experience was best for Higher Educational institutions and Private Education (OECD 2020; Delgado 2021b). Nevertheless, the closing of schools and institutes harmed the laboratory practices and work and research interactions compared to the pre-pandemic stage, despite the relatively well-implemented digital learning strategies.

Our research group in quantum information processing maintained, during the three years before COVID-19, a novel pyramidal approach (an organization where experienced researchers advise post-graduate students, who then advise undergraduate students) to attract and motivate students. We conducted an annual blended-learning workshop nationwide on our institution's 26 campuses, called "Semana I" (a yearly, mandatory, off-classes week for undergraduate students devoted to research and innovation activities). It included several derived one-year research stays for undergraduate students and graduate students developing original research (Delgado-Cepeda 2019; Delgado-Cepeda and Enríquez-Flores 2020). Such efforts have boosted and encouraged all students to publish original research work collaboratively. Although blended learning was previously present (our host institution is spread throughout Mexico), distance collaboration among several campuses became common in the last decade.

9.2.2   Changes in the Digital Strategy to Support Learning, Teaching, and Research in the COVID-19 Confinement

Students involved in the research group came from several entries. The majority of the undergraduate students have first attended the yearly nationwide workshops in quantum information. Even though most of the students were not completely involved in research, they purportedly learned the introductory concepts around quantum information and its applications. Around 40 students are expected each year. The first stage is delivered through a blended-learning approach. The second stage has been face-to-face in Mexico City (Delgado-Cepeda and Enríquez-Flores 2020) (with students from several campuses throughout the country). It is noteworthy that the delivery strategy changed during the pandemic; now, the workshop is done through distance delivery using virtual technologies such as the Zoom videoconference system. In this approach, new technologies were increasingly used, e.g., notes using iPad and i-Pencil, simulations using QUANTUM (an add-on developed by the research group and based on the Mathematica software), and distance demonstrative lab using 3DOptix.

Considering the latter mode of delivery, some students interested in a research stay decided to be added to the research group under the research modality, a series of optional courses letting those students research as part of their formal curricula. In the stay, they propose or are involved in a research project, working together with primary or established researchers, graduate students, or both. In specific seminars for each topic delivered two times a week, they advance in their development, which finally is published as a scientific collaboration. Videoconferencing and digital resources were again the main tools used to sustain such seminars. For group researchers, the experience began years before due to some students being in other far-off campuses. During the COVID-19 confinement, some adjustments and strategies were developed. For instance, a planned following of students three or four times a week was established and several weekly seminars by topic to reinforce the contact and research collaboration. Such efforts surely motivated students, partially far away from academic life.

Finally, graduate students followed a similar path during the pandemic, working on their theses, either with collaborators or alone with their advisers. Simulation work has been easily sustained through their equipment and supported through proxy connections to provide fast workstations. Some lab work was delayed as labs were closed, and some theses changed their focus to a complete simulation basis.

9.2.3 Organization, Strategies, and Population in a Short Timeline Through the COVID-19 Confinement

As explained in the previous section, videoconferencing was a central tool used to sustain the students' work. This had been already implemented in the group before the pandemic, and more efficient tools were used in areas where mathematical development is a daily basis or task. The use of iPad, i-Pencil, and Notability (an electronic handwriting application for iPad) effectively communicated real-time calculations and developments and the possibility to prepare animated physical and mathematical explanations designed to be posted asynchronously. Together, the increase in Mathematica and the QUANTUM add-on (Gómez Muñoz and Delgado 2016) during videoconferencing helped assess the students' developments until publication. Another helpful tool was Overleaf, an online tool to work collaboratively on scientific writing as shared projects using LaTeX. Due to the possibility of posting the developments, contributions, and collaborative elements, this practice became mandatory. In any case, the pyramidal organization was followed, but the forced digital presence and topics specialization made the collaboration easier.

The synthetic map or organization during the pandemic is shown in Fig. 9.1. There, three main integrating activities are reported together with the technological elements supporting them. The workshop organized yearly for the undergraduate students has as a secondary goal the attraction of interested students for one-year scientific stays in the research group through an insight proposal. During the research stay, each student must develop the research independently or collaborate with a graduate student. Such collaborations let those (undergraduate) students publish research work early in their

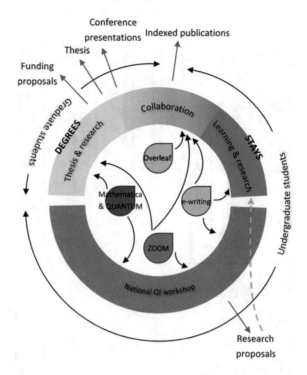

Fig. 9.1 Hierarchical elements in the students' inclusion within the research group, activities and tools supporting them in the lockdown, and products

academic lives. Graduate students work together on their theses, publications, writing funding and external proposals, and co-directing research work, all closely supervised by a primary adviser.

COVID-19 lockdown has been extended in Mexico from March 2020 to July 2021 (the current date of this article). During this period, the nationwide workshop was maintained (but reducing the number of participants because of the suspension of "Semana I," the natural space for that). During this time, the workshop has been organized externally and offered online, accepting only 30 students. In parallel, two students, S1 and S2, getting their master's degree (one of them, S2, collaborating from Spain) and two more, S4 and S5, obtaining their doctorate, were involved. Also, one undergraduate student, S3, performed a one-year research stay. Their main activities and collaborations are reported in the timeline depicted in Fig. 9.2 for the period reported. The activities revolved around indexed publications and collaborations, showing notable productivity. The articles reported have been labeled consecutively for each student as, for instance, S1.3 for the third article attributed to Student 1. The activities associated with each student have been colored differently to ease their identification.

As Fig. 9.2 depicts, intensive work in publications, proposals, and degrees represented around 1,000 h of videoconferencing from the primary researchers' group with the different groups of students. As a result, there were (a) five papers in Q1 or Q2 quartiles of Scopus in scientific research, (b) four indexed as conference papers

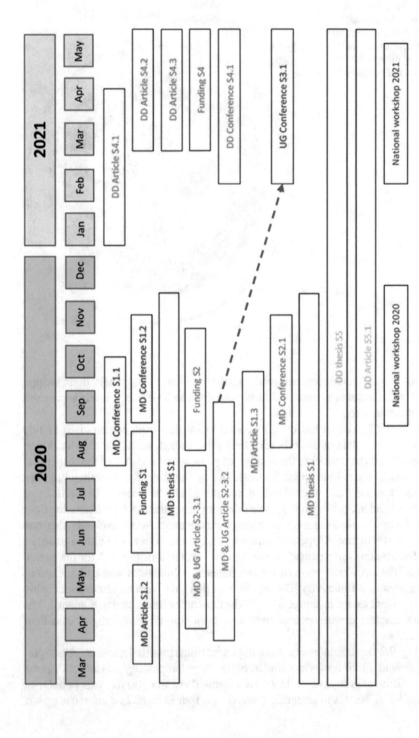

Fig. 9.2 Timeline of the leading student research activities corresponding to the COVID-19 lockdown (March 2020-May 2021)

in Q3 Scopus quartile, and (c) four more in Education in the Q1 and Q2 quartiles of Scopus. All of them related to the experiences of the students and the performed activities. In addition, three funding proposals were submitted to several international organizations. Also, during the period, two master's degrees were obtained. We describe those outcomes in more detail in the next section.

The current report deals with the documentation of actions to overcome the limitations imposed by the COVID-19 lockdown and research in education, particularly those related to the participating students, together with the possibilities to impact their attraction and promotion of research in science as a professional activity. As stated, these experiences during the COVID-19 confinement have been a rare educative topic, arousing the authors' interest. Thus, the objectives for this research were: (a) to account for the strategies followed during the lockdown, (b) to gather the main goals in research education in our group, and (c) to make a quantitative comparison of quality and quantity for research generated by our students during the period of the lockdown. Those objectives are addressed in the following sections.

9.3 Tangle, a Digital Approach, and the Global Effort

Tangle is an online suite to manage content, interactions, and collaboration of students participating diversely within the group (Delgado-Cepeda 2018). It was beneficial before the pandemic to provide ordered divulgation and formal resources to attract, teach, and integrate students in research (under research stays or graduate studies). Integrating essential contents and materials gives a roadmap for quantum information learning, clearly related to other areas such as quantum computation, communication, and other applications.

9.3.1 Tangle Design, Contents, and Utility

The Tangle suite is divided into four main sections. The first one is devoted to the basics of quantum mechanics, presenting the mathematical basis, the quantum mechanics postulates, and the central systems practical, as the first instance, in quantum information. The second section introduces the users to quantum information and quantum computation theories as presented by several authors. It presents the basic and intermediate topics on theoretical issues. The third section presents the main projects developed by the research group in the last ten years, containing discussions and papers owned by the group. It represents a transition between learning and research, letting the students select possible research lines followed by the primary researchers. The fourth section is a space of collaboration in the different ongoing projects, letting the students post contributions among the authors. It is also a platform to move into the Overleaf projects of writing. Commonly, the two first sections also divulge the lectures and scientific videos introducing each learning unit. Also, as an introduction to Tangle, the quantum information area is presented in economic, scientific, and social perspectives to engage the potential students. Figure 9.3 shows a collage of some aspects of the suite (Tangle), including the research projects' divulgation, videos, series, bibliography extracts, and interactive forums.

Tangle has become useful to ease the learning direction of students in several educational levels, including high school. A deeper description of their usage in terms of analytics has been reported for the pre-COVID-19 pandemic period (Delgado-Cepeda and Enríquez-Flores 2020). Through the nationwide workshops, those contents were superficially considered, by raising the possibility to guide, in the following years, students who could become fully and effectively involved in research in the immediate future together with the research group, mainly through

Fig. 9.3 Some elements of Tangle, involving introductory remarks, divulgation, visualization, bibliography, and collaboration

the research stays. During the pandemic, the online materials have become a natural constructed material for continuing the student guidance in those research stays and the introductory contents for the graduate students. This account provides an overview to cover our first research objective in terms of the initiatives, new technologies involved, and their relations with the goals achieved by the students. In the following sections, we cover the next two objectives.

9.3.2   Learning and Groups Involved

Integrated with Tangle, additional efforts during the COVID-19 lockdown have included using complementary technologies such as videoconferencing, electronic handwriting, and collaborative writing. For instance, in addition to the e-writing technology to ease the consideration of math writing and sharing, QUANTUM (Gómez Muñoz and Delgado 2016) allowed software scaffolding to automate calculations using the proper Dirac notation, basic in quantum mechanics and information. This tool connects the students' calculations with more complex representations: tables, figures, programming, and analyses. Interestingly, QUANTUM was created by the group around seven years ago. However, this add-on rapidly spread its usage to the worldwide scientific community and associated students. During the pandemic, prospectively, it was a useful tool to guide students to automate extensive calculations with quantum systems. Finally, in terms of online interactions, Zoom was used to facilitate contact with students. Notably, during the lockdown, one student was overseas, while most of the students were spread across the country's different states. Workshop webinars or individual collaborative sessions, as shown in Fig. 9.3, have contributed to the users' live experience of learning and collaboration.

9.3.3   Supporting Research and Collaboration

With the latest technologies, Overleaf (2021), a collaborative tool for scientific writing using LATEX (a commonly accepted language to prepare scientific documents), became extremely useful to write, review, collaborate, and publish journal articles about the research projects. Groups of collaborators can administrate the Overleaf projects via a link or invitation. In any case, collaborations remained restricted for each group of people involved. It allowed the users to work collaboratively and simultaneously on a publication by posting images and writing sections of related content for each member and subgroup.

9.3.4 Methods and Data Collection

The analyses presented to cover the research objectives have been performed with all students participating in at least one of the research activities within our university's quantum information-processing research group between March 2020 until June 2021 as a sample. The participation could be referred through several levels: workshop, research stays, and undergraduate studies, with 35 students in total. Data collection involves the detailed registers of activities across the last period giving research products as a result and the metadata of those products. We first perform a demography and accounting analysis to understand the sample and their products. Then, a conglomerate analysis for those products, numbers, and quality comprises the core of our research objective.

9.4 Outcomes of the Full Experience and Analysis

During COVID-19, the research group worked intensively with students to generate a series of research products and obtain their graduate degrees on time (when they applied for some of them). Table 9.1 presents a summary of the resultant products for each group involved. The first column corresponds to the number of students (St) in each group, dividing the population into Female (F) and Male (M) genders. The column labeled C refers to the number of states or countries involved during the distance interaction (only one student was overseas). For the section on products, the Research Proposals (RP), Conference Papers (CP), Journal Papers (JP), Thesis (T), and Conferences Attended (CA) are reported.

9.4.1 Groups, Collaboration, and Research Numbers During Lockdown

COVID-19 lockdown undoubtedly has introduced profound changes in all aspects of our lives. It changed Education drastically, migrating to a digital and distance

Table 9.1 Demography and summary of research products during the COVID-19 confinement

Groups	Demography				Products				
	St	C	F	M	RP	CP	JP	T	CA
Workshop	30	4	13	17	6	1	0	0	0
Research stay	1	1	0	1	0	2	1	0	1
Masters degree	2	2	0	2	0	2	3	2	3
Doctorate degree	2	2	0	2	1	2	2	2	0

modality, particularly in science (Usak et al. 2020). In fact, despite the strategies implemented by our research group, the research could barely be maintained during this period. The attraction of students became limited due to other priorities as part of changes in most of the educative policies of the institutions (UNDP 2020).

In our institution, the first impact of COVID-19 was the suspension of "Semana I" in 2020. Such activity (Semana I), mainly performed in a face-to-face learning setting, had constituted many activities for all students in our university, mainly directed toward research and innovation. Besides, some of the outcomes and projects were collaborations with industry, companies, and others in labs. The nationwide workshop in quantum information, except for the experimental sections, can be performed online for our activity. Nevertheless, due to the suspension of Semana I because of the lockdown, such a national workshop could not be carried out. Instead, the effort became diversified in several local activities. Workshops were organized locally, including only students in the lowest semesters. Also, a local lab in optics was offered on one of the campuses for Industrial Physics Engineers. The lab gave the participants the first insight into the optics lab by proposing new vision models, such as the human cornea and crystalline lens, using appropriate modeling. In addition, the analysis of the optical performance of the models proposed was performed using ray tracing computational simulations. In general, the pandemic has limited, especially during 2020, the possibility to invite students closer to the semesters where research stays are possible. Moreover, its effect could be seen as reducing the number of research group students participating in future years. This analysis exhibits the research goals, categorized by subgroups of students, activities, and products covering the second research objective.

9.4.2 Sensible Outcomes and Measurable Comparison Through the Period

The advancement in productivity generated by the students can be measured in terms of quality and number of publications. Particularly, considering the COVID-19 lockdown, a decrease, at least, in the number of publications could be expected. Nevertheless, Fig. 9.4 compares the last four years (when the national workshop was implemented to attract students to the research stays, including the graduate students) in both aspects: quality and number of publications. The information represented in Fig. 9.4 classifies the Q1, Q2, and Q3 publications, reporting the outcomes in color for each year (see the legends on the right; dot size corresponds to the number of articles). On the vertical axis, the average impact factor for each group of publications can be observed (dots has been slightly horizontally displaced in each class to avoid overlapping in the comparison). There is a consistent increase, as well as in quality and number of publications. Class for conference attendance (CA) reports the participation of students as presenters in national (N) or international (I) conferences. It is also noteworthy to mention that in the last four years, all participations

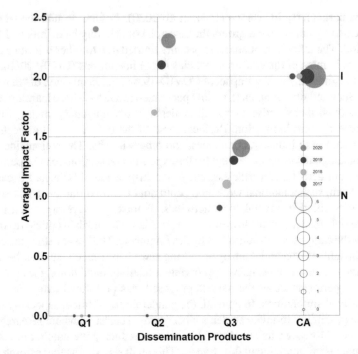

Fig. 9.4 A yearly summary of publications in Scopus Q1–Q3 quartiles colored in agreement with the right-upper scale (average impact factor on the left scale and number of items represented by the size disk on the right-lower scale). For conferences attended as speakers (CA), the number is also represented by the disk size and classified as International (I) or National (N)

have been international. Collectively, it can be said that all the outcomes illustrated in this paper show that the COVID-19 lockdown period did not affect the collaboration and scientific production, which has continued increasing. Using technological tools to facilitate the experience and learning of the participating students surpassed the absence of face-to-face work, provided a beneficial outcome, and increased their productivity in research.

The publications by some students in Q1 journals during their graduate and undergraduate studies are an outstanding goal and achievement. The exclusive participation in international conferences has promoted the students' work, forcing them to publish previous short works in Q3 journals. Also, there was a notable increase in the number of articles published, particularly in Q2 and Q3 journals. Additionally, during 2020, their reported areas of interest were spread across the fields of quantum communication, quantum chemistry, and quantum biology, associated with the underlying topic of quantum information.

9.5   Discussion and Conclusions

Online Education has upgraded its status during the COVID-19 lockdown. As never before, education has been open to technological solutions and new ways to deliver, administrate, evaluate, and assess the educational processes and goals (Dhawan 2020).

9.5.1   Discussion of Primary Outcomes Derived from the Research

Research is sometimes a silent education in the university. However, research institutes improve human resources and contribute to future scientific development. Research has had to survive with low attention during the COVID-19 crisis. Notably, it has not been the focus of support programs during the pandemic (except those closely connected to health and social priorities). In any case, such aspect of Higher Education has been affected with broad impact, its institutions and schools changed and scarred (Ghada-Refaat 2021).

In this work, we reported some efforts to maintain a permanent strategy toward attracting and training future researchers in quantum information and other related scientific areas of applied research and multidisciplinary science during the COVID-19 confinement. This effort provided successful experiences for the students and outcomes, particularly in theory, modeling, and simulation, where the use of labs was limited. Thus, it is noteworthy that limited outcomes were purportedly obtained in the experimental setup due to the closing of universities and labs. Prospectively, an uncertain outcome surrounds the attraction of new human resources for research, e.g., in quantum information, for the coming years during the "new normal" (post-COVID), not only in terms of slowing down but also due to the new economic, social, and political crises and rulings worldwide.

Notwithstanding, a critical outstanding fact is that in education, new technologies have boosted the scientific production of the students and our group context in the theoretical or simulation lines of research. Their use has opened new ways to effectively collaborate and boost scientific production during the COVID-19 contingency. The goals achieved by the students have surpassed the expectations. Notably, our integrative project for Education in quantum information research was recognized as a shortlisted project by the Reimagine Education 2020 initiative (QS 2021). This annual recognition rewards innovative pedagogies that focus on producing improved learning and employment outcomes for students. Due to the actions and decisions taken during Covid19, some graduate students effectively sustained scientific production and fulfilled their degree requirements on time and with high quality. Our analysis showed that the notable effort in design and organization improved outcomes in terms of quantity and quality, fulfilling the third research objective. Despite a limited call to recruit new students during this period, the research group seized on the immediate needs and leveraged an opportunity to improve.

9.5.2 Conclusions and Some Remarks for the Research Education Practice

In the broader spectrum of scientific research, the "new normal" is now arising in most countries worldwide. Schools and universities have begun to open secure protocols and conditions for learning, thus, ruling the comeback of the students under a new dynamic learning environment, which will change academic lives. As learned during the lockdown, distance collaboration can promote improved, effective, and outstanding ways to collaborate and broaden students' attraction. In the past, offering the nationwide workshop and research stays partially in distance modality served such objective. Now, during the new normal, the nationwide workshop described in this paper will be developed during the 2021 "Semana I" entirely online. In addition, it will be conducted in parallel with a biennial international workshop called "Quantum Fest 2021" (CINVESTAV 2021), which is organized by our group and other partners in other institutions in Mexico. It is the first time such an international conference will be carried out online, carrying out the hybrid experience left by the confinement period. Therefore, students can also gain an advantage in participating in the conference, especially to learn how to publish their research work in further editions of this or other conferences. It will be of great benefit to them and the scientific community at large. Alongside these efforts, science and scientific education must migrate to the new normal to re-instate the academic life with the premises set out in secure work zones, with new ways to share and collaborate using all the technology we have learned and developed during the lockdown. Notably, as Prof. David Payne (professor of photonics and Director of the Optoelectronics Research Center at the University of Southampton) has opined (Dhawan 2020), the scientific community should act resiliently to create new virtual academic communities, caring for the mental health of the stakeholders (teachers, students, education experts), and recovering (boosting) early career researchers for the future.

The current case study has shown that, with a limited population as sample, different aspects related to research and advanced studies have still been sustained through proper technologies and methodologies, but mainly with a sustained discipline to reach the desired research goals. Most technologies were inherited from continuing undergraduate studies during the COVID-19 lockdown. Notably, certain aspects of the experience should be particularized, mainly in terms of time, extension, complexity, flexibility, and tight collaboration. Despite the pyramidal structure, the support to each student from the adviser was critical to reaching their goals. Similar parallel analyses focused on students' social and mental health issues at the graduate level (Elmer et al. 2020) because of the exigence required. In other terms, an extended analysis about the multifactorial impact of lockdown on Higher Education in developing countries has been conducted (Said 2021), showing notable outcomes as in the present experience, mainly due to the efforts of students and advisers. This fact is an essential lesson from this period, whether the "new normal" restores or not the full presential teaching modality in the institutes.

9.5.3 Limitations and Future Work

The presented experience was limited to a small and reduced group of undergraduate and graduate students in science and engineering. Despite that the limitations of this case study cannot establish a universal, extendable model, it does report positive outcomes in scientific production and development of human resources in scientific research. Emergency Education will be with us for an indeterminate time, undermining our educative activities. The COVID-19 confinement has taught us new ways to approach education in a large variety of scenarios, levels, disciplines, and related activities. Literature on the impact of COVID-19 confinement on graduate students is sparse because they are still a minority immersed in the total population of Higher Education. Additional research should be conducted per discipline (regardless of separate disciplinary requirements) to collect and compare similar experiences already sustained. More extensive research about methodologies combined and supported by technologies should be developed to enrich graduate studies' management under similar conditions, particularly if they are scaffolding more exclusive research and collaborative activities in graduate studies supported by technology.

Acknowledgements The Quantum Information Processing Group of Tecnologico de Monterrey is grateful for each one of our students involved in learning and research in Quantum Information and their dedication during the Covid-19 crisis in 2020 and 2021. Thanks, mainly, because their participation contributed to deepening our knowledge about blended learning and research, providing successful experiences during this critical era for humankind.

The authors would like to acknowledge the financial support of the Novus 2019 Grant with PEP no. PHHT023-19ZZ00018 and the funding of scientific publications by the School of Engineering and Sciences.

Finally, the authors also acknowledge the technical support of the Writing Lab, Institute for the Future of Education, Tecnologico de Monterrey, Mexico, in the production of this work.

References

Balkhi F, Nasir A, Zehra A (2020) Psychological and behavioral response to the coronavirus (COVID-19) pandemic. Cureus 12(5):1–12
CINVESTAV (2021) Homepage of quantumfest. Retrieved from: http://eventos.fis.cinvestav.mx/quantumfest
Code J, Ralph R, Forde K (2020) Pandemic designs for the future: perspectives of technology education teachers during COVID-19. Inf Learn Sci 121(5/6):419–431

Delgado F (2021a) Teaching physics for computer science students in higher education during the COVID-19 pandemic: a fully internet-supported course 13(2):35

Delgado F (2021b) Transforming a blended learning course in numerical methods into a flexible digital course during the Covid-19 crisis. Future Internet 15(3):332–353

Delgado-Cepeda FJ (2018) Tangle: a blended educative suite for the quantum information education and development of research skills. In: e-Society 2018 conference proc, pp 23–29

Delgado-Cepeda FJ (2019) Blended learning in research-oriented education: Tangle, an educative suite for quantum information. IADIS Int J WWW/Internet 16(1):26–41

Delgado-Cepeda FJ, Enríquez-Flores MB (2020) Using mobile learning and research-based learning to attract students into quantum information research. In: Mob Learn 2020 Conf Proc 102–106

Dhawan S (2020) Online learning: a panacea in the time of COVID-19 crises. J Educ Technol 49(1):5–22

Elmer T, Mepham K, Stadtfeld C (2020) Students under lockdown: comparisons of students' social networks and mental health before and during the COVID-19 crisis in Switzerland. PLoS ONE 15(7):e0236337

El Said GR (2021) How did the COVID-19 pandemic affect higher education learning experience? an empirical investigation of learners' academic performance at a university in a developing country. Adv Human-Comput Int 2021:6649524

Ghada-Refaat ES (2021) How did the COVID-19 pandemic affect higher education learning experience? an empirical investigation of learners' academic performance at a university in a developing country. Adv Human-Comput Int 2021:6649524

Gómez Muñoz JL, Delgado F (2016) QUANTUM: a wolfram mathematica add-on for dirac Bra-Ket notation, non-commutative Algebra, and simulation of quantum computing circuits. J Phys: Confe Ser 698:012019

ITESM (2021) Homepage of photonics and quantum systems group. Retrieved from: https://tec.mx/en/research/where-research-carried-out/photonics-and-quantum-systems

nlU (2016) Quantum Europe 2016: a new era of technology. European Commission. Retrieved from: http://gdriqfa.unice.fr/IMG/pdf/quantumeurope2016_report.pdf

NSF (1999) Quantum information science: an emerging field of interdisciplinary research and education in science and engineering. Retrieved from: https://www.nsf.gov/pubs/2000/nsf00101/nsf00101.htm

OECD (2020) School education during covid-19: were teachers and students ready? Mexico, OECD Publishing, Paris. Retrieved from: http://www.oecd.org/education/Mexicocoronavirus-education-country-note.pdf

Overleaf (2021) Homepage of overleaf. Retrieved from: https://www.overleaf.com

QS (2021) Homepage of reimagine education. 2021. Retrieved from: https://www.reimagine-education.com

UNDP (2020) Policy brief: education during COVID-19 and beyond. UNDP, New York

Usak M, Masalimova AR, Cherdymova EI, Shaidullina AR (2020) New playmaker in science education: COVID-19. J Balt Sci Educ 19:180–185

Chapter 10
The Use of ICT in Times of Crisis: Evidence of the Earthquake of September 19, 2017

Noemí Vásquez-Quevedo and Jorge Mora-Rivera

10.1 Introduction

One of the most severe consequences of natural disasters to education is the closure of educational institutions and the suspension of the teaching process. Events of this nature leave millions of students without education. In Mexico City, an earthquake on September 19, 2017, damaged 2026 schools (Secretaría de obras y servicios 2021). The Tecnologico de Monterrey Campus Mexico City, with 5146 students enrolled at a professional level at the time of the earthquake, suspended classes for ten days and implemented technological strategies to continue educational services in that semester.

The aftermath of a natural disaster is full of challenges for civil society, the government, and educational institutions (Baytiyeh 2008). In education, the planning and execution of strategic teaching models, which rely on technological support for the didactic techniques, must be directed to generate innovative solutions to overcome the adversities of natural disasters (Basoo-Aránguiz 2018).

This research aimed to provide evidence that technological tools contribute positively to the teaching–learning process by analyzing and comparing the academic performance of a group of students before, during, and after the earthquake. This work's main contribution consists of statistically reliable evidence about the benefits of online learning after an earthquake, a topic that has been absent in previous studies in Mexico.

N. Vásquez-Quevedo (✉) · J. Mora-Rivera
Tecnologico de Monterrey, Business School, Department of Accounting and Finance, Mexico City, Mexico
e-mail: nvasquez@tec.mx

J. Mora-Rivera
Tecnologico de Monterrey, School of Social Sciences and Government, Mexico City, Mexico
e-mail: jjmora@tec.mx

S. Hosseini et al. (eds.), *Technology-Enabled Innovations in Education*,
Transactions on Computer Systems and Networks,
https://doi.org/10.1007/978-981-19-3383-7_10

10.2   Theoretical Framework

Natural disasters damage school facilities, causing suspension of educational services, and negatively affect people's health, causing numerous psychological effects (Esterwood and Saeed 2020). Some authors point out that disaster affects students' daily lives, impacting various educational factors and leading to low academic performance (Silverman and Greca 2002). In general, earthquakes can damage the infrastructure of vulnerable areas, put students at risk, and interrupt the educational system's activities (Naja and Baytiyeh 2004). In fact, of the three most damaged areas (physical, psychological, and educational), education has received the least academic research (Peek and Richardson 2010).

However, the existing research on natural disasters' impact on education focuses on two approaches: studies that analyze the psychological impact on students (post-traumatic stress disorder) and those that address the implementation of strategies such as online learning accompanied by technology. The latter research examines how the appropriate use of mobile technologies, cloud technologies, and social media contributes favorably to the safety of students and the continuity of education during and after a crisis (Baytiyeh 2019). Some studies in Asia show the role of mobile technologies in improving mental health before, during, and after a natural disaster (Sobowale and Torous 2016).

The lessons learned in recent years regarding disasters and emergencies in a global environment provide evidence that social networks serve as a comprehensive and meaningful component of emergency response (Simon et al. 2015). Implementing these tools supports the institutional communication strategy when the institution considers the implications of the social networks to which students have access (Dabner 2012). Additionally, studies have analyzed the impact of social networks in coordinating relief work to people in Mexico affected by the 2017 earthquake, especially how these networks minimized false or outdated information during the relief efforts (Flores-Saviaga and Savage 2021).

To face adverse situations, educational institutions must promote resilience. Social cohesion after an earthquake is also necessary among vulnerable communities for recovery processes, such as guaranteeing the structural safety of school buildings and giving continuity to education through an online teaching–learning modality (Ayebi-Arthur 2017; Baytiyeh 2017).

Some examples of proactive measures using mobile learning technologies to maintain the teaching and learning process during temporary school closings caused by crises are using WhatsApp groups, cloud storage technology, and private and free-access administration systems, such as Moodle, Edmodo, Google Apps for education, among others. In the absence of face-to-face interactions with their students, teachers use these tools to create groups, assign tasks, schedule evaluations, and publish summaries and short videos on a specific topic (Baytiyeh 2019).

Young people increasingly access and use mobile technology. One strategy has been to turn mobile games into effective learning technologies. The game-based learning project (mGBL) uses practical activities to develop skills and strategies to cope with crises, providing learning tools through mobile devices that are useful for hybrid learning models (Mitchell and Maxl 2007). These solutions are perceived of high value by international organizations, such as UNESCO and *Save the Children*, who promote solutions using smartphones to contribute to students' learning in times of crisis and invite teachers to be trained in mobile technologies (Baytiyeh 2019).

10.3   Methodology

10.3.1   Problem Statement

Technology is a crucial element for the continuity of education after a natural disaster. Online learning becomes the solution when educational institutions are forced to suspend activities in their facilities, allowing the teaching–learning process to continue.

Considering this perspective, we posed two research questions in this study:

1. Does using virtual tools favor learning in times of crisis?
2. Responding to the ravages of an earthquake, does a hybrid learning model improve academic performance in accounting and economics?

To answer these questions, we analyzed academic performance in different subjects and compared the results at two different moments (before and after the event) during the semester in which the earthquake occurred.

10.3.2   Method

The present investigation adopted a descriptive, qualitative approach following the methodology proposed by Álvarez and Gayou (2003). A virtual survey was applied at the end of the January-May 2018 academic period. The total sample was 191 undergraduate students: 70 from the economics program (LEC/LEF) and 121 from public accounting and finance (LCPF). The student's academic performance was measured taking the class mean in the following subjects: Corporate Accounting, Intermediate Accounting I and II, International Financial Reports, Theory and Policy of International Trade, Industrial Organization, and Econometrics II. The data used is from the semester when the earthquake occurred and the semesters before and after. Additionally, another virtual survey was applied to 58 students in the two-degree programs (Economics and Public Accounting and Finance) to obtain information related to (a) students' perception of the use of virtual tools; (b) their perception of using technological tools under adverse conditions; and (c) their perceived advantages in using ICT during the learning process.

10.4 Results

Table 10.1 shows the students' perception results on using ICT from the virtual survey. The figures in the first box indicate that 76% of the students considered the Zoom platform very useful in their learning, while 24% were indifferent. 85% of respondents said their progress in the learning process was due to virtual tools, regardless of the type. At the same time, 13% believed that these tools had no impact. Concerning the available technology tools, 31% of those surveyed answered that *Blackboard* gave them the most help, 19% said that *Zoom* significantly contributed, and 50% indicated that other e-learning tools positively influenced their learning.

The second box of Table 10.1 shows the students' opinions about the advantages of using digital tools. 85% of the students believed that immediate feedback was the main benefit of using these tools. The feedback tool (Blackboard or Zoom) gave the professor some flexibility to answer questions in real-time, especially helpful because the physical facilities did not allow on-site office hours because of the September 2017 earthquake. Additionally, 55% noted that homework review and pretests were essential, benefiting their future evaluations. Finally, 49% of students found the application of virtual exams practical because it facilitated assessment under conditions when direct contact between students and teachers was impossible.

Table 10.2 shows the results of the average academic performance for the three periods analyzed (before, during, and after the earthquake) in both degree programs. The above allows evaluating the impact of ICTs on the teaching–learning process in an adverse environment. The data indicate that the students in the bachelor's degree in public accounting and finance program did not have significant differences in

Table 10.1 Perception of the use of virtual tools in the period of the earthquake

Academic period with the adverse conditions

	Yes (%)	No (%)	Indifferent (%)	Total (%)
Virtual Tools Utility (Zoom)	76	0	24	100
Learning achievement through virtual tools	85	13	2	100
	Blackboard (%)	Zoom (%)	Other e-learning tolos (%)	
Tool with the most significant contribution to learning	31	19	50	

Advantages in the use of ICT

Immediate feedback	85
Review of previously completed assignments/exams	55
Identification of response options	57
Virtual exam application	49

Source Own work

Table 10.2 Descriptive statistics of academic performance by career and period of analysis

Semester	LCPF				LEC/LEF			
	Average	Std. Dev	Min	Max	Average	Std. Dev	Min	Max
2016–13 Semester	86.74	8.59	63.00	100.00	88.96	7.28** (0.038)	76.65	98.90
2017–13[a] Semester	85.54	9.03	64.00	99.00	90.44	4.65	81.78	96.58
2018–11[b] Semester	80.41** (0.026)	9.10	55.00	98.00	89.88	6.11	80.00	99.00

Source Own work

**Significant differences at 5%. Figures in parentheses represent *p*-values

[a]The academic period where the earthquake occurred was August-December 2017. This period represents the base category

[b]This period represents the semester immediately after the earthquake

academic performance before and during the earthquake (comparing the differences in means of the simple averages of their final grades in the two semesters). In other words, although the maximum and the average score achieved was slightly higher in the period before the earthquake, there were no statistically significant differences in their average values or the variance of these scores.

In the case of the undergraduate economics students, the results indicated similar final average grades without statistically significant differences in the periods analyzed. However, the existence of a significant difference at 95% confidence in the dispersion of the final grades should be noted, especially in the semester before the earthquake (see Fig. 10.1). This result shows that ICT use is positive; despite the earthquake, students' academic performance was not affected and had less dispersion.

On the other hand, when comparing the academic performance in the semester when the earthquake occurred with the subsequent period, no significant differences were found in the grades of the students pursuing the economics degree. However, for the accounting students, there were statistically significant differences in the final average grades (higher) in the semester of the earthquake. Likewise, the results showed that all the indicators (average grade, minimum and maximum values) were higher among the students enrolled in the semester of the earthquake (see Fig. 10.2). These results clearly indicate that ICT allows continuity of learning processes during crises and periods of uncertainty. Thus, the analysis shows that these tools are essential to the academic performance of students, which leads us to think that their adoption on a larger scale is necessary because they reduce costs and make teaching–learning processes more efficient.

10.5   Discussion

The results of this research show evidence of the need to promote technological tools, a promulgation of the Tec 21 Educational Model recently implemented at

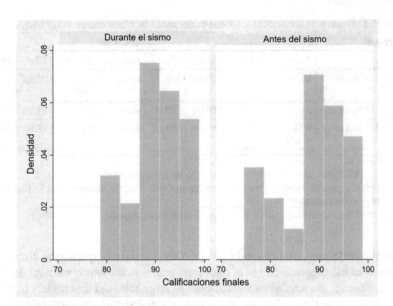

Fig. 10.1 LEC/LEF academic performance: during (durante) and before (antes) the earthquake (el sismo)

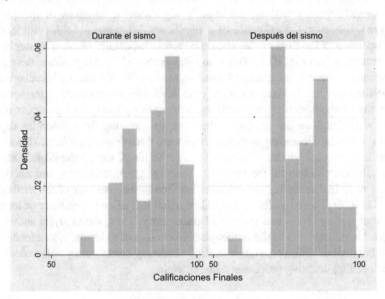

Fig. 10.2 LCPF academic performance: during (durante) and after (despues) the earthquake (el sismo). *Note* "Calificaciones Finales" means Final Grades

Tecnologico de Monterrey. Therefore, our findings support Basso-Aránguiz (2018) and Baytiyeh (2019). They emphasized that, under contexts of crisis and uncertainty, immersion in an environment heavily using technological tools facilitates the continuous training of teachers and students in the proper and efficient use of ICT (Basoo-Aránguiz 2018; Baytiyeh 2019; Sobowale and Torous 2016). International experience supports the urgent need to use technological tools to promote continuity and shape teaching–learning processes. At the national level, the experience of TEC-CCM after the earthquake is an example of what the research of international organizations suggests doing in times of crisis caused by natural disasters (Baytiyeh 2019; Sobowale and Torous 2016; Simon et al. 2015).

Our study expands on the results of authors, such as Simon et al. (2015) and Dabner (2012), about the importance of providing continuity to educational services after an earthquake. Although research addresses the emerging educational issues in crises (Ayebi-Arthur 2017; Baytiyeh 2017), we found no studies addressing the impact of technological tools on academic performance at a university level in Mexico, where the tools were used to monitor the teaching–learning process.

10.6   Conclusions

This study presents solid evidence gathered from the experiences of LCPF and LEC/LEF students using different technological tools, such as Blackboard and Zoom, among others. By measuring their academic performance during three periods (before, during, and after the September 19, 2017 earthquake), we found that the immersive use of technological tools positively impacted students' grades even in periods of crisis. These results can help bridge the adoption, use, and development of ICT with university teaching–learning processes, especially in countries with high vulnerability to natural disasters.

Although this research makes significant contributions to the literature, we point out some limitations. This study did not incorporate qualitative methodologies. Doing so would allow exploring in greater detail the main motivations of students to improve their academic performance through digital tools. Our study focused on two technological tools (Blackboard and Zoom). However, it would be desirable to incorporate other technological tools and social media use into the analyses of monitoring and assessing students and their academic achievement. These recommendations are beyond the scope of the present study, but they could undoubtedly be the subject of future research that expands the findings shown in this chapter.

References

Álvarez J, Gayou J (2003) Cómo hacer investigación Cualitativa: fundamentos y metodología, Paidós Educador, México

Ayebi-Arthur K (2017) E-learning, resilience and change in higher education: helping a university cope after a natural disaster. E-Learn Digital Med 14:259–274

Basoo-Aránguiz M (2018) Propuesta de modelo tecnologico para flipped classroom. Revista Electrónica Educare 22:1–17

Baytiyeh H (2008) Online learning during post-earthquake school closures. Disaster Prev Manage: Int J 27:215–227

Baytiyeh H (2017) Resilience should be critical for the post- earthquake recovery of communities in divided societies. Educ Urban Soc 51:1–19

Baytiyeh H (2019) Mobile learning technologies as a means of maintaining education delivery in crisis situations. Int J Inf Commun Technol Educ 15:1–10

Dabner N (2012) Internet and higher education' breaking ground' in the use of social media: a case study of a university earthquake response to inform educational design with facebook. Internet High Educ 15:69–78

Esterwood E, Saeed S (2020) Past epidemics, natural disasters, COVID19, and mental health: learning from history as we deal with the present and prepare for the future. Psychiatr Q 91:1121–1133

Flores-Saviaga C, Savage S (2021) Fighting disaster misinformation in Latin America: the #19S Mexican earthquake case study. Pers Ubiquit Comput 25:353–373

Mitchell A, Maxl E (2007) Mobile game-based learning—issues emerging from preliminary research and implications for game design [20th Bled eConference eMergence, 2007]

Naja M, Baytiyeh H (2004) Towards safer public school buildings in Lebanon: an advocacy for the seismic retrofitting initiative. Int J Disaster Risk Red 8:158–165

Peek L, Richardson K (2010) In their own words: displaced children's educational. Disaster Med Public Health Prep 4:63–70

Secretaría de obras y servicios, Concluyen obras de Rehabilitación y reconstrucción en el 97% de escuelas de nivel básico dañadas por el sismo 19-s, February 2021.

Silverman W, Greca A (2002) Children experiencing disasters: definitions, reactions, and predictors of outcomes, pp 10–33

Simon T, Goldberg A, Adini B (2015) Socializing in emergencies—a review of the use of social media in emergency situations. Int J Inf Manage 35:609–619

Sobowale K, Torous J (2016) Disaster psychiatry in Asia: the potential of smartphones, mobile, and connected technologies. Asian J Psychiatr 22:1–5

Chapter 11
Learning Perceptions of Traditional, Blended, and Flexible, Interactive, Technological ("FIT") e-Learning Courses

Blanca Bazán-Perkins

11.1 Introduction

An estimated 2.5 million articles are published each year in journals indexed in the Journal Citation Reports, most of which cover life and health sciences. It is estimated that the increase in Medline publications between 2003 and 2013 was 6.7% and continues to increase (Plume and van Weijen 2014). Incorporating this amount of new health sciences knowledge in the teaching–learning process makes necessary the continuous review of curricula to select relevant information while trying to avoid course overload (Verhoeff et al. 2018). Still, new generations are challenged to learn more information than previous ones, triggering the urgency to develop new learning strategies (Chen and Ni 2013).

11.2 Learning Strategies

The multifaceted learning process, its complexity, and the voluminous health sciences content present various challenges for both teachers and students in the teaching–learning process (Verhoeff et al. 2018; Fregni 2019). Various strategies have been created to achieve better assimilation of this knowledge, including the generation of videos (Cox 2011), computer simulations (Booth et al. 2021), and interactive digital resources (Kalogiannis et al. 2014) as support to teaching and learning. Our research group has determined that using gamification (Bazan-Perkins and Huesca-Juárez

B. Bazán-Perkins (✉)
School of Medicine and Health Sciences, Tecnologico de Monterrey, Mexico City, Mexico
e-mail: bbazan@tec.mx

Immunopharmacology Laboratory, Instituto Nacional de Enfermedades Respiratorias, Mexico City, Mexico

© The Author(s), under exclusive license to Springer Nature Singapore Pte Ltd. 2022 151
S. Hosseini et al. (eds.), *Technology-Enabled Innovations in Education*,
Transactions on Computer Systems and Networks,
https://doi.org/10.1007/978-981-19-3383-7_11

2016a), collaborative work, and elaborating integrative processes such as metabolic maps (Bazan-Perkins and Huesca-Juárez 2016b) increase students' learning gains. Also, our assessment of learning gain compared to students' preference in learning modalities shows the value of incorporating teaching experience and practice because students tend to prefer kinesthetic and multimodal learning, and these preferences are associated with a more significant gain in learning (Bazan-Perkins et al. 2017). This evidence has prompted us to seek new teaching strategies to support student learning.

11.3   Learning Challenges

Among the challenges of academic innovation is incorporating new content in the study plans resulting from the enormous progression in scientific knowledge. In particular, one of the fastest-growing areas in scientific knowledge is health sciences (Plume and van Weijen 2014). Thus, it is essential to identify the factors that promote obtaining, understanding, interpreting, organizing, and processing information among the new generations. In addition, it is fundamental to identify the threshold concepts in each course because its mastering denotes a transcendental understanding of a discipline without which the learner cannot progress (Loertscher et al. 2014).

The millennial generation has much experience with technology that accesses numerous information sources (Montenery et al. 2013), which leads to tools and design elements that converge to improve the teaching–learning process. Among the technological teaching–learning methodologies is blended learning, which has been defined as the combination of face-to-face classes with online content or other activities that support acquiring information and communication technologies (Picciano 2009). Blended learning utilizes various technologies and strategies, including recorded classes, flipped classes, online communication and tutorials, e-Portfolios, and wikis, all to improve the learning process (Francis and Shanon 2013). However, literature reports that blended learning affects students' intentions due to distraction problems (Marco et al. 2017). On the other hand, the totally remote courses allow synchronistic instruction from various cities and countries. Since 2017, the School of Medicine and Health Science (SMHS) of Tecnologico de Monterrey has developed an e-learning course that is flexible, interactive, and technological ("FIT"). It facilitates the interaction of teachers and students anywhere in the world (Membrillo-Hernández et al. 2019). Consequently, during the Covid-19 pandemic, blended and FIT courses have offered the necessary advantage of long-distance instruction using online resources (Biswas et al. 2021). However, a fundamental question is how to evaluate the effects on learning of online instruction through blended and FIT e-learning courses compared to traditional or face-to-face classes. We chose the learning gain (a term widely used to describe the tangible changes in learning achieved after a specific intervention) as the assessment measurement to know these effects (Pickering 2017).

11.4 Methods

We evaluated the impact of traditional face-to-face, FIT e-learning and blended courses on the learning gain compared with the perceptions of freshmen students in the School of Medicine and Health Sciences (SMHS).

This study was carried out among students taking the "Chemical Bases of Metabolism and Physiology" course between 2015 and 2019. They were randomly recruited from the SMHS Mexico City Campus of Tecnologico de Monterrey. The students were enrolled in Biomedical Engineering, Bachelor of Nutrition and General Well-being, and Medicine programs. All the students were invited to participate in the study voluntarily. They were informed about the processing of their personal data per the protection guidelines established by the Federal Institute for Access to Public Information in Mexico. This project is coordinated with the Instituto Nacional de Enfermedades Respiratorias (INER) and approved by the INER Research and Research Ethics Committees (S01-16).

For the blended and FIT e-learning sessions, the Zoom and CANVAS applications were used. The interactions for resolving questions and concerns and delivering tasks in all the courses occurred through the Remind application. The blended learning included one traditional face-to-face session per week. All courses were biannual and had the same content, instructional hours, and teacher. All FIT e-learning exams had fewer questions (40–50) than blended and traditional courses (100–120). In addition, FIT e-learning course exams were applied only at the middle and end of the course; the blended and traditional courses had three exams, one at the end of the course. In addition, the significant percentage of grades in FIT e-learning courses were assessed on activities. In contrast, in blended and traditional face-to-face courses, the majority of grading component was assessed on exams.

The online classes included the following rules:

(i)   Students and teachers must ensure good internet connections.
(ii)   The students must attend online classes in a well-lit place with little noise and no interruptions.
(iii) The students were encouraged to use headphones with a microphone for good concentration and avoidance of external sounds.
(iv)   The teacher should connect before the students to greet them when they connect. It is common for students not to respond immediately when greeted because the sound takes time, but the teacher needs to verify that they can hear one another.
(v)   The teacher must always have an alternative communication source in case of loss of connection with the students.
(vi)   To involve students during class, the teacher must ask them questions to maintain their attention and avoid distractions.

In all the courses, we applied a pre-test as a baseline for learning gain assessment. The post-test was carried out immediately after the last class without notifying the students so that they would not study. Both tests were not included in the students' grading. Subsequently, the data were processed with the Hake (2002) weighted gain Eq. (11.1).

$$(\Pi o \sigma \tau - \tau \epsilon \sigma \tau - \Pi \rho \epsilon \tau \epsilon \sigma \tau)/(M \alpha \xi - \Pi \rho \epsilon \tau \epsilon \sigma \tau) = \Lambda \epsilon \alpha \rho \nu \iota \nu \gamma \gamma \alpha \iota \nu \qquad (11.1)$$

Hake's equation for learning gain calculates the percentage of learning, taking the grades obtained in a process before (pre-test) and after (post-test) with respect to the maximum possible grade (max). This equation considers a pre-test–post-test process. In this case, the assessment questionnaire had 40 true–false questions (Brassil and Brian 2019), so, in the equation, Max has a value of 40.

Two additional open questions were included in the post-test questionnaire:

1. What do you perceive as positive about online lectures?
2. What do you perceive as negative about online lectures?

The changes between the groups were evaluated using the ANOVA followed by a post hoc test (Tukey). Statistical significance was established with a P-value < 0.05.

11.5 Results

Students taking the organic chemistry courses in the SMHS between 2015 and 2019 were invited to participate in the study. Those agreeing to participate included 62 in the traditional courses, 60 in blended, and 41 in FIT e-learning courses.

We observed a significant increase ($P < 0.01$) in the learning gain in the blended model (Fig. 11.1) in comparison to traditional and FIT e-learning courses. Notably,

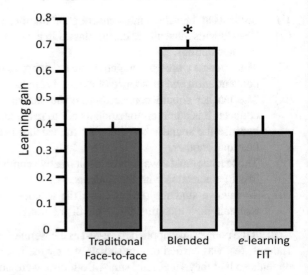

Fig. 11.1 Learning gain in face-to-face traditional ($n = 62$), blended ($n = 60$) and FIT e-learning courses ($n = 41$). One-way ANOVA, followed by Tukey. *$P < 0.01$ post-test, compared between all groups

Table 11.1 Positive perceptions of online instruction in blended courses

Answers to the question: What do you perceive as positive about online lectures?[a]			
Not having to travel, have class anywhere	Ability to study recorded lectures	Have more time	Nothing
10%	66%	22%	5%

[a]$n = 60$

the FIT e-learning course *grades* were higher than the blended and face-to-face traditional courses (data not shown).

Regarding the questions about the positive or negative perception of online instruction by Zoom application in blended and FIT e-learning courses, the open answers could be grouped because many students manifested the same concept.

Table 11.1 shows that most of the students perceived the positive aspects of recorded online sessions available for study in the blended courses. Table 11.2 shows that the primary negative perception related to distractors during the sessions.

Table 11.3 shows that in the FIT e-learning courses, most of the students considered that online advantages are similar to blended courses. Table 11.4 shows that

Table 11.2 Negative perceptions of online instruction in blended courses

What do you perceive as negative about online lectures?[a]				
Many distractors during the session	Connection failures	Lack of human interaction	Feel they do not learn	Course not suitable to be online
54%	36%	14%	3%	11%

[a]$n = 60$

Table 11.3 Positive perceptions of online instruction in FIT e-learning courses

What do you perceive as positive about online lectures?[a]			
Not having to travel, have class anywhere	Ability to study recorded lectures	Have more time	Nothing
5%	63%	15%	17%

[a]$n = 41$

Table 11.4 Negative perceptions of online instruction in FIT e-learning courses

What do you perceive as negative about online lectures?[a]			
Many distractors	Connection failures	Lack of human interaction	Feel they do not learn
56%	78%	14%	25%

[a]$n = 41$

internet connection failure was the most mentioned negative aspect of online sessions in FIT e-learning courses.

11.6 Discussion

The paradox of our time is that new technologies, on many occasions, instead of promoting effective teaching, have significantly distracted the students' attention (Francis and Shanon 2013). The present study shows that, although the student perceives that online instruction distracts him, the learning gain in blended courses is more significant than other strategies. A similar result has been observed in traditional and blended learning course comparisons where the blended course was demonstrated as feasible and effective (Koch and Brich 2020).

The combination of strategies will probably further benefit students, as observed in the blended model (Huesca and Reyes 2014). In fact, it has been observed that blended learning is continuously increasing in higher education worldwide because technological advantages and cost reductions have been prioritized (Twigg 2003).

This study aligns with previous ones reporting that the students' grades in the FIT e-learning course were higher than those of the traditional face-to-face course (Castillo-Reyna 2018). This probably occurs because the grades in FIT e-learning courses depend more on activities than exam grades, as opposed to blended and traditional face-to-face courses.

Poor internet connection in online courses has been a primary complaint and disadvantage for learning during the Covid-19 pandemic (Al Zahrani et al. 2021). Results show that connections failure was perceived more negatively in the FIT e-learning course, which depends on technology, more than the blended course. Although the students were encouraged to have good internet connections for the lectures, poor internet connections were sometimes inevitable.

Limitations of this study include that only one instructor for the three methods taught all the classes and that the FIT course exams differed from the other courses.

11.7 Conclusions

This study suggests that blended learning, which incorporates various learning tools, improves learning gain. In addition, the search for alternatives to reduce distractions must be undertaken to improve online courses. Finally, the problem of poor internet connections in online courses is the main problem to be resolved in the future.

Acknowledgements The authors would like to acknowledge the financial support of NOVUS (Grant number: 42-2019), Institute for the Future of Education, Tecnologico de Monterrey, Mexico, in the production of this work.

The authors acknowledge the technical support of the Writing Lab, Institute for the Future of Education, Tecnologico de Monterrey, Mexico, in the production of this work.

References

Al Zahrani EM, Al Naam Y, AlRabeeah S, Aldossary D, Al-Jamea L, Woodman A, Shawaheen M, Altiti O, Quiambao JV, Arulanantham Z, Elsafi S (2021) E-Learning experience of the medical profession's college students during COVID-19 pandemic in Saudi Arabia. BMC Med Educ 21(1):443

Bazan-Perkins B, Huesca-Juárez G (2016a) Gamification y trabajo colaborativo como herramientas para inducir el análisis y la ganancia en el aprendizaje. Memorias del Congreso de Internacional de Innovación Educativa, Dec 2016, pp 3182–3192

Bazan-Perkins B, Huesca-Juarez G (2016b) Evaluación de gamification como estrategia motivacional de apoyo al aprendizaje basado en problemas. Rev Educ Méd 5:132

Bazan-Perkins B, Huesca-Juárez G, Santibañez-Salgado A (2017) Ganancia del aprendizaje desde la perspectiva de los estilos de aprendizaje. Memorias del Congreso Internacional de Innovación Educativa, Dec 2017, pp 3726–3736

Biswas S, Dahan O, Solomonov E, Waksman I, Braun Benyamin O (2021) Advancing global health through engineering: a perspective on teaching an online global health course to engineers during a global pandemic. Biomed Eng Online 20(1):82

Booth CS, Song C, Howell ME, Rasquinha A, Saska A, Helikar R, Sikich SM, Couch BA, van Dijk K, Roston RL, Helikar T (2021) Teaching metabolism in upper-division undergraduate biochemistry courses using online computational systems and dynamical models improves student performance. CBE Life Sci Educ 20:1–16

Brassil CE, Brian AC (2019) Multiple-true-false questions reveal more thoroughly the complexity of student thinking than multiple-choice questions: a Bayesian item response model comparison. Int J STEM Educ 6:1–17

Castillo-Reyna J (2018) Teaching and learning microbiology for engineers in a digital world: the case of the FIT courses at the Tecnologico de Monterrey, Mexico. In: Auer M, Tsiatsos T (eds) The challenges of the digital transformation in education. ICL 2018. Advances in intelligent systems and computing, vol 916. Springer, Cham

Chen H, Ni JH (2013) Teaching arrangements of carbohydrate metabolism in biochemistry curriculum in Peking University Health Science Center. Biochem Mol Biol Educ 41:139–144

Cox JR (2011) Enhancing student interactions with the instructor and content using pen-based technology, YouTube videos, and virtual conferencing. Biochem Mol Biol Educ 39(1):4–9. https://doi.org/10.1002/bmb.20443

Francis R, Shanon SJ (2013) Engaging with blended learning to improve students' learning outcomes. Eur J Eng Educ 38

Fregni F (2019) Critical thinking in teaching & learning: the nonintuitive new science of effective learning

Hake RR (2002) Relationship of individual student normalized learning gains in mechanics with gender, high-school physics, and pre-test scores on mathematics and spatial visualization. In: Physics education research conference, Aug 2002, vol 8, pp 1–14

Huesca G, Reyes M (2014) Estudio comparativo sobre estilos de aprendizaje y ganancias de aprendizaje en la implementación de aula invertida. 1er Congreso Internacional de Innovación Educativa. Tecnológico de Monterrey, Dec 2014

Kalogiannis S, Pagkalos I, Koufoudakis P, Dashi I, Pontikeri K, Christodoulou C (2014) Integrated interactive chart as a tool for teaching metabolic pathways. Biochem Mol Biol Educ 42:501–506

Koch C, Brich J (2020) The feasibility and effectiveness of a blended-learning course for detecting and avoiding bias in medical data: a pilot study. BMC Med Educ 20:1–8

Loertscher J, Green D, Lewis JE, Lin S, Minderhout V (2014) Identification of threshold concepts for biochemistry. CBE Life Sci Educ 13:516–528

Marco LD, Venoit A, Gillois P (2017) Does the acceptance of hybrid learning affect learning approaches in France? J Educ Eval Health Prof 14:1–7

Membrillo-Hernández J, Molina-Solís E, Lara-Prieto V, García-García R (2019) Designing the curriculum for the 4IR: working the case of biology and sustainable development in bioengineering courses. In: International conference on interactive collaborative learning, Sept 2019. Springer, Cham, pp 306–315

Montenery SM, Walker M, Sorensen ME, Thompson R, Kirklin D, White R, Ross C (2013) Millennial generation student nurses' perceptions of the impact of multiple technologies on learning. Nurs Educ Perspect 34:405–409

Picciano AG (2009) Blending with purpose: the multimodal model. J Asynchronous Learn Netw 13:7–18

Pickering JD (2017) Measuring learning gain: comparing anatomy drawing screencasts and paper-based resources. Anat Sci Educ 10:307–331

Plume A, van Weijen D (2014) Publish or perish? The rise of the fractional author. Res Trends 38:16–18

Twigg CA (2003) Improving learning and reducing costs: new models for online learning. EDUCAUSE Rev 38:28–38

Verhoeff RP, Knippels M-CPJ, Gilissen MGR, Boersma KT (2018) The theoretical nature of systems thinking. Perspectives on systems thinking in biology education. Front Educ 3:1–11

Chapter 12
EDUDIGIT@L: An Open Laboratory for Educational Innovation

Marcela Georgina Gómez Zermeño and Lorena Alemán de la Garza

12.1 Introduction

The health contingencies and restrictions of COVID19 in Mexico have generated critical issues adding to the polarization of educational equity, which forces us to rethink the entire educational system. In the sudden, worldwide pandemic scenario, the virus has spotlighted the shortcomings of our educational systems, which have primarily utilized traditional face-to-face teaching. It also shows the inequality of access to technology because, in quarantine times, distance education is the primary modality that allows the educational system to continue functioning (United Nations Department of Global Communications 2020; UNICEF 2020).

One of the first measures taken to combat the COVID19 pandemic was to decree that children and young people should not attend day-care centers, schools, and universities; for fear that they might contract the disease. COVID19 generated a major global crisis for education because 1.5 billion students in 165 countries were affected by the closing of educational institutions (UNESCO 2020). The school closings caused more than 36.5 million elementary, middle, and high school students in Mexico to be out of school for a month, sheltered at home (SEP 2020).

For educators, COVID19 poses transformative challenges to educational practices. Therefore, educational leaders must take immediate steps to develop and implement strategies that mitigate the pandemic's impact on education. Thus, collaboratively linking the educational levels from K-12 through higher education is critical for developing and implementing post-crisis strategies. Knowledge co-creation

M. G. Gómez Zermeño (✉) · L. Alemán de la Garza
Tecnologico de Monterrey, Monterrey, México
e-mail: marcela.gomez@tec.mx

L. Alemán de la Garza
e-mail: lorena.aleman@tec.mx

© The Author(s), under exclusive license to Springer Nature Singapore Pte Ltd. 2022   159
S. Hosseini et al. (eds.), *Technology-Enabled Innovations in Education*,
Transactions on Computer Systems and Networks,
https://doi.org/10.1007/978-981-19-3383-7_12

and sharing what academic communities are doing at different levels to safeguard education during and after the pandemic are paramount (Álvares Mendiola 2020).

This discussion of knowledge co-creation strategies by educators from K-12 to higher education focuses on identifying the resources and competencies that must be strengthened to face the post-COVID19 crisis. It is the basis for the research question of this study, *"How can quality pedagogical improvements be made to an educational workshop about designing active learning experiences in digital environments?"*.

12.1.1 Quality, Inclusive, and Equal Education

Access to quality education for all is essential for the peace and sustainable development of societies worldwide (UN 2015; UNESCO 2007). Considering education to be not a privilege but a right of the people, Mexico promotes strategies to guarantee an education that offers opportunities to everyone (SEP 2019). This priority makes it essential to improve public policies and focus on guaranteeing quality education (Latapí Sarre 2009; Gómez-Zermeño 2010, 2017).

Quality in education is a concept that varies among educational stakeholders (INEE 2018). Building a school system offering equitable, quality education is complex. The challenge of the present inequity is that it is nurtured by single, uniform, standardized national educational policies that do not consider cultural, economic, and social diversity (Carneiro and Toscano 2009; Patera et al. 2020; Gómez-Zermeño 2018; Edwards Risopatrón 1991; Delors 1997).

Equity and justice pose multiple, complex challenges to overcome to improve the quality of education (Gómez-Zermeño 2017). In rural schools and marginalized communities in different states in Mexico, the fight against inequality must be at the center of educational policy. Mexico is a country where the most characteristic feature of its educational system is, precisely, inequality (UNESCO 2011).

12.1.2 Use of Technologies for Quality Education with Equity

In an interconnected world, technology in education supports new teaching trends that challenge the educational system, its programs, and the teachers' work in the classrooms (UNESCO—OREALC 2013). Fostering equitable, quality education and universal continuous learning requires developing skills using digital devices, communication applications, networks to access and manage information, creating and sharing digital content, communicating, collaborating, and problem-solving in life and work.

Digital skills assessments have highlighted significant inequalities in both developing and developed countries (UNESCO 2018). There is a need to promote paths of action that ensure inclusive education and enable all people to participate actively in learning. Hence, policies on using information and communication technologies

(ICT) must offer contextual and comprehensive approaches considering cultural diversity to be known and acknowledged as a pedagogical advantage (INEE 2018; Carneiro and Toscano 2009; Sunkel et al. 2013).

In Mexico, diversity is ubiquitous. Its significance and long historical process in the various social groups is rarely acknowledged. Since its origins, Mexican society has been a diverse group of people who possess and practice a specific culture (Gómez-Zermeño 2010, 2018). In the "new normality" generated by COVID19, the search for equity forces us to rethink the educational system almost in its entirety (Gómez-Zermeño 2017).

12.1.3 Use of Technologies for Quality Education with Equity

Numerous studies identify higher education institutions as privileged spaces for promoting educational innovation based on technology (Purcell et al. 2019). The results show that the complexity of the challenges faced by society has led academic communities to rethink how to interact and communicate knowledge. The aim is to provide collective responses to make educational transformations for the common good (Hosman 2014; Portuguez Castro et al. 2019; Williamson 2015).

Innovative educational research projects are needed to generate knowledge to face the challenges caused in K-12 education by the COVID19 pandemic. For Battisti, innovation can be studied in live laboratories, where ICT supports the learning among participants (Battisti 2014). Thus, laboratories can facilitate both research and educational innovation because they promote the co-creation of knowledge for solutions that meet the needs of the participants.

An "Open Laboratory for Educational Innovation (OPENLAB)" is a strategy for innovative research because it addresses socio-educational problems with openness, experimentation, inclusion, diversity, participation, and collaboration (Battisti 2014; Chesbrough 2011). In an OPENLAB, innovation involves the active participation of all members of experimentation, exchange, and creativity, affecting social reality with collective designs for more sustainable futures for and by communities (Ramírez-Montoya and García-Peñalvo 2018; BEPA 2014). For Schmitz, Matyók, Sloan, and James, human rights and social and educational justice are intertwined; all disciplines must collaborate to achieve innovations (Schmitz et al. 2012).

12.2 Method

A quantitative, case-study research design was chosen because of the methodological challenges of an OPENLAB as a strategy to generate knowledge to successfully face the post-COVID19 crisis period. For Walker, case studies are an appropriate way to study a phenomenon with intensity in a short time (Walker 1982). They are a technique to investigate various dynamics in unique contexts. Their potential lies in focusing on the object of study to analyze how it interacts (Eisenhardt 1989).

According to Boyer (cited in Mills, Durepos, and Wiebe), the quantitative approach applied in case research is a strategy to identify causal relationships among variables. It is inductive, exploring a single case to develop an in-depth theory or explanation about an object of study (Mills et al. 2012). In these cases, constructing foundations requires a systemic process that uses research instruments to collect data (Velázquez Sortino et al. 2017).

Although there is controversy about applying the quantitative approach in a case study, Yin argues that case studies can be based entirely on quantitative evidence (Yin 2009). He asserts that quantitatively collected data with complementary application of qualitative technical instruments are the key to delving into information that explains the phenomenon under study (Mertens 2005).

12.2.1 Research Instrument

An instrument designed by Gómez-Zermeño, adapted by Alemán, Sancho Vinuesa, and Gómez Zermeño and published by Alemán, was selected to generate information that would provide answers to the research question (Gómez-Zermeño 2012; Alemán De la Garza et al. 2015; Aleman and Gomez Zermeño 2019). "DIAPASON" is an instrument made up of 50 indicators that make it possible to collect quantitative data to assess an educational resource, examining the following parameters:

- *Pedagogical*: Nineteen indicators to assess the databases (contents), learning resources, teaching approach, suitability and adaptation to users, motivational capacity, tutoring, and evaluation.
- *Functional*: Six indicators to assess user control and autonomy, user-friendliness, and documentation functionality.
- *Technological*: Thirteen indicators to measure the visual environment, design, technology, versatility, navigation, interaction, and dialogues.
- *Temporal*: Six indicators to measure the timetable: the time provided to study the topics, carry out the activities, complete the exercises, take the exams, and participate in the discussion forums.
- *Global Perspective*: Six indicators comparing a face-to-face course with an online course, in terms of time required to learn a topic, carrying out different activities, time optimization, and diversity of resources to explain a topic, improve the teaching–learning process, and develop teaching skills.

12.2.2 Background

The "EDUDIGIT@L" OPENLAB was developed to promote the "*Compas Académicos*" ("Academic compass") initiative, inspired by the "Academic Buddy" strategy created by a higher education institution to ensure its academic continuity. Through this strategy, online course teachers volunteered to support face-to-face teachers using technological tools to develop their courses through a flexible digital teaching model.

During the EDUDIGIT@L OPENLAB, higher education teacher-researchers developed and taught a workshop entitled "Design of experiences for active learning in digital environments" to a group of teachers, supervisors, and technical-pedagogical advisors from Mexico City (CDMX). They volunteered to develop their knowledge of digital teaching and skills in using technological tools (Fig. 12.1).

This emergency initiative was based on the collaborative work of supervisors and teacher-researchers. Each supervisor oversees an average of seven public schools and two private schools in the same area of CDMX, each school having approximately 500 students. Since creating "Compas Académicos," approximately 80 schools have expressed their interest in participating in this initiative. It is estimated that it can benefit more than 40,000 students in preschool, elementary, and middle school.

Fig. 12.1 "EduDIGIT@L" OPENLAB videoconference session

12.3 Results Analisis

We applied the "DIAPASON" instrument to all participants to generate information to answer the research question. We then conducted focus-group interviews with a small group to delve into the results.

The DIAPASON instrument was applied based on a 5-point Likert scale: 4 = Strongly agree, 3 = Agree, 2 = Sometimes agree, 1 = Disagree, 0 = Strongly disagree. All indicators scored a mean of 2.94. The best result corresponded to the "Functional" parameter, which allows us to assess aspects related to user control and autonomy, user-friendliness, and documentation functionality (Fig. 12.2).

12.3.1 Pedagogical Parameter

For the 19 indicators linked to the "Pedagogical" parameter, a mean of 2.94 was scored, and the results range from 2.36 to 3.43. When analyzing each category, the highest mean corresponded to the indicators of "Resources" (3.14) and "Tutorial and evaluation" (3.12). In contrast, the lowest category was related to "Suitability and adaptation to users" (2.61).

As shown in Table 12.1, the indicators with the highest mean in the "Resources" category were "The activities introduce the topics" (3.43) and "The activities summarize the topics" (3.21). In the "Tutorial and evaluation" category, the highest results were achieved in the indicator that assesses "The exercises offer tutorials with guidance, help, and reinforcement to the participants" (3.36), followed by "The forums provide appropriate help to solve issues or questions" (3.14).

In the "Pedagogical Approach" category, 78.57% of the participants considered that "The activities and exercises develop self-learning," and 71.43% stated, "The activities and exercises develop skills." For the "Motivational Ability" category, 71.43% considered that "The activities and exercises motivate the participant to research," but only 50.00% considered that "The activities and exercises engage the participant."

The "Content basis" included indicators related to the structure of the workshop and its contents. 78.57% of the participants considered that "The topics of the units

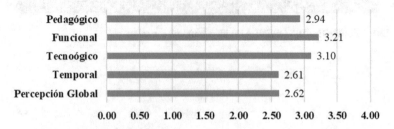

Fig. 12.2 DIAPASON assessment of parameters

Table 12.1 Results of the indicators for the "pedagogical" parameter

Category	Mean	Indicator	Mean
Contents	2.74	1. The topics in the units are explained in detail	2.93
		2. The topics are developed with clarity, using precise words	2.71
		3. The topics are well structured, and they have a logical order	2.57
Resources	**3.14**	**4. The activities introduce the topics**	**3.43**
		5. The activities summarize the topics	3.21
		6. The activities offer resources that facilitate the understanding of the topics	2.79
Pedagogical parameter	3.04	7. The activities and exercises focus on achieving the unit objectives	3.00
		8. The activities and exercises develop critical thinking	2.93
		9. The activities and exercises develop self-learning	3.14
		10. The activities and exercises develop skills	3.07
Suitability and adaptability to users	**2.61**	11. The length, structure, depth, and vocabulary of the topics are appropriate	2.86
		12. The activities addressed the knowledge, skills, interests, and needs of the participants	**2.36**
Motivational ability	2.87	13. The activities and exercises engage the participant	2.71
		14. The activities and exercises motivate the participant to research	3.14
		15. The activities and exercises stimulate creativity	2.93
		16. The tests are challenging, and they assess the participants' knowledge	2.71
Tutorial and evaluation	3.12	17. The tests give feedback	2.86
		18. The exercises offer tutorials with guidance, help, and reinforcement to the participants	3.36
		19. Discussion boards are an appropriate aid to solve questions and issues	3.14

Table 12.2 Results of the "functional" parameter for participants

Category	Mean	Questions	Mean
User control and autonomy	**2.72**	20. The activities have links to delve into the topics	3.00
		21. The exercise instructions are clear and easy to understand	**2.43**
User-friendliness	**3.61**	22. The instructions to access the course are clear and easy to understand	3.50
		23. It is easy to access the units, activities, exercises, evaluations, and resources	**3.71**
Documentation functionality	3.47	24. When presenting the topics, the references for the information are indicated	3.64
		25. The activities suggest using complementary documentation (open resources, library, blogs, wikis)	3.29

are explained in detail" and that "The topics are developed with clarity using precise words," while only 57.17% considered that "The topics are well structured and have a logical order."

12.3.2 Functional Parameter

The mean for the six "Functional" parameter indicators was 3.21, and the results ranged from 2.43 to 3.71. The highest mean corresponded to "User-friendliness" and the lowest to "User control and autonomy." Table 12.2 shows the data.

Most participants considered that "It is easy to access the units, activities, exercises, evaluations, and resources" and "When presenting the topics, the references for the information are indicated." For "User-friendliness," 92.85% of the participants considered that "The instructions for accessing the course are clear and easy to understand" and "The activities suggest using complementary documentation (open resources, library, blogs, wikis)."

12.3.3 Technological Parameter

The mean for the 13 indicators connected with the "Technological" parameter was 3.10, with responses ranging from 2.57 to 3.64. The highest mean of 3.64 corresponded to the categories "Communication and Interaction" and "Navigation," and the lowest mean (2.57) to the category "Design and technology." The data are shown in Table 12.3.

Most participants appreciated in the workshop that "Means of communication between participants and tutors are offered (forums, announcements, etc.)" and that "Means of communication between participants are offered." In the category "Navigation," it was valued that "There is a direct link to the home page from any page of the course," and 78.57% stated that "Navigation between units, activities, exercises, and resources is fast." Regarding the "Visual environment," 78.57% said that "The visual quality of the texts (typography, distribution, colors) is adequate," as was the

Table 12.3 Results of the "technological" parameter

Category	Mean	Questions	Mean
Visual environment	3.07	26. The visual quality of the texts is adequate (typography, layout, colors)	3.36
		27. The technical and aesthetic quality of the multimedia materials is adequate	2.93
		28. A variety of multimedia resources (videos, audio, images, animations, and texts) are integrated	2.93
Design and technology	**2.83**	**29. The graphic design of the pages is attractive, and the resources are dynamic**	**2.57**
		30. The activities use advanced technology (multimedia, animations, open resources, etc.)	2.64
		31. The use of the technological platform is reliable because it does not have technical glitches	3.29
Adaptability	2.97	32. The font size, colors, and resolution of the images can be adjusted	2.86
		33. Access to open educational resources is provided	3.07
Navigation	3.24	34. Page navigation is structured, simple, and ergonomic	2.79
		35. Navigation between units, activities, exercises, and resources is fast	3.29
		36. There is a direct link to the home page from any page of the course	3.64
Communication and interaction	**3.47**	37 Means of communication between participants are available (forums, announcements, etc.)	3.29
		38. Means of communication between participants and tutors (forums, announcements, etc.) are provided	**3.64**

Table 12.4 Results of the "time" parameter

Category	Questions	Mean
Calendar/Agenda	**39. The calendar helps to plan the time to be devoted to the course**	**3.29**
Study topics	40. The time established to study the topics in the units is enough	2.21
Carry out activities	**41. The time established to carry out activities is enough**	**2.14**
Carry out exercises	**42 The time established to carry out the exercises is enough**	2.21
Self-assessments	43. The time established for the self-assessments is enough	2.79
Discussion forums	44. The time established to participate in the discussion forums is enough	3.00

case with the "Versatility" category, where "Access to open educational resources is offered."

12.3.4 Time Parameter

The lowest mean (2.61) was calculated in the "Time" parameter, and the indicators ranged from 2.14 to 3.19. The highest mean corresponded to the category "Calendar/Agenda" and the lowest to the category "Carrying out activities." 85.72% of the participants considered that "The calendar helps to plan the time to be devoted to the course" and "The time established to participate in the discussion forums is enough." Only 35.72% considered that "The time established to carry out the activities is enough" and "The time established to carry out the exercises is enough." The data are shown in Table 12.4.

12.3.5 The Overall Perception of the Workshop Compared to Another Course

In the global perception expressed by the participants, an average of 2.62 was recorded, and the indicator with the highest average was found in the category "Time" (See Table 12.5). Also, 78.57% considered that "Compared to another course, this workshop allows me to optimize my time." Regarding the "Pedagogical approach," 71.43% valued that "Compared to another course, this workshop offers different resources to explain the topics."

Table 12.5 Results of the comparison between this workshop and other courses

Category		Questions	Mean
Time	2.45	**45. Compared to another course, this workshop requires less time to understand a topic**	**2.00**
		46. Compared with another course, this workshop allows me to carry out different activities simultaneously	2.36
		47. Compared to another course, this workshop allows me to optimize my time	**3.00**
Pedagogic approach	2.79	48. Compared to another course, this workshop offers different resources to explain the topics	2.79
		49. Compared to another course, this workshop improves teaching and learning	2.71
		50. Compared to another course, this workshop generates greater interest in strengthening teacher development	2.86

12.3.6   Results of the Interviews with a Small Group of EduDigit@al OPENLAB Participants

To delve into the information from the DIAPASON indicators of the pedagogical quality of the workshop, we conducted individual interviews with a sample of teachers, principals, technical-pedagogical advisors, and supervisors. Table 12.6 presents a summary of the questions/answers provided by the interviewees.

Table 12.6 Summary of the interviews with a small group of EduDigit@al OPENLAB participants

Questions	Answers
Did the COVID19 pandemic modify your perception of the use of technological tools in the teaching–learning process?	• Yes, it definitely opened up more expectations for me. I had never taken a technology course before; we had considered it as an "accessory." • It helped me to maintain interactions with my students' parents • I don't have an integrated chip like others, so I had to fully immerse myself, even asking my nephews and nieces about technology • Yes, a lot because there are many new things, and I have to adapt to this new way of life and change my habits educationally and personally • I think so. I learned to "unlearn" certain practices and habits • It helped me understand that the digital gap exists and that you don't need to go far to find it • "We're already in the pool, and we have to paddle."

(continued)

Table 12.6 (continued)

Questions	Answers
How have you acquired the digital skills and technological resources necessary to continue providing educational services to your students?	• I am very stubborn, and I like to innovate a lot. I throw myself 100% into using the tools. I'm one of those who click and click • I have to learn to use tools actively and pass on knowledge to teachers and learn with them; the parents were also surprised at how the technology works • With Webinars offered by SEP and other institutions, although they are very repetitive and tiring. A lot is explained, but nothing specific is achieved • Old school teachers don't use technology because we don't want to get out of our comfort zones. We are afraid of technology, and we lack the openness to learn something new
Do you prefer self-directed courses, with forum-based coaching, zoom session coaching, one-to-one coaching, or face-to-face courses to develop your ICT skills?	• Mixed environments because I can learn something different from everyone • I always thought it was better face-to-face, but now online is easier for me because I schedule my time and work better in the evenings • I have taken many online courses. I lean toward face-to-face or hybrid as I do now, but with personalized coaching • I took face-to-face courses for more than ten years, and now I like online more • I trained and armed myself with material to do it either online or face-to-face; hybrid courses are not something new because of COVID19 • Online, but all the questions come out after the sessions when the facilitators/trainers are not there
Do you prefer a course offering groups of participants from different levels or groups for each level of ICT skills?	• By different levels, although there will come the point where this distinction will not have to be made because generations are updating their skills and knowledge will be leveled • Different levels because currently there are two types of teachers: those who have a lot of innovation experience and those who want to retire preserving their traditional ways • Yes, I feel that something more specific for the advanced ones would be ideal • It is necessary to make a small test to accommodate by levels • Separation by levels so that each level feels at ease • Yes, it would be excellent by level because if you are a beginner and learn something new, you can get lost easily • It does have its advantages to bring everyone together, but in this particular case, it was not beneficial
Do you consider that higher education teachers can support K-12 education teachers in the post-COVID19 crisis?	• Yes, they can be supportive; they are a breath of fresh air • As long as a simple language is used to be understood. The language used is sometimes complicated and has to be translated and simplified • Yes, but without overwhelming. Focus on one or two tools only; I would end up forgetting a past tool because we were already on the next one • They should go to the frontlines to get to know the needs of K-12 education. Teaching a group of university students is not the same as teaching 40–50 children • Higher education professors do not know basic education needs and can fall into the same error of sending us information that is not being used • There is a gap between the professor and the teacher. There is a gap due to a lack of knowledge; the academic levels are different between them and us

12.4 Conclusions

It is necessary to turn difficulties into opportunities to transform the educational process through the open interaction between supervisors and principals. These interact with their teachers, and teachers with their students. Jointly defining educational innovation strategies that disrupt the traditional forms of teaching–learning at different educational levels is required. Through training resources based on digital pedagogy and technologies, it is possible to overcome the educational challenges posed by the COVID19 pandemic. It is also possible to value education as an act of freedom, awareness, and solidarity without neglecting progress toward the expected learning objectives.

An Open Laboratory for Educational Innovation that applies knowledge co-creation strategies among educators in K-12 through higher education contributes to the analysis of educational change processes. Successfully facing the post-COVID crisis means recognizing that both technology and quality in education are newly ascribed issues in a timeline of educational innovation and technological evolution. Within this new normality or reality, using technology in education entails analyzing its differential process of dissemination, correlation with social life, and educational change processes. In this disruptive context, the latter must not be isolated from social and technological advances. Technology must be a strategic tool in addressing inequity and exclusion in education.

For both the academic community and educational authorities, the COVID19 contingency posed the challenge of changing education. To make the appropriate changes, stakeholders in education must consider the pedagogical issue of adequately incorporating technology into school curricula, teacher training, and strategic educational planning. In addition, they must construct an adequate technological infrastructure. Adapting educational models will imply breaking with paradigms formed when technology was not part of the educational context. The adaptations demand innovative and flexible programs that do not limit educational practice to the classroom's physical space. Those who make educational policy decisions related to incorporating technology in the teaching–learning processes can preserve the actions of the past that have improved education. However, they must also be open and willing to address the transformations necessitated by the COVID19 pandemic, envisioning a sustainable future that offers equitable, quality education.

Acknowledgements The authors would like to thank Dr. Sofia Leticia Morales Garza for her contributions to teacher development through the "Compas Académicos" initiative. The authors also acknowledge the technical support of the Writing Lab, Institute for the Future of Education, Tecnologico de Monterrey, Mexico, in the production of this work.

References

Aleman L, Gomez Zermeño MG (2019) Analysis of the relation between teaching practices and academic performance. Int J Assess Eval 26(2):13–25. https://doi.org/10.18848/2327-7920/cgp/v26i02/13-25

Alemán De la Garza LY, Sancho-Vinuesa T, Gómez Zermeño MG (2015) Indicadores de calidad pedagógica para el diseño de un curso en línea masivo y abierto de actualización docente. RUSC Univ Knowl Soc J 12(1):104–118. https://doi.org/10.7238/rusc.v12i1.2260

Álvares Mendiola G (2020) Covid-19. Cambiar de paradigma educativo. Consejo Mexicano de Investigación Educativa A.C.

Battisti S (2014) Social innovation in living labs: the micro-level process model of public-private partnerships. Int J Innov Reg Dev 5(4/5):328. https://doi.org/10.1504/ijird.2014.064146

BEPA (2014) Social innovation: a decade of changes. https://doi.org/10.2796/27161

Carneiro R, Toscano JC (2009) Las TIC y los nuevos paradigmas educativos: la transformación de la escuela en una sociedad que se transforma, Roberto Carneiro … Los desafíos las TIC para el cambio Educ 15–28

Chesbrough H (2011) Open services innovation: rethinking your business to grow and compete in a New Era. Wiley

Delors J et al (1997) La educación encierra un tesoro: informe para la UNESCO de la Comisión Internacional sobre la Educación para el Siglo Veintiuno, UNESCO

Edwards Risopatrón V (1991) El Concepto de calidad de la educación. UNESCO Regional Office for Education in Latin America and the Caribbean, Chile

Eisenhardt KM (1989) Building theories from case study research. Acad Manag Rev 14(4):532–550

Gómez-Zermeño MG (2010) Competencias interculturales en instructores comunitarios que brindan servicio a la población indígena del estado de Chiapas. Rev Electron Invest Educ 12(1):1–25

Gómez-Zermeño M (2012) Digital libraries: electronic bibliographic resources on basic education. Comunicar 20(39):119–126. https://doi.org/10.3916/C39-2012-03-02

Gómez-Zermeño MG (2017) Sociedad, Internet y Cultura. Conceptos clave y nuevas tendencias. Porrua, Mexico

Gómez-Zermeño MG (2018) Strategies to identify intercultural competences in community instructors. J Multicult Educ 12(4):330–342. https://doi.org/10.1108/JME-12-2016-0062

Hosman L (2014) Improving partnerships: applying lessons learned to improve partnerships in innovative educational experiences. Partnerships A J Serv Civ Engagem 5(1):24–50

INEE (2018) El concepto de la calidad en la educación. Gac. la política Nac. evaluación Educ. en México 10(4):101

Latapí Sarre P (2009) El derecho a la educación.: Su alcance, exigibilidad y relevancia para la política educativa. Rev Mex Invest Educ 14(40):255–287

Mertens DM (2005) Research and evaluation in education and psychology: integrating diversity … SAGE Publications

Mills A, Durepos G, Wiebe E (2012) Encyclopedia of case study research. Sage Publications, Thousand Oaks

Patera S, Silva IS, Zavala FS (2020) Learn to learn in normative documents from the six countries participating in an international study. A critical depending from Ecuador and Mexico. Aula Abierta 49(3):225–244. https://doi.org/10.17811/rifie.49.3.2020.225-244

Portuguez Castro M, Ross Scheede CR, Gómez Zermeño MG (2019) The impact of higher education on entrepreneurship and the innovation ecosystem: a case study in Mexico. Sustainability 11(20):5597. https://doi.org/10.3390/su11205597

Purcell WM, Henriksen H, Spengler JD (2019) Universities as the engine of transformational sustainability toward delivering the sustainable development goals: 'Living labs' for sustainability. Int J Sustain High Educ 20(8):1343–1357. https://doi.org/10.1108/IJSHE-02-2019-0103

Ramírez-Montoya M-S, García-Peñalvo F-J (2018) Co-creation and open innovation: systematic literature review [Co-creación e innovación abierta: Revisión sistemática de literatura]. Comunicar 54:9–18. https://doi.org/10.3916/C54-2018-01

Schmitz CL, Matyók T, Sloan LM, James C (2012) The relationship between social work and environmental sustainability: implications for interdisciplinary practice. Int J Soc Welf 21(3):278–286. https://doi.org/10.1111/j.1468-2397.2011.00855.x

SEP (2019) Estrategia Nacional de Educación Inclusiva. Educación. Secretaria de Educación Pública

SEP (2020) 10 sugerencias para la educación durante la emergencia por Covid-19. Mejoredu

Sunkel G, Trucco D, Espejo A (2013) La integración de las tecnologías digitales en las escuelas de América Latina y el Caribe: una mirada multidimensional

UN (2015) Objetivo 4: Garantizar una educación inclusiva, equitativa y de calidad y promover oportunidades de aprendizaje durante toda la vida para todos

UNESCO (2007) Educación de calidad para todos: un asunto de derechos humanos. Chile, Santiago

UNESCO (2011) Compendio mundial de la educación 2011. Comparación de las estadísticas de educación en el mundo, Montréal, Québec

UNESCO (2018) Las competencias digitales son esenciales para el empleo y la inclusión social. UNESCO

UNESCO (2020) Preparación y recuperación de la vida escolar en la nueva normalidad por pandemia COVID-19

UNESCO—OREALC (2013) Enfoque Estratégico sobre Tics en Educación en América Latina y el Caribe

UNICEF (2020) Orientaciones para docentes y recursos digitales para atender a la diversidad en la educación a distancia en el contexto del COVID-19, Lima, Peru

United Nations Department of Global Communications (2020) Education and COVID-19: UN helps children continue their learning. Covid-19 Response

Velázquez Sortino M, Gómez-Zermeño MG, Alemán De La Garza L (2017) Interactions in a massive, online, open course (MOOC) for teacher's. Proposal for a model of analysis. Digit Educ Rev 31:149–175. https://doi.org/10.1344/der.2017.31.149-175

Walker R (1982) The use of case studies in applied research and evaluation. Soc. Sci. Educ. Stud. A Sel. Guide. Lit. Heinemann, London

Williamson B (2015) Governing methods: policy innovation labs, design and data science in the digital governance of education. J Educ Adm Hist 47(3):251–271. https://doi.org/10.1080/00220620.2015.1038693

Yin RK (2009) Case study research: design and methods, 4th edn. Can J Action Res 14(1):69–71. https://doi.org/10.33524/cjar.v14i1.73

Chapter 13
Design and Use of a Chatbot for Learning Selected Topics of Physics

José Rafael Aguilar-Mejía, Santa Tejeda, Carla Victoria Ramirez-Lopez, and Claudia Lizette Garay-Rondero

13.1 Introduction

Technological advancement has boosted new learning methodologies in physics education (Sarwi et al. 2019). The emerging technologies have been based on theories of student-centered learning. Some courses continue to use traditional methodologies within physics education, where the instructor assumes the active role, causing the benefits of technology not to be fully exploited (Hwang et al. 2015). For this reason, it is crucial to design didactic strategies that integrate emerging technologies with student-centered activities.

J. R. Aguilar-Mejía
Escuela de Ingeniería y Ciencias, Tecnologico de Monterrey, Monterrey, Mexico
e-mail: jraguilar@tec.mx

S. Tejeda (✉) · C. L. Garay-Rondero
Institute for the Future of Education, Tecnologico de Monterrey, Monterrey, Mexico
e-mail: stejeda@tec.mx

C. L. Garay-Rondero
e-mail: clgaray@tec.mx

C. V. Ramirez-Lopez
Vicerrectoría Académica y de Innovación Educativa, Tecnologico de Monterrey, Monterrey, Mexico
e-mail: carla.ramirez@tec.mx

© The Author(s), under exclusive license to Springer Nature Singapore Pte Ltd. 2022   175
S. Hosseini et al. (eds.), *Technology-Enabled Innovations in Education*,
Transactions on Computer Systems and Networks,
https://doi.org/10.1007/978-981-19-3383-7_13

13.2   Literature Review

One such recently implemented strategy is flipped learning, a pedagogical approach with two main characteristics (Nganji 2018; Scager et al. 2016). When applying the flipped learning methodology within physics education, it is necessary to consider two key points: (i) what emerging technologies support direct individual physics instruction? (ii) what type of active learning activities will reinforce and enrich student learning? For the first question, technological resources should be considered, letting the student address the issues individually at the time and space required. This exploration opens the possibility of using tools offering ubiquity, such as chatbots. Such tools can provide reliable information while adapting to the learner's need for information.

Active learning strategies have been employed in physics higher education. One acknowledged methodology is Tutorials in Introductory Physics (TIP) (McDermott and Shaffer 2001). The goal of TIP is to construct concepts and develop reasoning skills using various instructional strategies (McDermott 2013). Many tutorials are available for the purposes and topics. Their instructions provide worksheets for activities recommended to be carried out in teams of three or four people.

The literature discusses how learning must be personally relevant to be effective, such as self-regulated learning anywhere (Fitzgerald et al. 2018). Many works conclude with a reflection for the educational community about personalized learning focused on individual choice and control. Their perspectives contrast with Sarsar et al. (2018), who mentioned that digital learners have three types of expectations from mobile technologies in their courses, classified as pedagogical, personal/individual, and technological. All are disruptive educational approaches.

One disrupting approach could be using a chatbot, a technological tool to assist any user search for information. According to Gupta (2020), chatbots are conversational platforms focused on specialized activities. Chatbots can communicate through text or voice and use artificial intelligence and natural language processing to understand the user's message (Khanna et al. 2015). These characteristics allow them to be used as support tools at any time. On the other hand, Winkler and Söllner (2018) specified that chatbot's advantages are increasing user satisfaction due to their immediacy and their availability at any time, personalized attention to the user, and lower costs in service areas. Another advantage is that the data allows analyzing user needs to improve processes or services. Other uses are personalized interactions (Gonda et al. 2018), resources for tutorials, and cognitive skills development (Pogorskiy et al. 2018). For these reasons and the chatbot's adaptability in mobile devices, the education sector has begun implementing them.

Chatbots can enable or accelerate student learning (Becker et al. 2017), but it is necessary to know how to implement them to achieve the desired learning outcomes. Winkler and Söllner (2018) claim to research "the integration of chatbots in the different stages of learning processes with the help of learning theories" to resolve the lack of empirical evidence on how they influence learning. One of the learning outcomes necessary for first-year engineering students is understanding Newton's laws. Some investigations aim to develop technology strategies that help students improve their understanding of concepts in physics class (González et al. 2019; Pohan et al. 2020). These promote students' understanding of Newton's laws with the help of virtual laboratories. The emergence of technologies such as chatbots offers new ways to achieve learning outcomes. This research aimed to implement these tools within a physics class for understanding Newton's laws. We proposed an intervention integrating a chatbot with a tutorial-type activity. Another purpose was to gather empirical evidence of the impact that this type of implementation has on learning. Thus, this research is based on the following questions:

Q1. What is the learning gain of Newton's laws for first-year engineering students who carry out a tutorial-type activity with the "Professor Atom" chatbot? Q2. How does the chatbot's use impact groups with different characteristics? Q3. What are first-year engineering students' opinions about using the chatbot in the tutorial-like physics activity?

13.3 Design of the Chatbot

This project began in July 2018 to be integrated into Physics I through the modality of telepresence with a hologram. Telepresence is an educational innovation project of Tecnologico de Monterrey (Paredes and Vazquez 2019). It was complemented with artificial intelligence innovations designed and implemented for Physics I in 2017. This project evolved into the Professor Atom chatbot that could receive questions by voice and writing based on natural language and communicate with the student through dialogue. The help, explanations, exercises, criticisms, and discussions of a topic or problem were carried out through the system's dialogue with the student (Medina et al. 2016).

For instance, Professor Atom was created as a chatbot (Pai et al. 2020), developed with artificial intelligence based on natural language to receive questions or general inquiries from the students about basic Physics topics. This chatbot provides an immediate response, thus simulating an academic tutor with 24/7 attention. The students can use their mobile devices when and where they need to learn a concept, speeding up the learning experience, saving time searching for basic concepts, and being accompanied during their learning process.

From a pedagogical perspective, Professor Atom chatbot was designed with active learning strategies to promote students' learning by developing information search, analysis, and synthesis skills and motivating them to solve the problem examples presented (Friston et al. 2017; Ballen et al. 2017). The objective was authentic learning, in which the chatbot builds the students' knowledge by relating new information to add to their previous knowledge, readjusting and reconstructing it during their learning process (Riddell 2017).

It was intended that the student using Professor Atom could resolve questions, reinforce knowledge, review or update notes, study for an exam or exposition, carry out individual and team tasks, and delve deeper into a concept than it would be

Fig. 13.1 Examples of professor atom chatbot answers

done in the classroom (Docktor et al. 2016; Weliweriya et al. 2019). Considering the opinions of the Science and Engineering department professors and the Educational Innovation team, we decided that Professor Atom would address 129 basic physics concepts in four categories: definitions, formulas, examples, and video explanations. Some examples are shown in Fig. 13.1.

13.4 Method

This research method consisted of seven steps where 145 students participated from different campuses and engineering majors in a private educational institution in Mexico. First-year students were enrolled in five different groups (classes). Each group had characteristics as follows: 37% of students (groups 1 and 2) were within a traditional educational model, of which 48% (group 1) were in a face-to-face mode, and 52% (group 2) in a remote modality. The other 63% of the participants (groups 3–5) were in a face-to-face model to develop competencies through challenge-based learning. Group 2 had students from four different campuses and cities in Mexico. Groups 3, 4, and 5 belonged to the same campus, and group 1 students belonged to a single campus different from the other groups. Groups 1 and 2 had students in different engineering majors, while groups 3–4 studied engineering within the biotechnology area. All students in group 5 were studying in a program related to computer engineering and information technology. Moreover, groups 2–5 had the same instructor.

The first step was introducing the students to interact with the chatbot in the classroom. This stage aimed to characterize the chatbot and avoid false expectations

Table 13.1 Items by concepts of the HFCI

Concepts	Items
Free fall	1
Newton's third law	2, 14
Force motion	9, 11, 12
Circular motion	3, 4
Projectile motion	10
Kinematics	13
Force motion cluster	5, 6, 7, 8

regarding its use. The chatbot has to support student learning, and the experience with this technology affects the learning outcomes (Harrati et al. 2016).

Second, we administered a pre- and post-test using the Half Force Concept Inventory (HFCI) multiple-choice exam (Han et al. 2015). Since only a few aspects of Newton's laws were to be evaluated on the test, we chose the HFCI exam as a tool. The test had 14 questions about seven force concepts, as shown in Table 13.1. The focus of this research was most related to three of them, namely, Newton's third law, force motion, and force motion cluster, which represented 64% of the items in the test.

As a third step of the experimental design methodology, an individual tutorial activity based on TIP was implemented outside the classroom. During the exercise, the student was encouraged to interpret concepts about forces and Newton's laws. Then, TIP was implemented inside the classroom. These phases correspond to the implementation of flipped learning.

In the fourth step, a post-test was implemented to explore the change in the students' conceptual understanding through the normalized gain defined by Hake (1998). This variable measures the normalized learning gain after the students completed the methodology described in previous steps. The Hake's gain is calculated as shown in Eq. (13.1), where X_{post} represents the mean of the results obtained in the post-test and X_{pre} the mean of the diagnostic evaluation results.

$$g_{Hake} = (x_{post} - x_{pre})/x_{pre} \qquad (13.1)$$

Hake's gain was analyzed through a descriptive and statistical inference analysis. Moreover, data exploration and arrangement were directly observed in the physics courses in groups 1–5. The final step was to gather students' voluntary opinions on the chatbot to know their perceptions of Professor Atom's usability.

13.5   Analysis and Results

First, the quantitative data were collected from 145 students in the five different groups (described in the Method section) in person and via the Learning Management System. The group analysis of the diagnostic test later moved on to the final test. Then it was decided to observe the behavior of the data, differentiating the results by group, to have a more detailed analysis and examine if there was a different behavior in each one.

The mean of correct answers per student, per group, and the general average were calculated to analyze the results for the diagnostic evaluation (pre-test) and final (post-test). Figure 13.2 displays the distribution of the individual averages of the students in both tests on a scale of 0–100.

When comparing averages' distributions obtained by the participants in the pre-test and post-test, we observed that the maximum value increased from 79 to 93. The minimum values for both distributions presented a value equal to zero. It was also observed that the mean increased from 34 to 38, although the median remains at a value of 36. Likewise, there is more dispersion of the post-test data than the pre-test. An increase in the interquartile range was observed, going from 22 in the pre-test to 29 in the post-test.

Three different gains were calculated for the entire group of participants. In the first, the average of all the HFCI items was considered. Only the average of the items that evaluated the concepts addressed by Newton's laws was considered in the second. The third gain considered the averages of the items addressing other topics. The results are seen in Fig. 13.3a.

The students obtained an overall gain of 6.8%. If only the questions on the conceptual understanding of forces and Newton's laws were examined, a gain of 8.1% was obtained, and 3.8% in the other topics. Thus, there was a more significant gain in the topics developed in the intervention. According to Hake (1998), these gains are considered low since a value of less than 30% was obtained. For a focused analysis, normalized Hake's g was calculated for each of the different groups, considering

Fig. 13.2 Comparison of the score (0–100) distribution between the pre-test and the post-test

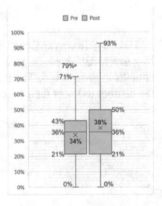

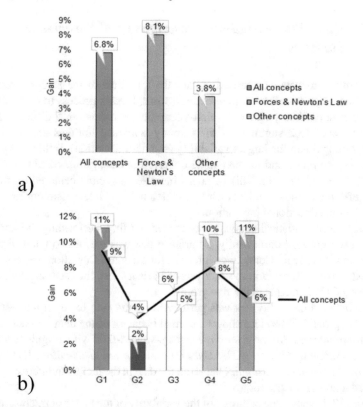

a)

b)

Fig. 13.3 a Hake's g by question type. **b** Hake's g per group considering only Newton's law concepts compared to Hake's g for all items

only the items of Newton's laws. These were compared with Hake's g calculated, considering all the items for each group. As shown in Fig. 13.3b, there is a greater Hake's g in three of the five groups versus Hake's g of all the concepts. Also, it has a bold black line that remembers the gain tanking account of all the items for each group. Groups of both study plans, groups 2 and 3, showed a Hake g in Newton's laws topics lower than all the items, with Hake g of 2% and 5%, respectively.

Next, the gain per student was calculated to know the results associated with the intervention. It was found that 50% of the students increased their conceptual understanding by showing a Hake's gain greater than zero, considering that zero represents a standard reference. On the other hand, it was found that 25% of the students obtained a Hake's gain equal to zero, and the other 25% scored a Hake's gain less zero.

13.5.1 Quantitative Analysis: Descriptive and Parametric Statistics

A descriptive analysis was carried out for the total data of the students receiving the methodology described in this research work. First, a process to clean the data and eliminate outliers yielded 145 first-year college students in 5 different groups (classes). Table 13.2 summarizes the primary statistical findings among the five groups. Group 3 had the largest variability (standard deviation), followed by group 4. Notably, the mode and median value observed in each group equal 0 due to the variable Y = Hake's gain. This behavior indicates a sample centered on the zero value, referring to those students who presented neither Hake's gain nor loss in this experiment in educational innovation.

A parametric statistical analysis was carried out first, performing the normality test for each group. Subsequently, a variance test was performed using Bartlett's method and Bonferroni Confidence Intervals for Standard Deviation (see Fig. 13.4). The next step was to perform the Analysis of Variance test, thus statistically proving the Hake's Gain behavior in the five groups.

Afterwards, a normality test was performed on the data for each interest factor named as "group." Table 13.3 shows a normal behavior of the data for each level of the factor of interest. All the groups present a p-value > 0.05 with a significance level of $\alpha = 0.05$. The hypothesis is H_0: *Data follow a normal distribution; H_1: Data do not follow a normal distribution.* That is, all the data in the factors of interest (groups) followed a normal distribution.

Figure 13.4a shows the behavior of the variability of the factor of interest through Bartlett's test for variances. The hypothesis result gave a p-value < 0.05 with a significance level of $\alpha = 0.05$ where H_0: *All variances are equal, H_1: At least one variance is different.* The conclusion was that there is not enough statistically significant evidence to accept H_0. Therefore, at least one group differed in their standard deviation due to the Y = Hake's gain.

Figure 13.4a shows that group 3 has the highest variance of all. Subsequently, Fig. 13.4b shows the result obtained by eliminating group 3 from the test. Then, on the right side, p-value > 0.05 with a significance level of $\alpha = 0.05$ can be observed. With this iteration, the test conclusion could be defined as the variances between groups 1, 2, 4, and 5 are significantly equal per Y = Hake's gain.

Table 13.2 Basic statistical analysis in groups

Group	Count	Mean	St. Dev.	Median	Mode	N mode
1	26	0.0221	0.1751	0	0	4
2	28	0.0321	0.1412	0	0	8
3	34	0.0326	0.3351	0	0	4
4	31	0.0584	0.2314	0	0	10
5	26	0.0221	0.1751	0	0	4

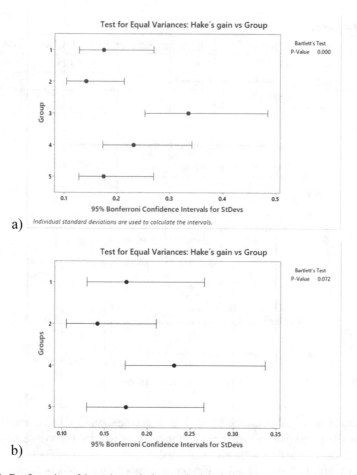

Fig. 13.4 Bonferroni confidence intervals for standard deviation for groups 1–5

Table 13.3 Normality test for groups of students

Group	N	p-value
1	26	0.342
2	28	0.218
3	34	0.774
4	31	0.138
5	26	

Immediately, an ANOVA test was performed for the groups with equal variances. The hypothesis defined was H_0: *All means are equal*; H_1: *Not all means are equal* with a significance level of $\alpha = 0.05$, obtaining $p > 0.05$. Furthermore, Table 13.4 indicates there is no significant evidence to reject H_0; all population means of groups

Table 13.4 Analysis of variance

Source	DF	Adjusted SS	Adjusted medium square	F-value	P-value
Group	3	0.02587	0.008622	0.25	0.861
Error	107	3.67814	0.034375		
Total	110	3.7040			

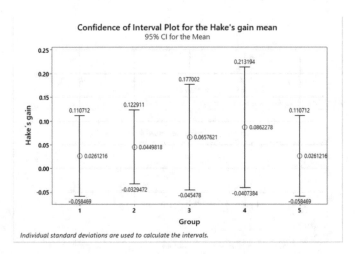

Fig. 13.5 Means interval plot of Y = Hake's gain and groups

1, 2, 4, and 5 are equal per Hake's gain. It is worth mentioning that a normal residual analysis was performed, where the assumptions of normality, homoscedasticity, and independence of the data were also validated.

Finally, Fig. 13.5 shows the Confidence Intervals for the mean, presenting similar behaviors per the variable Y = Hake's gain for each one of the groups (including group 3). Also, group 4 has the highest value due to the studied variable Y, referring to the chatbot and methodology proposed in this research. On the other hand, groups 1, 5, and 2 have the lowest values of loss in this variable Y.

13.5.2 Qualitative Analysis: Usability Expressed by the Students

After the intervention, 90 students voluntarily expressed their opinions on the use of the chatbot in writing. The research group collected and classified these opinions as positive and negative to improve the Professor Atom chatbot. This classification emerged from students' opinions. Table 13.5 shows that students preferred the technological and pedagogical functionalities of the chatbot, e.g.: (i) quick access to

Table 13.5 Feedback from students

	Topic	Aspect
Positive	1. Technological design	Quick access to information
	2. Pedagogical design/curatorship	Versatility of the chatbot's representations
	3. Technological/pedagogical design	Easy to use
Negative	1. Pedagogical design/curation	Synthesized information; suggest broader explanations
	2. Pedagogical/technological design	Identify the intentions and needs of the user
	3. Technological design	Disconnection after not using it for a few minutes

the content, (ii) ease of use, and (iii) the different (pedagogical) categories of each concept giving definitions and explanations. This feedback indicated that students appreciated the chatbot's representation versatility, which aligns with the experimental and practical postulates of Yuliati et al. (2018). Next, these opinions will be complemented with the other side of the coin.

The students gave negative feedback (see Table 13.5), mainly regarding the content and technological design. First, the participants mentioned that the number of topics and concepts were limited. Second, the information was synthesized, so they asked for more in-depth explanations. Third, the students perceived that interactions could be improved through natural language questions. The students proposed that the chatbot stay connected for longer in idle time to improve the user experience.

13.6 Discussion

Equal gains in the conceptual understanding of Newton's Law groups were observed among the groups. We conclude that the impact of the intervention was similar in the different groups despite the differences among them, such as the educational model, the teacher, the program curriculum, and the student campus.

To respond to research question *Q1*. *What is the learning gain of Newton's laws for first-year engineering students who carry out a tutorial-type activity with the "Professor Atom" chatbot?* We found that the intervention caused an increase in the level of conceptual understanding of Newton's laws because higher increases in Hake's g were obtained in the analysis of this topic. However, this value was low within the range considered by Hake (1998). Nevertheless, the effectiveness of chatbots depends on the students' perception of this tool (Winkler and Söllner 2018). This intervention realized that previous user experience with the chatbot could affect Hake's gain. Hence, future research suggests measuring the previous experience to see how it affects Hake's gain.

Regarding *Q2*. *How does the chatbot's use impact groups with different characteristics?* The ANOVA test validated an equal behavior in four of the five groups studied, related to the gain of the conceptual understanding of Newton's laws. Therefore, it can be concluded that a significant difference among groups was not observed.

Last but not least, *Q*3. *What are first-year engineering students' opinions about using the chatbot in the tutorial-like physics activity?* The students voluntarily expressed opinions, both positive and negative, about technological and pedagogical aspects of the user interaction; they requested more topics and concepts and versatility of representations.

For this research, how the students understand the technology and its impact on the learning outcomes was relevant. Students who perceived the merits of a chatbot showed greater interest in the activities carried out (Fryer et al. 2018). The chatbot's integration with the activity had a different impact on the students, evidenced by more dispersion of the results in the post-test compared to the pre-test. Likewise, the improvements of the chatbot that students suggested would affect their learning experience, according to Liu et al. (2019).

13.7   Conclusion

The literature review showed how integrating emerging technology with tutorials made it possible for some students to understand Newton's laws conceptually. In contrast, some other references provide findings of low values of conceptual understanding in students, which are also related to technology use. For this reason, this research brings elements to propose a novel method that incorporates chatbot technology and didactic methods to teach basic sciences to first-year students in engineering programs. With this in mind, the research group designed an experiment to collect qualitative and quantitative data to answer the research questions defined in Sect. 13.2.

The results from analyzing quantitative data indicated the equality of the population means of the groups for the Hake's gain, even with the peculiar characteristics of their teaching in the remote learning modality necessitated by COVID-19, the different campus locations of the professors and freshmen, and different teachers for the groups. These results provided statistically conclusive findings that the proposed methodology and the technological tool (Professor Atom chatbot) had the same significant impact on all the groups. Furthermore, the confidence intervals observed in Fig. 13.5 indicated a high probability that most of the students using this methodology and the chatbot obtained a positive Hake's gain.

The qualitative data came from the opinions of freshmen volunteers to answer the second research question. The information demonstrates the chatbot utility and effectiveness and the requirements to develop more elaborated content. The chatbot's limitations necessitated students' training to use it, and when this step was carried out, some students still had difficulties handling the chatbot tool.

In short, the low Hake's g indicated that the research objective was achieved by integrating emerging technology such as a chatbot with tutorials, typical in teaching physics. The findings also allow visualizing areas of opportunity for future work:

it is necessary to know the students' previous experience with the use of chatbots and establish if there is a relationship with the Hake's gain. Likewise, it would be preferable to increase the number of participants and extend the instructional design to public universities and high schools. The research group must generate an updated Professor Atom process analyzing unanswered questions and generating more content from our teachers, which the students value highly. This update will be implemented to achieve a better understanding of students' needs and uses.

Acknowledgements The authors acknowledge the technical support of Writing Lab, Institute for the Future of Education, Tecnologico de Monterrey, Mexico, in the production of this work.

References

Ballen CJ, Wieman C, Salehi S, Searle JB, Zamudio KR (2017) Enhancing diversity in undergraduate science: self-efficacy drives performance gains with active learning. CBE Life Sci Educ 16(4)

Becker SA et al (2017) NMC horizon report: 2017 higher education edition, Austin, Texas

Docktor JL et al (2016) Assessing student-written problem solutions: a problem-solving rubric with application to introductory physics. Phys Rev Phys Educ Res 12(1):1–18

Fitzgerald E, Jones A, Kucirkova N, Scanlon E (2018) A literature synthesis of personalized technology-enhanced learning: what works and why. Res Learn Technol 26(1063519):1–16

Friston KJ, Lin M, Frith CD, Pezzulo G, Hobson JA, Ondobaka S (2017) Active inference, curiosity and insight Karl. Neural Comput 29(10):2633–2683

Fryer LK, Nakao K, Thompson A (2019) Chatbot learning partners: connecting learning experiences, interest and competence. Comput Human Behav 93(June 2018):279–289

Gonda DE, Luo J, Wong YL, Lei CU (2019) Evaluation of developing educational chatbots based on the seven principles for good teaching. In: Proceedings of the 2018 IEEE International conference on teaching, assessment, and learning for engineering, TALE 2018, Dec, pp 446–453

González JD et al (2019) Implementation and evaluation of an effective computational method that promotes the conceptualization of Newton's laws of motion. J Phys Conf Ser 1247(1)

Gupta A (2020) Introduction to AI chatbots. Int J Eng Res V9(07):255–258

Hake RR (1998) Interactive-engagement versus traditional methods: a six-thousand-student survey of mechanics test data for introductory physics courses. Am J Phys 66(1):64

Han J et al (2015) Dividing the force concept inventory into two equivalent half-length tests. Phys Rev Spec Top Phys Educ Res 11(1):1–9

Harrati N, Bouchrika I, Tari A, Ladjailia A (2016) Exploring user satisfaction for e-learning systems via usage-based metrics and system usability scale analysis. Comput Human Behav 61:463–471

Hwang G-J, Lai C-L, Wang S-Y (2015) Seamless flipped learning: a mobile technology-enhanced flipped classroom with effective learning strategies. J Comput Educ 2(4):449–473

Khanna A, Pandey B, Vashishta K, Kalia K, Pradeepkumar B, Das T (2015) A study of today's A.I. through chatbots and rediscovery of machine intelligence. Int J u- e-Serv Sci Technol 8(7):277–284

Liu Q, Huang J, Wu L, Zhu K, Ba S (2019) CBET: design and evaluation of a domain-specific chatbot for mobile learning. Univers Access Inf Soc 19(3):655–673

McDermott LC (2013) Improving the teaching of science through discipline-based education research: an example from physics. Eur J Sci Math Educ 1(1):1–12

McDermott LC, Shaffer PS (2001) Tutorials in introductory physics and homework package. Prentice-Hall, Englewood Cliffs

Medina IIS, Medina JMC, Gaitan JEM (2016) Ayudas virtuales como apoyo al aprendizaje inclusivo en la ingeniería. Horizontes Pedagógicos 18(1):81–95

Nganji JT (2018) Towards learner-constructed e-learning environments for effective personal learning experiences. Behav Inf Technol 37(7):647–657

Pai K-C, Kuo B-C, Liao C-H, Liu Y-M (2020) An application of Chinese dialogue-based intelligent tutoring system in remedial instruction for mathematics learning 41(2):137–152. https://doi.org/10.1080/01443410.2020.1731427

Paredes SG, Vazquez NR (2019) My teacher is a hologram: measuring innovative STEM learning experiences. In: 2019 9th IEEE integrated STEM education conference, ISEC 2019, Mar 2019, pp 332–336

Pogorskiy E, Beckmann JF, Joksimovic S, Kovanovic V, West R (2019) Utilizing a virtual learning assistant as a measurement and intervention tool for self-regulation in learning. In: Proceedings of the 2018 IEEE International conference on teaching, assessment, and learning for engineering, TALE 2018, Nov, vol 44, pp 846–849

Pohan EH, Rambe A, Ariaji R (2020) Minimizing misconception and improving student's conceptual learning. J Phys Conf Ser 1477(4)

Riddell J (2017) Putting authentic learning on trial: using trials as a pedagogical model for teaching in the humanities. Arts Humanit High Educ 17(4):410–432

Sarsar F, Çakir ÖA, Bohórquez MJ, Van Leeuwen M (2018) Learners' and instructors' views on technology supported engineering education: initial outcomes in a cross-cultural study sample. Univ J Educ Res 6(12):2764–2771

Sarwi S, Ellianawati E, Suliyanah (2019) Grounding physics and its learning for building global wisdom in the 21st century. J Phys Conf Ser 1171(1)

Scager K, Boonstra J, Peeters T, Vulperhorst J, Wiegant F (2016) Collaborative learning in higher education: evoking positive interdependence. CBE Life Sci Educ 15(4):1–9

Winkler R, Söllner M (2018) Unleashing the potential of chatbots in education: a state-of-the-art analysis. In : Academy of management, annual meeting, A O M, Chicago

Weliweriya N, Sayre EC, Zollman D (2019) Case study: coordinating among multiple semiotic resources to solve complex physics problems. Eur J Phys 40(2)

Yuliati L, Riantoni C, Mufti N (2018) Problem-solving skills on direct current electricity through inquiry-based learning with PhET simulations. Int J Instr 11(4):123–138

Chapter 14
Impact of Interactive Tabletop Business Game on Learning and Building Competencies

Sonal Sahu

14.1 Introduction

The interactive tabletop game of our research is a blend of a board game and an online business simulator. Teams of 5 or 6 students play it, and up to 12 teams can play simultaneously. The board game allows us to visualize the tangible resources of a company and its processes. Students make every business decision while observing the flow of resources on the board, for example, inventories, fixed assets, sales, and human resources (employees).

The flow involves sales forecasting, analyzing the markets, buying raw materials, deciding whether to source market intelligence, investing money in employee development, hiring employees, managing marketing strategies, increasing the client base, and increasing returns on investment.

Students make all decisions with the support of an online simulator providing financial information such as financial statements, cash flow, income statements, financial ratios, and market information. Students also receive market research reports and information about changes in the external environment to improve a company's internal operations.

The objective for students is to connect what they have learned in the first four semesters of their business curriculum in separate class units or subjects such as finance, accounting, administration, marketing, human resources, logistics, and organizational behavior. They must understand how the interconnections can be used to make correct decisions in a business. '

S. Sahu (✉)
Finance and Accounting, Tecnologico de Monterrey, Zapopan, Mexico
e-mail: sonalsahu@tec.mx

S. Hosseini et al. (eds.), *Technology-Enabled Innovations in Education*,
Transactions on Computer Systems and Networks,
https://doi.org/10.1007/978-981-19-3383-7_14

Table 14.1 Benefits and disadvantages of board games and simulators

Benefits	Board games	Business simulators
Increase level of collaboration	Yes	No
Increase level of communication	Yes	No
Tangibly demonstrates company processes and resources to improve the understanding of abstract concepts and processes	Yes	No
Increase level of attention and motivation by connecting with childhood games	Yes	No
Exhibit dynamic business environments, close to reality	No	Yes
Generate realistic options involving various variables and different markets	No	Yes
Helps in acquiring detailed information to make informed decisions	No	Yes
Generates market and competition variables based on decisions made during the game	No	Yes
Information analysis is used to increase the level of critical thinking	No	Yes

14.2 Why It is Better

Board games and simulators are typically used separately in education. The methodologies have their benefits and disadvantages (see Table 14.1). Interactive tabletop games reap the benefits while eliminating the disadvantages of the other two methodologies.

The boards operate as a Balanced Scorecard (Kaplan and Norton 2007) and a Dashboard (Eckerson 2010) for measuring the company's strategies and outcomes. For this interactive tabletop game, we developed a board (Fig. 14.1) that helps students visualize the flow of resources in the company. For this, we used PHP to program the simulator and MySQL for the database. It was shared online, where teams made various analyses of the business flows.

14.3 Problem Statement

We developed the game because we observed while teaching the class that sometimes students had difficulty comprehending and visualizing:

- The flow and interconnectivity of concepts learned in different classes in the same discipline.
- How the learnings they acquired integrated with learnings of other disciplines.
- Which critical parameters in a real-time company facilitate decision-making.

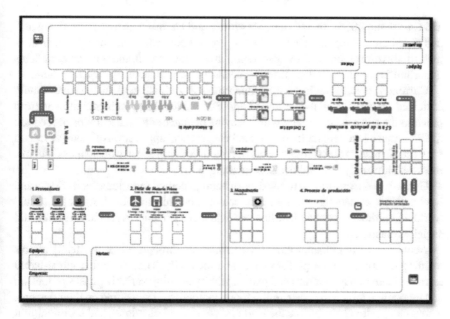

Fig. 14.1   Board used in the interactive tabletop game

14.4   Literature Review

Game-based learning is broadly discussed and used by teachers. Learning through games opens new opportunities for students (Yang et al. 2021).

According to research, *flow theory* derives from studies of an individual's state of mind during intense concentration and focus on activities that cause considerable pleasure; this generates intrinsic motivation (Csikszentmihalyi 1990). Flow theory is based on the correlation between the challenges individuals confront and their skills to accomplish specific activities (Csikszentmihalyi 1990). The authors of Csikszentmihalyi (1997) state that this balance between challenges and skills is fragile and can cause three reactions, depending on the students' skill level and challenges. When both challenges and skills are low, the student is likely to experience apathy; anxiety, when challenges are high and skills are low; and boredom when both the challenges and skills are high. Therefore, given the three mentioned possibilities in Van de Pol (2010), the teacher must adjust the demand levels through adequate strategies that strike a balance between skills and challenges, thus avoiding the feelings that could hinder students from reaching a state of optimal learning flow.

Games are beneficial for students to understand and learn abstract concepts, especially board games, which stimulate the students' attention and motivation (Chiarello and Castellano 2016). In addition, Mawhirter and Garofalo (2016) states that gamified simulations help students retain and apply knowledge and identify their abilities to solve problems. They also report that gamified simulations give students opportunities to identify their learning needs and simultaneously motivate them.

Currently, several studies (Casañ-Pitarch 2018; Zulfiqar et al. 2019) have heavily criticized universities that continue to apply educational and technical models from previous decades; these criticisms urge leaving behind traditional teaching to focus on methods that let students fully understand the practical application of theory. Pratikto et al. (2019) asserts that students, especially university graduates of business schools, must develop analytical and decision-making skills.

Game-based learning can be used as a teaching method in various fields. Sousa and Rocha (2019) argues that a training process can be enhanced by designing a virtual world that promotes content learning and immerses students in problem-solving and social interactions.

According to Teichmanna et al. (2020), learning through games positively affects learning outcomes, work performance, and creativity. They state that game-based learning increases motivation and excitement by creating variable phases of tension and relaxation, which makes learning more compelling. Depending on their designs, games can positively influence the learners' cognitive, behavioral, and socio-cultural engagement.

McCutcheon and Bray (2020) argues that the game context provides people with a discussion platform that they otherwise may not have been able to access. Further research by Johnson and Tiwari (2021) asserts that board games introduce choices that provoke thoughtful decision-making. Following the game rules develops emotional and social skills and behaviors necessary for academic success.

Regarding the impact of simulators, Zulfiqar et al. (2019) concluded that they help students learn in a fun way, promote critical thinking, and are productive for learning. They even facilitate experiences and dealing with failures and challenges in a risk-free environment.

14.5   Research Methodology

This research measured the impact of interactive tabletop games on student learning and competency development by using exploratory data techniques.

The methodology of this paper consisted of three steps. First, we designed two questionnaires, adapting the details of the instrument employed by Chai et al. (2015). Second, we decided the participants to play the tabletop game and from whom we would collect the data. Finally, the third step was to analyze the data collected. The rest of this section follows an outline structure.

14.5.1 Designing the Questionnaire

This study developed two questionnaires, pre- and post-game, to be applied before and after the tabletop interactive game to evaluate the student's perception of their learning and competency building. The questions also helped understand the transversal competencies that gamification helps them to develop.

The construction of the questionnaires was partially based on previous research and self-elaboration. Based on the literature review (Alshare and Sewailem 2018), we designed the questionnaire to analyze the competencies associated with making interdisciplinary connections, collaborative working, critical thinking, decision-making, problem-solving, and strategic thinking.

Both pre and post questionnaires had 17 questions applied in Qualtrics in the six categories listed below. To have conclusive results, we designed the questionnaires with a 5-point Likert scale (1 = strongly disagree to 5 = strongly agree). The description of the question categories follows:

- Interdisciplinary questions explored students' perceptions of how different streams like finance, human resources, and marketing are linked.
- Collaborative working questions measured students' perception of how each member contributed to the team.
- Critical thinking questions measured students' perception of applying the knowledge learned in previous semesters to real-life situations.
- Decision-making questions measured the confidence of students to resolve various challenges during the game to maximize the company's value.
- Problem-solving questions explored students' perception of dealing with real-time situations in the game generated by the simulator.
- Strategic thinking questions helped students assess when they could define plans for each area during the game and align them with the company's objectives.

14.5.2 Participants

The game was applied in a one-day workshop to the fourth-semester students taking the subject "Financial Analysis (CF-2015)." The participating students were from seven different study programs: LAE—Bachelors in Business Administration; LAF—Bachelors in Financial Administration; LCPF—Bachelors in Public Accounting and Finance; LCDE—Bachelors in Business Creation; LEM—Bachelors in Marketing; LIN—Bachelors in International Business, and LLN—Bachelors in Logistics. In total, 420 students participated in the game from August 2018 to January 2020.

At the start of the workshop, the pre-test questionnaire was applied to the participants individually. After completing the pre-test questionnaire, the students were put in teams of 5 or 6 members to play the game. The interactive tabletop game has a board game, as shown in Fig. 14.1, and an online simulator. The simulator continuously changes the market parameters, and the team must make decisions based on the financial parameters of the company. The team that wins the game is the one whose company has the maximum value at the end. Then, the post-test questionnaire is applied to measure students' perception.

14.5.3 Data Analysis

Before the final data was collected from the students, two rounds of a pilot study were conducted to test the validity of the questionnaires.

Statistical and graphical tests were performed for each study program separately to verify significant competency improvements of those students before and after the game. We also performed tests on all 17 questions to assess whether students improved in the areas intended by the game design. The data points were used to identify significant changes in the variation between the two scores. All statistical tests were performed with a confidence level of 95% in the population samples.

The following tests were performed to check the validity of the data:

- Anderson-Darling normality test.
- Paired t-test or t–t test.
- Mann-Whitney test.
- Box-plot analysis.
- Histogram.
- Individual interval plot.
- Two-variance test.
- Graphical summary and descriptive statistics.
- Spider chart.

14.6 Results

The results from the pre and post questionnaires formed the quantitative and qualitative parts of the study. The students' responses were analyzed to understand the impact of game-based learning on building competencies.

Table 14.2 Changes in the means and standard deviations, pre- versus post-game questionnaire, for each program in the scope of the study

Career	Parameter	Pre	Post	Change
LAE pre	Mean	3.966	4.347	0.381
LAF/LCPF pre	Mean	3.842	4.319	0.477
LCDE pre	Mean	3.752	3.974	0.221
Other pre	Mean	3.961	4.408	0.447
LAE pre	Standard deviation	0.303	0.140	−0.163
LAF/LCPF pre	Standard deviation	0.283	0.112	−0.171
LCDE pre	Standard deviation	0.307	0.113	−0.194
Other pre	Standard deviation	0.436	0.088	−0.348

14.6.1   Graphical Tests

Four different graphical tests were applied to check the differences in scores between pre- and post-tests among the various disciplinary programs participating.

Inference of the Graphical Analysis

In this study, the graphical analysis consisted of a histogram, interval plot, and box plot to analyze the results. Table 14.2 summarizes the output of all the graphical analyses, showing that the mean and standard deviation for each program stream improved when comparing pre- versus post-applications of the tabletop game.

Overall, the graphical analyses showed that the student results improved from pre- versus post-test in all the programs participating in the study.

14.6.2   Statistical Test for Each Career of Study

The Paired T-Test was conducted to check the differences in the mean for each study program (see Table 14.3).

Table 14.3 Paired T-test for pre- versus post-tests in the study programs

Career	Statistical test	T value	P-value @ 95% CI	Interpretation
LAE pre	Paired T-test	−5.83	0.000	Significant change in mean
LAF/LCPF pre	Paired T-test	−7.98	0.000	Significant change in mean
LCDE pre	Paired T-test	−2.96	0.009	Significant change in mean
Others pre	Paired T-test	−4.43	0.000	Significant change in mean

Inference of Paired T-Test Results
A Paired *T*-Test is a type of location test used when comparing two measurements to assess whether their population means differ. As depicted in Table 14.3, the *p*-value used was less than 0.05 (a 95% CI, confidence index) for all the study programs. With that CI, the *T*-test results indicated significant improvements in the mean scores of the students in pre- versus post-comparisons of the gamification applied in all the study programs.

14.6.3   Graphical Test for Impact on Each Question

A spider chart analyzed the change in each item of the questionnaire applied. There were 17 items (questions) in the pre- and post-tests for all students in the seven study programs. The purpose of this analysis was to check if there were any specific topics in each study program where there was no improvement after applying gamification.

   This analysis was carried out for all study programs, and it showed significant improvement in all the 17 questions.

Inference of the Spider Chart
The Spider chart is a chart plot with a sequence of equiangular spokes, called radii; each spoke represents one of the variables. The data length of a spoke is proportional to the variable data point's magnitude relative to the maximum variable magnitude across all the data points. In the Spider Chart depicted in Fig. 14.2, the radii are the

Fig. 14.2 Spider chart for the 17 questions, comparing pre- versus post-tests, LAE

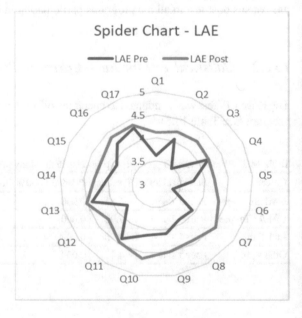

17 questionnaire items with a scale from 1 to 5. The mean score of each question improved for all items in the questionnaire. It showed that the students in all the study programs improved in every topic, as intended by the game design.

14.7 Discussion

The primary aim of this study was to examine the impact of the interactive tabletop game on the interdisciplinary concepts learned by Tecnologico de Monterrey Business School students in their first four semesters.

Playing interactive tabletop games provides a unique experience to students. Games help motivate the students to retain and apply the knowledge learned in the classrooms (Mawhirter and Garofalo 2016). The research findings show that the students' perceived value of learning increased after the game due to the understanding of interdisciplinary connections among all the study programs.

As asserted by other researchers (Zulfiqar et al. 2019; Sousa and Rocha 2019; Teichmanna et al. 2020), we also found in our study that the interactive tabletop game helps develop competencies like decision-making, problem-solving, strategic thinking, and collaborative work in students. The interactive tabletop game provides students with an opportunity to discuss with each other, brainstorm various ideas, and collectively agree to a single idea that can be applied to a real-life situation in a risk-free environment. These interactions give students an option to see the impact that certain decisions have on the company. The students can change their strategies in the game and seek better results.

According to Pratikto et al. (2019), it is crucial for university business school graduates to develop analytical and decision-making skills to understand what is happening in the industry and make correct decisions. The results of this study confirmed that the students perceived that their analytical, problem-solving, and decision-making skills improved after playing the tabletop game. They were able to analyze various variables simultaneously during the game, for example, a sudden increase in demand in the market, problems in procuring raw materials, and the lack of needed skilled labor. As these variables change, they must make decisions to improve the situation while maintaining the company's sound financial position.

14.8 Conclusions

The noted outcome of this study was the overall positive learning experience for the fourth-semester students of the business school. As the results indicated, the interactive tabletop game can be very effective in learning and building competencies. The game provided the students with a platform for discussion and helped them apply the concepts they learned in various classes and interlink them while making decisions.

References

Alshare K, Sewailem MF (2018) A gap analysis of business students' skills in the 21st century: a case study of Qatar. Acad Educ Leadersh J 22(1):1–22

Casañ-Pitarch R (2018) An approach to digital game-based learning: video-games principles and applications in foreign language learning. J Lang Teach Res (Online) 9(6):1147–1159

Chai CS et al (2015) Assessing multidimensional students' perceptions of twenty-first-century learning practices. Asia Pacific Educ Rev 16(3):389–398

Chiarello F, Castellano MG (2016) Board games and board game design as learning tools for complex scientific concepts: some experiences. Int J Game-Based Learn (IJGBL) 6(2):1–14

Csikszentmihalyi M (1990) The domain of creativity, pp 190–222

Csikszentmihalyi M (1997) Flow and the psychology of discovery and invention. Harper Collins, New York

Eckerson WW (2010) Performance dashboards: measuring, monitoring, and managing your business. Wiley

Johnson JE, Tiwari SR (2021) Handbook of developmentally appropriate toys, chapter: board games

Kaplan RS, Norton DP (2007) Usar el balanced scorecard como un sistema de gestión estratégica. Harv Bus Rev 1:75–85

Mawhirter DA, Garofalo PF (2016) Expect the unexpected: simulation games as a teaching strategy. Clin Simul Nurs 12(4):132–136

McCutcheon V, Bray G (2020) What have games got to do with me? Patterns 1(1):100002

Pratikto H, Prabowo SW, Murdiono A, Basuki A (2019) The role of business simulator games implementation in improving the ability of analysis and business decision making independently for students (literature research). KnE Soc Sci 1005–1010

Sousa MJ, Rocha Á (2019) Leadership styles and skills developed through game-based learning. J Bus Res 94:360–366

Teichmanna M, Ullricha A, Knosta D, Gronaua N (2020) Serious games in learning factories: perpetuating knowledge in learning loops by game-based learning. In: 10th Conference on learning factories, vol 45, pp 260–261

Van de Pol J, Volman M, Beishuizen J (2010) Scaffolding in teacher-student interaction: a decade of research. Educ Psychol Rev 22(3):271–296

Yang K-M, Lee L-C, Chiu C (2021) The effects of a self-designed tabletop game and learning achievement. J Comput 32(1):174–182

Zulfiqar S et al (2019) An analysis of the influence of business simulation games on business school students' attitude and intention toward entrepreneurial activities. J Educ Comput Res 57(1):106–130

Chapter 15
The e-Portfolio as a Learning Evaluation Tool: Main Benefits and Challenges

María Guadalupe Siqueiros Quintana,
Gloria del Carmen Mungarro Robles, and Heidi Sacnicté Robles Tarazón

15.1 Introduction

Schools cannot separate from societal progress; especially, they cannot distance themselves from information and communication technologies (ICTs). This possibility and others have been at the head of discussions about what happens in school institutions. Even on many occasions, schools' performance and methods are called into question (Díaz 2005). The most questioned methods are those related to three of the main activities carried out and promoted by the school: teaching, learning, and assessment. In the case of evaluation methods, these are changing at different educational levels depending on the institution's context and the capacity of the educational actors.

Electronic portfolios as an evaluation tool in the new constructivist learning models have become a trend in recent years. Some studies have shown that this tool facilitates reflection (Arancibia et al. 2017; Chávez Ávila 2017; Mostafa 2020), allows better work organization and establishing professional goals (Beka and Kulinxha 2021), facilitates the establishment of objectives and assessment of learning (Bertolotti and Beseghi 2016), and promotes awareness of one's knowledge, practical thinking, professional skills, and comprehensive assessment (Muñoz and Soto 2019). Furthermore, it improves writing performance—especially when using Facebook—(Barrot 2021) and contributes to high attendance rates and reductions of failure rates (Gómez and Arellano 2019).

This rapid expansion of electronic portfolio assessment, which has been generated throughout the world (at all levels, especially in higher education), creates the need to continue evaluating the results of its use and to know, from the students' perspective, the benefits or challenges these bring to their academic training.

M. G. Siqueiros Quintana (✉) · G. C. Mungarro Robles · H. S. Robles Tarazón
Benemérita y Centenaria Escuela Normal del Estado de Sonora, Hermosillo, Sonora, Mexico
e-mail: enesmarilu@gmail.com

S. Hosseini et al. (eds.), *Technology-Enabled Innovations in Education*,
Transactions on Computer Systems and Networks,
https://doi.org/10.1007/978-981-19-3383-7_15

199

15.2 Development

For Camacho (2008), the most relevant constructivist evaluation of learning involves the cognitive and socio-affective processes that the student must develop to achieve autonomy, creativity, and decision-making skills. Camacho comments that self-evaluation and co-evaluation drive this construction process. There must be spaces for the assessment of this process to know the results of students learning. The electronic portfolio is a good space for this purpose.

15.2.1 Problem Statement

The new pedagogical approaches, such as constructivism development of competencies, bring significant challenges for teachers, generating the need for a change of logic and understanding to arrive at acceptance and appropriation of educational innovations. Change in the classroom is not easy because of the complexity of these approaches (Díaz-Barriga et al. 2012).

The 2012 Curriculum of the Normal Schools in Mexico adopts the constructivist and sociocultural conception of learning, competencies, and student-centered learning. The base document of the Ministry of Public Education proposes an evaluation perspective oriented toward self-regulation and reflection on what has been learned (Díaz-Barriga and Barroso 2014).

Many teachers deploy a diversity of pedagogical methods that, in some cases, are implemented without their knowing the impact or students' perspective of these strategies. In the new models, such as the student-centered one, it is crucial to know the students' opinions and experiences under the new strategies. Thus, the interest of this study lies in the following research questions: What are the characteristics of the e-portfolios used by the first semester students? What is their perception of the electronic portfolio implementation? What are the advantages and disadvantages from the students' perspective of its use as an evaluation and learning tool?

In this research, two objectives were established: the first was to describe the characteristics of the e-portfolios prepared by teachers in training in a specific course. The second objective was to know the students' perception of the electronic portfolio as a learning and evaluation tool.

15.2.2 Theoretical Framework

Díaz-Barriga (2008) highlights the portfolio and rubrics as promoters of reflection and self-assessment among the main evaluation strategies (congruent with the new approaches). The portfolio is a selection or collection of evidence of the learning achieved by its author, showing his effort, progress, and achievements (Barrett 2001; Díaz Barriga Arceo 2006; Murillo 2012).

According to Díaz (2005), the advantages offered by portfolio development are the following: intellectual autonomy, self-evaluation, an improvement over the traditional evaluation, better student knowledge, and comprehensive assessment. It is especially suitable for organizing and facilitating the student's autonomous training (Díaz-Barriga 2008); it helps structure knowledge, adapts to the students' diversity, and enhances the processes required to acquire knowledge and learn autonomously (Colén et al. 2006).

Electronic portfolios (or e-portfolio) use ICTs, which incorporate different media (images and video, for example), inserting hyperlinks and relating evidence to reflections. E-portfolios are characterized by online storage space, file backup, easy portability, and accessibility, and they promote developing technological skills (Barrett 2001).

Danielson and Abrutyn (2002) describe three types of portfolios: work, evaluation, and presentation. The work program functions as a repository for all the evidence made during a study program; the assessment section shows mastery of curricular content, and the presentation demonstrates the highest level of achievement attained by the student.

15.2.3 Methodology

To achieve the research objectives, we designed a mixed research approach with a descriptive scope to detail the students' experiences and perceptions when using the e-portfolio. The study was carried out in two phases: First, the e-portfolio was elaborated and reviewed for its evaluation. In the second phase, the students expressed their evaluations about various aspects of the e-portfolio (see Table 15.1).

Two first-semester classes (groups A and D) assigned to the same teacher participated. The professor designed and implemented this evaluation strategy in the "Child Development Psychology" course (i.e., children aged 0–12), belonging to the psychology path of the curriculum for the Bachelor's Degree in Primary Education to teach in a normal school in the state of Sonora, Mexico. The classes were arranged to have 26 students each. However, in both, a student dropped out at the time of this research. Furthermore, in one of the classes, a student did not make their

Table 15.1 Methodological elements of this research

Methodological elements	Phase 1	Phase 2
Investigation type	Case analysis	Non-experimental
Scope	Qualitative	Mixed
Participants	49 students	41 students
Dates	Nov. 3–8, 2017	Dec. 12–15, 2017

e-portfolio. Although the same classes were considered for the two phases, participation varied: 49 portfolios were reviewed, but in the end, only 41 students participated in the questionnaire.

To make the e-portfolio, we adapted the evaluation rubric used by Díaz-Barriga et al. (2012), which was presented to the students and adjusted before making the e-portfolio. The content and structure were integrated into the activities developed for the course. In this case, the portfolio modality solicited was the work portfolio, which included qualitative self-evaluation reflections of each learning evidence. In other words, it was emphasized to the students not to limit themselves to describing the evidence, but also they should reflect on it, commenting on what they learned from producing it. In total, there were nine pieces of evidence organized into four learning units.

The questionnaire with six questions was used for the second phase: four Likert-scale items with five response levels (1 = disagree to 5 = agree) and two open questions. The latter were related to the advantages and disadvantages of the e-portfolio. The questionnaire was applied electronically through the Google Forms platform during the last week of classes via a link shared in a Facebook group started at the beginning of the semester for each class. For the closed questions, an Excel program (quantitative) was used. For the open questions (qualitative), the Atlas ti program was used to analyze the advantages and disadvantages that the students expressed and to interpret them by creating open categories and families.

15.3 Results

Phase 1

The students built a website on the suggested digital platform (https://es.wix.com), which allowed them to learn to use a new online tool for hypermedia, audio, and video resources. The students incorporated an autobiography, an essay, videos, presentations, an infographic, and an intervention project with their respective reflections.

Most of the students demonstrated incipient management of both the portfolio and the technological tools to carry it out (the e-portfolio). Despite this, it was considered that good results were obtained, as the students showed autonomy in their performance. The few questions that arose were resolved in class in the scheduled period. There was a diversity of designs and ways to present the portfolio. The most representative design was a portfolio specifically for the requested course.

Exceptional designs were also found that exceeded expectations. In some cases, the students thought about linking all the courses in which the professors requested portfolios. Although this was suggested to them, the decision to contemplate one or more portfolios for their educational path was entirely up to the student. Some decided to use one page in the same portfolio to organize their learning evidence

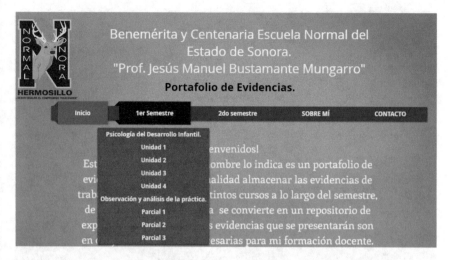

Fig. 15.1   Updated e-portfolio example (http://17260006.wixsite.com/evidenciastc)

presented in their training path. An example of this is seen in Fig. 15.1, which the student has continued updating.

Because it was the students' first experience in making an e-portfolio, we considered that only essential elements of the suggested platform would be used. However, some students added comments about specific elements (an essential aspect of co-evaluation, which was not promoted in the first instance of this research). See the example in Fig. 15.2.

Phase 2

Regarding their experience making the electronic portfolio in the Child Development Psychology course, 95% of the students fully agreed and agreed that it encourages autonomous learning, 96% that it stimulates creativity and imagination, and 92% that the use of the portfolio interested them. Regarding perceiving it as simple, there was less agreement: 73% agreed and fully agreed, 17% were undecided, and 9% disagreed and completely disagreed (see Fig. 15.3).

When analyzing the two open questions related to the advantages and disadvantages of portfolios, the students expressed a diversity of answers. Regarding the advantages, there were four leading categories referring to the adjectives they gave to the portfolio, their repercussions from learning and evaluation, and the use of ICTs (Fig. 15.4). The main advantages mentioned had to do with learning, facilitation of work organization, and the flexibility provided by ICTs, to return and work on the e-portfolios at different times.

The disadvantages mentioned by the students included the difficulties of the page, perhaps because it was new to them, problems related to internet connectivity, and the time required to complete their designs. Some expressed that there was no downside to these portfolios (Fig. 15.5).

204   M. G. S. Quintana et al.

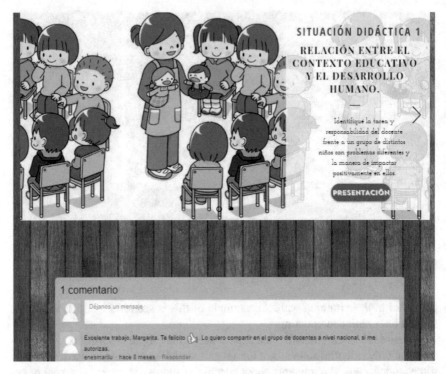

Fig. 15.2 Example of e-portfolio with the option to comment (https://maguimmlm.wixsite.com/portafolio)

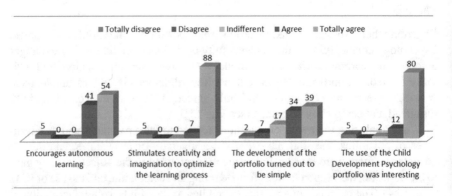

Fig. 15.3 Percentage of students corresponding to each statement and response levels

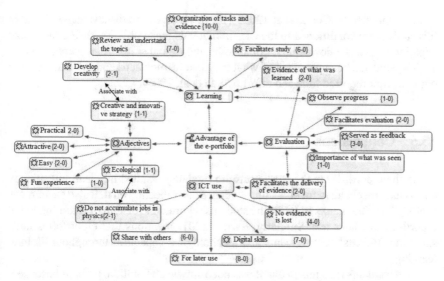

Fig. 15.4 Families and categories of answers about the advantages of the e-portfolio

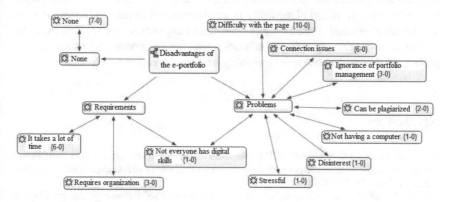

Fig. 15.5 Families and categories created about the disadvantages of the e-portfolio

15.4 Discussion

The e-portfolio design was developed through personal creativity, according to students' personalities, tastes, and abilities. As in other studies like Díaz-Barriga et al. (2012), the e-portfolios allowed the recovery and systematization of production and experiences. They could become a powerful instrument for monitoring and learning reflections by the participants. Based on what was reported by the students themselves, the portfolio model allowed recording the acquisition of professional skills in the development process during their training journey at the university.

As mentioned by Cortés et al. (2015), the advantages and disadvantages found in this study were conditioned to the uses individuals make of ICTs, their educational experience, and the development of specific and digital skills. As reported in other studies, students became aware of what they had learned and reported that carrying out this work required time and effort (Colén et al. 2006).

15.5 Conclusions

Using the e-portfolio in the work portfolio modality resulted in a learning strategy and a study mechanism for collecting evidence and reflecting on it. It also encourages lifelong learning thanks to ICTs: the students reported the benefit of returning to the e-portfolio for later use. Similarly, Barret (2001) mentions that e-portfolios must show the students' achievements and technological capacities throughout lifelong learning.

Some students recognized that it was not a simple elaboration, perhaps because it was their first experience. It was not only a matter of recording their evidence; it also required interpreting the various assessments with a self-critical look. Their project had to be conceptualized didactically as continuous and dynamic construction, not as a terminal product. Based on this educational experience, we suggest using the e-portfolio from the beginning of education training and continuing as a long-term project, an essential element in continuing lifelong education as a teacher.

References

Arancibia ML, Halal C, Romero R (2017) Valoración y barreras en la integración del e-portafolio en el proceso de práctica inicial por parte de docentes y estudiantes de educación superior. Píxel-Bit Rev Medios Educ 51:151–164

Barrett HC (2001) Electronic portfolios—a chapter in educational technology; An encyclopedia to be published by ABC-CLIO, 2001. In: Electronic portfolios in educational technology encyclopedia, pp 1–6

Barrot JS (2021) Effects of Facebook-based e-portfolio on ESL learners' writing performance. Lang Cult Curriculum 34(1):95–111. https://doi.org/10.1080/07908318.2020.1745822

Beka A, Kulinxha G (2021) Portfolio as a tool for self-reflection and professional development for pre-service teachers. Int J Learn Teach Educ Res 20(2):22–35. https://doi.org/10.26803/ijlter.20.2.2

Bertolotti G, Beseghi M (2016) From the learning diary to the ELP: an e-portfolio for autonomous language learning. Lang Learn High Educ 6(2):435–441. https://doi.org/10.1515/cercles-2016-0023

Camacho I (2008) La evaluación constructivista contribuye a marcar la dirección en el proceso educativo. Rev Cienc Educ 1(32):136–142

Chávez Ávila P (2017) El portafolio digital como instrumento de reflexión y autoevaluación docente en la educación superior. Aleth Rev Desarro Humano Educ Soc Contemp 9(1):76–97. https://doi.org/10.11600/21450366.9.1aletheia.76.97

Colén T, Giné N, Imbernón F (2006) La carpeta de aprendizaje el alumno universitario. La autonomía del estudiante en el proceso de aprendizaje

Cortés OF, Pinto AR, Atrio SI (2015) E-portafolio como herramienta construccionista del aprendizaje activo en tecnología educativa. Rev Lasallista Invest 12(2):36–44

Danielson C, Abrutyn L (2002) Una introducción al uso de portafolios en el aula

Díaz JJ (2005) El potafolio de desempeño: una práctica reflexiva para lograr éxito en la formación y el aprendizaje

Díaz-Barriga F (2008) La innovación en la enseñanza soportada en TIC. Una mirada al futuro desde las condiciones actuales - Educrea. https://educrea.cl/la-innovacion-en-la-ensenanza-soportada-en-tic-una-mirada-al-futuro-desde-las-condiciones-actuales/. Accessed 02 June 2021

Díaz-Barriga F, Barroso R (2014) Diseño y validación de una propuesta de evaluación auténtica de competencias en un programa de formación de docentes de educación básica en México. Perspect Educ Form Prof 53(1):36–56. https://doi.org/10.4151/07189729-Vol.53-Iss.1-Art.210

Díaz-Barriga F, Romero E, Heredia A (2012) Diseño tecnopedagógico de portafolios electrónicos de aprendizaje: una experiencia con estudiantes universitarios. Rev Electrón Invest Educ 14(2):103–117. [Online]. Available: http://www.scielo.org.mx/scielo.php?script=sci_arttext&pid=S1607-40412012000200008

Díaz Barriga Arceo F (2006) La evaluación auténtica centrada en el desempeño: una alternativa para evaluar el aprendizaje y la enseñanza. In: Enseñanza situada: vínculo entre la escuela y la vida. McGraw Hill, pp 125–164

Gómez VE, Arellano OM (2019) Portafolio reflexivo: una propuesta para la enseñanza de la Metodología Cualitativa. Zo Próxima 31:87–106

Mostafa H (2020) Using e-portfolio to enhance reflective instructional practices and self-efficacy of EFL student-teachers. J Educ 76(Part 1):1–35. https://doi.org/10.12816/EDUSOHAG

Muñoz LDLC, Soto E (2019) El portafolio digital ¿Una herramienta para aprender a ser docentes críticos? Un estudio de casos, vol 19, no 3

Murillo G (2012) El portafolio como instrumento clave para la evaluación en educación superior. Actual Invest Educ 12(1):1–23. https://doi.org/10.15517/aie.v12i1.10266

Chapter 16
Adapting the Eclectic Method to a Graphic Adventure Video Game to Improve Student Literacy

Carlos Miranda-Palma and Rosa María Romero González

16.1 Introduction

The Ibero-American Intergovernmental Network for the Education of People with Special Educational Needs (RIINEE) (RIINEE 2017) report mentions that technological resources to support education and adapted to different learning levels have been gradually incorporated into traditional systems. It states that almost half of Latin American and Caribbean countries have a significant deficit in accessing and using these resources. The countries with the most progress in introducing and using these learning tools have more access to adapted teaching resources. These include Brazil, Chile, Costa Rica, Mexico, Peru, and Uruguay, which stand out for their incorporation of information and communication technologies (ICTs) and teaching materials.

Nowadays, playing video games is the primary social practice mediated by digital technologies in which new generations of students participate. Some studies have focused on their role in developing cognitive skills and enhancing learning environments. These studies have concluded that video game environments captivate, engage, and motivate students (Garrido 2013).

Psychiatrist Guillermo Peñaloza Solano (Milenio 2020) mentions that in these Covid-19 pandemic times, technological tools have increased in Mexico, including video games.

He mentions that video games have mental health benefits, stimulating memory, strengthening learning, improving reaction quality, and promoting decision-making.

R. M. Romero González
Universidad Autónoma de Querétaro, Campus Juriquilla, Juriquilla, México
e-mail: rossyrg04@yahoo.com.mx

C. Miranda-Palma (✉)
Universidad Autónoma de Yucatán, Unidad Multidisciplinaria Tizimín, Tizimín, México
e-mail: cmiranda@correo.uady.mx

© The Author(s), under exclusive license to Springer Nature Singapore Pte Ltd. 2022   209
S. Hosseini et al. (eds.), *Technology-Enabled Innovations in Education*,
Transactions on Computer Systems and Networks,
https://doi.org/10.1007/978-981-19-3383-7_16

They also entertain in a safe environment, despite the pandemic, and generate a sense of belonging.

This research adapts the eclectic method, a methodology used to improve the skills of students with learning disabilities in reading and writing, in a video game that entertains and includes learning scenarios. We present the adaptation of the method in the structure of the video game and its different levels of cognitive complexity. Some figures of this adaptation and images of its use are also presented.

16.2 Development

As the video game serves a Special Educational Need (SEN), a methodology for the development of learning activities must be used. The eclectic approach is a methodology used to improve the skills of children with learning disabilities in reading and writing. This approach (Salavarrieta 2015) comprises the other methods' most significant and valuable aspects (Syllabic, Alphabetic, Global, and everyday words). It was selected because the activities it offers are more feasible to implement in a video game and offer different degrees of difficulty. It also offers entertaining activities for a video game, because as mentioned above, it takes the most significant and valuable features of other methods.

Likewise, the graphic adventure video game must have a plot where the involved user advances and solves challenges or problems. However, to advance to higher levels, the user must satisfactorily complete the learning activities posed by the SEN attention methodology. Therefore, a SEN expert is necessary for the flexibility to create, modify, or exchange the game's learning activities. If another SEN attention methodology is desired, the expert's support can help avoid recreating the whole entertainment part of the video game. However, this flexibility requires a methodology adaptable to change and a design that permits adjustments and changes at a relatively low cost.

16.2.1 Theoretical Framework

The RIINEE report (RIINEE 2017) mentions that, notwithstanding the diverse origin and age of the official data presented by each country, the sample shows that around 8.5% of the Latin American population has special education needs. The percentage of women with SEN is higher (4.5%) than that of men (4%). The information provided shows that people with SEN are an essential social group in qualitative and quantitative terms. They are plural in their social, political, economic, and cultural characteristics.

Caballero (2014) mentions that children with learning difficulties in reading or writing may have socializing problems, aggressiveness, shyness, loneliness at school, or experience school violence, and lack of understanding from the teacher, classmates, or parents. They may also be scolded or verbally or physically abused by their parents. They may also be uninterested in classes.

Alfageme and Sanchez (2002) mention that video games improve performance, reeducation, or recovery of physical or psychological skills or abilities.

Graphic adventure video games (Torrente et al. 2011) are participatory and have a more evident plot as the problems and challenges arising during the game are solved. They promote exploration and problem-solving skills and help establish connections between concepts. The approach and resolution of problems favor both entertainment and learning. The Graphic Adventures video game has the most appropriate characteristics for this study.

Most studies examine video games designed mainly for entertainment purposes but have been given an educational approach for the classroom, although this is not their primary purpose. Examples of these works are Morales (2018), Trejo (2019), and Brazo et al. (2018). In this present study, the purpose of the video game is superseded by design for a teaching purpose.

Sommerville (2011) mentions that the software includes the activities and processes comprising the development and evolution of a software system. In this project, Design-Based Research (DBR) was used for the software development process. DBR aims to analyze learning contextually by systematically designing and studying particular forms of learning, teaching strategies, and tools responsive to the systemic nature of learning, teaching, and assessment. All this makes it a powerful methodological paradigm in learning and teaching research (Molina et al. 2011).

16.2.2 Problem Statement

The term "Special Educational Needs" (SEN) was introduced in the late 1970s in the Warnock Report (Warnock 1981). This report emphasized the support to students with SEN from an inclusive point of view, eliminating the barriers between students who required special education and those who received regular education.

In Mexico, attention to students with SEN is one of the most critical issues in the educational field. Specifically, the 1st and 2nd-grade elementary school teachers have problems with students who do not want to read. They also have problems with students who have learning difficulties in reading and writing that prevent them from reading and writing at the same level as children without learning difficulties. As teachers have many children in the classroom, they cannot attend to each of them and their difficulties, nor can they afford to fall behind in teaching since they have a school program and limited time. Moreover, they have children who learn to read before others, and they cannot afford to have several or all of them fall behind because of one child. Thus, teachers have to ask parents for support at home so that their children do not fall behind.

Currently, referring students with problems in reading and writing for personalized attention is not allowed. Instead, they receive assistance in the same daily learning environment (the classroom) with their classmates. The idea is for them not to have an excluding education. Within this context, teachers must use all their creativity and resourcefulness to achieve this goal. However, the type and amount of resources and materials to carry out such strategies are limited, so they must manually create resources. Furthermore, these activities or strategies must be developed for all students, not only students with learning disabilities. The aim is for all students to improve their skills, mainly cognitive and reading skills.

As a result, this research aimed to adapt the eclectic method as a learning activity in a graphic adventure video game that improves reading and writing skills in elementary school students with learning disabilities.

16.2.3 Method

First, using the DBR, an iterative and incremental methodology was designed to create a graphic adventure video game to support SEN care, as shown in Fig. 16.1.

The DBR was divided into five stages: problem analysis, solution design, construction, validation, and evaluation. Five discrete stages were defined for the development process.

Figure 16.1 shows that the evaluation stage is implemented transversally in the DBR. It is carried out in each stage to verify that its activities have been executed correctly.

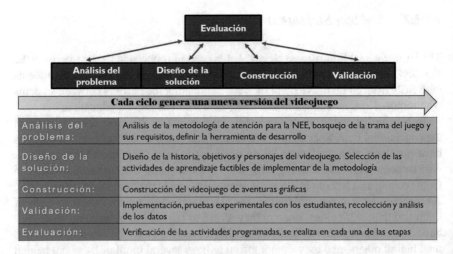

Fig. 16.1 The five stages of DBR

(a) *Problem analysis*: The SEN situation to be addressed with the video game was analyzed in this stage. The video game requirements were determined, and a detailed study of the eclectic method was made. Likewise, the development tool to build the video game was defined.

For the evaluation, the most relevant characteristics and factors of the target group with SEN were defined. It was also verified that the characteristics and activities of the SEN methodology were defined, and the video game requirements and development tools were also established.

(b) *Solution design*: In this stage, the video game design document was prepared. This document describes the main idea of the video game, its objective and key features, and the game mechanics. It also describes the inputs and outputs of the game, the story protagonists interacting with the user within the game, and the artwork requirements, among others. Likewise, the eclectic-method-learning activities feasible to implement in a digital tool were selected since not all activities were feasible.

We used the eclectic-method-learning activities recommended by García and Escrig (cited in Cristóbal Muñoz (2013)), which define each activity with its corresponding purpose.

For the evaluation, the logic and structure of the use cases of the video game were verified, and the elaboration progress in the video game design document. The feasibility of the learning activities selected from the SEN methodology was also verified.

(c) *Construction*: In this stage, the software development model was incremental. Figure 16.2 shows the construction stage in detail. Each increment in this stage has to comply with four activities: requirements, analysis, design and coding, and testing. An increment can be an entertainment or learning activity, and the number of increments depends on the game design.

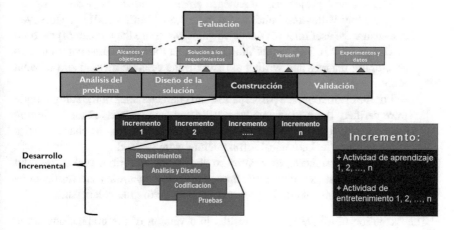

Fig. 16.2 Construction stage

At this stage, the video game advances according to the increments made in entertainment and learning activities. This form of development enables a preliminary version to be examined by the SEN expert for feedback before the full version of the video game is finalized. These increments of entertainment scenarios or learning activities are not limited. The magnitude of a video game is limited by the SEN it intends to address.

For the evaluation, the functionality of the video game's implemented use cases was verified. The functionality of the entertainment and learning activities described in the flow diagrams developed for each use case was also verified. This was performed in each increment of the trial activity of this methodology.

(iv) *Validation*: In this stage, the video game would undergo a trial period with the SEN students it intends to address and those who do not have SEN. At this stage, the involvement and participation of the SEN expert and researcher are critical during the development of the class sessions because it is where the analysis begins (Fig. 16.2).

In this same stage, instruments are administered to obtain data and compare the progress in the skills that the video game is intended to address. These instruments will be applied to the children who have SEN and their class-mates who do not have special needs. The results are expected to show a slight to moderate improvement in children with SEN and moderate to excel-lent improvement in children without SEN. To measure these improvements, we perform the testing at the beginning (pre) and the end (post) of the exper-imentation. Another comparison that would help measure the usefulness of the game is to apply the evaluation instrument (post) to the children who used the video game and a group of children who did not use it (in the same school level or grade). A comparison could be made between the children who used the video game and those who did not.

This research project uses the measurement instruments to assess progress suggested by Valles and Vallés (cited in Cristóbal Muñoz (2013)). Moreover, to measure the usefulness of the video game, we chose the indicators proposed by Ortega (2009). The results validate whether the video game contributes to developing reading and writing skills with the eclectic method and to what extent.

For the evaluation, the participation and characteristics of the study sample were verified, the instruments were validated, and the tests at the beginning (pre) and end (post) of the experiment were applied. Also, the characteristics of the required technological infrastructure were verified.

(v) *Evaluation*: Evaluation, as mentioned above, was described and carried out throughout all stages of the DBI. In each of these stages, data and verifications provided certainty about the progress in constructing the video game.

The execution of all DBR stages results in a version of the graphic adventure video game that can be used as a tool to address a SEN.

16.2.4 Results

Once the methodology was designed, the graphic adventure video game was developed using the eclectic method for the learning activities. The result of the video game structure can be seen in Fig. 16.3. The game is divided into two parts: Sierra Gorda and Secret Island.

The video game development was completed, and three versions were generated: Windows, Android, and HTML5. Figure 16.4 shows an example of an entertainment activity.

Figure 16.5 shows an example of the use of an eclectic approach to learning activities.

The project is currently in the validation (experimentation) stage. However, given the current circumstances of the Covid-19 pandemic, this experimental stage is being carried out remotely (distance education). It has the support of the parents and teachers of each participating group. One first-grade and one second-grade elementary school class are participating. This stage will last six months, and we are currently halfway through the experimentation period.

Figure 16.6 shows images of some of the children currently using the video game.

Table 16.1 describes the adaptation of the eclectic method activities suggested by García and Escrig (cited in Cristóbal Muñoz (2013)) to learning activities that can be implemented in a digital tool, in this case, a video game. For each of these adapted activities, the pedagogical purpose intended to be developed with these activities is stated. These activities are presented in ascending order of cognitive complexity intended to be developed in the video game.

The learning activities of Table 16.1 are intended to influence the indicators suggested by Ortega (2009). These indicators allow measuring the usefulness of the

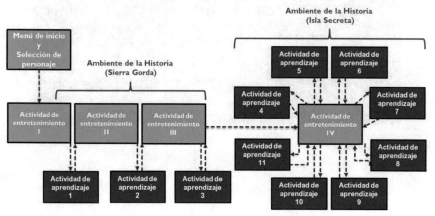

Fig. 16.3 Video game structure

Fig. 16.4 Entertainment activity

Fig. 16.5 Learning activity

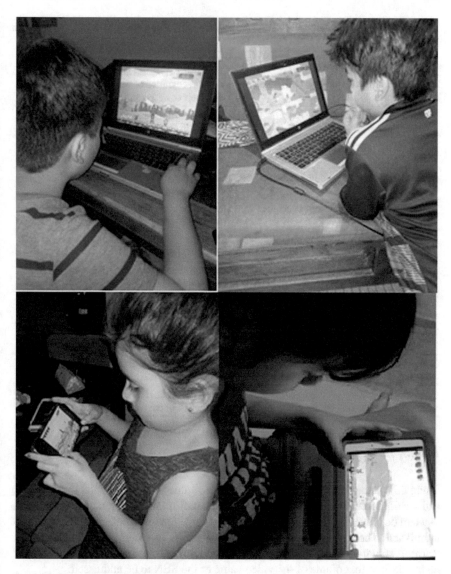

Fig. 16.6 Video game validation stage

video game to validate if it contributes to the development of reading and writing skills using the eclectic method. The indicators are the following: word segmentation, word formation with the given syllables, selecting the syllable (visual-graphic discrimination), completing the word with the correct syllable (visual-graphic discrimination), image-word association, selection of the word corresponding to the given image, verification of correct sentences with the given words, and use of capitalization.

Table 16.1 Pedagogical purpose of each of the learning activities according to the eclectic approach

Learning activity	Educational purpose (eclectic method)
Matching words to words	Visual recognition of words
Matching words with pictures (write the name of the picture)	Visual recognition of words by associating them with their corresponding picture
Select the words that have the ("pr" o "pl") syllable	Visual discrimination of words that include the spelling in any position of the word
Select the pictures that have the syllables ("pr" o "pl")	Discrimination and visual association of the spelling worked on
Select the missing syllable in each word	Recognition of the missing syllable, thus working the phonological route
Sort the scrambled letters and select the correct word	Recognize and understand the letters to form a meaningful word
Order the scrambled syllables and select the correct word	Recognize and understand the syllables to form a meaningful word
Complete the sentences with the missing word	Recognize and understand the words to form a meaningful sentence
Observe the drawing and complete the sentences of the story with the correct word	Visual discrimination, comprehension, and association of the right word
Match the drawing with the correct story	Visual discrimination, comprehension, and association of the correct sentences
Look at the picture and select the correct sentence	Visual discrimination, comprehension, and association of the correct sentence
After reading a story, choose true or false for each sentence (reading comprehension)	Visual discrimination, comprehension, and association of the correct sentence

16.2.5 Discussion

Using this methodology to develop a SEN video game (in this particular case, reading and writing problems), it is possible to have a preliminary version of a video game that can be played by an expert in SEN and receive feedback before its development is finished. There would be no limit to the number of entertainment scenarios or learning activities using this proposed methodology. Any limitation would depend on the desired magnitude of the video game or the SEN to be addressed.

This design methodology can be adapted to other SENs. In addition, once the video game is finished, it could be tested with another methodology to address the same SEN. The eclectic method is used for this research, but another methodology that supports this area could be used. To test another method, one only needs to design and develop the new learning activities and replace those that already exist without altering the structure of the video game.

A SEN expert (and supporting material) supported the design and development of the learning activities adapted from the eclectic method to enable a useful product that addresses the SEN.

16.3 Conclusions

This research project has presented the adaptation of the eclectic method in learning activities for a graphic adventure video game whose purpose is not only entertainment but from its design, also aims to support or assist a SEN.

The eclectic method is designed to support the improvement of literacy skills in children with learning disabilities. In this process of adapting the eclectic-method-learning activities, the challenge was designing and adapting each digital activity in a video game to meet the objectives and purposes of the original activities. The learning activities adapted into technological and entertainment activities were designed to be friendly, fun, dynamic, playful, and instructional.

The benefits of using this methodology to create graphic adventure video games include naturally combining entertainment activities with learning activities. These activities can be created incrementally, unlimited, and can be substituted by other activities. This allows flexibility since the activities (learning and entertainment) are handled as independent and interchangeable modules.

Using this methodology to create video games is impactful because more digital tools (video games) can be created for schools. As mentioned at the beginning of this paper, in schools in Mexico and Latin America, there is a significant deficit in the access and use of technological resources to support education and adapted to different levels of learning. This methodology can be used to create video games for any educational area.

Finally, a graphic adventure video game to support reading and writing is an area that has not been explored and offers research opportunities. Romero et al. (2018) highlight the idea that, although work has been done on SEN, there is still a long way to go for schools to incorporate educational technology as a regular resource for students with SEN. Orozco et al. (2017) mention the need to raise awareness among researchers to continue innovating specific teaching resources for SEN. Therefore, this proposal can contribute to the construction of digital tools that support SEN and reduce the gap between students who have SEN and those who do not.

Acknowledgements The authors would like to thank the *Programa para el Desarrollo Profesional Docente para el Tipo Superior* (PRODEP) for its support to carry out this research.

The authors acknowledge the technical support of Writing Lab, Institute for the Future of Education, Tecnologico de Monterrey, Mexico, for the production of this work.

References

Alfageme MB, Sánchez PA (2002) Learning skills with videogames. [Aprendiendo habilidades con videojuegos]. Comunicar 19:114–119
Brazo AI, Muñoz JM, Castro de C (2018) Aprendiendo léxico y ortografía francesa en la universidad mediante el videojuego SCRIBBLENAUTS. EDMETIC 7(2):18–36

Caballero GL (2014) Dificultades de aprendizaje en lecto-escritura en niños y niñas de 6 a 8 años. Estudio de casos: Fundación "Una escuela para Emiliano". Universidad Autónoma del Estado de Hidalgo

Cristóbal Muñoz S (2013) La metodología de lectoescritura en educación en educación infantil y su influencia en el aprendizaje lectoescritor de los alumnos. Universidad de Valladolid

Garrido JM (2013) ¿Por qué los estudiantes juegan con videojuegos de estrategia?: algunos principios para la enseñanza. Revista Electrónica de Investigación Educativa 15(1):62–74

Milenio, Videojuegos favorecen a la salud mental de menores durante la pandemia. Milenio Diario (2020). https://www.milenio.com/ciencia-y-salud/sap-videojuegos-favorecen-salud-men tal-ninos-pandemia

Molina M, Castro E, Molina JL, Castro E (2011) Un acercamiento a la investigación de diseño a través de los experimentos de enseñanza. Enseñanza de las ciencias 29(1):75–88

Morales M (2018) Viabilidad del uso del videojuego en el aula: opiniones prácticas de los maestros en pre-servicio. EDMETIC 7(2):78–91

Orozco GH, Tejedor FJ, Calvo MI (2017) Meta-Análisis sobre el efecto del Software Educativo en alumnos con Necesidades Educativas Especiales. Revista de Investigacion Educativa 35(1):35–52

Ortega RM (2009) Estudio y análisis del método ecléctico de lectoescritura en las escuelas de la SAFA.Departamento de Didáctica y Organización Escolar, Universidad de Granada

RIINEE, Informe Final. Estudio sobre el estado de la implementación del artículo 24 de la Convención sobre los Derechos de las Personas con Discapacidad en países de la Red Intergubernamental Iberoamericana de Cooperación de Personas con Necesidades Educativas, Red Intergubernamental Iberoamericana de Cooperación de Personas con Necesidades Educativas Especiales (2017)

Romero SJ, González I, García A, Lozano A (2018) Herramientas tecnológicas para la educación inclusiva. Revista Tecnología Ciencia y Educación 9(1):83–112

Salavarrieta FM (2015) Aprendiendo a leer, Cartilla de lectura

Sommerville I (2011) Ingeniería de Software, 9th edn. Pearson

Torrente J, Marchiori E, Blanco A, Sancho P, Martinez I, Mellini B, … Delli Veneri A (2011) Fomentando la Creatividad: Creación de Escenarios de Aprendizaje Basados en Juegos

Trejo H (2019) Recursos tecnológicos para la integración de la gamificación en el aula. Tecnología Ciencia y Educación 13(2):75–117

Warnock M (1981) Meeting special educational needs. London

Chapter 17
YouTube as a Reinforcement Tool for Learning Differential Calculus

Martha Guadalupe Escoto Villaseñor, Juan Manuel López Villalobos, Rosa María Navarrete Hernández, De Jesús Rodríguez Luisa Paola, and Rosa Estela Russi García

17.1 Introduction

The implementation of technological tools in the educational field brings teaching challenges. Adapting to change fundamentally implies responsibility among all educators. Using technology invites teachers to experiment, create, make mistakes, and share. When incorporating technology in the teaching–learning processes, observing students' behavior and responses to the pedagogical methods is of utmost importance.

This work discusses some open educational materials created and presented through a YouTube channel as reinforcement resources for a differential calculus learning unit. This content is helpful for teachers, students, and the interested general public. These resources can be shared or reused according to the training needs in any of the proposed topics.

YouTube can complement learning in the differential calculus unit and any curricular subject because it generates open digital educational access for the entire academic community. Its introduction inside and outside of class strengthens the contents by presenting them in a novel way and being available as a resource students can consult whenever and as frequently as they need. It is also a space where they express their opinions about the educational content.

Among the objectives to be achieved is increasing the passing rate of students taking the differential calculus learning unit, considering their diverse capacities and

M. G. Escoto Villaseñor (✉) · J. M. López Villalobos · R. M. Navarrete Hernández · D. J. R. L. Paola · R. E. Russi García
Instituto Politecnico Nacional, Centro de Estudios Científicos y Tecnológicos No 1, Ciudad de México, México
e-mail: mgescoto@ipn.mx

J. M. López Villalobos
e-mail: jmlopezv@ipn.mx

© The Author(s), under exclusive license to Springer Nature Singapore Pte Ltd. 2022   221
S. Hosseini et al. (eds.), *Technology-Enabled Innovations in Education*,
Transactions on Computer Systems and Networks,
https://doi.org/10.1007/978-981-19-3383-7_17

interests. Another was creating digital repositories inside and outside the "Gonzalo Vázquez Vela Center for Scientific and Technological Studies No 1" through the active participation of both students and teachers to develop competencies.

YouTube has demonstrated an increasing influence on teaching and learning. On the teaching side, educators must now have higher technological skills related to spreading technology. In this regard, YouTube is an educational support tool presenting the opportunity to acquire and transmit knowledge.

Using a YouTube channel adds professional value to the teacher (Semich and Copper 2016); it takes the professor beyond a "classroom methodology" to enter a space to configure a new educational system that meets the unique needs of the digital native generation.

17.2 Theoretical Framework

YouTube in the classroom allows the teacher to create a virtual library of videos with select content for a particular learning community.

The students can create their virtual library with videos they select or produce their own. The library lets students review videos of interest, share them with others, and assemble evidence of their progress and professional evolution (Ramírez 2016).

Rodríguez and Fernández (2017) showed that implementing videos on YouTube as support material in a statistics course for Latin American students pursuing an online master's degree positively impacted their grades because it improved their content understanding of the subject.

We found that YouTube videos have a more significant impact than the students' high school educational background. This implies that using ICT can improve equity and reduce students' socioeconomic gaps, which affect their education and social mobility (Cuecuecha 2017).

Digital platforms have become preferred spaces to interact and establish communication. However, digital competence means more than just sending WhatsApp messages or sharing videos on Facebook; it also has to do with the critical thinking behind using these tools (Garcia 2019).

Arguedas and Herrera (2018) state that YouTube has tremendous educational potential in both face-to-face and distance education because it is a free resource that provides the flexibility to learn autonomy. However, many of its benefits have not yet been explored. Moreover, the authors assure that since the launch date of YouTube, the site has been an invaluable tool for teachers worldwide in all teaching disciplines.

It should be clarified that this proposal does not intend to replace one learning with another but proposes using the resources and tools available to motivate students positively. Thus, we must constantly seek and use new technologies to teach in the classroom or support ongoing teaching–learning strategies and methods.

Lucero (2016) states that new technologies and the Internet have changed how we communicate and interact and how our children and young people learn. Therefore, today's teachers must know and apply new methodologies to bridge the gap between students and the traditional teaching method that is textbook-based.

In this project, videos and the YouTube platform enhance and reinforce teaching, presenting content clearly, simply, and concisely. Our work is about visualizing the potential that using these resources provides and the creativity developed.

17.3 Problem Statement

The mathematics student enters a complex and abstract world full of axioms; its study involves numbers, formulas, graphs, symbols, and geometric figures and requires logical reasoning.

We are presented with an opportunity for change. We can access various sources and use software as tools. We can create, modify, add or delete, take or contribute different resources to implement reflective strategies that allow the transformation, modification, design, and appropriation of the information.

As the society we live in becomes more complex, we must approach thinking, learning, and knowledge holistically, comprehensively, and, above all, experimentally.

On many occasions, we hear that social networks and new technologies provide a perfect opportunity to complement learning in a generation familiar with these. Incorporating them in class can help students by offering unique content. Nevertheless, will the creation of a YouTube channel have a positive impact as a reinforcement tool in learning differential calculus? Will it be possible to combine mathematical knowledge with other types of knowledge?

YouTube's user-friendliness provides an educational resource allowing the teacher to search, select, and save videos that they consider helpful in their class regardless of the subject they teach.

By creating an account or channel, teachers can store their videos and build their virtual libraries. Both students and teachers can access this material at the time required. The videos are easily shared on electronic or social media using various technological devices, thus facilitating the reinforcements of learning units.

17.4 Method

We selected four classes from the "Gonzalo Vázquez Vela Center for Scientific and Technological Studies No 1" (167 members) to develop this experiment. The units of analysis were not randomly assigned, and there was no total control over the variables. The process was configured with five phases of the experimental project:

- *Research planning*: To define the basis of this research, we analyzed the context of previous research on the web platform and considered multimedia tools, which allowed defining the research problem, the objectives of the study variables, the operation of the YouTube platform, and the selection, preparation, and design of the materials to monitor the capture of the information.

- Design and development: Depending on the topics in the differential calculus learning unit, we developed the materials and videos for four classes (sample $N = 167$) in the upper-middle level of the "Gonzalo Vázquez Vela Center for Scientific and Technological Studies No 1 (CECyT No 1)." We also designed the assessment tests associated with the didactic unit.

  The didactic unit put into operation to reinforce learning was based on a sequence of competencies found in the study program of the National Polytechnic Institute.

- Presentation: From the beginning of the semester, the YouTube platform was used as a tool to reinforce the topics seen in class. The channel created allowed viewing the statistics, the opinions of those who consulted it, the number of students enrolled, and the number of visits to each video. We did not require the students to register with YouTube and consult; the material was only for reinforcing the differential calculus learning unit.

- Analysis of the results: The results are consults on the YouTube platform. Every time a topic video was uploaded, we did a follow-up, analysis, or correction. This channel allowed us to monitor the increase of students interested in the topics, their queries, time, visits per day, gender, age, duration of visit, and impressions. Thus, YouTube integrates qualitative and quantitative characteristics for study.

- Dissemination of the results obtained: The results were presented to the Directors of the Center for Scientific and Technological Studies No 1 as a proposal for a digital repository. We invited them to view the videos' contents, presentations, designs, utility, and issuances of proposals for use. (Proposals ignored or not considered, but accepted by some teachers who teach the learning unit.)

17.5 Results

Open educational resources are digital resources created with an educational purpose that is free and open. YouTube is an Internet portal that allows its users to upload and view videos.

When we associate Open Educational Resources (OER), a YouTube channel, and mathematics, we agree with what Hewlett Foundation expresses: "Knowledge is a public good. Technology in general, and the Internet in particular, offer an extraordinary opportunity for anyone, anywhere, to share, use, and leverage this knowledge."

The proposal was to use a YouTube channel as an open educational resource for learning mathematics, in this case, the Differential Calculus learning unit, as a dynamic to share and reinforce knowledge.

YouTube's open educational resource facilitates teachers and students searching, selecting, and saving helpful videos; it allows virtual library access to the chosen material when required.

Among the results obtained, we highlight that the creation of the YouTube channel brought continuity to the face-to-face classes disrupted by the pandemic health contingencies through tutorial videos.

The health contingency accelerated and modified the designed work plan. However, the YouTube channel made it easier for us to continue four high school classes (167 students studying a differential calculus unit) at the "Gonzalo Vázquez Vela Center for Scientific and Technological Studies No 1" of the Polytechnic National Institute.

The videos that were reinforcement material for the students became support material for the teacher giving continuity to the classes. The simplicity was that all the students knew the channel and were subscribed to it.

Migrating an entire face-to-face class to an online modality became a real challenge. Finding, adapting, and incorporating various resources turned out to be not a straightforward task.

Figure 17.1 shows the 26 topic videos uploaded to the YouTube platform to continue the course through the health contingency.

Fig. 17.1   Videos on the YouTube platform for differential calculus. *Source* Own elaboration (2020)

The video tutorial presented in Fig. 17.2 contains multimedia elements shared with the students as the informative part of the dynamic teaching process. The videos allowed the subject to be reviewed until the student understood the process and attained the desired knowledge or competency. The videos were created with multimedia resources that integrated various basic types of content, such as text, audio, images, animation, and graphics. Using the various multimedia components allowed students to learn skills on many different levels.

In the four sample classes (167 students), 84% demonstrated the usefulness of open digital resources for acquiring knowledge through videos. They used technological resources to present the evidence required in the course.

The increased actions in this health contingency enhanced the development, usability, and impact of these resources on education.

The YouTube channel provides different types of graphical and numerical statistics, broken down, either by video or general. Statistics show the user's age, gender, dates, user status, video impressions, number of video views, and increased visits after posting it.

Figure 17.3 shows the visits received in the created YouTube channel from April 4 to July 2, 2020.

Figure 17.4 shows the visits received in the past 90 days. This YouTube channel report shows the video visits each and which were the most viewed.

Some of the student comments on YouTube about the reinforcement of learning integral calculus were the following:

- Excellent video. It made it easier for me to understand the subject.
- How it solves and addresses the issue is of great help; the examples are well explained. It helps me be able to reinforce and clarify questions on the subject.
- The videos are beneficial for all the public. Thanks to all these videos, we reinforce the knowledge obtained in class. We also resolve the questions remaining from class. This video is very well explained step-by-step and is very helpful; thank you.

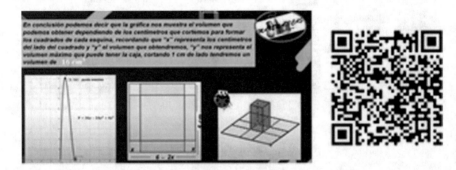

Fig. 17.2 Video of the YouTube platform for differential calculus. *Source* Own elaboration (2020)

Tu canal recibió 8,855 vistas en los últimos 90 días

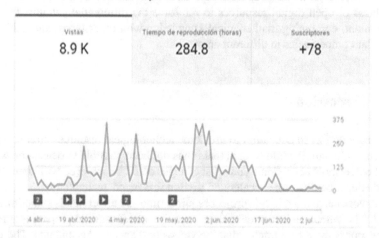

Fig. 17.3 Number of visits received on the YouTube channel. *Source* Elaboration of the YouTube channel (2020)

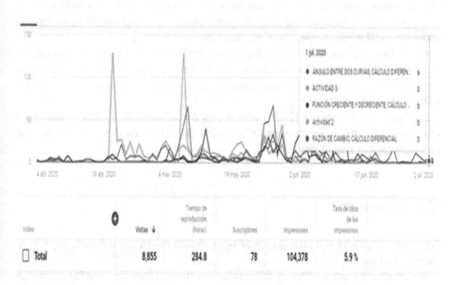

Fig. 17.4 Number of visits received on the YouTube channel per video. *Source* Elaboration of the YouTube channel (2020)

- Teacher, thanks for the video. It is much easier to understand the subject by analyzing how the exercises are solved in your videos. Your videos are well done. By the way, thank you for all the effort you put into them.

We consider that the proposed objectives were achieved, demonstrating the usefulness of open digital resources to reinforce the differential calculus learning unit content, combining mathematical knowledge with other types, and achieving curricular competencies in different areas.

17.6 Discussion

The pandemic forced education to use some technological resources circulating on the web. Although, it could be said that it has not been possible to determine which would be the most appropriate and what changes could be achieved with their use to evolve educationally at the accelerated rhythm that marks technology.

The work carried out in this project requires time and effort that is sometimes not valued. The video can last three minutes, but the time it takes to prepare it is much greater; nor is there a guarantee that the videos will engage the students. The work of change in education is not easy.

What can be assured is that creating a YouTube channel allows teachers to create a virtual library and helps students reinforce the topics seen in class. The videos can be accessed when required and offer the convenience of being shared by electronic media or social media through various technological devices.

According to Pérez and Cuecuecha (2019), recent research has shown that using YouTube videos as didactic material improves students' grades. This is a notable observation since students are more interested in audiovisual content than in the process of traditional teaching.

Posligua and Zambrano (2020) affirm that a tool such as YouTube facilitates reflection, improves understanding, and positively influences the construction and reconstruction of knowledge.

17.7 Conclusion

The results highlight the importance of open digital resources and their support to students and teachers.

The students participating in this project confirmed that the YouTube channel videos reinforced learning and allowed continuing the differential calculus learning unit topics.

The unforeseen circumstances caused by the epidemic forced teachers to modify and diversify their work.

All the work to continue the courses and migrate to an online modality required knowledge, dedication, creativity, and effort. However, the resources available on the web allowed adopting technology to create and expand their access to knowledge with flexibility of time and space.

The conversation about technology and network usage must go beyond device availability and connectivity issues. It is crucial to focus on content and the learning implications of usage.

The use of videos is possible to reinforce the differential calculus learning unit. The four classes in the sample obtained passing grades from 88 to 90%; thus, we invite teachers to corroborate this achievement with this methodology in their classes.

References

Arguedas C, Herrera E (2018) Un canal en YouTube como herramienta de apoyo a un curso de física en educación a distancia. Ensayos Pedagógicos 13(1):107–130

Cuecuecha MA (2017) El impacto del origen socioeconómico sobre las características del primer empleo y de las trayectorias laborales en México. Un estudio basado en la EMOVI 2011. México: Centro de Estudios Espinoza Yglesias

Garcia AL (2019) Necesidad de una educación digital en un mundo digital, 22. RIED. Revista Iberoamericana de Educación a Distancia

Lucero J (2016) Del libro de texto a YouTube; una aproximación a las nuevas tecnologías y a las nuevas formas de aprendizaje. Revista De Estudios Socioeducativos: RESED 2(4):185–187

Pérez J, Cuecuecha A (2019) El efecto de usar YouTube como apoyo didáctico en calificaciones de microeconomía. Apertura: Revista de Innovación Educativa 11(2):22–39

Posligua R, Zambrano L (2020) El empleo del YouTube como herramienta de aprendizaje. Rehuso 5(1):10–18

Ramírez MI (2016) Posibilidades del uso educativo de You Tube. Ra Ximhai, 12

Rodríguez MC, Fernández J (2017) Uso del recurso de contenido en el aprendizaje en línea: YouTube. Apertura 9(1):22–31

Semich G, Copper J (2016) Instructional videos as ICT for teacher professional development: transitioning from the traditional classroom to YouTube. In: Exploring the new era of technology-infused education, pp 317–331

Chapter 18
A Correlation Analysis Between MOOCs and Scholarly Performance, Emphasizing Scientific Peer Review Journal Publication

An Evidence-Based Comparison Among Several Countries

Mohammadreza Amiri, Samira Hosseini, and Ana E. Sosa-Flores

18.1 Introduction

Academia has dramatically benefited from emerging digital technologies (DT) in the last decade. Massachusetts Institute of Technology (MIT) was one of the first higher education universities to implement DT (Briggs and Crompton 2016). Among the various DTs, the Massive Open Online Courses (MOOCs, first offered by the University of Manitoba, Canada) are online platforms offering courses without registration restrictions (Adair 2014). MOOCs followed the philosophy that knowledge should be freely and equally accessible to all keen learners (Bali 2014a). MOOCs started with no charges, but some companies now offer course certificates for a fee (e.g., Coursera and edX) (Briggs and Crompton 2016).

M. Amiri (✉)
KITE Research Institute, Toronto Rehabilitation Institute – University Health Network, Toronto, Canada
e-mail: reza.amiri@uhn.ca

School of Pharmacy, Taylor's University, Subang Jaya, Malaysia

S. Hosseini
Escuela de Ingenieria y Ciencias, Tecnologico de Monterrey, Monterrey, Mexico
e-mail: samira.hosseini@tec.mx

S. Hosseini · A. E. Sosa-Flores
Writing Lab, Institute for the Future of Education, Tecnologico de Monterrey, Monterrey, Mexico

A. E. Sosa-Flores
UAS Technikum Wien, Vienna, Austria

© The Author(s), under exclusive license to Springer Nature Singapore Pte Ltd. 2022   231
S. Hosseini et al. (eds.), *Technology-Enabled Innovations in Education*,
Transactions on Computer Systems and Networks,
https://doi.org/10.1007/978-981-19-3383-7_18

Patru and Balaji (2016) highlighted the importance of the DTs for the developing countries' policymakers to ensure these nations benefit from the growing quality and the timeless and placeless characteristics that distinguish technology-supported education from traditional education. With the dawn of the MOOCs, a vast ocean of information became available to keen learners in developing countries (DCs) who previously were bereaved of collaborative learning and sharing opportunities with experts internationally, innovative learning technologies, and learning resources (Christensen 2013; Warusavitarana et al. 2014). The MOOCs became "proof" of the internet's promise to democratize education (Hoy 2014). Although the availability of MOOCs to financially deprived people who lack computers, electricity, or full internet access is questionable, the hope is that one who seeks education will find the resources (Bali 2014a, b).

To our best of knowledge, the possible correlation between MOOCs and scholarly output measurements, such as the numbers of publications in scientific peer-reviewed journals and the emergence of new authors, has not been studied in the context of developing nations. Therefore, in this study, we focused on three developing countries, namely Malaysia, Mexico, and Iran, compared to the United States (US) and Canada to analyze the impact of MOOCs on increasing numbers of academic production.

18.2 Methods

18.2.1 Data Collection

18.2.1.1 SciVal

To access the research performance of the scholars in three developing countries and the comparison to the US and Canada, we queried SciVal (Colledge and Verlinde 2014; Elsevier Research Intelligence 2018) as it provides comprehensive data regarding research publications and collaborations of over 9700 institutions and their associated researchers from 230 nations worldwide (Elsevier Research Intelligence 2018). We queried the countries individually to search for the number of publications, citations, citations per publication, and authors between 2013 and 2017.

18.2.1.2 Google Trends

We used Google Trends (GT; Google Inc., California, United States) to discover the searched terms about MOOCs (Google Inc. 2018). GT offers information about the interests in a search term and its associated keywords or topics relative to the total national or international search volume (Google Inc. 2018). In our query about search interest in MOOCs, GT provided from 13 to 25 related topics (e.g., Massive Open Online Courses, Online Courses, online certificate, online learning, Coursera, edX) based on the country of interest. This tool is highly modifiable for time, location (i.e., countries, regions, sub-regions), and topics/keywords. For each country, the queries obtained the weekly data in the requested timeframe. To match the frequency with SciVal, we transformed the series to annual data, considering the maximum value in the weekly distributions as 100 and the other values proportional to this value. Note that GT does not provide absolute volume; instead, it shows interest relative to the peak in the selected period, i.e., peak interest would be indexed as 100, and volumes would be calculated as a relative ratio.

18.2.2   Data Analysis

(1) *Normality tests*: The Shapiro-Wilk normality test was used to identify the normally distributed variables. We selected this test because the number of our samples was lower than 2000. Also, the variables' normality was tested by selecting a proper parametric or non-parametric test, e.g., Pearson correlation for normally distributed data and Spearman correlation for non-normally distributed data.

(2) *Correlation coefficient*: We employed two-tailed Pearson or Spearman Correlation Analysis to assess the possible association between the scholarly variables and their directions. We also made scatter plots categorized by countries for further identification of the associations.

18.3   Results

Scholarly Variables

Table 18.1 provides detailed information about the scholarly output variables stratified by countries between 2013 and 2017. This information provides patterns throughout this period and is a comparison tool of scholarly activities in the nations.

Between 2013 and 2017, the scholarly output in Mexico and Iran increased steadily, while the US and Canada had a seesaw pattern. The number of publications in Malaysia dropped in 2015 but has hiked up since then. Comparing the three developing nations, we observe that the publication numbers were consistently higher in Iran compared to the other two developing countries. Mexico produced the least among the three; the number of publications in Mexico steadily increased but at a slower pace.

Citation counts are expected to be lower for more recent publications, and in all the countries, the citation counts decreased since 2013. However, Iran had the lowest rate of citation counts compared to all other countries since 2015 (Table 18.1). Between 2013 and 2014, Malaysia had the smallest decreasing rate (-6.0%) compared to Iran

Table 18.1 Scholarly variables stratified by country

(i)	2013	2014	2015	2016	2017
Scholarly output					
US and Canada	734,690 (NA)	728,614 (−0.83)	731,287 (0.37)	727,400 (−0.53)	733,142 (0.79)
Mexico	19,558 (NA)	21,100 (7.88)	21,220 (0.57)	22,781 (7.36)	23,899 (4.91)
Malaysia	25,221 (NA)	28,305 (12.23)	27,385 (−3.25)	29,905 (9.2)	31,952 (6.85)
Iran	42,057 (NA)	44,642 (6.15)	44,684 (0.09)	52,262 (16.96)	56,476 (8.06)
Citation counts					
US and Canada	10,167,316 (NA)	8,007,353 (−21.24)	5,720,513 (−28.56)	3,315,781 (−42.04)	1,180,233 (−64.41)
Mexico	167,702 (NA)	141,694 (−15.51)	107,959 (−23.81)	70,604 (−34.6)	26,354 (−62.67)
Malaysia	178,600 (NA)	167,919 (−5.98)	132,260 (−21.24)	83,988 (−36.5)	31,103 (−62.97)
Iran	344,618 (NA)	316,872 (−8.05)	249,904 (−21.13)	185,359 (−25.83)	79,461 (−57.13)
Authors					
US and Canada	1,024,215 (NA)	1,045,908 (2.12)	1,074,987 (2.78)	1,101,374 (2.45)	1,133,489 (2.92)
Mexico	36,667 (NA)	41,064 (11.99)	42,049 (2.4)	46,331 (10.18)	48,677 (5.06)
Malaysia	33,752 (NA)	37,919 (12.35)	38,267 (0.92)	44,001 (14.98)	48,912 (11.16)
Iran	66,058 (NA)	69,574 (5.32)	71,031 (2.09)	82,172 (15.68)	86,358 (5.09)
Citation per publication					
US and Canada	13.8 (NA)	11 (−20.29)	7.8 (−29.09)	4.6 (−41.03)	1.6 (−65.22)
Mexico	8.6 (NA)	6.7 (−22.09)	5.1 (−23.88)	3.1 (−39.22)	1.1 (−64.52)
Malaysia	7.1 (NA)	5.9 (−16.9)	4.8 (−18.64)	2.8 (−41.67)	1 (−64.29)
Iran	8.2 (NA)	7.1 (−13.41)	5.6 (−21.13)	3.5 (−37.5)	1.4 (−60)

The figures in brackets are the percent change from the previous year

(−8.1%). Between 2015 and 2017, Iran's citation counts dropped at lower rates of −21.1, −25.8, and −57.1% consecutively compared to Malaysia (−21.2, −36.5, and −63.0), Mexico (−23.8, −34.6, −62.7), and the citation counts of US and Canada (−28.6, −42.0, and −64.4).

Comparing developing countries, in 2015, all experienced the lowest incremental rate in the number of authors (i.e., 2.4% in Mexico, 0.9% in Malaysia, and 2.1% in Iran), while their highest increment compared to the previous year was in 2016 for Malaysia (15.0%) and Iran (15.7%), and in 2014 for Mexico (12.0%) (see Table 18.1). Nonetheless, since 2013, the number of authors in all the nations has been increasing. The highest number of authors was in Iran and the lowest in Malaysia except for 2017 when Mexico and Malaysia had approximately the same number of authors producing publications.

The quality of papers can be assessed by the citations per publication variable. Even though the figures in this variable diminished through the period, among the developing countries, Mexico had the highest quality ratio in 2013. Iran leapfrogged to first place in the subsequent years.

Figure 18.1 shows the scatter plots of the MOOCs' search interest, publications, and authors' numbers in all the countries (see color codes below) and the histograms of the scholarly variables to illustrate the distribution. Among the developing countries, the search interest in MOOCs through the years had a positive association with authors and publication numbers in Malaysia (green triangles) and Mexico

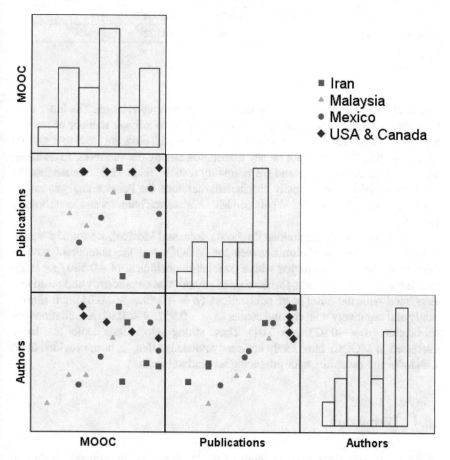

Fig. 18.1 Relationship between MOOC search and scholarly variables stratified by countries

Table 18.2 Normality test

Variable	Shapiro-Wilk statistic	Normal distribution
Publication	0.934	Yes
Citation counts	0.898	Yes
Citation per publication	0.912	Yes
Authors	0.928	Yes
MOOC	0.933	Yes

Table 18.3 Correlation coefficient

	MOOCs	Authors	Publications	Citation counts
Authors	0.580^*	**(ii)**	0.892**	−0.952**
Publications	0.238	0.892^{**}		-0.904^{**}
Citation counts	−0.478	-0.952^{**}	-0.904^{**}	
Citations per publication	−0.476	-0.961^{**}	-0.922^{**}	0.994^{**}

* $p < 0.05$
** $p < 0.01$

(red circles), unlike Iran (blue squares) with a negative correlation. The latter indicates that MOOCs' search interests were attributed to a fewer number of authors and publications. The US and Canada (violet diamonds) plots are close to a straight line, indicating there may not be any association among the variables. In addition, the histograms in Fig. 18.1 and the normality tests in Table 18.2 indicate that the scholarly variables are normally distributed; therefore, the Pearson analysis can be employed to test the correlation between MOOCs' search interests and the scholarly variables.

In the three developing nations (Malaysia, Iran, and Mexico), we found a significant and positive correlation between the MOOCs and the number of authors throughout the analyzed period with a correlation coefficient of +0.580 ($p < 0.05$) (see Table 18.3). In addition, the number of authors was significantly and positively associated with the number of publications ($\rho = +0.892$; $p < 0.01$) and significantly and negatively with citation counts ($\rho = -0.952$; $p < 0.01$) and citations per publication ($\rho = -0.922$; $p < 0.01$). These strong associations depict that those interested in MOOCs have likely acquired knowledge that, in turn, provided them with tools and capabilities for producing scholarly outputs.

18.4 Discussion

MOOCs learners have various motivations to complete the courses, including personal enjoyment (Loizzo et al. 2017), gaining skills to do jobs better

(Venkataraman 2014), professional development (Loizzo et al. 2017), and institution and instructor-related motivations (Hakami et al. 2017). MOOCs are considered learner-centered instructional environments that improve the learning process and the overall outcomes (Blumberg 2008). Although MOOCs provide educational opportunities, they are beneficial if blended with other educational methodologies (Briggs and Crompton 2016) and thus may transcend and support principles of learner-centered education (Li et al. 2015). This blended learning is seen as a "logical solution" for individual needs and a natural pedagogical evolution (Liyanagunawardena et al. 2013).

MOOCs have emerged as powerful tools to provide education and essential content to a wide range of learners. Like many other technologies, MOOCs also have downsides. Not all course topics have available and capable experts for course development. Some topics cannot be taught through institutions available by MOOCs but lack physical equipment and the educator's presence (Hoy 2014). A median MOOC completion rate of 13% indicates that many who start the course never finish because there is no obligation to complete the course (Jordan 2015). More dramatically, many who register never start taking the lessons (Lewin 2013). Also, there is no "guarantee" that those who have completed the courses have "mastered" the materials (Hoy 2014). Even though this statement characterizes MOOC users, it could also be the case for university graduates. This statement might be accurate, but since there is a significant and positive correlation between MOOCs and authorship, one may claim that serious learners who seek knowledge shall find and employ it. Therefore, the assumption that MOOCs may influence the capabilities of the learners to become an author may not be unreasonable. Ultimately, MOOCs lead to higher numbers of publications, enhancing academic performance.

Perhaps one of the significant beneficial features of MOOCs is the immediate feedback to the participants, allowing them and the trainers to identify whether any concept is not well received. (Hoy 2014; Davies 2013) found that highly educated learners benefit extensively from personalized feedback that facilitates social comparisons with previously successful learners. Online discussions are another positive aspect of MOOCs where participants can share opinions, clarify ambiguous topics, and participate in an academic community with others who have the same interests (Hoy 2014). Although courses have deadlines for submitting the assignments/quizzes, the participants in the same cohort may not finish their drills synchronously (Hoy 2014); however, enjoying discussions over topics, one should go with the flow. Moreover, MOOCs have user-friendly formats and inherent openness, facilitating the learning process for committed learners (Hoy 2014). This ensures the accessibility of traditional education to enthusiastic candidates who have not enjoyed the privileges of consistent education. As a blended learning strategy, MOOC has impacted education by providing improved test scores and higher class attendance and offering better assessment approaches (Davies 2013).

18.5 Conclusion and Future Works

No scientific text is flawless, including our presented study in this paper. First, we do not claim we found a robust causality among the studied variables; rather, we identified possible existing relationships. Second, the studied period is limited because the advent of MOOCs is only a few years more than half a decade; furthermore, data about individual respondents are not available to the public. Even if the data were available, the struggle to sample individuals and track their accomplishments in research would be tediously difficult. Last, choosing developing countries was the interest of the authors to possibly advise future educational policymakers in those countries to further emphasize the MOOCs in higher education.

Nevertheless, this study clearly indicates a direct correlation between MOOCs' influence and academic performance regarding the number of publications, citations, citations per publication, and authors. This work will not be limited to the presented data. Our future investigations will address the mentioned viewpoints and further advance our study to provide a comprehensive analysis of such correlations.

Acknowledgements The authors would like to acknowledge the technical and financial support of Writing Lab, Institute for the Future of Education, Tecnologico de Monterrey, Mexico, and School of Pharmacy, Taylor's University, Malaysia, in producing this work.

References

Adair D, Alman SW, Budzick D, Grisham LM, Mancini ME, Thackaberry AS (2014) Many shades of MOOCs. Internet Learn

Bali M (2014a) MOOC pedagogy: gleaning good practice from existing MOOCs. J Online Learn Teach 10(1):44

Bali M (2014b) Going beyond the good MOOC/bad MOOC debate (An observation on the special issue). J Glob Literacies Technol Emerg Pedagogies 2(3):261–266

Blumberg P (2008) Developing learner-centered teaching: a practical guide for faculty. John Wiley & Sons

Briggs S, Crompton H (2016) Taking advantage of MOOCs in K-12 education. In: Advances in mobile and distance learning, pp 297–309

Christensen G, Steinmetz A, Alcorn B, Bennett A, Woods D, Emanuel EJ (2013) The MOOC phenomenon: who takes massive open online courses and why? SSRN Electron J

Colledge L, Verlinde R (2014) SciVal: SciVal metrics guidebook

Davies E (2013) Will MOOCs transform medicine? BMJ 346(1):f2877–f2877

Elsevier Research Intelligence (2018) SciVal. Available: https//www.scival.com

Google Inc. (2018). About google trends. Available: https://support.google.com/trends/answer/624 8105?hl=en-GB&ref_topic=6248052

Hakami N, White S, Chakaveh S (2017) Motivational factors that Influence the use of MOOCs: learners' perspectives—a systematic literature review. In: Proceedings of the 9th international conference on computer supported education

Hoy MB (2014) MOOCs 101: an introduction to massive open online courses. Med Ref Serv Q 33(1):85–91

Jordan K (2015) Massive open online course completion rates revisited: assessment, length and attrition. Int Rev Res Open Distrib Learn 16(3)

Lewin T (2013) Colleges adapt online courses to ease burden. The New York Times, 29

Li Y, Zhang M, Bonk CJ, Guo N (2015) Integrating MOOC and flipped classroom practice in a traditional undergraduate course: students' experience and perceptions. Int J Emerg Technol Learn (iJET) 10(6):4

Liyanagunawardena TR, Adams AA, Williams SA (2013) MOOCs: a systematic study of the published literature 2008–2012. Int Rev Res Open Distrib Learn 14(3):202

Loizzo J, Ertmer PA, Watson WR, Watson SL (2017) Adult MOOC learners as self-directed: perceptions of motivation, success, and completion. Online Learn 21(2)

Patru M, Balaji V (2016) Making sense of MOOCs: a guide for policymakers in developing countries

Venkataraman B (2014) Who are the learners in MOOCs? Available: http://oasis.col.org/handle/11599/2331

Warusavitarana PA, Dona KL, Piyathilake HC, Epitawela DD, Edirisinghe MU (2014) MOOC: a higher education game-changer in developing countries. In: Rhetoric and reality: critical perspectives on educational technology, Proceedings Ascilite Dunedin, pp 359–366

Chapter 19
Gamification and Improvement of Teaching in Engineering Courses at the Federico Santa María Technical University

Cristian Carvallo and Hugo Osorio

19.1 Introduction

Some teaching and learning methodologies are breaking long-held paradigms maintained by teachers, among them the belief that students' positive course evaluations are due to low academic demands. However, it could be the result of good teaching, especially when the teaching is carried out with adequate planning, taking as input the learning results that arise at the beginning of the semester and the teaching and learning methodologies then directed to the profile of the students.

Traditional teacher-centered education has become a thing of the past (López-Fernández et al. 2019); the student has become the center of the educational process, where active learning methods have taken center stage, especially in engineering education, which employs these as essential, practical components of the training. This is especially true in the second cycle of the degree programs, where students manage technologies and systematic study better.

The active teaching methodologies can influence the acquisition of competencies achieved by final-year or graduates through projects, course assignments, research, and laboratory sessions that develop most of the required 21st-century competencies (Lavi et al. 2021).

In addition, in engineering courses for sophomores and juniors, students must often think about applying math and science courses in more realistic and tangible contexts to develop their problem-solving skills (Díaz-Ramírez 2020).

C. Carvallo (✉)
Academy of Aeronautical Sciences, Universidad Técnica Federico Santa María, Santiago, Chile
e-mail: cristian.carvallo@usm.cl

H. Osorio
Postgraduate Director, Universidad San Sebastián, Santiago, Chile
e-mail: hugo.osorio@uss.cl

© The Author(s), under exclusive license to Springer Nature Singapore Pte Ltd. 2022   241
S. Hosseini et al. (eds.), *Technology-Enabled Innovations in Education*,
Transactions on Computer Systems and Networks,
https://doi.org/10.1007/978-981-19-3383-7_19

The work presented below presents innovations in Industrial Civil Engineering and Commercial Aviation Engineering courses at the Federico Santa María Technical University. The cases indicated that these innovations improved student assessments and teacher evaluations, generated motivational learning environments, and helping the teacher obtain quick feedback from their students.

The above is framed within the concept of gamification as a teaching and learning technique. This methodology had positive results (Putz et al. 2020) where gamification positively affected the retention of students' knowledge, regardless of age and gender.

For their part, (Göksün and Gürsoy 2019) also suggested that gamification positively affects academic performance and student engagement in scientific research methods courses.

Research conducted by Díaz-Ramírez (2020) showed that students obtained a higher pass rate than students who did not engage in a gamified activity. In addition, those involved in gaming were highly engaged in problem-solving activities, perceived that the game contributed to a better learning process, felt that teamwork activities improved their learning, and commented about other impacts.

However, gamification does not just have positive impacts. Some studies did not show statistically significant differences between gaming and other methodologies. Such is the case of Aras and Çiftçi (2021), and, similarly, (Sanchez et al. 2020) concluded in their research that gamification could have positive effects in the short term but not the long term. It also shows that interpersonal differences can influence the positive effects of gamification, indicating that these positive effects can be short-lived and could be beneficial for higher-performing individuals.

19.2 Development

19.2.1 Theoretical Framework

The term gamification can be confused with other teaching techniques and strategies, including applying "serious games." These correspond to technological games designed with a purpose beyond mere entertainment, for example, created for educational and informational purposes, like simulators or games to raise awareness (Dicheva et al. 2015).

On the other hand, recreational teaching games serve the purposes of game-based learning (GBL). This disruptive educational practice leverages the intrinsic motivational aspects of certain video games to capture learners' attention (Del Moral et al. 2016). Some examples are using the game "Angry Birds" to learn parabolic movement and "Monopoly" to acquire negotiation skills.

The aforementioned does not obey the concept of gamification. Gamification is the application of game resources (design, dynamics, elements) in non-playful contexts to modify the behaviors of individuals through motivation (Teixes 2015).

As an example of a non-playful context, Waze is a mobile phone application used daily to visualize the best routes and avoid traffic congestion. The user can earn points by giving feedback about their travel experience to the application. Sports applications encourage users to compete and compare themselves with other users, such as Runtastic or Strava (Fig. 19.1).

In this work, the non-playful context refers to the courses with some tools implemented and establishes the following definition of gamification: "Application of game principles and elements in a learning environment to influence behavior, increase motivation, and increase student participation" (Tecnológico de Monterrey 2016).

It is not about using games per se, but taking some of their principles or mechanics, including:

- Points or incentives.
- Immediate feedback.
- Recognition.
- Freedom to make mistakes.

It is also thought that when gamifying a class, it is not necessary to consider all the elements but to take those that may be most valuable for the learning experience. Some applications and websites can support gamification, some having free access and others with paid membership. The best known are Classbadges, Classcraft, Rezzly, BookWidgets, FlipQuiz, Socrative, Kahoot, Mentimeter, and Symbaloo.

As stated in Seaborn and Fels (2015), there are questions about gamification due to the lack of empirical work with significant evidence that validates it as an effective tool to motivate and engage users in non-entertainment contexts. However, recent studies have shown that gamified teaching processes using challenges positively impacted university students in Engineering and Business programs (Legakiab et al. 2020). Distance university education has also had compelling evidence that gamification increases interactions in that modality and decreases the dropout rate (Peña et al. 2021).

Fig. 19.1 Example of mobile applications. Images from Runtastic and Waze, applications available in the iTunes store and Google Play Store

University-level mathematics courses can leverage intelligent tutoring systems (ITS) and gamification tools to elevate students' confidence and offer different approaches to problem-solving. An essential part of system design is considering the fun elements and giving students choices to learn how to cope with problems. This can be accomplished by using background music that can be turned on or off, audios or voice messages, making students laugh, using real-life examples, and inserting surprise events in games linked to student activities (Faghihi et al. 2014).

Göksün and Gürsoy (2019) also argued that gamified activities more positively impacted academic performance and student engagement than non-gamified activities in other classes.

An interesting conclusion about the long-term effects of gamification is raised by Sanchez et al. (2020), who indicates that the positive effect of gamification on motivation and performance may be short term and recommends that teachers not always use the same techniques. They add that gamification could increase the gap between the best-performing and worst-performing students to a great extent.

19.2.2 Problem Statement

Students tested in traditional courses tend to memorize readings in engineering courses, and traditional evaluations mainly contemplate individual work. Also, student progress tests become complex instruments due to the diversity and extension of the responses. In addition, individual evaluations do not offer the student opportunities to share what is understood, debate, and see if the learning is similar to his or her peers.

Nancy et al. (2020) notes the opportunity to explore new techniques that support teaching using technologies.

Considering different learning categories (active, self-regulated, and constructive) (Huber 2008), one sees the need to improve traditional engineering teaching to improve student performance, using some of the gamification techniques.

19.2.3 Method

To determine the influence of gamification methodologies in engineering courses, we developed the following stages:

- Analyze the State of the Art of gamification concepts in Education.
- Select feasible tools to use in Engineering courses.
- Implement tools in content development and evaluation.
- Design specific proposals for the implementation of gamification elements.
- Validate the proposal through a case applied to the Quality Management course.

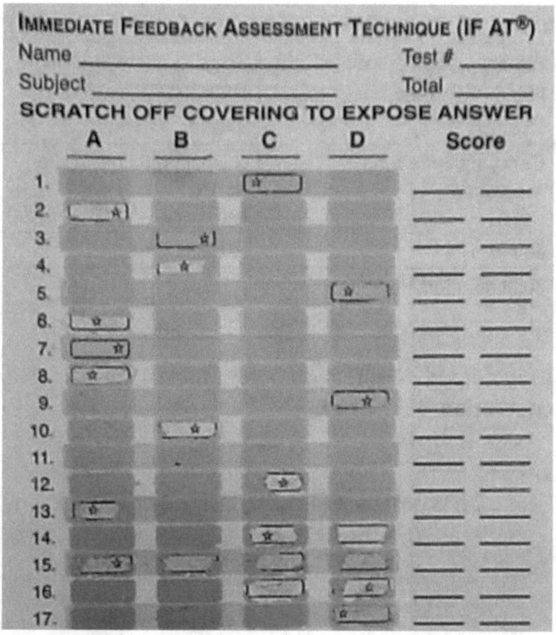

Fig. 19.2 Image of an IF AT card used by the author

To evaluate the pilot, we implemented two techniques that partially covered the learning objectives of the Quality Management course. The tools used were IF AT ® (Immediate Feedback Assessment Technique) and Kahoot. The first one consists of a system using scratch cards (Fig. 19.2) complemented with individual activities before the class (papers, real cases, research on the web), which the student must carry out individually or collaboratively.

At the beginning of class, the student answers an evaluation with multiple-choice questions, then answers the same evaluation in a group. When selecting an alternative answer, the student must scratch the corresponding option on their group card. The score depends on the number of scratches in each question, with 4, 2, and 1 point scores.

In this way, the traditional class structure in Table 19.1, when modified, appears as shown in Table 19.2.

Another tool used corresponds to interactive evaluations using Kahoot (https://kahoot.com/). In this free application, the teacher creates an account and designs activities, which he later presents to his students to answer using their devices, such

Table 19.1 Chair scheme with traditional evaluation

Teacher-centered class Questions from the students. Teacher's responses	Assessment associated with the previous reading
45 min	45 min
Total duration: 90 min	

Table 19.2 Chair scheme applying team-based learning and IF-AT® technique

Plenary session associated with pre-class reading	Carrying out individual assessment	Formation of work teams
15 min	20 min	5 min
Carrying out a team assessment	**General plenary of the course** **Feedback**	**Calculation of individual and group evaluations** **Feedback**
30 min	10 min	10 min
Total duration: 90 min		

as mobile phones (smartphones, tablets) or personal computers having an internet connection (Fig. 19.3).

Fig. 19.3 Example of use of Kahoot application made by the author

Kahoot can be used to review students' knowledge and also as a formative assessment. It is designed for social learning, with students gathered around a shared screen, a projector, or a computer monitor (Nancy et al. 2020).

The use of Kahoot may positively affect learning compared to other tools and approaches, as evidenced by the literature review conducted by Wang and Tahir (2020).

19.2.4   Results

Table 19.3 shows the first applications carried out and how the average evaluation (scale from 0 to 100) increased from the second half of 2012 to the second half of 2013 using the IF AT technique.

Figure 19.4 shows that the results improved and the variability decreased in the second semester of 2013, group evaluation with IF AT.

Table 19.3 Author's results obtained in first applications of the IF-AT technique

Statistics	2nd semester 2012 (traditional evaluation)	2nd semester 2013 individual (IFAT)	2nd semester 2013 group (IFAT)
Amount of data (N)	51	42	42
Media	74.9	77.1	91.7
σ	15.4	12.1	8.9
Minimum	30	50	69
1er Q	68	67	88
Median	75	77	95
3er Q	90	89	97
Maximum	100	94	100

Fig. 19.4 Initial results in evaluations using the IF-AT technique

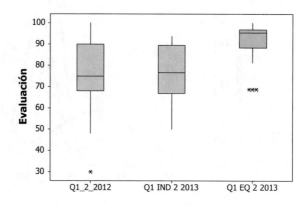

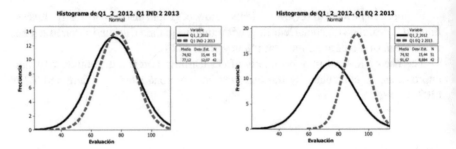

Fig. 19.5 Comparison of traditional individual assessment with assessment using the IF AT technique

Therefore, it can be affirmed that group activity and the IF AT technique improved student performance (Fig. 19.5).

This methodology continued to be used with similar results in the second half of 2016, where four evaluations carried out are shown (Fig. 19.6), of which three were using IF AT.

In Fig. 19.6, it can be seen that in evaluation 3 [Control 3 Trad], using traditional methodology (development questions), students decreased more than 15 points on average and with more significant variability than evaluations 1, 2, and 4, where the IF-AT methodology was applied.

The other tool used was the Kahoot tool. This technique was used mainly in activities in the first semester of 2017. Table 19.4 synthesizes the evaluations carried out on 24 students, where the maximum grade was 100 and the minimum 55.

Finally, in Fig. 19.7, a clear difference of more than five points in the mean can be seen in the course. Some learning objectives were evaluated in a gamified way (continuous line) and compared to the traditional methodology course.

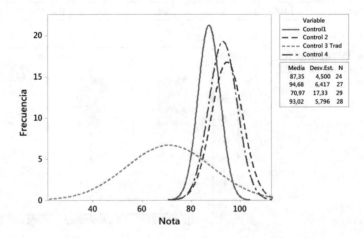

Fig. 19.6 Comparison of traditional evaluations and those with the IF AT technique

Table 19.4 Extract of evaluation results using Kahoot

Student	Total score (points)	Correct answers	Incorrect answers	Kahoot grade
1	4395	5	4	59
5	7732	7	2	78
6	11,616	9	0	100
7	7276	7	2	75
10	7699	7	2	78
11	9571	8	1	88
12	5819	6	3	67
16	6092	6	3	68
17	3736	4	5	55
18	7039	7	2	74
24	6898	6	3	73

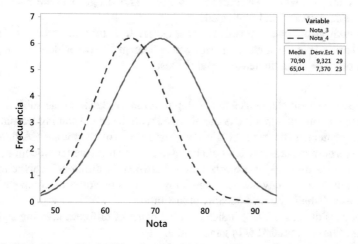

Fig. 19.7 Comparison of final results of traditional and gamified evaluations (Kahoot, IF AT)

Concerning students' attitudes about the effectiveness of the methodology to promote motivation, we present below some comments from the teacher evaluation surveys of these courses:

2016 2nd Semester:

- Very good, the games that the teacher makes, the games on the webpage, and the way to correct the controls are all excellent, and they force us to learn.
- It is an excellent subject. I loved the field and how it was presented. The teacher gives good classes. It is a pleasure to attend them and participate. In every class I attended, I learned new things.

2017 1st Semester:

- Excellent teacher, explicit material, and didactic and entertaining methods (Kahoot and IF-AT).
- Excellent teacher, the activities in class complement what was taught very well, and Kahoot is an innovative and entertaining way to learn.
- The teacher entertainingly conducts the classes and motivates the students to attend his lectures.

The previous answers confirm research reports in other publications, where active methodologies help student learning. (López-Fernández et al. 2019) indicates that another active learning technique, project-based learning (PBL), positively impacted Aerospace Engineering students. They had greater motivation to achieve the objectives, a better disposition toward the learning process, a better perception of the effort-reward relationship, and it improved the students' perception of the teachers, among other things.

Göksün and Gürsoy (2019) also reported positive impacts when applying gamification techniques, which reinforced the students' knowledge. The students attended classes more prepared and motivated.

This study also showed a positive impact, especially in the reinforcement of knowledge, measured per the students' performance. The qualitative evidence of improved motivation came from the teacher evaluations.

Discussion

There are several challenges to develop in future research on the subject; one of them is to measure whether the grade obtained with the active gaming learning techniques is greater than the grade obtained with traditional methodologies. Although the evaluations demonstrate this, it would be interesting to measure the student's perception of their learning and make correlations between the different levels of learning using Bloom's taxonomy and the definitions of the objectives or competencies to achieve established by each educational institution.

Also, as (Putz et al. 2020) indicated, the impact of different learning styles can be included and correlated with gamification.

Applying other interactive tools or techniques that promote student-centered training to compare which ones have the most significant impact would be an interesting challenge, as was done by Göksün and Gürsoy (2019) when comparing the Kahoot tools with Quizizz.

Using these two techniques to gamify the activities omits exploring other techniques and evaluating if there are better methodologies that positively impact learning performance and motivation. Also, measuring the duration of the impact of gamification on the student, as indicated by Sanchez et al. (2020), suggests that there may be specific ways to gamify learning that works better for people with higher cognitive abilities. Another interesting analysis would be to examine the effect that different gamification elements have, for example, in the classification tables to investigate the impacts on people's competitiveness.

Another question that arises is the role or influence that a teacher can have on student performance. The teacher's ability to motivate may affect how their students perform, positively or negatively, in the courses. An active methodology based on gamification could be surpassed by a traditional teacher who is a great motivator and leader in front of their students. However, as shown in other studies (López-Fernández et al. 2019), active methods positively impact students' perception of their teachers.

19.3 Conclusions

The pilot plan developed during the periods reported in this work achieved the expected results, improving student performance, benefiting collaborative work, providing immediate feedback to the student, and reducing the delivery time of partial evaluation results. Results are also confirmatory by Díaz-Ramírez (2020) with positive effects on academic performance, a sense of belonging, and teamwork.

It is also possible to confirm other impacts coinciding with (Putz et al. 2020), who reported social and practical skills improvements, such as problem-solving, collaborative work, and communication.

Sanchez et al. (2020) argued that gamification might be viable for short-term tasks, suggesting that the positive impact may be the effect of novelty. For this reason, they recommended that teachers not use the same gamification method permanently and added that gamification might not have positive effects on low-achieving students.

It remains a concern if the learning result is met in the student. The student can have a great time and be entertained in classes. However, it is necessary to design an instrument that measures the level of gamified learning achievement explicitly.

It should be noted that gamification does not ensure student motivation since teacher motivation is also essential.

Other challenges to consider are knowing the characteristics of the students, deciding whether to gamify a topic or the entire class, verifying that the required physical and technological infrastructure exists, defining the objectives of gamifying, documenting the experience, and measuring the impacts.

Finally, what has been done helps to confirm the benefits of gamified activities in university-level students (López-Fernández et al. 2019; Lavi et al. 2021; Díaz-Ramírez 2020; Putz et al. 2020); the difficulties that appear are more associated with infrastructure than the methodology itself. There were no difficulties and aspects mentioned as disadvantages of gamification in the cases studied, such as the time in which the technique is applied (Sanchez et al. 2020), which was not observed. However, attention should be paid to the techniques used and how they can be varied to maintain students' attention (Sanchez et al. 2020; Zainuddin et al. 2020; Fernández-Vega et al. 2020).

In this study, the active learning gaming methodology was repeated over time and continued to have positive impacts. This confirms the benefits of the technique to improve students' performance, motivation, and the evaluation that the teacher receives at the end of the teaching period.

Acknowledgements The authors acknowledge the support of the Universidad Técnica Federico Santa María in the development of this work. In particular, the Director of the Directorate of Teaching and Learning, Mr. Hugo Alarcón, his pedagogical advisor Ms. Teresita Marín, and the person in charge of Didactic Resources, Ms. Cecilia Ritchie. Likewise, the General Director of Teaching, Mr. Gonzalo Fuster, and the Director of the Academy of Aeronautical Sciences, Mr. Osvaldo Sarabia V.

The authors acknowledge the support of Writing Lab, Institute for the Future of Indication, Tecnologico de Monterrey, Mexico, in the production of this work.

References

Aras G, Çiftçi B (2021) Comparison of the effect of reinforcement with question-answer and Kahoot method on the success and motivation levels of nursing students: a quasi-experimental review. Nurse Educ Today 102

De la Peña C, Lizcano D, Martinez-Alvarez I (2021) Learning through play: gamification model in university-level distance learning. Entertainment Comput 39(100430):1–24

Del Moral ME, Fernández L, Guzmán A (2016) Proyecto game to learn: Aprendizaje Basado en Juegos para potenciar las Inteligencias Lógicomatemática, Naturalista y Lingüística en Educación Primaria. Pixel-Bit Revista de Medios y Educación, n°49, julio

Díaz-Ramírez J (2020) Gamification in engineering education—an empirical assessment on learning and game performance. Heliyon 6(9)

Dicheva D, Dichev C, Agre G, Angelova G (2015) Gamification in education: a systematic mapping study. Educ Technol Soc

Faghihi U, Brautigam A, Jorgenson K, Martin D, Brown A, Measures E et al (2014) How gamification applies for educational purpose especially with college algebra. Procedia Comput Sci 41:182–187

Fernández-Vega I, Jiménez JS-J, Quirós LM (2020) Uso de la app Kahoot para cuantificar el grado de atención del alumno en la asignatura de Anatomía Patológica en Medicina y evaluación de la experiencia. Educación Médica

Göksün D, Gürsoy G (2019) Comparing success and engagement in gamified learning experiences via Kahoot and Quizizz. Comput Educ 135:15–29

Huber GL (2008) Aprendizaje Activo y Metodologías Educativas. Revista de Educación, número extraordinario, pp 59–81

Lavi R, Tal M, Dori Y (2021) Perceptions of STEM alumni and students on developing 21st-century skills through methods of teaching and learning. Stud Educ Evaluation 70

Legakiab N-Z, Xib N, Hamari J, Karpouzisa K, Assimakopoulosa V (2020) The effect of challenge-based gamification on learning: an experiment in the context of statistics education.Int J Hum Comput Stud 144(102496):1–14

López-Fernández D, Ezquerro J, Rodríguez J, Porter J, Lapuerta V (2019) Motivational impact of active learning methods in aerospace engineering students. Acta Astronaut 165:344–354

Nancy W, Parimala A, Merlin Livingston LM (2020) Advanced teaching pedagogy as an innovative approach in the modern education system. Procedia Comput Sci 172:382–388

Putz L, Hofbauer F, Treiblmaier H (2020) Can gamification help to improve education? Findings from a longitudinal study. Comput Hum Behav 110

Sanchez D, Langer M, Kaur R (2020) Gamification in the classroom: examining the impact of gamified quizzes on student learning. Comput Educ 144

Seaborn K, Fels D (2015) Gamification in theory and action: a survey
Tecnológico de Monterrey (2016) EduTrends. Gamificación. Revista completa. Septiembre
Teixes F (2015) Gamificación: fundamentos y aplicaciones, Editorial UOC, edición digital
Wang A, Tahir R (2020) The effect of using Kahoot! for learning—a literature review. Comput
    Educ 149
Zainuddin Z, Chu SKW, Shujahat M, Perera CJ (2020) The impact of gamification on learning and
    instruction: a systematic review of empirical evidence. Educ Res Rev 30

Chapter 20
Dropout Reduction in MOOCs Through Gamification and Length of Videos

**Manuel Medina-Labrador, Sebastian Martinez Quintero,
David Escobar Suarez, and Alejandra Sarmiento Rincón**

20.1 Introduction

The MOOCs include many challenges such as identifying students, evaluating qualitative responses, and developing technological strategies to increase the completion rates. One of the main disadvantages that MOOCs face is attrition (Dalipi et al. 2018). *Dropout* is defined as the decrease in the number of students at the end of a specific learning program. It depends on multiple factors such as interactions, motivation, accessibility, course design, teachers, commitment, and technologies used during the development and implementation of the course (Chen et al. 2020). According to Zhou and Xu (2020), the desertion rate on multiple platforms was around 90% by 2020.

The literature highlights various approaches to analyzing online dropouts, looking at different themes, the study focuses, and models. Some major approaches follow.

(a) *Prediction*: Predictive analysis and retention indicators, including characterization of the students, identification and data concordance with the participants, and the students' academic interests (Mohamad et al. 2018). (b) *Intent to continue*: The technology acceptance model (TAM) establishes the effects of perceived ease-of-use, satisfaction, and usefulness on the intention to continue the course (Joo et al. 2018).

M. Medina-Labrador (✉) · S. Martinez Quintero · D. Escobar Suarez · A. Sarmiento Rincón
Industrial Engineering, Pontificia Universidad Javeriana, Bogota, Colombia
e-mail: manuel_medina@icloud.com

S. Martinez Quintero
e-mail: jmartinezq@javeriana.edu.co

D. Escobar Suarez
e-mail: david-escobar@javeriana.edu.co

A. Sarmiento Rincón
e-mail: monica.sarmiento@javeriana.edu.co

© The Author(s), under exclusive license to Springer Nature Singapore Pte Ltd. 2022   255
S. Hosseini et al. (eds.), *Technology-Enabled Innovations in Education*,
Transactions on Computer Systems and Networks,
https://doi.org/10.1007/978-981-19-3383-7_20

Others are the information system continuity model (IS) and adequacy of task technology (Jo 2018) and the interest in learning and metacognition model (Tsai et al. 2018), where the positive correlations among liking, enjoyment, and commitment to the intention of using MOOCs are known. (c) *Motivation*: The course completion correlates with the students' determination and goal orientation before starting the MOOC (Wang and Baker 2018). (d) *Attraction*: Student support, course content, and interactions among students and teachers are associated with retention (Gregori et al. 2018). Finally, (e) Attrition model for open learning environment setting (*AMOES*) (Gütl et al. 2014; Rizzardini and Amado-Salvatierra 2018). AMOES proposes understanding dropout through three factors: (1) dropout and permanence, (2) grouping of course participants, and (3) participation funnel in the learning environment.

According to El Said (2017), students abandon MOOCs through dissatisfaction with interactivity, technology implementation, course design, and perceived value. According to Eriksson et al. (2017), the factors influencing dropout are content, MOOC design, student situation, social characteristics, and time management. On the other hand, based on Khalil et al. (2014 and Antonaci et al. (2018), gamification increases motivation and reinforces student engagement, explaining 61.9% of the variations in MOOC retentions.

"Gamification" refers to applying games in environments where this activity is not usual (Aparicio et al. 2019). The main theoretical objective of gamification is fun, where festive activities change people's behavior and increase engagement (Huang and Hew 2015). Based on Hamari et al. (2014) and the SI Success Theory (DeLone and McLean 2003), gamification is viewed with three perspectives: (a) *motivation and reinforcement*: resulting from the elements (such as points and badges) that cause the participant to enjoy the game experience (Wigfield and Eccles 2000); (b) the *feelings* acquired by the player-student, and (c) the student's *behavior* through gamification.

20.1.1 Theoretical Framework

Research shows that students receive various benefits from gamification, including academic performance (Grant and Betts 2013; Landers et al. 2015), motivation (Gooch et al. 2016; Hakulinen et al. 2015), commitment (Kyewski and Krämer 2018), attitude toward gamification (Aldemir et al. 2018), collaboration (Knutas et al. 2014), and social conscience (Christy and Fox 2014). It is essential to identify the suitable reinforcer for each gamification element to achieve the desired behavior. (Notaris et al. 2021) listed the reinforcing elements of gamification: points, leaderboards, badges, levels, objectives, rewards, progress, and challenges. Gamification can employ many reinforcement mechanisms, such as (a) virtual goods which are not physical objects or money for use online (i.e., avatars, powers, social "likes," progress bars, and weapons) (Chang and Wei 2016; Krause et al. 2015); (b) redeemable points that students earn to exchange virtual items and rewards (Huang and Soman 2013); (c) team leaderboards in which the winning teams are recognized (Kuo and Chuang

2015); (d) "Where is Wally," where students are challenged to find a specific learning object hidden on the platform (i.e., bright star or exclamation point) (Armstrong and Landers 2017), and (e) badges, which are reinforcing elements in games, (i.e., cups, medals, and trophies) (De-Marcos et al. 2016; Tenorio et al. 2016). The above reinforcements strengthen the learning process and motivate students to stay connected to the course and not drop out.

Based on Yamba and Luján (2017), videos and gamification stimulate participation within a MOOC. According to Yalagi et al. (2021), videos open up new interactive possibilities in education; videos with a 10–12 min duration reported 83% satisfaction and 30% engagement with the course. Moreover, Alvarado et al. (2020) reports that Generation Z students preferred long videos (40–45 min) over 10–12 min short videos. This finding aligns with the research (Guo et al. 2014); they found that video duration is the factor that most influences student engagement in a MOOC. In their study, the average time in which students committed to watching a video was six minutes, and the shorter videos were the ones that most attracted the participants, as students' attention decreased considerably over time after a threshold of 5–10 min. According to Pérez (2015), the videos in MOOCs should not exceed 15 min, especially those requiring high concentration compared to those more informative than challenging. Likewise, Hildebrand and Ahn (2018) showed that the students who watched the course videos improved their grades and participated more thanks to questioning involving the teacher and the other classmates. Moreover, the videos containing more complex information, like equations, mathematical terms, and engineering expressions, were very popular with students because they can be viewed multiple times, especially before exams. For the above reasons, video duration impacts different generations and ages and academic levels; videos can reduce dropouts during the weeks of the MOOC course.

MOOC students must decide to view course videos as support materials; thus, it is relevant to know how the duration of the videos affects abandonment. The decision to view is a confirmation of an election (Kahneman 2003). However, many of the decisions can be made based on cognitive errors, called biases. According to Loewenstein (2010), most errors in decision making can be caused by exaggerating the specific benefits. However, if some biases reduce the quality of decision making, others can counteract overstatement or undervaluation through the minutiae effect. The minutiae effect refers to the tendency to downplay minimal results, whether they profit or lose; it includes the tendency to underestimate the consequences and often delay. For this reason, when applying the minutiae effect, individuals could underestimate the effort they must make. It is better to make small efforts now to have significant future benefits. Based on Medina-Labrador et al. (2019), the minutiae technique analyzed in previous MOOC research showed a positive effect through a few evaluative questions at the beginning of the course and small increments until the final week of the course; the use of this bias decreased attrition to 86%, an improvement over using a fixed number of questions throughout the MOOC. Furthermore, the minutiae effect can be represented in different variables, such as short videos, employed to achieve a change in students' behavior when they consider the option of dropping out of the course.

20.1.2 Problem Statement

Dropout analysis offers a solution that could help decrease attrition rates, predict student progress, optimize teaching techniques, and improve decision making on the platform. This study aimed to reduce attrition through gamification/reinforcement and evaluate the minutiae effect by employing short-length videos. Our research considered the effect of the variables gender, previous experience, educational level, and age on dropping out during the four-week course. The questions in this research were: (A) Is gamification, represented in our study as "fill in the blank," associated with the decrease in MOOCS attrition? (B) Can the length of the videos negatively influence the dropout from MOOCs? (C) What are the best predictors of dropout among the factors analyzed? (D) Is it possible that gamification with a reinforcer influences weekly survival during a MOOC? In this study, we used survival and risk analysis to answer the above questions presented. Our main objective aimed to determine the combined effect of gamification ("fill in the blank") and the duration of the videos on MOOC attrition and risk abandonment.

20.2 Method

Three stages were carried out: (a) Exploratory, (b) Quasi-experimental, and (c) Experimental. The exploratory stage used the log-linear test to determine the reinforcer of the game, considering nine possibilities, 19 colors, and the emotions produced in the participants. In the second stage (quasi-experimental), we analyzed different factors in two MOOCs. In the first, we examined the correlation between video duration and attrition. In the second, we found the influence of the minutiae effect on dropping out, considering the number of weekly reinforcers. In the experimental stage, we developed a 2×2 factorial design, using the factors of video duration and the number of reinforcers. The levels of the video times were (without video and with video 180 s.). The reinforcer levels were (without reinforcers and four reinforcers each week). Finally, a longitudinal analysis was performed on survival and the risk of attrition. The study used IBM SPSS Statistics version 27 in all MOOCs, sales forecasts, and analyses. The independent variables were gender, age, amount of previous experience, and educational level. The game "fill in the blank" was used in all studies as it has shown more significant commitment and lower dropout rates (Browne et al. 2014). The final certificate was free and awarded both for completing the four weeks of the course and answering the questions in each module.

20.2.1 Participants

The analyzed population was divided based on the proposed stages: exploratory ($N = 376$), quasi-experimental ($N = 103$), and experimental ($N = 192$). Children under 18 years of age and students who stated that they took the course at their own pace were excluded from the study. The nationality was mainly Colombian, and the subjects were randomly assigned and participated in only one research stage. The students were recruited through digital advertising for three months (Table 20.1).

20.2.2 Instrument

The data were collected using three forms: (a) Characterization of the reinforcer (shape, color, and emotion evoked); (b) Quasi-experimental and experimental phase registration, with the students' demographic information; (c) Evaluation of weekly questions. The characterization of the reinforcer used an instrument adapted from Padrón-Mercado and Barreto (2011) (REC) with nine items that evaluated the symbol of the reinforcer, the emotion it produced, and color. The form included demographic aspects, possible reinforcers (avatar, cup, crown, sword, star, medal, redeemable points, exclamation point, and leaderboard) (Chang and Wei 2016), eight emotions (anger, disgust, fear, joy, desire, happiness, interest, and wonder), and 19 different colors. The weekly question form was submitted on the last day of the week, with only one opportunity to respond and no possibility of going back. All courses (quasi-experimental and experimental) had the same reinforcer from the exploratory phase.

The experimental phase used the evaluation form of Medina-Labrador et al. (2019), consisting of four initial questions, increasing weekly by one or two questions until reaching 12 questions in the last week. That achieved a dropout of 83.3%.

20.3 Results

The exploratory phase aimed to find the appropriate reinforcer to be used in the following phases. The (REC) instrument used in this phase was subjected to a reliability test evaluating the items' clarity, coherence, relevance, and sufficiency. The survey was validated by experts whose final result was Cronbach's alpha $\alpha = 0.88$; later, and the survey was applied to the participants. The results of the log-linear model showed that the effects of K, $K = 1$, and interaction by pairs of the main variables $K = 2$ could be eliminated. The analysis determined that there is an association between the variables Crown-joy, Gender (indistinct), Color-Purple (# 822B7F); χ^2 (gl $= 49$, $N = 376$) $= 75.46$, $p = .01$, ($R2 = 0.99$). This result served to apply this reinforcement in the quasi-experimental phase without distinction to the participants.

Table 20.1 Participants in the different stages of the research

Phase	Variable	Attributes	M	SD
Exploratory	Gender	Male (47%), female (53%)		
	Previous experience in MOOCs	None (22.6%), 1 (21.5%), 2 (23.1%), 3 (7.2%), 4 or more (25.5%)	1.92	0.39
	Educational level (years of study)	8 (0.3%), 10 (2.1%), 12 (4.5%), 14 (8.5%), 16 (25.8%), 18 (30.3%), 20 (15.4%), 22 (7.4%)	16.47	1.95
	Age	18–28 (68.4%), 28–38 (9%), 38–48 (7.7%), 48–58 (11.4%), 58–68 (1.9%), 68–78 (0.3%)	24.53	4.41
Quasi-experimental	Gender	Male (50%), female (50%)		
	Previous experience in MOOCs	None (26.8%), 1 (33.9%), 2 (10.7%), 3 (12.5%), 4 or more (16.1%)	1.57	0.23
	Educational level (years of study)	8 (4.9%), 10 (1.0%), 12 (2.9%), 14 (14.6%), 16 (34.0%), 18 (22.3%), 20 (17.5%), 22 (1.0%) and 24 (1.9%)	16.51	2.01
	Age	18–28 (83.5%), 28–38 (5.8%), 38–48 (4.9%), 48–58 (3.9%), 58–68 (1.9%) and 68–78 (0%)	21.49	5.65
Experimental	Gender	Male (51.3%), female (48.7%)		
	Previous experience in MOOCs	None (84.6%), 1 (7.7%), 2 (3.4%), 3 (1.7%), 4 or more (2.6)	1.3	0.83
	Educational level (years of study)	8 (9.9%), 10 (1.0%), 12 (7.3%), 14 (14.1%), 16 (27.6%), 18 (21.9%), 20 (13.0%) and 24 (5.2%)	15.84	1.55
	Age	18–28 (74%), 28–38 (7.8%), 38–48 (6.3%), 48–58 (8.9%), 58–68 (2.6%) and 68–78 (0.5%)	24.01	4.74

Note Students 100% Colombian and enrolled for a period of three months

20.3.1 Quasi-Experimental Phase

The first course of this phase had 103 students, and its objective was to find the number of reinforcers that influence dropout. The booster (crown # 822B7F) was awarded each week to the student for remaining and passing all five multiple-choice questions. The number of reinforcers was incremental (i.e., in the first week, the participant received one crown and four in the last). The number of reinforcers with which a subject did not pass the MOOC was ($M = 1$, SD $= 1.44$) and those who passed ($M = 4$, SD $= 1.16$). The results indicated that dropout was 85.40% and that there were no associations between dropout and the variables of gender, educational level, previous experience, and age range. However, relationships were found between the number of four reinforcers with attrition, U ($1; N = 103$) $= 30.50, p = .01$.

The second MOOC followed the same conditions as the first course regarding duration, content, and tests. This course had 56 participants. Its objective was to determine the relationship between the amount of time viewing the video and attrition. Each week, the students freely watched a video with a duration between 30 and 240 s. The final attrition was 89.3%. The analysis of repeated means showed differences between the means of the viewing time of the videos in each week F ($3, N = 56$) $= 22.15, p = .01$. The viewing time in week two was the most viewed with $M = 0.65$ and interval (42.33–88.66 s.). The average time of the videos in which students did not dropout was between 151.75 and 209.75 s. Associations were found between having previous MOOC experience and attrition χ^2 ($4, N = 56$) $= 10.34, p = .03$ and with the number of videos U ($1; N = 56$) $= 0.0, p = .02$. Those who did not watch any videos dropped out, and those who saw four did not drop out. Also, those students who had no experience in virtual courses dropped out of the MOOC. No differences were found with the other independent variables.

20.3.2 Experimental Phase

The experimental phase determined the effect of the reinforcer and the time of the video. A 2 × 2 factorial design was conducted, analyzing video time factors and the number of reinforcers. The levels of the video times were without video and with video (151.75–209.75 s), ($M = 180$ s). For the number of reinforcers, the levels were without reinforcers and four reinforcers each week. The results indicated that the survival weeks were affected by the reinforcer F ($1; N = 56$) $= 17.68, p = .01$ and by the intersection of the reinforcer * video F ($1; N = 56$) $= 18.71, p = .01$. The lowest attrition was found at a value of 81.8% in the reinforcing factorial position * video. A relationship was found between the number of videos viewed and attrition t ($190, N = 192$) $= -22.15, p = .01$. Students who watched two or less dropped out 100%. No relationship was found between age and years of schooling with dropout (Fig. 20.1).

Fig. 20.1 Experimental
colour enhancer # 822B7F
with own development

Survival analysis was performed in all the experimental groups. The survival graph indicated that the highest survival rate was found in the group with Crown enhancement (see Fig. 20.2). There was a 47% probability of attrition between weeks 0–1, 28% between weeks 2–3, and 17% between weeks 3–4. The lowest survival rate was found in the group without video and reinforcers. The multivariate analysis of the Cox regression showed that none of the independent variables (age, years of schooling, and previous experience) significantly affected the model χ^2 (13, $N = 56$) $= 16.27$, $p = .07$. However, regarding the number of videos viewed, there was a correlation with attrition χ^2 (Wald $= 53.78$, df $= 4$, $p = .02$). The highest hazard

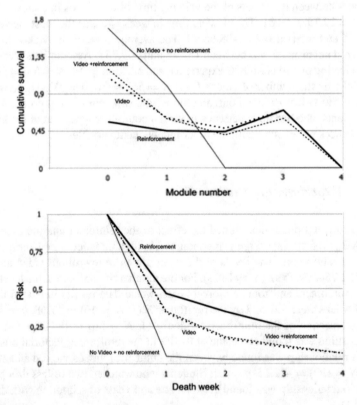

Fig. 20.2 Survival function with 95% confidence interval (UP) and risk function of the reinforcer group, video time group, final group and contra group with 95% confidence interval (down)

ratios were found in the number of videos (1) Exp $\beta = 3597$ and number of videos (2) Exp $\beta = 195$; the above indicates that the students who have only watched between 1 and 2 videos have between 195 and 3,597 times more risk to dropout (see Fig. 20.3).

Regarding the risk function, the graph shows that the group without video and reinforcement has the highest risk of attrition between weeks 0 and 1 (100%). In the case of the group with only videos, the risk of attrition for the first week was 75%, 48% for week two, and 83% for week three. Thus, the above results present the effect of the videos and reinforcers from another perspective.

Fig. 20.3 Cox regression. Survival function with 95% and risk function (1 and 2 videos)

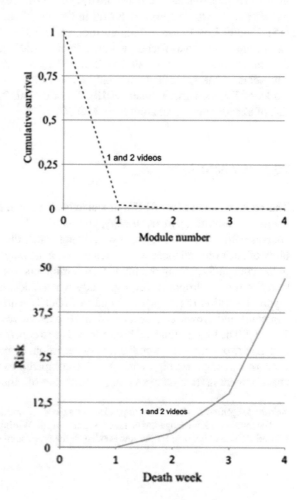

20.4 Discussion

Very similar results were reported by El Said (2017) Hone and El Said (2016), who indicated that desertion occurs within the first week. The results obtained regarding the influence of "minutiae bias" verify the hypothesis of this study and align with (Loewenstein 2010) in areas other than online learning, and they improve the results found by Medina-Labrador et al. (2019). MOOC students are prone to underestimate the results of small numbers, favoring the cost–benefit ratio prospectively. The gamification factors expressed as "fill in the blank" and the duration of the videos (151.75–209.75 s.) decrease the attrition of MOOCs. These results are consistent and improve what was found by Alvarado et al. (2020); Guo et al. 2014), who had determined the video times of 10–12 min. This research delved into the power of enhancers in the game and especially Crown Figure # 822B7F. This extends the works of Kyewski and Krämer (2018); Tenorio et al. 2016), which determined the risk of abandonment probability in a MOOC.

20.5 Conclusions

This research shows that 81.8% of students abandon a MOOC in the presence of a gamification/reinforcement strategy, and 89.3% when participants are subjected to courses with videos. Participants who do not watch the videos have a higher probability of attrition, and those who watch between the range of 151.75–209.75 s remain in the course. Regarding the number of reinforcers, the incremental strategy effectively mitigated dropping out, especially when students received four. The lowest reported attrition (81.8%) was found in MOOCs with gamification/reinforcement strategies and crown enhancers # 822B7F plus videos with durations of 151.75–209.75 s. The longitudinal analysis allowed us to conclude that the number of videos less than two increases the probability of desertion. Opportunities for future research concern investigating high attrition rates compared to the first week, the risks of abandonment in the first weeks, and the number of reinforcers received.

Acknowledgements The authors appreciate the support of Javeriana University.

The authors acknowledge the technical support of the Writing Lab, Institute for the Future of Education, Tecnologico de Monterrey, Mexico, in the production of this work.

References

Aldemir T, Celik B, Kaplan G (2018) A qualitative investigation of student perceptions of game elements in a gamified course. Comput Hum Behav 78:235–254

Alvarado M, Basinger K, Lahijanian B, Alvarado D (2020) Teaching simulation to generation Z engineering students: lessons learned from a flipped classroom pilot study. In: 2020 winter simulation conference (WSC). Simulation Drives Innovation IEEE, UK, Dec 2020

Antonaci A, Klemke R, Kreijns K, Specht M (2018) Get Gamification of MOOC right! Int J Serious Games 5(3):61–78

Aparicio M, Oliveira T, Bacao F, Painho M (2019) Gamification: a key determinant of massive open online course (MOOC) success. Inf Manage 56(1):39–54

Armstrong MB, Landers RN (2017) An evaluation of gamified training: using narrative to improve reactions and learning. Simul Gaming 48:513–538

Browne K, Anand C, Gosse E (2014) Gamification and serious game approaches for adult literacy tablet software. Entertainment Comput 5(3):135–146. https://doi.org/10.1016/j.entcom.2014.04.003

Chang JW, Wei HY (2016) Exploring engaging gamification mechanics in massive online open courses. Educ Technol Soc 19(2):177–203

Chen C, Sonnert G, Sadler PM, Sasselov DD, Fredericks C, Malan DJ (2020) Going over the cliff: MOOC dropout behavior at chapter transition. Distance Educ 41(1):6–25

Christy KR, Fox J (2014) Leaderboards in a virtual classroom: a test of stereotype threat and social comparison explanations for women's math performance. Comput Educ 78:66–77

Dalipi F, Imran AS, Kastrati Z (2018) MOOC dropout prediction using machine learning techniques: review and research challenges. In: 2018 IEEE global engineering education conference (EDUCON). Emerging trends and challenges of engineering education IEEE, UK

DeLone WH, McLean ER (2003) The DeLone and McLean model of information systems success: a ten-year update. J Manage Inf Syst 19(4):9–30

De-Marcos L, Garciá-López E, Garciá-Cabot A, Medina-Merodio JA, Domínguez A, Martínez-Herraíz JJ, Diez-Folledo T (2016) Social network analysis of a gamified e-learning course: small-world phenomenon and network metrics as predictors of academic performance. Comput Hum Behav 60:312–321

De Notaris D, Canazza S, Mariconda C, Paulon C (2021) How to play a MOOC: practices and simulation. Entertainment Comput 37:100–395

El Said GR (2017) Understanding how learners use massive open online courses and why they drop out: thematic analysis of an interview study in a developing country. J Educ Comput Res 55(5):724–752. https://doi.org/10.1177/0735633116681302

Eriksson T, Adawi T, Stöhr C (2017) "Time is the bottleneck": a qualitative study exploring why learners drop out of MOOCs. J Comput High Educ 29(1):133–146

Gooch D, Vasalou A, Benton L, Khaled R (2016) Using gamification to motivate students with Dyslexia. In: Proceedings of the CHI conference on human factors in computing systems (CHI' 16), San Jose, CA, USA

Grant S, Betts B (2013) Encouraging user behaviour with achievements: an empirical study. In: Proceedings of the IEEE international working conference on mining software repositories, San Francisco, CA, USA

Gregori EB, Zhang J, Galván-Fernández C, de Asís Fernández-Navarro F (2018) Learner support in MOOCs: identifying variables linked to completion. Comput Educ 122:153–168

Guo PJ, Kim J, Rubin R (2014) How video production affects student engagement: an empirical study of MOOC videos. In: Proceedings of the First ACM conference on Learning@ scale conference, NY, USA, Mar 2014. https://doi.org/10.1145/2556325.2566239

Gütl C, Chang V, Hernández R, Morales M (2014) Must we be concerned with the massive dropouts in MOOC? An attrition analysis of open courses. In: Proceedings of the international conference interactive collaborative learning, ICL, Dubai, United Arab Emirates, Dec 2014

Hakulinen L, Auvinen T, Korhonen A (2015) The effect of achievement badges on students' behavior: an empirical study in a university-level computer science course. Int J Emerg Technol Learn 10:18–30

Hamari J, Koivisto J, Sarsa H (2014) Does gamification work? A literature review of empirical studies on gamification. In: 2014 47th Hawaii international conference on system sciences (HICSS), USA, Jan 2014. https://doi.org/10.1109/HICSS.2014.377

Hildebrand J, Ahn B (2018) Student video viewing habits in an online mechanics of materials engineering course. Int J Eng Pedagogy 8(3):40–59. https://doi.org/10.3991/ijep.v8i3.7948

Huang B, Hew KF (2015) Do points, badges, and leaderboard increase learning and activity: a quasi-experiment on the effects of gamification. In: Proceedings of the 23rd international conference on computers in education, Hangzhou, China, Nov 2015

Huang WHY, Soman D (2013) Gamification of education. Research report series: behavioural economics in action. Rotman School of Management, vol 7, no 5, pp 227–232.https://doi.org/10.4236/jss.2019.75019

Jo D (2018) Exploring the determinants of MOOCs continuance intention. KSII Trans Internet Inf Syst (TIIS) 12(8):3992–4005

Joo YJ, So H-J, Kim NH (2018) Examination of relationships among students' self-determination, technology acceptance, satisfaction, and continuing intention to use K-MOOCs. Comput Educ 122:260–272. https://doi.org/10.1016/j.compedu.2018.01.003

Kahneman D (2003) Maps of bounded rationality: psychology for behavioral economics. Am Econ Rev 93(5):1449–1475. https://doi.org/10.1257/000282803322655392

Khalil H, Ebner M (2014) MOOCs completion rates and possible methods to improve retention—a literature review. In: EdMedia: world conference on educational media and technology 1305-1313. Association for the Advancement of Computing in Education (AACE), Austria, June 2014. Recuperado de https://www.learntechlib.org/primary/p/147656/

Kuo MS, Chuang TY (2015) How gamification motivates visits and engagement for online academic dissemination—an empirical study. Comput Hum Behav 55:16–27

Knutas A, Ikonen J, Nikula U, Porras J (2014) Increasing collaborative communications in a programming course with gamification. In: Proceedings of the 15th international conference on computer systems and technologies (CompSysTech' 14), Ruse, Bulgaria, June 2014

Krause M, Mogalle M, Pohl H, Williams JJ (2015) A playful game changer: fostering student retention in online education with social gamification. In: Proceedings of the 2nd ACM conference on Learning@Scale (L@S'15), Vancouver, BC, Canada

Kyewski E, Krämer NC (2018) To gamify or not to gamify? An experimental field study of the influence of badges on motivation, activity, and performance in an online learning course. Comput Educ 118:25–37

Landers RN, Bauer KN, Callan RC (2015) Gamification of task performance with leaderboards: a goal setting experiment. Comput Hum Behav 1–8

Loewenstein G (2010) Aprender de los errores de los consumidores para ayudarles a tomar mejores decisiones. Harvard Deusto Bus Rev 190:31–38

Medina-Labrador M, Vargas GRG, Alvarado J, Caicedo M (2019) Survival and risk analysis in MOOCs. Turk Online J Distance Educ 20(4):149–159

Mohamad N, Ahmad NB, Jawawi DNA (2018) Malaysia MOOC: improving low student retention with predictive analytics. Int J Eng Technol 7(2.29):398–405. https://doi.org/10.14419/ijet.v7i2.29.13662

Padrón-Mercado CM, Barreto I (2011) Social representations associated to hedonic food intake in restaurants. Rev Latinoam de Psicología 43(3):487–496

Pérez A (2015) Herramienta para la autoría de visualizaciones interactivas de vídeos académicos. (tesis de grado). Universidad Pompeu Fabra, Barcelona. Recuperado de http://hdl.handle.net/10230/25411

Rizzardini RH, Amado-Salvatierra HR (2018) Towards full engagement for open online education. A practical experience from MicroMasters at edX. In: Software data engineering for network eLearning environments. Springer, Cham, pp 161–177. https://doi.org/10.1007/978-3-319-683 18-8_8

Tenorio T, Bittencourt II, Isotani S, Pedro A, Ospina P (2016) A gamified peer assessment model for online learning environments in a competitive context. Comput Hum Behav 64:247–263

Tsai Y-H, Lin C-H, Hong J-C, Tai K-H (2018) The effects of metacognition on online learning interest and continuance to learn with MOOCs. Comput Educ 121:18–29. https://doi.org/10. 1016/j.compedu.2018.02.011

Yalagi PS, Dixit RK, Nirgude MA (2021) Effective use of online teaching-learning platform and MOOC for virtual learning. In: Journal of physics: conference. IOP Publishing, India

Yamba M, Luján S (2017) MOOCs: factors that decrease desertion in students. Enfoqute 8(1):1–15. https://doi.org/10.29019/enfoqueute.v8n1.124

Wang Y, Baker R (2018) Grit and intention: why do learners complete MOOCs? Int Rev Res Open Distance Learn 19(3):20–42. https://doi.org/10.19173/irrodl.v19i3.3393

Wigfield A, Eccles JS (2000) Expectancy–value theory of achievement motivation. Contemp Educ Psychol 25(1):68–81. https://doi.org/10.1006/1999.1015

Zhou Y, Xu Z (2020) Multi-model stacking ensemble learning for dropout prediction in MOOCS. In: Journal of physics: conference series, vol 1607, no 1. IOP Publishing, China, p 012004, Aug 2020

Chapter 21
Proposal for a Game to Promote Leadership and Collaboration

Maria Camila Bermeo-Giraldo, Miguel D. Rojas-López, and Susana María Valencia-Rodríguez

21.1 Introduction

Leadership is a process of interaction between individuals in which one of them leads (Mughal 2020). It is a quality that inspires, promotes learning, and potentializes the members of a group or work team established to achieve a common goal, contributing to the organization and the people collaborating in it (Klaic et al. 2020).

According to Alfaro (2020), there has been a worldwide increase in corruption practices in governmental institutions, organizations, and society in general. This has led to the construction of an international corruption ranking, where organizational trust is measured using statistical criteria (Brito 2016).

Hence, leadership ethics observed by upright leaders has become essential to control and combat corruption in organizations (Pliscoff and Lagos 2021). However, this has not yet attracted the scientific community's attention because research on ethics in the specialized literature on leadership is limited.

As a method to approach leadership in teaching, we recommend serious games as a practical learning and teaching tool for workgroups' formation and analyses in the business sector (Buzady 2017). Each work team member must have a high capacity for collaboration, skills achievement, and desirable humanistic behaviors.

M. C. Bermeo-Giraldo (✉)
Centro de Investigaciones Escolme, Institución Universitaria Escolme, Medellin, Colombia
e-mail: cies2@escolme.edu.co

M. D. Rojas-López · S. M. Valencia-Rodríguez
Departamento de Ingeniería de las Organización, Universidad Nacional de Colombia, Medellin, Colombia
e-mail: mdrojas@unal.edu.co

S. M. Valencia-Rodríguez
e-mail: sumvalenciaro@unal.edu.co

Thus, considering the benefits of game design methodologies to teach concepts such as cooperation and collaboration (Maurer et al. 2021), we propose in this paper a game to promote cooperation among team members to acquire the ethical values of leaders.

21.2 Theoretical Framework

21.2.1 Leadership

Leadership is a human and natural necessity of society. Its origin in literature dates back to around 1904 when it addressed managerial positions in World War I, but during the last decades, research has been interested analyzed leadership during social changes and its influence on subordinates or followers (Serrano and Portalanza 2014).

Leadership (Samimi et al. 2020) is defined by the guidelines and functions that individuals at the highest levels of an organization follow to guide and influence followers or employees. It includes abilities, competencies, and aptitudes of human behavior to influence a work team to achieve a goal or accomplishment (Romero-Rodriguez and Castillo-Abdul 2019).

For Lupano and Castro, leadership is a complex construct defined as a natural process of exerting influence on another person. The influenced persons are recognized as followers (Lupano and Castro 2013). Another concept from Rocafuerte's perspective is the ability of an individual to contribute positively to the workgroup so that the members can make the best decisions for others. Then, their cooperative decisions help the team fulfill the established objectives (Rocafuerte 2016).

Therefore, a team needs to cooperate since the consequences, good or bad, are the responsibility of everyone involved, not proceeding from the individual action of one member. Figure 21.1 shows some of the elements that are considered essential to develop leadership.

Fig. 21.1 Essential elements of leadership

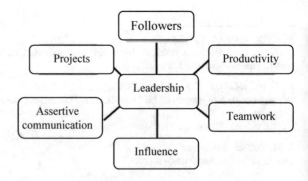

(1) *Organizational ethics*

Organizational ethics arises as a response to employees' needs for fairness, trust, and integrity in organizations (Abbas Ibrahim and Mohammed 2020) due to scandals and corruption within companies, which have saturated all institutional levels, affecting corporate credibility and image before society (Rodríguez 2020).

Consequently, organizations have been forced to make decisions to implement socially responsible practices that could positively influence the behavior and attitudes of employees. As a result, organizational ethics have become an instrument to reduce corruption in organizations (Tafolli and Grabner-Kräuter 2020).

More specifically, the reasons for the development of organizational ethics are (Ruiz et al. 2016):

- The unethical actions of companies lead to corruption, abuse of power, scams in the banking industry, and lack of corporate responsibility, generating distrust.
- Globalization, the growth of corporate power, and the relocation of companies make laws insufficient.
- In recent years, corporate image and reputation have become a competitive advantage for companies. Companies are striving to link themselves with ethical values and to win the consumers' trust.

Figure 21.2 shows the problems arising from ethics in organizations.

(2) Ethical Leadership

The current economic situation and global market require constant updating, cooperation, collaboration, and a qualified and motivated workforce. Therefore, organizations have focused on ensuring that the competencies of directors and managers have ethical and collaborative characteristics.

The great challenge is identifying an effective leader, i.e., one who strives to obtain the maximum benefit for the organization while behaving ethically. To achieve good leadership, one must be morally (ethical) and technically sound (effective) (Ciulla 2020).

Not all leadership theory analyses mention the traits of a true leader. Some refer to behaviors that every leader must have or the different situations that make a

Fig. 21.2 Organizational ethical issues

Internal ethical problems	External ethical problems
• Discrimination and inequality • Immoral harassment or mobbing • Unfair compensation • Lack of confidentiality and privacy of information	• Truthfulness and transparency of information • Misleading advertising • Lack of environmental respect • Corruption • Poor product quality

person a leader. Nevertheless, all agree that leadership must include vision, mission, coordination, and change. At the same time, it must encourage cooperation among the different team members to achieve the proposed goals.

Rocafuerte also states that ethical leadership is similar in certain aspects to transcendent leadership. It must be based on virtues, which will entail minor but essential modifications in the concept of leadership (Rocafuerte 2016).

Among the virtues on which ethical leadership should be based are the following:

- **Prudence**: Is the virtue of moral excellence. Ethical leadership is considered a source of well-being and trust for collaborators, bringing out wisdom in decision making, the ability to face change whenever necessary, and objectively analyze the possible consequences of team actions (Hendriks et al. 2020).
- **Integrity**: This virtue gives leadership its ethical and honest quality. Honesty is essential for ethical leadership and cooperation in a team to exist. It is the quality most valued by employees, as it influences their commitment to the organization and puts moral principles before personal economic benefits derived from unethical actions (Nangoli et al. 2020).
- **Temperance**: The leaders must know how to control themselves, always keeping calm, especially in difficult moments when the team loses its calm. The leader must demonstrate strength of character, expressing concepts appropriately, and motivating his followers to achieve the established goals (Sosik et al. 2020).
- **Fortitude**: Working with a vision of the future requires leaders to be strong-minded. Leaders must be faithful to their ideas and beliefs and not change them as soon as the first obstacles appear. Fortitude is closely linked to patience and perseverance and is essential in ethical leadership and in the concept of cooperation. In a team where fortitude prevails, the problems that may arise are challenges that team members can face (Kline 2020).
- **Fairness**: A fair leader will be virtuous. If subordinates observe that the leader gives each one their due without being influenced by preferences, the leader will gain credibility, and the team members' performance will generate better results. Acting with rectitude makes the leader trustworthy and reliable in the eyes of others.
- **Tolerance**: The ethical leader is the one who recognizes the humanity in others and respects their dignity. He or she also helps the team to promote this value among themselves when conflicting opinions arise.

21.2.2 Serious Games

Games are structures that use established compulsory rules to provide entertainment opportunities. In addition to entertaining, serious games impact training by influencing the players' cognitive, emotional, and social aspects (Larson 2020), as in education.

Serious games, however, also have several other definitions. They can be video games, simulators, and microworlds that have the main objective of training rather than entertaining (Hurtado 2018). It is important to note that the adjective "serious" in this context refers to developments in military defense, education, scientific research, health care, emergency management, urban planning, engineering, religion, and politics.

Silva (2020) indicates that the main characteristic of serious games is that they are used for more than entertainment since they can increase the motivation and commitment of students in the teaching process, compared to traditional methods.

Likewise, due to the efficiency of these games for training, Calabor, Mora, and Moya consider the use of serious games important in accounting and other core subjects that incorporate competencies and strategies to improve the performance of employees in business sectors (Calabor et al. 2018). Thus, managerial games have significantly developed in recent years, rapidly becoming one of the most critical training tools at the corporate level and in the most important universities.

Lastly, serious games feature noteworthy characteristics:

- They are intended for education, training in specific skills, understanding of complex processes, and a workgroup tool for observing shortcomings or mistakes when the concepts of cooperation and collaboration are not included in the work plan (Jiménez et al. 2019).
- They link the player to reality through simulation in the virtual environment, e.g., in the game, the student assumes the role of a manager who must make difficult decisions that jeopardize the position of other collaborators (González-Acosta et al. 2020).

21.2.3 Background

The publications on the promotion of collaboration and cooperation in games are very prolific. Several works conceptually analyze the design of serious games (Buchinger and Silva Hounsell 2018) and the relationship between game type and the acquisition of competencies in the organizational environment. Examples include digital tools (Sandí 2019), business training for executives (Robles 2020), collaborative and competitive reinforcement training for employees (Sekhavat 2020), and others.

An empirical analysis of students' perception of tools used in the classroom, such as video games for teaching educational content, has been carried out in Mojena Wilce and Salcines-Talledo (2021). The findings revealed that students consider these games as a strategy that increases motivation, creativity, knowledge, cooperative learning, collaboration, and problem solving.

Additionally, a role-playing game simulating a business situation was designed for students of accounting programs (González-Acosta et al. 2020). Among the results, a correlation was found between the students' high grades and the role-playing game that incorporated the subject's content.

Similarly, the use of serious games in the business sector was analyzed to explore corporate awareness and the level of adoption of purposeful games (Amod and Roodt 2020). The results showed that corporate employees use and adopt technologies related to serious games, especially for training and e-learning, and collaborative tools and simulation tools.

21.3 Methodology

To fulfill the objective of this research, we designed a game to teach and reinforce the concepts of leadership and cooperation among students in the final semester of programs connected with administrative sciences. From this experience, we suggest that the validation stage is carried out through pilot test sessions with at least 20 students.

The research methodology used for design and development included the following steps:

- Identifying characteristics: Detailed analysis of information and identification of the main characteristics of leadership and cooperative processes in organizational environments.
- Relationships understood regarding leadership, organizational ethics, existing collaboration, and individual characteristics involved in decision making, considered in light of ethical leadership and cooperation.
- Game design: Design an educational game as a support tool to highlight individual characteristics that influence ethical leadership, cooperation and collaboration at the organizational level.

To design the game with an educational purpose, we used the ten-step methodology proposed by Gómez (2012):

(1)   Identify the theme of the game.
(2)   Establish the game's purpose.
(3)   Establish the instructional objectives of the game.
(4)   Identify and define general concepts of the subject matter.
(5)   Select candidate techniques.
(6)   Select the most appropriate technique(s) according to characterization.
(7)   Incorporate specific knowledge into the game.
(8)   Develop pilot sessions.
(9)   Consolidate the game.
(10) Develop evaluation survey.

21.4 Design the Game

The objective was to design a game to teach ethical values and the concepts of cooperation and collaboration, following the games methodology described above. The following points were defined in this methodology:

The *game objective* was to rescue the group of people stranded on the island by collecting leadership and collaboration points from each participant.

Number of players: Between 2 and 4 people.

Subject: Leadership and cooperative situations in organizational environments.

Purposes: Teaching and reinforcement.

Instructional objectives: The instructional objectives of the game were as follows:

- Recognize the importance of ethical leadership and cooperation in organizational relationships.
- Identify the participants' position in situations that require decision making related to leadership and how they collaborate with each other.
- Deliberate the influence of ethics in leadership decisions in different situations, working as a team.

After these points, the next step was to define the candidate technique. The game's keywords were established, among them: leadership, cooperation, collaboration, organizational ethics, and leadership virtues.

With this information, three techniques were selected that included all the aspects previously established. The idea of constructing Jeopardy-type quiz games, role-playing games, or monopoly-type board games resulted from this analysis.

To select the best option, we developed the characterization questions shown in Table 21.1.

The highlighted questions were the differentiating questions. Subsequently, per the calculations defined in the methodology for game design, the following results materialized (Gómez 2012):

JEOPARDY = 13/22 = 0.59

Does not meet the criterion.

MONOPOLY = 16/22 = 0.72

Meets the criterion "Chosen Technique."

Table 21.1 Characteristics

Number	Questions
1	Is the objective of the game to score the most points?
2	Do the defined dynamics allow the development of pre-planning techniques?
3	Does the game have a beginning and an end?
4	Does the game create representations and situations to define strategies?
5	Do external events depend on random situations?
6	Do players accumulate points throughout the experience?
7	Is it necessary to have losers and winners?

Table 21.2 Game material

Name	Amt.	Description
BOARD Is-LEAD	1	24-square board decorated with scenarios divided into four zones: north, south, east, and west, representing different areas of the island through which the participants advance: • 1 START Box • 5 South Zone Boxes (Green-Forest) • 5 West Zone Boxes (Red-Mountain) • 5 North Zone Boxes (Yellow-Plains) • 5 East Zone Boxes (Blue-Coast) • 3 RELAX Boxes
Dice	1	6-sided standard die, each side contains a different number from 1 to 6
Colored tokens	4	1 token of a different color is assigned to represent each participant
Laptop	1	Loaded with Is-LEAD.xls file
Instructions sheet	1	Instructions of the game

ROLE-PLAY = 18/22 = 0.81

Meets the criterion "Chosen Technique."

The formalized game idea was developed at this stage of the game design (see Table 21.2).

The next step was to validate the game through pilot sessions that allowed a survey to measure students' perceptions and evaluate possible improvements to the game.

21.5 Conclusions

Leadership and cooperation are concepts that have been studied and documented since ancient times in disciplines such as management, psychology, and economics, among others. Therefore, it was necessary to identify who had these capabilities to strengthen decision making and teamwork within the organizations.

The ethical leader must have solid virtues and values to support decisions and interactions with people. Specific values that could be lost within a crisis include justice, integrity, temperance, and tolerance, replaced by speculation, discouragement, corruption, and desire for wealth gain ground. People show their virtues when they play a game and how they would act. Importantly, they must rely on cooperation, a fundamental concept in teams and in the thinking of each individual team member.

In the organizational environment, recovering values is difficult, but the safest formula is through example, going beyond ethical codes and codes of conduct. The example becomes internalized. Leaders are not born; they are made and potentiated. Therefore, the game design must structure a way to promote the virtues of a leader, which will reflect in the work team that begins playing.

Through the practice of serious games, the necessary skills and abilities can be acquired to perform successfully in the organizational and digital environments permeating all fields of today's society with increasing intensity. In addition, the games are efficient and economical learning modalities within companies or workgroups.

The significance and impact of this study lie in a serious game design for teaching the concepts of cooperation and leadership to senior students in programs related to administrative sciences.

This study also constitutes a basis for future research for the adoption and implementation of serious games. It may be of great interest for universities and companies considering using serious games as a motivational facilitator of teaching.

21.6 Future Work

Organizations evolve due to external forces, including technology, competition, and changes in environment, among others. The leaders of the organizations are exposed to external and internal influences that affect the criteria for decision making. These are not always in the positive interest of the organization or society. When the leaders are prone to be negatively influenced, their decisions are not cooperative or efficient and gravely affect their work teams' performances.

This work is a first approach to analyzing how leaders' decisions can be influenced through a game where players reflect on the ethical choices made in real life. It is possible to build models, simulators, and other tools that allow executives to evaluate their decision-making process and the effects of these decisions, both at a personal and group level. It is also possible to assess the influences or causes experienced in the organization through the teamwork carried out and the goals achieved.

References

Abbas Ibrahim U, Mohammed S (2020) Relationship between organizational ethics and employee performance in airlines industry: evidence from Nigeria. Sci J Bus Manag 8(1):41. https://doi.org/10.11648/j.sjbm.20200801.16

Alfaro (2020) ¿La ética se gestiona? análisis y reflexión sobre las prácticas de gobierno corporativo, compliance y responsabilidad social en empresas del sector construcción. Pontificia Universidad Católica Del Perú

Amod S, Roodt S (2020) How corporates in South Africa are using serious games in business. In: Lecture notes in computer science (including subseries Lecture notes in artificial intelligence and lecture notes in bioinformatics), April 2020, vol 12066 LNCS, pp 288–298. https://doi.org/10.1007/978-3-030-44999-5_24

Brito JG (2016) La ética y los estilos de liderazgo. INNOVA Res J 1(2):41–48. https://doi.org/10.33890/innova.v1.n2.2016.11

Buchinger D, da Silva Hounsell M (2018) Guidelines for designing and using collaborative-competitive serious games. Comput Educ 118:133–149. https://doi.org/10.1016/j.compedu.2017. 11.007

Buzady Z (2017) Flow, leadership and serious games—a pedagogical perspective. World J Sci Technol Sustain Dev 14(2/3):204–217. https://doi.org/10.1108/wjstsd-05-2016-0035

Calabor MS, Mora A, Moya S (2018) Adquisición de competencias a través de juegos serios en el área contable: un análisis empírico. Rev. Contab. 21(1):38–47. https://doi.org/10.1016/J.RCSAR. 2016.11.001

Ciulla JB (2020) Ethics and effectiveness: the nature of good leadership. In: The search for ethics in leadership, business, and beyond. Springer, Cham, pp 3–32

Gómez MC (2012) Método para el Diseño de Juegos Orientados al Desarrollo de Habilidades Gerenciales. In: Método para el Diseño de Juegos Orientados al Desarrollo de Habilidades Gerenciale. Juegos gerenciales, Medellin, pp 1–20

González-Acosta E, Almeida-González M, Torres-Chils A, Traba-Montejo YM (2020) La gamificación como herramienta educativa: el estudiante de contabilidad en el rol del gerente, del contador y del auditor. Form Univ 13(5):155–164. https://doi.org/10.4067/S0718-50062020000500155

Hendriks M, Burger M, Rijsenbilt A, Pleeging E, Commandeur H (2020) Virtuous leadership: a source of employee well-being and trust. Manag Res Rev 43(8):951–970. https://doi.org/10.1108/MRR-07-2019-0326

Hurtado AJ (2018) Niveles Cognitivos de los Docentes sobre Softwares Educativos para el proceso Enseñanza-Aprendizaje Virtual en los CEBA de Gestión Pública de la Provincia de Arequipa. Arequipa 2017. Universidad Nacional de Educación

Jiménez JF, Maris S, Rodríguez GF (2019) Los videojuegos como excusa para la articulaciÃ³n entre docencia, investigaciÃ³n y extensiÃ³n. E-Tramas 4:35–45

Klaic A, Burtscher MJ, Jonas K (2020) Fostering team innovation and learning by means of team-centric transformational leadership: the role of teamwork quality. J Occup Organ Psychol 93(4):942–966. https://doi.org/10.1111/joop.12316

Kline TJB (2020) Teams that lead. Psychology Press

Korzynski P, Kozminski AK, Baczynska A, Haenlein M (2021) Bounded leadership: an empirical study of leadership competencies, constraints, and effectiveness. Eur Manag J 39(2):226–235. https://doi.org/10.1016/j.emj.2020.07.009

Larson K (2020) Serious games and gamification in the corporate training environment: a literature review. TechTrends 64(2):319–328. https://doi.org/10.1007/s11528-019-00446-7

Lupano LM, Castro A (2013) Estudios sobre el liderazgo. Teorías y evaluación. Rev. Psicodebate 6, Psicol. Cult. y Soc. 107–122

Maurer M, Cheong C, Cheong F, Gütl C (2021) C2ELT2S—a competitive, cooperative and experiential learning-based teamwork training strategy game: design and proof of concept. In: Advances in intelligent systems and computing, 26 February 2021. https://doi.org/10.1007/978-3-030-52575-0_83. Accessed 31 May 2021

Mojena Wilce Y, Salcines-Talledo I (2021) Percepciones de los estudiantes de Educación Secundaria sobre el valor educativo de los videojuegos y su diseño como estrategia pedagógica. Rev. Virtual Univ. Católica del Norte 5821(64):5–40. https://doi.org/10.35575/rvucn.n64a2

Mughal MU (2020) The impact of leadership, teamwork and employee engagement on employee performances. Saudi J Bus Manag Stud 1–12. https://doi.org/10.36348/sjbms.2020.v05i03.008.

Nangoli S et al (2020) Perceived leadership integrity and organizational commitment. J Manag Dev 39(6):823–834. https://doi.org/10.1108/JMD-02-2019-0047

Pliscoff C, Lagos N (2021) Efecto de las capacitaciones en la reflexión sobre ética y corrupción. Rev. Adm. Pública 1–27. Accessed 28 May 2021. [Online]. Available http://bibliotecadigital.fgv. br/ojs/index.php/rap/article/view/83103.

Robles E (2020) Implementación de un modelo de gamificación para mejorar la capacitación comercial de ejecutivos de una entidad financiera peruana. Universidad Peruana de Ciencias Aplicadas (UPC)

Rocafuerte DE (2016) El liderazgo transformacional: una aproximación conceptual. Universidad Espíritu Santo Ecuador

Rodríguez LM (2020) El binomio política–corrupción en América Latina. Rev. Derecho electroal 20:157–175. Luis Mario Rodríguez Rodríguez** https://doi.org/10.35242/RDE_2020_29_9

Romero-Rodriguez LM, Castillo-Abdul B (2019) Comunicación para la motivación. Claves de la asertividad y del trabajo en equipo en las organizaciones. In: Happiness management and creativity in the XXI century. Intangible capitals as a source of innovation, comptetitiveness and sustainable development, pp 41–53

Ruiz E, Gago ML, García C, López S (2016) Recursos humanos y responsabilidad social corporativa. McGraw Hill, Madrid, España

Samimi M, Cortes AF, Anderson MH, Herrmann P (2020) What is strategic leadership? Developing a framework for future research. Leadersh Q 1–22. https://doi.org/10.1016/j.leaqua.2019.101353

Sandí JC (2019) Desarrollo de competencias digitales en el profesorado a través de juegos serios: un estudio de caso aplicado en la Universidad de Costa Rica (UCR). e-Ciencias la Inf 10(2):1–29. Accessed 4 January 2021. [Online]. Available https://www.scielo.sa.cr/pdf/eci/v10n2/1659-4142-eci-10-02-046.pdf

Sekhavat YA (2020) Collaboration or battle between minds? An attention training game through collaborative and competitive reinforcement. Entertain Comput 34:100360. https://doi.org/10.1016/j.entcom.2020.100360

Serrano BJ, Portalanza A (2014) Influencia del liderazgo sobre el clima organizacional. Suma Negocios 5(11):117–125. https://doi.org/10.1016/s2215-910x(14)70026-6

Silva FGM (2020) Practical methodology for the design of educational serious games. Information (Switzerland) 11(1):14. https://doi.org/10.3390/info11010014

Sosik JJ, Chun JU, Ete Z (2020) Character and leadership. In: The Wiley encyclopedia of personality and individual differences. Wiley, pp 505–510

Tafolli F, Grabner-Kräuter S (2020) Employee perceptions of corporate social responsibility and organizational corruption: empirical evidence from Kosovo. Corp Gov 20(7):1349–1370. https://doi.org/10.1108/CG-07-2020-0274

Chapter 22
Open Innovation Laboratory to Foster Skills and Competencies in Higher Education

Daniel Cortés, José Ramírez, and Arturo Molina

22.1 Introduction

Today's society is undergoing constant shifts at various social, economic and environmental levels. Price Waterhouse Coopers, in a study entitled "The World in 2050," stated that by the middle of the twenty-first century, there would be significant changes in the so-called emerging nations (E7) as they achieve better social and financial conditions (Hawksworth and Chan 2015; Boiardi et al. 2013). The paradigm shift in the global economic balance will increase the consumption of goods and services. Promoting economic development in the different productive sectors will be necessary by creating innovative tools, models, and structures that meet the growing population's needs (Mauricio-Moreno et al. 2015). This increased integration will allow all sectors to benefit from the accelerated evolution of technology, driven primarily by increased computational power, such as artificial intelligence, robotics, data analytics, cloud computing and the internet of things. The growing adoption of technologies, mainly in industry, makes it possible to reinvent, redesign, and integrate models that have led to a crucial evolution in manufacturing processes called Industry 4.0 (Drath and Horch 2014). There are numerous paths to integration in the medium and long term. Higher education institutions must integrate their programs with industries' technologies, tools, and objectives to achieve this necessary transformation in the academic field. The productive sectors are constantly evolving and require professionals to address current problems and future challenges through

D. Cortés · J. Ramírez · A. Molina (✉)
School of Engineering and Sciences, Tecnologico de Monterrey, Mexico City, Mexico
e-mail: armolina@tec.mx

D. Cortés
e-mail: a01655708@itesm.mx

J. Ramírez
e-mail: a00995924@itesm.mx

specific skills and competencies, enabling them to propose innovative solutions that disrupt current paradigms.

Education also is undergoing a profound revolution as coming generations of professionals adopt new learning techniques to cope with the transformation of industry and services (Mourtzis et al. 2018). Thus, there is a continued effort by schools worldwide to transform their curricula to develop the skills and competencies demanded of graduating students by the labour market (Martin et al. 2011). This radical transformation in learning, Education 4.0, is the first giant leap from traditional education in decades. Integration is a fundamental part of this transformation; the various productive sectors and governments have developed different initiatives with educational institutions to generate models and projects that benefit both parties. This two-way collaboration is a fundamental pillar of the growing adoption of the Open Innovation (OI) culture. In this regard, this work describes the approach taken by Tecnologico de Monterrey to lead educational transformation through its Open Innovation Laboratory.

This work is structured as follows. Section 22.2 briefly explores the concept of Education 4.0 and how advances in technology applied to industry impact future professionals. Section 22.3 is about Open Innovation Laboratories (OIL) from the academic perspective and its structure to boost scholars' skills and competencies. Section 22.4 details how OIL at Tecnologico de Monterrey is a learning environment to foster experiences in Education 4.0 and Open Innovation. Last but not least, Sect. 22.5 elaborates on three OIL case studies that illustrate a real-life deployment of the concept at Tecnologico de Monterrey.

22.2 Education 4.0 Overview

Education 4.0 has multiple definitions. One of them explores this concept as the adoption of novel methodologies and cutting-edge instructional spaces that completely alter the paradigm of traditional education. This notion fosters better development of hard skills and further refining of soft skills (Aziz Hussin 2018). On the one hand, there is intense research covering that covers the skills needed in college students; on the other hand, there are different methodologies and learning techniques to develop them. The industry's transformation has given way to defining the specific skillset to be promoted in the third decade of the twenty-first century (Şahin 2009). However, these defined workforce skills will change as new technologies are integrated.

Thus, it is essential to note that various organizations, such as the 2016 World Economic Forum, have made great efforts to publicize the industrial trends in skills and competencies for this decade (Forum 2016). Their survey collected data from over ten million people and dozens of corporations. The findings demonstrate the growing need to develop soft skills as technology reduces the need to perform repetitive, highly technical tasks. Higher education institutions are aware of these trends and seek to train students to meet the expectations demanded by modern industry. Modern learning models will strengthen the technologies, methodologies and tools that facilitate the integral development of students. Some of these allow customizing teaching to accommodate students' different learning styles. Active-based learning and problem-based learning are strategies that leverage the main features of new educational methodologies and spaces.

This paradigm shift has significantly improved compared to traditional areas for developing skills and competencies. Communication software through broadband internet has enabled continuous and flexible education. Thanks to these tools, many physical classrooms have been exchanged for virtual spaces that allow the students and teachers to be in ubiquitous remote classes and courses. These make it possible to reach worldwide audiences with online platforms such as massive online open courses (MOOC). As a critical strategy (West et al. 2008), Open Innovation also takes advantage of the new trends in education to provide an environment of participation among different entities (government, industry and academia), thus allowing the development of the skills required by students.

22.3 Open Innovation Laboratory

Open Innovation is a powerful concept, contributing to the flow of knowledge among entities; hence, ideas can come equally from internal or external actors participating in the same project with different perspectives on the same development (Faems 2008). Higher education institutions have played an increasingly important role and work closely with Industry to create new research agendas. However, this collaboration falls flat if no infrastructure and framework are provided. In this regard, academic institutions have created collaboration hubs where facilities, technologies, innovative tools, and experts from academia and industry come together in spaces known as Open Innovation Laboratories (OIL). These provide the infrastructure to raise, shape and integrate ideas, offering a unified approach to design, development, testing and launching.

Due to the complexity and technological resources required for complex projects, OIL provides a cost-effective solution compared to the performance of a single entity: Development times and costs are reduced, and implementations have higher success rates. Compatible with technological parks worldwide, OIL aims to establish collaboration to solve novel societal challenges, exploit market niches in short periods, and develop applied research with industry participation. OIL improves student competencies by enriching their knowledge in a daring environment where attitude, skills, knowledge and participation are boosted through Challenge-Based learning and Project-Based learning. Thus, for academia and research institutions, three pillars sustain the collaboration and deployment projects with third parties: (i) Learning Methods and Techniques, (ii) Design Methodologies, and (iii) Rapid Product Realization Platforms (see Fig. 22.1).

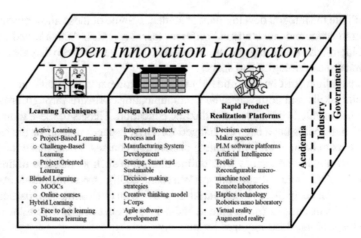

Fig. 22.1 Open Innovation Laboratory. Schematic representation of participating entities and the three OIL pillars

22.3.1 Learning Techniques

Learning techniques are a series of practices to improve the profile and competencies of scholars. Among the learning techniques found in the literature, active learning improves the most desired competencies in 21st-century scholars (Chesbrough 2003). Multidisciplinary teams, knowledge, and hard and soft skills are necessary to develop innovative solutions to real-life problems and challenges. Also, developing individual competencies, blended and hybrid learning aim to enhance skills previously acquired, allowing students to learn about external topics and implement solutions through the project. When developing projects using the OIL infrastructure, participants have improved at least the following competencies: communication, critical thinking, creativity and innovation, collaboration, and cooperation. They provide the foundation to deal with real-life problems requiring commitment, active participation, communication, information sharing, innovative solutions and multidisciplinary teams to attain a feasible solution. Emerging technologies support and enrich learning techniques (Moirano et al. 2020). Notwithstanding, the implementation of OIL requires that participants understand and follow these principles: (i) comprehend the central problem and goal of the project, (ii) communicate, share, and contribute interactively to elevate the understanding of the group and (iii) voluntarily participate, to arrive at a faster, better, and more structured solution.

22.3.2 Design Methodologies

During project development, the series of steps and structure determine the solution's perspective, activities, tools and assessment. The project's multidisciplinary and complex nature allows participants to uncover new necessities during the development, resulting in multiple solutions requiring additional resources. Wandering is undesirable; thus, to prevent deviations, it is necessary to identify the structure that allows the idea to move from the beginning of the project and guides it to implementation. In this infrastructure are the design methodologies. Their purpose is to provide the actions to be followed during the endeavor, with recommended activities, toolboxes, and tollgates defining a roadmap and setting the project's duration. The general structure of the methodology should encourage participants to explore opportunities (divergence), analyze options (synthesis), and materialize solutions (convergence). There are multiple methodologies for project fulfillment, such as standardization, industry best practices, and literature review to analyze the setbacks that preceded research groups. Therefore, during the beginning of the project, participants must define the approach to document the problem and reach a solution within the defined budget.

22.3.3 Rapid Product Realization Platforms

These tools stand as the backbone of the OIL. They include a blend of hardware and software from both emerging and traditional technologies and approaches. They promote participant collaboration and supporting the innovation process during the project. The platforms rely on involved parties' application, transmission, and training to exploit the resources for design, manufacturing, testing, simulating, and evaluating proposed solutions. The synergy of learning techniques and methodologies occurs in this pillar, coming together in a physical space to shape ideas. Rapid product realization platforms include (i) laboratories, (ii) machinery and equipment, and (iii) facilities.

Laboratories include a wide variety of spaces, physical and virtual laboratories to test CAD, CAM, CAE, PLM, and ergonomics technologies. Other activities involve computer sciences, include data analysis, programming, cloud analysis, and social media analysis. There are science laboratories for physical, chemical, thermodynamics and mechanical testing; creative spaces for arts, audio, photography and video production; and electronics labs for PCB design, electrical analysis and test benches. According to the project's necessities, multiple laboratories accommodate needs, which could vary during the implementation.

Machinery and equipment support a wide variety of processes. They consist of basic and advanced manufacturing techniques and include traditional, and Computer Numerical Control centers for large-scale or precision volumes. Also, there are additive processes, such as sintering and 3D printers; and subtractive processes to execute lathe, milling, and drilling; and transformative processes for trimming, shaping, marking, etching, soldering, melting, painting, and sanding.

Facilities correspond to physical spaces where participants interact. Decision theatres, video conference rooms, and Gesell chambers, among others, are used for interactive purposes. However, implementing of ICTs has allowed innovative spaces that thrive in digital domains and can be ubiquitously accessed remotely. Virtual facilities allow participants to share ideas in real-time to shape design and execution strategies. Both physical and virtual environments aim to increase the collaboration and cooperation of participants; thus, OIL relies upon these spaces to increase productivity during project development, but above all, to foster competencies and skills in scholars.

22.4   Open Innovation Laboratory Deployment

OILs turn to the three pillars to develop joint projects with internal and external entities working for a common agenda. There are no rigid guidelines on what an OIL should include. Each project aims to be multidisciplinary, with flexible timetables in different areas and different purposes depending on the interested parties. In this combined effort, academic institutions align traditional courses to fit challenges, projects, or case studies. While institutions have dedicated laboratories or specialized departments, it is still necessary to establish a collaborative process because OIL spaces (third pillar) require availability and accessibility for external actors to participate. Thus, to show an OIL, it is paramount to define: (i) adequate workspaces, (ii) laboratories' capabilities, processes' definition with a directory of available technologies in defined spaces, and (iii) design methodologies to align efforts.

OIL deployment at Tecnologico de Monterrey derives from an initiative to provide laboratories for students, industry, and government to create projects in the same space. Nevertheless, the backbone of the projects comes from design methodologies (second pillar) that focus on developing products, processes, manufacturing systems, promotion, and marketing. A commonly used method brings together efforts for rapid product development (represented at the top of Fig. 22.2): The Product Path Development (PPD) has four colour stages: (i) ideation, (ii) conceptual design, (iii) detailed design, and (iv) prototyping. It includes three sub-paths that parallel the progress for mechanics, electronics, and the informatics system. It also considers the underlying impact of S3 (Sensing, Smart and Sustainable) characteristics on defining a viable product according to current social, technological and environmental trends. Each activity is carried out using OIL physical spaces located at the CEDETEC building on the campus. At the bottom of Fig. 22.2, a brief schematic represents the location of some physical laboratories for the PPD.

The above resources aim to develop integrated learning techniques (first pillar) to boost skills and competencies, thus completing the desired professional profile of students. The three main reasons for constructing and implementing this OIL from

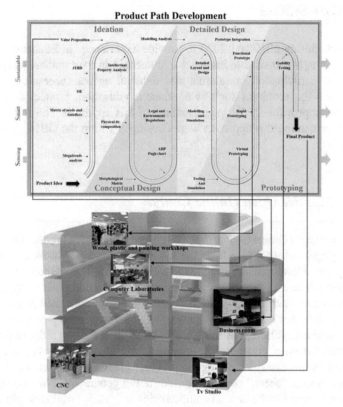

Fig. 22.2 Tecnologico de Monterrey's OIL. Methodology for product development carried out at CEDETEC building

the academic viewpoint will be summarized in the following aspects. (i) Promote desirable skills among digital native collaborators. In Tecnologico de Monterrey's OIL, the skills presented in section three that correspond to relevant competencies for the twenty-first century professional are promoted. (ii) Improve the learning experience. Due to the dynamics involved in working on projects, students develop capacities and abilities that traditional techniques do not offer. OIL's infrastructure broadens the students' vision to propose solutions to current real problems and positively impacts their professional training. (iii) Consolidate knowledge. The lecturer is a facilitator as massive amounts of information are broadly available in various sources. OIL encourages students to play an active role with available resources to seek and deepen practical solutions through collaborative and multidisciplinary projects.

22.5 Case Studies

Joint efforts during 2019 and 2020 to provide experiences in Education 4.0 environments brought remarkable instances documented in case studies, where collaboration and participation of internal and external agents successfully deployed attended real-life problems such as continuous education, product development, and lecture improvement. Taking advantage of this approach. The following case studies documenting this approach were developed within the OIL at Tecnologico de Monterrey.

22.5.1 Massive Open Online Course

The Massive Open Online Course (MOOC) "Rapid Innovative Product Development for Emerging Markets" arose from the Integrated Product, Process and Manufacturing System Development reference framework, a design methodology that has been applied in face-to-face courses. It belongs to the second pillar of the OIL. This MOOC introduces participants to the design methodology and drives them to develop innovative ideas that materialize quickly following a structured procedure.

The course uses different learning techniques within the first pillar of the OIL by encouraging the users' creativity and guiding them with descriptive videos and documents with the necessary knowledge to progress gradually. The proposed activities are graded among "peers," possibly from different geographical locations, encouraging them to develop the desired competencies and receive multidisciplinary feedback. The MOOC is held in eight weeks. Through specific tasks and weekly exercises, students advance through the three phases of developing the product: imagination, conceptualization, and design. This course has a nontechnical approach to encourage the adoption of its principles among different persons with variety of geographic locations, areas of study, ages, among others. The course has had an excellent reception in the Latin American community; most users come from Mexico, Colombia and Peru. Nearly twenty thousand students have enrolled since its launch in 2016, and course statistics have quite favourable ratings, 4.6 out of 5 stars. Comments are primarily positive and are considered by the designers to improve students' experience in the future.

22.5.2 Integrated Manufacturing System Course

The Integrated Manufacturing Systems Course (IMS) is offered to undergraduate sixth-semester students in the Industrial Engineering major at Tecnologico de Monterrey, Mexico City campus. It has a duration of four months in a three-hour scheme per week. In a physical course, students attend the classroom to share information, sources, and techniques provided by the lecturer. The method has been adapted as a Challenge-Based Learning course; therefore, a final project is required for the final grade, demanding five extra hours of individual active learning per week. IMS uses the OIL third pillar to shape proposed ideas into physical prototypes. Tollgates (delivery points) are defined along the course, and students are responsible for their coordination; thus, collaboration is needed to accomplish all activities on time.

In the end, documentation on the four stages of the IMS is delivered. These are Stage one: generate ideas considering manufactured articles available in the market. The product and information model, as well as product attributes, are developed with engineering tools. Stage two: identify necessary manufacturing processes for their products considering the material properties such as roughness, volume, finishing, tolerances, and shape. Schematize an optimal process path showing suppliers, manufacturing cycles, and availability for a given time of production. Stage three: Simulate and optimize the system's operation, considering all resources needed, using plant design software, and including machines and processes times to distribute their facility. Stage four: Conceptualize the enterprise to define the best strategy for proposing a business model to commercialize the products. Expected learning outcomes are developing competencies such as critical thinking, collaborative work, problem-solving and increased active learning. Also, according to the ABET accreditation program focused on students' competencies, expected outcomes include a global vision, leadership, and entrepreneurial spirit within the OIL ecosystem.

22.5.3 Summer Research Stays

Summer research "boot camp" stays are held each year at the Tecnologico de Monterrey between June and August. Public and private institutions participate in collaborative exchange research projects as part of Open Innovation initiatives. Students involved belong to the last semesters of an undergraduate program and come from different formation areas; thus, the participants form a multidisciplinary group. These boot camps are held in the OIL and take advantage of the design methodologies, facilities, and technologies. Hence, participants are challenged for seven weeks to create a product. This methodology integrates the participants' knowledge to elaborate the product, process, manufacturing system, and business model. Participants use spaces and tools to generate the ideas, basic design, detailed design, and functional product prototypes.

It is an intensive stay; other OIL instances boost students' performance, such as the MOOC from the first case study, which provides the necessary insight into the product design. The result is knowledge of how a product is developed when participants enter their stay. The course design has proven high success rates, appropriately adapting to different engineering areas such as mechanical, electrical, electronics, mechatronics, industrial, and textile, to mention a few.

Even if participants start with a vague idea of the product to develop, the intensive course and methodology encourage them to solve existing societal problems. For example, "Attachable garments" arose during the 2018 summer as a product that came from collaborating participants in Textile, Industrial, Mechatronics and Industrial Chemical Engineering. The project contributed to supplying garments in developing countries to people with scarce resources. A wide variety of solutions were studied, and finally, the production of clothing products assembled by end-users was chosen, thus reducing costs without losing sight of the product utility and resistance. It was created using rapid product realization platforms (third pillar) such as reconfigurable micromachines as a prototyping tool. The attachable garments project developed the processes, manufacturing system, and business model aiming for viable commercialization. This OIL instance generated a change of thinking among the participants. In their words: "This project provided the tools, steps, and guidance through engineering, process and economic analysis to develop and launch products."

22.6   Findings and Conclusions

This work presents the OIL's schematic approach and delves into the methodology deployed at Tecnologico de Monterrey. It presents three cases, referring to the implementation of the concepts raised in practical projects developed inside the institution and involving the participation of internal and external actors. The participants' skills development and knowledge reinforcement in various periods and contexts were observed using the OIL ecosystem. Improvement in at least the following competencies was observed: collaboration, cooperation, critical thinking, communication, creativity, and innovation. Design methodologies play a fundamental role in how projects are structured, while learning strategies motivated students to take advantage of available resources for project development. Finally, technologies, laboratories, and spaces promoted interaction, testing, and development of innovative projects.

OIL deployment in higher education has positively impacted how students perceive knowledge, interact and develop practical skills to fulfil projects in conjunction with the industrial sector. In this way, not only does knowledge become practical and prevail for a longer time, but prompt interaction with the industrial sector promotes exchange and understanding of needs in both directions. Future work will focus on an OIL's achievement and learning measurement.

Acknowledgements   The authors would like to acknowledge the technical support of the Writing Lab, Institute for the Future of Education, Tecnologico de Monterrey, Mexico, in the production of this work.

Also, the students who attended DELFIN XXIII from other university campuses in Mexico, students at Tecnologico de Monterrey from ISE class 20201.

References

Aziz Hussin A (2018) Education 4.0 made simple: ideas for teaching. Int J Educ Lit Stud 6(3)

Boiardi P, Hehenberger L, Gianoncelli A (2014) European Venture Philanthropy and Social Investment 2013/2014 The EVPA Survey

Chesbrough HW (2003) Open innovation: the new imperative for creating and profiting from technology. Harvard Business Press

Drath R, Horch A (2014) Industrie 4.0: Hit or Hype? [Industry Forum]. Ind Electron Mag 8:56–58. IEEE

Faems D (2008) In: Chesbrough H, Vanhaverbeke W, West J (eds) Open innovation: researching a new paradigm. Creat Innov Manag 17(4):334–335

Forum WE (2016) The future of jobs: employment, skills and workforce strategy for the fourth industrial revolution. Global Challenge Insight Report. World Economic Forum Geneva

Hawksworth J, Chan D (2015) The world in 2050: will the shift in global economic power continue?

Martin S, Diaz G, Sancristobal E, Gil R, Castro M, Peire J (2011) New technology trends in education: seven years of forecasts and convergence. Comput Educ 57(3):1893–1906

Mauricio-Moreno H, Miranda J, Chavarría D, Ramírez-Cadena M, Molina A (2015) Design S3RF (Sustainable × Smart × Sensing-Reference Framework) for the future manufacturing enterprise. IFACPapersOnLine 48(3):58–63

Moirano R, Sánchez MA, Štěpánek L (2020) Creative interdisciplinary collaboration: a systematic literature review. Think Ski Creat 35:100626

Mourtzis D, Vlachou E, Dimitrakopoulos G, Zogopoulos V (2018) Cyber-physical systems and education 4.0—the teaching factory 4.0 concept. Procedia Manuf 23:129–134

Şahin M (2009) Instructional design principles for 21st-century learning skills. Procedia Soc Behav Sci 1:1464–1468

West J, Vanhaverbeke W, Chesbrough H (2008) Open Innovation: a research agenda. 285–307

Chapter 23
Assessment for Learning in a Virtual Computer Science Course

Lorenza Illanes Díaz Rivera and Roberto Retes Rodríguez

23.1 Introduction

Assessment is undoubtedly a crucial aspect of the learning process, and there are several practical approaches. Assessment for learning delves into learning capabilities and the appropriate steps to promote it; it is oriented toward dynamic teaching and learning processes. Learning assessment shows what has already been achieved and assimilated in an overview of the actual situation. Feedback guides students towards their academic goals and, over time, clarifies the goals (Sadler 1989; Caceres Mesa and Suarez Monzon 2021; Jimenez-Garcia et al. 2020). Thus, our research investigated whether learning assessment (Gibbs and Simpson 2005; Popescu 2019) with feedback (Nicol and Macfarlane-Dick 2006; Suhendi et al. 2018) improved student achievement in a Java Computing course.

To describe this research, we have divided this paper into the following sections: the introduction, the development of the research consisting of: the theoretical framework that supported the study, the problem statement, the method used to carry out the experimentation, the results obtained and its analysis, and the discussion of the research. Finally, we present the research conclusions and the references.

L. I. . Díaz Rivera (✉)
Intelligent System Center, Tecnologico de Monterrey, Monterrey, México
e-mail: l_illanes@tec.mx

R. . Retes Rodríguez
Department International Degrees, Universidad Peruana de Ciencias Aplicadas, Lima, Perú
e-mail: pcmarret@upc.edu.pe

© The Author(s), under exclusive license to Springer Nature Singapore Pte Ltd. 2022   293
S. Hosseini et al. (eds.), *Technology-Enabled Innovations in Education*,
Transactions on Computer Systems and Networks,
https://doi.org/10.1007/978-981-19-3383-7_23

23.2 Development

To investigate assessment for learning in a virtual computer science course, we developed a theoretical framework to support our constructs: an assessment for learning, feedback, and the problem situations of the activities and evidence. We determined the problem to be investigated: What kinds of assessments for learning supported by feedback lead to higher student academic performance? We constructed rubrics for each activity to determine these assessments, allowing moving to the experimentation stage to test which feedback-supported assessments of learning yield the best academic performance. Students received feedback on the 13 activities and the three pieces of evidence analyzed; the results are presented in the sections below. We begin with the theoretical framework supporting this research.

23.2.1 Theoretical Framework

There are many definitions of educational evaluation (Leyva 2010; Maccario 1989; Maquillón and Alonso 2014). Reviewing them highlights three crucial elements of the evaluation process: collecting information, forming value judgments, and decision-making. What dominates the objectives of evaluations is the assessment of learning (Shepard 2000). Gibbs, Graham and Simpson (2005) and Popescu (2019) attempt to justify a set of conditions under which assessments support learning. Educators can examine and improve teaching practices by using assessments to monitor and promote individual learning (Shepard 2000, Sudewa 2020). Moreover, feedback can provide information about the outcome of an activity or process (Lara Sierra 2006; Chagas 2016). As Mogollón (2007) and Alvarado et al. (2016) point out, continuous descriptive communication provides students with information about their progress in the teaching–learning process.

Seven principles of good feedback practice are distinguished by Nicol and Macfarlane-Dick (2006) and Suhendi et al. (2018). Assessment in higher education is commonly undertaken to contribute to student feedback and certification of student achievement. This approach should be balanced over the long term for learning-oriented assessment that fosters future learning (Boud and Falchikov 2006; Jin 2016). The benefit of lifelong learning in higher education has been recognized through the focus on learning outcomes (Hussey and Smith 2010; Mazo et al. 2018) and skills development (Sudewa 2020; Stephenson and Yorke 1998). In the long term, lifelong learning has shown the value of using assessment to learn and not just to verify what has been learned (Moreno 2012; Barreira et al. 2017). Preparing students for lifelong learning involves training them to make complex judgements about their own and others' work and make decisions under uncertainty, which they will experience in the future (Boud and Falchikov 2006; Jin 2016). Other conditions are required to ensure that assessment benefits learning (Jin 2016; Fernández 2009). Virtual assessments generate several advantages for learners (Alvarado et al. 2016;

Graff 2003). They are available at any time. The main characteristic of valuable assessment for learning is that students view it as a real help in more and better learning while at the same time developing positive expectations. On the other hand, many of the deficiencies identified in university courses are related to assessment practices (Boud and Falchikov 2006; Jin 2016). The research problem is set out below.

23.2.2 Problem Statement

This study investigated whether assessment for learning supported by feedback benefits students' academic performance in an online computer science course. With this intention, the impact of feedback in higher education through formative activities was measured, and the positive impact on students' self-regulation was identified. Consequently, this paper has the specific objective of examining whether assessment for learning through continuous feedback on activities can improve students' academic outcomes. This research arises from the desire to improve student achievement of the subject of Computing in Java. Thirteen evaluation rubrics were created as part of the feedback, leaving room for comments within the spaces of the rubric. Instructors provided general feedback on their work, including screenshots of the processes. Once the rubrics were created, it was necessary to know if they led to better student learning by allowing them to correct their activities throughout the course. Below, we describe the appropriate methodology to establish the levels achieved by the students and analyze the results obtained.

23.2.3 Method

The research method was mixed, i.e. having both qualitative and quantitative analyses. The online course analyzed was a professional-level JAVA Computing course consisting of 13 activities and evidence consisting of three exams. We investigated whether assessment for learning (Gibbs and Simpson 2005; Popescu 2019) through feedback (Nicol and Macfarlane-Dick 2006; Suhendi et al. 2018) improves student achievement throughout the semester of January to May 2018. Students in four courses participated in this research: one semester and three tetra-monthly (quarterly) courses. Table 23.1 presents the sample.

Throughout the semester and quarterly courses, instructors provided feedback on all the activities submitted by the students. They were allowed to correct errors and resubmit the activity, revising as many times as necessary to obtain a 100 grade. The students had a timetable for the course topics, activity deliveries, progress evidence, and final evidence. The course is a cumulative knowledge course, so the difficulty increases. Given that programming is an active learning exercise (Becker 1997) using trial and error, this course is appropriate to apply assessment for learning. In

Table 23.1 Sample for the quantitative and qualitative research

Courses	Quantitative research	Qualitative research
Semester course	14 students	3 students
Tetra-monthly course	13 students	
Summer course		3 students

this research, we wanted to expose the results obtained by applying assessment for learning (Gibbs and Simpson 2005; Popescu 2019) supported by feedback (Nicol and Macfarlane-Dick 2006) and measure the impact on the students' learning.

23.2.4 Findings

To fulfill the research objective, we captured assessment data (see examples in Tables 23.5 and 23.6) for each activity delivered (feedback had been provided). Once this data had been captured, we purified the file by removing the students who had dropped the course for various reasons. Subsequently, the frequency of feedback per activity and evidence per student was obtained for the semester course (Table 23.2) and the quarterly courses (Table 23.3).

In the semester course frequencies table, it can be seen that the maximum feedback used by students is four, with the mode being one feedback.

Once we had the feedback frequencies, it was interesting to know if the assessment for learning with feedback improved student achievement. Each student's assessment by activity and evidence was obtained for their original and final assessments for the semester class (Fig. 23.1) and the tetra-monthly classes (Fig. 23.2).

Table 23.2 Frequency of feedback by activities and evidence of a semester course

No		1	2	3	4	5	6	7	8	9	10	11	12	13	EV1	EV2	EVTOT	Total
								Curso Tetramestral										
1	A	1	1	1	3	3	4	2	2	2	3	3	0	0	2	2	0	29
2	A	1	1	5	5	2	2	2	2	2	2	2	2	2	2	2	3	42
3	A	2	2	3	2	2	2	2	2	2	7	7	3	3	3	2	0	44
4	A	3	3	1	3	3	2	2	2	2	2	2	1	1	1	1	1	30
5	A	2	2	2	4	4	2	2	2	2	11	11	5	5	1	1	4	60
6	A	1	1	4	2	2	3	3	3	3	2	2	6	6	1	0	0	39
7	A	1	1	2	5	5	3	3	3	3	3	3	2	2	3	2	1	42
8	A	2	2	1	5	5	3	3	3	3	5	5	3	3	2	4	2	51
9	A	2	2	3	3	3	3	3	3	3	2	2	1	1	3	2	4	40
10	A	1	1	2	2	2	1	1	1	1	2	2	2	2	2	2	0	24
11	A	1	1	4	2	2	1	1	1	1	0	0	1	1	1	0	0	17
12	A	1	1	3	2	2	2	2	2	2	4	4	2	2	1	1	1	32
13	A	1	1	1	3	3	0	0	0	0	1	1	0	0	3	1	0	15
		1	2	3	4	5	6	7	8	9	10	11	12	13	EV1	EV2	EVTOT	Total
0		0	0	0	0	0	1	1	1	1	1	1	2	2	0	2	6	18
1		8	8	4	0	0	2	2	2	2	1	1	3	3	5	4	3	48
2		4	4	3	5	5	5	6	6	6	5	5	4	4	4	6	1	73
3		1	1	3	4	4	4	4	4	4	2	2	2	2	4	0	1	42
4		0	0	2	1	1	1	0	0	0	1	1	0	0	0	1	2	10
		0	0	1	3	3	0	0	0	0	3	3	2	2	0	0	0	17

Table 23.3 Frequency of feedback by activities and evidence of a tetra-monthly course

No	AC	1	2	3	4	5	6	7	8	9	10	11	12	13	EV1	EV2	EVTOT	Total
1	A	1	1	2	2	1	1	3	2	2	2	1	1	1	1	1	0	22
2	A	1	1	2		1		1	1	1	1	0	0	0	1	1	0	13
3	A	1	1	1	1	1	1	0	1	0	0	0	1	0	1	1	0	10
4	A	1	2	1	2	3	4	2	2	4	1	3	3	1	1	4	1	35
5	A	1	1	1	1	1	1	3	1	1	0	0	0	0	1	1	0	13
6	A	1	2	3	1	2	2	2	3	3	2	3	2	1	1	1	2	31
7	A	1	1	2	2	2	3	3	1	1	0	2	1	1	0	2	0	22
8	A	1	1	1	1	1	1	3	0	1	0	0	0	0	1	1	0	12
9	A	1	2	1	1	2	2	1	1	1	1	2	1	1	1	1	2	21
10	A	2	1	1	1	1	2	1	2	2	2	1	1	1	1	1	1	21
11	A	1	1	1	1	1	0	1	1	1	1	0	1	1	1	1	1	14
12	A	1	1	1	1	1	1	1	3	0	1	1	3	1	2	1	1	1	20
13	A	1	1	1	2	2	3	1	2	2	2	1	1	1	2	2	1	25
14	A	1	1	0	1	1	1	0	1	2	2	1	1	1	1	2	0	16
	AC	1	2	3	4	5	6	7	8	9	10	11	12	13	EV1	EV2	EVTOT	Total
	0	0	0	1	0	0	2	1	3	1	4	4	4	3	1	0	7	31
	1	13	11	9	10	9	8	6	6	7	6	5	8	10	12	10	9	139
	2	1	3	3	4	4	3	2	4	4	5	2	1	1	1	2	2	42
	3	0	0	1		1	1	5	1	1	0	3	1	0	0	0	0	14
	4	0	0	0	0	0	0	1	0	0	1	0	0	0	0	1	0	3

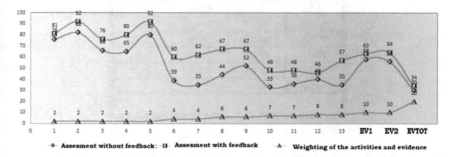

Fig. 23.1 Evaluation of activities and evidence with and without feedback in the semester course

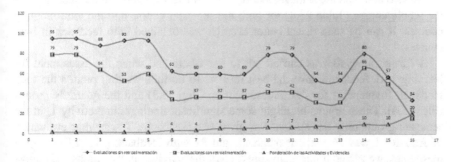

Fig. 23.2 Evaluation of activities and evidence with and without feedback in the tetra-monthly courses

With this, we could determine how much use was made of each activity with and without feedback on average. It can be seen that feedback was used more by the tetra-monthly students than the semester students. In both groups, feedback was

Table 23.4 Student achievement during the semester and quarterly courses with or without feedback

Semester Course		Tetra-monthly courses	
33.43	50.27	33.16	42.88
39.1	40.62	61.24	69.62
26.33	26.53	23.82	61.98
63.57	84.81	61.88	71.92
39.42	39.42	29.12	77.2
50	76.58	36.6	60.44
35.31	40.24	55.26	87.5
27.78	30.58	47.94	79.12
69.94	75.6	43.86	73.92
57.48	70.26	39.36	40.4
37.48	37.48	25.08	26.1
68.31	81.63	63.54	73.98
68.16	89.84	23.8	35.7
28.3	36.3		

used more in the initial and intermediate activities than in the final ones (Figs. 23.1 and 23.2).

We also obtained the achievement of each student with and without feedback for the whole course (Table 23.4) for both the semester course and the tetra-monthly courses. It can be seen that a better average was obtained with feedback in both courses.

A further analysis was carried out to see where and when the assessment for learning with feedback gave the best results. To do this, we first plotted the total feedback frequencies for the semester group (Fig. 23.3) and the quarterly groups (Fig. 23.4). These graphs highlight some significant findings. In Activity 1, in the semester group, only one student was given two feedbacks. The average evaluation of Activity 1 was 76 without feedback and 81 with feedback (Fig. 23.1). Along these lines, we can continue analyzing each of the activities in the graphs and realize that the students did not leverage the feedback as they should have. Therefore, we decided to make a graphical analysis of students' feedback frequencies in the semester (Fig. 23.5) and quarterly (Fig. 23.6) programs.

Examining these two graphs (Figs. 23.5 and 23.6), we see that the semester course students used feedback about half as often as the tetra-monthly students. Does this have something to do with maturity? The tetra-monthly students were working people, older in general than the semester students and all their courses were online.

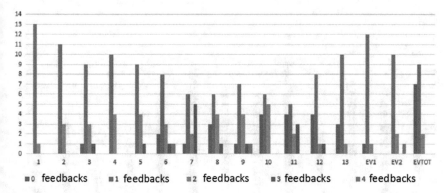

Fig. 23.3 Frequency of feedback by activity and evidence for a semester course

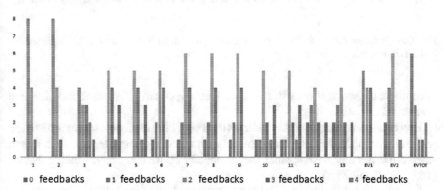

Fig. 23.4 Frequency of feedback by activity and evidence for a tetra-monthly course

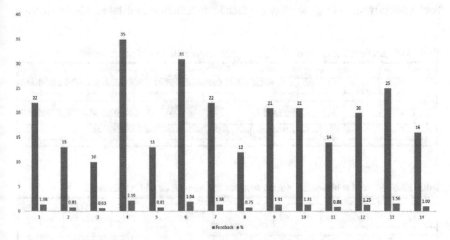

Fig. 23.5 Frequency of feedback and the feedback's percentage of the sixteen activities per student in the semi-annual course

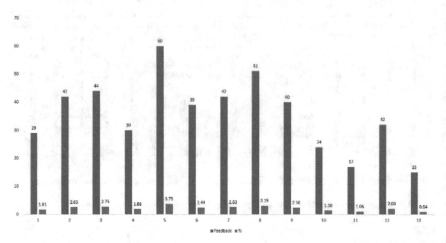

Fig. 23.6 Frequency of feedback and the feedback's percentage of the sixteen activities per student in the tetra-monthly course

In contrast, the younger semester students learned primarily face-to-face, with some courses taken online.

However, some tetra-monthly students used very little feedback, so a more detailed analysis was made. We had three students who took the semester course and then entered the summer course; since they dropped out, we can analyze their behavior (Tables 23.5 and 23.6).

It can be seen that student 1 (Table 23.5) dropped out of the activities at number 6, and although he was doing well, he did not continue. Student 2 did not use the feedback correctly up through activity number 5 and then made mistakes when uploading

Table 23.5 Student achievement during semester course with or without feedback

No		1	2	3	4	5	6	7	8	9	10	11	12	13	EV1	EV2	EVTOT
															Semester course		
1	A	95	100	100	100	84											
	B																
	C																
2	A	93	100	52	56	100	0	0	0	0	0	87	52	52	50	60	
	B			100	100			5	80	54	68						
	C						55										
3	A	90	100	24	90	84	16	80	80	50	50				30	50	41
	B			100													
	C																

Table 23.6 Student achievement during summer course with or without feedback

No		1	2	3	4	5	6	7	8	9	10	11	12	13	EV1	EV2	EVTOT
										Summer course							
1	A	100	100	100	100	100	41	50	50	40	76	61	40	100	75	75	68
	B						100	50	50		100	100			84		71
	C						100										
2	A	81	66	100	85	100	44	100	74	68	75	100	50	25	90	48	76
	B	81	100		100		74		74	75	75		50		100	100	84
	C	100							74								87
3	A	100	100	50	100	100	40	0	74	75	40	60	30	50	50	58	68
	B			100							68	60	30			75	76
	C												40				79

activities 6, 7, 8, 9 and 10. However, he was provided feedback and uploaded activities 7, 8, 9 and 10 correctly, but with errors, and was given feedback again. Then, he only used this second feedback in Activity 7. He never corrected Activity 6, and from Activity 11 onward, he did not use the feedback and did not present his final evidence. Student 3 only used the feedback for Activity 3 and did not do activities 11, 12, and 13.

Table 23.6 presents the behavior of the same three students in the summer course. All three used feedback up to Activity 5. Student 1 used feedback except in six activities: 8, 9, 12, EV1, EV2, and EV3. The same happened with the other two students, except they used feedback until the end; each used feedback three times. Below, a short discussion about the analysis of the researched data follows.

23.3 Discussion

It was established that learning assessment with continuous feedback improved students' academic performance in the Java Computing course. Academic improvements were evidenced and identified as motivational factors, and students found the impact of their efforts to improve their contributions reflected in their grades. On the other hand, it must be noted that the teacher's workload with this form of evaluation is very demanding. Thus, this workload consideration should be in the planning at the beginning of each academic period to avoid implementation time difficulties. Also, how assessments can affect students' motivation and self-esteem require special attention (Moreno 2012).

There is still much research to be done: the educational spaces of online students are different. The times, moments, and spaces still need to be investigated.

This research reveals that learning assessment supported by feedback improves academic achievement and describes how students in this particular course improved their achievement (Gibbs and Simpson 2005; Popescu 2019).

23.4 Conclusions

From the findings, we conclude that students improve their grades as long as they correct their contributions, usually in the short term. This was evident in the few weeks of the quarterly and the semester programs. In our research, the motivation of the learners decreased as time progressed. However, given the results, it is clear that this assessment approach benefited the average performance of the students by 10%. It favours those who are more mature and committed to their academic tasks, regardless of the study plan (semester or quarterly) or the format it is delivered (face-to-face or virtual).

As teachers, we have to be increasingly expert in offering the opportunity for our students to improve their learning or, even more importantly, regulate their self-learning in their various educational spaces (Shepard 2000). Of course, the application of more effective feedback to support learning remains to be researched (Nicol and Macfarlane-Dick 2006). Other critical areas for research include how to provide peer feedback that promotes learning in this subject and, finally, how to extend the scope of this work to any online subject (Maquillón and Alonso 2014). The students must be aware of the assessment rules before they are applied and the course's timeline to pass the course without difficulties (Maquillón and Alonso 2014; Alvarado et al. 2016). It will also be important to provide feedback within the course on how each student's learning process is going, not just feedback on the activities.

References

Alvarado JV, Alfaro AF, Rivas MC, Rodriguez CG (2016) Collaborative logical framework: an e-learning assessment tool. In: LRN platform. Proceedings—2016 11th Latin American conference on learning objects and technology, LACLO 2016

Barreira C, Bidarra G, Monteiro F, Vaz-Rebelo P, Alferes V (2017) Assesment of learning in higher education. Perceptions by teachers and students in Portuguese universities, Avaliação das aprendizagens no ensino superior. Perceções de professores e estudantes nas universidades Portuguesas. Revista Iberoamericana de Educacion Superior, vol 8(1)

Becker W (1997) Teaching economics to undergraduates. J Econ Lit 35(3):1347–1373

Boud D, Falchikov N (2006) Aligning assessment with long-term learning. In: Assessment and evaluation in higher education, vol 31(4). University of Technology, Sydney. Australia, pp 339–413

Caceres Mesa ML, Suarez Monzon N (2021) Understanding the educational dimension in the context of the Bachelor of Science in Education degree program of the Universidad Autónoma del Estado de Hidalgo ICT-based learning assessment. Las prácticas de evaluación de los aprendizajes mediadas por las TIC. Su comprensión desde la dimensión formativa en el contexto de la licenciatura en ciencias de la educación de la Universidad Autónoma del Estado de Hidalgo. Universidad y Sociedad 13(2)

Chagas JM (2016) Replication of fluid mechanical discipline in fully PBL focusing on student learning evolution assesment, Replicação da disciplina mecânica dos fluidos totalmente em PBL com o foco na evolução do aprendizado e avaliação plena do aluno. In: International symposium on project approaches in engineering education, vol 6

Fernández J (2009) Evaluación de los aprendizajes en la Universidad: Nuevos enfoques. Instituto de Ciencias de la Educación. Universidad Politécnica de Valencia, España

Gibbs G, Simpson C (2005) Conditions under which assessment supports student's learning. In: Learning and teaching in higher education, vol 1. Oxford University, United Kingdom, pp 3–31

Graff M (2003) Cognitive style and attitudes towards using online learning and assessments methods. Electron J e-learn 1(1):21–28. University of Glamorgan, United Kingdom

Hussey T, Smith P (2010) The uses of learning outcomes: teaching in higher education. 8(3):357–368

Jimenez-Garcia E, Redondo-Duarte S, Ruiz-Rosillo MA, Rodriguez-Martin JJ (2020) Institutional learning assessment plan at the Universidad Europea de Madrid, Plan institucional de evaluación de aprendizajes en la Universidad Europea de Madrid. Formacion Universitaria 13(6)

Jin H (2016) Concept maps: learning through assessment. In: The creative enterprise of mathematics teaching research: elements of methodology and practice— from teachers to teachers

Lara Sierra J (2006) Evaluación continua: Reportaje exclusivo para el Cartagena Heraldo

Leyva Y (2010) Evaluación del aprendizaje: Una guía práctica para profesores. UNAM, México
Maccario B (1989) Teoría y práctica de la evaluación de las actividades físicas y deportivas. Bs.As.
    Ed. Lidium
Maquillón J, Alonso J (2014) Experiencias de Innovación y formación en Educación. Universidad
    de Murcia, España
Mazo EA, Agudelo YG, Medina LMT, Montoya BMC (2018) The evaluation of academic learning
    in the special education degree of the university of antioquia, La evaluación de los aprendizajes
    académicos en la licenciatura en educación especial de la Universidad de Antioquia. Publicaciones
    de la Facultad de Educacion y Humanidades del Campus de Melilla, vol 48(2)
Mogollón I (2007) El chat y otros procedimientos de evaluación a distancia aplicables en sistemas
    mixtos
Moreno T (2012) Evaluación para el aprendizaje: Perspectivas internacionales. Revista de evalu-
    ación educativa, vol 1, no. Consultado en: http://revalue.mx/revista/index.php/revalue/issue/cur
    rent
Nicol D, Macfarlane-Dick D (2006) Formative assessment and self-regulated learning: a model and
    seven principles of good feedback practice. In: Studies in higher education, vol 31(2). University
    of Strathclyde, United Kingdom, pp 199–218
Popescu CD (2019) The assessment process of various types of education in terms of the roles
    involved in the teaching and learning processes. In: Case study, vol 30(1). Annalee Universiteit
    Ovidius Constanta, Seria Filologie
Sadler DR (1989) Formative assessment and the instructional design systems. Instr Sci 18:119–144
Shepard L (200) The role of assessment in a learning culture. Educ Researcher 29(7):4–14
Stephenson J, Yorke M (1998) Capability and quality in higher education. Kogan Page, London
Sudewa PH, Nur M, Wasis (2020) Needs assessment for development of inquiry-based learning
    materials using PhET media to enhance students' science process skills. J Phys Conf Ser 1521(4)
Suhendi HY, Ramdhani MA, Irwansyah FS (2018) Verification concept of assessment for physics
    students learning outcome. Int J Eng Technol (UAE) 73(3)

Chapter 24
Augmented Reality in Collaborative Learning

Elizabeth Griselda Toriz García, Andrés David García García, and Marcelino Aparicio Ponce

24.1 Introduction

Currently, collaborative group work is essential in all learning activities. Innovative educational techniques focus on the individual's training and learning outcomes.

The development of human mental capacity is facilitated by the socialization of training, i.e., collaborative group learning.

Communication within groups strengthens their work, develops the mind, and fosters skills mastery. The ability to interpret content manifests differently: others' words, actions, and productions allow us to understand and learn.

The construction of knowledge occurs through the adaptation of minds, so it is vital to reinforce collaborative learning. Creating teams and performance expectations is one of the most complex tasks faced in the classroom and work–life; therefore, we applied augmented reality to improve teamwork skills. In this article, we present the results of this initiative to transform work groups into collaborative teams.

E. G. Toriz García (✉) · A. D. García García
Escuela de Ingeniería y Ciencias, Tecnológico de Monterrey, Campus Estado de México, Estado de México, México
e-mail: etoriz@tec.mx

A. D. García García
e-mail: garcia.andres@tec.mx

M. Aparicio Ponce
Sociedad Interactiva de Capacitación y Educación Para El Desarrollo Sustentable, Estado de México, México
e-mail: marceaparicio4@gmail.com

© The Author(s), under exclusive license to Springer Nature Singapore Pte Ltd. 2022   305
S. Hosseini et al. (eds.), *Technology-Enabled Innovations in Education*,
Transactions on Computer Systems and Networks,
https://doi.org/10.1007/978-981-19-3383-7_24

24.2 Development

Traditional teaching methods tend to be boring for students. Most of them have at least one mobile device, and, during classes, they become distracted looking for information not required for the subject study or checking their social networks. This often occurs when the work is entrusted to a team because the student can think that another colleague is already doing the work.

However, mobile devices can be an ally of learning, attracting students' interest while applying available emerging technologies (Cai et al. 2017). In this work, augmented reality on mobile devices was used to capture students' attention in an emotional experience to connect them with the subject in a fun and exciting immersion. They performed interactive tasks that increased their collaboration and teamwork skills (Ismail 2019). Instead of reading theory, they saw it in action.

This innovative teaching–learning process combined interactive augmented reality with the Media Scape Learn Lab (MSLL) rooms, whose work tables contain a screen for each computer, allowing visualization of the progress of the activities and projects assigned. Using this approach, the students could debate and make decisions collaboratively.

This new educational space made it possible to provide effective and innovative feedback to each team and support their project. This proposal verifies that all these tools work together to impact learning positively, which has not been reported in other investigations.

24.2.1 Theoretical Framework

Teamwork is essential in the development of a country and its organizations. Undoubtedly, collaborative, self-sufficient, dynamic, and successful teams accomplish the task entrusted with higher performance.

Team-based learning is a pedagogy designed to maintain a stimulating learning environment through small interactive groups of students (Álvarez et al. 2018). Although collaborative learning (CL) brings to mind small group activity carried out in the classroom, it is more than simple teamwork, i.e., students form "small teams" after receiving instructions from the teacher. They then exchange information and work on a task within a team until all members understand and finish it, learning through collaboration (Álvarez et al. 2018; Adams et al. 2017).

Comparative analyses of this approach with traditional learning models have shown that students learn more when using CL. They remember the content longer, develop superior reasoning and critical thinking skills, and feel more self-confident and accepted by others (Cabero and Fernández 2018).

This pedagogy has been successfully introduced in several schools with high satisfaction rates from students and teachers (Martínez and Fernández 2018). Its ability to engage a large classroom in learning complicated concepts makes it an attractive option for addressing today's challenges in education. In an energetic and competitive learning environment, teams of four to eight students apply knowledge and concepts to challenging problems.

Terms such as passive, memorization, individual, and competitive are not associated with CL (Fernández 2018). Instead, the essential elements always present in this learning are cooperation, responsibility, communication, self-assessment, and teamwork. Students solve problems together, developing leadership skills, communication, trust, decision making, and conflict resolution.

Many activities have increased active participation, teamwork skills, and the opportunity to learn from each other (Affendy and Wanis 2019). These include focused listening, guided and reciprocal questioning of peers, puzzles, one-minute documents, annotations in pairs, round table, structured problem solving, think-and-share in teams, out-loud problem-solving, and three-step interviews.

However, a significant challenge to overcome is that the tasks require the integrated work of all team members. The work must not be done individually or divided among the group members to become merely the sum of isolated individual pieces that produce a very complex final product. Another challenge can be the dissatisfaction of the team members with the functions they perform. Among the most common dissatisfactions is the lack of equitable workload distribution. Teamwork mediocrity is observed when one member is literally "carried" by other team members.

Also critical is the indifference shown by team members to integrate themselves into the tasks entrusted because they check their social networks. Therefore, in our work, we implemented augmented reality to achieve better results in collaborative learning.

Augmented reality in learning transmits information while offering new memorization methods, fun, action, and expression of emotions (Blas Padilla et al. 2019). Augmented reality (AR) is a rising technology due to its innovation in multiple areas (Alexander et al. 2019). Its use makes it possible to capture the participants' attention by provoking their emotions to connect them with the topic to be learned. It also provides the feeling of immersion in a specific learning environment (Akcayir et al. 2016). Virtual reality and augmented reality are beneficial for students who find it difficult to maintain attention and concentrate on the thematic contents; they keep the student busy and amused while learning. In the same way that the Internet has changed how we communicate information, these tools have changed how we share experiences (Zheng et al. 2018).

24.2.2 Problem Statement

Individual commitment to a collaborative effort makes teams, companies, and societies succeed, sustaining civilizations. Having excellent multidisciplinary teams is essential to achieve high performance in any project. The ability to work collaboratively is highly valued by many employment recruiters today. However, creating work teams is one of the most overwhelming issues confronting contemporary organizations (Riebe et al. 2017).

In organizational terms, it is tough for an individual to meet all the objectives of an organization working alone; for this, teams are needed (Dunn et al. 2021).

One element making teamwork difficult is contradictory cultural philosophy. On the one hand, individuality, the value of solo effort, the accumulation of personal wealth, and the importance of competition are encouraged. On the other, collaboration and combining forces to achieve specific objectives are promoted.

Other challenges are the dissatisfaction of the members with their functions and inequitable workload. To these must be added that most students have at least one mobile device, which forces teachers to use them as a work tool during classes so as not to lose their students' engagement.

Even so, students are easily distracted, looking for information not required for the study topic or checking their social networks.

This study presents the results of applying augmented reality on mobile devices and in the TEC21 Media Scape Learn Lab (MSLL) classrooms (ITESM 2019). The objective was to capture students' full attention through realistic interactions with holograms and real-life everyday objects, superimposing holographic images on the natural world and manipulating three-dimensional models with their hands. These actions provoke their emotions to connect with the subject, immerse them in a specific learning environment, and acquire collaborative work skills. The experiences help train them for success in their professional practices.

24.2.3 Method

This mixed methods research (Creswell and Plano Clark 2017) allowed the collection, analysis, and linking of qualitative and quantitative data in the same study.

The following were designed: Activities assigned as homework that guaranteed individual responsibility and considered the difficulties of students to meet outside of class time; and class activities extending that individual work with a complexity requiring the cooperation of all students and the integrated and joint work of all team members.

The following were also designed and validated: An evaluation instrument to guarantee that the final product was indeed developed as a team with all members involved in the content; a self-evaluation and co-evaluation instrument to assess the teamwork dynamics; an observation guide to evaluate teamwork, and an instrument to assess attitudes toward work.

Educational resources with augmented reality technology were designed with the blender tool and made compatible with mobile devices.

We observed students' performance in the work team. We assessed qualitative aspects such as acceptance, interest, and mastery of the didactic tools and conducted quantitative and comparative analyses of their grades (Sendjaya et al. 2019).

The experimental study was carried out with 200 students enrolled in the climate change and energy use course. The control consisted of evaluating the collaborative work before applying augmented reality. The impact of the immersive pedagogical tool was measured after having applied it with the same students. Data were collected sequentially (in different periods) and concurrently (simultaneously) (Gericke et al. 2019).

The following were applied: (a) Questionnaires before and immediately after applying the proposed tools to measure learning activities (Arctic Climate Impact Assessment (ACIA) 2018); (b) Likert-type surveys; (c) interviews with students; (d) focus groups, and (e) evaluation rubrics. Activities to evaluate teamwork (integration of INTC knowledge) were developed in parallel with content learning (acquisition of ADQC knowledge) and project development (application of APPC knowledge) as the primary face-to-face components of biannual research activities and proposal development.

The validation of the evaluation instruments and the data were analyzed using the Statistical Package for Social Sciences (SPSS).

24.3 Results

Initially, 80% of students (160 out of 200) completed their assigned individual work (IW). It was a vital requirement to follow the puzzle technique to deliver the individual work (IW) to join a team and perform the activity applying augmented reality (ARA). Forty students who did not meet the requirement were not allowed to work with their team until completion. They were given time to do so.

The time taken to complete the ARA activity by the teams whose members performed the individual activity was recorded and compared with the time taken by the teams that did not meet this initial requirement. It took the latter group up to twice as long to complete the ARA activity.

From these actions, students became aware of the value of doing individual work for the achievements of the team and the entire class. After a quarter of this study, one hundred per cent IW compliance was achieved.

Using AR, the students observed the problem and proposed the respective solutions. Cards were used; at the time of activating the first one through the smartphone camera, a city appeared. Other activated cards presented environmental problems. By activating the cards, they designed a clean city, free of atmospheric pollutants in soil, water, and air, and they also promoted the use of clean energy.

The results obtained indicate that augmented reality influences students' behavior, increasing their interest and level of learning, notably improving their participation in work teams, and learning of the course content. It was found that students can propose solutions to environmental problems to make decisions about sustainable development and quality of life.

All the instruments to evaluate collaborative learning were applied before and after applying augmented reality to measure its impact. The results are displayed in Table 24.1.

The final assessment grades evidenced strong motivation and engagement (see Table 24.2).

Table 24.1 Opinions of the participants about the collaborative learning and augmented reality methodologies

Semester/actions August 2017–December 2018	% Collaborative learning CL	% Augmented reality AR	% Higher impact
Excellent tool for learning	85	90	5
Stimulates learning compared to the traditional methodology	89	93	4
Build enthusiasm for the course material	90	94	4
Improves teamwork	88	98	10
Pre-assigned activities affect the learning of the course	70	80	10
Greater motivation to work as a team	88	93	5
Increase in knowledge of the course	90	94	4
Must be applied in other courses	80	95	15
Adjective strengths	Stimulating and interactive	Great and total participation	
Adjective weaknesses	Slow. Long activities "Easy not to participate"	Students want more interaction time Short activities	

Source Own work

Table 24.2 Average grades obtained during the study applying collaborative learning and augmented reality methodologies

Semester/methodology August 2017–December 2018	% Passing students	Grade $\pm$ SD
Traditional	50	77 ± 1.6
Collaborative learning	80	85 ± 1.3
RA/Media Scape LearnLab	92	89 ± 1.2

Source Own work

24.3.1 Results Analysis

Teams were formed having four to eight students (the maximum work-table capacity in the Media Scape Learn Lab (MSLL) classrooms). To ensure that all team members work, we designed the activities so that the result would have to be accomplished by all members' integrated and joint works.

The work must not be done individually or divided among the group members to become merely the sum of isolated individual pieces that produce a very complex final product. It is necessary to guarantee prior individual work (IW), so individual tasks were assigned that only scored as delivered or not. Zero points were awarded if students did not turn in the assignment and one if they did. IW was homework, and the time allotted to the class was used to obtain the product by teams.

To guarantee individual responsibility in teamwork, we used puzzle technique logic. Each individual has to work on a "piece," ensure that others understand it, and then add the various pieces together to produce a new, more complex final product. In this way, the final product cannot be elaborated without each member's prior individual work.

Students not completing their IW were not allowed to work with their teams. They were ordered to carry out the individual task while all the complied team members began to work. The work time of the compliance teams was compared with the non-compliant teams. There was a notable difference in the time to reach the result. Students could see how not completing IW affected the times of the other team members who did comply. Thus, they became aware of the importance of doing individual work.

To ensure that all the participants handled the contents through teamwork, interacted, and worked together, we devised a random integrating question (of several areas of the work) for one of the team members. If they did not know how to answer correctly, someone else was given the opportunity. If they did not know the answer either, the job was returned. This practice was established as a condition to receive the work and influenced the final product grade.

To evaluate the dynamics of group work, we used self-evaluation and co-evaluation of their performance in teamwork, applying criteria with assigned values (from 0 to 2) to each of their team members for each criterion. The scores were 0 if it never meets the criterion established), 1 if it partially meets it, and 2 if it always meets it.

Among the criteria considered were: (1) Attends all scheduled meetings on time; (2) Completes their part of the job on time within the stipulated deadlines; (3) Performs work with an optimal level of quality; (4) Proposes ideas to develop the work; (5) Does not impose ideas on the other team members of the team, and (6) Complies with group agreements and norms.

To evaluate teamwork, we designed an observation guide with a series of criteria to be observed regarding group work in the classroom. We elaborated a file per group in which the criteria translated into observable behaviors so that the assigned score was as objective as possible. Each observed aspect was assigned a score from 0 to 2.

Observable behaviors: (1) All members are present; (2) Before carrying out the task, they discuss the best way to carry it out; (3) Only one person participates in the discussion and/or task; (4) They actively listen to each other (attend to the other while speaking, accept the questions of others, debate assertively, and criticize the ideas and not the people); (5) They adequately handle conflicts (explicitly clarifying, discussing possible solutions, and making decisions about them); (6) They promote a friendly team climate of tolerance, respect, and good treatment; (7) Before handing in the task and/or product, all team members review it and propose modifications and suggestions; (8) They divide the work proportionally so that all members perform part of the activity. These criteria were also applied to individual behaviors when necessary.

To measure the impact of augmented reality on collaborative learning, we applied all the evaluation instruments to the participants before and after using the tool.

Before applying AR, the most common adjectives used by students when asked about the strengths of CL were "stimulating" and "interactive." Several of them felt that CL "facilitated understanding the concepts" and "gives rise to discussion." When asked about the weaknesses of the CL course, the shortcomings identified were a slow time and the long and detailed activities. Some students thought that their classmates found it "easy not to participate."

Before applying AR, we designed educational resources with the Blender tool and made them compatible with mobile devices, enabling the possibility that this approach can be scaled to web platforms. Thus, the student explored and interacted with the environment and proposed situations, focused on the content of the class, and became aware of the causes of climate change and global warming.

The developed application was installed on the devices in the Media Scape LearnLab (MSLL) classrooms. The activity was timed and required that all team members work to achieve the objective in the estimated time (5 min). Cards were used; at the time of activating the first one through the smartphone camera, a city appeared. Other activated cards presented environmental problems.

During the development of the experiment, it was observed that the participants focused their attention entirely on the activity. Their faces were relaxed and smiling, enjoying the dynamics and fun practice.

After applying AR, the most common adjectives used by students when asked about the strengths of AR and its impact on their teamwork were "great" and "total." Several students considered that working with AR "made it easier to understand the concepts" and provided "better evidence to participate in a debate." When asked about the weaknesses of the CL course, the flaws identified by the students were that they wanted to have more time with AR and the activities were too short. All the students participated.

The students observed the problem through the AR and proposed solutions by activating the cards; they designed a clean city, free of atmospheric pollutants in soil, water and air, and promoted clean energy.

The results obtained indicated that augmented reality influences students' behavior positively. It increases their interest and level of learning and notably improves their work team participation and knowledge of the course content. Students can propose solutions to environmental problems to make decisions about sustainable development and quality of life.

The final assessment grades evidenced strong motivation and engagement. Students expressed that this educational technology facilitates and motivates learning.

24.4 Discussion

In the qualitative analysis to evaluate the impact of augmented reality on collaborative learning, we observed a "tunnel vision" of the participants. They focused their attention on the material presented in the holograms and made little use of other learning tools available to them, such as brochures and posters. This contrasted with the activities where AR was not applied where they frequently used these tools, partially coinciding with the conclusion that the users' attention is strongly attracted by the "holograms" of the AR system, leading them to neglect other sources of information (Radu and Schneider 2019). This indicates that the increase in learning is directly linked to the visualization of the concepts.

The students were observed aware and confident of their learning, demonstrated by the grades obtained. In contrast, another study published indicated that AR can give people a false sense of confidence (Unahalekhaka et al. 2019).

This study shows that learning times were shorter when AR was applied and communication was more efficient, in line with the findings found by researchers from Harvard University (Radu et al. 2020). Concerning teamwork, a high level of cooperation and interaction was observed among the participants, aligning with observations in other investigations (Grandi et al. 2019; Griffith et al. 2021).

24.5 Conclusions

Augmented reality in university teaching realizes a true acceptance for its use in teaching–learning processes.

This technology is perceived by students as being of real utility for training. The user-friendliness of augmented reality facilitates innovative practices. Students can control the training activities through interactions with the object, determining the relational location to the object they want to observe and the moment of interaction with it. A significant increase in learning and disciplinary competencies was observed among the students learning collaboratively compared with those taking the subject under the traditional methodology. The reasons are excellent content supported by AR, acquisition of curricular and transversal knowledge, and the development of effective teamwork and communication capacity. AR positively impacts learning. Interactive AR lessons increase the collaborative capabilities of students, enhancing their teamwork skills.

Acknowledgements The author wishes to acknowledge the financial support of the Novus Initiative, TecLabs, Tecnológico de Monterrey, Mexico, in the production of this work.

The author acknowledges the technical support of Writing Lab, Institute for the Future of Education, Tecnologico de Monterrey, Mexico, in the production of this work.

References

Adams B, Cummins M, Davis A, Freeman A, Hall C, Ananthanarayanan V (2017) The NMC horizon report: 2017 higher education edition. INTEF, Madrid. http://educalab.es/documents/10180/38496/Resumen_Informe_horizon_2017/44457ade-3316-418e-9ff9-fd5e86fc6707

Affendy NMN, Wanis IA (2019) IOP Conf Ser Mater Sci Eng 551:012050

Akcayir M, Akcayir G, Pektas H, Ocak M (2016) Augmented reality in science laboratories: the effects of augmented reality on university students' laboratory skills and attitudes toward science laboratories. Comput Hum Behav 57:334–342. https://doi.org/10.1016/j.chb.2015.12.054

Alexander D, Ashford-Rowe K, Barajas-Murphy N, Dobbin G, Knott J, McCormack M, Pomerantz J, Seilhamer R, Weber N (2019) EDUCAUSE horizon report: 2019 higher education. EDUCAUSE, Louisville Co

Álvarez JF, López C, Hafner A, Gonzalo P, González E, Portero M, Llopis B (2018) Informe ODITE sobre tendencias educativas. http://odite.ciberespiral.org/comunidad/odITE/recurso/informe-odite-sobre-tendencias-educativas-2018/23109971-25e2-4833-8507-c4da7acfe822#Informe%20completo

Arctic climate impact assessment (ACIA) reports. Cambridge University 2018

Barroso-Osuna J, Cabero-Almenara J, Gutiérrez-Castillo J-J (2018) La producción de objetos de aprendizaje en realidad aumentada por estudiantes universitarios. Grado de aceptación de esta tecnología y motivación para su uso. Revista mexicana de investigación educativa 23(79):1261–1283

Blas Padilla D, Vázquez-Cano E, Morales Cevallos MB, López Meneses E (2019) Uso de apps de realidad aumentada en las aulas universitarias. Campus Virtuales 8(1):37–48

Cabero J, Fernández B (2018) Las tecnologías digitales emergentes entran en la Universidad: la Realidad Aumentada y la Realidad Virtual. RIED: Revista Iberoamericana de Educación a Distancia 21(2):119–138

Cai S, Chiang FK, Sun Y, Lin C, Lee JJ (2017) Applications of augmented reality-based natural interactive learning in magnetic field instruction. Interact Learn Environ 25(6):778–791. https://doi.org/10.1080/10494820.2016.1181094

Creswell J, Plano Clark V (2017) Designing and conducting mixed methods research. Sage, Thousand Oaks, CA

Dunn SS, Dawson M, Block B (2021) Teaching teamwork in the business school. J Educ Bus 96(6):381–386. https://doi.org/10.1080/08832323.2020.1840322

Fernández B (2018) La utilización de objetos de aprendizaje de realidad aumentada en la enseñanza universitaria. Int J Educ Res Innov 9:90–104

Gericke N, Boeve-de Pauw J, Berglund T, Olsson D (2019) The sustainability consciousness questionnaire: the theoretical development and empirical validation of an evaluation instrument for stakeholders working with sustainable development. Sustain Dev 27(1):35–49. https://doi.org/10.1002/sd.1859

González-Pérez LI, Ramírez-Montoya MS, García-Peñalvo FJ (2018) Instrumento para medir la usabilidad de los repositorios institucionales. Technical report GRIAL-TR-2018-007. Grupo GRIAL, Salamanca, España

Grandi JG, Debarba HG, Maciel A (2019) Characterizing asymmetric collaborative interactions in virtual and augmented realities. In: 2019 IEEE conference on virtual reality and 3D user interfaces (VR), pp 127–135. https://doi.org/10.1109/VR.2019.8798080

Griffith AE et al (2021) Discovering co-creative dialogue states during collaborative learning. In: Roll I, McNamara D, Sosnovsky S, Luckin R, Dimitrova V (eds) Artificial intelligence in education. AIED 2021. Lecture notes in computer science, vol 12748. Springer, Cham. https://doi.org/10.1007/978-3-030-78292-4_14

Ismail AW (2019) A review of the collaborative learning environment across virtual and augmented reality technology. IOP Conf Ser Mater Sci Eng 551:012050

ITESM (2019) Plan Estratégico 2030. D.R.©, Instituto Tecnológico y de Estudios Superiores de Monterrey, Av. Eugenio Garza Sada Sur No. 2501, C.P. 64849, Monterrey, N.L. 2019

Martínez S, Fernández B (2018) Objetos de realidad amentada: Percepciones del alumnado de Pedagogía. Pixel Bit, Revista De Medios y Educación 53:207–220. https://doi.org/10.12795/pixelbit.2018.i53.14

Radu I, Schneider B (2019) What can we learn from augmented reality (AR)? Benefits and drawbacks of AR for inquiry-based learning of physics. In: 2019 CHI conference on human factors in computing systems proceedings (CHI 2019), 4–9 May 2019, Glasgow, Scotland, UK. ACM, New York, NY, USA, p 12. https://doi.org/10.1145/3290605.3300774

Radu I, Tu E, Schneider B (2020) Relationships between body postures and collaborative learning states in an augmented reality study. In: Bittencourt II, Cukurova M, Muldner K, Luckin R, Millán E (eds) AIED 2020. LNCS (LNAI), vol 12164. Springer, Cham, pp 257–262. https://doi.org/10.1007/978-3-030-52240-7_47

Riebe L, Girardi A, Whitsed C (2017) Teaching teamwork in Australian university business disciplines: evidence from a systematic literature review. Issues Educ Res 27(1):134–150. http://www.iier.org.au/iier27/riebe.html

Sendjaya S, Eva N, Butar Butar I, Robin M, Castles S (2019) SLBS-6: validation of a short form of the servant leadership behavior scale. J Bus Ethics 156(4):941–956. https://doi.org/10.1007/s10551-017-3594-3

Unahalekhaka A, Radu I, Schneider B (2019) How augmented reality affects collaborative learning of physics: a qualitative analysis. Comput-supported Collaborative Learn. Retrieved from https://par.nsf.gov/biblio/10101504

Zheng L, Xie T, Liu G (2018) Affordances of virtual reality for collaborative learning. In: 2018 international joint conference on information, media and engineering (ICIME), pp 6–10. https://doi.org/10.1109/ICIME.2018.00011

Chapter 25
Determinants of Satisfaction of Tecnologico de Monterrey Students with the Implementation of the Flexible-Digital Model During the COVID-19 Crisis

Jorge Mora-Rivera and Noemí Vásquez-Quevedo

25.1 Introduction

The current health emergency caused by the COVID-19 pandemic and the restrictions on mobility suddenly transformed the educational system (Erstad et al. 2021). The confinement caused online educational modalities to become essential to continue the teaching–learning process. In many universities, this task was not overly arduous because their online educational offerings have grown in a sustained manner in the last two decades. Some academicians consider that this growth has been a golden age (Eom and Ashill 2016). Recent literature has analyzed the potential benefits of virtual learning, its strategic importance, and its academic quality. In particular, this latter has become essential in the current state of the art of distance education because it focuses on the students' perception of learning results and their satisfaction.

In this context, our study's motivation was to evaluate the effectiveness of online learning to identify the main satisfaction factors among students who experienced our university's Flexible-Digital Model (FDM) during the period of confinement caused by the COVID-19 pandemic. Therefore, our research aimed to analyze pedagogical strategies that combine didactics with technology to solve educational crises (Basoo-Aránguiz 2018).

J. Mora-Rivera
Tecnologico de Monterrey, Escuela de Ciencias Sociales y Gobierno, Departamento de Economía, Ciudad de México, México
e-mail: jjmora@tec.mx

N. Vásquez-Quevedo (✉)
Tecnologico de Monterrey, Escuela de Negocios, Departamento de Contabilidad y Finanzas, Ciudad de México, México
e-mail: nvasquez@tec.mx

© The Author(s), under exclusive license to Springer Nature Singapore Pte Ltd. 2022   317
S. Hosseini et al. (eds.), *Technology-Enabled Innovations in Education*,
Transactions on Computer Systems and Networks,
https://doi.org/10.1007/978-981-19-3383-7_25

25.2 Theoretical Framework

The conceptual framework of the present study is based on investigations of three of the predominant themes in the current literature: first, those works that lay the foundations for distance education (Peltier et al. 2003); second, studies that analyze student satisfaction, specifically university students (Weerasinghe et al. 2017), and third, the research identifying the critical factors contributing to online university education systems (e-learning) (Eom and Ashill 2016; Eom et al. 2006). This present study focuses precisely on the latter. The literature about this perspective indicates that the online learning results depend on two essential factors: humans and design. The human factors are the students and instructors, whereas design depends on the technology, course contents, interactions, and follow-up in learning (Piccoli et al. 2001).

Some authors use constructivist learning theories as a conceptual framework to propose models that analyze the success factors of online learning (Eom and Ashill 2016; Piccoli et al. 2001; Alavi and Leidner 2001). These models are strengthened by a structure in which the required inputs are students, instructors, and learning management systems. The results are identified through student satisfaction and learning outcomes attributes that some authors have considered as dependent variables in their modeling (Nichols 2020; Eom 2019). Therefore, our study considered the following educational variables as essential elements in determining student satisfaction in a virtual learning environment:

1. *Course content and design.* This references the quality of the course in general (Aldemir and Gülcan 2004; Menchaca and Bekele 2008) and the technical structure and technological design, in particular, to motivate students to study and fulfill specific course demands (Kukreja et al. 2021).
2. *Teacher performance.* Refers to students' perception of their teachers' performance, including feedback and response time, mastery of the content, and teacher motivation (Freeman and Urbaczewski 2019).
3. *Feedback and interaction.* One of the main challenges of online education has been to provide tools that allow interaction and feedback between teachers and students on a par with those of a face-to-face environment. Several studies have identified how interactions supported by communication tools boost students' social presence and satisfaction in online learning (Park and Kim 2020).
4. *Learning style.* Refers to the coexistence of different learning styles that demand online activities that balance and promote learning (Menchaca and Bekele 2008).
5. *Self-motivation.* Refers to a student's self-regulation, an indicator of intrinsic motivation, a significant predictor of a favorable e-learning outcome. Intrinsic motivation is the psychological characteristic that makes an individual do an activity for personal satisfaction, fun, or challenge (Eom 2019; Zimmerman 1990).

25.3 Methodology

25.3.1 Problem Statement

The current health and economic crises have highlighted the indispensable role technology plays in ensuring the continuity of education during total or partial confinements. In this scenario, online learning and the implementation of new educational models represent the only alternative to continuing the teaching–learning process in educational institutions. Faced with this situation, Tecnologico de Monterrey implemented an innovative educational model called the Flexible-Digital Model (FDM) that provided educational continuity to its students during 2020 and the first semester of 2021 on its 26 campuses throughout the Mexican territory.

In this context, and to identify areas for improvement in continuing FDM, we posed the following research questions: (1) In the opinion of the students, was the academic quality of the courses under the FDM on par with the face-to-face courses? (2) What are the main factors that contributed to student satisfaction with the implementation of the FDM?

We applied a virtual survey and implemented an econometric model described in greater detail in the next section to answer these questions.

25.3.2 Econometric Model

This quantitative research uses a conceptual perspective to identify the main factors of student satisfaction within a virtual learning model. This approach is similar to Eom and Freeman (Eom 2019) and Urbaczewski (Freeman and Urbaczewski 2019). To achieve the study's primary purpose, we applied a virtual survey to 315 students in different semesters and educational programs on the CDMX and Estado de Mexico campuses of Tecnologico de Monterrey. The survey aimed to capture the students' perception and satisfaction of learning under the FDM, including a section on the educational context (teacher performance, course content, learning style, self-motivation, and interaction of students with teachers) and specific questions related to the perception of the FDM. In addition, it asked questions to get sociodemographic information at the individual and family levels.

To achieve our objective, we employed a logistic econometric model with binary dependent variable. The model assumed that the students' satisfaction would be determined by maximizing their utility for perceiving the quality of the face-to-face courses compared to courses under the FDM. The above can be expressed in the following equation:

$$y_{i0}^* = X_{i0}\beta_0 + \varepsilon_{i0} \tag{25.1}$$

where X_{i0} represents a set of independent variables such as sociodemographic characteristics, digital skills, and aspects of the educational environment. β_0 is the vector of coefficients to be estimated and ε_{i0} is the random error term. Although it is not possible to determine the total utility of the students, we can observe their opinions. Therefore, y_{i0} is the result of the students' decision-making influenced by the explanatory variables X_{i0}. Thus, when $y_{i0} = 1$ the student stated that the academic quality of the FDM was at least similar to that of the face-to-face courses; when $y_{i0} = 0$ the student stated that the academic quality of the virtual model was lower. So that $y_{i0} = 1$ if $y_{i0}^* > 0$, and $y_{i0} = 0$ if $y_{i0}^* \leq 0$ (Cameron and Trivedi 2010).

25.4 Results

Table 25.1 shows the average values of our main variables of interest differentiated by gender. The figures in the table show that some variables present significant differences between men and women, while others indicate similar behaviors. For

Table 25.1 Descriptive statistics for the variables of interest

Variables	Sample total	Women	Men
Demographic data			
Quality in the FDM equal or superior	0.33	0.32	0.34
Age	20.74	20.51	21.03**
PrepaTec	0.56	0.59	0.52
Last semester GPA	88.56	89.35	87.80**
Digital tools are useful	0.82	0.87	0.78**
Number of computers at home	3.70	3.44	3.94**
Number of income earners in the household	1.98	1.90	2.05
Number of family members	4.27	4.21	4.32
Number of school attendees	1.86	1.83	1.88
Educational context			
Teachers	0.787	0.784	0.789
Course contents	0.721	0.710	0.731
Feedback	0.790	0.789	0.790
Self-motivation	0.781	0.800	0.762**
Learning style	0.721	0.733	0.709
Interaction	0.704	0.705	0.704
Observations	315	154	161

Source Own elaboration based on the virtual survey applied to Tec de Monterrey students at the end of the February-June 2020 semester

Note The asterisks represent those variables that, in the test of the hypothesis of the difference of means between men and women, are statistically significant at 5%

example, the percentage of men who consider that academic quality was maintained under the FDM is slightly higher than that of women, although both are above 30%. On the other hand, a higher percentage of females came from Prepa Tec (the high school) and reported a higher average last semester than the males. Regarding digital tools, 87% of women considered them useful for learning, compared to 78% of men. Finally, regarding the family context variables, no significant differences were observed between men and women. For the total sample, the average number of computers in the home was 3.7, while the average number of household members was 4.27, and 1.86 attended school.

The lower part of Table 25.1 shows the means of the students' opinion variables corresponding to the educational context experienced with the FDM. To facilitate the interpretation of these variables, we standardized their values in a range that goes from 0.2 to 1. The analysis of this information reveals two interesting things. First, the students' opinion regarding the teachers' performance and mastery is practically the same between men and women; something similar happens with the student–teacher interaction and the feedback under the FDM. Second, males indicated that they value the content and design of the courses more than women, who gave greater weight to variables that indicate individual characteristics such as self-motivation and learning style.

In Table 25.2, we show the Logistics model results that allowed us to identify the variables influencing the students' satisfaction with the academic quality of the FDM compared to the face-to-face educational model. The dependent-variable $y_{i0} = 1$ identifies whether the student stated that the academic quality of the FDM was at least similar to that of the face-to-face courses. In order to show robust results, we carried out two regressions with different specifications. Furthermore, robust standard errors were used in each of the regressions. The coefficients β_0 are presented as marginal effects. Column (1) shows the regression results that only incorporate variables related to the educational context, possibly the most interconnected with the FDM. As a robustness measure, the coefficients in column (2) incorporate individual control variables and those of the family environment, in addition to the educational context variables. Although the coefficients vary slightly, the results generally remain stable; therefore, in the rest of the text, we refer only to the figures in the second column of Table 25.2, which shows the results, including the individual and sociodemographic controls.

The results in the second column of Table 25.2 suggest that human factors such as teacher performance, self-motivation, student learning style, and course design and content have a positive and significant impact on student learning satisfaction of Tecnologico de Monterrey students under the FDM. Along the same lines, the interaction between teachers and students positively impacted students' perception of quality of learning. Among the sociodemographic variables, only age and favorable opinion of digital tools improved student satisfaction scores. The rest of the sociodemographic variables did not seem to influence satisfaction levels.

Table 25.2 Determinants of student satisfaction under the flexible-digital model

Dependent-variable: FDM was on par with face-to-face courses = 1

Variables of the educational context	(1)	(2)
Teachers	0.5513 [1.91]*	0.4518 [1.97]**
Course content	0.0697 [1.93]*	0.0693 [1.84]*
Feedback	−0.0226 [−0.49]	−0.0342 [−0.71]
Self-motivation	0.0691 [1.71]*	0.0681 [1.74]*
Learning style	0.0529 [1.87]*	0.0511 [1.80]*
Interaction	0.0503 [1.67]*	0.0616 [1.98]**
Demographic variables		
Age		0.0447 [2.89]**
Gender		0.0008 [0.02]
Prepa Tec		−0.0639 [−1.14]
Digital tools are useful		0.2088 [3.59]***
Number of school attendees		0.0090 [0.30]
Number of income earners in the household		0.0084 [0.26]
Observations	315	315
Log-likelihood	−187.89	−178.05
$\chi 2$ of the model	23.27	35.52
Pseudo R^2	0.0596	0.1088

Source Own elaboration based on the virtual survey applied to Tec de Monterrey students at the end of the February-June 2020 semester

Note The numbers in brackets are the z-values. ***, **, *: values significant at 1%, 5% and 10%, respectively.

25.5 Discussion

The challenge of academic continuity presented by the economic and health crises of the COVID-19 pandemic resulted in distance educational models that became indispensable, moving from a complementary educational modality to one satisfying a real and urgent need (Eom and Ashill 2016; Park and Kim 2020; Lockee 2021).

Authors such as Kukreja et al. (2021), Eom and Ashill (2016), and Eom et al. (2006) point out that continuous dialogue between teachers and students, the teacher's knowledge, and the course designs have a significant influence on students' opinion of distance courses. Our results similarly indicated that these factors influenced the Tec de Monterrey students' opinion of the academic quality received with the FDM (Eom and Ashill 2016; Eom et al. 2006; Kukreja et al. 2021). Likewise, our study's findings echo those investigations that suggest the only alternative to continuing the teaching–learning process in crisis scenarios is to implement pedagogical strategies that combine traditional didactic elements with technological tools, as recently pointed out by Lockee (2021), Park and Kim (2020) and Sun et al. (2020).

25.6 Conclusions

Since the closure of educational institutions due to the COVID-19 pandemic, virtual instruction became the only way to continue training programs worldwide. In this research, we identified those factors that influenced the satisfaction of Tecnologico de Monterrey students under a flexible-digital model that allowed the teaching–learning process to continue. Our results showed that both human factors and the course design and content positively influenced the satisfaction of Tecnologico de Monterrey students with the implementation of the FDM. Likewise, the findings of this study suggested that, in general, the students were satisfied with the use of the FDM. Although they considered that the academic quality of the online courses was not better than the face-to-face ones, at least 33% of the respondents did believe that the quality was maintained. By analyzing the variables and contrasting them by gender, we identified that men highly value feedback and course content. Females prefer characteristics such as self-motivation and learning style.

Although this research provides statistically reliable evidence on the factors that impact student satisfaction with a distance education model, it is necessary to mention some limitations of this study. First, it would be convenient to have longitudinal information; that is, consider data from different periods to assess the consistency and robustness of the variables influencing student satisfaction. Second, it is possible to suggest that future research uses complementary quantitative and qualitative methods to assess course design, self-motivation, interaction, and level of engagement in learning activities. In addition, it would be helpful to identify the critical success factors to improve the quality of virtual learning using different quantitative models to complement or contrast the findings reached in this study. However, none of these limitations reduces the value of the results of this research; they only show the need for future analyses that could be strengthened by including new data and alternative methodological approaches.

References

Alavi M, Leidner D (2001) Research commentary: technology-mediated learning—a call for greater depth and breadth of research. Inform Syst Res 12:1–10

Aldemir C, Gülcan Y (2004) Student satisfaction in higher education: a Turkish case. J Higher Educ Manage Policy 16:109–122

Basoo-Aránguiz M (2018) Propuesta De Modelo Tecnologico Para Flipped Classroom. Revista Electrónica Educare 22:1–17

Cameron A, Trivedi P (2010) Microeconometrics using Stata: revised edition, 2nd edn. Stata Press, Texas, U.S.A.

Eom S (2019) The effects of student motivation and self-regulated learning strategies on student's perceived e-learning outcomes and satisfaction. J Higher Educ Theor Prac 19:29–42

Eom S, Ashill N (2016) The determinants of students' perceived learning outcomes and satisfaction in university online education: an update. Decis Sci 14:185–215

Eom S, Wen H, Ashill N (2006) The determinants of students' perceived learning outcomes and satisfaction in university online education: an empirical investigation*. Decis Sci 4:215–235

Erstad O, Miño R, Rivera-Vargas P (2021) Educational practices to transform and connect schools and communities [Prácticas educativas para transformar y conectar escuelas y comunidades]. Comunicar 66:9–20

Freeman L, Urbaczewski A (2019) Critical success factors for online education: longitudinal results on program satisfaction. In: Communications of the association for information systems, vol 44

Kukreja V, Sakshi S, Kaur A, Aggarwal A (2021) What factors impact online education? A factor analysis approach. J Eng Educ Transform 34:365–374

Lockee B (2021) Online education in the post-COVID era. Nat Electron 4:5–6

Menchaca M, Bekele T (2008) Learner and instructor identified success factors in distance education. Distance Educ 29:231–252

Nichols D (2020) Study of the perceptions and attitudes regarding online student services

Park C, Kim D (2020) Exploring the roles of social presence and gender difference in online learning. Decis Sci 18

Peltier J, Drago W, Schibrowsky J (2003) Virtual communities and the assessment of online marketing education. J Mark Educ 25:260–276

Piccoli G, Ahmad R, Ives B (2001) Web-based virtual learning and research framework environments: a preliminary assessment of effectiveness in basic IT skills training. MIS Q 25:401–426

Sun L, Tang Y, Zuo W (2020) Coronavirus pushes education online. Nat Mater 19:687–687

Weerasinghe I, Lalitha R, Fernando S (2017) Students' satisfaction in higher education literature review. Am J Educ Res 5:533–539

Zimmerman B (1990) Self-regulated learning and academic achievement: an overview. Educ Psychol 25:3–17

Chapter 26
Virtual Learning Checkpoints: Autonomy and Motivation Boosters in the English Flipped Classroom

Diana Angélica Parra Pérez and María Catalina Caro Torres

26.1 Introduction

Technological developments and new educational trends are opening questions about pedagogical practices and evaluation processes. Evaluation in teaching and learning environments has been an essential component of institutional curricula for years. It has been contextually designed and adapted to various learning scenarios. Therefore, those who evaluate experiences are primary in determining the effectiveness of assessment in a learning process. These include the views of professors who design and administer the evaluations and the students, both sharing the purpose of verifying the performance levels.

The systematization of experiences has been used to construct or validate pedagogical methods (Barrera Quiroga 2019). The initiative has been to create a self-assessment resource from systematizing the experiences of students and professors in higher education engaged in assessment practices in hybrid learning and the flipped English classroom model. The social representations made by the participating subjects of the self-assessment resource have made it possible to characterize it and determine its functionality within the English teaching–learning process.

D. A. P. Pérez
Escuela de Idiomas, Universidad de Antioquia, Medellín, Colombia
e-mail: diana.parra2@udea.edu.co

M. C. C. Torres (✉)
International Center of Foreign Languages and Cultures, Universidad de La Sabana, Chía, Colombia
e-mail: maria.caro1@unisabana.edu.co

© The Author(s), under exclusive license to Springer Nature Singapore Pte Ltd. 2022   325
S. Hosseini et al. (eds.), *Technology-Enabled Innovations in Education*,
Transactions on Computer Systems and Networks,
https://doi.org/10.1007/978-981-19-3383-7_26

26.2 Theoretical Framework

26.2.1 Hybrid Learning and Flipped Classroom

Hybrid learning (or "blended learning") concepts combine face-to-face teaching with technological support; the technology allows students to access learning on their own time and from a different place than the face-to-face setting (Hockly 2018). Among the benefits of the hybrid approach to learning is personalized learning that can be achieved using pre-recorded class videos available in the virtual environment. Another strength of the hybrid model is the increased interaction possibilities among students beyond the face-to-face encounter (Doman and Webb 2016). In teaching and learning English as a foreign language, the face-to-face component complements the virtual component by enabling students to participate in social interactions in the classroom that foster the development of their communicative competence (Some-Guiebre 2020).

The flipped classroom approach within the hybrid learning framework involves presenting course content before the face-to-face meeting, using class time for active learning experiences (Birgili et al. 2012). For English language learning specifically, hybrid, flipped-classroom learning benefits include more exposure to course materials to increase practice opportunities. This gives professors more opportunity to see each student's progress and identify possible areas of reinforcement or skills that need further development. Another advantage is that students can learn from their mistakes and receive feedback from their peers and the professor before coming to class, thus becoming aware of what needs to be studied in greater depth before the face-to-face meeting (García Sanz 2018).

26.2.2 Self-assessment

The pedagogical approach of making the student the center of the English learning process is a focused challenge of researchers. Self-assessment has been studied summatively from a training perspective (Kambourova 2017). It can be conceived merely as a way to assess and quantify learning. However, beyond this measurement, it can be considered a pedagogical action that opens diverse opportunities for students to observe their learning process in detail and make decisions for improvement. Furthermore, Sevilla and Gamboa (2016) and García (2018) co-relate self-assessment as a pedagogical strategy to develop autonomy in English learning. Creating self-evaluation mechanisms, which measure student engagement in foreign language learning in hybrid environments, must consider each student's emotional factors, motivation, and commitment to their learning.

26.2.3   Social Representations

The research practices defined as systematization of experiences "obey intentions and purposes, some particular, such as data organization and others more general such as the reconstruction of cultural and social scripts" (Barrera Quiroga 2019). These practices are suggested as a type of qualitative research to describe formative processes oriented to the critical interpretation of observed experiences. In educational contexts, several participants interact through teaching–learning activities. Professors, for example, in academic meetings have the opportunity to co-construct pedagogical actions based on their teaching experiences and the learning experiences of their students. According to Barrera (2019), one social representation is the information that the participants give about an object of analysis. This information becomes a text that arises from discursive interactions. These texts are polyphonic because they are constructed from several emerging opinions. In this study, the academic committee's views made it possible to construct the representations of a self-assessment resource used in the hybrid learning of English. One of the reasons for exploring social representations is that they seek to reconstruct experiences analytically and reflectively for interpretation and understanding (Jiménez-Quintero 2020). In this case, the goal was to reconstruct what this self-assessment resource represents in the English teaching–learning process in a higher education context.

26.3   Research Problem

Based on systematizing experiences as a qualitative research process, we describe below the critical moments from which the problem statement arose. The academic committee members, the Director of the Resource and Research Center, the coordinator of the English program, and the professors met regularly to continuously monitor and improve the ongoing teaching–learning processes. In 2017, the academic committee reflected on evaluation, leading to the systematization of the experience with four key moments: The first was the results' analysis of the program evaluation surveys carried out every semester during the two previous years (2015 and 2016). The purpose was to identify the students' views of the learning experience and the evaluation processes.

The second moment was constructing a narrative by the academic committee that recorded the program's formative and summative evaluation practices. The third pivotal moment was linked to one of the discussions of the academic committee about assessment in the program, specifically the students' performance results in the virtual activities.

The fourth moment focused on structuring and designing the pedagogical strategy to meet the needs identified by the participants in the first three moments. The "learning checkpoint" was born in the virtual environment: a self-assessment activity open and free to be done as many times as the student requires to validate his learning.

It includes automatic feedback with correct and incorrect answers and is structured with questions similar to those on the formal tests of the course.

After systematizing the experience described above, a validation of the pedagogical, self-assessment "learning checkpoint" in the English language program was initiated, and the following research objective was established:

• To describe students' and professors' social representations of a self-assessment task (the learning checkpoint) to show how it links to their English learning.

26.4 Method

To reconstruct the practice implemented in this systematization, we took a hermeneutic approach, which is fundamentally associated with interpreting the facts from the researcher's reality. In our qualitative research, we followed the Grounded Theory proposed by Glaser and Strauss and their procedures for obtaining data through constant comparison analysis to codify information and create concepts (Hunger et al. 2016). The ATLAS.ti software was used for the analysis and coding of the data collected. The study followed a cycle of four phases in an action-research approach (Table 26.1).

Finally, the data collected were analyzed, compared, and codified to conceptualize social representations.

Table 26.1 Phases and research instruments

Phase	Activities	Research instrument
I Identification of needs	Analysis of documentary records. Triangulation of information to identify the need for evaluation	• Documentary record (2015 and 2016 program evaluation survey, Narrative on evaluation, and meeting minutes)
II Planning	Design of the evaluation activity. Digitalization and upload to the virtual platform	
III Action	Implementation of the "learning checkpoint" resource during the 2017-2nd semester	• Semi-structured interviews • Student survey • Professors' survey
IV Reflection	Identification of the social representations of professors and students concerning the purpose of the implemented "learning checkpoints," their relationship with the learning process, and with the concept of self-assessment, its advantages, and disadvantages	

26.5 Results

During phase I (Identification of needs), the documentary review process was used. The analysis and triangulation of the information collected from the participants were carried out. This information was gathered from important sources within the experience, coming from students and each academic committee member. In the program evaluation surveys, the students expressed concern for their learning, wanting to be more prepared for the formal tests and the level of demand of these tests of their learning, and they indicated an interest in access to tools to do their follow-up:

Excerpt 1: "There should be an initial section that allows you to self-assess your level of progress and learning."

The director and program coordinator of the program elaborated in the narrative the need for strategies to reduce students' anxiety, nervousness, or frustration when taking objective-formal tests and improve their perception of preparing for them. The following excerpt is taken from the conclusions section of the narrative:

Excerpt 2: "Provide spaces or support alternatives that let students use and practice self-direction strategies to reduce anxiety, nervousness, and frustration."

The professors expressed their interest in tracking the success and failure of the students' work on the platform to prepare a class that responds to their actual learning needs.

Excerpt 3: "It is vital to make learning visible, to be able to track successes and failures, and to reflect on these results to prepare a class that responds to the students' real needs.

The results described and exemplified above allowed determining the needs of the academic community. These needs were the basis for the academic team planning and designing the Learning Checkpoint self-assessment activity (planning phase II). There were 84 learning checkpoints designed for the hybrid-flipped English program, 12 for each course offered by the institution from levels 1 to 7, which correspond to levels A1–B2 in the Common European Framework (Europa 2018).

After implementing the "learning checkpoint" (Phase III, Action), new data were collected to determine the social representations of all the program members who took part in this evaluative practice. The process of constantly comparing the data collected was done in this third phase, using the open coding method of Grounded Theory for data analysis (Hunger et al. 2016). This coding process consolidated all the data collected from the research instruments, interviews, and surveys, conducted in Phase III. The data collected were interpreted and contrasted to find relationships and trends (open coding). For example, Table 26.2 illustrates the family of codes called "purpose-of-learning checkpoints." It shows the codes with the highest trends.

The objective of Grounded Theory is to develop a model based on empirical data systematically collected and analyzed. The code correlations and continuous comparisons followed the process of axial and selective coding, which led to constructing the conceptual category and subcategories (see Table 26.3).

Table 26.2 Example of codes

Family of codes	Codes	Instrument and question
Purpose of learning checkpoints	To consolidate, strengthen or improve self-learning Raise awareness of learning/performance Identify progress or achievement Learning support	Student Survey Question 1: What do you think is the purpose of the Learning Checkpoints?
	Verify, validate, or test learning/comprehension Identify strengths and weaknesses for professors to verify learning Improve performance, learn concepts, and improve the level Prepare for midterms	Student Survey Question 2: What has motivated you to do them?
	Measuring the effectiveness of independent work Self-feedback Reflect on learning	Professor Survey: Question 4 How are Learning Checkpoints linked with learning?

Table 26.3 Conceptual category and subcategory

Subcategory	Category
Consolidation of learning through constant self-assessment	Self-assessment: an autonomy and motivation trigger for the consolidation of English learning
Development of autonomy and reflection of self-assessment	
Persistence, commitment, and motivation in self-assessment	

26.6 Discussion

This study examined students' and professors' social representations about a self-assessment resource called a learning checkpoint in a hybrid-flipped English program. The social representations of the main participants in this assessment practice defined the learning checkpoint as a voluntary mechanism, tool, or interactive strategy to promote English language learning. This assessment experience was seen positively, fostered autonomy and motivation, and facilitated the consolidation of English learning.

26.6.1   Consolidation of Learning Through Continuous Self-assessment

Zhengdong mentions that the feedback surrounding the evaluation processes in the English classroom involves motivational and self-determination factors (Zhengdong 2020), and evidence of this was found in this study. The data provided by the students, professors, coordinator, and board of directors were analyzed. The analysis made it possible to determine that the functions of the learning checkpoint include reinforcing, strengthening, or improving the learning process, especially with English grammar and vocabulary. This finding was consolidated through the usefulness of the learning checkpoints for continuously verifying the understanding of the contents and skills development. Thus, the students could direct their actions effectively to improve their performance. In addition, Kulprasit points out that self-assessment experiences are part of the "assessing to learn" type of evaluation. This type focuses not only on measuring but also on developing cognitive, metacognitive, affective, and social learning skills (Kulprasit 2021). Thus, self-assessment activities before, during, and after learning lead to selecting strategies that improve future learning.

Another vital function of the self-assessment resources was that they followed the structure of international standardized test-type questions, like the formal course evaluation tests. This allowed students to prepare and repeat the questions as many times as necessary, without feeling the pressure that their results would affect their course averages. Such representations were evidenced in responses such as "They are similar to the quizzes we do in class (student survey, question 2, P4) or "To prepare for the midterm" (student survey, question 2, P4). Such information allowed the program researchers to confirm that the need expressed by the students in the analysis phase to have training for formal tests was successfully met.

Meanwhile, professors found the functionality of this evaluative practice in verifying the students' learning before the face-to-face meetings, focusing the classes to consolidate concepts, and improving performance in the areas of difficulty. This result was also considered valuable by the students: "This information allows professors to determine in which topics I have deficiencies" (student survey, question 2, P4)."

26.6.2   Development of Autonomy and Self-assessment Reflection

One of the features that the learning checkpoints offered students was the opportunity to repeat them as many times as they required, at their discretion and decision. This allowed the students to find their learning successes and failures and try again to check their improvement and progress. This was interpreted as the development of metacognitive strategies through which students self-review, self-monitor, and self-regulate their evidence of learning (Kulprasit 2021). The following is evidence of some students' representation of this functionality: "I really like to try until I get the highest grade because by trying several times, I learn more" (student survey E38). "I repeat it to get a better grade" (student survey E39). "Repeating to correct mistakes and understand the mistakes" (student survey E42).

Thus, self-assessment motivated students to perform the learning checkpoints and accurately identify their strengths, weaknesses, and progress in the learning process. This continuous assessment brought reflection on self-learning and verification of the effectiveness of independent work. In the framework of a flipped classroom, hybrid course, the self-assessment becomes a valuable element to promote autonomy. Some professors depicted the purpose of this learning checkpoint functionality as: "To strengthen the student's autonomous learning" (Teacher survey P1). "…they aim for students to follow-up on their process and identify the aspects that need to be improved" (Teacher survey P5).

26.6.3 Persistence, Commitment, and Motivation in Self-evaluation

The social representations of the participants, teachers, and students clarified the importance of self-assessment as a trigger for students' persistence and commitment to their learning. Kim and Kim's (2016) research reports that persistence plays a crucial role in second language learning processes (Kim and Kim 2017). This study provided evidence that the self-assessment process using the learning checkpoint evoked student persistence, commitment, and motivation. Being able to verify learning several times until obtaining the desired result demonstrated their persistence. One student reported that she found "completing it several times" an advantage (student survey E5). We also found statements that demonstrated motivation to learn English, as completing the learning checkpoint meant having no pressure, as expressed by the following student: "I can do a self-assessment without the pressure of getting a bad grade" (Student survey E7). Finally, elements were determined through which self-assessment was associated with commitment to learning. Students found that the checkpoint allowed them to identify a pathway for "self-knowledge" (Student survey E68) and "… carrying out a self-assessment of my performance" (Student survey E70). Each student decided to complete these actions. The learning checkpoint, as initially mentioned, had no impact on the students' grades. It was a voluntary participative resource for those who might find it helpful. Thus, we conclude that students' manifestations and social representations demonstrate their willingness and commitment to their learning.

26.7   Conclusions

The systematization of this evaluation practice to consolidate this research allowed us to create a self-evaluation instrument called a "Learning Checkpoint." This study focused on exploring the social representations of the participants, students, and professors, who had the experience of voluntarily using the Learning Checkpoint while studying English in the hybrid-flipped program.

The social representations of students and professors about the learning checkpoints indicated that these were devised to consolidate foreign language learning through continuous and repetitive use as many times as the student wanted. Likewise, since the checkpoints were activities completed before class attendance (flipped classroom), they made planning the face-to-face sessions even more assertive, focusing on the students' learning needs indicated by their results at each checkpoint.

A second result was the contribution of the Learning Checkpoints to the development of self-monitoring and self-regulation skills. This result allowed us to confirm the correlation between fostering self-assessment processes to develop autonomy in English learning, self-monitoring and self-regulation skills.

The third outstanding result was that the Learning Checkpoints fostered persistence and commitment to improve English language skills and performance among the trainees. In addition, their social representations showed they felt motivated to learn.

This research allowed us to clarify the importance of self-evaluation through implementing the Learning Checkpoints. We find it essential to highlight that the evaluative practices responding to community needs and the continuous reflection and discussion by the participants (management, coordinator, professors, and students) consolidated this pedagogical method as a significant alternative classroom experience.

Acknowledgements We thank the Universidad de La Sabana for all their support to carry out this research process. We also thank the professors of the Plan Umbrella English program for their contributions to creating the learning checkpoints and their participation in this research project.

The authors acknowledge the technical support of Writing Lab, Institute for the Future of Education, Tecnologico de Monterrey, Mexico, in the production of this work.

References

Barrera Quiroga DM (2019) La sistematización de experiencias, una estrategia de la investigación antihegemónica. El Ágora USB 19(2):547–557. https://doi.org/10.21500/16578031.4389

Birgili B, Seggie FN, Oğuz E (2018) The trends and outcomes of flipped learning research between 2012 and 2018: a descriptive content analysis. J Comput Educ 2021:1–30. https://doi.org/10.1007/s40692-021-00183-y

de Europa C (2018) Marco común europeo de referencia para las lenguas: aprendizaje, enseñanza, evaluación. MECD y Anaya. https://rm.coe.int/cefr-companion-volume-with-new-descriptors-2018/1680787989

Dakhi O, Jama J, Irfan D, Ambiyar I (2020) Blended learning: a 21st-century learning model at college. Int J Multi-Sci 1(7):547–557. Recuperado de https://multisciencejournal.com/index.php/ijm/article/view/92/72.

Doman E, Webb M (2016) The flipped experience for Chinese university students studying English as a foreign language. TESOL J 8:102–141. https://doi.org/10.1002/tesj.264

García Sanz E (2018) La autoevaluación en la comprensión y expresión oral: análisis de sus criterios desde la perspectiva del discente. Marcoele. Revista de Didáctica Español Lengua Extranjera 26:1–19

Hunger I, Müller J (2016) Glaser BG, Strauss AL (eds) The discovery of grounded theory. Strategies for qualitative research. In: Salzborn S (ed) Klassiker der Sozialwissenschaften. Springer VS, Wiesbaden, pp 259–262. https://doi.org/10.1007/978-3-658-13213-2_59

Hockly N (2018) Blended learning. ELT J 72(1):97–101. https://doi.org/10.1093/elt/ccx058

Jiménez-Quintero AM (2020) Sistematización de prácticas pedagógicas significativas en la carrera de licenciatura en educación infantil. Formación Universitaria 13(4):69–80. https://doi.org/10.4067/S0718-50062020000400069

Kambourova M (2017) Acerca de la autoevaluación de los aprendizajes en educación superior o sobre el estado de la cuestión. Global Knowledge Academics, Colombia, South America

Kim T-Y, Kim Y-K (2017) The impact of resilience on L2 learners' motivated behaviour and proficiency in L2 learning. Educ Stud 43(1):1–15. https://doi.org/10.1080/03055698.2016.1237866.

Kulprasit W (2021) Assessment for learning (AFL): its role in L2 writing contexts. New English Teach 15(1):1–13. http://www.assumptionjournal.au.edu/index.php/newEnglishTeacher/article/view/4314

Sevilla Morales H, Gamboa Mena R (2016) Student self-evaluation and autonomy development in EFL learning. Revista de Lenguas Modernas 25:199–222. https://doi.org/10.15517/rlm.v0i25.27695

Some-Guiebre E (2020) Foreign language classroom interaction: does it promote communicative skills? Int J Educ Methodol 6(3):497–505. https://doi.org/10.12973/ijem.6.3.497

Zhengdong G (2020) How learning motivation influences feedback experience and preference in Chinese university EFL students. Front Psychol 11:1–14. https://doi.org/10.3389/fpsyg.2020.00496

Chapter 27
Gamification and Development of Informational Competencies in Higher Education

Daniel Flores-Bueno and Cesar H. Limaymanta

In the last five years, the scientific community's interest in gamification in higher education has grown, as evidenced by the increasing number of articles published since 2017 in the primary bibliometric databases: Scopus and Web of Science. However, the number of articles dedicated to using this pedagogical strategy in developing information competencies is still scarce, presenting an opportunity to contribute research to this field of study. The authors of Galbis-Córdova et al. (2017) point out that "there is still no research that has delved into the students' beliefs that a positive attitude toward using gamification contributes to developing their skills" (p. 132). Toward this end, this work investigates students' perspectives of the relationship of two variables (gamification and information competencies) in a quasi-experimental study with a quantitative approach. For this purpose, the data were collected in two moments (pre and post) at the course's beginning and end.

This study aims to contribute three results: a review of the literature, a replicable pedagogical proposal for gamification to develop information competencies, and an empirical study to analyze the size of the effect between these two variables. We used the ALFIN-Humass questionnaire (Pinto 2011) to collect the information, assessing three dimensions from an internal perspective (motivation, self-efficacy, and learning habits). The questionnaire had 26 items, grouped into four categories, measuring information competencies in search, evaluation, processing, and communication-dissemination of information.

D. Flores-Bueno (✉)
Department of Humanities, Universidad Peruana de Ciencias Aplicadas, Lima, Peru
e-mail: pcpedflo@upc.edu.pe

C. H. Limaymanta
Department of Library and Information Sciences, Universidad Mayor de San Marcos, Lima, Peru
e-mail: climaymantaa@unmsm.edu.pe

S. Hosseini et al. (eds.), *Technology-Enabled Innovations in Education*,
Transactions on Computer Systems and Networks,
https://doi.org/10.1007/978-981-19-3383-7_27

Finally, this research sought to answer the research question: What are the students' perceptions of the effect of gamification on their development of information competencies at the Universidad Nacional Mayor de San Marcos (in 2019)?

The sample consisted of students from a university in Metropolitan Lima who were evaluated from May to June 2019. To answer the research question, we present the following sections covering the literature review, the definition of the variables, an explanation of the method and design of the investigation, the materials used, the procedures carried out in collecting the information, and the results, discussion, and conclusions.

27.1 Literature Review

27.1.1 Gamification in Education

Gamification in higher education is a recent topic with no more than eight years of academic research. It arises from the development of the digital media industry (Deterding et al. 2011). In the last five years, gamification in education has been investigated in its variant modalities: face-to-face, blended, and online. The definition of gamification in this research is the use of game elements in contexts that are not games (Deterding et al. 2011).

It must be noted that other concepts have emerged in recent years that confuse the term "gamification." A couple of examples are game-based learning and serious games. The former refers to video games aimed at learning, and the latter refers to computer games for educational purposes (Escamilla et al. 2016). However, it must be remembered that gamification is an experience of the game's narrative, challenges, and rules, and technology may or may not be present (Kapp n.d.). Currently, the demand to increase students' commitment to learning (Buckley and Doyle 2016) and simultaneously deal with many students in the classroom (Schofer and Meyer n.d.) leads teachers to seek new active learning strategies. One of these is gamification, which has multiple advantages in developing soft skills such as effective communication, time management, and stress management (Huang and Yeh 2017). However, this strategy also has detractors who criticize the way people relate to learning, feeling that it is not linked to intrinsic motivation but is conditioned on external stimuli (Roy and Zaman 2018). One theory that helps us understand gamification is experiential learning, developed by David Kolb, who expresses learning as a holistic process of adapting to the world, where knowledge is created not through experience but by reflecting on the experience (Kolb 2015). His main ideas are summarized in his experiential learning cycle. Everything begins with substantial experience, followed by reflective observation, abstract conceptualization, and active experimentation, which allows the learner to explore, analyze, decide, and act. This process was carried out in the gamified experience in the "Information Resources" course taught at the Universidad Nacional Mayor de San Marcos from May to June 2019. An educational and immersive gamification technique called "Breakout Edu" (ScolarTIC 2019) was implemented in that intervention. To complete the course, the students had to solve team challenges in a certain period to open virtual locks connected to a spy story set during World War II.

27.1.2   Information Literacy

This research adopted the concept of competencies defined as "knowing how to be," "knowing how to do," and "knowing how to know" within a framework of continuous improvement and ethical commitment to personal and social development (Tobón 2008). Regarding information literacy, the definition proposed by the Chartered Institute of Library and Information Professionals (CILIP) of the United Kingdom was used because it simply synthesizes other definitions. Thus, "information literacy is knowing when and why you need information, where to find it, and how to evaluate, use, and communicate it ethically" (Boden et al. 2004). The three dimensions of information competencies adopted in this study were selected from the ALFIN HUMASS instrument proposed by Pinto (2011): (a) search for information, (b) evaluation of information, and (c) communication and dissemination of information.

27.2   Problem Statement

What is the effect of gamification on the perception of information competencies among students at the Universidad Nacional Mayor de San Marcos in 2019?

27.3   Method

The research took a quantitative approach with a pre and post-test, quasi-experimental design applied to two groups of students (experimental group and control group) taking an already existing subject in a public university in Lima, Peru. The quasi-experimental design was based on the proposal by Hernández Sampieri et al. (2006):

$$G1 \ O1 \ X \ O2$$
$$G2 \ O3 - O4$$

G1 is the experimental group, G2 is the control group, O1 and O3 are the pretests, and O2 and O4 are the post-tests of students' perception of their information competencies. X represents the gamification intervention with the experimental group. The

Table 27.1 ALFIN-Humass instrument reliability

No	Variable/Dimension	Alpha
	Overall scale	0.927
1	Information search	0.903
2	Information evaluation	0.790
3	Information processing	0.620
4	Information communication/dissemination	0.748

Source Own elaboration

inclusion criterion for the study is that both groups of students were studying the same subject with content on information literacy. In addition, those chosen from the experimental group must attend the scheduled sessions regularly; if a student did not take one of the tests, they were automatically removed from the study. The mean age of the students in the control group was 20 years ($s = 7.4$ years), while for the experimental group, it was around 21.3 years ($s = 2.4$ years).

27.3.1 Materials

Data were collected twice from both the control and experimental groups with the ALFIN-Humass questionnaire (Pinto 2011), i.e., at the beginning of the investigation (pretest) and the end of the gamification strategy (post-test). The instrument included 26 items in three categories. After adjusting to the study context with gamification and the reliability analysis using Cronbach's α, 15 items remained and were distributed in four categories. One of these, "information processing," did not have the appropriate reliability index because the value was less than 0.7. An index greater than 0.7 indicated acceptable dimension reliability (Nunnally 1978). Table 27.1 shows the reliability analysis results, which ultimately indicated the information search, evaluation, and communication/dissemination dimensions as acceptable.

27.3.2 Procedure

The response variable was the perception of informational competencies; its evaluated dimensions were search, evaluation, and communication/dissemination of information. The independent variable was gamification applied through the programmed activities integrated into a narrative named "Enigma Code." This game was inspired by the movie *The Imitation Game* by director Morten Tyldum. The students were presented with a narrative taking place during the World War II. Its protagonists are a team of encryption experts who work for British intelligence and whose opponents are the German army. Gamification involves the missions that several five-student teams must carry out to solve three-course challenges per session. In all these actions, the game's strategy deployed variants of Breakout Edu with challenges where students opened virtual locks each time they successfully solved a mission to achieve the course objectives. Students unlocked virtual locks, salvaged valuable assets, earned medals, and achieved in-game objectives, which they redeemed for points in the course. For greater game immersion, a video was prepared explaining the rules, the narrative, and the penalties.

Regarding the axiological aspects applied during the data collection process, these were based on five ethical principles: voluntary participation by the students with full respect for their fundamental rights and freedoms; beneficence and non-maleficence, ensuring participants well-being; fairness to all participants; scientific integrity, respect for honest actions, and truthfulness in the use and conservation of data; and, finally, responsibility, considering the implications of conducting and disseminating the research.

27.4   Results

To answer the research question and test the hypothesis, we conducted a descriptive and inferential analysis.

27.4.1   Descriptive Analysis

In the pretest, the near-equivalence of scores in both student groups are shown in Table 27.2 (mean scores of 86.18 and 85.6, respectively). On the other hand, the post-test averages indicated a slight advantage in the experimental group over the control group, with 98.6 and 86.09 means, respectively. Regarding the score for the development of information competencies in the experimental group, their average score was 86.5 and 98.6 in the post-test, thus showing a significant increase. This statement is tested using the statistical hypothesis displayed in Table 27.4.

Table 27.2   Average and dispersion of informational competency scores

Group	Pretest		Post-test	
	Mean	CV (%)	Mean	CV (%)
Control	86.18	26.2	86.09	27.1
Experimental	85.6	20.2	98.6	18.2

Source Own work

27.4.2   Inferential Analysis

To carry out the inferential analysis, we carried out the normality test t because the use of parametric or non-parametric inference depends on it. Table 27.3 shows the results of the inferential analysis. A comparison of the perception of informational competencies scores was conducted in the pretest and post-test. In the case of the pretest, it was concluded that there is no difference in the information competencies of the students in the control and experimental groups ($p = 0.694$). On the other hand, in the post-test, there was a difference in the score of the experimental group over the control group; the said difference is not significant at 0.05, but at 0.10, it is. It was affirmed with a 10% significance level that there is a difference in the perceived information competencies scores between the control group and the experimental group after applying gamification as an active learning strategy to students in the experimental group.

Likewise, a before-and-after comparison test was carried out to check if gamification positively influenced the development of information competencies from the students' perception. The Wilcoxon test for dependent samples was used because the data do not have a normal distribution. The student's t-test was also used because the data follow a normal distribution. According to Table 27.4, the control group did not improve in developing informational competencies ($p = 0.878$). On the contrary, the experimental group did improve in developing information competencies after applying gamification as an active learning strategy during the learning sessions ($p < 0.01$).

Table 27.3 Test for independent samples: pre and post-test

Type of test	Normality		Statistical test	Average range	P-value
	Group	P-value			
Pretest	Control	0.005**	Mann	16.86	0.694
	Experimental	0.96	Whitney-U	15.53	
Post-test	Control	0.025*	U de Mann	12.23	0.087
	Experimental	0.498	Whitney	18.08	

Source Own elaboration

Table 27.4 Test for dependent samples in the control and experimental group

Type of test	Normality		Statistical test	Average	P-value
	Group	P-value			
Pretest	Control	0.005**	Wilcoxon	86.18	0.878
	Experimental	0.025*		86.09	
Post-test	Control	0.096	Student's t-test	85.8	0.000**
	Experimental	0.498		98.6	

Source Own work

27.5 Discussion

This research analyzed the correlation between developing information competencies and gamification as a pedagogical strategy. Gamification has proven to be a means for students to participate in their educational process. Through competition, time management, and teamwork, students actively learn. They go from being passive subjects to people with higher self-determination to make decisions, allowing them to solve the challenges posed in the classroom at a specific time. This change can positively impact different aspects of their performance, including increased class attendance and participation, as reported by the research of Pinter et al. (2020).

Another critical aspect of learning is the role that motivation plays (Buckley and Doyle 2016; Werbach and Hunter 2014). In the proposal for the development of this research, motivation appears in different stages. In the first instance, promoting the students' autonomy to act increases their intrinsic motivation (Deci and Ryan 1985). Second, competition with other teams where the challenge is not so complex that it is unattainable or so easy that it is boring is a motivator (Csikszentmihalyi 2009). The social aspect also plays a vital role because class members can measure where they are vis a vis their peers. Finally, the accumulation of points and the tasks feedback are extrinsic motivators. The adaptation process has accelerated in this last stage thanks to previous trial and error, allowing learning (Kolb 2015).

Despite the benefits of this pedagogical strategy, not everything was positive. Some questions were highlighted in the literature. One of the main ones was the trivialization of learning when there are extrinsic rewards; the better motivator would be intrinsic, brought on by the pleasure of learning (Werbach and Hunter 2014). Some authors also point out that more significant commitment and motivation do not necessarily translate into improved learning outcomes (Domínguez et al. 2013).

Regarding the development of information competencies and gamification, we point out that instructional design with gamification demands extra work from the teachers, which is not necessarily taken on in the same way by all teachers. When creating the game, planning for the class dynamics, the evaluation system, and the points recording takes more time than planning a conventional class. This factor must be studied to understand why some experiences are successful and others are not.

Finally, this topic's relevance and pertinence should be highlighted due to the importance of this competency in higher education, as (González Flores 2014) notes. There is still little research in this regard. In some cases, gamification is understood as a narrative put at the service of learning (Pun 2017), as postulated in this research. On other occasions, it falls under the controversial understanding of gamification inside a family of serious games and game-based learning constructs.

27.6 Conclusion

The means and score dispersions of students' perceptions of their information competencies in the control and experimental groups were similar in the pretest (86.18 vs. 85.6). However, in the post-test, significant growth was registered in the experimental group (86.09 vs. 98.6), affirming that the main hypothesis was fulfilled. The application of gamification positively influenced students' perception of informational competencies at the Universidad Nacional Mayor de San Marcos in 2019. Likewise, in the test for dependent samples in the control and experimental groups, an increase in their perception of developing information competencies was observed (from 85.8 to 98.6). This study agrees with (Hew et al. 2016), who conducted an Asian investigation indicating that a gamified strategy can be a powerful incentive for learning. The design of a rubric validated by experts is pending for our future research, which will allow measuring the students' information competency by analyzing the learning outcomes evidence. Qualitative research focused on analyzing the experience and measuring incidences in the learning sessions is also pending.

Acknowledgements The authors acknowledge the Research Directorate of the Peruvian University of Applied Sciences for the incentive provided for this research.

The authors also acknowledge the technical contribution of the Writing Lab, Institute for the Future of Education, Tecnologico de Monterrey, Mexico, in the production of this work.

References

Boden D, Woolley M, Armstrong C, Webber JS, Abell A (2004) Alfabetización en información: la definición de CLIP (UK). Bol Asoc Andaluza Bibliotecarios 19(77):79–84. Accessed at http://dialnet.unirioja.es/servlet/articulo?codigo=130226
Buckley P, Doyle E (2016) Gamification and student motivation. Interact Learn Environ 24(6):1162–1175. https://doi.org/10.1080/10494820.2014.964263
Csikszentmihalyi M (2009) Flow theory and research. Oxford University Press
Deci LE, Ryan MR (1985) Intrinsic motivation and self-determination in human behavior. 49:6221
Deterding S, Dixon D, Khaled R, Nacke L (2011) From game design elements to gamefulness. In: Proceedings of the 15th international academic MindTrek conference on envisioning future media environments—MindTrek '11. ACM Press, New York, p 9. Accessed at https://doi.org/10.1145/2181037.2181040
Domínguez A, Saenz-de-Navarrete J, De-Marcos L, Fernández-Sanz L, Pagés C, Martínez- Herráiz JJ (2013) Gamifying learning experiences: practical implications and outcomes. Comput Educ 63:380–392. https://doi.org/10.1016/j.compedu.2012.12.020
Escamilla J, Fuerte K, Venegas E, Fernández K et al (2016) EduTrends Gamificación. Observatorio de Innovación Educativa, pp 1–36. Accessed at http://observatorio.itesm.mx
Galbis-Córdova A, Martí-Parreño J, Currás-Pérez R (2017) Higher education students use of gamification for competencies development. J E-Learn Knowl Soc 13(1):129–146
González Flores I (2014) Necesidad de la alfabetización informacional en la Educación Superior. Vivat Academia 0(121):65. https://doi.org/10.15178/va.2012.121.65-76
Hernández Sampieri R, Fernández Collado C, Baptista Lucio P (2006) Metodología de la investigación. McGraw Hill

Hew KF, Huang B, Chu KWS, Chiu DKW (2016) Engaging Asian students through game mechanics: findings from two experimental studies. Comput Educ 92–93:221–236. https://doi. org/10.1016/j.compedu.2015.10.010

Huang L-Y, Yeh Y-C (2017) Meaningful gamification for journalism students to enhance their critical thinking skills. Int J Game-Based Learn 7(2):47–62. https://doi.org/10.4018/IJGBL.201 7040104

Kapp KM (n.d.) The gamification of learning and instruction: game-based methods and strategies for training and education

Kolb DA (2015) Experiential learning: experience as the source of learning and development, 2a edn. Pearson Education, New Jersey

Nunnally JC (1978) Psychometric theory. Accessed at https://books.google.com.pe/books/about/ Psychometric_theory.html?id=WE59AAAAMAAJ&redir_esc=y

Pinter R, Čisar SM, Balogh Z, Manojlović H (2020) Enhancing higher education student class attendance through gamification. Acta Polytechn Hung 17(2):13–33. https://doi.org/10.12700/ APH.17.2.2020.2.2

Pinto M (2011) An approach to the internal facet of information literacy using the IL-HUMASS survey. J Acad Librariansh 37(2):145–154. https://doi.org/10.1016/j.acalib.2011.02.006

Pun R (2017) Hacking the research library: Wikipedia, Trump, and information literacy in the escape room at Fresno State. Libr Q 87(4):330–336. https://doi.org/10.1086/693489

ScolarTIC (2019) Introducción a la Gamificación para Docentes [Archivo de vídeo]. Accessed at https://www.scolartic.com/web/introduccion-a-la-gamificacion-para-docentes

Schofer E, Meyer JW (n.d.) The worldwide expansion of higher education in the twentieth century. American Sociological Review. American Sociological Association. https://doi.org/10.2307/414 5399

Tobón S (2008) La formación basada en competencias en la educación superior: El enfoque complejo. Accessed at http://cmapspublic3.ihmc.us/rid=1LVT9TXFX-1VKC0TM-16YT/For mación basada en competencias (Sergio Tobón).pdf

Van Roy R, Zaman B (2018) Need-supporting gamification in education: an assessment of motivational effects over time. Comput Educ 127:283–297. https://doi.org/10.1016/j.compedu.2018. 08.018

Werbach K, Hunter D (2014) Gamificación: revoluciona tu negocio con las técnicas de los juegos. Pearson Educación

Chapter 28
Design of a Technological Platform for the Implementation of the Pyramid Education Model

Carlos Aguirre Ayala, Juan Manuel García Chamizo, Omar Otoniel Flores-Cortez, and Verónica Idalia Rosa

28.1 Introduction

Education is a fundamental pillar of developing societies. The scenarios that drive innovation are built on knowledge, which has its origin in research. Thanks to technological contributions, the barriers that reduce access to training courses and professional careers are lower because various services offer curricular programs. Skills are developed more quickly in flexible learning environments because they do not depend on schedules or physical location.

To apply the Pyramid Education methodology, we used the Moodle e-learning platform and the Joomla CMS, leveraging the potential of both through an extension called Joomdle. Moodle is used to teach virtual courses; however, it presents some difficulties due to its flat and bland design. However, its limitations are minimized when integrating it with Joomla, a CMS well known for its showiness and power. By merging both platforms, Moodle can realize its full potential and present a friendly and professional environment.

C. . Aguirre Ayala · V. I. Rosa
Escuela de Informática, Universidad Tecnologica de El Salvador, San Salvador, El Salvador
e-mail: carlos.aguirre@utec.edu.sv

V. I. Rosa
e-mail: veronica.rosa@utec.edu.sv

J. M. . García Chamizo
Departamento de Tecnología Informática Y Computación, Universidad de Alicante, Alicante, España
e-mail: juanma@dtic.ua.es

O. O. Flores-Cortez (✉)
Escuela de Ciencias Aplicadas, Universidad Tecnologica de El Salvador, San Salvador, El Salvador
e-mail: omar.flores@utec.edu.sv

© The Author(s), under exclusive license to Springer Nature Singapore Pte Ltd. 2022   345
S. Hosseini et al. (eds.), *Technology-Enabled Innovations in Education*,
Transactions on Computer Systems and Networks,
https://doi.org/10.1007/978-981-19-3383-7_28

28.2 Development

28.2.1 Background

The technological revolution subjects all spheres of social life to changes, including the education sector. According to the World Summit for Innovation in Education (WISE), schools will become interactive environments in the next 15 years, and the prototype of the school, as it is known today, will change. The master class will disappear, and the teacher will become the student's guide. WISE believes that learning will be personalized, lifelong, and more expensive. According to research published on the networks, the internet will be the primary access source and English the majority language; educational systems worldwide will continue undergoing significant changes due to the technological revolution (Ally 2019).

E-Learning (or Online Learning) is a teaching–learning modality where designing, implementing, and evaluating a course or training plan are carried out in computer networks. It can be defined as an education or training offered to geographically dispersed or distant learners, some interacting in deferred times, using computer and telecommunications resources (Velazco Flórez et al. 2017).

For the implementation of online learning, computerized platforms offer a virtual learning space to facilitate the distance training experience, both for companies and educational institutions. These allow the creation of virtual classrooms, where interactions between tutors and students and among the student peers occur. The interactions include assessments, file exchanges, participation in forums, chats, and other educational exchanges (Verdezoto Rodríguez and Chávez Vaca 2018).

Online Learning platforms have the characteristics of interactivity, flexibility, scalability, standardization, usability, ubiquity, durability, and accessibility. The most used platforms include Dokeos, Ilias, Atutor, Moodle, Claroline, E-doceo, WebCT, Blackboard, and Skillfactory (Aguirre Ayala and Hernández Montoya 2016).

A content administration system is a computer application to create, edit, administer, and publish information in an easy, organized way, not requiring specialized knowledge of digital publishing. Generally, the administrative interface is user-friendly and straightforward, allowing anyone to manage web content without the need for technical knowledge or HTML. Among the main advantages of these applications are website organization, content publication, scalability, implementation of new functionalities, user administration, design and aesthetic appearance of the site, navigation and menu, image manager, flexible arrangement of modules, automated publication, archive and history, reading formats, and comment management (Notario and Reinoso 2016).

28.2.2   *Current Situation*

The purpose of educational systems is learning, which requires investment in technological and human resources to achieve the quality it deserves. We must be aware that the future of society depends on the new generations. Therefore, educators must work carefully and be committed to the educational system, seeking methodologies that use Information and Communication Technologies (ICT) to optimize education and learning quality and achieve expected results (Hernandez 2017).

The internet has considerably changed the traditional educational system. However, the internet alone does not produce better, more efficient students or professionals; their teachers' training and educational institutions must be responsibly in tune with the times (Viñals and Cuenca 2016).

There is growing consensus of the potential of the internet and related ICTs, such as electronic games, social networks, virtual environments, blogs, wikis, videos, among others, which play essential roles in less formal education and learning. ICTs facilitate the search, extraction, access, organization, treatment, transmission, and use of the information managed in educational contexts (La educación superior propende una formación para la vida en un mundo cambiante 2018).

Digital media and the internet contribute to the accelerating accumulation of data and information. Some sites have large volumes of data with no quality control to ensure that the content is reliable, adequate, and factual.

In response to this problem, interest in finding a teaching–learning methodology that strengthens educational systems has arisen.

Thus, considering current educational needs and the benefits of ICT, we developed the Pyramid Education model (Rosa et al. 2019). It is a collaborative education model to strengthen the teaching–learning process in any area of knowledge. Using the model, the teacher and student roles coexist on an online learning platform where knowledge is stratified in levels. The platform can be accessed from anywhere using the internet.

The proposed model uses a stratified or hierarchal teaching–learning process personalized to each student's level of knowledge, as shown in Fig. 28.1.

The participant roles must coexist. A member may be a teacher at one level and also a student at another level. In their role as a teacher, they will be able to create, transmit, and impart content to those who are playing the role of learner. As a learner, they will be able to access learning content produced by a higher-level teacher. Therefore, each member acts as a designer, coordinator, organizer, tutor, evaluator, and learner from the different user levels, according to Fig. 28.2. The model proposes that a Ph.D. student is in charge of tutoring two masters students; each masters student is in charge of two Engineering students and each Engineering student two Technical students.

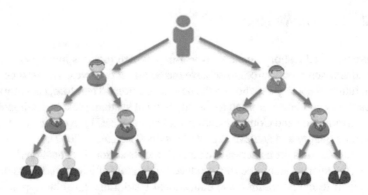

Fig. 28.1 Stratified pyramid levels

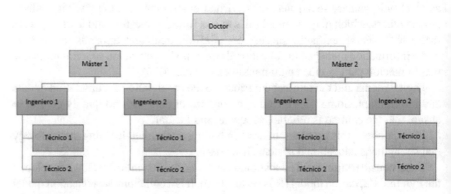

Fig. 28.2 Proposed design of the education pyramid

28.3 Method

The research will be descriptive-experimental. A description will be made of the characteristics of the elements in the study related to the development of the Joomla, Moodle, and Joomdle solution and the proposed educational model.

The method of carrying out the project reproduces the causal method. It is proposed to develop the computational platform, which, as shown in Fig. 28.3, coincides with the experimental method of science and the top-down method of design engineering (Méndez-Porras et al. 2015).

28.4 Results

The necessary processes were carried out for the development of the computing platform integrating Joomla and Moodle according to the following order:

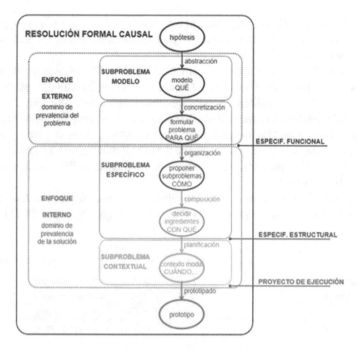

Fig. 28.3 Formal causal resolution design for problem-solving

Joomdle Installation: To download the Joomdle installation files, visit http://sou rceforge.net/projects/moodle-joomla/files/, the official site of the project (Fig. 28.4).

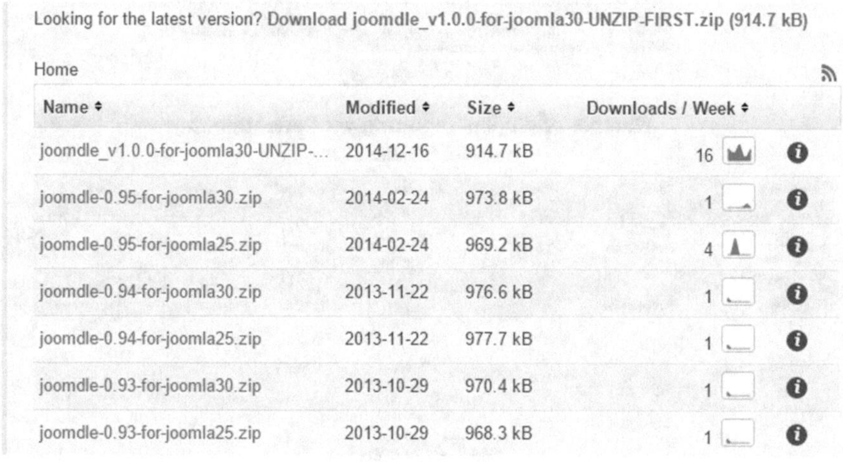

Looking for the latest version? Download joomdle_v1.0.0-for-joomla30-UNZIP-FIRST.zip (914.7 kB)

Home				
Name ⬍	Modified ⬍	Size ⬍	Downloads / Week ⬍	
joomdle_v1.0.0-for-joomla30-UNZIP-…	2014-12-16	914.7 kB	16	
joomdle-0.95-for-joomla30.zip	2014-02-24	973.8 kB	1	
joomdle-0.95-for-joomla25.zip	2014-02-24	969.2 kB	4	
joomdle-0.94-for-joomla30.zip	2013-11-22	976.6 kB	1	
joomdle-0.94-for-joomla25.zip	2013-11-22	977.7 kB	1	
joomdle-0.93-for-joomla30.zip	2013-10-29	970.4 kB	1	
joomdle-0.93-for-joomla25.zip	2013-10-29	968.3 kB	1	

Fig. 28.4 Download latest verion from Joomdle download site

The downloaded file is unzipped, and then the *auth_joomdle* and *enroll_joomdle* folders found in the unzipped folder are copied into the *auth* and *enroll* folders inside the Moodle directory (Fig. 28.5).

Open Moodle, as administrator, from the URL http://localhost/moodle/admin/, and proceed to the activation of the Joomdle extension in Moodle, as shown in Figs. 28.6 and 28.7, in addition to enabling the corresponding Web, Fig. 28.8.

XML-RPC protocols are activated in Moodle; Joomdle uses XML-RPC to connect to Moodle. The option "Enable protocols" must be selected from the list and activate XML-RPC. Some servers may also require the SOAP protocol to be enabled. For the configuration, follow the path *Site Administration-Extensions-Web services-Manage protocols* (Fig. 28.9).

User permissions to connect with Joomdle are checked; for this, follow the path *Site Administration-Users-Permissions-Define roles* (Figs. 28.10 and 28.11).

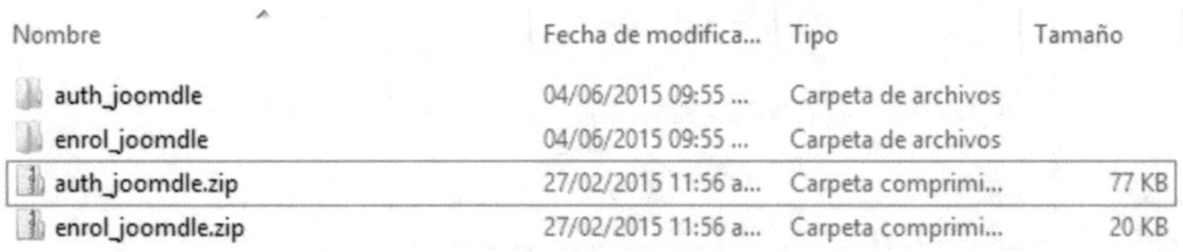

Nombre	Fecha de modifica...	Tipo	Tamaño
auth_joomdle	04/06/2015 09:55 ...	Carpeta de archivos	
enrol_joomdle	04/06/2015 09:55 ...	Carpeta de archivos	
auth_joomdle.zip	27/02/2015 11:56 a...	Carpeta comprimi...	77 KB
enrol_joomdle.zip	27/02/2015 11:56 a...	Carpeta comprimi...	20 KB

Fig. 28.5 Zipped installation file from Joomdle download site

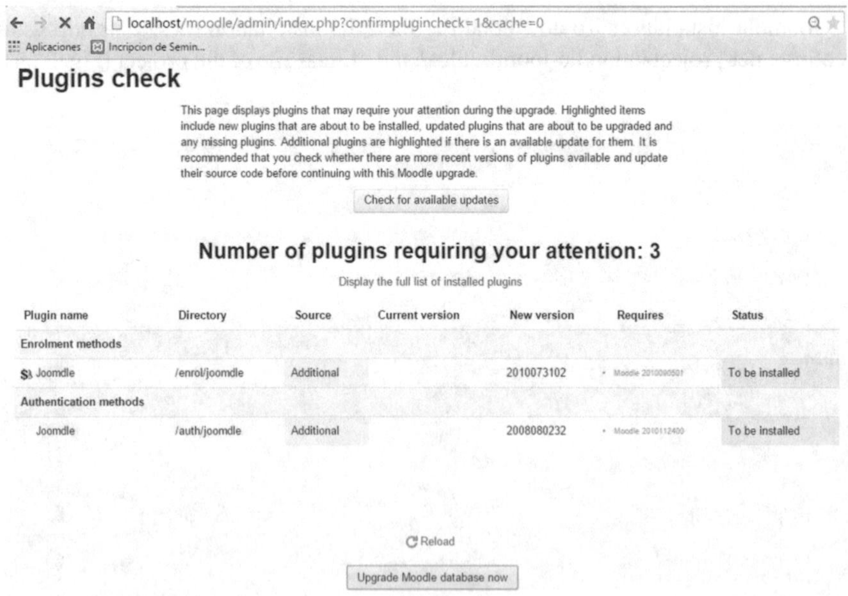

← → ✕ 🏠 localhost/moodle/admin/index.php?confirmplugincheck=1&cache=0   Q ☆
⠿ Aplicaciones 🔲 Incripcion de Semin...

Plugins check

This page displays plugins that may require your attention during the upgrade. Highlighted items include new plugins that are about to be installed, updated plugins that are about to be upgraded and any missing plugins. Additional plugins are highlighted if there is an available update for them. It is recommended that you check whether there are more recent versions of plugins available and update their source code before continuing with this Moodle upgrade.

Check for available updates

Number of plugins requiring your attention: 3

Display the full list of installed plugins

Plugin name	Directory	Source	Current version	New version	Requires	Status
Enrolment methods						
$▸ Joomdle	/enrol/joomdle	Additional		2010073102	• Moodle 2010080501	To be installed
Authentication methods						
Joomdle	/auth/joomdle	Additional		2008080232	• Moodle 2010112400	To be installed

↻ Reload

Upgrade Moodle database now

Fig. 28.6 Update Joomdle database

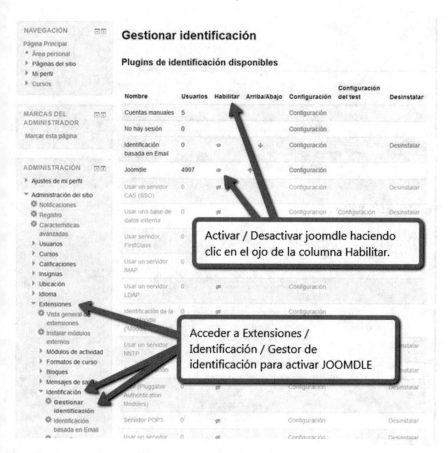

Fig. 28.7 Manage plugins from Joomdle database

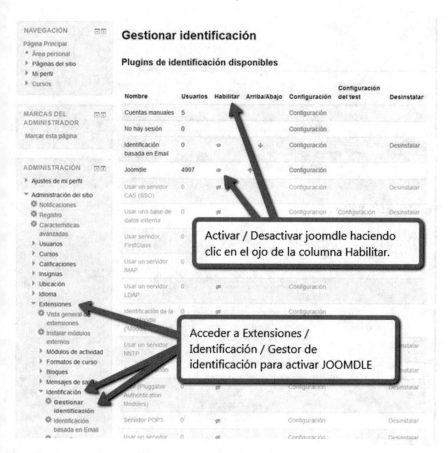

Fig. 28.8 Web services update

The following capabilities of the role are enabled for the user: Use XML-RPC protocol webservice/xmlrpc. Use SOAP web service/soap protocol. See debatesmod/forum view discussion (Fig. 28.12).

Fig. 28.9 XML-RPC protocol

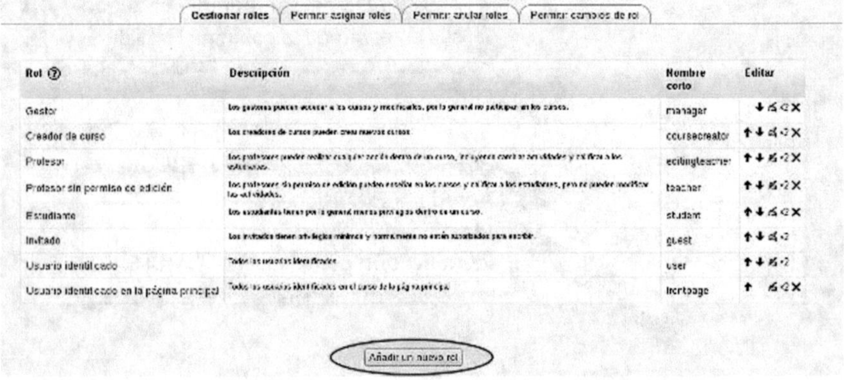

Fig. 28.10 User permissions

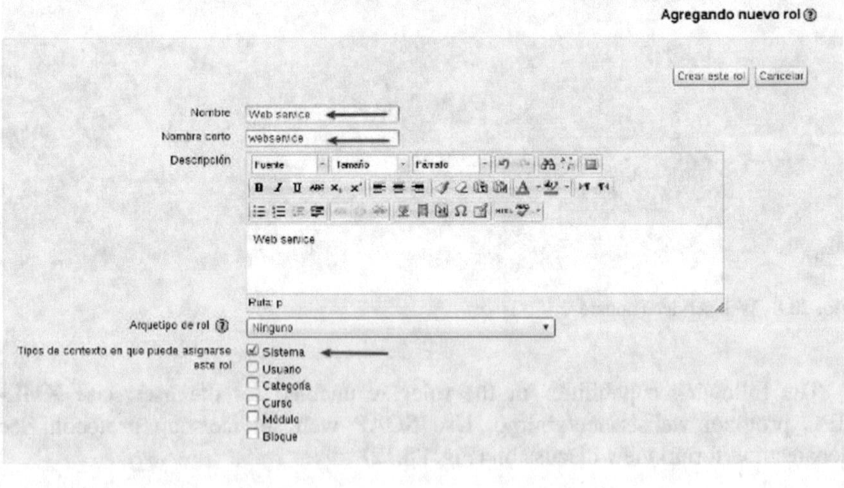

Fig. 28.11 Define roles

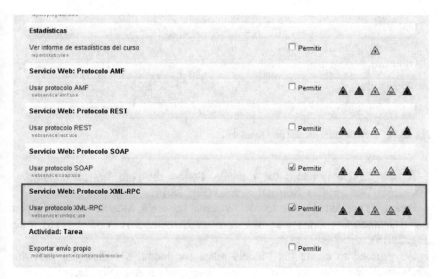

Fig. 28.12 Role capabilities for the user

The user who will be assigned Joomdle is added to the new role created, Web Services. Follow the path *Site Administration-Users-Permissions-Assign Global Roles* (Fig. 28.13).

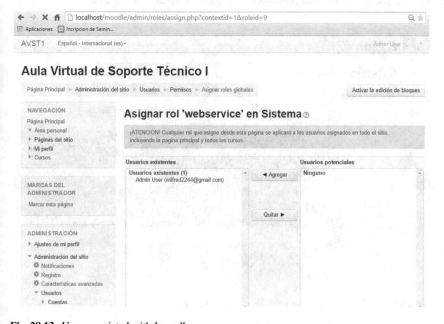

Fig. 28.13 User associated with Joomdle

Servicio externo

Nombre* Joomdla
Habilitado ☑
Únicamente usuarios ☑
autorizados ⑦

Agregar servicio   Cancelar

En este formulario hay campos obligatorios*

Fig. 28.14 Add external service into Joomdle

A new service is added for Joomdle. Follow the path *Site administration-Extensions-Web services-External services* (Fig. 28.14).

Functions are added to the Joomdle external service in Moodle. Follow the path *Site Administration-Extensions-Web Services External Services-Roles-Add Roles* (Fig. 28.15).

We proceed to create the Moodle token for Joomdle. Follow the path *Site administration-Extensions-Web services-Manage tokens-Add* (Fig. 28.16).

Identification is managed in Moodle, and the Joomla URL is assigned. To do this, follow the path *Site Administration-Extensions-Identification-Manage identification*, click on "Joomdle Configuration," and then type the URL on which Joomla is installed (Figs. 28.17 and 28.18).

Setting up Joomdle in Joomla: To do this, enter the URL of the administration module where Joomla is installed. In this case, http://localhost/administrator/. Specify the username and password (Figs. 28.19, 28.20 and 28.21).

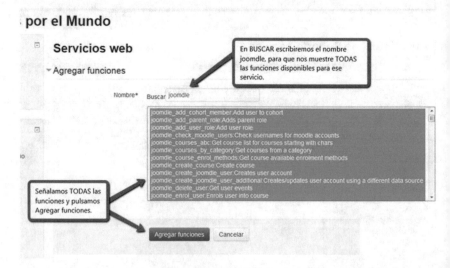

Fig. 28.15 Add functions to the Joomdle external service

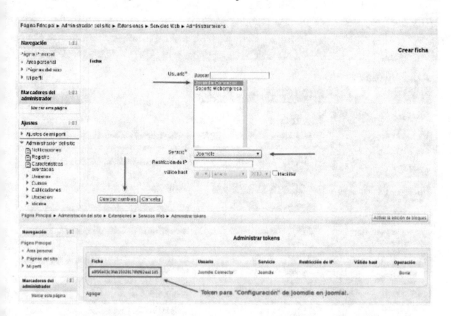

Fig. 28.16 Add more functions to the Joomdle external service

Fig. 28.17 Manage Moodle ID

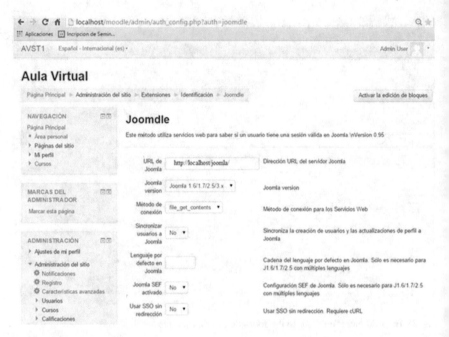

Fig. 28.18 More manage Moodle ID

Fig. 28.19 Administrator credentials

After installation, proceed to configure the installed Joomdle component. To do this, search the menu bar of the administration panel for the Components option and click on Joomdle and then on Control Panel (Fig. 28.22).

In Settings, enter the URL where Moodle is installed, as well as the authentication token (Fig. 28.23).

More configurations can be made, depending on the need of the administrator user and what he wants to show to the end-user.

The process is finished by checking that Joomla and Moodle can communicate. If any indicator appears in red, the entire process will have to be reviewed again to identify what was not done correctly (Fig. 28.24).

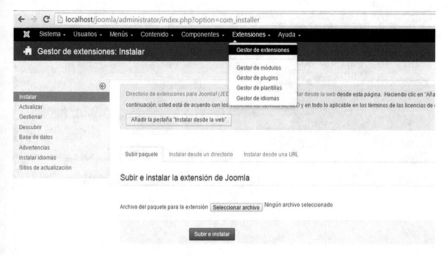

Fig. 28.20 Installing Joomdle plugin

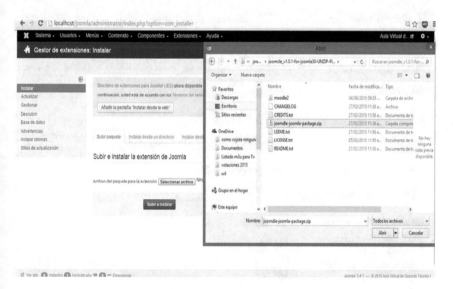

Fig. 28.21 Installing more Joomdle plugin

To display the portal, configure the main menu as a *Moodle Wrapper*. The application will be displayed within a frame, as seen in Fig. 28.25.

Fig. 28.22 Joomdle component configuration

Fig. 28.23 Joomdle settings

Fig. 28.24 More Joomdle component configuration

Fig. 28.25 Wiks portal

28.5 Discussion

At the end of the implementation, it is possible to verify that Moodle and Joomla are perfectly integrated through the Joomdle extension. With this, it is possible to obtain greater flexibility of the corporate portal and a multiplatform site that can be viewed on any device or computer without losing the significance and usability of the website.

The platform provides a pleasant experience to users. It is an excellent tool for managing classes, courses, and diplomas in the virtual mode because it provides the student with grade history and specific task events.

The virtual platform developed has been called Wiks, a solution that starts from the conceptual basis of Moodle, which is based on the pedagogical principles of social constructivism. It has a modular design which allows the teacher to add content with relative ease. The Wiks platform provides a collaborative, flexible, and friendly space where students experience the teaching–learning process.

The users on the platform are:

- Administrator
- Teacher with editing permissions
- Tutor
- Student.

The URL to access this website is https://yadaline.com/jwiki.

The implementation of this platform in a natural environment remains for future work, which will provide data for validating the proposed model.

28.6 Conclusions

Using the Education Pyramid model through an Online Learning platform provides many benefits:

- In the technological field, it is a user-friendly and valuable platform to receive and share knowledge of a specific topic.
- It is a framework for integrating ICT and education, promoting participant responsibility and collective commitment for the topic to be developed on the platform.
- It facilitates database creation with significant digital resources to develop application methodologies that generate knowledge from the data in any discipline.
- The model can be massively extended to different areas of knowledge and societal sectors; in education, it can be adapted to the academic structure of each educational institution.
- The proposed model is low cost, mainly because it relies on the participants' collaboration and coexistence of various roles. Thus, it does not incur teacher fees or high technological infrastructure costs, given that the platform is open source and no licensing is paid.

References

Aguirre Ayala CA, Hernández Montoya ME (2016) Implementación de un entorno de aprendizaje virtual integrando herramientas de e-learning y CMS. Entorno 61. https://doi.org/10.5377/entorno.v0i61.6132

Ally M (2019) Competency profile of the digital and online teacher in future education. Int Rev Res Open Distance Learn 20(2). https://doi.org/10.19173/irrodl.v20i2.4206

Bergmann, M., Gutow, L., Klages, M. (2015). Marine anthropogenic litter. https://doi.org/10.1007/978-3-319-16510-3.

Boucher, J., Billard, G., Simeone, E., & Sousa, J. (2020). *The marine plastic footprint*. Gland, Switzerland: IUCN. Viii + 69 pp.

Hernandez R (2017) Impact of ICT on education: challenges and perspectives. J Educ Psychol 5(1) La educación superior propende una formación para la vida en un mundo cambiante. Ingenio Magno 9(1)

Méndez-Porras A, Nieto Hidalgo M, García-Chamizo JM, Jenkins M, Porras AM (2015) A top-down design approach for an automated testing framework. In: Lecture notes in computer science (including subseries lecture notes in artificial intelligence and lecture notes in bioinformatics), vol 9454. https://doi.org/10.1007/978-3-319-26401-1_4

Notario Ó, Reinoso AJ (2016) Sistema de gestión de contenidos y Tienda online sincronizada con ERP. Tecnol Desarro XVI(14)

Pew Charitable Trusts and SYSTEMIQ. (2020). Breaking the plastic wave. https://www.systemiq.earth/breakingtheplasticwave/

Rosa I, Aguirre CA, Flores OO, Chamizo JMG (2019) Pyramidal Education: a collaborative learning style to support teaching in any area of knowledge. In: XLV Latin American computing conference, pp 1–6. https://doi.org/10.1109/CLEI47609.2019.235062

Velazco Flórez SY, Abuchar Porras A, Castilla I, Rivera K (2017) e-Learning: Rompiendo fronteras. Redes Ing. https://doi.org/10.14483/2248762X.12480

Verdezoto Rodríguez RH, Chávez Vaca VA (2018) Importancia de las herramientas y entornos de aprendizaje dentro de la plataforma e-learning en las universidades del Ecuador. Edutec Rev Electrónica Tecnol Educ 65. https://doi.org/10.21556/edutec.2018.65.1067

Viñals A, Cuenca J (2016) El rol del docente en la era digital The Role of Teachers in the Digital Age. Rev Interuniv Form del Profr 86(2)

Williams, A. T., & Rangel-Buitrago, N. (2019). Marine litter: Solutions for a major environmental problem. *Journal of Coastal Research*, *35*(3), 648–663. Coconut Creek (Florida), ISSN 0749-0208.

Chapter 29
DidacTIC: Strategy Based on Gamification that Seeks to Contribute to the Solution of Desertion in Virtual Education

Julieth Katherin Acosta-Medina, Martha Liliana Torres-Barreto, and Maira Camila Paba-Medina

29.1 Introduction

Education is essential for society; it is a country's primary growth driver, training people to acquire knowledge and cognitive, emotional, and communication skills to lead organizations and create relevant environments. There are different phases of educational training: primary, high school, undergraduate, and higher, and different modalities: face-to-face, semi-face-to-face, and virtual. Virtual pedagogical projects in virtual education close the inequitable gaps of access to the educational system because they allow various population groups from different regions the opportunity to increase their knowledge, complement their education, and develop new skills convenient to their schedules and space (Crisol-Moya et al. 2020).

This educational modality is accelerating worldwide, supported by technological advances due to the enforced confinements of the Covid-19 pandemic. However, a high percentage of students drop out of their online courses or careers due to multiple factors, including low motivation (Rodríguez-Pineda and Zamora-Araya 2021). To address this, we present a strategy called DidacTIC, based on gamification and machine learning principles and artificial intelligence techniques, as a possible solution to this problem. In addition, the initial results of the implementation of this strategy in a higher education institution in northwestern Colombia are described.

J. K. Acosta-Medina (✉) · M. L. Torres-Barreto · M. C. Paba-Medina
Escuela de Estudios Industriales y Empresariales, Universidad Industrial de Santander, Bucaramanga, Colombia
e-mail: katheacosta19@gmail.com

M. L. Torres-Barreto
e-mail: mltorres@uis.edu.co

M. C. Paba-Medina
e-mail: mairacami28@gmail.com

© The Author(s), under exclusive license to Springer Nature Singapore Pte Ltd. 2022   363
S. Hosseini et al. (eds.), *Technology-Enabled Innovations in Education*,
Transactions on Computer Systems and Networks,
https://doi.org/10.1007/978-981-19-3383-7_29

29.2 Theoretical Framework

Virtual education refers to the training programs whose teaching and learning rely on virtual media and environments. This modality has rapidly spread worldwide due to the changes brought about by the Covid-19 pandemic. This situation forced millions of students out of their classrooms to virtual learning environments to avoid the contagion of this virus. Among the advantages of virtuality are the non-geographic restrictions, cost reductions, and access flexibility (García Sánchez et al. 2018). However, a high proportion of these students have abandoned their virtual training program, making dropping out one of virtual education's main problems currently researched (Jara Contreras 2020).

"Dropout" refers to the students dropping out of school caused by a combination of various factors. Its study can be approached from two perspectives: time and space. Regarding time, pre-matriculation dropout occurs before the enrollment process, early desertion in the first academic periods, and late dropout in the last semesters. Concerning space, desertion depends on the educational institution or the academic program (González Castro et al. 2017).

Gamification is an educational innovation that can be used to counteract dropout. This Anglo-Saxon term originated in business in reference to the attraction and retention of customers. However, in the context of this educational innovation, it refers to the use of game elements that increase the concentration and commitment of the students, motivating them, and, therefore, promoting learning, problem-solving, and positively impacting their academic performance (Pascuas et al. 2017).

For this reason, the use of gamification in the context of dropping out is very appropriate because the gaming elements of this methodology characteristically increase emotions and the generation of dopamine during the learning process, making it more effective and motivating (Acosta-Medina et al. 2020).

29.3 Problem Statement

The incidence of Covid-19 has boosted virtual education, but one of its major problems is academic dropouts. For Latin American countries such as Bolivia, dropouts in 2020 in universities reached 35%; in Peru, 18.6%; and in Mexico, 38%. Colombia is no exception. Even though Colombian universities decided to grant tuition discounts ranging from ten to 80%, about 16% of students still dropped out of higher education (Perez Rodriguez 2021).

Regarding the causes of this student dropout, no reason has been found that predominates. It may be due to the sum of many circumstances, such as financial or personal aspects, displeasure with the methodology, poor communication, little support, and problems with time organization (González Castro et al. 2017).

These causes associated with desertion can be classified as internal, personal, and external. The internal factors are related to the institution's situations, such as interpersonal relationships, academic processes, poor accompaniment, and teachers' lack of experience. Personal causes refer to the low commitment of students, the lack of time organization, intellectual capacities, study habits, and technological skills. External causes include family situations, financial factors, and the work context (González Castro et al. 2017).

In the case of Colombia, different studies indicate that the risks of desertion in virtual programs can be classified into five categories: ignorance, dissatisfaction, lack, poor communication, and absence (González Castro et al. 2017). A common factor is low student motivation, which is the main challenge for teachers and educational institutions (Rueda Ramírez et al. 2020; Rodríguez Urrego 2019).

Therefore, it is necessary to apply strategies that act on causes, so balance and greater motivation are provided to the student to counteract this problem.

29.4 Method

The mixed descriptive method used in this research was semi-experimental and cross-sectional in nature. It was intended to develop and validate a gamified tool to reduce attrition. The study began with a documentary review of gamification in educational settings and its influence on dropouts. Subsequently, gamification was used to develop a strategy to boost student motivation and reduce the dropouts in our virtual programs. Finally, the initial results of implementing this strategy in the virtual programs of this university n in northwestern Colombia were analyzed.

29.5 Results

29.5.1 The Role of Gamification in Virtual Education

The results of the documentary review indicated that in the current context, improving student motivation is essential in virtual training. In the development of virtual learning environments, one must consider not only theories of educational pedagogy but also the motivation variable as a cross-sectional factor (Candia García 2016). Likewise, to perform well in virtual teaching and learning environments, users require the competencies of autonomy, self-discipline, good study habits, organization, efficiency at work, and willingness to learn. These can be developed and enhanced through motivational strategies that increase students' interest in their academic progress (González Castro et al. 2017).

One of the strategies that can be used in virtual environments is gamification. It directly stimulates intrinsic motivation, awakening curiosity, interest, or satisfaction. The extrinsic motivation from gamification comes from using external elements such as rewards or prizes to attract the participants (Acosta-Medina et al. 2020). These gamified technological tools are relevant in the virtual modality because they add to engaging experiences and support the development of social skills necessary to interact online (Melo-Solarte and Díaz 2018).

In recent years, gamified environments have been created that demonstrate the benefits of incorporating game concepts into the educational process. These include increased knowledge retention, improved social skills, and decreased student dropouts (Moreno Guerrero et al. 2021). However, to implement them successfully, it must be considered that motivation goes hand in hand with participation, so it is crucial to establish an efficient connection between students and teachers (Landers et al. 2017).

29.5.2 "DidacTIC" Gamified Strategy

Our work proposes the joint development of a communication platform and motivational didactic tool based on gamification principles and supported by Information and Communication Technologies (ICT). The strategy rests on two pillars: (1) play as a support element and (2) constant and effective communication between students and teachers on a study platform (see Fig. 29.1).

1. A game called "Didactic City" was designed, which focuses on teaching citizenship skills. The construction of Didactic City considered an ethnographic analysis of the students and characteristics of the virtual programs for a Colombia intervention. As a result, we created a narrative with a futuristic environment and gameplay requiring building mechanics and collecting. The player must gather resources and solve missions described by multiple-choice questions presenting moral dilemmas with an open, single-answer response that promotes argumentation and writing. The problem situations seek to potentiate systemic thinking and multi-perspectivism.

2. The communication platform was developed as a Knowledge Management System (KMS) to extract information from the Didactic City game interactions and the Learning Management System (LMS) used by the virtual programs. These data were the basis for establishing the communication means and student messaging. It used email, text messages, and calls to inform students of their level of progress in the "Didactic City" tool. They were congratulated

Fig. 29.1 DidacTIC gamified strategy

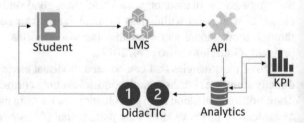

for their academic achievements and reminded of the delivery dates for work or exam presentations in the different subjects. These communications were achieved thanks to computational cognitive models based on machine learning, combining neural networks and decision trees, which determined the students' motivational level. We analyzed connection frequency, days of highest use, and activities that generated a more significant presence.

The game "Didactic City" was developed using the C# programming language in the Unity 3D video game engine. It connected with the communications platform through API REST and JSON coding that facilitated the storage and distribution of text, configuring a front-end and back-end infrastructure. In the front-end were the direct player interactions with "Didactic City," the communication messages to the students, and the interactive board with the student motivation and desertion probability in each course. The back end was the information management from one end to the other, allowing the content of the missions to be modified, the prediction history analysis, the frequency configuration, and the message communications.

29.5.3   "DidacTIC" Implementation

The DidacTIC strategy was implemented in 15 courses at a Colombian university with 100% virtual academic programs. The students who used this strategy were between 18 and 25 years old; 50.7% were men, and 49.3% were women (see Fig. 29.2).

On a scale of 1–5, where 1 corresponds to disagree and 5 to agree, on average, students found the experience of using Didactic City pleasant (with an overall score of 4.12), an easy-to-use tool (4.17) that allowed them to increase their knowledge of citizenship skills (4.07), and kept them motivated in their virtual classes (3.96) (see Fig. 29.3). Likewise, when using Didactic City, the students felt motivated to use the knowledge acquired thanks to this tool (4.03) because it increased their interest in learning (3.89) and made them happy (3.66) (see Fig. 29.4).

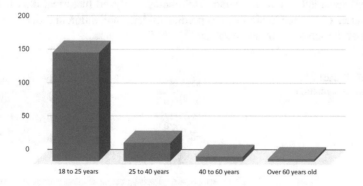

Fig. 29.2   Age of students who used DidacTIC

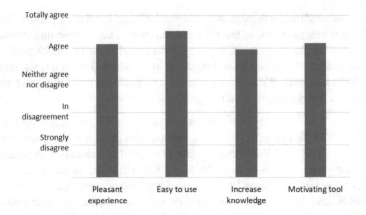

Fig. 29.3 Students' perception about DidacTIC

Fig. 29.4 Student emotions when using DidacTIC

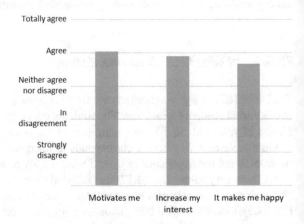

The computational cognitive model that measures student motivation was analyzed separately in each course. This model analyzed historical data from the first quarter of the academic term to predict student motivation and dropout in the middle of the school term, as shown in Fig. 29.5.

Fig. 29.5 DidacTIC motivational prediction model

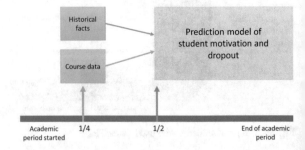

Table 29.1 Students' motivation level course 1

Student	Status	Probability
17,373		41.06
16,088		99.74
19,146		99.83
19,097		99.83
19,092		89.87
19,562		41.44
19,816		99.83
19,136		99.59
19,568		99.83
19,107		99.83

As shown in Table 29.1, each teacher could visualize their students' motivation level on an interactive board. When the probability had a value less than 50, that student had low motivation, reflecting a high risk of dropping out of the course. On the contrary, if the probability had a value greater than 50, this student had high motivation, reflecting a low risk of dropping out of the course.

Based on the student motivation levels, each teacher could make decisions, such as providing more significant support to the students, answering their questions, or referring them to university wellness programs (psychology, pedagogical support, financial benefits, etc.) Currently, this strategy is still being implemented, and its data is compared with historical data of the institution, making it possible to measure the impact of the DidacTIC game.

29.6 Conclusions and Discussion

It should be noted that learning is a continuous process requiring continuous motivation. Although students have will initially, it usually decreases as the topics progress and the complexity of the course increases (García Sánchez et al. 2018). Therefore, it is essential to use innovative tools that promote commitment and increase student motivation.

On the other hand, virtual education requires careful planning and execution because any weakness harms the teaching and learning process and can cause student dropouts. Therefore, in developing virtual learning platforms, it is essential to consider motivational strategies that achieve student commitment and help them develop social skills such as autonomy and time organization.

These strategies can be included in virtual environments through gamification, which contributes to the permanence of students because the game elements promote creativity and a dynamic, pleasant environment of playful spaces for interactions among participants and conditions that facilitate knowledge retention. Although it should be noted that to successfully implement these gamified technological tools, there must be effective connection mechanisms that improve communication and user participation.

For future studies, it is recommended to analyze the connectivity of the impacted students and develop tools that do not require the internet, thus extending access to a more significant number of the population. In addition, we expect to continue developing research related to DidacTIC, using the databases derived from the tool and the platform, to continue analyzing the incidence and impact of this strategy in education.

Acknowledgements Special thanks for the financial support received for the realization of this project to the General System of Royalties funds of CTel of the Government of Antioquia administered through the Autonomous Heritage National Fund of Financing for Science, Technology and Innovation Francisco José de Caldas—MINCIENCIAS-, and the Galea educational innovation laboratory of the Industrial University of Santander.

The authors acknowledge the technical support of the Writing Lab, Institute for the Future of Education, Tecnologico de Monterrey, Monterrey, Mexico, in the production of this work.

References

Acosta-Medina JK, Torres-Barreto ML, Álvarez-Melgarejo M, Paba-Medina MC (2020) Gamificación en el ámbito educativo: un análisis bibliométrico. I+D Rev Investig 15(1):28–36. https://doi.org/10.33304/revinv.v15n1-2020003
Acosta-Medina JK, Torres-Barreto ML, Alvarez-Melgarejo M (2020) Literature mapping about gamification in the teaching and learning processes. Rev Espac 41(11):26. Available: https://www.revistaespacios.com/a20v41n11/a20v41n11p26.pdf
Candia García F (2016) Diseño de un modelo curricular E-learning, utilizando una metodología activa participative. RIDE Rev Iberoam para la Investig el Desarro Educ 7(13):147–182

Crisol-Moya E, Herrera-Nieves L, Montes-Soldado R (2020) Educación virtual para todos: una revisión sistemática. Educ Knowl Soc 21:13. https://doi.org/10.14201/eks.23448

García Sánchez MR, Reyes Añorve J, Godínez Alarcón G (2018) Las Tic en la educación superior, innovaciones y retos/The ICT in higher education, innovations and challenges. RICSH Rev Iberoam Ciencias Soc Humanísticas 6(12):299–316. https://doi.org/10.23913/ricsh.v6i12.135

González Castro Y, Manzano Durán O, Torres Zamudio M (2017) Riesgos de deserción en las universidades virtuales de Colombia, frente a las estrategias de retención. Libr Empres 14(2):177–197. https://doi.org/10.18041/1657-2815/libreempresa.2017v14n2.3038

Jara Contreras EA (2020) Deserción estudiantil en educación superior tecnológica: causas e implicancias socioeconómicas e institucionales. Universidad César Vallejo

Landers RN, Armstrong MB, Collmus AB (2017) How to use game elements to enhance learning: applications of the theory of gamified learning. In: Serious games and edutainment applications. Springer International Publishing, Cham, pp 457–483

Melo-Solarte DS, Díaz PA (2018) El Aprendizaje Afectivo y la Gamificación en Escenarios de Educación Virtual. Inf Tecnológica 29(3):237–248. https://doi.org/10.4067/S0718-076420180 0300237

Moreno Guerrero AJ, Trujillo Torres JM, Aznar Diaz I (2021) Metodologías activas para la enseñanza universitaria. Editorial GRAOS, Barcelona, España

Pascuas Y, Vargas E, Muñoz J (2017) Experiencias motivacionales gamificadas: una revisión sistemática de literatura. Innovación Educ 17(75):63–80

Perez Rodriguez FJ (2021) La deserción universitaria en América Latina, por Covid-19. Coordinación de la Investigación Científica. https://www.cic.umich.mx/coronavirus/123-la-desercion-universitaria-en-america-latina-por-covid-19.html. Accessed 04 Aug 2021

Rodríguez Urrego M (2019) La investigación sobre deserción universitaria en Colombia 2006–2016. Tendencias y resultados. Pedagog Saberes 51. https://doi.org/10.17227/pys.num51-8664

Rodríguez-Pineda M, Zamora-Araya JA (2021) Abandono temprano en estudiantes universitarios: un estudio de cohorte sobre sus posibles causas. Uniciencia 35(1):19–37. https://doi.org/10.15359/ru.35-1.2

Rueda Ramírez SM, Urrego Velásquez D, Páez Zapata E, Velásquez C, Hernández Ramírez EM (2020) Perfiles de riesgo de deserción en estudiantes de las sedes de una universidad colombiana. Rev Psicol 38(1):275–297. https://doi.org/10.18800/psico.202001.011

Chapter 30
Challenges to Technology-Enhanced Collaborative Learning in a Disability-Inclusive Research Partnership: The Case of the PIRL Project

Julius Nganji, Ellen Murray, Soomin Lee, Deb Cameron, Lynn Cockburn, Anika Chowdhury, Jane A. Davis, Lesley Lepawa Sikapa, Louis Mbibeh, and Mahadeo Sukhai

30.1 Introduction

Both research partnerships and communities of practice (CoPs) are vital to the conduct of high-quality research. CoPs promote knowledge sharing and collaborative learning among members with a common interest (Wenger 1996). In academia, CoPs can create research opportunities with varying levels of member engagement

J. Nganji (✉) · S. Lee · D. Cameron · L. Cockburn · J. A. Davis
Department of Occupational Science and Occupational Therapy, University of Toronto, Toronto, Canada
e-mail: j.nganji@utoronto.ca

S. Lee
e-mail: soominn.lee@mail.utoronto.ca

D. Cameron
e-mail: deb.cameron@utoronto.ca

L. Cockburn
e-mail: l.cockburn@utoronto.ca

J. A. Davis
e-mail: ja.davis@utoronto.ca

M. Sukhai
Research and IDEA Teams, Canadian National Institute for the Blind, Department of Ophthalmology, Faculty of Health Sciences, Queens University, Kingston, Canada
e-mail: mahadeo.sukhai@cnib.ca

E. Murray
E Murray Consulting, Toronto, Canada

© The Author(s), under exclusive license to Springer Nature Singapore Pte Ltd. 2022   373
S. Hosseini et al. (eds.), *Technology-Enabled Innovations in Education*,
Transactions on Computer Systems and Networks,
https://doi.org/10.1007/978-981-19-3383-7_30

(Smith et al. 2017; Chien 2021). Eventually, this engagement can lead to more formal collaborations and the development of research teams and partnerships (Demers and Tremblay 2021).

In CoPs, a key determinant of successful learning is developing reflexivity and cultural intelligence among their members (Tharapos and O'Connell 2020). Cultural intelligence refers to an individual's ability to harness the "three interdependent strengths of thinking, energizing, and acting" (Earley and Mosakowski 2004) in ways that recognize the uniquely complex intersectional nature of each group member so that strong working relationships can be maintained. CoPs have internal cultural norms and values, for example, the inclusion of members with disabilities. Very few studies exist on CoPs comprised of researchers with and without disabilities. When persons with disabilities (PWDs) are part of the CoP, technologies must be accessible to them (Marques et al. 2016; Mortier 2020) and implemented by *all* group members. Parity of technology access (Gallardo et al. 2021) is fundamental to creating full participation and equity within CoP activities. Without these cultural and technological considerations, full participation in the CoP will be compromised for members with disabilities.

Within both local and global CoPs, communication has become progressively mediated by digital technologies, such as cellphones, laptops, and media platforms (e.g., MS Teams, Slack, Facebook, WhatsApp) (Home—G3ict 2018; Gilbert 2016; Harniss et al. 2015; Willemse 2015). Examining how information and communication technologies (ICT) are used is critical for determining assumptions about barriers to accessibility and learning in various populations.

ICT accessibility for people with disabilities must also be considered. Further research is needed to understand how researchers in low-income countries learn about the relationship between disability and ICT access (Harniss et al. 2015; Barlott et al. 2016; Gould et al. 2015; Matter et al. 2017; Samant et al. 2013). One program that aims to further understand this complexity is the World Health Organization's (WHO) Global Cooperation on Assistive Technology (GATE) (WHO 2021). Most of this work focuses on PWDs as recipients or respondents rather than as researchers and contributors of knowledge (Hughes 2020). Given the limited literature on CoPs comprised of researchers with and without disabilities, it would be beneficial to understand the process of forming and maintaining such groups, their challenges, and how these challenges are addressed.

The Partnerships for Inclusive Research and Learning (PIRL) is a CoP of about 100 members in Canada, Cameroon, and several other countries. One aim of the PIRL

L. L. Sikapa
Faculty of Arts and Science, University of Toronto, Toronto, Canada
e-mail: lesley.sikapa@utoronto.ca

A. Chowdhury
Master of Public Service, University of Waterloo, Waterloo, Canada
e-mail: anika.chowdhury@uwaterloo.ca

L. Mbibeh
University of Bamenda, Bamenda, Cameroon

CoP is to expand the sparse literature on researchers with disabilities, especially in the Global South, including their use of ICTs. The CoP's actions focus on strategies to build inclusive research teams that include researchers living with disabilities. Together, PIRL members examine how ICTs contribute to the collaborative learning of researchers within research teams and their ICT challenges.

To address the existing knowledge gap about disability inclusion in CoPs, this paper presents preliminary findings of a survey aimed at identifying the ICT challenges that CoPs such as the PIRL face in fostering equitable participation of its members. Our work is relevant to other research groups working within the context of the global COVID-19 pandemic and the resulting shift to mostly technology-mediated interactions and learning.

30.2 Literature Review

30.2.1 CoPs and Collaborative Learning

CoPs are based on the principles of collaborative learning, which involves at least two people learning together. One of the advantages of collaborative learning is that group members improve their understanding of the subject matter through the collaborative construction of knowledge (Wenger 1996; Zhong 2021; Herrera-Pavo 2021).

In technology-enhanced collaborative learning, those who would have otherwise felt shy or unable to speak in a face-to-face meeting can send their contributions digitally and contribute to online discussions (Medaille and Usinger 2018). Social media can facilitate collaborative learning because learners use their cell phones and computers to share content (Sungkur et al. 2020). WhatsApp is an effective collaborative learning platform, especially in resource-limited settings. For example, in Cameroon, where there are frequent power outages and poor internet connections, WhatsApp is often preferred; it uses phone connections rather than more expensive data-facilitated connections (Pacholek et al. 2021).

Members of a CoP need to interact actively with others to contribute and engage in the project (Qureshi et al. 2021). Previous research has suggested that collaborative learning can lead to improved success and cultural intelligence (Hei et al. 2019). Similarly, one could expect that collaborative learning and interaction of members in a disability-inclusive research team could increase awareness of all team members' strengths, needs, and contributions, leading to better research outcomes and uptake.

30.2.2 Technology and Learning During a Pandemic

During its first year, the PIRL CoP used a hybrid approach to learning where members participated in virtual and in-person meetings. Members gathered in person for team meetings and annual institutes (Hammad et al. 2020; Mbibeh et al. 2021). With the COVID-19 pandemic, all activities shifted to an online-only format. Studies have shown that pandemics disrupt collaborative teamwork (Wildman et al. 2021) as individuals and the team face challenges.

Teaching and research are two sectors that have been greatly affected by the pandemic, requiring immediate shifts to online delivery (Cen et al. 2020; Stanković et al.). During this pandemic, mobile devices with data access are also playing a crucial role in collaborative learning, both formally and informally (Salas Rueda et al. 2021). Good access to technological devices and the internet positively impacts how people contribute to a CoP.

The digital divide is the gap between those who have access to ICTs and those who do not or do not have as much access as they need. For example, studies in the USA found that those more affected by the digital divide were low-income persons, people of color, older people, indigenous persons, PWD, and rural residents (Gallardo et al. 2021; Sanders and Scanlon 2021). International studies, including a series of six regional reports released by the International Telecommunication Union of the United Nations, confirm these digital divides by gender, income, age, and geography (Rowntree and Shanahan 2020; International Telecommunications Union 2021).

When examined in the context of the Global South, factors influencing the complexities of the digital divide are beginning to emerge. In the African continent, for example, it has been found that low infrastructure sharing, which refers to the "sharing of telecommunications networks to transmit services to end-users," contributes to widening this divide (Arakpogun et al. 2020). Also, affordability and digital literacy are key determinants of access to and internet use in Africa (Aikins 2019). The digital divide appears wider in rural areas, which usually have less infrastructure than urban areas (Lembani et al. 2020). A study in Cameroon found that significant portions of low-income populations do not have access to the internet and ICT tools (Kuika Watat and Jonathan 2020). Regarding mobile phone usage in some low-income countries, when the African continent was compared to Asia, a study found a broader digital divide in Asia (Vimalkumar et al. 2020).

Within the digital divide, another often overlooked is the disability divide (Dobransky and Hargittai 2016; Tsaliki and Kontogianni 2014; Aranda-Jan and Boutard 2019; Pal et al. 2016). This divide widens every time technologies are not designed with accessibility in mind; however, it can be bridged through collaborative efforts such as the GATE initiative (WHO 2021).

While the above studies have focused on primary aspects of interest, very few have examined collaborative learning within inclusive research teams. Thus, this study examined the challenges faced by members of a diverse CoP to become more inclusive and provide recommendations for addressing identified challenges. The overarching research question was "When, how, and why are information and communication technologies (ICT) used in communities of practice (CoP) that focus on disability-inclusive development?".

30.3   Methodology

This study used a survey methodology. Surveys are well suited for gathering specific information across a large group of people from diverse locations. Before conducting this study, ethical clearance was obtained from the University of Toronto, Canada (Ref: 39308) and the University of Bamenda, Cameroon (Ref: 2019/0124H/UBa/IRB).

30.3.1   Data Collection and Management

An online SurveyMonkey questionnaire was designed and administered by PIRL members. The survey contained some questions from the Canadian Internet Use Survey (CIUS), which measures access to the internet and devices. A convenience sampling technique was used. The survey was sent to members of the PIRL CoP between September–November 2020. The survey contained both closed and open-ended questions related to individual access to mobile phones, computers, and the internet and individual use of ICT and the costs of online communication. There were questions on individual characteristics, including the Washington Group Questions (The Washington Group 2021) on functioning and disability self-identification.

Responses to the survey were reviewed, and invalid (incomplete) results were omitted. Two team members coded personally identifiable information to ensure confidentiality. The completed results were downloaded in Excel format for collaborative analysis by PIRL members.

30.3.2   Data Analysis

Our team collectively analyzed the survey data using descriptive statistical analyses, including frequencies and percentages, to glean preliminary interpretations from the data to answer the research question. These survey questions were developed to help respond to the PIRL CoP aim of "improving the inclusion of persons with disabilities in research teams." Microsoft Excel was used to analyze the data while the figures were generated using Prism GraphPad, a graphing and statistical analysis software.

30.4 Results

Over 70 respondents completed at least some part of the survey, with a final dataset of 60 respondents. Of the 60 respondents, 11 (18%) self-identified as living with a disability, 23 identified as female, and 25 identified as male. No respondents selected the "other" gender category, and 12 people did not respond to this question.

There were 33 respondents from Africa and 15 from North America and Europe; 12 did not provide their location. Respondents ranged in age from 25 to 65. We coded income ranges as high, medium, and low to address differences in absolute income relative to each location. Not all respondents disclosed their reported income range. Of the Global South respondents, 12 were in the high-income category, four in medium, and 12 in low income. The Global North respondents included nine in the high category, zero in medium, and five in low income.

We identified three themes during this preliminary analysis: (1) access to devices, (2) individual access to the internet, and (3) technology infrastructure. In addition to describing each theme, we included challenges related to finances, living with disabilities, and digital literacy where information was available.

Access to devices: All 60 survey respondents had access to a mobile phone and could use it to access the internet. When asked if they owned a computer, 83% of the respondents said yes. They were asked if they had a desktop, laptop, or tablet computer. Table 30.1 shows the distribution of ownership of computer devices by geographic location, with 18% of African respondents not owning a computer and none owning all three types of computers. In comparison, all Global North respondents owned a computer, and 20% owned a desktop, laptop, and tablet. Unlimited access to a computer also differed significantly by geographic location. Figure 30.1 shows that over 40% of Global South respondents could not use a computer as much as they wanted. This limitation of access to a computer was not seen in the Global North respondents.

Fifteen people responded when asked, "What prevents you from having a computer?" Thirteen comments referred to financial constraints. A more general question asked why respondents did not have as much access to technology as they desired. The top three reasons provided were cost (22 responses), limited access to a computer (7 responses), and lack of skills or training (4 responses).

Table 30.1 Counts of desktop, laptop, and tablet computers owned by respondents

Location	Do you own a desktop? A laptop? A tablet? (Yes/No)				
	Zero devices	One device	Two devices	Three devices	Grand total
Africa	6	17	10	0	33
North America and Europe	0	6	6	3	15
Location unknown	2	7	2	0	12
Total responses	8	30	18	3	60

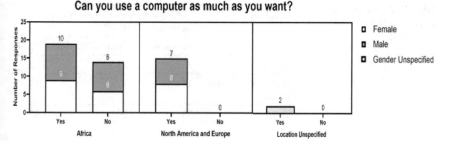

Fig. 30.1 Access to a computer by gender and location

Individual access to the internet: Respondents in Africa did not have as much internet access as those outside Africa. They could not use the internet as much as they wanted, whereas those in North America and Europe reported using it as much as they desired (see Fig. 30.2). The high financial costs associated with internet access were noted by many of the African respondents, with and without disabilities.

Most respondents indicated that their internet access at work could be used for professional development. Many in Africa were not allowed to use the work internet connection for PIRL activities because, although PIRL collaboration was professional development, it was not directly part of their employment.

Technology Infrastructure: The survey data showed that respondents in North America and Europe had consistent internet connections all the time, compared to those in Africa who usually had intermittent connections (see Table 30.2). Fisher's exact test statistic value is <0.00001. The result is statistically significant at $p < 0.05$.

One respondent commented, "Access is further challenged by poor internet connectivity in Cameroon. This is due to bad business from service providers who do not care about customers [and] government manipulation of connectivity as a tool of control and oppression." Other comments were, "To have reliable internet, I am

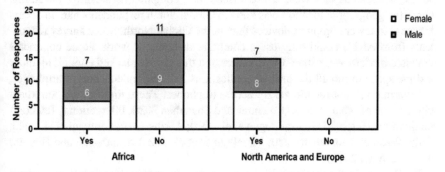

Fig. 30.2 Access to the internet by gender and location

Table 30.2 Access to a consistent internet connection by location

Location	Do you have access to a consistent internet connection?		
	All the time	Some of the time	Total
Africa	7	25	32
North America and Europe	13	1	14
Total	20	26	46

obliged to use all four providers… [and] I still cannot guarantee internet access;" the network "is sometimes very slow and unstable." A second major infrastructure challenge for numerous respondents from Africa was intermittent electricity, with comments about blackouts and trouble charging phones, their primary way to access the internet.

30.5 Discussion

This paper presented the preliminary findings identifying the challenges that an inclusion-oriented CoP, such as PIRL, faces when fostering equitable member participation. Overall, the findings indicated a digital divide between PIRL members in Africa and those in Europe and North America. Our preliminary review of the data (not presented here) indicates that the divide is even more apparent among PWD living in Africa, which will be further explored in our ongoing research.

In this synthesis, we highlight challenges to collaborative learning and participation in knowledge co-construction, a key goal of partnership research. Difficulties with using devices and access to the internet impact all aspects of research processes for all team members, regardless of geographic location.

Challenges Associated with Access and Use of Devices: Respondents in North America and Europe had access to computers, tablets, and mobile phones that they can use as much as they want. The distribution of computer ownership showed that where the geographic location was known, Global South respondents had no access or access to fewer computer devices than in the Global North. Some survey respondents from Africa could only use a computer at home or work. Some comments indicated devices were shared with others and that devices lacked enough memory or drive space to run all the desired applications. All respondents had smartphones, and sharing was not mentioned for access to phones. These findings are congruent with a range of other studies (Rowntree and Shanahan 2020; International Telecommunications Union 2021; Arakpogun et al. 2020; Aikins 2019; Lembani et al. 2020; Kuika Watat and Jonathan 2020; Vimalkumar et al. 2020; Aranda-Jan and Boutard 2019; Pal et al. 2016).

For PIRL CoP members to fully participate in collaborative learning, they need full access to technological devices to facilitate interaction. When the technology is not available or is available but not accessible, the members are excluded. This exclusion has repercussions not only for the excluded individual but the entire team. This digital divide obviously precludes PIRL members in the Global South; this divide is also a barrier to full collaboration for all PIRL members who want to share knowledge with colleagues in the Global North and Global South. For example, during meetings, CoP members with visual impairments have indicated that they use devices with screen readers and other applications. Some indicated limitations in obtaining applications relevant to their purposes and that documents and resources were shared among team members using non-accessible formats. Many members of the CoP have informally indicated that they wanted more digital literacy and accessibility training.

Some of the challenges associated with the access and use of computers are:

Financial constraints: All respondents in this survey could afford and own a smartphone, and most had access to a computer. The majority of those who indicated that they do not use a computer as much as they wanted to, cited limited access as the main reason. Some indicated that access to financial resources is very limited for women with disabilities. It was evident that reasons for limited access included not owning a computer, which for some respondents was due to a lack of financial means.

Lack of ICT skills: Some respondents indicated that they do not use computers regularly due to a lack of digital literacy skills; it can be challenging to learn how to use a computer if one must rely on a communal device.

Disability: Another reason some respondents indicated for not using a computer regularly was disability. These findings align with Dobransky and Hargittai (2016) and Wedasinghe and colleagues (2014), who found that the disability divide, including the lack of affordable assistive technology, inhibits the participation of PWDs. PWDs have additional financial barriers to surmount to be fully included.

30.5.1 Challenges with Access to the Internet

The lack of internet access at workplaces for professional development through CoPs has impactful implications. For example, PIRL members reported relying on their personal wireless, cable, or mobile internet connections to participate in PIRL activities. The lack of workplace support for connectivity meant that some of those who could not afford an internet connection at home might not fully participate in PIRL activities, negatively and inequitably impacting collaborative learning and knowledge co-construction within the partnership.

30.5.2 Challenges with Inconsistent Internet Connections

Even if an individual has a device and access to the internet, the broader infrastructure needs to be available to fully participate in the PIRL CoP. A weak and unstable internet connection hinders effective participation and contribution in an inclusive research team, affecting all CoP members.

Respondents in Africa reported frequently experiencing power outages that interfered with their participation and contributions to PIRL activities because they could not charge their devices or the internet service was down. These disruptions impacted all members of the CoP in a variety of ways, not only those members who had limited access.

30.6 Conclusion and Recommendations

CoPs provide members with the opportunities to interact and work toward a common goal. In a large international CoP, there may be different challenges. These are even more profound for a disability-inclusive CoP that requires using various technologies to interact inclusively and aims for full collaboration among members from the Global South.

This study set out to understand the challenges members of an international disability-inclusive research partnership face when using technology for collaborative learning and knowledge co-construction. The results indicated a North/South digital divide. Those members in the Global North generally have more access to technological devices, a stable connection to the internet, and reliable power. On the other hand, many in the Global South lack access to ICT devices and experience frequent power outages and have weak and unstable internet connections, limiting participation in collaborative learning. The lack of reliable access to ICT and inclusiveness among members of the Global South hinders collaboration and learning for all CoP members. Global South members want to participate and share their knowledge, and the Global North members need their perspectives and knowledge sharing to achieve the goals of the CoP.

Based on these findings, we present initial recommendations to help improve participation in international disability-inclusive research teams.

- Participants in the Global North need to carefully and reflectively examine their privileges and responses regarding technology access and develop patience and openness to alternative ways to engage in collaborative learning.
- When budgeting for the project, provide access to technological devices for those without access, including funds to purchase devices, required software, and internet access regardless of geographic location.
- When purchasing equipment or choosing a collaboration platform, ensure it is accessible to everyone on the team. Choose software with low data usage for online tasks.
- Encourage the use of surge protectors for areas with unstable electricity to protect the equipment.
- When scheduling meetings in unstable internet connection zones, try to schedule them during low data usage periods when connections might be more reliable.

- Allow extra time for learning by all team members. At the beginning and throughout the project, provide collaborative learning opportunities for those with limited digital skills to acquire the digital knowledge and competencies required to fully participate in the project, and for those who are not familiar with working in these inequitable spaces to adjust their practices.

This paper only examines a limited portion of the survey data and does not provide an in-depth understanding of the responses. Our ongoing and future research will continue to explore these themes. The use of interviews, document reviews, and focus groups with CoP members will provide a better understanding of the issues to provide greater insight into the challenges of a disability-inclusive research CoP.

Acknowledgements The authors are thankful to the Social Sciences and Humanities Research Council of Canada (SSHRC) for a grant that has enabled the PIRL partnership to be established and maintained. The authors acknowledge the technical support of Writing Lab, Institute for the Future of Education, Tecnologico de Monterrey, Mexico, in the production of this work.

References

Aikins S (2019) Determinants of digital divide in Africa and policy implications. Int J Public Adm Digit Age 6:64–79. https://doi.org/10.4018/IJPADA.2019010104

Arakpogun EO, Elsahn Z, Nyuur RB, Olan F (2020) Threading the needle of the digital divide in Africa: the barriers and mitigations of infrastructure sharing. Technol Forecast Soc Change 161:120263. https://doi.org/10.1016/j.techfore.2020.120263

Aranda-Jan C, Boutard A (2019) Understanding the mobile disability gap. [Online]. Available: https://www.gsma.com/mobilefordevelopment/resources/understanding-the-mobile-disabi lity-gap/

Barlott T, Adams K, Cook A (2016) Increasing participation in the information society by people with disabilities and their families in lower-income countries using mainstream technologies. Univers Access Inf Soc 15(2):189–198

Cen X et al (2020) The online education mode and reopening plans for Chinese schools during the COVID-19 pandemic: a mini-review. Front Public Health 8:566316–566316. https://doi.org/10.3389/fpubh.2020.566316

Chien C-W (2021) Electronic notes as a tool in emergent researchers' communities of practice. Technol Pedagogy Educ 1–15. https://doi.org/10.1080/1475939X.2021.1878053

de Hei M, Tabacaru C, Sjoer E, Rippe R, Walenkamp J (2019) Developing intercultural competence through collaborative learning in international higher education. J Stud Int Educ 24(2):190–211. https://doi.org/10.1177/1028315319826226

Demers G, Tremblay D (2021) Des communautés de pratique en milieu universitaire: quels défis et quelle valeur pour l'innovation dans l'organisation ?

Dobransky K, Hargittai E (2016) Unrealized potential: exploring the digital disability divide. Poetics 58:18–28. https://doi.org/10.1016/j.poetic.2016.08.003

Earley P, Mosakowski E (2004) Toward culture intelligence: turning cultural differences into a workplace advantage. Acad Manag Exec 18:151–157. https://doi.org/10.5465/AME.2004.285 61784

Gallardo R, Beaulieu LB, Geideman C (2021) Digital inclusion and parity: implications for community development. Community Dev 52(1):4–21. https://doi.org/10.1080/15575330.2020. 1830815

Gilbert S (2016) Learning in a Twitter-based community of practice: an exploration of knowledge exchange as a motivation for participation in #hcsmca. Inf Commun Soc 19(9):1214–1232. https://doi.org/10.1080/1369118X.2016.1186715

Gould M, Leblois A, Cesa Bianchi F, Montenegro V (2015) Convention on the rights of persons with disabilities, assistive technology and information and communication technology requirements: where do we stand on implementation? Disabil Rehabil Assist Technol 10(4):295–300

Hammad R, Khan Z, Safieddine F, Ahmed A (2020) A review of learning theories and models underpinning technology-enhanced learning artefacts. World J Sci Technol Sustain Dev 17(4):341–354. https://doi.org/10.1108/WJSTSD-06-2020-0062

Harniss M, Samant Raja D, Matter R (2015) Assistive technology access and service delivery in resource-limited environments: introduction to a special issue of Disability and Rehabilitation: Assistive Technology. Disabil Rehabil Assist Technol 10(4):267–270 [Online]

Herrera-Pavo MÁ (2021) Collaborative learning for virtual higher education. Learn Cult Soc Interact 28:100437. https://doi.org/10.1016/j.lcsi.2020.100437

Home—G3ict: The global initiative for inclusive ICTs. http://g3ict.org/. Accessed 08 Nov 2018

Hughes D, Beekman L, Boyd L (2020) Pushing past pedagogy: improving inclusivity in research. In: Critical disability workshop, CHI conference on human factors in computer systems, Honolulu, HI, USA

International Telecommunications Union (2021) Digital trends reports. [Online]. Available: www.itu.int:443/en/ITU-D/Conferences/WTDC/WTDC21/Pages/RPM/Digital-Trends-Reports-2021.aspx

Kuika Watat J, Jonathan GM (2020) Breaking the digital divide in Rural Africa. [Online]. Available at: https://aisel.aisnet.org/amcis2020/global_dev/global_dev/2/

Lembani R, Gunter A, Breines M, Dalu MTB (2020) The same course, different access: the digital divide between urban and rural distance education students in South Africa. J Geogr High Educ 44(1):70–84. https://doi.org/10.1080/03098265.2019.1694876

Marques LFC et al (2016) Accessibility in virtual communities of practice under the optics of inclusion of visually impaired. In: Universal access in human-computer interaction. Methods, techniques, and best practices. Springer, Cham, pp 14–26. https://doi.org/10.1007/978-3-319-40250-5_2

Matter R, Harniss M, Oderud T, Borg J, Eide AH (2017) Assistive technology in resource-limited environments: a scoping review. Disabil Rehabil Assist Technol 12(1748–3107):105–114. https://doi.org/10.1080/17483107.2016.1188170

Mbibeh L, Nganji JT, Cockburn LB et al (2021) The PIRL Project: a case study of learning how to do disability-inclusive research. In: Global inclusion workshop, CHI conference on human factors in computer systems, Yokohama, Japan (virtual), pp 1–10. Accessed 15 May 2021. [Online]. Available: https://cdn.disabilityinnovation.com/documents/CHI-Workshop_submission_14.pdf

Medaille A, Usinger J (2018) 'That's going to be the hardest thing for me': tensions experienced by quiet students during collaborative learning situations. Educ Stud 1–18. https://doi.org/10.1080/03055698.2018.1555456

Mortier K (2020) Communities of practice: a conceptual framework for inclusion of students with significant disabilities. Int J Incl Educ 24(3):329–340. https://doi.org/10.1080/13603116.2018.1461261

Pacholek K et al (2021) A WhatsApp community forum for improving critical thinking and practice skills of mental health providers in a conflict zone. Interact Learn Environ 1–19. https://doi.org/10.1080/10494820.2021.1890622

Pal J et al (2016) An accessibility infrastructure for the global south. In: Proceedings of the eighth international conference on information and communication technologies and development, Ann Arbor MI USA, pp 1–11. https://doi.org/10.1145/2909609.2909666

Qureshi MA, Khaskheli A, Qureshi JA, Raza SA, Yousufi SQ (2021) Factors affecting students' learning performance through collaborative learning and engagement. Interact Learn Environ 1–21. https://doi.org/10.1080/10494820.2021.1884886

Rowntree O, Shanahan M (2020) The mobile gender gap report 2020. GSMA. Accessed: 28 Mar 2021. [Online]. Available: https://www.gsma.com/r/gender-gap/

Salas Rueda RA, Castañeda Martínez R, Ramírez Ortega J, Garcés Madrigal AM (2021) Educators' opinion about technology and web platforms during the Covid-19 pandemic (in Spanish). Rev Gest Las Pers Tecnol 14(40):21–37

Samant D, Matter R, Harniss M (2013) Realizing the potential of accessible ICTs in developing countries. Disabil Rehabil Assist Technol 8(1):11–20. https://doi.org/10.3109/17483107.2012.669022

Sanders CK, Scanlon E (2021) The digital divide is a human rights issue: advancing social inclusion through social work advocacy. J Hum Rights Soc Work. https://doi.org/10.1007/s41134-020-00147-9

Smith SU, Hayes S, Shea P (2017) A critical review of the use of Wenger's Community of Practice (CoP) theoretical framework in online and blended learning research, 2000–2014. Online Learn 21(1). https://doi.org/10.24059/olj.v21i1.963

Stanković M, Nejić K, Stojiljković N Level of fear, opinion and quality of study during the coronavirus pandemic (Covid-19). How hard is it to get back to daily commitments? p 8

Sungkur RK, Sebastien O, Singh UG (2020) Social media as a catalyst for distant collaborative learning: trends and concerns for small Island states. J Knowl Econ 11(4):1454–1469. https://doi.org/10.1007/s13132-019-00613-4

Tharapos M, O'Connell BT (2020) Transnational communities of practice: their development, operation, and contribution. J Stud Int Educ 1028315320964314. https://doi.org/10.1177/1028315320964314

The Washington Group (2021) Resources for data users. Washington Group on Disability Statistics. [Online]. Available: https://www.washingtongroup-disability.com/resources/resources-for-data-users/

Tsaliki L, Kontogianni S (2014) Bridging the disability divide? Young children's and teenagers with disability internet experiences in greece. J Child Media 8(2):146–162. https://doi.org/10.1080/17482798.2013.823878

Vimalkumar M, Singh JB, Sharma SK (2020) Exploring the multi-level digital divide in mobile phone adoption: a comparison of developing nations. Inf Syst Front. https://doi.org/10.1007/s10796-020-10032-5

Wedasinghe N, Wicramaarchchi R (2014) Web, mobile and computer related model to bridge the disability digital divide in Sri Lanka. In: International conference on electrical engineering and information and communication technology, pp 1–6. https://doi.org/10.1109/ICEEICT.2014.6919120

Wenger E (1996) How we learn. Communities of practice. The social fabric of a learning organization. Healthc Forum J 39(4):20–26

Wildman JL, Nguyen DM, Duong NS, Warren C (2021) Student teamwork during COVID-19: challenges, changes, and consequences. Small Group Res 52(2):119–134. https://doi.org/10.1177/1046496420985185

Willemse JJ (2015) Undergraduate nurses reflections on WhatsApp use in improving primary health care education. Curationis 38(2):1–7

World Health Organization (2021) WHO—Global Cooperation on Assistive Technology—About us [Online]. Available: http://www.who.int/phi/implementation/assistive_technology/phi_gate/en/

Zhong Q (2021) Fostering group autonomy through collaborative learning in an online environment. Stud Self-Access Learn J 79–91. https://doi.org/10.37237/120106

Chapter 31
Requirements for the Production of Digital Learning Material and Results of Its Implementation with First-Year Medical Students

Samuel Xavier Pimienta Rodríguez and Mónica María Díaz-López

31.1 Introduction

The fourth industrial revolution (or digital revolution) reached the educational field. Now, the generations of "digital natives" demand educational environments that generate compelling educational experiences (Oke and Fernandes 2020). Accordingly, students from higher education institutions use innumerable digital technological tools to improve their academic performance. Nevertheless, even in this era of "pandemic virtuality," they often find themselves presented with lecturing professors following the model of unidirectional master classes, where the teacher transmits standardized knowledge to a mass of students, making the educational experience insufficient (Reaves 2019).

If the teacher does not know how to use, design, construct, and implement digital technological tools, he cannot aim for optimal expected learning outcomes, exciting class dynamics, and student enjoyment of educational activities (Binnewies and Wang 2019).

31.1.1 Digital Learning Materials

Educational and technological tools are among the digital learning materials (DLMs), classified into drills and practices, tutorials, multimedia, simulations, educational

S. X. Pimienta Rodríguez (✉)
M Sc Informática Educativa, Universidad de la Sabana, Chia, Colombia
e-mail: samuelpiro@unisabana.edu.co

M. M. Díaz-López
Departamento de Educación Médica, Universidad de la Sabana, Chía, Colombia
e-mail: monicadl@unisabana.edu.co

© The Author(s), under exclusive license to Springer Nature Singapore Pte Ltd. 2022   387
S. Hosseini et al. (eds.), *Technology-Enabled Innovations in Education*,
Transactions on Computer Systems and Networks,
https://doi.org/10.1007/978-981-19-3383-7_31

games (serious games), and computer tools (databases and encyclopedias, electronic performance support systems [EPSS], communications and cooperative environments and new tutees) (Berg et al. 2004). This classification of DLMs allows us to understand the importance of these didactic tools in a virtual learning environment, especially their effect on students (Amhag et al. 2019).

There are two essential aspects the teacher must consider when creating a pedagogically efficient DLM. First, the neurobiology of learning (NL), and second, the technological, technical, and pedagogical requirements for the design and development of a DLM (Friedlander et al. 2011; Rintamäki 2020).

31.1.2   Neurobiology of Learning and Gamification

The neurobiology of learning encompasses the intrinsic elements of the cognitive system of the individual who wishes to learn. These elements determine the efficiency of learning and the type of experience the student has. The essential elements of NL include attention, long-term memory, motivation, stress, and the emotional system (Thinking and in Teaching Learning: The Nonintuitive New Science of Effective Learning—Kindle edition by Fregni, Felipe).

Therefore, to leverage NL elements in the DLMs, we need optimal planning of its design and development. Gamification is one mechanism to integrate game elements, mechanics, and infrastructure for purposes and scenarios not designed for gaming and entertainment (Pettit et al. 2015). Integrating these principles in learning generates a variety of effects on the elements of NL and the student's brain structures involved in the learning process, such as the striatum, the production of brain-derived neurotrophic factor (BDNF), the amygdala (emotional processing), and the dorsolateral prefrontal cortex (decision making) (Landers et al. 2015; Denny 2013; Domínguez et al. 2013).

Therefore, before designing and developing a DLM, we must consider the seven elements of gamification: objectives, challenges, feedback, reinforcement, comparison, social connectivity, and fun (Ismail et al. 2019). These are necessary for valuable student experiences and efficient learning.

31.1.3   Design and Development of a DLM

The design and development of a DLM depend on various factors such as the instruction or target audience, the course subject to be taught, the learning modality, the teaching methodology, the learning objectives, and the type of digital technology to be used (Amhag et al. 2019).

First, we must identify the target audience and the instruction since it can be for undergraduate (Pettit et al. 2015; Ohn et al. 2020) or postgraduate students (McAuliffe et al. 2020), and the methodological conceptions will be different.

The course subject must also be considered because some contain purely theoretical aspects, for example, courses in the basic sciences (Prochazkova et al. 2019; Felszeghy et al. 2019), while others contain practices and procedures, such as clinical or surgical courses (Scaffidi et al. 2019; Lamb et al. 2017).

Depending on how the DLMs are delivered, we can classify the learning modality by location, such as face-to-face, online (virtual), or blended learning. Courses can also be classified by timing (synchronous or asynchronous). It is also essential to identify the teaching methodology, whether cooperative, collaborative, or individual. These aspects dictate the structural planning of the DLM from the technological perspective (Liu and Pu 2020; Ossiannilsson 2017).

Ultimately, we must consider the learning objectives to be pursued to develop the students. These may require training for higher-order thinking skills that have to do with analyzing clinical cases and developing critical thinking (Geng 2021). Thus, the DLM must have a structured database (content), assessment process, and various digital learning resources (multimedia or non-multimedia) that facilitate achieving the learning objectives (Nilson and Goodson 2021).

Considering all the above factors, especially the latter, one must decide which type of digital technology to use to support the design and development of the DLM.

31.2 Methods

31.2.1 Design and Development of Cardiac Cycle DLM

We aimed to develop a digital learning material (DLM) for undergraduate students (instruction) in "Cardiovascular Physiology—Cardiac Cycle" (the course subject) delivered via an online synchronous modality. We chose an individual teaching methodology. The learning objective was to remember, understand, and apply cardiac cycle concepts and comprehend their correlation with pathologically healthy patients (Rintamäki 2020).

The digital technology used was a web application with a student registration system. Each student had a profile and the digital learning resources and evaluation system designed to achieve the proposed learning objective (Figs. 31.1 and 31.2). The first step was to create a storyboard with all the instructions for the developer team, including the elements of the user interface (UI) and user experience (UX) with all the detailed contents, text, videos, sections, activities, and interactions.

It was essential to assess the student's knowledge to determine whether the learning objectives were met (Thoma et al. 2019). We designed a question bank with various questions that evaluated student's remembering structures, processes of the cardiac cycle, and understanding the concepts. The more complex questions assessed how they applied the concepts in clinical cases and other patient's scenarios.

Once the developer team received the storyboard, it went into production. When the production stage was finished and the DLM was ready, we performed a pilot test

Fig. 31.1 Home page, showing the registration option and the MED's presentation. *Source* www. sepriori.com

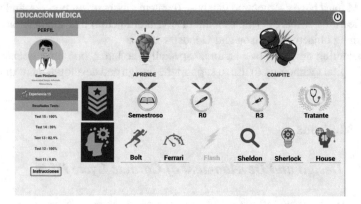

Fig. 31.2 Profile page with didactic resources and gamification elements, badges, leaderboards, and experience. *Source* www.sepriori.com

to determine its functionality and identify production errors and bugs. These errors were corrected, and the DLM was ready for implementation.

31.2.2 Implementation

For the DLM's implementation, we scheduled 120-min sessions with a maximum of 15 students per session. Each session began with an explanation of the platform and gamification process (ten minutes), and then the students had time for the pre-test (30 min). Afterward, the students reviewed cardiac cycle theory in the "Connect" mode, which contained conceptual maps linked to the graphic expression of the volume and pressure curves during the cardiac cycle (20 min). Then the "Video" mode (20 min) explained these concepts. Once the students completed these steps, there was discussion, and students' questions were addressed (10 min). In the end, they took the post-test (30 min).

Data collection was handled with a standardized instrument created in Microsoft OneDrive. It contained variables such as age, group, pre-test score (%), post-test score (%), and students' comments on the didactic activities. Subsequently, we applied the Wilcoxon SR Test in the IBM SPSS statistical software to analyze the quantitative variables. For the qualitative analysis, we used the QDA Miner software.

31.3 Results

We implemented the DLM for 116 students taking the Morphophysiology course at the University of La Sabana in Bogotá-Colombia, obtaining 102 complete feedback (87.93%). Of the 102 students, 66.67% were women, and 33.33% were men. The median student age was 18 years old (IQR 18–19). The median score of the pre-test was 58.5% (IQR 45.7–73.8%) and 82.9% on the post-test (IQR 73.2–95.1%). There was a statistically significant difference between the pre and post-tests, with a median difference of 22.6% (IQR 8.3%–36.6%, $p < 0.001$).

In the qualitative analysis, we defined three categories: positive comments, student suggestions, and technical difficulties. There were 67.58% positive comments, divided into three subcategories: pleasant learning experience (31.05%), preference for multimedia content (19.17%), and reinforcement or consolidation of knowledge (17.35%). 22.37% of the students made suggestions related to the need for effective feedback, the desire for expansion and scaling of the DLM to other course subjects, the need for advanced demonstration of the DLM before using it, and improving the DLM appearance and colors. The last category of technical difficulties was only 10.05% of the comments, mainly related to incompatibilities with the web browser.

31.4 Discussion

The digital world has taken us by surprise in the educational field; thus, pedagogical aspects must be considered to achieve student's effective learning and enjoyment of didactic activities. Digitalization, automation, and application of artificial intelligence algorithms to different DLM components is no longer something seen in a few educational sectors; to the contrary, it is extending to many scenarios. In medical education (Masters 2019; Siang and Zary 2019), it is shifting from a possibility to a priority in the academic curricula of health sciences (Paranjape et al. 2019; Tuomi 2018).

To achieve effective and fun learning and automate assessments and DLM contents, educators must consider the neurobiology of learning (Landers et al. 2015) and all the steps mentioned above to design and develop the DLM.

For an effective cardiac cycle DLM, we had to carefully plan its design and development. In the end, the DLM significantly improved student's knowledge of the cardiac cycle and demonstrated effective learning. Also, another relevant finding was that the students enjoyed the activities. The positive comments on the DLM demonstrated that the students had a playful experience and enjoyed and engaged with the material. There were some study limitations, reflected in the difficulties the students mentioned, mainly incompatibility with the Safari browser and the need for effective feedback from the tutor. We think these were due to a defect in the production stage, which is the most challenging stage to coordinate since it needs a broad knowledge in web development. Nevertheless, these limitations did not affect the effective learning and enjoyment of the student. To improve these limitations in the future, we need to be more careful with this point of convergence between the technological, pedagogical, and medical fields (Soto et al. 2021).

Understanding various theoretical concepts, the development of new educational strategies, and the attitudinal adjustments of teachers and students are essential for constructing knowledge. This knowledge is built from observation, experimentation, analysis, generation of models, construction of arguments, and communication of ideas. In this project, these were evident in the gamification process, which, in the end, increased meaningful learning (Geng 2021).

Generating and implementing new teaching strategies redefine the role of teachers, accomplished by expanding the quality of instructional content and using digital tools, instruments, and assessment formats to generate a considerable impact on how the student participates in the experience (Kuiper and Pesut 2004). The students developed specific skills through collaborative and interdisciplinary work, stimulated by effective communication, reflective thinking, and self-regulated study.

31.5 Conclusion

The DLM of the cardiac cycle demonstrated effective learning by significantly improving student's knowledge in this topic. Their interest, motivation, engagement, enjoyment, and active participation in the learning process were evident. This project provides a starting point to transform medical education.

This transformation needs an institutional model providing a framework for contemporary pedagogical thinking and well-defined expected learning outcomes. The optimal integration of digital technologies, didactic strategies, and thematic knowledge can elevate the quality of teaching and learning while making it enjoyable for the student.

References

Amhag L, Hellström L, Stigmar M (2019) Teacher educator's use of digital tools and needs for digital competence in higher education. 35(4):203–220. https://doi.org/10.1080/21532974.2019.1646169

Binnewies S, Wang Z (2019) Challenges of student equity and engagement in a hyflex course. Blended Learn Des STEM High Educ 209–230

Critical Thinking in Teaching & Learning: The Nonintuitive New Science of Effective Learning—Kindle edition by Fregni, Felipe. Professional & Technical Kindle eBooks @ Amazon.com

Denny P (2013) The effect of virtual achievements on student engagement. In: Conference human factors computing systems—proceedings, pp 763–772

Domínguez A, Saenz-De-Navarrete J, De-Marcos L, Fernández-Sanz L, Pagés C, Martínez-Herráiz JJ (2013) Gamifying learning experiences: practical implications and outcomes. Comput Educ 63:380–392

Felszeghy S et al (2019) Using online game-based platforms to improve student performance and engagement in histology teaching. BMC Med Educ 19(1)

Friedlander MJ et al (2011) What can medical education learn from the neurobiology of learning?. Acad Med 86(4):415–420

Geng H (2021) Redefining the role of teachers in developing critical thinking within the digital era. pp 18–21. ago

Ismail MA-A, Ahmad A, Mohammad JA-M, Fakri NMRM, Nor MZM, Pa MNM (2019) Using Kahoot! as a formative assessment tool in medical education: a phenomenological study. BMC Med Educ 19(1):230

Kuiper RA, Pesut DJ (2004) Promoting cognitive and metacognitive reflective reasoning skills in nursing practice: self-regulated learning theory. J Adv Nurs 45(4):381–391

Lamb LC, DiFiori MM, Jayaraman V, Shames BD, Feeney JM (2017) Gamified Twitter microblogging to support resident preparation for the American board of surgery in-service training examination. J Surg Educ 74(6):986–991

Landers RN, Bauer KN, Callan RC, Armstrong MB (2015) Psychological theory and the gamification of learning. Gamification Educ Bus 165–186 ene

Liu N, Pu Q (2020) Factors influencing learner's continuance intention toward one-to-one online learning. https://doi.org/10.1080/10494820.2020.1857785

Masters K (2019) Artificial intelligence in medical education. 41(9):976–980. https://doi.org/10.1080/0142159X.2019.1595557

McAuliffe JC, McAuliffe RHJ, Romero-Velez G, Statter M, Melvin WS, 2nd Muscarella P (2020) Feasibility and efficacy of gamification in general surgery residency: preliminary outcomes of residency teams. Am J Surg 219(2):283–288

Nilson LB, Goodson LA (2021) Online teaching at its best : merging instructional design with teaching and learning research, pp 276

Ohn MH, Ohn KM, Yusof S, D'Souza U, Iswandono Z, Mchucha I (2020) Development of novel gamified online electrocardiogram learning platform (GaMED ECG@TM). In: Lecture notes in electrical engineering, vol 603. pp 719–729

Oke A, Fernandes FAP (2020) Innovations in teaching and learning: exploring the perceptions of the education sector on the 4th industrial revolution (4IR). J Open Innov Technol Mark Complex 6(2):31. abr

Ossiannilsson E (2017) Promoting active and meaningful learning for digital learners. pp 294–315

Paranjape K, Schinkel M, Panday RN, Car J, Nanayakkara P (2019) Introducing artificial intelligence training in medical education. JMIR Med Educ 5(2)

Pettit RK, McCoy L, Kinney M, Schwartz FN (2015) Student perceptions of gamified audience response system interactions in large group lectures and via lecture capture technology approaches to teaching and learning. BMC Med Educ 15(1)

Prochazkova K, Novotny P, Hancarova M, Prchalova D, Sedlacek Z (2019) Teaching a difficult topic using a problem-based concept resembling a computer game: development and evaluation of an e-learning application for medical molecular genetics. BMC Med Educ 19(1)

Reaves J (2019) 21st-century skills and the fourth industrial revolution: a critical future role for online education. Int J Innov Online Educ 3(1)

Rintamäki O (2020) Gamifying the teaching of neurobiology and EEG basics

Scaffidi MA et al (2019) Protocol for a randomized trial evaluating the effect of applying gamification to simulation-based endoscopy training. BMJ Open 9(2)

Siang K, Zary N (2019) Applications and challenges of implementing artificial intelligence in medical education: integrative review. JMIR Med Educ 5(1):e13930. https//mededu.jmir.org/2019/1/e13930

Soto TJ, Soto TJ, Tillman DA, An SA (2021) Applying TPACK to medical education. In: Society for information technology and teacher education international conference, vol 1. pp 1632–1637

van den Berg E, Blijleven P, Jansen L (2004) Digital learning materials: classification and implications for the curriculum. en Curriculum Landscapes and Trends, Springer Netherlands, pp 237–254

Thoma B, Turnquist A, Zaver F, Hall AK, Chan TM (2019) Communication, learning and assessment: exploring the dimensions of the digital learning environment. 41(4):385–390. https://doi.org/10.1080/0142159X.2019.1567911

Tuomi I (2018) Informe Resumen: el impacto de la Inteligencia Artificial en el aprendizaje, la enseñanza y la educación. Intef, n.º November, pp 47

Chapter 32
Constructing Virtual Learning Communities Through Social Media in Pathophysiology Courses

Nancy de los Ángeles Segura-Azuara, José Guillermo Guzmán-Segura, Juan Pablo Guzmán-Segura, and Nancy María Guzmán-Segura

32.1 Introduction

In the twenty-first century, learning transcends classroom walls, especially evident in these pandemic times (Pérez-Escoda et al. 2020). The use of remote interactive platforms for recreational or educational purposes allows people to remain in contact with one another despite the social distancing and confinements of the current health crisis. People seek to stay in touch and relate to each other in various ways, including social media. They have collaborated in constructing information networks that result in rapid and effective communication among individuals from different circles, causing the emergence of interactions for purposes not previously conceived. In this way, the teaching–learning processes have become possible without the limitations of time and space. The interactions of social group members have different purposes, but always to keep in touch.

Various digital resources support collaborative synchronous and asynchronous learning among peers despite the distance. In the face-to-face format, individuals

N. Á. Segura-Azuara (✉)
Basic Medical Sciences, School of Medicine and Health Sciences, Tecnologico de Monterrey, Monterrey, Mexico
e-mail: nsegura@tec.mx

J. P. Guzmán-Segura
Economics, School of Social Sciences and Government, Tecnologico de Monterrey, Monterrey, Mexico
e-mail: A01039810@itesm.mx

J. G. Guzmán-Segura
PrepaTec Cumbres, Tecnologico de Monterrey, Monterrey, Mexico
e-mail: A01039811@itesm.mx

N. M. Guzmán-Segura
Chemical Engineering, School of Engineering, Tecnologico de Monterrey, Monterrey, Mexico
e-mail: A01039812@itesm.mx

© The Author(s), under exclusive license to Springer Nature Singapore Pte Ltd. 2022   395
S. Hosseini et al. (eds.), *Technology-Enabled Innovations in Education*,
Transactions on Computer Systems and Networks,
https://doi.org/10.1007/978-981-19-3383-7_32

interact differently than in online modalities. On social networks in the remote format, the social group members build the content that is shared. This content is related to the tastes, tasks, and problems of each individual. Others participate either by reacting to interactions or content shared or by creating new content that can lead to a new line of interactions. This study identified the types of resources and contents contributed by students in physiopathology courses in the medical surgeon program of a Latin American university; the students' perception of their peers' contributions was also analyzed. Detecting the types of interactions among students in social networks leads us to select the best teaching–learning tools.

32.2   Theoretical Framework

32.2.1   Social Media

For several decades, virtual interactions among people from different circles have occurred the same amount or more than person-to-person (Pérez-Escoda et al. 2020). Virtual interactions are supported by the wide use of social networks worldwide, in different areas: among friends, family, co-workers, service providers, i.e., among people who have some relationship. However, not everyone recognizes the usefulness or the importance of incorporating them within educational settings (Ansari and Khan 2020). There are even circles in which social networks have been classified as harmful, and attempts have been made to eliminate them because of the negative impact on young people (Boulianne and Theocharis 2020).

The emergence of the COVID-19 pandemic worldwide forced interactions through digital platforms, enhancing the activities and adding value due to their continuity in different urban and rural contexts, such as labor, school, family, and recreation. The interactions among fellow students could not be the exception. Various authors have recognized social networking sites (SNS) for their usefulness in formal and informal learning. It is recognized that three out of four millennials have a social media profile on their smartphone (Koranteng et al. 2019). For several authors (Chan and Leung 2018), a social network site allows building a profile and network connections with other users. The types of interactions among members include text, images, and documents. Each SNS has its degree of popularity and prevailing age profile, so that different social groups tend to prefer one SNS over another (Clark et al. 2018). The ties established among the group members make it possible to build and strengthen these networks (Ansari and Khan 2020).

Nowadays, interactions through the different social networking sites (for example, Facebook, Twitter, Instagram, and TikTok) transcend leisure to penetrate and embed in the daily tasks of people who have a smart devices or a computer. Thus, contacts with other people occur without space or time barriers because these interactions occur in real-time (synchronously) and asynchronously. People's interactions occur according to their needs, so it is increasingly challenging to stay on the sidelines and resist change. Different age groups adapt to using SNS thanks to the ease of using the formats (Gazit et al. 2020).

We know that education is an eminently social process among its agents and stakeholders, including teachers, students, administrative staff, parents, and the community. Many build work networks to make work and tasks more efficient, streamline procedures, and establish agreements, among others. Therefore, some authors consider social networks a critical tool in the teacher-student binomial to promote learning (Ansari and Khan 2020). According to several authors, these networks contribute to constructing attitudes, values, knowledge, and skills and directly influence learning among physicians in training (Escobar-Mamani and Gómez-Arteta 2020). Thus, students commit to learning, partly attributable to the capacity for immediate feedback and the development of collaborative competencies among peers using such networks (Manca and Ranieri 2016).

Most SNS offer mechanisms for constructing practice communities for peer learning, and sharing information in different formats. Also, shy learners interact more frequently on these platforms. Communication in this manner encourages learning because information is shared in a simple, dynamic, and easily accessible way. Participants develop various competencies and acquire knowledge, critical thinking, the ability to analyze and synthesize, and written communication skills.

Facebook is a highly popular SNS that facilitates immediate peer or teacher-student feedback. Likewise, it allows establishing models for collaborative interactions within particular open or closed groups (Facebook Groups) (Clark et al. 2018). SNS offers spaces for reflection, dialogue, and practice for some authors, contributing to individuals' self-regulation (Badri et al. 2017). On the other hand, Twitter is an SNS that develops the capacity for synthesis and analysis because individual communications are limited to 280 characters (Valdez et al. 2020; Masciantonio et al. 2021); thus, communication must be brief, concise, direct, and relevant.

32.2.2 Virtual Learning Communities

Learning is a phenomenon that occurs individually; however, it is promoted through social interactions. In the past, students had individualized learning with little communication among peers. This individualistic approach promotes competition to a greater extent than collaboration. Currently, the information is available to everyone at any time and place (Alonso et al. 2018).

The construction of virtual or online communities facilitates interactions among individuals by breaking down socio-cultural and economic barriers. Internet access plus having an interactive device are required. Bi-directional communication strengthens the bonds of the group members, making learning grow exponentially. The sharing element in virtual communities works as a catalyst for learning by triggering questions, conclusions, discussions, and reflections among their members. Likewise, it works as a source of inspiration to continue interacting, to build the learning community. The resources in images, videos, links to pages, and articles add dynamism to studying a particular subject and creativity to the virtual community. The practicality of having them on hand in a portable device boosts learning well beyond the limitations of the classroom.

Some authors have investigated how medical students perceive social networks and their role within medical schools (Ibarra-Yruegas et al. 2015; Sattar et al. 2016). Most consider that social networks are necessary daily to share health information among colleagues, patients, health institutions, and service providers. Several prefer social networks mainly for their ease of access, availability, and speed in the transmission of information. However, other authors have certain reservations regarding its indiscriminate use, mainly due to the shared information's security and sources. Some attribute responsibility for the actions or decisions relying on these sources to the person who receives it, not the issuer.

32.2.3 Development of Competencies

Some authors have studied interactive models from the perspective of the competencies involved, classified as instrumental, interpersonal, and systemic (Sanson-Fisher et al. 2019). The first refers to using strategies individually, according to the person's purposes and interests. "Interpersonal" involves interactions between at least two agents or people. In these, the motivation and emotions of the individuals involved are essential in determining the degree and depth of interactions. In the last classification (systemic), individuals are integrated into a particular system. Information technologies generally have an eminently instrumental function in the system, incorporating aspects of information management, orderly administration, and computers for interactions.

Several organizations (Farnsworth et al. 2016) have described the conceptual roles that a doctor in training is expected to assume to achieve competencies to practice their profession, as described by CanMeds. Being an effective and efficient communicator is necessary, from their point of view; also, having respect for diversity, competencies of interaction and empathy with others, documentation of information and security incidents, and activities carried out.

The health professional must have the necessary skills to communicate efficiently, with clear, understandable language, to the level of their audience, brief and direct. Establishing this communication is crucial with patients, their families, other health team members, and authorities; in short, each agent participates in patients' health care and environments. Creating online learning communities fosters students' developing collaborative, motivational, and challenging skills to prepare for professional practice.

Based on these concepts, the present study uses the Facebook and Twitter social networks as the SNS resources for a virtual learning community and assesses students' perceptions regarding the network and the contents of the interactions among peers.

32.3   Problem Statement

This study used the Twitter and Facebook social networks to promote learning among the participants. The process of metacognition, argumentation, and the exchange of information was promoted. The study's objective was to evaluate the interactions among the participants and compare the interactions between both social networks and the student's perception of the contents of the interactions.

32.4   Method

A descriptive, mixed, transectional method was used (Hernández Sampieri and Mendoza Torres 2018). The voluntary sample consisted of 115 medical students studying pathophysiology at a private university in Mexico. The Twitter and Facebook social interaction platforms were used. On Twitter, a hashtag was used to identify related communications. On Facebook, a closed group was created to safeguard the privacy of the participants. The closed group required each of the participants to enroll individually (Tables 32.1 and 32.2).

The students received instructions regarding their interactions in these SNS. The communications should not be repeated or be identical to any made by other participants. Respect and tolerance should prevail. Each participant had to contribute communications of different types throughout the course, relevant to the concepts, processes, causes, conditions, and consequences of topics discussed in the classroom. The duration of the interactive project was one academic semester. The course tutor counted and classified the interactions that occurred in each of the social networks. Subsequently, a questionnaire was applied to the participant's perception of the communications within the SNS.

This end-of-the-course student survey was designed to determine their perception of the usefulness of shared resources and the utility it represented for them. We obtained 49 responses in this survey (see Tables 32.3 and 32.4).

32.5   Results

During the development of the study, multiple contributions flowed to both social networks. However, the students made a more significant number of communications on Facebook than on Twitter. Table 32.1 reflects some statistical data regarding the contributions made by the medical students. Images were the most used medium for contributions on social networks, followed by text messages and videos. The least used means to share information with their colleagues were PowerPoint presentations (where some did not share even one in the semester), followed by webpage entries (where the maximum that someone shared during the semester was 4).

Table 32.1 Descriptive statistical analysis of the contributions

	Average	Std. Dev	Max	Min
Contributions on both platforms				
Articles	2.31	1.95	9.00	1.00
Images	8.08	4.99	22.00	1.00
Web pages	1.56	0.91	4.00	1.00
PowerPoint Presentations	0.86	0.36	1.00	0.00
Text messages	4.95	4.49	18.00	1.00
Videos	2.65	2.17	12.00	1.00
Facebook contributions				
Articles	2.32	2.02	9.00	1.00
Images	9.02	4.65	22.00	1.00
Webpages	1.54	0.93	4.00	1.00
PowerPoint Presentations	1.00	0.00	1.00	1.00
Text messages	3.47	3.93	18.00	1.00
Videos	2.88	2.25	12.00	1.00
Twitter contributions				
Articles	2.25	1.49	5.00	1.00
Images	6.65	5.17	19.00	1.00
Webpages	1.58	0.90	4.00	1.00
PowerPoint Presentations	0.00	0.00	0.00	0.00
Text messages	5.91	4.58	16.00	1.00
Videos	1.93	1.74	8.00	1.00

However, when we segmented this information per social network, we found that, on average, a student was more likely to share an image or a video on Facebook than on Twitter. On the latter, they shared text messages more.

The use of web pages and PowerPoint presentations were similar on both platforms. There was a more significant difference in the number of images and text messages contributed on Twitter, and there was greater use of empirical articles on Facebook.

Table 32.2 highlights valuable information by comparing the total use of resources to make contributions. In total, 41% of the contributions made by the participants were images on Facebook, 19.9% images on Twitter, and 15.7% were text messages, also on Twitter. Most of the total contributions (23.5%) were images posted by female participants on Facebook. The least used means of contribution by male participants were PowerPoint presentations on Twitter (0%), followed by Web Pages (0.2%) on Twitter, PowerPoint presentations on Facebook (0.2%), and empirical articles on Twitter (0.3%). Facebook was used more than Twitter: 61.3% of the contributions were made on that platform.

Table 32.2 Heat map of contributions by gender

Social Network Site	Contribution	Male	Female	Total
FB	Image	0.174	0.235	0.410
	Text	0.025	0.035	0.060
	Video	0.026	0.057	0.083
	Webpage	0.004	0.008	0.012
	PowerPoint presentation	0.002	0.002	0.004
	Article	0.018	0.026	0.044
TW	Image	0.078	0.121	0.199
	Text	0.069	0.088	0.157
	Video	0.004	0.014	0.018
	Webpage	0.002	0.004	0.006
	PowerPoint presentation	0.000	0.000	0.000
	Article	0.003	0.003	0.006

FB = Facebook; TW = Twitter

Table 32.3 The usefulness of the course and the contributions of their peers—student's perception:

Categories	Female	Male
Organize thoughts and understand better	67% (19)	32% (9)
Helped organize differential diagnoses	43% (12)	14% (4)
Helped to understand pathophysiology better	57% (16)	21% (6)
Seeing cases allows for the understanding and integration of theory	4% (1)	0%
I saw the pathology from another point of view which helped me understand it better	14% (4)	7% (2)

The chi-square values for the gender variables of the contributions in each SNS were 12.83 and 11.76 for Facebook and Twitter, respectively. An alpha significance level of 0.05 with 5 degrees of freedom gives us a value in the x^2 table of 11.07. Therefore, having obtained a value higher than the confidence interval, the null hypothesis is rejected. It is concluded that there is no dependence between the variables; that is, gender and type of contribution in both SNS are dependent.

Table 32.4 Categorization according to the Usefulness of the contributions—student's perception

Categories	Female	Male
Complex information is easily integrated	71% (30)	29% (12)
It is easier to integrate pathophysiology processes with algorithms	19% (8)	21% (9)
Easier to integrate pathophysiology processes with imaging	2% (1)	0%
Easier to integrate pathophysiology processes with videos	10% (4)	0%
It is easier to integrate clinical manifestations with images	5% (2)	0%
It is easier to integrate the clinical manifestations and diagnosis with algorithms	2% (1)	0%
It is easier to remember a process with the use of images	2% (1)	0%
It is easier to remember a mnemonic	14% (6)	7% (3)
Tables are used as a comparison tool	2% (1)	0%

32.6 Discussion

The most used resource by both groups on Facebook were images, followed by videos, possibly because both allow information to be communicated in a small space, paying particular attention to the main points to be highlighted. The videos manage to explain processes and can have audio, which improves the understanding of the information. The current generation of students tries to find tools that allow them to be more efficient in terms of time and space, which can influence their preferences, consistent with what has been described in other studies (Jordan and Weller 2018; Ali 2016).

On Twitter, images were the most frequent contributions, followed by text. This suggests that users are more familiar with videos on Facebook than on Twitter. At the same time, they tended to prefer text and were limited to 280 characters maximum in this second social network. Likewise, on Facebook, the video is usually displayed when scrolling the page, while on the second social network, the video must be clicked to view it. The findings regarding students' academic development are similar to those found in another study (Mansour and Mansour 2019).

On the other hand, the least used resource in both social networks was the slide presentation, followed by the web pages. We consider the time factor crucial since building a slide presentation takes much time from the student and the reader. On the other hand, web pages are an option that may contain little detailed and technical information for the course content; as such, it was not one of the most frequently used by students.

From the chi-square analysis for the variables of gender and type of contribution in each social network, it appears that the amount of contributions depends on gender, which is very interesting and may give rise to further analysis concerning the causes of this dependence.

According to the student perception survey results, most of them highly valued the SNS for helping them organize better and understand the processes related to the course, consistent with other studies (Aldahdouh et al. 2020). This aligns with the central point of pathophysiology courses since most of them are processes that trigger situations that are evidenced as clinical manifestations, alterations in laboratory or cabinet tests, etc. The contributions of their colleagues allowed them to improve their understanding of the course content.

From the student's perception, most agreed that the formats presenting complex information simply are the most valuable for them, as described in prior studies Al-Qaysi et al. (2020). In second place were the formats related to pathophysiology, whether in algorithms, videos, or images.

32.7 Conclusions

In our study, the most frequently shared types of communication on educational topics on social networks were multimedia (images and videos). When separated by gender, we see a significant difference. The female gender contributed more resources than the male; despite maintaining the relative distribution frequency between both groups. We believe the cause is that it is easier for females to establish frequent communication in their social networks, or they feel a greater degree of responsibility to participate in the learning community. However, we do not have the mechanisms to elucidate this phenomenon, which could be investigated in a subsequent study.

This study can be easily transferred to other health sciences courses, allowing students to use resources to create learning communities that they can extend to their patients and colleagues. The students have had the experience to evaluate the contributions that provide the most outstanding efficiency according to their objectives. Likewise, the methodology can be scaled to other curricula, undergraduate and graduate professional programs, and other universities and educational levels.

One of the limitations of our study is that it is applied in physiopathology courses, so the results must be validated in other types of courses and in other educational contexts, which would require future research. Also, the average participant age of 20 in our study might represent a degree of maturity in the discipline of their study program; this may not be equally represented in other age groups, so validation in those is required.

Acknowledgements We thank the physiopathology students for their enthusiastic participation in the social networks and the directors of our institution for the opportunity to conduct educational research. We acknowledge the technical support of the Writing Lab, Institute for the Future of Education, Tecnologico de Monterrey, Mexico, in the production of this work.

References

Aldahdouh TZ, Nokelainen P, Korhonen V (2020) Technology and social media usage in higher education: the influence of individual innovativeness. SAGE Open [Internet]. 10(1) 2020 Jan 1 [cited 2021 Jul 5].https://doi.org/10.1177/2158244019899441

Ali A (2016) Medical student's use of Facebook for educational purposes. Perspect Med Educ 5(3):163–169

Alonso CM, do C, Béguin PD, Duarte FJ, de CM (2018) Work of community health agents in the family health strategy: meta-synthesis. Revista de Saude Publica 52:14. https://doi.org/10.11606/s1518-8787.2018052000395

Al-Qaysi N, Mohamad-Nordin N, Al-Emran M (2020) Employing the technology acceptance model in social media: a systematic review. Educ Inf Technol 25(6):4961–5002

Ansari JAN, Khan NA (2020) Exploring the role of social media in collaborative learning the new domain of learning. Smart Learn Environ [Internet] 7(1):9. Available from: https://slejournal.spr ingeropen.com/articles/https://doi.org/10.1186/s40561-020-00118-7

Badri M, Alnuaimi A, Al Rashedi A, Yang G, Temsah K (2017) School children's use of digital devices, social media and parental knowledge and involvement—the case of Abu Dhabi. Educ Inf Technol 22(5):2645–2664

Boulianne S, Theocharis Y (2020) Young people, digital media, and engagement: a meta-analysis of research. Soc Sci Comput Rev 38(2):111–127

Chan WSY, Leung AYM (2018) Use of social network sites for communication among health professionals: systematic review [Internet]. J Med Internet Res JMIR Publications Inc 20:e8382 [cited 2021 Jul 5]. Available from https://www.jmir.org/2018/3/e117

Clark JL, Algoe SB, Green MC (2018) Social network sites and well-being: the role of social connection. Curr Dir Psychol Sci [Internet] 27(1):32–7 2018 Feb 1 [cited 2021 Jul 5]. Available from: https://journals.sagepub.com/doi/full/https://doi.org/10.1177/0963721417730833

Escobar-Mamani F, Gómez-Arteta I (2020) WhatsApp for the development of oral and written communication skills in Peruvian adolescents. Comunicar 28(65):111–120

Farnsworth V, Kleanthous I, Wenger-Trayner E, Wenger E, Farnsworth V, Farnsworth V et al (2016) Communities of practice as a social theory of learning: a conversation with Etienne Wenger. Br J Educ Stud 64:1–22

Gazit T, Aharony N, Amichai-Hamburger Y (2020) Tell me who you are, and I will tell you which SNS you use: SNSs participation. Online Inf Rev 44(1):139–161

Hernández Sampieri R, Mendoza Torres C (2018) Metodología de la Investigación, Las rutas cuantitativa, cualitativa y mixta. MCGRAW-HILL, México, McGraw Hill

Ibarra-Yruegas BE, Camara-Lemarroy CR, Loredo-Díaz LE, Kawas-Valle O (2015) Social networks in medical practice. Medicina Universitaria 17(67):108–113. https://doi.org/10.1016/j.rmu.2015.01.008

Jordan K, Weller M (2018) Communication, collaboration and identity: factor analysis of academic's perceptions of online networking. Res Learn Technol 10:26

Koranteng FN, Wiafe I, Kuada E (2019) An empirical study of the relationship between social networking sites and student's engagement in higher education. J Educ Comput Res [Internet] 57(5):1131–59. Available from: http://journals.sagepub.com/https://doi.org/10.1177/073563311 8787528

Manca S, Ranieri M (2016) Facebook and the others. Potentials and obstacles of Social Media for teaching in higher education. Comput Educ 95:216–30

Mansour I, Mansour A (2019) An analysis of student's attitudes towards Twitter use for academic purposes: a case of Saudi undergraduate female students. Int J Qual Assur 2(2):211–218

Masciantonio A, Bourguignon D, Bouchat P, Balty M, Rimé B (2021) Don't put all social network sites in one basket: Facebook, Instagram, Twitter, TikTok, and their relations with well-being during the COVID-19 pandemic. PLoS One [Internet] 16:e0248384 2021 Mar 1;(3 March). Available fromhttps://doi.org/10.1371/journal.pone.0248384

Pérez-Escoda A, Jiménez-Narros C, Perlado-Lamo-de-espinosa M, Pedrero-Esteban LM (2020) Social network's engagement during the COVID-19 pandemic in Spain: Health media versus healthcare professionals. Int J Environ Res Public Health [Internet]. 17(14):1–17. Available from: /pmc/articles/PMC7400399/

Sanson-Fisher R, Hobden B, Carey M, MacKenzie L, Hyde L, Shepherd J (2019) Correction: interactional skills training in undergraduate medical education: ten principles for guiding future research. BMC Medical Education 19(1):1–7. https://doi.org/10.1186/s12909-019-1566-2

Sattar K, Ahmad T, Abdulghani HM, Khan S, John J, Meo SA (2016) Social networking in medical schools: medical student's viewpoint. Biomed Res 27(4):1378–1384. Retrieved from http://www.alliedacademies.org/articles/social-networking-in-medical-schools-medical-students-viewpoint.html

Valdez GFD, Cayaban ARR, Al-Fayyadh S, Korkmaz M, Obeid S, Sanchez CLA et al (2020) The utilization of social networking sites, their perceived benefits and their potential for improving the study habits of nursing students in five Countries. BMC Nurs [Internet]. 19(1):1–14. Available from https://doi.org/10.1186/s12912-020-00447-5

Chapter 33
Analysis of Educational Innovation Applying Gamification at the Universidad Politécnica de Madrid

Susana Sastre-Merino, José Luis Martín-Núñez, and María Cristina Núñez-del-Río

33.1 Introduction

Worldwide, higher education institutions are immersed in transformations of pedagogical methodologies motivating students to give greater prominence and commitment to their learning process. In the case of Europe, since the Declaration of Bologna (June 1999), different strategies supporting educational innovation (EI) have been promoted in universities to encourage the faculty to reinvigorate activities and tasks to be carried out and incorporate active methodologies in the subjects taught. Some of these initiatives include calls for educational innovation projects (EIPs), the creation of educational innovation groups (EIGs), teacher training in active methodologies, awards for teaching innovation, and services with support staff for EI (De los Ríos-Carmenado et al. 2021).

We have recently witnessed the educational paradigm shift from the teacher-centered model to the student-centered model. The focus is on what the student must do to develop and demonstrate competencies in the subjects he takes. The measure does not focus on the professor's teaching time but on the estimated time to dedicate to the activities carried out by the students. The apprentice's autonomy and involvement require active methodologies, among which gamification stands out.

Gamification in higher education has attained more prominence in the last decade. Its pedagogical value has consistently been recognized in early childhood education and the first years of primary education; playful tasks are the core of the learning

S. Sastre-Merino (✉) · J. L. Martín-Núñez · M. C. Núñez-del-Río
Instituto de Ciencias de la Educación, Universidad Politécnica de Madrid, Madrid, Spain
e-mail: susana.sastre@upm.es

J. L. Martín-Núñez
e-mail: joseluis.martinn@upm.es

M. C. Núñez-del-Río
e-mail: mc.nunez@upm.es

© The Author(s), under exclusive license to Springer Nature Singapore Pte Ltd. 2022
S. Hosseini et al. (eds.), *Technology-Enabled Innovations in Education*,
Transactions on Computer Systems and Networks,
https://doi.org/10.1007/978-981-19-3383-7_33

activity of schoolchildren. However, as age increases, it seems that "playing is a child's thing" was a wide held belief. Thus, playing was long discarded as an alternative for university studies; it was not seen as an acceptable way for adults to learn.

In the XXI century, numerous studies have provided evidence of the benefits and advantages of playfulness: superior results, increased motivation and competency, and commitment and involvement by students in their learning process (Johns 2015; Perea Moreno et al. 2018; Pérez-López and Rivera 2017; Soler et al. 2018; Yien et al. 2011). Thus, gamification becomes a recurring tool that mobilizes the student and energizes the classes, offering contextual situations and spaces for practice, application and exercises that reinforce student's motivation. Hence, it is seen as an exciting and effective didactic proposal, even taking video games as an example (Prieto et al. 2014).

Research has highlighted the impact of this educational strategy on the effective use of time in the classroom, increasing educational results, improving student's motivation and commitment to tasks, and promoting a climate favorable to learning in the classroom. It offers an environment of cooperation and collaboration, developing transversal skills of great utility for the future professional (teamwork, social skills) while respecting student's rhythms and personal learning styles (Aretio 2016; Cortizo et al. 2011; Oliva 2016).

Studies highlight the need to design and plan recreational activities rigorously to meet student's learning objectives and adapt to their development level (Martínez García 2016; Ortiz-Colón et al. 2018). The 5Es (Engage, Explore, Explain, Elaborate, and Evaluate) model of Karplus and Thier (1967) offers a great starting framework that describes the phases for teachers to consider, generating training actions through constructivist and active learning.

Committed to the quality and improvement of training, aware of the responsibility of the teaching staff in this regard, the Universidad Politécnica de Madrid (UPM), from its Department for Quality and Educational Innovation Service, incorporated the gamification line in its annual call for EIPs. The response of the teaching staff offers the possibility of analyzing their essential characteristics and progress, providing a framework in which to detect training opportunities and needs.

Considering that gamification has become very relevant in the university environment and is consolidated as a motivating methodology for students, it was felt necessary to analyze its incorporation in a Spanish technical university. Therefore, this work aims to:

- Analyze the number of EIPs carried out at UPM in the Gamification category, assessing their presence in the various training areas of the university centers and the level of studies.
- Identify the primary needs to address the different gamification EIPs in the various training areas of the university centers.
- Determine the methodologies used to implement gamification in EIPs.
- Describe the technologies used to implement gamification in EIPs.

33.2 Methodology

To respond to the objectives set out in this research, we conducted a systematic analysis of educational innovation projects within the line of gamification. Accessible information was considered and published on the Technical University of Madrid web portal (Universidad Politécnica de Madrid 2020a). These projects corresponded to calls by the Quality and Educational Innovation Service to update teaching methodologies at the university. Specifically, the gamification line began in the 2016–2017 academic year and has been maintained through the 2019–2020 academic year, the last for which data is available. It must be noted that the projects awarded in this last call were extended by one year if they could not be developed due to the pandemic situation. Of 577 teachers who participated in the EIPs, 212 were women, and 365 were men. As for the coordinators of these EIPs, 17 were women, and 41 were men. Relating these values to the entire university teaching staff (26.4% women, 63.3% men, (Universidad Politécnica de Madrid 2020b)), we observe that they represent similar proportions among the coordinators. In the case of the participants, the percentage of women was 10 points higher than their proportion in the total.

Table 33.1 shows the number of gamification projects approved in the calls for the implementation of educational innovation projects.

From each EIP published file, we extracted a series of analysis variables from a database. The variables considered are:

- The school of the university that proposes the EIP. The schools have been classified into five major training areas for analysis: A&F—Agronomy and forestry, I&T—Informatics and telecommunications, C&A—Civil engineering and architecture, IT—Industrial technologies, and SC- Social sciences.
- Target audience: bachelor's/master's/doctoral students, foreigners, professors.
- The identified needs to be resolved by the EIP.
- The applied didactic methodologies.
- The technologies used.

A process of analysis, codification, and categorization was used to determine the values of the variables *Identified needs, Didactic methodologies,* and *Technologies employed.* The type of categorization was open or ad hoc, typical of the first phase of grounded theory. It was inductive because the categories were constructed from

Table 33.1 Gamification projects analyzed

Call year	Approved projects in the gamification line	Total approved projects in the call	Percentage of gamification projects to total (%)
2016–2017	11	82	13.4
2017–2018	11	113	9.7
2018–2019	20	85	23.5
2019–2021	16	79	20

the collected data (Strauss 1987). Concerning the collection and coding of data, it is noteworthy that the same EIP may employ various methodologies and technologies or seek to solve different needs. This implies that the summation of frequencies for each variable does not correspond to the total of EIPs analyzed.

33.3 Results

The results are presented below, organized according to the four objectives of the study.

33.3.1 Characterization of the Gamification EIPs

Figure 33.1 shows the number of projects approved in EI calls according to the training areas of the university departments. As can be seen, the two areas with the most projects are computing and telecommunications and civil engineering and architecture. If the departments are taken into account separately, the Civil Engineering School (8 projects) and the Telecommunications School (8 projects) had more EIPs in gamification, followed by the Industrial Engineering School (7 projects).

Concerning the recipients of the gamification EIPs (Fig. 33.2), we observe that most were aimed at undergraduate students classes. They were twice the next highest category, corresponding to master's students. The EIPs aimed at professors, foreign students, and Ph.D. students constituted a minority.

Fig. 33.1 Gamification projects in IE-UPM calls

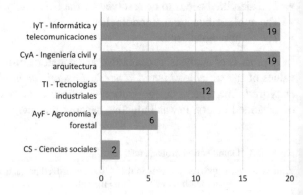

Fig. 33.2 Recipients of the gamification EIPs at the UPM

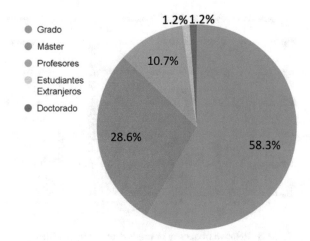

- ● Grado
- ● Máster
- ● Profesores
- ○ Estudiantes Extranjeros
- ● Doctorado

1.2% 1.2%
10.7%
28.6%
58.3%

33.3.2   Identified Needs to be Met

Table 33.2 reflects what intention was behind the elaborated proposals. Altogether 155 needs were identified. Considering that EI must improve some specific aspect of the educational process, the faculty involved must first intend to garner the student's commitment and achieve higher motivation, leading to better academic grades, reflecting more significant learning. Facilitating the task and the faculty training and developing new resources and materials for the subjects taught require an outstanding level of commitment. The development of transversal skills, crucial for the comprehensive training of students, must be addressed without losing sight of how to link training and professional practice. Also, though perhaps not as significant, personalized educational processes focusing on student's characteristics are probably linked to greater awareness about diversity.

   When reviewing the needs detected by training areas (Fig. 33.3), differences in their relative distribution can be seen. It is shown that the main focus is directed

Table 33.2 Needs detected and addressed by the EIPs (frequencies)

	A&F	I&T	C&A	IT	SC	Total
Increase the motivation and active participation of the students	6	16	18	14	1	55
Improve academic results	6	9	9	6	0	30
Provide resources and training for teachers	1	12	5	6	3	27
Improve transversal skills	4	2	9	3	0	18
Bring professional practice/reality closer to the classroom	0	5	6	4	1	16
Personalize learning	1	3	3	1	1	9
TOTAL	18	47	50	34	6	155

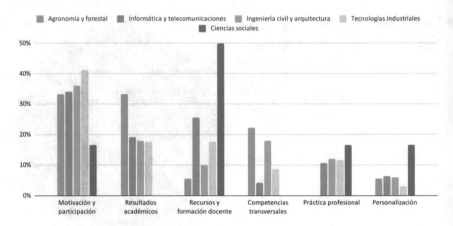

Fig. 33.3 Relative frequency of needs detected by the EIPs

to improving student's motivation, followed by the improvement of their academic results, which is consistent with the sense of gamification as an educational strategy. The increased sensitivity toward faculty training in the area of social sciences is striking. It is crucial to remember that the number of EIPs in this area is minimal (6).

33.3.3 Didactic Methodologies Proposed in the EIPs

The professors included in their proposals a variety of methodologies to be applied in the different EIPs (Table 33.3). They constitute different alternatives for student learning, providing different approaches.

The most frequent methodologies correspond to the collaborative tasks of various types, including information searches, projects, cases, virtual practices, reports, and investigations. Next came face-to-face classes, in which Kahoot, Socrative, and other tools were applied without affecting other aspects of the sessions.

Table 33.3 Proposed didactic methodologies in the EIPs (frequencies)

	A&F	I&T	C&A	IT	SC	Total
Collaborative tasks	4	2	11	5	2	24
Face-to-face classes	1	8	7	6	0	22
Individual tasks	1	6	8	2	1	18
Laboratories	0	4	0	3	0	7
Field trips/excursions/visits	1	0	3	0	0	4
Total	7	20	29	16	3	75

Fig. 33.4 Relative frequency of didactic methodologies in EIPs

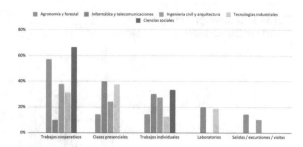

It stands out that the proposal for divergent activities outside the classroom, such as visits, gymkhanas, and contests that broaden the context of student learning, had the lowest frequencies (Fig. 33.4).

Considering the training areas, even with more collaborative activities and face-to-face classes, there were apparent differences in selecting the methodologies to be used. It is plausible that the specific characteristics of the competencies to be developed in each of them justified such results. The data revealed that gamification is not done with the same methodologies in different degree programs.

33.3.4 Technologies Included in the EIPs Proposals

The different EIPs advocate the use of various technologies for the development of gamification (Table 33.4). The proposals involve different levels of complexity, probably reflecting the expertise of the teachers involved.

Lastly, analyzing the technologies used to implement gamification in EIPs (Fig. 33.5) shows that the IT and Telecommunications areas tended to propose solutions with tailor-made gamification applications. In contrast, Civil Engineering and Architecture tended to have more traditional solutions, such as Moodle.

Table 33.4 Technologies used in the EIPs (frequencies)

	A&F	I&T	C&A	IT	SC	Total
Resources developed by the teachers	1	18	4	5	0	28
Web content	3	7	8	7	1	26
Moodle	3	8	10	3	2	26
Video creation	2	3	5	4	1	15
Immediate response systems—IRS	1	2	3	5	0	11
Other tools	1	0	2	1	0	4
None	0	2	1	0	0	3
Total	11	40	33	25	4	113

Fig. 33.5 Technologies to implement Gamification in EIPs

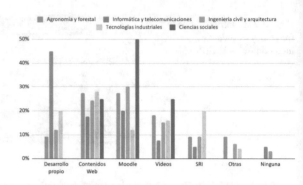

33.4 Discussion

Gamification is consolidating as an educational innovation line at the UPM. It facilitates improvements in educational results, motivation, and performance (Yien et al. 2011; Aretio 2016; Cortizo et al. 2011; López-Pernas et al. 2019), which lead to reduced dropouts and more active student participation.

Regarding assessing student performance, it is essential to establish mechanisms to verify academic results (Pérez-López and Rivera 2017). The strategy will be successful if it impacts grades or the nature of the student's learning.

Gamification penetration by area is not homogeneous, being more visible today in Civil Engineering-Architecture and Telecommunications-Informatics programs. Neither is it homogenous in the level of studies, with EIPs aimed more frequently at improving the learning conditions of undergraduate students. This may be a mere reflection of the referenced enrolled population (Universidad Politécnica de Madrid 2020b).

The faculty's general interest was to generate resources, evidence, or promising practices to share with other colleagues, undoubtedly aligned with the spirit of an EIP (Pérez-López and Rivera 2017; Soler et al. 2018). Specifically, their proposals reinforced aspects less prevalent in the subject's curricula, such as developing transversal or language skills. Their planning also reinforced teaching methodologies, establishing alternative paths to traditional teaching (Martínez García 2016), aiming to homogenize student's learning levels, and promote autonomous and personalized learning.

In their proposed methodologies, the technologists approached didactic situations with their solutions, developing proposals aligned with their training areas (López-Pernas et al. 2019). Undoubtedly, this boosts related professional competencies, which could perhaps be completed with perspectives from other areas. Gamification without technology can promote and facilitate analysis and actions that are remote from standard practice in the professional area and could achieve even more impact. The specific cases in which gamification was used in person without computers are very suggestive: gymkhanas, logic boxes, etc.

Videos and content on web pages or social networks must essentially accompany gamification. For these, immediate response systems (IRS) may be added, which become solutions in themselves for gamification (Perea Moreno et al. 2018; Bravo-Ramos et al. 2019).

In light of the analyzed data, higher education educational institutions should promote gamification as a strategy and didactic tool and implement EIPs in the subject curricula of different degree programs. Increasing their presence orderly will favor the achievement of better educational results, as has already been demonstrated.

33.5 Conclusions

The current social and educational context calls for updating methodologies that reinforce student's involvement in their learning process. Gamification has been positioned as a valid option and an excellent methodological alternative to apply in the university world, motivating students and serving as a lever to improve academic performance and increase student participation, as confirmed by recent studies (Pegalajar Palomino 2021).

The universities' calls for educational innovation projects encourage innovation in the classrooms and establish the necessary mechanisms for a structured transfer of the findings to the community. However, it is imperative to define the indicators and criteria that lead to a more in-depth understanding of the results obtained in the different EIPs.

Gamification's penetration as a teaching methodology has not been homogeneous in the training areas where it has been applied nor in its implementation in terms of technologies and methodologies.

Faculty training must reinforce and level the application of gamification, leveraging the technological potential and taking special care of the pedagogical background.

Acknowledgements The study has been carried out with the support of the UPM's Call—IE1920.9101. Teaching "co-obser-action": learning strategies in other classrooms.

The authors would like to acknowledge the financial and technical support of Writing Lab, Institute for the Future of Education, Tecnologico de Monterrey, Mexico, in the production of this work.

References

Aretio LG (2016) El juego y otros principios pedagógicos. Su pervivencia en la educación a distancia y virtual. RIED. Revista Iberoamericana de Educación a Distancia 19(2):9–23
Bravo-Ramos JL, Martín-Núñez JL, Pablo-Lerchundi I, Caravantes Redondo A (2019) Evaluación en el contexto de la clase presencial utilizando Sistemas de Respuesta Inmediata. Investigación

comprometida para la transformación social. [XIX Congreso Internacional de Investigación Educativa. Madrid, 2019]. pp 938–944

Cortizo JC, Carrero FM, Monsalve B, Velasco A, Díaz LI, Pérez J (2011) Gamificación y docencia: lo que la universidad tiene que aprender de los videojuegos. Retos y oportunidades del desarrollo de los nuevos títulos en educación superior [VIII Jornadas de Innovación Universitaria, Villaviciosa de Odón, Madrid, 2011]

De los Ríos-Carmenado I, Sastre-Merino S, Díaz Lantada A, García-Martín J, Nole P, Pérez-Martínez JE (2021) Building world class universities through innovative teaching governance. Stud Educ Evaluat 70

Johns K (2015) Engaging and assessing students with technology: a review of Kahoot! Delta Kappa Gamma Bulletin 81(4):89–91

Karplus R, Thier HD (1967) A new look at elementary school sciem~e. Rand McNally, Chicago

López-Pernas S, Gordillo A, Barra E, Quemada J (2019) Examining the use of an educational escape room for teaching programming in a higher education setting. IEEE Access 7:31723–31737

Martínez García C (2016) La senda del maestro: experiencias de gamificación en el aula universitaria. Grandes transformaciones sociales, nuevos desafíos para la sociología [XII Congreso Español de Sociología. Gijón, 2016]

Oliva HA (2016) La gamificación como estrategia metodológica en el contexto educativo universitario. Realidad y Reflexión 16(44):108–118

Ortiz-Colón AM, Jordán J, Agredal M (2018) Gamificación en educación: una panorámica sobre el estado de la cuestión. Educ Pesqui 44:1–17

Pegalajar Palomino MC (2021) Implicaciones de la gamificación en Educación Superior: una revisión sistemática sobre la percepción del estudiante. Revista de Investigación Educativa 39(1):169–188

Perea Moreno AJ, Aguilera Ureña MJ, Laguna Luna AM, de la Cruz-Fernández JL, Torres Roldán M, Torres Castro J, Sol Prieto MC, Guzmán Díaz MG, de la Cruz-Lovera C, Martínez Valle JM, Manzano Agugliaro F, Salmerón Manzano EM, Gil Montoya F, Alcayde García A (2018) El uso de los sistemas de respuesta interactiva como herramienta para favorecer el aprendizaje proactivo en ingeniería. Revista de Innovación y Buenas Prácticas Docentes 5:91–96

Pérez-López I, Rivera E (2017) Formar docentes, formar personas: análisis de los aprendizajes logrados por estudiantes universitarios desde una experiencia de gamificación. Signo y Pensamiento 36(70):112–129

Universidad Politécnica de Madrid (2020a) Portal de innovación educativa. https://innovacioned ucativa.upm.es/

Universidad Politécnica de Madrid (2020b) Portal de transparencia. https://transparencia.upm.es/

Prieto A, Díaz D, Monserrat J, Reyes E (2014) Experiencias de aplicación de estrategias de gamificación a entornos de aprendizaje universitario. ReVisión 7(2):76–92

Soler MG, Cárdenas FA, Hernández-Pina F (2018) Enfoques de enseñanza y enfoques de aprendizaje: perspectivas teóricas promisorias para el desarrollo de investigaciones en educación en ciencias. Ciência and Educação (bauru) 24(4):993–1012

Strauss AL (1987) Qualitative analysis for social scientists. Cambridge University Press, Cambridge

Yien J, Hung C, Hwang G, Lin Y (2011) A game-based learning approach to improving student's learning achievements in a nutrition course. Turkish Online J Educ Technol-TOJET 10(2):1–10

Chapter 34
The Role of ICTs in Selected Secondary Schools in Fako Division, Cameroon

Kfukfu Nsangong and Julius Nganji

34.1 Introduction

Information and communication technologies (ICTs) are essential in our world today, permeating every sector of the economy, including education (Asongu et al. 2021). In the education sector, many educators believe that technology is essential for school restructuring and curriculum reform as it is needed to improve the educational system (Oyediran-Tidings et al. 2021; Ergado et al. 2021). The quality of accomplishment depends on the school administration's leadership, cooperation, and competencies, as reported by Latchem et al. (2001), who suggested that, in the quest for increased access to education, considerable emphasis should be placed on potentiating ICTs.

School leaders motivate teaching and non-teaching staff to become interested and learn ICTs to perform their various roles for effective school success. In the technological age, the school administrator's functions have become increasingly challenging. They need computer literacy skills to locate, access, evaluate, and analyze information in the workforce (Carroll and Broadhead 1995). This challenge has become even more profound with the current and sudden need to move to online teaching and learning during the COVID-19 pandemic.

The lack of ICT skills, poor attitude toward ICT use, and limited and outdated computers present problems for ICT use in schools with limited resources. Even though ICTs effectively facilitate school administration, the lack of sound and reliable technological infrastructure in some countries in Sub-Saharan Africa, such as

K. Nsangong
Department of Educational Administration and Leadership, St. Cloud State University, St. Cloud, USA
e-mail: knsangong@go.stcloudstate.edu

J. Nganji (✉)
Department of Occupational Science and Occupational Therapy, University of Toronto, Toronto, Canada
e-mail: j.nganji@utoronto.ca

© The Author(s), under exclusive license to Springer Nature Singapore Pte Ltd. 2022   417
S. Hosseini et al. (eds.), *Technology-Enabled Innovations in Education*,
Transactions on Computer Systems and Networks,
https://doi.org/10.1007/978-981-19-3383-7_34

Cameroon, hinders these efforts (Nganji and Nggada 2014). Also, the lack of support from school administration (Ngajie and Ngo 2016) and a lack of vision (Mbangwana 2008) have hindered the quality and success of ICT implementation, which is vital for school success. Against this backdrop, this study sought to investigate the use of ICTs to improve the quality of secondary school administration.

This study aimed to investigate how information and communication technologies are used to improve the quality of secondary school administration in the Fako Division of Cameroon. To achieve the primary goal of this study, we developed the following specific objectives to guide the study:

1. Determine the extent to which the use of ICT facilitates the functions of school administrators.
2. Investigate the extent to which the use of ICT encourages the professional development of teaching and non-teaching staff.
3. Assess the degree to which ICT facilitates teaching and learning in schools.

Thus, to achieve the above objectives, the following questions were asked:

1. To what extent does the use of ICT facilitate the functions of school administrators?
2. To what extent does the use of ICT encourage the professional development of teaching and non-teaching staff?
3. To what extent does the use of ICT facilitate teaching and learning in schools?

The study also proceeded by formulating null (Ho) and alternative (Ha) hypotheses that would be either accepted or rejected based on statistical analyses of the findings. The hypotheses for question 1 were:

- Ho1: The use of ICT does not facilitate the functions of school administrators.
- Ha1: The use of ICT facilitates the functions of school administrators.

The hypotheses for question 2 were:

- Ho2: The use of ICT does not encourage the professional development of teaching and non-teaching staff.
- Ha2: The use of ICT encourages the professional development of teaching and non-teaching staff.

The hypotheses for question 3 were:

- Ho3: The use of ICT does not facilitate teaching and learning in secondary schools.
- Ha3: The use of ICT facilitates teaching and learning in secondary schools.

The following section presents a brief literature review on various uses of ICTs in the educational sector, specifically for administration and teaching/learning. The study methodology is then discussed, and the study results and analysis of the findings are presented. The paper ends with some specific recommendations for educational institutions in Cameroon, which could apply to similar low-resource settings.

34.2   Review of ICT Use in Education

34.2.1   ICT Use for Administration and Professional Development

We noted earlier that ICTs had permeated different sectors of the economy. Technological advances have also led to the development of new management techniques (Mbua 2002) that benefit the education sector. The efficient use of ICTs helps guide decision making. School administrations must support this adoption to benefit teachers by integrating technology into their classrooms (Sandholtz et al. 1997; Bennett 1995). In addition, good interpersonal skills are essential as the administrator works with people.

To improve teacher performance and professional growth, school administrators must provide basic teaching materials (Mbua 2003). For effective professional development, the focus should be on the administration's leadership and commitment, as the school fosters collaborative working, providing quality assistance and support.

34.2.2   ICT Use in Learning

ICT often takes a learner-centered approach to instruction, helping to guide learners in their educational journey (Nganji 2018). In technology-enhanced learning, the responsibility for learning falls on the learner, and the instructor acts as a coach, facilitator, and tutor (Perrucci et al. 2020). Many students are motivated by feeling they are in control of their learning (Barak 2010).

Although computers can improve learning outcomes for students, this can only come about if they are appropriately used (Dede 1998). Designing learning environments so that students can effectively manage their learning can motivate them to interact positively with learning systems (Nganji 2018). Thus, the use of ICT empowers students to be more independent and actively control their learning process. When this learning is online, there is also flexibility as to when and where learning occurs.

34.2.3   ICT Use in Teaching

Today, technology offers alternative ways to deliver instruction and is fast becoming essential, primarily due to the COVID-19 pandemic. Several studies have documented this shift to online learning in situations like pandemics when people cannot meet in a physical location (Marchlik et al. 2021; Pozo et al. 2021).

Although technological developments have driven educational systems mainly in the global North, most educational systems in Sub-Saharan Africa seem to be left behind due to lack of infrastructure. Due to many inequalities in higher education in low- and middle-income countries, online education has been touted as one of the solutions (Reinders 2021). Thus, it is crucial to investigate this.

34.2.4 Access to ICTs in Schools in Sub-Saharan Africa

Although ICTs are beneficial for schools, sub-Saharan Africa (SSA) still faces significant challenges to adopting their widespread use in schools. For instance, (Tilya et al. 2018) noted some of the challenges were insufficient budget and inadequate ICT infrastructure, with the unavailability of electricity as a significant hindrance to ICT growth. Samarakoon, Christiansen, and Munro (Samarakoon et al. 2017) corroborate these challenges with their study in Sierra Leone. Asongu and Odhiambo (2019) argue that this lack of infrastructure makes education in SSA sub-standard compared to other world regions.

Another critical challenge to online learning is the unreliable Internet infrastructure. A survey of 2341 lecturers and students from Ghana, Kenya, and South Africa (Porter et al. 2016) recorded extremely low satisfaction with Internet connection, cost, and reliability.

In Cameroon, the challenge to ICT adoption and use in schools has been related to inadequate access to ICTs, poor infrastructure, and the lack of skills to use the ICTs (Samarakoon et al. 2017). Although there are challenges with access to computers in schools, mobile phone use is rising (Haji et al. 2017) in Africa. It is positively utilized to drive other sectors in Cameroon, such as agriculture (Nzie et al. 2018). Also, in the Cameroon education sector, studies have recommended adopting social media in education (Kuika Watat et al. 2020).

34.3 Methodology

The survey research design was descriptive, with a questionnaire as the data collection tool. The questionnaire used a five-point Likert scale as follows: Strongly agree (SA) = 5, agree (A) = 4, neutral (N) = 3, disagree (D) = 2, and strongly disagree (SD) = 1. The items in the questionnaire were developed from the research questions and review of related literature. The questionnaire was divided into two sections, A and B.

Section A aimed at collecting demographic data. Section B focused on the various research questions, the problems of ICT implementation and its utilization in schools, and suggested solutions. The questionnaire had open-ended and closed-ended questions. Both face and content validity were ensured before data collection. The printed questionnaires were administered directly to the respondents after obtaining ethical clearance and approval for data collection. A total of ninety (90) questionnaires were administered, and ninety (90) returned, giving a return rate of 100%.

34.3.1   Study Population

The study was carried out in the Fako Division, an English-speaking region with four sub-divisions; it is one of the six divisions of the Southwest Region of Cameroon. The target population consisted of 128 administrators (mainly principals and vice-principals) in the 73 schools in the Fako Division. The schools included 25 public (25 principals and 38 vice-principals), 18 denominational (18 principals and 11 vice-principals), and 30 lay private (30 principals and six vice-principals) schools. Of the 128 administrators in all the schools, we randomly selected a sample of 90 administrators for the study.

34.3.2   Data Collection and Analysis

Descriptive statistics based on frequencies and percentages were used for analyses. The Statistical Package for Social Sciences (SPSS) was used to analyze the data, and the analysis of variance (ANOVA) was used to verify the hypotheses.

34.4   Results

In this section, the survey results are first presented then discussed, considering other studies conducted in Cameroon. This helps provide insight into whether there is progress in adopting ICTs in schools in Cameroon. The discussion paves a way to look to the future of technology-enhanced learning in Cameroon.

34.4.1   Demographic Data

The results collected showed 73.33% males (66) and 26.67% females (24), reflecting a gender imbalance of school administrators. Also, 88.89% of respondents were administrative heads of secondary and high schools (80), while 11.11% were administrative heads of secondary Schools (10) only.

This implies there are more administrators in secondary and high schools than in secondary schools only. Most administrators (57.78%) were vice-principals (52); 42.22% were principals (38). The largest number (29) of administrators had a Bachelor's degree as their highest educational qualification (32.22%). In contrast, others (21) had as highest qualification the DIPES II /Equivalent (23.64%), the DIPES I/Equivalent (20), and Master's degree (20), the latter two being 22.22%. DIPES is a diploma obtained from a teachers training college in Cameroon. There were 55.56% of school administrators with working experience of 0–5 years, 33.33%

with working experience of 11–15 years, 6.67% between 16–20 years, and none had working experience more than 20 years.

A close examination of the results shows that more than half of the respondents had a working experience of 0–5 years. All the respondents had knowledge of ICT use in their schools.

34.4.2 The Extent to Which the Use of ICT Facilitates the Functions of School Administrators

During this study, the first question was, "To what extent does the use of ICT facilitate the functions of school administrators?" The results are presented in Fig. 34.1. From the statistical analysis of the individual responses, we observed that the mean decreases in descending order from the first variable (strongly agree) to the last (strongly disagree). The standard deviations decrease from the first variable to the second, then increase with the third variable, and subsequently decrease from the fourth variable.

The total mean (17.89) is greater than the total standard deviation (14.55). The null hypothesis is therefore rejected, and the alternative hypothesis is accepted. Thus, it can be concluded that the use of ICTs facilitates the functions of school administration within this study population.

Fig. 34.1 How ICT facilitates school administration

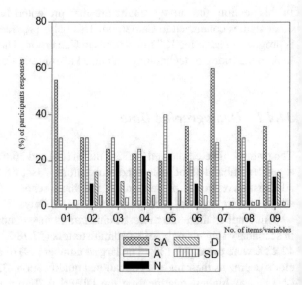

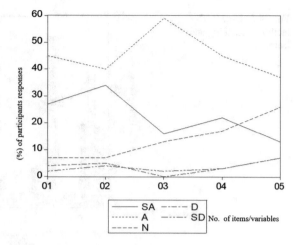

Fig. 34.2 How ICT facilitates professional development

34.4.3   The Extent to Which the Use of ICT Encourages Professional Development of Teaching and Non-teaching Staff

This research also sought to answer the question, "To what extent does the use of ICT encourage the professional development of teaching and non-teaching staff?" The results are presented in Fig. 34.2.

Statistical analysis of the responses revealed that the mean of the entire variables (17.89) is greater than the standard deviation of all the variables (14.55). The mean increases from the first variable (strongly agree) to the second (agree) and then decreases from the third variable (neutral) to the last (strongly disagree); the standard deviation decreases from the first variable to the last. Thus, the null hypothesis is rejected, and the alternative hypothesis is accepted: The use of ICTs encourages the professional development of teaching and non-teaching staff.

34.4.4   The Extent to Which the Use of ICT Facilitates Teaching and Learning in Schools

This research also sought to answer the question, "To what extent does the use of ICTs facilitate teaching and learning in secondary schools?" The results are presented in Fig. 34.3.

Based on a statistical analysis of the responses, we observed that the value of all means (17.89) is greater than the value of all standard deviations (13.77). Also, the mean values and standard deviations fluctuate with variables from the first (strongly agree) to the last (strongly disagree). The null hypothesis is therefore rejected, and the alternative hypothesis is accepted.

Fig. 34.3 How ICT
facilitates teaching and
learning

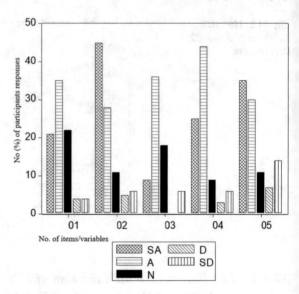

The results show that the use of ICTs facilitates teaching and learning in secondary schools.

34.4.5 Challenges to ICT Implementation and Use in Secondary School Administration

When asked the major challenges faced in implementation, the top reasons given were the following:

1. Budgetary constraints in purchasing and maintaining ICT equipment (44%).
2. Most administrators, teachers, support staff, and students are not computer literate (22.2%).
3. Lack of qualified ICT personnel for laboratory sessions (11.11%).
4. Small computer laboratory with a high student-per-computer ratio (8.90%).
5. Many schools have not yet grasped the importance of ICT (7.78%).
6. Nonchalant attitude toward ICT (3.33%).
7. The absence of Internet in some schools (2.22%).

34.5 Discussion

This study shows that ICTs facilitate the functions of school administrators, professional development, teaching, and learning. It is worth discussing these findings and how they compare to others conducted in Cameroon.

34.5.1   ICTs Facilitate the Functions of School Administrators

Analyzing the data from our study about the role of ICTs in administration reveals that computers are gradually being adopted into the secondary education sector in the Fako Division. For the schools with access, ICTs play an essential role in facilitating teaching and learning and helping to facilitate the duties of school administrators. With technology, humans are more efficient and faster. Preparing reports and managing recruitment and human resources are easier with ICTs.

Although the importance of ICTs has been acknowledged and most schools want to adopt them, a similar study on their use in secondary school administration in Buea, Cameroon, found limited use (Njouny 2021). This could be attributed to the lack of adequate financial resources to purchase the equipment and, in some cases, low digital literacy among secondary school administrators and teachers.

34.5.2   ICTs Facilitate Professional Development

The results from our survey show that the use of ICTs encourages the professional development of teaching and non-teaching staff. This involves using the ICTs to gain new skills, which also opens the staff to new content and opportunities. A connection to the Internet facilitates communication with other colleagues elsewhere, which can also help their professional development.

Despite these benefits, a study conducted in Bamenda in the Northwest Region, the second of only two English-speaking regions in Cameroon, found that many teachers still oppose incorporating technologies into classrooms (Mbakwa 2019). A survey administered to 34 secondary school students and 13 teachers through WhatsApp, Facebook, and Telegram showed that most schools were still practicing the "chalk and talk" system where students rely on teachers for lectures in a physical classroom, and there is no online component. Although the teachers still prefer this teaching method, that study also found that financial constraints were one of the causes hindering adoption of technology-enhanced education.

34.5.3   ICTs Facilitate Teaching and Learning

The adoption of ICTs has proven to be very beneficial in facilitating teaching and learning. The current global COVID-19 pandemic has shown how important this is, especially when students and teachers cannot be in the same physical classroom. The move to online learning gives the student some autonomy and allows the teacher to guide the student.

Responses from the respondents in our study showed that ICTs facilitate teaching and learning. Although a study in Cameroon reported that some teachers were less favorable to adopting ICTs in teaching, students, on the other hand, have generally been in favor of using ICTs in education (Mbah 2010). However, the challenge is that most people do not own a personal computer and rely on access via internet cafes.

34.5.4 Toward Mobile Learning (M-Learning) in Cameroon

Considering these findings, it is worth discussing the types of devices being used and the potential for broader adoption of technology-enhanced learning in Cameroon. A survey of ten schools in Yaoundé in the Central Region, which is French-speaking, examined the types of devices used in schools (Ngoungouo 2017). The study found that some schools mainly used computers, telephones, and projectors with minimal use of learning management systems for course delivery.

Nevertheless, given the current need to adopt technology-enhanced education during the COVID-19 pandemic, some studies have focused on how Cameroon has responded to this challenge. Through document analysis, interviews, and observations, the study by Béché (2020) found various initiatives to adapt during the pandemic, albeit with little infrastructure. The national television was used to deliver courses for students who were preparing for their final examinations. Selected teachers delivered the courses while students all over the country watched and took notes and received support from parents. One of the challenges with such delivery was the unreliable electricity supply in a country with frequent power outages. University students were reportedly using other technologies such as WhatsApp, Skype, and Zoom for learning and a limited number of learning management systems.

Given the high rate of mobile phone penetration (Stork et al. 2012) and the limited availability of affordable personal computers, school administrators and educational developers must start moving toward mobile learning (m-learning), which might be more effective. This requires the government to collaborate with telecommunication providers to lower the cost of providing mobile Internet to students. Affordability will encourage more learners to engage in technology-enhanced learning.

34.6 Conclusion and Recommendations

This study aimed to investigate how information and communication technologies can facilitate administration in secondary schools in the Fako Division of Cameroon. Based on the study's findings, it can be concluded that the use of information and communication technologies facilitates school administrators' functions, encourages the professional development of teaching and non-teaching staff, and facilitates teaching and learning in secondary schools.

Given that the data in this study only focused on selected schools and only analyzed information collected from 90 respondents, care should be taken when interpreting the results. Further studies in a broader population are encouraged. Nevertheless, the results provide valuable insights that we can recommend to other schools looking to incorporate ICTs.

The recommendations are as follows:

- Due to financial constraints, the government should purchase ICTs for schools and ensure frequent maintenance for continuous use. Provisions could be made directly from government coffers or indirectly through foreign aid and Non-governmental Organizations (NGOs).
- ICT instructors available in schools should be well trained or highly recommended by the government and other organizations.
- ICT training should be offered to leaders and staff on using ICTs in schools effectively for success in attaining the institutions' goals.

This study was restricted to administrative heads (principals and vice-principals) of secondary schools in the Fako Division. Future studies should be extended to other school administrators and cover the entire Southwest Region to obtain a better picture and impact of technology on administration in secondary schools.

References

Asongu S, Amari M, Jarboui A, Mouakhar K (2021) ICT dynamics for gender-inclusive intermediary education: minimum poverty and inequality thresholds in developing countries. Telecommun Policy 45(5):12, Art no. 102125. https://doi.org/10.1016/j.telpol.2021.102125

Asongu SA, Odhiambo NM (2019) Enhancing ICT for quality education in sub-Saharan Africa. Educ Inf Technol 24(5):2823–2839. https://doi.org/10.1007/s10639-019-09880-9

Barak M (2010) Motivating self-regulated learning in technology education, (in English). Int J Technol Design Educ 20(4):381–401. https://doi.org/10.1007/s10798-009-9092-x

Béché E (2020) Cameroonian responses to COVID-19 in the education sector: exposing an inadequate education system. Int Rev Educ 66:755–775

Bennett N (1995) Managing professional teachers. Paul Chapman Publishing, London, p 166

Carroll J, Broadhead R (1995) Canadian internet handbook—educational edition, Prentice-Hall Canada

Dede C (1998) Evaluating the effectiveness of technology initiatives. The High School Magazine, 1 (September), vol 6. pp 16–20

Ergado AA, Desta A, Mehta H (2021) Determining the barriers contributing to ICT implementation by using a technology-organization-environment framework in Ethiopian higher educational institutions (in English). Educ Info Technol 26(3):3115–3133. https://doi.org/10.1007/s10639-020-10397-9

Haji SA, Moluayonge GE, Park I (2017) Teacher's use of information and communications technology in education: cameroon secondary schools perspectives. The Turkish Online J Educ Technol 16(3):147–153

Kuika Watat J, Jonathan GM, Ntsafack Dongmo FW, Zine El Abidine NEH (2020) Social media impact on academic performance: lessons learned from Cameroon. In: Information systems, Cham, pp 370–379. https://doi.org/10.1007/978-3-030-63396-7_25

Latchem C, Walker D (2001) Perspectives on distance education telecenters: case studies and key issues. The Commonwealth of Learning, Vancouver

Marchlik P, Wichrowska K, Zubala E (2021) The use of ICT by ESL teachers working with young learners during the early COVID-19 pandemic in Poland. Educ Info Technol; Early Access, pp 25. https://doi.org/10.1007/s10639-021-10556-6

Mbah TB (2010) The impact of ICT on student's study habits. Case study: University of Buea, Cameroon. J Sci Technol Educ Res 1(5):107–110

Mbakwa PN (2019) The state and challenges of technology enhanced learning in Cameroon's english subsystem of education: case study of colleges. In: International conference on online and blended learning 2019 (ICOBL 2019)

Mbangwana (2008) Introduction of ICT in SCHOOLS AND CLASSROOMS in Cameroon. In: Toure K, Tchombe TMS, Karsenti T (eds) ICT and changing mindsets in education, Bamenda, Cameroon, Langaa, Bamako, Mali, ERNWACA/ROCARE

Mbua FN (2002) In: Educational planning: issues and perspectives. Limbe, Presprint

Mbua FN (2003) In: Educational administration: theory and practice. Limbe, Presprint

Ngajie BN, Ngo MMC (2016) Integration of ICTs into the curriculum of Cameroon primary and secondary schools: a review of current status, barriers and proposed strategies for effective Integration. Int J Educ Developm Using Inform Commun Technol (IJEDICT) 12(1):89–106

Nganji JT (2018) Towards learner-constructed e-learning environments for effective personal learning experiences. Behav Infor Technol 37(6). https://doi.org/10.1080/0144929X.2018.147 0673

Nganji JT, Nggada SH (2014) Adoption of blended learning technologies in selected secondary schools in Cameroon and Nigeria: challenges in disability inclusion. In: Olulube N (ed) Advancing technology and educational development through blended learning in emerging economies, Hershey, PA, Information Science Reference, pp 159–173

Ngoungouo AB (2017) The use of ICTs in the Cameroonian school system: a case study of some primary and secondary schools in Yaoundé. Int J Educ Developm Using Info Commun Technol (IJEDICT) 13(1):153–159

Njouny EM (2021) Evaluating the use of ICTs in secondary school administration in Cameroon: the case of some secondary schools in the Buea municipality. IJER-Int J Educ Res 4(02):62–75

Nzie JRM, Bidogeza JC, Ngum NA (2018) Mobile phone use, transaction costs, and price: evidence from rural vegetable farmers in Cameroon. J Afr Bus 19(3):323–342. https://doi.org/10.1080/152 28916.2017.1405704

Oyediran-Tidings SO, Nekhwevha FH, Ondari-Okemwa EM, Salubi O (2021) Access to educational information enabled by ICT tools in the Fort Beaufort Education District (FBED), Eastern Cape, South Africa. Information Development, Article; Early Access pp 15. Art no. 0266666921995232. https://doi.org/10.1177/0266666921995232

Perrucci V, Khanlari A, Cacciamani S (2020) The role of the instructor and the tutor in the discoursive interaction in a blended university course: a case analysis. Qwerty 15(2):85–104. https://doi.org/ 10.30557/qw000032

Porter G et al (2016) Mobile phones and education in Sub-Saharan Africa: from youth practice to public policy. J Int Dev 28(1):22–39. https://doi.org/10.1002/jid.3116

Pozo JI, Echeverria MPP, Cabellos B, Sanchez DL (2021) Teaching and learning in times of COVID-19: uses of digital technologies during school lockdowns. Frontiers in Psychol 12:13 Art no. 656776. https://doi.org/10.3389/fpsyg.2021.656776

Reinders S, Dekker M, Falisse JB (2021) Inequalities in higher education in low- and middle-income countries: a scoping review of the literature. Developm Policy Review, Review Early Access, pp 25. https://doi.org/10.1111/dpr.12535

Samarakoon S, Christiansen A, Munro PG (2017) Equitable and quality education for all of Africa? the challenges of using ICT in education. Perspectives on Global Developm Technol 16(6):645–665. https://doi.org/10.1163/15691497-12341454

Sandholtz JH, Ringstaff C, Dwyer DC (1997) Teaching with technology: creating student-centered classrooms. Teachers College Press, New-York

Stork C, Calandro E, Gillwald A (2012) Internet going mobile: internet access and usage in eleven African countries. In: 19th Biennial conference of the international telecommunications society (ITS): "Moving forward with future technologies: opening a platform for all", Bangkok, Thailand, 18th-21th November 2012, International Telecommunications Society (ITS), Calgary

Tilya F (2018) Information and communication technology and educational policies in the Sub-Saharan African Region. In: Voogt J, Knezek G, Christensen R, Lai K-W (eds) Second handbook of information technology in primary and secondary education. Springer International Publishing, Cham, pp 1–19

Chapter 35
Discussing the Meaning of Innovation: A Collaborative Activity for Engineering Education

Julian "Iñaki" Goñi

35.1 Introduction

Engineering is often seen as a tool to make our world better (Ettridge and Sharma 2020). Engineering students can be very passionate about using their natural sciences and engineering design knowledge to tackle some of the "Grand Challenges" of our times (Wetmore 2018). Moreover, engineers are involved in problems with profound socio-political roots, such as conflict, crisis, disasters, human rights, economics, and political oppression (Tan et al. 2019). This perspective of the power of engineering is not coincidental. Technology is perceived as one of the critical drivers of societal change, and this particular historical moment is one of a solid technological innovation bias (Godin 2020).

As Sheila Jasanoff asserts, "through technology, human societies articulate their hopes, dreams, and desires while also making material instruments for accomplishing them" (Jasanoff 2016, p. 242). In this sense, technological decisions are always connected to our understanding of "the good life" and our value systems (Vallor 2016). Technological choices are also intrinsically political: "they order society, distribute benefits and burdens, and channel power" (Jasanoff 2016, p. 243].

Technology is also political in the sense that it impacts society. Of course, the typical examples of technology "failing" in Chernobyl and "succeeding" in the Manhattan Project come to mind. However, since then, the cases exposing the social implications of technology have only increased. The Cambridge Analytica scandal darkened the interrelationships of information technologies, privacy, and democracy (Wagner 2021). Predictive policing raises questions on the extent of public power (Karppi 2018). Social media has been shown to produce echo chambers and filter bubbles that form public opinion (Kitchens et al. 2020). Gene-editing technology

J. Goñi (✉)
DILAB School of Engineering, Pontificia Universidad Católica de Chile, Santiago, Chile
e-mail: jvgoni@uc.cl

© The Author(s), under exclusive license to Springer Nature Singapore Pte Ltd. 2022   431
S. Hosseini et al. (eds.), *Technology-Enabled Innovations in Education*,
Transactions on Computer Systems and Networks,
https://doi.org/10.1007/978-981-19-3383-7_35

touches on the very nature of life, triggering intense public scrutiny, especially when framed as decisions about "designer babies" (Coller 2019). The examples are plentiful, but the conclusion always points to the public impact of technology. The "hard impacts" (Boenink et al. 2010) expose us to observable risks in terms of health, environment, and safety, and the "soft impacts" (Boenink et al. 2010) to changes in our moral routines, social practices, and subjectivity).

Even when projects are initially considered successful, it is not clear which criteria measure success. For instance, the LifeStraw (a personal water purification device aimed at communities with no access to potable water) is often seen as an exemplar of socially responsible design, as it helps underserved people, particularly in Africa, from a humanitarian point of view (Vere et al. 2011). However, it also reproduces dependency dynamics as the communities cannot manufacture the product; they must import it (Melles et al. 2011). Considering product, the historical background of dependency in Africa, and the alternative of conventional water supply infrastructure that the rest of the world uses, can we call this technological solution a success? How do we define success, and why?

In this context, it is problematic that the engineering education curricula lack a more reflective approach to engineering practices (Wetmore 2018; Dym et al. 2005). Moreover, it is problematic that ethics courses are scarce and typically focus on specific ethical scenarios (Wetmore 2018) rather than developing a critical mindset to analyze how technology and society are strongly intertwined (Ortiz-Revilla et al. 2020). We must consider that engineers de facto use social tools when they frame problems, interpret data, and conceptually construct the very problems they aim to solve (Gray and Fernandez 2018). However, undergraduate engineering students tend to adopt a passive role regarding the social implications of their work, as engineering education still tends to promote the idea that technical considerations are more important than social ones (Cech 2013).

Acquiring "techno-moral wisdom" (Vallor 2016) is, of course, not solely a task for engineers. As Shannon Vallor (Vallor 2016) argues, all individuals and communities should strive for shared values of a global community, intercultural understanding, global justice, human security, and collective human wisdom to navigate this complex socio-technical age. For engineers, these values should be translated into educational experiences of "putting our hands on our hips (criticality), pausing before we act (humility), moving our bodies toward others (openness), and standing up when we know something is wrong (action)" (Tomblin and Mogul 2020, p. 118].

Despite the increasing interest in the social studies of technology and the so-called science, technology, and society (STS) within engineering education literature (Neeley et al. 2019a), there is still a need for educational translations of the socio-technical tensions inside the engineering classroom. It seems particularly relevant to promote a more reflective and critical mindset in engineering students toward the concept of innovation which is often surrounded by uncritical, cult-like, and often irresponsible views of socio-technical change (Winner 2018; Russell et al. 2019).

This article presents the methodological characteristics of an educational activity called "Meaning of Innovation Dialogue" that critically and collaboratively explores the meaning of innovation for engineering students. Through this activity, it is expected that students have an opportunity to reflect on the philosophical, ethical, and political challenges of innovating, with a particular focus on imagining alternative visions for more reflective innovation.

35.2 The "Meaning of Innovation" Dialogue

35.2.1 Overview

The Meaning of Innovation Dialogue (MID) is a two-step collaborative activity in which engineering student teams are asked to reflect on the concept of innovation through dialogue. The activity is organized into two phases:

- Critical case studies phase: In this stage, teams of three to four students discuss a selection of STS-related publications and analyze two case studies of emergent technologies with salient social implications.
- Socratic dialogue phase: In this stage, teams of five to eight students have a structured conversation about the meaning of innovation through one of the three guiding questions: What is innovation? What should be the purpose of innovation? How should innovation be governed?

Through this activity, it is expected that engineering students can explore the concept of innovation through three distinct analytical levels: *pragmatic* (uses and definitions), *ethical* (normative, axiological, and deontological aspirations), and *political* (democratic, responsible, and anticipatory mechanisms).

35.2.2 Methodological Foundations

The MID is based on two different argumentative educational activities, which serve to structure the conversations.

The primary methodological foundation of this pedagogical proposal is the Socratic Seminar (Castellano-Reyes 2020). The Socratic Seminar is a collaborative activity where students reason together in a complex scenario or with complicated information. The Socratic Seminar is typically used for analyzing text-based information under established discussion norms, organizing students in a fishbowl (concentric circle) arrangement (Griswold et al. 2017). In a Socratic Seminar, instructors aim to guide and provoke student's debate with open and engaging questions that can be literal (e.g., what does this data show?), interpretative (e.g., what are the implications of this data?), or evaluative (e.g., how does this data apply to you?) (Griswold et al. 2017).

The Socratic Seminar focuses on questions designed by the instructor rather than given answers (Castellano-Reyes 2020). Through this technique, much of the regulation is still teacher-centered as instructor questions are the driving force of the conversation (the teacher is still Socrates, the central figure). Even though there are several different guidelines for conducting a Socratic Seminar, most argumentative guides are designed for the instructor rather than students, who would self-regulate the conversation.

The second main activity is the Critical Debate Model (Fuentes and Goñi 2021; Fuentes 2011). This model is based on Leitao's (2007) idea of argumentation as a dialogical and social process rather than an intra-psychological operation. Under a sociocultural approximation, argumentation is a discursive negotiation process, a specific set of utterances that propose and oppose, not necessarily individuals who are proponents and opponents (Leitao 2007). In this sense, one person can perfectly argue with himself, as long as the utterance uses the dialogical pattern of proposing and opposing. More specifically, argumentation is based on three building blocks; a point of view (thesis), elements that support the acceptance of this point of view (support elements), and elements that restrict its acceptance (counterarguments) (Leitao 2007).

Based on these three elements of argumentation, the Critical Debate Model (CDM) proposes a rearrangement of the classical British Parliamentary debate model. In the CDM, instead of two opposing teams, there are three groups of students. Two groups of students interchange proposing and opposing specific controversial statements, while the third group is in charge of reviewing pertinent evidence. Additionally, students are given a scaffolding structure to develop their arguments. It must include three elements: A point of view (e.g., "We believe/assert/propose that the Chilean healthcare system must be replaced") plus a justification (e.g., "because it is unfair by nature") plus evidence (e.g., "as supported by the newly published study of X foundation that states that…") (Fuentes and Goñi 2021). At the end of the initial rounds of arguments, students can freely choose to support their initial position or oppose it based on emerging arguments of the debate.

The CDM's strength is that it provides relevant scaffolding to construct arguments and decouples the idea that students must rigidly adopt a debate stance (being pro or contra a statement that is typically assigned randomly). However, it preserves the idea of argumentation as being adversarial and not best suited when instructors seek to emphasize collaboration.

Drawing from both the Socratic Seminar and the Critical Debate Model, the MID aims at organizing a collaborative experience in which students self-regulate a conversation not guided by instructor-led questioning. Instead, it seeks to provide a dialogical structure that specifies what argumentative interventions can be made; it views the argumentative stances of proposing, supporting, and opposing as fluid among students. Additionally, it seeks to shift the preparation phase from the teacher to the students through guided case analysis.

35.2.3 Critical Case Studies Phase

Before participating in the main dialogue, smaller groups of students are asked to prepare by discussing and sharing highlights from the mandatory readings and, through the lens of those readings, analyze two cases studies from a pool of documented cases selected by the instructor beforehand. After watching or reading the available material in each case, students must answer these two questions collectively: (1) How is innovation used in that context? (2) What would be a more responsible use of innovation in that context?

The mandatory reading material of this activity changes from semester to semester, but some examples of readings used are:

- The Ethics of Invention (2016) by Sheila Jasanoff (mainly from the section "How Technology Rules US" to "Standpoint and Method")
- Who's Driving Innovation? (2019) by Jack Stilgoe (particularly Chaps. 1 & 2).
- Technology and the Virtues (2016) by Shannon Vallor (particularly Part 2.6 "Techno-moral Wisdom for an Uncertain Future: 21st-Century Virtues").
- The Idea of Technological Innovation: A Brief Alternative History (2020) by Benoit Godin (particularly the Introduction and Part 1)
- The Innovation Delusion (2020) by Lee Vinsel and Andrew Russell (particularly Part 1).

On the other hand, the case studies are also very frequently updated based on the current technological climate. Some examples used for discussion were:

- Amazon's Alexa & NHS partnership to give citizens medical advice (see https://youtu.be/1bOVKSFZlds)
- Facial recognition used for giving fines to uncompliant citizens (see https://youtu.be/0oJqJkfTdAg)
- Algorithmic bias in facial recognition software (see https://youtu.be/TWWsW1w-BVo)
- Fears of a surveillance state in Smart Cities (see https://www.bbc.co.uk/ideas/videos/welcome-to-the-smart-city-of-the-future/p07q2q3t/player)

Overall, the reading selection criteria either provide a rich historical or current contextualization of the uses of innovation, a normative perspective to evaluate innovation practices or provocative and exciting views about innovation that may help shake students from their comfort zone. The selection criteria for the study cases is that it reflects an emerging technology with foreseeable positive impact but can be critically interpreted as controversial and containing serious risks (hard impacts) or affecting our subjectivity outside of democratic deliberation (soft impacts). Cases with available and engaging audiovisual or reading material are preferred.

In teams, students select and divide reading material and choose shared case studies to discuss. This discussion has now been recorded through a video call app and uploaded to the course site.

The assessment criteria for this phase are presented in Table 35.1.

Table 35.1 Assessment criteria for the critical case studies

Criteria	Scoring		
	Description	% of final grade	Score (out of 7)
Conceptual accuracy	Students present the main concepts of each text correctly, without defining or using concepts in a manner different from what is directly expressed in the text	20%	
Case reconstruction	Students can reconstruct the leading technical and social elements of the case study in a way in which a controversy is identified	20%	
Point of view	While discussing the case studies, students formulate at least one clear point of view regarding the controversial aspects of the technology	20%	
Justification	Each point of view presented contains clear, consistent, and pertinent reasons as to why accept the asserted point of view	20%	
Support	Each point of view and/or its justification is supplemented with conceptual references or empirical evidence	20%	

35.2.4 Socratic Dialogue Phase

After students complete and submit their case study analysis, they are randomly mixed, and groups of five to eight students are formed. These students participate in a structured conversation about the "meaning" of innovation itself. In this conversation, students are assigned a participation order to add to the collective argumentation by turns. These turns are fixed, circular (the first turn starts again after the last turn), and repeat until the time is over. Typically, depending on the number of students, each round lasts about 20–30 min.

In a student's turn, they are expected to produce a time-bounded argumentative movement out of the available options:

- Propose: Add a point of view and a brief justification of that point of view.
- Oppose: Add a restriction to the acceptability of a point of view.
- Support: Provide evidence or conceptual support of a proposition or an opposition.
- Ask: Produce a Socratic question to provoke a clarification, interpretation, or evaluation of a point of view.
- Summarize: Produce a summary of the state of the conversation per the main question being explored.

The idea is that students produce a brief addition to the conversation, not directed at anyone in particular, following the rule of "one turn, one idea." In other words, it is expected that students only choose one possible argumentative move to express just one bounded idea in each of their turns. This way, the conversational fluidity increases and the monopolization of speech gets avoided. It is important to note that students should not explicitly tell what argumentative move they are doing; rather, it should be clear by itself. However, during practice rounds before the actual exercise, I suggest having students state their argumentative move for metacognitive reasons.

The idea of "the meaning" of innovation is structured into three main questions relating to different aspects of innovation. Each group of students dialogues about a different main question, and the instructor may add follow-up questions only if the conversation starts to flatten in terms of new ideas. The main questions of the dialogue are:

- What is innovation? This is the pragmatic dimension of innovation. In this question, students are meant to explore the different uses of innovation (descriptive analysis) and its defining characteristics (prescriptive analysis). Possible follow-up questions are: Is innovation a process, characteristics of a product, or a person's mindset? (This question relates to Godin's (2020) reconstruction of the history of innovation). Does something/someone need to be practical in order to be innovative? Can something/someone need to make an impact to be innovative?
- What should be the purpose of innovation? This is the teleological/deontological/axiological dimension of innovation. In this question, students are meant to explore what innovation should aspire to be, either through its ultimate purpose (teleological analysis), its normative duties (deontological analysis), or its guiding values (axiological analysis). Possible follow-up questions are: Is innovation good in itself? What would be a more responsible vision for innovation? What should be the shared ethics of innovation?
- How should innovation be governed? This is the political dimension of innovation. In this question, students are meant to explore how innovation should be controlled (policy analysis) and by whom (democratic analysis). Possible follow-up questions are: Is innovation democratic? What should be the role of experts in innovation? What should be the role of citizens in innovation? What should be the role of government in innovation? What should be the role of private companies in innovation?

Ideally, the instructor will not play any role during the whole round (besides taking notes). However, having follow-up questions is good if the conversation starts to flatten. A flat conversation occurs when no new points of view emerge and/or too many successive turns tend to just accept a particular point of view and add support. It is essential to mention that students are also told that they can (and probably will need to) express points of view they do not personally share. The idea of the conversation is not necessarily to reflect their belief system but to explore a topic through engaging and collaborative argumentation.

To assess and grade each conversation, we recommend a form of "360 feedback" (Rose 2019b). It is best to assess this activity by combining peer assessment, self-assessment, and instructor assessment. In all cases, the conversation should be graded as a whole and not particular individual. This is because the activity aims to produce a socially shared regulation (Panadero and Järvelä 2015) of the conversation in which the argumentation process is truly distributed across actors. Making this explicit to students also helps them understand that the point is not for them to stand out but to contribute to the team and expand on what others have done.

The fishbowl arrangement can be used when conducted onsite to have students give personal feedback to others about the quality of the conversation and what they can do individually to improve the team dynamics. This idea can also be used online, assigning each student to another student to mutually coach each other when they are part of the dialogue. I usually make a short break after 10–15 min for students to be coached by other students who were observing and taking notes.

The assessment criteria for this phase are presented in Table 35.2. These criteria are explained before the activity and observed by all graders (instructors, peers, and team members).

Table 35.2 Assessment criteria for the Socratic dialogue

Criteria	Scoring		
	Description	% of final grade	Score (out of 7)
Fluidity	The conversation flows in terms of the response time among turns, the length of each intervention, and the use of the "one turn, one idea" rule	25%	
Controversiality	The conversation contains opposing points of view, questions with no clear answers, and new points of view emerge	25%	
Progressive elaboration	Emerging points of view are explored, supported, and questioned by the team before acceptance or rejection. The conversation does not just jump from one viewpoint to another. The issues explored echo past interventions and tend to become more complex over time	30%	
Support	Critical points of view and/or justification of the point of view are supplemented with conceptual references or empirical evidence	20%	

35.3 My Experience Using This Activity

The Meaning of Innovation Dialogue is an educational proposal that I have been developing and iterating over time. I teach an undergraduate course for engineering design students about critical approximations to the entrepreneurial mindset and innovation. What I like about this activity is that it is both very structured and very open. It is very structured because the argumentative nature of the speech is heavily determined and does not correspond with natural conversation. This is by design to promote equal participation, teamwork, confrontation of ideas, and hearing what others have to say.

On the other hand, the content of the conversation is entirely open and very receptive to the students' subjectivity. Thus, the content of the conversation drastically changes from one application to the other. In some groups, the dialogue centers on issues of sustainability and social impact. In contrast, other dialogues focus on inclusivity (gender, social position, age) or interdisciplinary frontiers (the arts, social science, humanities).

One persistent central topic of conversation is the notion of "practicality." In my experience with engineering students, innovation as something oriented to solve problems seems to be very rooted. This is, of course, linked with traditional narratives of engineers as problem solvers (Siller et al. 2021). Prompts about the value of exploration per se are usually ineffective. However, questioning "practicality" from the social and ethical sensibilities in framing a problem and a solution is usually well received and leads to interesting conversations.

Other frequent topics of conversation that organically arise are the distinctions among innovation, creativity, invention, and entrepreneurship, or normative conversations about whether a clearer and consensus definition of innovation is desirable. The point of view that innovation equals progress is often disregarded quite quickly. However, the question of whether any positive change should be regarded as innovation tends to lead to an exciting conversation. This may sound strange at first, but it relates to the speaker's modal attitude that can implicitly change from descriptive analysis (what innovation has been) to normative (what innovation should be).

Finally, the topics of conversation are greatly affected by the content of the course itself. For instance, one semester, I was writing a paper on how the design process alone does not incorporate responsibility, and responsibility is often treated as complementary or used unsystematically. I used some of the material to create a new presentation for the course. That semester, a significant portion of the dialogue about the governance of innovation was dedicated to how the design process is not responsible by itself. Beyond the possible interpretation that students, motivated by grades, sought to appease instructors, the most important insight for me was understanding how conversations situate in a particular historical moment and evolve based on the subjectivities and systems involved (students, student–teacher relationships, direct communities, and the current political climate).

35.4 Discussion

This article explores the methodology of an educational activity meant to promote critical reflection by engineering students about the socially complex notion of "innovation." This activity, called the Meaning of Innovation Dialogue (MID), seeks to explore the different philosophical and sociological aspects of innovation through three major questions: What is innovation? What should the purpose of innovation be? How should innovation be governed? Through these questions and a structured argumentation format, engineering students are prompted to collaborate and identify controversial and opposing points of view while elaborating and supporting other student's ideas.

Engineering and technology have a profound impact on society. Also, society has a profound impact on technology. As Thomas Hughes so beautifully describes it, we should look at technology as part of a "seamless web" in which physical artifacts are intertwined with economical, social and political structures (Hughes 1986). Making engineering students explore critical cases of technological disasters or evident ethical tensions is necessary for more responsible engineering. However, there is a need to push forward to grasp the more subtle and systematic ways technology and society are co-constructed to form socio-technically wise students. In other words, as educators, we should seek to look past "the big cases" that can sometimes feel alien to most students who will not participate in creating a transformative social network or military bomb. However, these students should consider how society affects their future work, role models, and aspirations, and integrating their citizenry into their identity as future engineers. It is the purpose of this activity to move in that direction.

This article only exhibits the educational methodology of the MID and its theoretical foundations. In this sense, it provides no systematic empirical evidence regarding how this tool mediates students learning experiences and how and if it promotes a more reflective vision of innovation. The future steps of this project are to use this educational tool contextually to provide such evidence. This empirical examination can be conducted under the framework of conceptual change theory (Boshuizen et al. 2020). As a process of conceptual change, empirical research should capture student's cognitive processes, mainly how they identify inconsistencies in their existing framework theories and reorganize their mental models using the new arguments from the MID.

Framework theory predicts that students will likely create synthetic models (Vosniadou 2012) in which they integrate previously held beliefs about innovation with this more reflective vision of innovation. Capturing these intermediate models can prove to be very insightful for educators seeking to promote meaningful change, as synthetic models have intense assimilatory properties that may resist new evidence and require additional efforts. Changing student's views at an ontological level (Chi 2005) requires processes of conceptual change well beyond a specific educational activity to more extensive educational experiences at the curricular level. For these reasons, the next step of this research project will focus on capturing student's synthetical models to draw inferences on how to sustain engineering student's embracing of innovation throughout their studies and beyond.

References

Boenink M, Swierstra T, Stemerding D (2010) Anticipating the interaction between technology and morality: a scenario study of experimenting with humans in bionanotechnology. Stud Ethics Law Technol 4(2). https://doi.org/10.2202/1941-6008.1098

Boshuizen HPA, Vosniadou S, Lehtinen E (2020) Conceptual changes for and during working life. Int J Educ Res 104:101682. https://doi.org/10.1016/j.ijer.2020.101682

Castellanos-Reyes D (2020) Socratic seminar. In: The student's guide to learning design and research, EdTech Books

Cech EA (2013) The (Mis)Framing of social justice: why ideologies of depoliticization and meritocracy hinder engineer's ability to think about social injustices. In: Lucena J (ed) Engineering education for social justice. Philosophy of Engineering and Technology, Dordrecht, Springer, pp 67–84

Chi MTH (2005) Commonsense conceptions of emergent processes: why some misconceptions are robust. J Learn Sci 14(2):161–199. https://doi.org/10.1207/s15327809jls1402_1

Coller BS (2019) Ethics of human genome editing. Annu Rev Med 70(1):289–305. https://doi.org/10.1146/annurev-med-112717-094629

de Vere IJ, Melles G, Kapoor A (2011) An ethical stance: engineering curricula designed for social responsibility. In: Proceedings of the 18th international conference on engineering design (ICED 11), Impacting society through engineering design, pp 216–225

Dym CL, Agogino AM, Eris O, Frey DD, Leifer LJ (2005) Engineering design thinking, teaching, and learning. J Eng Educ 94(1):103–120

Ettridge M, Sharma S (2020) Engineering a better world: lessons from the royal academy of engineering's international development activities. J Int Dev 32(1):85–95. https://doi.org/10.1002/jid.3447

Fuentes C (2011) Elementos para o desenho de um modelo de debate crítico na escola. In: Argumentação na escola: o conhecimento em construção, Leitão S, MDC (eds) Campinas, SP, Pontes Editores, pp 225–250

Fuentes C, Goñi J (2021) Online critical debate model: designing and analyzing deliberation for the digital age. In: Cattani A, Mastroianni B (eds) Competing, cooperating, deciding: toward a model of deliberative debate. Firenze, Firenze University Press

Godin B (2020) The idea of technological innovation. Edward Elgar Publishing Limited, Cheltenham

Gray CM, Fernandez TM (2018) When World(view)s collide contested epistemologies and ontologies in transdisciplinary education. Int J Eng Educ 34(2):574–589. [Online]. Available: https://dialnet.unirioja.es/servlet/articulo?codigo=6874326

Griswold J, Shaw L, Munn M (2017) Socratic seminar with data: a strategy to support student discourse and understanding. Am Biol Teach 79(6):492–495. https://doi.org/10.1525/abt.2017.79.6.492

Hughes TP (1986) The seamless web: technology, science, etcetera, etcetera. Soc Stud Sci 16(2):281–292. https://doi.org/10.1177/030631278601600 2004

Jasanoff S (2016) The ethics of invention: technology and the human future. W.W. Norton & Company, New York

Karppi T (2018) 'The Computer Said So': on the ethics, effectiveness, and cultural techniques of predictive policing. Soc Media + Soc 4(2):205630511876829. https://doi.org/10.1177/205630 5118768296

Kitchens B, Johnson SL, Gray P (2020) Understanding echo chambers and filter bubbles: the impact of social media on diversification and partisan shifts in news consumption. MIS Q 44(4):1619–1649. https://doi.org/10.25300/MISQ/2020/16371

Leitao S (2007) La dimensión epistémica de la argumentación. In: Carlos Saez J (ed), Ciencias de la Mente: Aproximaciones desde Latinoamerica, Santiago de Chile, pp 5–32

Melles G, de Vere I, Misic V (2011) Socially responsible design: thinking beyond the triple bottom line to socially responsive and sustainable product design. CoDesign 7(3–4):143–154. https://doi.org/10.1080/15710882.2011.630473

Neeley K, Wylie C, Seabrook B (2019) In search of integration: mapping conceptual efforts to apply STS to engineering education. In: 2019a ASEE annual conference and exposition proceedings, June, pp 19. https://doi.org/10.18260/1-2--32954

Ortiz-Revilla J, Adúriz-Bravo A, Greca IM (2020) A framework for epistemological discussion on integrated STEM education. Sci Educ 29(4):857–880. https://doi.org/10.1007/s11191-020-00131-9

Panadero E, Järvelä S (2015) Socially shared regulation of learning: a review. Eur Psychol 20(3):190–203. https://doi.org/10.1027/1016-9040/a000226

Rose DS (2019b) 360 feedback versus alternative forms of feedback. In: Handbook of strategic 360 feedback, Oxford University Press, pp 409–426

Russell AL, Vinsel L (2019) Make maintainers: engineering education and an ethics of care. In: Wisnioski M, Hintz ES, Kleine MS (eds) Does America need more innovators? MIT Press, Cambridge & London, pp 249–269

Siller T, Johnson G, Korte R (2021) Broadening engineering identity: moving beyond problem solving. In: Pirtle Z, T. D, M. G (eds) Engineering and philosophy. Philosophy of engineering and technology, Cham, Springer, pp 181–195

Tan E, Calabrese Barton A, Benavides A (2019) Engineering for sustainable communities: epistemic tools in support of equitable and consequential middle school engineering. Sci Educ 103(4):1011–1046. https://doi.org/10.1002/sce.21515

Tomblin D, Mogul N (2020) STS Postures: responsible innovation and research in undergraduate STEM education. J Responsible Innov 7(sup1):117–127. https://doi.org/10.1080/23299460.2020.1839230

Vallor S (2016) Technology and the virtues. Oxford University Press, Oxford

Vosniadou S (2012) Preconceptions, misconceptions and synthetic models. In: Fraser B, Tobin K, McRobbie CJ (eds), Second international handbook of science education, vol 2. Springer International Handbooks of Education, pp 119–130

Wagner P (2021) Data privacy—the ethical, sociological, and philosophical effects of Cambridge Analytica. SSRN Electron J. https://doi.org/10.2139/ssrn.3782821

Wetmore JM (2018) Reconnecting engineering with the social and political sphere. In: Engineering a better future, Cham, Springer International Publishing, pp 15–19

Winner L (2018) The cult of innovation: its myths and rituals. In: Engineering a better future, Cham, Springer International Publishing, pp 61–73

Chapter 36
Technological Tools for the Training of Mentor Teachers: Learnings from a Chilean Program

Verónica Cabezas, Sebastián Pereira Mardones, Catalina Figueroa Iglesias, and Camila Straub Barrientos

36.1 Introduction

Mentoring and teacher support has a broad presence in literature and public policy, mainly due to the benefits reported for mentor teachers (MT), those accompanied, and the schools in which they work. Among these benefits are improvements in teacher retention, an increased sense of companionship, a reduced sense of isolation, and other critical elements to attract and retain teachers in classrooms. Despite its relevance, the formation of MT has not been the focus of in-depth study within academic research (Aspfors and Fransson 2015; Fransson 2016). Therefore, there is no consensus in the literature on training mentors; this varies significantly between countries (Abell et al. 1995) in content, duration, and teaching methods (Aspfors and Fransson 2015). However, a widespread consensus is that being a good teacher is not equated to being a good mentor (Gardiner and Weisling 2018).

In this context of lack of consensus regarding training MT, there is little evidence on MT training courses in b-learning and distance modalities (Fransson 2016). This is accentuated by the fact that, although technological tools in teacher training are increasingly common (Philipsen et al. 2019), there is still little knowledge of how participating teachers perceive these tools in continuous training experiences

V. Cabezas (✉)
School of Education, CEPPE UC, Pontificia Universidad Católica de Chile, Santiago, Chile
e-mail: vcabezag@uc.cl

S. Pereira Mardones · C. Figueroa Iglesias · C. Straub Barrientos
CEPPE UC, Pontificia Universidad Católica de Chile, Santiago, Chile
e-mail: sapereira@uc.cl

C. Figueroa Iglesias
e-mail: catalinafigueroa@uc.cl

C. Straub Barrientos
e-mail: cpstraub@uc.cl

© The Author(s), under exclusive license to Springer Nature Singapore Pte Ltd. 2022   443
S. Hosseini et al. (eds.), *Technology-Enabled Innovations in Education*,
Transactions on Computer Systems and Networks,
https://doi.org/10.1007/978-981-19-3383-7_36

(Parsons et al. 2019). This situation's relevance is accentuated by the scenario of the pandemic health crisis and the innovations necessary for the training of teachers. Considering this, we present this study to describe the participant perceptions and evaluations of a mentor teaching training course in b-learning modality, which sustains its virtual character with two technological platforms: Sibme and Canvas.

36.2 Background

36.2.1 Definition and Benefits of Mentoring and Teacher Support

Until now, the literature on mentoring has failed to provide a clear and universal definition of this practice. It is often used interchangeably with the concept of induction (Spooner-Lane 2016). More traditional definitions conceive mentoring as the accompaniment process that a teacher with more experience and age brings to a beginning teacher (Schatz-Oppenheimer 2016). Recently, more symmetrical conceptualizations of this relationship have emerged, emphasizing reciprocity and collaboration, understanding the mentoring process as one in which the mentor and mentee learn and build knowledge together (Burgess 2007; Smith 2011). Although diffuse in their definitions, an assortment of practices usually associated with the role of mentors includes joint planning, observation, feedback from classes, and reflection on the practice itself (Spooner-Lane 2016).

Regarding the benefits of teacher mentoring and accompaniment, the literature reveals advantages for mentors, mentees, and schools due to improving teacher performance (Fountain and Newcomer 2016; Robson and Mtika 2017), retention (Smith 2011; Callahan 2016), teacher well-being (Kessels et al. 2008; Richter et al. 2013), and teacher commitment (Rozelle and Wilson 2012), among others (Ingersoll and Strong 2011). Particularly in the case of mentors, the exercise of this role increases collegiality among teachers (Squires 2019), productivity (Fountain and Newcomer 2016), professional development and growth (Fountain and Newcomer 2016; Hudson 2013), reduces the feeling of isolation (Heider 2005), renews enthusiasm for teaching (Callahan 2016), consolidates their knowledge, and promotes self-realization and leadership (Hudson and Hudson 2010). Schools benefit from increased organizational stability and the quality of the teaching staff and student learning (Fountain and Newcomer 2016; Ingersoll and Strong 2011). Thus, mentoring for teachers is a mutually beneficial relationship that can be an effective strategy to face the challenges of attracting and retaining teachers.

36.2.2 Background on Mentoring

Although the induction processes, in general, and the mentoring processes, in particular, have grown in popularity and relevance, strategies that ensure that the mentors in charge of accompanying are properly trained have not been developed (Aspfors and Fransson 2015; Fransson 2016). The evidence indicates that the MTs' professional knowledge has emerged from their professional experiences, abilities, initial teacher training, and personal experiences (Clarke et al. 2013; Aspfors and Fransson 2015). Although it might be thought that an experienced teacher could be suitable to accompany a new teacher, the literature indicates that to be a "teacher of teachers," one must go through a gradual and conscious reorganization of skills to become a mentor suitable for their new role (Orland-Barak 2005). Along these lines, the literature reports that MTs who do not have adequate training are more likely to face difficulties in exercising this role (Sandvik et al. 2019).

The literature also suggests that MTs who have been trained show better communication skills and are more likely to share their experiences with their companions than those not trained (Evertson and Smithey 2000). Furthermore, MT training increases critical thinking and reflection (Fransson 2016; Koballa et al. 2010; Sinclair 2003; Tang and Choi 2005; Ulvik and Sunde 2013), clarifies role awareness, and reduces their beliefs that mentoring is a critical and evaluative process (Lejonberg et al. 2015). Even when this information comes from studies with self-reporting from mentors (Aspfors and Fransson 2015), it undoubtedly sheds light on the importance of training and educating those who assume these roles in educational systems. In short, MT training is essential to acquire skills such as generating relationships of trust (Medrano Ureta 2009), effective communication (Constantinescu 2015), timely feedback (Medrano Ureta 2009), reflection on their teaching impact on others professionally (Gagen and Bowie 2005), and role effectiveness (Hudson 2013).

Within the scarce literature about MT training, (Wang and Odell 2002), three models of mentor training stand out, which differ according to the understanding that the mentor is expected to have: (i) knowledge transfer model; (ii) theoretical-practical model; and (iii) collaborative research model (Aspfors and Fransson 2015). The second of these models is the one used in this study, as detailed in the problem statement section, considering that learning is generated through practice, which a mentor supports.

36.2.3 Continuous Remote Teacher (and Mentor Teachers) Training

The most effective forms of teacher professional development result from strategies employed in situ, i.e., in the same school where teachers work and during their working hours (Darling-Hammond et al. 2017), nonetheless the rise of Information Technologies (ICT) and hybrid and remote professional teacher development (PTD) in recent years have enabled new forms of development (Philipsen et al. 2019). ICT and PTD are cost-effective (Philipsen et al. 2019), provide greater schedule flexibility (Parsons et al. 2019; Elliott 2017; Dede et al. 2009), and eliminate geographic barriers, making it possible to expand opportunities (Philipsen et al. 2019). This is essential for teachers, considering that one of the main obstacles to accessing PTD is the high workload (Elliott 2017) and the shortage of time.

In particular, the remote modality has grown exponentially due to the internet's expansion and the development of platforms designed to support pedagogical objectives (Gárate and Cordero 2019). Among the available options are web pages with open resources, where educators can access the content of their interest. Similarly, they may initiate formal tutorials through massive and open online courses (MOOCs), videoconferencing platforms like Zoom, Skype, or Google Meet, and collaborative platforms such as blogs, wikis, or Google Docs (Parsons et al. 2019; Elliott 2017).

In addition to the advantages above, remote education allows collaboration and learning without a specific physical place or time restrictions (Parsons et al. 2019; Elliott 2017; Gárate and Cordero 2019). This allows participants to process the course content at their own pace and revisit it when necessary (Parsons et al. 2019; Wynants and Dennis 2018). These programs also allow choosing how to provide learning, synchronous or asynchronous, or both (Parsons et al. 2019; Yoon 2020).

Among the challenges of these programs described in the literature is that the participants must have the necessary technological tools and digital skills (Gárate and Cordero 2019). Others are collaboration and the construction of online learning, which can affect the participants' satisfaction (Yoon 2020). Thus, the interaction among participants is one of the critical variables for the success of remote programs, indicating that program designs should consider the interactions between students, students, and teachers, and students and the program content (Parsons et al. 2019; Elliott 2017). Finally, the positive, continuous presence of the program instructor is essential for the participants to feel more motivated to participate; they have higher levels of satisfaction with these programs when they have this type of instructor (Parsons et al. 2019).

Regarding MT training, most of the research has focused on face-to-face courses, with little evidence available for remote courses (Schaefer 2021), possibly because this type of MT course is not the most common (Fransson 2016). In this area, and following (Schaefer 2021), three studies can be identified that cover the formation of remote MT. One was conducted by Fransson (2016), whose main result was that those training remotely value it because the absence of transfers allowed them to have more time to participate in the course seminars. The modality's other positive factors included self-paced studying and listening to the sessions more than once and pausing the recordings to take notes or reflect. On the other hand, the author reported participant concern about using technological tools; this anxiety dissipated as the program progressed. McCrary and Mazur (2010), for their part, investigated the design and functionality of narrative strategies and online dialogical reflection using a platform called Staying Past Dark. Even though the simulation was not studied as training for MTs (Fransson 2016), it concluded that the narrative strategies and dialogic reflection seemed to facilitate reflection and decision-making by the six experienced mentors studied; communication with the platform designers was one of their challenges. On the other hand, Sinclair (2003) conducted a study on a b-learning program for MT, resulting that, although technology does not replace face-to-face interactions, it can expand the experience of those who participate in the activities.

36.3   Problem Statement

Our research was developed in the context of evaluating an MT training course offered by the Fundación Impulso Docente (Teacher Impulse Foundation).[1] The course aims to train MTs capable of developing competencies to observe and provide feedback to other teachers, manage specific strategies to generate environments conducive to the learning of all students, and design a mentoring plan considering the diversity and context of the educational establishment they work.

Initially, the course is hybrid and uses a theoretical-practical methodology based on the MT accompanying another teacher from the same school. It has a duration of 5 months of work, which translates into 100 chronological hours, of which 72 are remote and 28 are face-to-face, divided into three mandatory meetings. The accompaniment occurs mainly through observation and feedback to the accompanied teacher, in which the MT must apply what they learned during the theoretical sessions.

In addition to the theoretical sessions, the MT receives periodic feedback from a Foundation tutor on the MT's work with his/her companion. The course uses two platforms to support the virtual component: (i) Canvas and (ii) Sibme. The first platform corresponds to the theoretical component of the methodology, and the second supports the practices (see Fig. 36.1). Canvas, in particular, facilitates developing online courses, managing content, encouraging collaborative work, interacting with other participants through forums, providing feedback on tasks, and keeping track of course participants and their grades. Thus, this platform allows a repository for course documents and, also, following the progress of students' activities and grades. For its part, Sibme is a mobile application that allows the generation of audiovisual records of class observations and the feedback of the MT to the accompanied teacher, which the Foundation's tutor subsequently evaluates. In this way, potential mentors develop their learning process by carrying out practical tasks, i.e., teaching through supervised activities (Bambrick-Santoyo 2012). Due to the pandemic health crisis, the course adjusted its activities to be carried out remotely, maintaining the structure, methodology, and platforms.

The context of the study and the course is in Chile. This country has reported problems in teacher training, mainly due to the lack of a link between training activities and teaching practice (Pedraja-Rejas et al. 2012) and that it does not provide the necessary skills to perform in the classroom (Rodríguez and Castro 2014). In addition,

---

[1] For more information: https://impulsodocente.com/programas/mentoria-y-colaboracion-doc ente/.

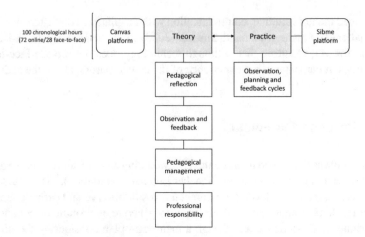

Fig. 36.1 Mentor teacher training course outline

Chile approved a 2016 law that contemplates, among other measures, the institution-alization of the induction and mentoring of novice teachers as a right, which supports and facilitates their insertion into the profession. Therefore, the course stands as a vehicle to face the challenge of training MTs to serve beginning teachers. It uses a modality that exposes students to greater regional diversity with a methodology that incorporates innovative tools, such as teacher support and platforms.

In this context, this study aims to describe the assessments made by teachers trained as mentors in a course in b-learning modality, concerning the theoretical-practical methodology, specifically, the platforms used (Canvas and Sibme) and the feedback received from their tutors throughout the course.

36.4 Methods

To study the MTs' perceptions about their experiences in the course, we chose a mixed-method design. Mixed methods are defined as those research designs charac-terized by data collection, analysis, and integration using quantitative and qualitative sources. Precisely, a sequential explanatory design model was followed (Creswell 2014), which implies that the data collection and analysis were carried out consec-utively, starting with quantitative data and ending with the collection of qualitative information. The study participants were in two MT cohorts, one that participated in the hybrid course (2019) and another that did it remotely (2020).

The collection of quantitative data was carried out through online surveys directed to each cohort at the end of their participation in the course. The objective of the survey was to investigate the evaluation of the modality, methodology, and evalu-ations of the course. The self-elaborated survey was based on the course structure and program and the review of the national and international literature on mentoring.

The characteristics of effective professional development and distance mentoring programs and attributes that promote online learning were identified. In the first cohort, 98 surveys were applied and 75 in the second. Due to adjusting the course modality because of the health crisis, the questionnaire applied to the second cohort (2020) varied slightly from the first instrument (2019). However, both instruments had modules of common questions about the course. All question items were on a Likert scale with a range of responses between 1 (Strongly disagree) and 5 (Strongly agree).

The survey structure had seven main modules aimed at knowing the evaluations of the MTs. These modules were (1) course structure (timely communication of dates and time dedicated to the course, among others); (2) course content (clarity of the delivered material, correspondence of the material to the course); (3) course modality and methodology (assessment of the b-learning/e-learning modality and the peer accompaniment in the training process); (4) the platforms (their ease of use and relevance to the training process); (5) course evaluations (course workload, relevance of evaluations); (6) link with the tutor and team in charge of the course (frequency and relevance of feedback from the tutor); and (7) the competencies associated with participating in the course (opinion on skills acquired in the training process). In this study, survey modules 3, 4, and 6 were mainly used.

For the qualitative survey, 11 semi-structured interviews were conducted with MTs, accompanied teachers, and their management teams from three schools throughout the country. The interviews sought to investigate the experiences after the course and complement the survey information about the course opinions and perceptions. The interview guidelines considered dimensions common to the interviewees, divided into three main objectives: (i) investigate the continuity of mentoring practices after they participated in the course; (ii) describe the factors that enabled or impeded the development of mentoring processes within the schools, and (iii) identify the advantages and disadvantages of the modality and methodology of the course. In this study, the interviewees' responses on this last point were a reference, with questions such as, "What are the advantages of the course's modality?" and "What are the advantages and disadvantages of the course's methodology?". The selection of schools, the region, the year of participation in the course, and the administrative unit was considered to ensure the greatest possible diversity. Due to the health contingency, the approximately one-hour interviews were conducted via Zoom. The qualitative information was analyzed using content analysis; the objective was to capture, evaluate and synthesize the discourses expressed in the interviews, processing relevant data on the conditions that could arise for its subsequent use in light of a specific problem (Piñuel Raigada 2002). In the first instance, open coding was carried out; the participants' speeches were reduced to codes or units of meaning, in line with the dimensions of the interview pattern. After that, the comments were analyzed per the nature of the opinions, distinguishing positive, neutral, and negative opinions on the elements studied. After this analysis, we triangulated the qualitative and quantitative results to summarize the results.

The information collection occurred in January, November, and December 2020, respectively, for each instrument. All study subjects were invited to participate voluntarily via email, and signing an informed consent in which the anonymity and confidentiality of the information collected were established. Therefore, all the data presented safeguards the identity of the participants, maintaining a strict confidentiality protocol. Due to the nature of the data, the results were valid references for some cases, but they are not intended to make statements that are generalizable to the entire population.

36.5   Results

In general, from the analysis of the surveys and interviews, four main results could be extracted. Table 36.1 shows the degree of agreement of the respondents with the statements of interest in the study.

First, the Canvas platform was rated positively by respondents from both cohorts. In the 2019 group, 85% agreed or strongly agreed with the statement that the Canvas platform allowed them to be aware of their progress as mentors by providing access to their learning outcomes. In addition, around two-thirds of the sample (69%) stated that they agreed or strongly agreed that this platform allowed them to interact efficiently with the other mentors in training. It should also be noted that in the results of the 2020 cohort, satisfaction with the training on the use of the platform was very high, with 89% declaring that they agreed or strongly agreed that the training was clear, easy to understand, and sufficient to use the platform well. Although some teachers expressed some resistance or difficulty in using the platforms in the open questions of both surveys (8 in the 2019 cohort survey and 1 in the 2020 survey), most participants rated them well. Some even mentioned Canvas among the reasons for recommending the program because it allows organizing the theoretical contents, making the time for each task transparent, and having the precise reading for each, which, in the end, led to tools and implementation strategies in the classroom.

Second, the valuation of the Sibme platform was also high. In both cohorts, the vast majority (92% and 84%) strongly agreed that it allowed them to effectively observe and provide feedback to the mentee teacher. In particular, recording the class and receiving feedback was among the most highly valued, as can be seen in the comment of one of the interviewees:

> I agree with my colleagues that there is a great advantage to be able to record when one wanted to provide the feedback and have the evidence, and also to rewatch the video calmly [...] looking at specific details, helped make the feedback more complete

In addition, 80% of those surveyed agreed or strongly agreed that the training to use the platform was satisfactory. As with the Canvas platform, a minority of the participants were not satisfied with the platform. Of the 2019 cohort, 16% stated that they disagreed that the Sibme platform was easy to use and did encounter any problems. Even though it is a lower percentage, it showed that some participants did not feel comfortable with the introduction made to this platform. This sheds light on

Table 36.1 Cohort survey results in 2019 and 2020

Question	Strongly disagree (%)	Disagree (%)	Neutral (%)	Agree (%)	Strongly agree (%)
2019 Cohort survey results					
The methodology of the course allowed me to learn to observe effectively and give productive feedback	1	2	4	48	46
The methodology of the course allowed me to practice how to be an effective mentor with my Impulso Docente tutor	3	4	10	46	38
The CANVAS platform allowed me to interact effectively with the other mentors in training	2	13	17	45	24
The CANVAS platform allowed me to be aware of my progress as a mentor	4	2	10	47	38
The SIBME platform helped me to observe classes and effectively give feedback to the mentee teacher	1	2	5	41	51
The feedback received from my Impulso Docente tutor allowed me to maintain and enhance aspects that I already had developed	3	5	11	36	46

(continued)

Table 36.1 (continued)

2020 Cohort survey results

I believe that anyone could use the course platforms without much difficulty	3	8	13	33	43
The training to use the CANVAS platform was easy to understand	3	4	4	36	53
The training to use the CANVAS platform was sufficient to use it correctly	3	1	8	37	51
The training to use the SIBME platform was easy to understand	3	7	7	33	51
The training to use the SIBME platform was sufficient to use it correctly	4	9	7	32	48
The SIBME platform helped me to observe classes and give effective feedback to the mentee teacher	4	4	8	35	49
My tutor's feedback guided me towards improvement, showing possible actions to implement	1	4	1	13	80
My tutor's feedback on my performance was constructive	1	3	1	16	79
My tutor's feedback on my performance was specific and detailed	1	0	1	17	80

[a]N 2019 cohort: 98. N 2020 cohort = 75. Due to rounding, percentages may not always appear to add up to 100%

the importance of having ways to solve technical questions with the platforms in this type of course so that all participants can leverage the tools offered by the program.

As a whole, these results show that the use of these platforms was positively valued by the participants and considered as essential elements in their training process, allowing, on the one hand, more awareness of their training process, and on the other, support to the practical component of the course. Thus, 76% of the participants in the 2019 cohort agreed or strongly agreed that anyone could use the course platforms without great difficulty, highlighting the incorporation of tools of this type in the training of teachers and MTs.

Third, the feedback received by course participants from their tutors appears as another relevant finding. The results showed that having this support from an external actor made it possible to enhance previous skills and enhance weaknesses in the opinion of the participants in both cohorts. 82% of the respondents in the 2019 cohort agreed or strongly agreed that this feedback allowed them to enhance skills they already had, which is similar to what was stated by the participants in the 2020 cohort, with 93% affirming agreement or strong agreement that this feedback was constructive and improvement-oriented. The importance of social presence, having a relationship and feedback between peers and establishing critical dialogues align with the literature on mentoring in *e-learning* contexts (Jonassen et al. 1998; Huang 2002).

Fourth, a final finding related to the high assessment from the participants in both cohorts of the theoretical-practical methodology of the course. When consulted about it, a consensus among the respondents of the 2019 cohort declared it allowed them to learn to observe and give feedback to another teacher effectively (93% agreed or strongly agreed with this statement). Similarly, from the interview comments, it is clear that the course differed from other training experiences. It allowed connecting with other teachers and putting into practice what was learned during the course. An example of the above can be observed in the comment of one of the interviewees:

> (…) I think the reflective process we had with the teachers was very significant for me. We could analyze and reflect on situations much more because, deep down, we were both in the same situations, all living new processes, so the process of reflection that each one had was very similar. Alternatively, we would find similar edges, and we could modify certain things together. That was super significant, building this new way of teaching together.

Possibly due to the latter point, only 2% of the respondents in the 2019 cohort stated that they did not feel capable of accompanying another teacher, which is consistent with the high percentage of participants who would recommend this training experience to another teacher. Ultimately, this provides keys for the design of this type of program, realizing the relevance that contextualized practice and feedback from an external agent may have for learning the skills and competencies necessary to be a mentor teacher.

36.6   Conclusions

The program's evaluation findings reveal that the b-learning modality can be helpful in training mentors. This modality allows teachers to sustain significant learning insofar as they allow them to connect and thus collaborate with peers, and at the same time, be adaptable to the particular contexts of each.

In line with the literature, this study's results show that the participants highly valued combining theoretical and practical elements in the course design. The theoretical component allowed, in the words of the teachers, to expand their *"pedagogical vocabulary."* Likewise, the importance of having a tutor with whom to dialogue and who supervises the feedback emerged, which is connected with the findings of Parsons et al. (2019) on the importance of the positive and continuous presence of the program instructor. In conclusion, learning by doing allows the participants to end the course with a valuable experience.

As Fransson (2016) and Sinclair (2003) mentioned in their research, the results of the qualitative work indicated that several teachers had some resistance or fear of using the platforms. However, these fears dissipated with the training. In particular, the Sibme platform's ease-of-use was well evaluated among mentors-in-training, who highlighted the practicality of recording the class and providing feedback in one place.

Finally, it can be concluded that the introduction of platforms in continuous training can improve the experiences in these instances, both for the course designers and participants, especially considering that the future proliferation of hybrid teaching–learning environments is likely.

36.7 Discussion

Our research aimed to contribute to the scarce literature on the training of MTs (Aspfors and Fransson 2015; Fransson 2016), addressing from a particular case the opinions and perceptions of the participants in two cohorts in an MT training course in a b-learning format. Although our results have limitations in terms of the selection and number of participants, the findings are relevant to those who form MTs using technological platforms and for decision-makers.

In the first instance, our research reveals the importance of training for MTs, with only 2% of MTs participating in the course declaring that they do not feel capable of accompanying another teacher, in line with Hudson (2013). Although our data do not allow us to determine if MTs are more effective in the exercise of their role, they do show that MT training can build teaching skills for both MT and accompanied teachers (Hudson 2013). Second, aligning with (Parsons et al. 2019), our findings reveal that incorporating technological elements in the teacher training can be helpful and beneficial for learning, as long as an expert supervises the process. In line with Fransson (2016), some participants in this study were apprehensive about using the technology initially, but this dissipated during the course, showing that its incorporation can be well valued by teachers; this finding contributes to the results of Parsons et al. (2019). This is particularly relevant in a post-pandemic scenario, in which the emergence of hybrid learning environments could proliferate as viable learning alternatives. Finally, our results showed that MT training using a practice-based model (Aspfors and Fransson 2015) could benefit MT, even when there is a lack of evidence and insight into the real impacts of this training.

The question remains open about the impacts that MT training processes might have on the effectiveness of mentoring (i.e., retention, teacher development) and whether there are differences between MTs who have received training and those who have not. However, it is clear that, in a scenario such as the current one of mentoring expansion, it is essential to promote studies in this line and continue exploring the contribution of technological tools in the remote training of MTs.

Acknowledgements We thank the Fundación Impulso Docente for its collaboration to evaluate its program and Fundación Colunga for funding this study.

The authors acknowledge the technical support of the Writing Lab, Institute for the Future of Education, in the production of this work.

References

Abell SK, Dillon DR, Hopkins CJ, McInerney WD, O'Brien DG (1995) Somebody to count on: mentor/intern relationships in a beginning teacher internship program. Teach Teach Educ 11(2):173–188

Aspfors J, Fransson G (2015) Research on mentor education for mentors of newly qualified teachers: a qualitative meta-synthesis. Teach Teach Educ 48:75–86

Bambrick-Santoyo P (2012) Leverage leadership: a practical guide to building exceptional schools. John Wiley & Sons

Burgess KR (2007) Mentoring as holistic online instruction. New Directions Adult Continuing Educ 2007(113):49–56

Callahan J (2016) Encouraging retention of new teachers through mentoring strategies. Delta Kappa Gamma Bulletin 83(1):6

Clarke M, Killeavy M, Moloney A (2013) The genesis of mentors' professional and personal knowledge about teaching: perspectives from the Republic of Ireland. Eur J Teach Educ 36(3):364–375

Constantinescu RS (2015) Defining elements of the mentor teacher as a professional. Procedia Soc Behav Sci 197:1610–1613

Creswell JW (2014) A concise introduction to mixed methods research. SAGE publications

Darling-Hammond L, Hyler ME, Gardner M (2017) Effective teacher professional development. Learning Policy Institute. Palo Alto, CA. Recuperado de. https://files.eric.ed.gov/fulltext/ED606743.pdf

de Medrano Ureta CV (2009) Competencias del profesor-mentor para el acompañamiento al profesorado principiante. Profesorado, Revista De Currículum y Formación Del Profesorado 13(1):209–229

Dede C, Jass Ketelhut D, Whitehouse P, Breit L, McCloskey EM (2009) A research agenda for online teacher professional development. J Teach Educ 60(1):8–19

Elliott JC (2017) The evolution from traditional to online professional development: a review. J Digital Learn Teacher Educ 33(3):114–125

Evertson CM, Smithey MW (2000) Mentoring effects on proteges' classroom practice: an experimental field study. J Educ Res 93(5):294–304

Fountain J, Newcomer KE (2016) Developing and sustaining effective faculty mentoring programs. J Public Affairs Educ 22(4):483–506

Fransson G (2016) Online (web-based) education for mentors of newly qualified teachers: challenges and opportunities. Int J Mentor Coach Educ 5(2):111–126

Gagen L, Bowie S (2005) Effective mentoring: a case for training mentors for novice teachers. J Phys Educ Recreation Dance 76(7):40–45

Gárate M, Cordero G (2019) Apuntes para caracterizar la formación continua en línea de docentes. Revista de estudios y experiencias en educación 18(36):209–221. https://dx.doi.org/https://doi.org/10.21703/rexe.20191836garate10

Gardiner W, Weisling N (2018) Challenges and complexities of developing mentors practice: insights from new mentors. Int J Mentor Coach Educ

Heider KL (2005) Teacher isolation: how mentoring programs can help. Curr Iss Educ 8(14)

Huang HM (2002) Toward constructivism for adult learners in online learning environments. Br J Edu Technol 33(1):27–37

Hudson P (2013) Mentoring as professional development:'growth for both mentor and mentee. Prof Dev Educ 39(5):771–783

Hudson P, Hudson S (2010) Mentor educators' understandings of mentoring pre-service primary teachers. Int J Learn 17(2):157

Ingersoll RM, Strong M (2011) The impact of induction and mentoring programs for beginning teachers: a critical review of the research. Rev Educ Res 81(2):201–233

Jonassen DH, Carr C, Yueh HP (1998) Computers as mindtools for engaging learners in critical thinking. Tech Trends 43(2):24–32

Kessels C, Beijaard D, Veen KV, Verloop N (2008) The importance of induction programs for the well-being of beginning teachers. In: Paper presented at the annual meeting of the American educational research association. New York, NY

Koballa TR Jr, Kittleson J, Bradbury LU, Dias MJ (2010) Teacher thinking associated with science-specific mentor preparation. Sci Educ 94(6):1072–1091

Lejonberg E, Elstad E, Christophersen KA (2015) Mentor education: challenging mentors' beliefs about mentoring. Int J Mentor Coach Educ 4(2):142–158

McCrary NE, Mazur JM (2010) Conceptualizing a narrative simulation to promote dialogic reflection: using a multiple outcome design to engage teacher mentors. Educ Technol Res Dev 58(3):325–342

Orland-Barak L (2005) Lost in translation: mentors learning to participate in competing discourses of practice. J Teach Educ 56(4):355–366

Parsons SA et al (2019) US teachers' perceptions of online professional development. Teach Teacher Educ Int J Res Stud 82(1):33–42

Pedraja-Rejas LM, Araneda-Guirriman CA, Rodríguez-Ponce ER, Rodríguez-Ponce JJ (2012) Calidad en la formación inicial docente: evidencia empírica en las universidades chilenas. Formación Universitaria 5(4):15–26

Philipsen B, Tondeur J, Roblin NP, Vanslambrouck S, Zhu C (2019) Improving teacher professional development for online and blended learning: a systematic meta-aggregative review. Educ Tech Res Dev 67(5):1145–1174

Piñuel Raigada JL (2002) Epistemología, metodología y técnicas. Estudios de Sociolingüística, pp 1–42

Richter D, Kunter M, Lüdtke O, Klusmann U, Anders Y, Baumert J (2013) How different mentoring approaches affect beginning teachers' development in the first years of practice. Teach Teach Educ 36:166–177

Robson D, Mtika P (2017) Newly qualified teachers' professional learning through practitioner enquiry. Int J Mentor Coach Educ 6(3):242–260

Rodríguez C, Castro V (2014) Calidad en la formación inicial docente: los déficits de las competencias pedagógicas y disciplinares en Chile. Revista Electrónica" Actualidades Investigativas en Educación" 14(2):1–25

Rozelle JJ, Wilson SM (2012) Opening the black box of field experiences: how cooperating teachers' beliefs and practices shape student teachers' beliefs and practices. Teach Teach Educ 28(8):1196–1205

Sandvik LV, Solhaug T, Lejonberg E, Elstad E, Christophersen KA (2019) Predictions of school mentors' effort in teacher education programmes. Eur J Teach Educ 42(5):574–590

Schaefer JM (2021) In sync: a qualitative study of asynchronous online teacher mentor training (Doctoral dissertation, Capella University)

Schatz-Oppenheimer O (2016) Being a mentor: novice teachers' mentors' conceptions of mentoring prior to training. Prof Dev Educ 43(2):274–292

Sinclair C (2003) Mentoring online about mentoring: possibilities and practice. Mentor Tutor 11(1):79–94

Smith ER (2011) Faculty mentors in teacher induction: developing a cross-institutional identity. J Educ Res 104(5):316–329

Spooner-Lane R (2016) Mentoring beginning teachers in primary schools: a research review. Prof Dev Educ 43(2):253–273

Squires V (2019) The well-being of the early career teacher: a review of the literature on the pivotal role of mentoring. Int J Mentor Coaching Educ 8(4)

Tang SYF, Choi PL (2005) Connecting theory and practice in mentor preparation: mentoring for the improvement of teaching and learning. Mentor Tutor Partnership Learn 13(3):383–401

Ulvik M, Sunde E (2013) The impact of mentor education: does mentor education matter? Prof Dev Educ 39(5):754–770

Wang J, Odell SJ (2002) Mentored learning to teach according to standards-based reform: a critical review. Rev Educ Res 72(3):481–546

Wynants S, Dennis J (2018) Professional development in an online context: opportunities and challenges from the voices of college faculty. J Educators Online 15(1):n1

Yoon SA, et al (2020) Encouraging collaboration and building community in online asynchronous professional development: designing for social capital. Int J Comput-Support Collaborative Learn 1–21

Chapter 37
Flipgrid for Social Interaction and Collaborative Learning in a Virtual Learning Environment

Adriana Pérez, Alana F. Roa, and Nayibe Rosado-Mendinueta

37.1 Introduction

made its impact evident (Organización Mundial de la Salud, 2020), proposals have sprung forth from higher education institutions to continue student training by integrating technological tools that enhance learning and generate autonomy: tools that facilitate teaching and student-centered learning while enhancing digital technology strengths.

The changing world and its resulting needs led to exploring a range of technological possibilities that are currently well known and have diverse uses in educational environments. In Latin America, there was a unification of efforts and resources. Examples include: Colombia, with *Colombia Aprende* knowledge network and the Colombian University Association (ASCUN); in Mexico, with RIE 360, the Educational Innovation Network and the National Association of Universities and Institutions of Higher Education (ANUIES); in Chile, with the Council of Deans of Chilean Universities (CRUCH) and the Corporation of Private Universities (CUP); in Venezuela, with the Venezuelan Association of University Deans (AVERU); and in Brazil, with the Brazilian Association of Deans of State and Municipal Universities (ABRUEM), among others. In May 2020, this effort included dialogues with university deans, the Inter-American Development Bank, and Universia Banco Santander to discuss the region's universities' challenges due to the pandemic. All these initiatives ensured the continuity of teaching and student learning during the contingency.

A. Pérez (✉) · A. F. Roa · N. Rosado-Mendinueta
Departamento de Español, Universidad del Norte, Barranquilla, Colombia
e-mail: aderamirez@uninorte.edu.co

A. F. Roa
e-mail: alanafarrahr@uninorte.edu.co

N. Rosado-Mendinueta
e-mail: nrosado@uninorte.edu.co

© The Author(s), under exclusive license to Springer Nature Singapore Pte Ltd. 2022   459
S. Hosseini et al. (eds.), *Technology-Enabled Innovations in Education*,
Transactions on Computer Systems and Networks,
https://doi.org/10.1007/978-981-19-3383-7_37

In this context of continuity, the priority was to ensure that the face-to-face interactions between teachers/students and between students/students that took place in the classroom were not lost. Therefore, universities had to learn and adapt to respond to new needs.

Geroge (2021) and Dávila (2021) reported that digital competencies are essential and necessary to guarantee the continuity of academic activities interrupted by COVID19. These authors took an innovative perspective that integrated virtual training with digital technology to generate quality learning environments for students. These students have incipient skills in managing technologies; their self-regulation and autonomy that are also in initial development, as reported by Canales and Silva (2020). Similarly, Cabero-Almenara (2021) points out that students "have had problems adapting to learning situations mediated by technologies; among other reasons, these situations require having strong competency to self-regulate their learning." This competency enables them to master digital knowledge (Saavedra et al. 2019), which they need to meet the challenges of professional training that have been transformed by the coronavirus contingencies (Salazar et al. 2021).

The COVID19 reality offers the opportunity to understand it is possible to develop and strengthen these digital competencies. An emerging alternative is Flipgrid. It is "a tool that enhances audiovisual communication for student–teacher, teacher–student, and student–student. It enriches the teaching–learning process through debate, discussion, and feedback, especially outside the classroom" (Serrano et al. 2019). This technological tool makes it possible to leverage the students' strengths in managing networks and foster the use of technologies for interactions and academic learning as autonomous processes.

Therefore, we developed this research to describe how using Flipgrid can potentiate students' social presence and collaborative learning.

37.2 Theoretical Framework

37.2.1 Digital Learners and Transmedia Literacy

The term "digital native" (Prensky 2001) refers to the first generations to grow up with the digital language of computers, video games, cell phones, video cameras, and the Internet. Now about 20 years later, the term has generated many controversies and deconstructions (Bennett et al. 2008). These have resulted in the concept of "digital learners": young people who have been born and raised in a media environment that allows them to acquire transmedia competencies ranging from playing video games and video and photo production to managing social networks (Masanet et al. 2019).

According to Masanet et al. (2019), teenagers learn and solve their problems according to their personal motivations primarily and independently through social media, exhibiting great closeness with it. In what can be considered a form of collaborative learning, adolescents rely on imitation strategies (learning by doing), with new actors such as influencers, and "learn by teaching" strategies, transmitting knowledge to peers to master a skill or acquire new ones.

For Scolari (2018), transmedia competencies are the "skills, practices, priorities, sensibilities, learning strategies, and ways of sharing that are developed and applied in the context of new participative cultures." However, these competencies are developed at different levels, coinciding with what Prensky (2009) would call "digital wisdom," which both students and teachers can build, whether digital natives or digital immigrants. Above all, these skills are enhanced in informal learning spaces outside of school, so the challenge is to bring the daily practices of teens and their skills acquired in digital environments to the classroom and formal learning.

In this context of transmedia competencies, it is necessary to conceptualize what is meant by transmedia literacy. Traditional literacy is concerned with books, inspired by linguistics, and media literacy with television, focusing on media effects. Transmedia literacy focuses on digital networks and interactive media experiences within the cultural studies and media ecology framework (Scolari 2018).

37.2.2 Interaction and Learning in Virtual Environments

One of the main concerns of teachers when migrating the contents and activities of their courses to virtual environments due to the health emergency caused by COVID19 was how to keep their students engaged and motivated in their classes while ensuring deep and meaningful learning. The lack of face-to-face interactions and socialization and networking spaces made the scenario more challenging. It necessitated investigating the findings of studies of virtual teaching environments produced to date.

For Garrison and Cleveland-Innes (2005), interaction is a fundamental focus of the online educational experience and learning. However, to achieve defined learning outcomes and influence critical and reflective thinking, this interaction must be structured and systematic. They argue that interaction is no guarantee that students will be cognitively engaged in an educationally meaningful way. Therefore, they see the need to integrate three types of presence to address the qualitative nature of a community of inquiry (CoI). According to Garrison et al. (1999), these are teaching presence, cognitive presence, and social presence.

Teaching presence refers to instructional design. It includes planning, activities, parameters, and delivery times. It also places the responsibility on the teacher to monitor and manage collaboration and reflection, "moving the discussion forward" to create a positive learning environment. Finally, Anderson et al. (2001) state that direct instruction confirms understanding through assessment and explanatory feedback, ensuring that the community achieves the intended learning outcomes.

Cognitive presence reflects the learning process in a CoI in four phases: (1) defining a problem or task as a triggering event, (2) exploring relevant knowledge or information through brainstorming, questioning, and information sharing, (3) integrating ideas to construct meaning, and finally, (4) testing possible solutions (Garrison et al. 2001).

The third central element of a CoI is *social presence*. Participants can project their personal characteristics onto the community and present themselves as "real people" (Garrison et al. 1999). Its importance lies in the fact that participants will feel motivated to continue if their interaction with the group is pleasant and personally satisfying; this also supports cognitive presence. This element is vital because it allows establishing a connection and an environment of trust among the community, despite not having the visual contact characteristic of face-to-face interactions.

Social networks, the place par excellence for interactions and sociability among young people in the West, have developed a clear tendency for audiovisual content in recent years. Besides Instagram and YouTube, platforms such as Facebook and Twitter have incorporated images and videos as an essential part of relating to each other, the world around us, and the construction of identity (Garrison et al. 2001). To this extent, introducing a platform that fosters interactions between student/student and student/teacher with images and videos could leverage social presence to support cognitive presence. Thus, students' daily and motivated use of media and social media networks can facilitate the transition to formal learning activities.

37.2.3 Flipgrid and Discursive Social Interactions

Flipgrid is a Microsoft tool for distance learning, allowing interactions on various topics organized in different student groups with multiple applications in educational contexts. Russmann and Svensson (2017), Huertas-Abril (2021), Connor and Peter (2021), Casañ-Núñez (2020), and Bartlett (2018) agree with this assumption. In addition, the Flipgrid web portal (Microsoft 2021) states, "it helps educators see and hear all students in the class and foster fun and supportive social learning."

At a technical level, this tool makes it possible for students to record their videos as many times as necessary until sure they are ready to publish them. This implies self-evaluation, preparation, and rehearsal and considering their digital skills and linguistic skills (oral expression, speech, time, image, among others) during the creation of videos (Keiper et al. 2021).

Flipgrid works as a closed student social network, which is "contagious" and resonates with the social learning theory proposed by Bandura (1977). According to this theory, people can learn by observing the behavior of other people or the influence of models through processes of attention, retention, motor reproduction, and motivation. Likewise, the platform favors perceiving the academic activity as a continuum of the activities they perform in their social networks, promoting a social climate that fosters engaged and meaningful learning.

37.3   Methodological Framework

This research is part of a larger project investigating student and teacher perspectives on emergent design, ICTs, and different applications in pandemic contexts. This report investigates how Flipgrid enhances students' social presence and collaborative learning in distance education. The research uses an action research methodology (Hernández-Sampieri et al. 2014; Yuni y and Urbano 2015), in which an area of interest is identified, planned, implemented, evaluated, and reflected upon to enrich future implementations.

The first step was a review of the literature on the advantages of Flipgrid and its different pedagogical applications in academic contexts. This led to designing various activities to integrate Flipgrid in the teaching–learning process of academic communication skills. Subsequently, it was implemented in three social learning activities during the second semester of 2020 in an academic Spanish course called "Communication Competency 1" (CC1).

This implementation was done at different times during the course through an exploratory social forum, an academic forum focused on homework, and a collaborative learning forum. Once these forums were developed, we assessed their implementation by analyzing the students' interactions as they performed the activities designed with Flipgrid. This helped us to discern whether using Flipgrid enhanced their social presence and collaborative learning.

In this research, we also analyzed students' perceptions of Flipgrid by analyzing the answers to two open-ended questions related to applying ICTs in this course designed to conform to the contingencies of the coronavirus (Reguera 1987).

37.3.1   Characteristics of the Participants

The students who participated in this study were young people between 16 and 20 years old who took the academic Spanish course (CC1) during their first university year. They were undergraduate students enrolled in different majors at a private university in Barranquilla, Colombia.

37.3.2   Design, Instruments, and Procedures

- *Activities designed with Flipgrid:* Three types of activities in which *Flipgrid* was used are described below:

(1)   *Presentation forum:* This general exploratory forum was informal. Each student introduced themself in a two-minute-or-less video indicating their name, the program they were studying, and a brief description of themself.

A. Pérez et al.

(2) *Collaborative learning forum:* This forum aimed to develop a collaborative task linked to the bibliographic research of academic sources: writing an expository text on a given topic. Students reported their reflections and difficulties during the research in a maximum of two-minute video. They also shared, through video responses, solutions to their classmates' experiences while comparing them with their own.

(3) *Academic forum:* This forum involved a reading task about orality on "what I learned about oral presentations in the university environment and how readings relate to the program I am studying." This video presentation had a one-and-a-half-minute limitation.

The three forums were designed progressively to facilitate transitioning the students' daily use of their transmedia skills to more scholarly practices. The first recording was informal with a personal, non-academic topic to promote the social climate and connection in the learning community. In the second step, the recording continued to be informal, but students were encouraged to share and exchange knowledge related to the subject matter. Finally, they moved on to academic content, but this time with a formal video, perfectly aligned with the university context.

After implementation, a qualitative analysis described the interactions in the forums and the teaching, cognitive, and social presence elements (instructional design, task comprehension and execution, and social climate, respectively), and other elements identified in the same data.

- *Survey:* A general survey validated by experts was applied to CC1 students and teachers on the contingency class design, ICTs, and their different applications in the pandemic context. The comprehensive survey included 13 items with a Likert scale rating inquiring about the emergent technological design of the course, its activities, and resources. The open-ended responses to questions 12 and 13 are reported in this article. The first part was used to obtain demographic information (age, sex, the program of study, class group, etc.).

The survey was designed in QuestionPro, and its distribution was online due to the COVID19 crisis. In addition, it was administered through Blackboard, a platform used in all CC1 courses. The invitation regarding this instrument was sent by institutional e-mail to guarantee access per user and password assigned by the university. The survey was answered voluntarily.

37.4 Results

37.4.1 Forum Experience

The teachers who taught the CC1 courses helped their students use Flipgrid during their social learning processes and present the oral expression projects. These students were confronting a new experience in their Spanish classes when developing the

Table 37.1 List of activities, purposes, interaction registers, and topic

Forum	Relation			
	Activity	Purpose	Recording	Topic
Presentation forum	Individual personal	Describe	Informal	Non-academic
Collaborative learning forum	Individual collaborative	Present resolve	Informal	Academic
Academic forum	Individual collaborative	Argument debate	Formal	Academic

Self-developed

forums. They constructed their speeches considering the context, the video recording, the task objective, and all the implications of preparing a video in which oral expressions, emotions, and discursive interactions, among others, are displayed.

Table 37.1 shows the relationship between the activities, their purposes, the level of the register (recording) managed by the students, and the topic in the different interactions. It is possible to observe the progressive design that leads students from the personal activity to a collaborative one, from an informal to a formal recording, and from a non-academic to an academic topic. They ended up leveraging their initial interest and spontaneity with the platform to achieve a transition to formative purposes. The Table shows how each of the forums promoted the evolution from lower-order cognitive processes to higher-order ones, according to Bloom's taxonomy (1971).

The possibility for all students enrolled in the course to contribute to the discussion through video comments asynchronously promoted equitable participation. In addition, by observing and imitating peers who did the activity first or better, those students who were not inclined to participate could experiment by rehearsing and recording several times before posting their responses. They also interacted with their peers, got to know each other, and applied their knowledge to teach others, reinforcing their own.

In this way, the teaching presence, built into the instructional design provided by the teacher, helped the student's cognitive development. However, the social presence, interacting with peers, kept the students motivated during the activities, promoted collaborative work, and normalized efforts as a regular part of learning.

Other findings related to the experience with using *Flipgrid* in the forums are presented below.

When analyzing the interactions in the *presentation forum*, we observed that it was an icebreaker activity that created a favorable social environment, decreasing their fear of being judged and the discomfort of an individual synchronous presentation (Syahrizal and Pamungkas 2021). The students managed the time, place, and attempts to share their first impression with their peers, doing it from home because of the pandemic contingency. This forum achieved other purposes: collecting spontaneous oral samples to analyze students' communicative competency upon arrival at the university and introducing a social-network-like technology into their classroom interactions.

The *collaborative learning forum* encouraged peer-to-peer feedback on an academic topic. This activity benefited student/student interaction, enhanced social and collaborative learning, and helped improve classroom connectivity in the context of distance education (Microsoft 2021). Likewise, creativity was observed in the students' responses. The activity provided an opportunity for formative evaluation and revealed the "learning by teaching" strategies that students employed to transmit knowledge to other peers and acquire new skills (Masanet et al. 2019).

Regarding the *academic forum*, students followed instructions to pay attention to the aspects learned about language and oral expression, both in the content of their comments and the checklist available on Blackboard. This oral debate forum allowed them to build, exchange and discuss content related to the subject. Consequently, the activity fulfilled the transactional purpose of strengthening communication through knowledge-sharing by all the participants.

Moreover, using discussion forums as a tool for asynchronous communication and interactions fostered deeper reflection than synchronous communications, for example, in the chat or online class. The use of oral debate had these components, plus the development of academic speaking.

It is important to note that the student's need to submit a speech in a length of time set by the teacher (who can use the Flipgrid platform to control that this time is not exceeded) requires the student to plan the most important points or topics to be addressed and organize them. In other words, to complete the task, students had to read, reflect, summarize or synthesize the information within the presentation time limit. In terms of academic speaking, this represents the knowledge and application of structure to order the discourse. In addition, they rehearsed or repeated the recording until they were satisfied with the result, observing themselves in this process, which led to auto-criticism of their oral expression.

The migration of face-to-face courses to distance learning modalities provided a valuable opportunity to include more technologies to enhance learning. In our study, in the academic Spanish courses, we could use videos asynchronously to see and hear the students and generate close interactions when both students and professors were not yet accustomed to meeting through a camera and a screen due to the confinement mandated by COVID19 restrictions. This coronavirus presented this challenge to all educational systems (Daniel 2020; Banco Interamericano de Desarrollo 2020).

37.4.2 Student Perceptions

The students formulated their opinions about the use of technologies in their learning of reading, writing, and academic speaking during the COVID19 confinement period, especially their views about *Flipgrid*.

Below are excerpts from the students' open-ended responses revealing their perceptions of Flipgrid. They highlight the key concepts and meaningful insights for the qualitative analysis:

Making the videos is **very easy,** and it is easy to share them (E3).

It is **easy to use** and **fun** (E7).

I did not know it, and it was **very helpful**. I liked it a lot, and I will continue using it. (E121).

I liked using it for some videos. I feel it is a **very good platform** to carry out these assigned tasks. (E18).

…because of how **easy it is to use and submit** assignments. (E305).

They are **easier** and **more fun** to use (E32).

It is very **easy to handle** and **very recreational** (E56).

It was **dynamic and easy to use** (E11).

…because it was **easy and pedagogical.** (E66).

It was simple to create and upload **videos** to the platform (E179).

You can make presentations, questions, and **interactive videos** for your learning (E210).

A good learning tool to interact with the teacher and classmates (E364).

When analyzing the answers, we found a positive perception of *Flipgrid*. Several common aspects were identified, such as its ease of use and the perception that it is an attractive and fun tool for creating, which undoubtedly contributed to strengthening their digital competencies.

On the other hand, the experience led them to connect a face with a name and see and listen to their classmates as they are. This was shown in the following student comments: *"With Flipgrid, I can see and hear others," "It is a tool by which I can get to know my classmates; thanks to that, it makes me feel more comfortable in class, making that resource different from the others," "This means that there is a real person behind the screen."*

Likewise, it led them to connect with others; for example, as quoted in the following student comments: *"I liked Flipgrid more because it is not something that tends to be monotonous; it is not the same to do an assignment on Word as to record a video and upload it to the platform. As we are in a virtual age, it is not bad at all to see my classmates or teacher's face;" "… it was a very dynamic tool in which I could know more about my classmates, and I could feel them being themselves because of the very free manner in which they recorded these."*

Finally, when analyzing the students' responses, we did not find any negative comments about the tool. Most of them agreed that they liked or preferred Flipgrid. Consequently, it is not surprising that they responded that they liked Flipgrid and its various applications in the Spanish class. Therefore, this preference leads us to predict its continuance in CC1.

In summary, Flipgrid made it easier to teach and participate in CC1. Including it in academic contexts promoted social learning through different discursive interactions. In this sense, the researchers agree with the students' view that Flipgrid is a simple, practical, and easy-to-use tool.

37.5 Final Thoughts

With *Flipgrid*, we implemented strategies that favored a social environment, inquired about the learners' moods, and invited sharing concerns and achievements. At the same time, they promoted listening to the experiences of their peers, empathy, and the integration of a course or community of inquiry. This led to collaborative learning by providing students with a space for experimenting and searching for solutions to their peers' problems. This taps into the youth trend of "learning by teaching," as mentioned by Masanet et al. (2019). On the other hand, by introducing technological platforms that integrate audio visualization of all interactions (similar to a social network), we leveraged the innovative element to increase students' interest and motivation to connect and participate in peer-to-peer interactions.

Students perceive some fundamental aspects of the teaching process, such as practice and feedback, positively when the experience can be shared in a social environment, developing their skills, working on mistakes, and strengthening their abilities. Moreover, open-ended questions in the forums can stimulate more meaningful use of language and argumentation due to their very nature of not presenting a single correct answer. This favors student creativity and critical thinking. These practices allowed us to examine the students' knowledge and thought processes and, in this way, help them advance in their learning and autonomy.

The results suggest that Flipgrid is a tool that balances participation, provides spaces for interaction, reflection, self-reflection, and learning. It also contributes to the structuring of the discourse and organization of the training process. Possibilities open up to further explore the potential of Flipgrid to facilitate students' collaborative learning and as a device to understand the areas of improvement as learning opportunities. There is also the possibility for research on the "learning by teaching" that young people perform in these activities.

Acknowledgements We thank the professors and students who participated in this study and the Universidad del Norte, Colombia, for their support. This work is part of the research project "La pedagogía de géneros en la enseñanza y aprendizaje de la competencia comunicativa académica en la Universidad del Norte," registered by the Research Directorate, Development and Innovation (code 2020-005). In addition, this work was presented at the V International Congress: Reading and Writing in Global Society (CILESG), Barranquilla, Colombia, in June 2021.

The authors acknowledge the technical support of the Writing Lab, Institute for the Future of Education, Tecnologico de Monterrey, Mexico, in the production of this work.

References

Anderson T, Rourke L, Garrison D, Archer W (2001) Assessing teaching presence in a computer conferencing context. J Asynchronous Learn Network 5:1–17
Banco Interamericano de Desarrollo, Banco Santander and Universia (2020) La educación superior en tiempos de COVID-19. Banco Interamericano de Desarrollo, New York
Bartlett M (2018) Using Flipgrid to increase students' connectedness in an online class. eLearn 9

Bandura A (1977) Social learning theory. General Learning Press, New York City

Bennett S, Maton K, Kervin L (2008) The 'digital natives' debate: a critical review of the evidence. Br J Edu Technol 39:775–786

Bloom B (1971) Taxonomía de los objetivos de la educación. Editorial El Ateneo, México

Cabero-Almenara J (2020) Aprendiendo del tiempo de la COVID-19. Revista Electrónica Educare 24:4–6

Canales R, Silva J (2020) De lo presencial a lo virtual, un modelo para el uso de la formación en línea en tiempos de Covid-19. Educ rev 36:1–20

Casañ-Núñez J (2020) Pros y contras de Flipgrid en la enseñanza del inglés según estudiantes del máster de profesorado. INNODOCT 1:751–755

Connor E, Peter L (2021) Facilitating student interaction: the role of flipgrid in blended language classrooms. Comput Assisted Lang Learn Electron J 22:26–39

Daniel SJ (2020) Educación y la pandemia COVID-19. Perspectivas 49:91–96

Dávila S (2021) Caracterización de las competencias digitales en estudiantes universitarios de Chiclayo a raíz de la Covid 19. Ciencia Latina Revista Científica Multidisciplina 5:3823–3834

Garrison D, Cleveland-Innes M (2005) Facilitating cognitive presence in online learning: interaction is not enough. Am J Distance Educ 19:133–148

Garrison D, Anderson T, Archer W (1999) Critical inquiry in a text-based environment: computer conferencing in higher education. Internet Higher Educ 2:87–105

Garrison D, Anderson T, Archer W (2001) Critical thinking, cognitive presence and computer conferencing in distance education. Am J Distance Educ 15:7–23

Geroge C (2021) Competencias digitales básicas para garantizar la continuidad académica provocada por el Covid-19. Apert 13:36–51

Hernández-Sampieri R, Fernández-Collado C, Bautista-Lucio P (2014) Metodología de la investigación, 6ta ed. Mc Graw Hill, México

Huertas-Abril C (2021) Developing speaking with 21st century digital tools in English as a foreign language classroom: new literacies and oral skills in primary education. Aula Abierta 50:625–634

Keiper M, White A, Carlson C, Lupinek J (2021) Student perceptions on the benefits of Flipgrid in a HyFlex learning environment. J Educ Bus 96:343–435

Masanet M, Guerrero-Pico M, Establés M (2019) From digital native to digital apprentice. A case study of the transmedia skills and informal learning strategies of adolescents in Spain. Learn Media Technol 44:400–413

Microsoft (2021) "Flipgrid" página web

Organización Mundial de la Salud (2020) Medidas de protección básicas contra el nuevo coronavirus. página web

Prensky M (2001) Digital natives, digital immigrants. On Horizon 9:1–6

Prensky M (2009) H. sapiens digital: from digital immigrants and digital natives to digital wisdom. Innov J Online Educ 5

Reguera A (1987) Metodología de la investigación lingüística. Prácticas de escritura. Editorial Brujas, Argentina

Russmann U, Svensson J (2017) Introduction to visual communication in the age of social media: conceptual, theoretical and methodological challenges. Media Commun 5:1–5

Saavedra C, Casillas M, Ramírez A (2013) Saberes digitales: un desafío para los maestros de hoy. Revista electrónica de Investigación e Innovación Educativa 4:84–91

Salazar M, Aguilar L, Alcántara T, Braun A (2021) La incorporación de los saberes digitales durante la pandemia por COVID-19. Observatorio del Instituto para el Futuro de la Educación

Scolari C (2018) Introducción. Del alfabetismo mediático al alfabetismo transmedia. In: Scolari C (ed) Adolescentes, medios de comunicación y culturas colaborativas. Aprovechando las competencias transmedia de los jóvenes en el aula, vol I. Universitat Pompeu Fabra, Barcelona, pp 14–23

Serrano R, Casanova O (2020) Social learning. Posibilidades didácticas de Flipgrid. In: Buenas prácticas en la docencia universitaria con apoyo de TIC. Experiencias en 2019, J. Alejandre, Coord. España, Universidad de Zaragoza, pp 147–154

Syahrizal T, Pamungkas M (2021) Revealing students' responds on the use of flipgrid in speaking class: survey on ICT. Acuity: J English Lang Pedagogy Literature Culture 202:96–106

Yuniy JA, Urbano A (2015) Mapas y herramientas para conocer la escuela: investigación etnográfica e investigación-acción". Editorial Brujas, Argentina

Chapter 38
REUNI+D: An Online Network for Research, Training, and Professional Development in Innovation and Educational Technology

Ana García-Valcárcel Muñoz-Repiso, Sonia Casillas Martín, and Marcos Cabezas González

38.1 Introduction

The REUNI+D university network (University Network for Educational Research and Innovation), coordinated at this time by the GITE-USAL group of the University of Salamanca and funded by the Ministry of Science and Innovation of Spain,[1] brings together eleven research groups from various relevant Spanish universities in education, educational technology, and innovation in teaching–learning processes. These groups are: (1) Research and innovation group in educational technology (GITE-USAL), (2) Subjectivities, visualities and contemporary educational environments (ESBRINA) of the University of Barcelona, (3) Research on the curriculum and teacher training (ICUFOP) of the University of Granada, (4) Laboratory of education and new technologies (EDULLAB) of the University of La Laguna, (5) STELLAE of the University of Santiago de Compostela, (6) Inclusion, diversities, universal design for learning, curriculum and technology (INDUCT) of the Complutense University of Madrid, (7) Educational Node of the University of Cáceres, (8) Research, evaluation and educational technology (GIETE) of the University of Seville, (9) Faculty,

---

[1] Project financed by the Ministry of Science and Innovation of Spain. Revitalization actions "Research Networks", 2018 (Ref. RED2018-102439-T).

A. G.-V. Muñoz-Repiso (✉) · S. C. Martín · M. C. González
Department Didáctica, Organización y Métodos de Investigación, Universidad de Salamanca, Salamanca, España
e-mail: anagv@usal.es

S. C. Martín
e-mail: scasillasma@usal.es

M. C. González
e-mail: mcabezasgo@usal.es

© The Author(s), under exclusive license to Springer Nature Singapore Pte Ltd. 2022   471
S. Hosseini et al. (eds.), *Technology-Enabled Innovations in Education*,
Transactions on Computer Systems and Networks,
https://doi.org/10.1007/978-981-19-3383-7_38

communication and educational research (PROCIE) of the University de Málaga, (10) Educational Innovation with digital technologies: technological change and cultural and educational transformations (ELKARRIKERTUZ) of the University of the Basque Country, and (11) Citizenship, learning ecologies and expanded education (CEAEX) of the University of Valladolid.

The collaboration between the groups that make up the network dates to 1992. It enables more than 100 researchers from different universities to participate in joint projects, organize scientific events, and provide postgraduate training, serving as a basis for the professional development of all its members. The REUNI+D interuniversity educational research network has allowed the collaborative construction of knowledge and strives to offer open and accessible content (García-Valcárcel Muñoz-Repiso 2018) and aims to promote open science as a milestone in the universal construction of knowledge. At the same time, the development of new research perspectives in education is proposed. This text will present the objectives, the initiatives implemented, and the primary results to encourage the development of similar networks with which fruitful connections could be established soon. The connectivity offered by the Internet allows creating synergies among educational research networks in different parts of the world.

38.2 Online Work

38.2.1 Collaboration and Flexibility

Networking is built on trust, collaboration, and flexibility. It requires establishing objectives by all member nodes and planning joint work to enrich the entire community that forms the network, the active involvement of all groups, and the shared assumption of responsibilities (Almuiñas and Galarza 2016). Digital communication tools facilitate the necessary flexibility of spaces and times to share information through synchronous and asynchronous communication strategies. However, flexibility is also essential in working, envisioning research and reality, and connecting with others to continue learning (Navarro et al. 2017). It allows us to strengthen and broaden our work environment beyond our research group and create a community of practice. In this sense, the connection with other groups helps us question our epistemological practices and conceptions. All learning in the search for new perspectives and answers to the problems addressed.

38.2.2 Line of Action in the University of the XXI Century

Experiences in different countries have shown the benefits of networking in enhancing innovation and research production, highlighting the positive effects of online connections on decision-making (Katona et al. 2011) and increasing learning (Penuel et al. 2012). It has also been shown that teacher learning communities have strengthened knowledge and resources for practice (Baker-Doyle and Yoon 2011). In addition, social service is demanded from university institutions, which has led the universities to bet on the networking of teachers and researchers to connect with the rest of society. Such networks promote research and educational innovation beyond a particular institution to address social needs; hence, there is great importance in transferring the results of scientific research to develop new services, ideas, and products that impact the population's well-being. This line of action has led to financing these types of initiatives to promote research of excellence. In this way, REUNI+D was established as a network of excellence in the educational field in 2014, receiving funding from the State Research Agency.

38.3 The Objectives of the REUNI+D Network

The Network's interest focuses on the profound changes brought about by the impact of digital technologies at multiple levels: informational (learning), professional, personal, social, and civic (empowerment of citizens). We identify ourselves with the objective of the Strategy for the Digital Single Market (Comisión Europea 2018), which proposes a single connected market for all in Europe to achieve a fair, open, and secure digital environment. This implies a continuous updating to address the challenges, including online platforms, data management, and cybersecurity. Concerning these challenges, it is stated, "Platforms have become key guardians of the Internet, as intermediaries for access to information, content, and online commerce. Online platforms organize the Internet 'ecosystem,' which constitutes a profound transformation of the World Wide Web that brings with it new opportunities, but also challenges" (p. 9) (Comisión Europea 2017). This situation reaffirms our conviction about the importance of research groups in virtual environments and the need to join forces to create robust research networks that combine the various groups' knowledge, allow open access to research processes and results, foster innovation, and create communities of practice. In this sense, REUNI+D assumes the objective of the European Commission to safeguard a fair, sustainable, and trust-inspiring digital environment based on freedom of expression, responsibility, and innovation.

38.3.1 Promote Open Knowledge and Open Science

Open, universal, and accessible knowledge is the basis of knowledge societies. Strengthening more sustainable and inclusive knowledge societies is increasingly connected to expanding Internet access (UNESCO 2014). Concepts such as "open scientific resources" and "open educational resources" are increasingly present at the tables of decision-makers on public policies. Open Science represents an approach to research in a collaborative, transparent, and accessible way (Open Science "Wheel"). REUNI+D plans to develop skills related to Open Science (O'Carroll et al. 2017) among its researchers, which means:

- *Publication in Open Access.* This implies abilities to make correct decisions about where and how to publish research results, self-archive, and communicate the results to have academic and social impact.
- *Open Data.* Capabilities related to research data, data production, management, analysis/use/reuse, dissemination, and a paradigm shift from "data protected by default" to "open data by default," respecting legal and other restrictions. The ethical standards necessary for social science research, such as the informed consent of the participants and ensuring the anonymity of sensitive data, among others, deserve special mention.
- *Professional behavior from the researcher.* Research management skills, particularly leadership, management, and soft skills, are required to build positive and trustworthy work environments. They also include knowledge of the legal aspects of using data and copyright, ethical conduct in the appointment of authors, attribution of the research, and sensitive data.
- *Citizen Science.* This relatively new concept implies the need for researchers to interact with citizens, including communicating with other stakeholders, not just members of the scientific and/or academic community. The goal is to achieve better user participation and dissemination of research results.

We align ourselves with the European Commission by encouraging «research data» to be findable, accessible, interoperable, and reusable (FAIR). It is about achieving the necessary balance between openness and protection of scientific information, commercialization, and intellectual property rights or aspects related to security. To this end, general-purpose data repositories are emerging that accept a wide range of data types in various formats, with no intention of integration or harmonization and with few requirements on their descriptors (Wilkinson et al. 2016).

38.3.2 Create a Community of Practice and Research on Innovation and Educational Technology of National and International Prestige

This seeks to articulate a common and diversified work plan among all the groups in the network to promote research and development activities and contribute to advancing knowledge. It is intended to create a dynamic community of practice, an environment for reflection and professional growth, and higher quality research with potential for internationalization. At the same time, we seek connections with related research networks, both national and international, that may be complementary and enriching.

In addition, the REUNI+D website (http://reunid.eu) aims to promote the dissemination of training practices and the processes and results of research generated on the network, promoting educational research from critical and open perspectives.

38.3.3   Contribute to the Training of Future Researchers in the Field of Innovation and Educational Technology

The groups that comprise REUNI+D share their interest in exploring and disseminating alternative educational research methods. In this sense, it is pertinent for a network of these characteristics to adopt a corporate identity dynamic, understood as the effort to give coherence to the research discourse and practice by each research group involved, always respecting diversity.

The experience in educational research and innovation of the groups that participate in the network is disseminated through various training activities aimed at Ph.D. students and practicing professionals with a strong international projection. In this sense, it is intended to assert the role of educational research in decision-making processes, seeking synergies among research, educational policies, and educational practice.

38.4   Actions Taken and their Results

REUNI+D has carried out multiple actions to achieve the planned objectives over two decades of joint work. Here are some actions and results that deserve to be highlighted for their social transfer.

38.4.1   Connection with Other Research Networks

REUNI+D has established fruitful alliances with other entities and consolidated educational research networks both nationally and internationally. At the national level, the network participates in the development of RETINDE (Transdisciplinary Network of Educational Research) as one of the active nodes, promoting horizontal collaboration strategies with other relevant Spanish networks and associations in the educational field, such as the Spanish Pedagogy Society (SEP), Ibero-American Society of Social Pedagogy (SIPS), Interuniversity Association for Pedagogical Research (AIDIPE), University Association for Teacher Training (AUFOP), University Network of Educational Technology (RUTE), Research Network on Leadership and Educational Improvement (RILME), IARTEM, etc. At the international level, the relationship has been strengthened with some networks that will allow expanding and increasing in its influence, such as the National Center for Research Methods (Great Britain), The Center for the Learning Sciences (Germany), and Cátedra UNESCO/ICDE Open Educational Movement for Latin America (Mexico).

38.4.2 Training Activities for Researchers in Open Format

One of the most exciting training activities offered has been a MOOC called "*Alternative trends in educational and social research*," in which all the research groups of the network have participated. The MOOC was developed through the MIRIADAX platform in 2017. This open training course addressed emerging epistemologies and approaches to educational research, considering feminist epistemology, the epistemology of reflective subjectivity, and practical epistemology. Participatory and collaborative research designs (Kochanek et al. 2015), sociocultural approaches (Hickey-Moody and y Page 2016), and design-based arts (Leavy 2009) were analyzed.

For several years, the network has also organized "summer schools" in different universities for training purposes and networking between the doctoral students of the groups in the REUNI+D network.

Along the same lines, two virtual seminars (webinars) were organized and offered for researchers in education, which are available on YouTube:

(1)   *Looking for alternatives: Paths to other educational research (2020).* https://www.youtube.com/watch?v = ufpwMQbDiYw
(2)   *Growing Together: Educational Research and Open Knowledge (2021).* https://www.youtube.com/watch?v = Cu8knoQ3dCI

The evaluation of these training activities is very positive, both for the network members and for external participants. The learning of the course and seminar contents and the shared experiences in constructing knowledge were valued. These activities projected essential international interactions, mainly among European and Latin American researchers. Another notable consequence of this network connection is the exchange of experts from the different groups in master's and doctorate courses, facilitating stays of network members in different universities, and offering collaborative options and post-doctorate contracts.

38.4.3 Design of Coordinated Research Projects

Joint research projects are those made up of several sub-projects that complement each other. Two or more research groups participate so that each sub-project has its own identity and objectives and its research team and coordinator. In this case, the joint project may be more ambitious. However, the coordination between the sub-projects must be perfectly planned and justified based on the project's general objectives.

The network groups have obtained funding from national and international entities to carry out several collaborative projects (More information at https://reunid.eu/cat egory/proyectos/).

38.4.4   Organization of Scientific Events

The groups in the network participate in the organization and development of different events of national and international relevance to disseminate research activity in the field of innovation and educational technology. We highlight some that are held regularly:

(1)   International Conference ieTIC.
(2)   Ibero-American Congress of University Teaching.
(3)   University Conference on Educational Technology.
(4)   National and International Congress of Pedagogy.

38.4.5   Creation of a REUNI+D Space in an Open Repository

To implement the Open Science budgets after analyzing the platforms and repositories available to share research documentation on the network, we are opening a REUNI+D site in the OSF platform, chosen for its simplicity in information management. The address of the REUNI+D space in this repository is https://osf.io/hdg4u/.

The site is in the initial phase of development. However, progressive development is foreseen, allowing sharing with the entire educational community research resources of interest, such as fieldwork protocols, projects, reports, and data in different formats.

38.4.6   Dissemination of Content Created on the Network

The network website mentioned above allows the dissemination of information on the activities and events organized by the network. In addition, the articles section (https://reunid.eu/category/articulos/) aims to disseminate the results of the research carried out and reflections on current issues.

Also, through the REUNI+D research portal (https://reunid.portalcientifico.es/), the scientific publications of the members of the Network are disseminated. This portal allows access to bibliometric data of researchers, group research, and the entire network, facilitating open access to publications.

38.5 Social Impact of the Network

REUNI+D's activity facilitates developing new research proposals that integrate and potentiate the various research groups, contributing to methodological innovation from the perspectives created by analyzing educational reality. Through various training actions, both virtual in an open format (webinar, MOOC) and face-to-face (conferences, congresses, summer school), novel methodological research proposals (alternatives) are constructed and disseminated by network groups, in all cases with a strong international projection.

REUNI+D disseminates its research activity through an open and accessible virtual platform that increases the visibility of research groups and, specifically, educational research carried out within the network's framework. The various actions converge in creating networked interuniversity working groups and a REUNI+D space in an open repository that allows sharing research processes and resources and the data and results obtained in educational technology and innovation. In this way, REUNI+D contributes to the development of Open Science strategies in our field of knowledge.

The work of researchers from the various groups that make up REUNI+D has been strengthened thanks to the potential provided by the network, increasing the social influence of researchers in various social spheres, especially those in which relevant educational policy decisions affect the entire educational fabric of a country. The work of the network is disseminated in formats adapted to the needs of the different sectors of the educational community, from teachers linked to educational practice (through workshops or meetings) to the highest educational policy-making positions (reports with the endorsement of the network, publications). An increasingly cohesive research network, capable of sharing discourses and research processes, will have increasing scientific weight at the national and international level, increasing its prestige and ability to set trends and guide educational policy actions. If connections with other relevant research networks are also initiated, these aspects will be strengthened, and the network may become an international benchmark for educational research.

The prestige of REUNI+D also increases interest in the training activities promoted by the network aimed at training researchers internationally. These activities will impact the methodological innovations of the scientific community working in the field of education, resulting in a greater repertoire of research strategies and epistemological foundations of the various frameworks that address educational realities. The intended internationalization of the network will have an added effect on disseminating the regulated training activities offered in the universities linked to the network groups, leading to reevaluating the postgraduate degrees in which the researchers participate, which could be very positive for the recruitment of international students.

On the other hand, a positive image of the network in the educational field can facilitate the connections between academic institutions and the private sector. There is a growing interest in the business sector to access the educational market and offer very diverse services. In this sense, the network groups have long-established strategic alliances with various sectors interested in educational innovation. These links will continue to be extended throughout Europe and Latin America through new contracts and research projects.

38.6   Conclusion

The activity of the REUNI+D network aims to impact the strengthening and advancement of educational research within the framework of the Europe 2030 Strategy and contribute to the development of the Spain 2030 Agenda, in line with the priority axes of the network's strategy. One of its objectives is to guarantee universal access to quality health and education services. Specifically, it is committed to transferring and managing the knowledge generated by the network participants through Open Science actions, internationalization of educational research, and promotion of a scientific culture of open, participatory, and innovative educational research.

References

Almuiñas JL, Galarza J (2016) Las redes académicas como ejes de integración y cooperación internacional de las instituciones de educación superior. Revista Cubana De Educación Superior 35(1):18–29

Baker-Doyle KJ, Yoon SA (2011) In search of practitioner-based social capital: a social network analysis tool for understanding and facilitating teacher collaboration in a US-based STEM professional development program. Prof Dev Educ 37(1):75–93

Comisión Europea (2018) Right environment for digital networks and services. https://ec.europa.eu/digital-single-market/node/78516

Comisión Europea (2017) Un mercado único digital conectado para todos. https://ec.europa.eu/transparency/regdoc/rep/1/2017/ES/COM-2017-228-F1-ES-MAIN-PART-1.PDF

García-Valcárcel Muñoz-Repiso A, González Rodero LM, Gómez-Pablos VB; Martín del Pozo M (2018) REUNI+D: una red universitaria para la construcción colaborativa de conocimiento RIED. Revista Iberoamericana de Educación a Distancia 21(2) https://doi.org/10.5944/ried.21.2.20605

Hickey-Moody A, y Page T (eds) (2016) Arts, pedagogy and cultural resistance: new materialisms. Rowman & Littlefield, London, England

Katona Z, Zubcsek PP, Sarvary M (2011) Network effects and personal influences: the diffusion of an online social network. J Mark Res 48(3):425–443

Kochanek JR, Scholz C, Garcia AN (2015) Mapping the collaborative research process. Educ Policy Anal Arch 23(121). http://dx.doi.org/https://doi.org/10.14507/epaa.v23.2031

Leavy P (2009) Method meets art: arts-based research practice. Guilford Press, New York

Navarro MJ, López A, Hernández MEE (2017) Trabajo colaborativo en red impulsor del desarrollo profesional del profesorado. Revista Brasileira De Educação 22(70):651–667

O'Carroll C, Kamerlin CL, Brennan N, Hyllseth B, Kohl U, O'Neill G, Van Den Berg R (2017) Providing researchers with the skills and competencies they need to practise open science. European Commission—Publications Office of the European Union, Luxembourg

Penuel WR, Sun M, Frank KA, Gallagher HA (2012) Using social network analysis to study how collegial interactions can augment teacher learning from external professional development. Am J Educ 119(1):103–136

UNESCO (2014) La información y el conocimiento abierto en el contexto de la cooperación multilateral. http://unesdoc.unesco.org/images/0023/002309/230986s.pdf

Wilkinson MD, Dumontier M, Aalbersberg IJ, Appleton G, Axton M, Baak A, Mons B (2016) The FAIR Guiding Principles for scientific data management and stewardship. Sci Data 3:160018. https://doi.org/10.1038/sdata.2016.18

Chapter 39
Teacher Adoption of a Hybrid Learning Model in Vulnerable Secondary Schools

Camila Barahona, Luis Lippi, María Fernanda Rodríguez, Gabriel Astudillo, and Isabel Hilliger

39.1 Introduction

In the context of the COVID-19 emergency, the incorporation of technologies for teaching became accelerated to continue offering education and learning experiences to all students in times of confinement (Videla et al. 2020). Given this situation, schools had to adopt new teaching methodologies such as the hybrid learning model (*blended learning*), an alternative to adapt education to the diverse needs of students and their families. It combines synchronous and asynchronous workspaces remotely.

The *blended learning* model is a reflective integration of asynchronous and synchronous learning experiences (Rasheed et al. 2020). On the one hand, in asynchronous learning experiences, students must self-regulate access to the proposed content through a learning management system (LMS) (Rasheed et al. 2021). To achieve this, formative assessment activities are usually offered to motivate student

---

I. Hilliger
School of Engineering, Pontificia Universidad Católica, Santiago, Chile
e-mail: ihillige@ing.puc.cl

L. Lippi · G. Astudillo
Santiago, Chile
e-mail: luis.lippi@usach.cl

G. Astudillo
e-mail: gabriel.astudillo.l@usach.cl

M. F. Rodríguez
Facultad de Educación, Psicología y Familia, Universidad Finis Terrae, Santiago, Chile
e-mail: maria.rodriguez@uft.cl

C. Barahona (✉)
Intituto de Éticas Aplicadas, Pontificia Universidad Católica, Santiago, Chile
e-mail: cebaraho@uc.cl

© The Author(s), under exclusive license to Springer Nature Singapore Pte Ltd. 2022   481
S. Hosseini et al. (eds.), *Technology-Enabled Innovations in Education*,
Transactions on Computer Systems and Networks,
https://doi.org/10.1007/978-981-19-3383-7_39

participation and monitor their progress through questionnaires, peer reviews, or gamified activities (Ticker 2020).

On the other hand, synchronous learning experiences create opportunities for students to actively participate, promoting higher-order skills such as problem-solving, analysis, critical thinking, and creativity. By active learning activities, we refer to practices that have become fundamental to promote meaningful learning, alluding to project-based learning, problem-based learning, and case studies, among others (Anthony et al. 2020).

To date, most studies on the *blended learning* model focus on the benefits perceived by higher education students, which are associated with improving learning outcomes and promoting self-regulatory skills, among others. However, more studies are needed to know how to adopt the *blended learning* model by teachers in school contexts (Apandi and Raman 2020a), particularly in cases like vulnerable schools. Along this line, this article presents a case study in vulnerable schools in Chile, whose focus is to describe the factors that affect the learning of a *blended learning* model imparted by secondary school teachers.

39.2 Case Study

39.2.1 Context

The participants of this study were five public high school teachers in vocational-technical education. The five schools work with students in a high condition of school vulnerability, which average 91% according to the School Vulnerability Index (IVE-SINAE) prepared by the National Board of School Aid and Scholarships (JUNAEB), an institution in the State of Chile.

The sample comprised 108 teachers, of which 81 were in general education (humanistic, scientific education) and 27 in differentiated training (professional technician).

39.2.2 Research Question

This research aimed to analyze the factors that explain the learning experience of secondary education teachers (high school) using a blended learning model. Thus, the research question emerged: What factors could favor the adoption of a blended learning model by secondary school teachers?

39.2.3   Description of the Blended Learning Model

The *blended learning* model considered the development of asynchronous and synchronous resources and activities (Stöhr et al. 2020). The asynchronous resources were produced by assistant teachers and implemented with the Canvas platform. All contents were designed and aligned with the learning objectives of the national curriculum.

The general model consisted of two stages, an asynchronous stage and a synchronous stage (a class session). Resources for the asynchronous stage were available to students one week before the corresponding synchronous class. Each asynchronous stage had the following four steps: (1) Introduction: presentation of the session content, (2) Explanation of the content through interactive videos (3) Challenge with the use of ICT; (4) Formative assessment activity through a questionnaire in Canvas to monitor the understanding of the content.

Teachers reviewed the performance of their students in the asynchronous stage through formative assessment activities. This questionnaire allowed them to obtain information to evaluate the students' learning, both in a group and individually. From this information, teachers planned their synchronous classes according to the students' needs. Therefore, each class had particular dynamics that could be modified according to needs (Mehring 2016).

The resources used in the synchronous classes were designed by the teacher of each subject. They could adapt their classes according to the results of the formative evaluation activities (exit ticket). Each synchronous class was held virtually through the Google Meet platform and was recorded to be available to all students. Each synchronous class had the following seven steps: (1) Warm-up; (2) Collaborative review of the report; (3) Canvas formative assessment feedback; (4) Recovery activity; (5) Deepening activity; (6) Resolution of questions and (7) Synthesis.

39.2.4   Data Collection

For the development of this study, a questionnaire was designed for data collection, which considered the following dimensions: teacher characteristics, instructional design of the blended learning model, initial teacher training needs, and benefits of the *blended learning model.*

When designing the questionnaire, the proposal of Aldunate and Nussbaum (2013) on technology adoption was considered to construct the items of the teaching characterization dimension. In this regard, the authors defined four categories of teachers according to how they used ICTs in the classroom, the effort involved in using them and the ICT learning process. The categories were adapted to the Spanish language and are as follows: (1) Innovative, (2) Early adopters, (3) Follower of the masses, (4) Late adopters.

The instructional design dimensions and the benefits of the *blended learning* model emerged from the literature by identifying the need to understand the factors that influence the learning process in this type of model (Apandi and Raman 2020b). These dimensions were evaluated on a 5-point Likert scale. Each dimension considered 5 items.

The dimension of initial teacher training raises proposals to guide vocational training institutions' decisions regarding the curricula they currently teach. This dimension is evaluated on a 5-point Likert scale and has five items.

The dimensions and questionnaire items were reviewed by two experts in educational technology and an expert in the design of measuring instruments, who made modifications in the writing of some items. Once these changes were incorporated, the instrument was sent to the institutional management team, who sent the questionnaire to the teachers in digital format.

39.2.5 Data Analysis

The analysis was conducted in two phases. The first consisted of an exploratory factor analysis, which investigated the underlying structure of the questionnaire, where different dimensions of the adoption of the blended model could be observed. The second phase of analysis consisted of developing a multiple linear regression model to estimate the effect of the identified dimensions and other teacher aspects on the difficulties of adopting the *blended* model.

Data processing was performed in R, using the Psych package (Revell and Ayotte 2020) for exploratory factor analysis and the R base package for regression models.

Exploratory factor analysis is an information reduction technique that identifies latent variables that explain the information shared by a set of observed variables. Factor analyses are divided between their exploratory and confirmatory applications, depending on the degree of knowledge, and the hypotheses about the factorial structure of the phenomenon studied. In this case, exploratory factor analysis was chosen because, although there were hypotheses about adopting the blended model, these were not theoretically elaborated to submit for verification. Instead, it was decided to observe the emergence of a structure from the data.

Since the variables measured in the questionnaire were ordinal scales, the polycóric correlation matrix was used, which is the appropriate procedure for this type of variable, also available in the Psych package. The Maximum Likelihood method was used to extract the factors, and a Varimax rotation was applied. The KMO obtained $(0.8; p < 0.05)$ is acceptable, indicating that factor analysis is relevant.

The multiple linear regression model aims to study the relationship between two or more variables when seeking to explain the variation of a dependent variable as a function of the variation of one or more independent variables (Jeffrey 2010). In the latter case, it is also possible to estimate the specific impact of each of the predictor variables over the dependent variables and control if the observed relations are robust

(Vivanco 1999). There, it can be noted that those aspects related to formative assessment obtained the highest scores (equal to or greater than 4.00), while items related to learning activities appear with slightly lower scores.

39.3   Results

Table 39.1 presents the teacher characteristics. Most of the Teachers declare themselves as early adopters or innovators.

Table 39.2 presents the time that teachers estimate have dedicated to incorporating technology into their pedagogical work. More than half of the teachersrespondents perceive having dedicated a high amount of time, followed by those who perceive to have invested a médium amount of timework.

Table 39.3 shows the sample mean for the score of the different items of the scale of perceived benefits of the Blended model. The aspects with the highest score are the Deepening Activity, the Resolution of Questions, and the Recovery Activity.

Table 39.4 presents the sample means obtained on the perception-of difficulty-scale in the instructional design stages.

Table 39.1 Teacher characteristics

Type of teacher			
Innovator	Early adapter	Follower of the masses	Late adapter
32	48	14	12

Source The teachers self-classified from the question, "In regards to using technology in your classes, which of the following describes you best?"

Table 39.2 Time invested by the teachers to incorporate technology

	Time invested	
High	Mid	Low
61	46	1

Table 39.3 Perception scale of the benefits of the blended model

Question	Mean
Using the canvas exit ticket report	3.91
Ice-breaker activity (warm-up)	3.91
Question resolution	4.19
Recovery activity	4.18
Deepening activity	4.30

Table 39.4 Perception of difficulty in the instructional design stages of the blended model

Question	Mean
Review the formative assessment report of each class	4.28
Adapt my synchronous class, based on the report of the formative evaluation	3.95
Feedback from the formative assessment report	4.00
Recovery activity	3.83
Deepening activity/application	3.97
Resolution of questions	3.97
Using tools in the synchronous class	3.47
The formative evaluation permits me to make informed decisions about the learning process of my students	4.23

Table 39.5 Needs scale of initial teacher training

Question	Mean
Learning to integrate technology in the classes	4.59
Active learning methodologies like blended learning, project-based learning, gamification	4.45
Formative evaluations in virtual contexts	4.43
Timely feedback	4.70
Data analysis for making evidence-based decisions	4.62

Table 39.5 shows the sample averages obtained concerning the different needs of initial teacher training. In this regard, it is observed that there are no notable differences between the items since all have averages of around 4.50 points.

Table 39.6 presents the factorial loads of the analysis carried out. There it can be observed that three latent factors clearly emerge from the variables, which, in addition, corresponded to the scales that organized the questionnaire.

Factor 1 corresponds to the didactic sequence that constitutes the *blended learning* model. The most significant factorial loads appear in the items *Feedback* and *Adaptation of the class*, both depending on the Canvas formative evaluation results.

In second place, there is a factor that groups the questions related to the needs of initial training that teachers identified from their experience with the *Blended* model, where timely feedback skills and technological integration were highlighted.

Finally, a factor emerges that explains the questions related to the perception of benefits of the *blended* model. The most significant factorial loads are in the *Resolution of questions* and the *Recovery activity*.

Table 39.7 shows the three regression models performed to explain the difficulty of adopting the *blended* model. Model 1's predictor variable is the type of teacher. It can be observed that those who self-classified as innovators presented a significant reduction in the difficulty in implementing the blended model.

Table 39.6 Factorial loads

item	Factor 1	Factor 2	Factor 3
9. Feedback	0.94		
9. Adapting my class	0.90		0.33
9. Recovery activity	0.67		0.40
9. Deepening activity	0.61	0.42	
9. Reviewing report	0.58	0.31	
9. Resolving questions	0.54		0.50
9. Using tools	0.47		
8. Evidence-based decicions	0.45		0.37
12. Timely feedback		0.92	
12. Integrating technology		0.80	
12. Analyzing data		0.78	0.39
12. Virtual formative evidence		0.75	
12. Metodologías activas de aprendizaje		0.73	
7. Resolving questions			0.92
7. Recovery activity		0.37	0.73
7. Deepening activity			0.67
7. Icebreak activity			0.62

Note F1: Instructional design of blended learning model; F2: Initial teacher training needs; F3: Benefits of blended learning model

Model 2, in addition to the type of teacher, considers as a regressor variable the three dimensions that emerged in the factor analysis. Of these, only the instructional design presents a significant decrease in the difficulties of adoption by teachers. In contrast, the needs of initial training and the perceived benefits of the *blended* model do not present statistically significant effects. On the other hand, although the introduction of this block of variables slightly reduces the effect of the innovative teacher profile, it is still statistically significant. It is evidenced as a different effect of instructional design of the *blended* model.

Finally, Model 3 incorporates as control variables the school and the training plan to which the teachers belong. Both variables are statistically non-significant, so the effects observed in the previous models remain: innovative teaching profile and the instructional design of the *blended* model.

When interpreting these two analyses, it is observed that the instructional design of the *blended* model is the critical aspect and that the most significant elements of this factor are the feedback and the adaptation of the class made by the teacher. This indirectly indicates that these two aspects of teaching practice would be of first importance when implementing a hybrid learning model.

Table 39.7 Linear regression

Dependent variable: Difficulty of adopting the blended model	Model 1	Model 2	Model 3
Teacher type 1: early adopter	0.126	0.017	0.060
	(0.244)	(0.247)	(0.249)
Teacher type 2: innovator	-0.566^{***}	-0.466^{**}	-0.452^{**}
	(0.183)	(0.185)	(0.186)
Teacher type 3: follower of the masses (Category of reference: late adopter)	0.340	0.226	0.259
	(0.251)	(0.251)	(0.256)
Instructional design		-0.217^{***}	-0.230^{***}
		(0.080)	(0.084)
Training needs		-0.069	-0.057
		(0.076)	(0.078)
Benefits of the model		-0.062	-0.054
		(0.078)	(0.079)
E1			-0.420
			(0.303)
E2			-0.516^{*}
			(0.269)
E3			-0.256
			(0.273)
E4			-0.385
			(0.233)
(Category of reference: E5)			0.234
General training (Category of reference: training in a specialty)			(0.188)
Constant	2.660^{***}	2.657^{***}	2.796^{***}
	(0.114)	(0.112)	(0.269)
Observations	109	107	107
R^2	0.135	0.209	0.258
Adjusted R^2	0.110	0.161	0.173
Residual Std. error	0.806 (df = 105)	0.788 (df = 100)	0.783 (df = 95)
F statistic	5.471^{***} (df = 3; 105)	4.393^{***} (df = 6; 100)	3.011^{***} (df = 11; 95)

Note $^* p < 0.1;$ $^{**} p < 0.05;$ $^{***} p < 0.001.$ $E =$ School

39.4 Discussion

This article sought to analyze the factors that explain the adoption of a *blended learning* model by secondary school teachers. Based on the questionnaire results, we identified two factors (Table 39.7) that affect incorporating this type of strategy.

The first factor that affects the adoption of a *blended* model corresponds to the teacher's profile (Table 39.7). This result is consistent with previous studies by Aldunate and Nussbaum (2013), who indicated that the teacher's profile will positively or negatively impact the success of educational innovation. Likewise, Almerich et al. (2016) pointed out that teachers are crucial in introducing ICT into educational practice. The study by Kim et al. (2020) indicates that teachers who are familiar with ICTs will positively adopt the use of ICTs in their instruction.

The second factor that affects adopting a *blended* model corresponds to the proposed instructional design (Table 39.7).

This result is in line with other studies that indicate that teachers can be more effective when they can easily incorporate the instructional design guidelines of the teaching model proposed by their leaders (Toquero et al. 2021). On the other hand, the study by Persico and Pozzi (2015) indicates that to speed up the adoption process in *blended learning* educational scenarios, it is necessary to socialize the instructional design among all the actors involved, particularly the teachers.

Inside of this factor, we can confirm that the majority of the teachers who adopted the *blended learning* model had the flexibility of adapting the synchronous class as a function of the results obtained by the students in the activities of evaluation training (Table 39.6), which is in line with those proposed by Albo and Hernandez-Leo (2021). who indicated that instructional design improves teaching practices through evidence-based decision-making.

In the context of the COVID-19 emergency, the incorporation of technologies for teaching was accelerated. In the context of this study, it was observed that the time investment (Table 39.2) to adapt to the *blended learning* model was high. As Allen et al. (2020) indicate, the adaptation of transforming teaching in confinement contexts involved great efforts by teachers. To decrease the effort and amount of time to incorporate ICTs, there must be initial teacher training addressing different models of ICT integration for hybrid learning. The training should delve into the instructional design required for asynchronous stages and how the results of that design feed into synchronous class planning. Previous studies have shown that if initial teacher training provides little instruction in technology integration into the classroom, the use of ICTs in the teaching exercise will be lower than expected (Graziano 2017).

39.5   Conclusions and Future Work

The objective of this study was to answer the research question, "What factors could favor the adoption of a blended learning model by secondary school teachers?" Our results allowed us to conclude that to ensure the success of an educational innovation, the teachers must have the skills to incorporate ICTs into teaching and have at their disposal an instructional design known by all the actors involved.

Among the contributions of this study, we highlight that it is crucial to bring technology closer to teachers. On the one hand, we suggest that educational institutions that train teachers incorporate a high offering of experiences with technology to teachers being trained. Also, it is suggested that, for practicing teachers, their schools generate systematic training in technology through continuous learning experiences.

In addition, this study specifies which elements of instructional design have the most significant impact: *synchronous class adaptation* and *feedback*. For decision-makers in the school environment, this implies the priority of efforts when implementing blended learning models should be to generate teaching capacities to provide feedback to students and adapt synchronous classes based on the evidence provided by formative assessment.

As future work, the need arises to work with teachers who identify as mass followers and late adopters, with whom knowledge gaps about ICTs and preconceptions about the blended learning model could be counteracted. The results associated with initial teacher training have to be deepened with teachers-in-training and higher education institutions to adapt the study programs to society's needs.

39.6   Limitations

Finally, one of the limitations of this research corresponds to the sample size with which we worked in this case study. Although this was not an obstacle to finding statistically significant relationships, it does not allow us to rule out relevant effects that have not appeared in this research. This is the case with the benefit perception factor of the model, where no statistically significant relationships were found in the difficulty of adopting the *blended* model.

In the same vein, the fact that this is a case study implies that we worked with a limited number of subjects, activities, and skills in a limited period. Thus, future research should test the blended model more extensively in sample size and greater heterogeneity of experiences in implementing *blended models* in different subjects, school contexts, and educational levels.

Acknowledgements We thank the teachers of the five schools involved in this study for their valuable participation, and we recognize the work of all teachers during the pandemic.

The authors acknowledge the technical support of Writing Lab, Institute for the Future of Education, Tecnologico de Monterrey, Mexico, in the production of this work.

Annexes

Factorial loads table https://drive.google.com/file/d/1DcTy2Lb1ibEcZnw3Tv_ysQg
z0nV_eVhs/view?usp=sharing
  Polycoric correlation matrix https://drive.google.com/file/d/1ERZC8KepMVU
2MgQkvYWIYdU1ru7F1JKm/view?usp=sharing

References

Albo L, Hernandez-Leo D (2021) EdCrumble, a data-enriched visual authoring design tool for blended learning. IEEE Trans Learn Technol 14(1):55–68. https://doi.org/10.1109/TLT.2020.3040475

Aldunate R, Nussbaum M (2013) Teacher adoption of technology. Comput Hum Behav 29(3):519–524. https://doi.org/10.1016/J.CHB.2012.10.017

Allen J, Rowan L, Singh P (2020) Teaching and teacher education in the time of COVID-19 48(3):233–236. https://doi.org/10.1080/1359866X.2020.1752051

Almerich G, Orellana N, Suárez-Rodríguez J, Díaz- García I (2016) Teachers' information and communication technology competences: a structural approach. Comput Educ 100:110–125. https://doi.org/10.1016/J.COMPEDU.2016.05.002

Anthony B et al (2020) Blended learning adoption and implementation in higher education: a theoretical and systematic review. Technol Knowl Learn 2020:1–48. https://doi.org/10.1007/S10 758-020-09477-Z

Apandi AM, Raman A (2020a) Factors affecting successful implementation of blended learning at higher education. Int J Inst Technol Soc Sci 1(1):13–23. Accessed: 08 Aug 2021. [Online]. Available: https://ijitsc.net/journal/index.php/home/article/view/12

Apandi AM, Raman A (2020b) Factors affecting successful implementation of blended learning at higher education. Int J Instr Technol Soc Sci 1(1):13–23. [Online] Available: https://ijitsc.net/journal/index.php/home/article/view/12. Accessed 09 Aug 2021

Graziano KJ (2017) Peer teaching in a flipped teacher education classroom. TechTrends 61(2):121–129. https://doi.org/10.1007/s11528-016-0077-9

Jeffrey. Wooldridge, Introducción a la Econometría. 4e., 4°. Cengage Learning Editores S.A. de C.V

Kim MJ, Lee CK, Preis MW (2020) The impact of innovation and gratification on authentic experience, subjective well-being, and behavioral intention in virtual tourism reality: the moderating role of technology readiness. Telemat Inf 49:101349. https://doi.org/10.1016/J.TELE.2020.101349

Mehring J (2016) Present research on the flipped classroom and potential tools for the EFL classroom 33(1):1–10. http://dx.doi.org/https://doi.org/10.1080/07380569.2016.1139912

Persico D, Pozzi F (2015) Informing learning design with learning analytics to improve teacher inquiry. Br J Edu Technol 46(2):230–248. https://doi.org/10.1111/BJET.12207

Rasheed RA, Kamsin A, Abdullah NA (2020) Challenges in the online component of blended learning: a systematic review. Comput Educ 144:103701. https://doi.org/10.1016/J.COMPEDU.2019.103701

Rasheed RA, Kamsin A, Abdullah NA (2021) An approach for scaffolding students peer-learning self-regulation strategy in the online component of blended learning. IEEE Access 9:30721–30738. https://doi.org/10.1109/ACCESS.2021.3059916

Revell AJ, Ayotte BJ (2020) Novel approaches to teaching aging and disability: active learning through design and exploration. Int J Aging Human Dev 91415020912944. https://doi.org/10.1177/0091415020912944

Stöhr C, Demazière C, Adawi T (2020) The polarizing effect of the online flipped classroom. Comput Educ 147:103789. https://doi.org/10.1016/J.COMPEDU.2019.103789

Ticker C (2020) Balance with blended learning: partner with your students to reimagine ... Catlin R. Tucker—Google Libros. Corwin, SAGE

Toquero CMD, Sonsona DA, Talidong KJB (2021) Game-based learning: reinforcing a paradigm transition on pedagogy amid COVID-19 to complement emergency online education. Int J Didact Stud 2(2):10458. https://doi.org/10.33902/IJODS.2021269730

Videla CGB, Meneses EL, Diaz JM (2020) Teachers' perception of educational challenges in the face of the COVID 19. New Trends Issues Proc Humanities Soc Sci 7(3):224–234. https://doi.org/10.18844/prosoc.v7i3.5256

Vivanco M (1999) Análisis Estadístico Multivariable. Editorial Universitaria, Santiago

Chapter 40
Design, Development, and Evaluation of a Predictive Model for Regular School Dropout in the Chilean Educational System

Patricio Rodríguez and Alexis Villanueva

40.1 Introduction

School failure or exclusion is central in analyzing school systems due to their long-term effects on students' lives during their school years and subsequent integration into adult life. This phenomenon is manifested when the school system fails to ensure that students reach certain levels of schooling, experiencing situations such as grade repetition and temporary or permanent dropout (OECD 2010). This results in training future adults with low qualifications or students who do not complete their school training at the secondary level.

In this work, we designed, developed, and evaluated predictive models for school dropout in the Chilean educational system using administrative data configured in school trajectory format to understand the behavior of student withdrawal over time and identify the factors that most affect it.

The administrative data come from multiple sources, at the individual level and with much detailed breakdown (schools, territories, among others), describing the students' passage through the educational system from 2004 to 2019.

A predictive binary classification approach with decision trees [*Decision Tree* (M. Jena y S. Dehuri 2020), *XGBoost* (Bentéjac et al. 2021), *LightGBM* (Bentéjac et al. 2021), and *CatBoost* (Bentéjac et al. 2021)] was used, together with specific mitigation measures for the class instability problem.

P. Rodríguez (✉)
Institute of Education and Center for Advanced Research in Education, University of Chile, Santiago, Chile
e-mail: prodriguez@uchile.cl

A. Villanueva
Center for Advanced Research in Education, University of Chile, Santiago, Chile
e-mail: alexis.villanueva@ciae.uchile.cl

40.2 Background

40.2.1 Relevance of Studying School Dropout

According to Valenzuela et al. (2019), school exclusion has moved from the perspective that views dropout as a problem of the student's context, trajectory, and responsibility to one that understands the problem as systemic, for which the school and society as a whole are responsible.

Thus, the causes of dropout are found at different levels associated with the student, their family, school, context, and social environment (Bellei and Contreras 2003; Christenson and Thurlow 2004; Torres et al. 2015; Weybright et al. 2017; Witte et al. 2013). As exclusion is a gradual and cumulative process, some indicators warn of future disengagement even from the early years of the school trajectory (Christenson and Thurlow 2004).

International evidence indicates that dropping out of school permanently penalizes students (Valenzuela et al. 2019) in aspects such as obtaining jobs with low value and prospects, fewer skills to face the work world, lower-income, and lower pensions (OECD 2010; Dussaillant 2017). In social terms, the consequences include lower tax revenue, the significant economic burden on the State for social programs, higher crime rates (OECD 2010), and lower social cohesion (Christenson and Thurlow 2004; Torres et al. 2015).

In the case of Chile, the economic impact of school dropouts on lifetime earnings for a cohort of 15-year-old dropouts in 2011 was estimated at $ 1.8 billion US, that is, 0.88% of the GDP for that year; unemployment costs of $893 million US (0.42% of GDP) and lower tax revenues of $267 million US (0.13% of GDP) (Kokkidou et al. unpublished).

40.2.2 Risk Factors for School Dropout

According to international literature (Valenzuela et al. 2019), there are three theoretical approaches to understanding school dropout reasons, which can be (1) from the outside (*pull-out*), with external factors that cause students to drop out (such as family, classmates, or "the economic climate") (Doll et al. 2013; Stearns and Glennie 2006), (2) from within (*push-out*), due to poor academic support or mismatch between student level of instruction and student skills (Doll et al. 2013; Stearns and Glennie 2006; Ecker-Lyster and Niileksela 2016), or (3) a progressive process of student distraction and disenchantment with the educational system (*fall-out*) (Doll et al. 2013). Therefore, the multiple factors influencing the path to school dropout are multidimensional (Valenzuela et al. 2019). Prevalent **individual** factors include school grade repetition causing students to be overaged in their classes (Bornsheuer et al. 2011), poor school attendance (Şahin et al. 2016), low performance (Fortin et al. 2013), and specific learning needs (Gonzalez and Cramer 2013). **Socioemotional** factors are attitudes toward learning (Zaff et al. 2017), non-academic problem behaviors (Weybright et al. 2017; Witte et al. 2013) and school mobility (Herbers et al. 2013; Gasper et al. 2012). **Sociodemographic** ones include gender, ethnicity, and nationality issues (Rumberger 1995; Witte and Rogge 2013). **Family-related** factors relate to socioeconomic status and parental involvement (Strom and Boster 2014; Adelman and Székely 2017). **School-related** ones include the characteristics of the school (Witte and Rogge 2013), its resources (Dussaillant 2017; Ecker-Lyster and Niileksela 2016), the relationship between students and teachers (Winding and Andersen 2015), participation in school activities (Román 2013), and community aspects (such as geographic location and urbanity of the environment) (Witte et al. 2013; Zaff et al. 2017). Finally, the **contextual** issues are understood as potential "pull factors" that encourage early job placement (Kattan and Székely 2017).

40.2.3 Predicting School Dropout Using Machine Learning

A meta-analysis in the academic literature and case studies on machine learning applications to predict school dropouts between 2013 and 2017 found that algorithms such as neural networks or decision trees are primarily used. These consider dropout prediction as a binary classification exercise through a dropout vs. non-dropout dichotomy (Mduma et al. 2019).

In line with that, Sorensen (2019) elaborated a decision tree model to predict the dropout during the second period in the last year of primary education, obtaining 75% precisión for the dropout cases using academic and individual indicators without considering institutional factors. However, she does not indicate the false-positive rate of her model.

Since, substantially fewer students drop out than graduate, this imbalance must be remedied (Mduma et al. 2019). Thus, reporting performance evaluation metrics for both cases is necessary and considering specific training solutions with data about the imbalances.

A practical approach to dealing with data imbalance is subsampling training data (Márquez-Vera et al. 2016). In this way, Márquez-Vera et al. (2016) used a geometric mean between the rate of true positives and true negatives of 0.891 through a decision tree using individual, academic, and school indicators to predict dropout the following year among 419 secondary school students in Mexico. Additionally, Márquez-Vera et al. (2016) presented their results in the form of a *glass box*. The predictions allowed informed decision-making and specific interventions for the diagnosed needs of the student. Regarding the above, Lundberg et al. (2019) proposed, in the case of assembled tree algorithms, using SHAP (*Shapley Additive Explanation*) values to quantify the contribution of each variable individually toward the total predicted value.

40.3 Methodology

To develop the predictive model, we used data obtained from secondary sources; namely, those collected, organized, and published by the Chilean Ministry of Education since 2004 in its open data platform, and to a lesser extent, data related to SIMCE[1,2,3] made available by the Agency for Quality in Education.

The minimum information unit available in this data is the student, identified anonymously utilizing a masking method on each student's Unique National Role (MRUN) identifier. In this way, the different data sets can be crossed, and we can temporally trace each individual's trajectories.

These data sets are available in the form of file series by year and, in some cases, measurement level by the results of standardized census tests and SIMCE surveys.

The use of administrative data to reconstruct the school trajectories of all students is an excellent opportunity to identify trends and patterns that lead to dropouts. However, some limitations must be considered since certain factors identified as relevant in the literature but challenging to measure or non-existent in administrative data are excluded, such as contextual factors or problematic non-academic behaviors.

40.3.1 Construction of School Paths

The reconstruction of trajectories consists of a series of steps to produce a temporally ordered sequence of the transit of each student from the first level of regular primary education to the last reported period.

Thus, trajectory tables with ordered sequences are generated for each student and year. All the available data are included, and the student's situation regarding their trajectory is described: enrollment status and dropout incidence, among others. With the data thus ordered, new variables relevant to the model are calculated, including significant switches and school changes between years or within the same year, among others. The procedure is the following:

First, the available information on enrollment and performance was homologated, articulating the axes of the trajectories and cementing their traceability. Then, we assigned the information from other sources, which complements the student's information.

Second, each student was assigned to a cohort (i.e., having the same year of entry to the first level of regular primary education). We excluded trajectories before the

---

[1] Sistema de Medición de la Calidad de la Educación: https://www.agenciaeducacion.cl/simce/.

[2] The results of surveys for parents and students are also linked to the SIMCE measurement process.

[3] These data include the Personal and Social Development Indicators (IDPS from its name in Spanish), whose objective is to measure quality in education more broadly, including non-academic aspects, specifically: self-esteem and school motivation, school coexistence environment, participation, and citizen training and hygiene habits and healthy life (Agencia de la Calidad de la Educación 2017).

first available period (2004) since there was not enough data to trace these trajectories from the beginning.

Third, once each student's cohort information was assigned, the base trajectories were reconstructed to contain only the enrollment and student performance data, matching available enrollment-performance pairs for each year and MRUN. When some enrollments or returns lacked an opposite, fictitious enrollment and return data were constructed by doubling the available case and filling in the unavailable columns with null values.

Fourth, when a student had more than one enrollment or annual performance data, we established criteria to identify the enrollment-performance pairing that should represent the period within the trajectory, considering that only one of the multiple possible combinations should prevail.

After this procedure, we could trace the trajectory of each student in the cohorts since 2004, totaling **3,847,469** trajectories. However, because assigning each trajectory to a cohort was necessary, it was only possible to construct trajectories of students who entered the first year of primary education in the first reported period (i.e., 2004). Therefore, the number of students with reconstructed trajectories increased each successive year and stabilized after 12 years (when the students in the 2004 cohort reached the last grade level).

Even after 12 years, it was not possible to reconstruct the trajectory of all students because the cohort of origin was unknown, which happens, for example, in the cases of foreigners who do not start school education in the country.

40.3.2   Summary of the Trajectories

Given the amount of data available, we opted for traditional supervised machine learning methods to generate the predictive model over larger-scale alternatives traditionally used in forecasting exercises, such as models based on neural networks. This is because such models work with training samples much larger than those available to us, and their interpretability, in contrast to traditional classification methods, is much lower.

Thus, the trajectories of each student must be reduced to a single observation that summarizes and describes their passage through school education. To do this, we generated a **summary table** in which variables built from grouping the trajectories were added, describing the final situation of the student, their most frequent data, and other additional elements available in the data. These variables were related to factors identified in the literature and other descriptors of the trajectory.

Each trajectory summary operationalizes regular dropout, which is measured considering situations such as a student who, being enrolled in a grade level for children and young people one year, is out of this educational system the following year and may be out of the school system or in an adult learning modality. Consistency descriptors are also included to control the quality with which the trajectories

Table 40.1 Count of variables according to risk factor

Risk factors type	Number of variables
Individual	28
Socioemotional	11
Sociodemographic	7
Family[a]	1
School	32
Community	7
Contextual	0
Consistency	5
Additional	22

[a]The socioeconomic level calculated as the mean between the standardized reported household income and the standardized maximum parental education is included. Additionally, a multi-level imputation was carried out to deal with the high number of missing cases.

related to the methods described are presented to treat multiple enrollments or inconsistencies in the data. Thus, 113 variables ended up being grouped according to the factors (Table 40.1).

Using administrative data limits the availability of contextual or family variables compared to the more widely available individual and school data.

40.3.3 Preparation of Training Sample

In the training sample information that allows comparing the summary variables of trajectories heading toward regular dropout with those that do not, we created a set of **counterfactual summaries** for each observation of a student who drops out. For this, we truncated the school trajectory summaries of students who do not drop out or do so at a later year and grade level. Thus, these were abbreviated on multiple occasions based on their counterfactual similarity (evaluated by year and level reached) to a case of desertion.

However, the above procedure produces a severe imbalance in the training sample. To avoid adjusting a model to a sample in which the relevant class is substantially a minority, we chose a stratified subsampling per the student's gender, dependency[4] of the last school, the last year, and registered grade level, thus modifying the balance of classes to generate a proportion of 1:1, reducing the negative class (does not drop out) from **26,793,262** counterfactuals to **345,874**, a number equal to that of dropouts.

---

[4] In Chile, a student can enroll in 4 types of schools described according to how they are financed: public, subsidized, private paid, and delegated administration.

40.3.4   *Training and Validation of Machine Learning Models*

Algorithms from the decision tree family were used to produce machine learning models. Specifically, the basic decision tree algorithm was the base model and then a set of decision trees with gradient enhancement using *XGBoost*, *LightGBM*, and *CatBoost*.

The test sample was built with data up to 2018, with stratified and balanced sampling per the criteria stated in the previous section. Then, the results were validated in an unbalanced test sample using summaries of trajectories that reached the year 2019 and were or were not dropouts in 2020, totaling **2,802,156** trajectories of which **47,632** (1.7%) were attrition.

Given the natural imbalance of the phenomenon, the following were used as performance metrics of the models: the *recall*[5] and *precision*[6] of both classes, the geometric mean between the *sensitivity*[7] and the *specificity*[8] (GM-score), and the f1 *score*[9] of the positive class.

To deal with the cases lost due to missing indicators of personal and social development (IDPS) and the decision not to impute these variables, we developed three different models: One without considering the IDPS indicators, one with them and eliminating the cases not available in their entirety and, finally, one with three of the four indicators because the indicator of hygiene habits and healthy life was measured one year after the previous ones and had a greater amount of non-existent data.

40.4   Results

The results of the four algorithms on the test sample and not including the IDPS indicators are in Table 40.2.

The performance of the tree algorithms with gradient enhancement is superior to the traditional tree, with *LightGBM* slightly superior to *CatBoost* in the geometric mean between *sensitivity* and *specificity*. This indicates that although *CatBoost* achieves a higher performance in accuracy for class 1 (meaning fewer false positives) globally, this improvement is not enough to establish effectively higher performance.

---

[5] Value between 0 and 1 is the hit rate of the binary classifier of a given class concerning the total number of cases belonging to that class. The false-negative rate is 1 − *recall*. This rate is essential because minimizing false negatives ensures that all students who could drop out receive support and are not undetected.

[6] Value between 0 and 1 is the hit rate concerning the total predictions that the binary classifier makes for a given class. The false-positive rate is 1 − *precision*.

[7] *Recall* of the positive class in a binary classifier.

[8] *Recall* of the negative class in a binary classifier.

[9] Harmonic mean between the *precision* and the *recall* of a class, in this case, the positive one.

Table 40.2 Resultados iniciales

Algorithm	Class 0 (DOES NOT dropout)		Class 1 (DOES dropout)		GM-Score	Time (s)
	Recall	Precision	Recall	Precision		
Decision tree	0.7995	0.9959	0.8112	0.0654	0.8053	70.70
XGBoost	0.9391	0.9967	0.8201	0.1888	0.8776	284.82
LigthGBM	**0.9317**	**0.9970**	**0.8397**	**0.1754**	**0.8845**	**67.18**
CatBoost	0.9211	0.9972	0.8488	0.1569	0.8842	407.24

Since the counterfactuals were randomly selected in the training sample to balance the cases, the stability of the results in 100 different samples was evaluated using the model already mentioned and training only with the *LightGBM* algorithm (Fig. 40.1).

Therefore, with multiple samples, stable results were maintained with a variation that, in the worst case, had a range of variation of approximately 0.014. Therefore, the randomness of stratified and random subsampling did not significantly affect performance.

The models that consider IDPS factors are shown in Table 40.3 using only *LightGBM*.

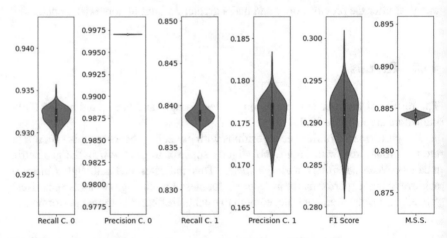

Fig. 40.1 Violin diagram showing the stability of results in multiple samples

Table 40.3 Results with idps samples

Sample	Class 0		Class 1		GM-Score
	Recall	Precision	Recall	Precision	
Base	0.9317	0.9970	0.8397	0.1754	0.8845
with IDPS	0.9237	0.9972	0.8611	0.1745	0.8919
Partial IDPS	**0.9266**	**0.9971**	**0.8613**	**0.1847**	**0.8934**

Although the performance is slightly higher with the IDPS (totally and partially), it should be considered that, on the one hand, of 2,802,156 summaries of trajectories evaluated in the base model, only 1,654,577 had information on the IDPS and, at the same time, not considering the IDPS with lagging students, this value increased to 1,664,253. On the other hand, the percentage of dropouts was 1.70, 1.84, and 1.89%, respectively. This performance made it impractical to include IDPS in a dropout prediction model, given the cost of obtaining these data versus the marginal improvement it produces.

Finally, the initial *LightGBM* model (Table 40.2) was tested in specific test samples according to dependency and grades (Table 40.4).

As Table 40.4 indicates, performance tends to improve at higher grade levels and in public school dependency. The best performance is in the 3rd cycle plus public dependency; the worst is in primary education plus private school individuals.

There is an apparent relationship between the predictive performance and the percentage of reported dropouts, which also maintains the trends by grade level and public school dependency since in the 1st cycle, the proportion of dropouts is 0.71% among the subsidized schools and increases to 1.60% for paid private school students. In contrast, in the 3rd cycle, this is 1.44% among students in paid private schools vs. 4.52% in public schools, the latter being the segment with the highest dropout in percentage terms.

Table 40.4   Results in sub-samples without IDPS

Level	Dependency	Class 0		Class 1		GM-Score
		Recall	Precision	Recall	Precision	
1st cycle (1st–4th grade)	Pub	0.9364	0.9981	0.8525	0.1387	0.8935
	P.S	0.9223	0.9979	0.7309	0.0627	0.8210
	P.P	0.8742	0.9927	0.6048	0.0726	0.7272
2nd cycle (5th–8th grade)	Pub	0.9444	0.9975	0.8202	0.1609	0.8801
	P.S	0.9377	0.9979	0.7596	0.0923	0.8440
	P.P	0.8984	0.9934	0.5110	0.0578	0.6776
3rd cycle (9th–12th grade)	**Pub**	**0.9361**	**0.9953**	**0.9058**	**0.4018**	**0.9208**
	P.S	0.9372	0.9969	0.8939	0.2819	0.9153
	P.P	0.9486	0.9949	0.6689	0.1601	0.7966
Primary (1st–8th grade)	Pub	0.9404	0.9978	0.8358	0.1492	0.8865
	P.S	0.9297	0.9979	0.7458	0.0755	0.8327
	P.P	0.8854	0.9930	0.5680	0.0666	0.7092
7th–12th grade	Pub	0.9342	0.9957	0.8885	0.3298	0.9110
	P.S	0.9374	0.9970	0.8708	0.2343	0.9035
	P.P	0.9385	0.9944	0.6143	0.1212	0.7593

Pub. = Public; P.S. =Subsidized private; P.P. = Private

Table 40.5 Contribution of risk factors according to type

Risk factor type	Quantity	Relevant variables	Added contribution	Average contribution
Individual	28	17	0.6493	0.0382
Socioemotional	11	4	0.0282	0.0070
Sociodemographic	7	3	0.0381	0.0127
Family	1	1	0.0078	0.0078
School	32	14	0.0938	0.0067
Community	7	2	0.0076	0.0038
Contextual	0	0	0.0000	0.0000
Consistency	5	3	0.0173	0.0058
Additional	22	12	0.1470	0.0122

Table 40.5 shows the contribution of the risk factors identified in Table 40.1, considering two values: (1) The aggregate contribution, which is the sum of the importance of each variable.[10] in the set and (2) the average contribution, which is the aggregate contribution divided into the number of variables by type. Those variables whose contribution to the summed model was less than 0.001 were not considered. This discarded 57 of the 113 variables and provided an average contribution of greater interest.

Individual factors have the most significant contribution to predictions, consistent with what is observed in the international literature. However, each trajectory's community, sociodemographic, and consistency factors are also relevant. Of the variables with importance greater than 0.01, two are socioemotional (changes in the school between and within the year), and two are school variables (dependency and number of teachers in the school). Therefore, in contrast to previous studies, including non-individual dimensions results in a substantive contribution to predicting school dropout.

40.5 Discussion

In this work, we designed, developed, and evaluated a predictive model of regular school dropout based on administrative data from the Chilean educational system, using what the literature indicates as factors associated with school dropout.

We constructed 3,847,469 summaries of student trajectories in the cohorts between 2004 and 2019, synthesizing their passage through the school system using 113 variables. In contrast to previous studies, variables at the family or community school level contributed significantly to the prediction.

---

[10] The importance of a variable is calculated as the mean (standardized between 0 and 1) of the absolute value of its SHAP values.

Comparatively, this is a first study that uses a quasi-census sample of cohorts followed throughout the school year, both in primary and secondary education, which identifies the most critical risk factors for dropping out throughout the education cycle and the protective factors to stay in the school system after 12 years.

This represents a significant increase over the samples used in previous work. As expected in problems of this type, the low prevalence of the phenomenon forced us to decide which aspects of the prediction to prioritize. In this case, it was preferred to minimize false negatives using the GM- score as a performance metric in the model. The best results were obtained in public schools (grades 9–12 and 7–12) and charter schools (grades 9–12 and 7–12).

The performance of the model is stable in the selection of counterfactuals. The SIMCE standardized test results and IDPS do not produce significant performance improvements. This is noteworthy because it reflects that the variables of lagging behind in school are more relevant to explaining the risk of dropping out than students' performance in specific disciplines.

40.6 Conclusions

School failure, as a general phenomenon, and dropout as a specific event are well-studied and well-known areas in the literature. However, the local effort to obtain a broad and global vision of its behavior and evolution to prevent and anticipate it is still a pending challenge requiring data and systemization. The correctness and consistency of the data is a challenge since the data collection in previous years was manual and decentralized, generating problems that can be managed.

We hope that the methodology and the case presented in this article will help professionals and public officials in data systematization and those designing and developing their prediction models for school failure. The proposed strategy makes it possible to correctly predict more than 93% of the students who will remain throughout the 12-year educational cycle in Chile and almost 84% of those who will drop out of school at some point, results that are better than comparable studies in other countries.

The development of a model such as the present one has implications for public policies. It makes it possible to identify specific schools and individuals on which to focus resources to manage risk and understand from a quantitative perspective which factors have the most significant impact on school dropout over time. Thus, long-term policies can be generated to manage these factors, such as academic lag, so that the dropout prevalence in future cohorts of students is lower than in previous ones. At the same time, the model's results allow school communities to identify with high precision in each school's specific grade level those students most at risk of dropping out and who require support and protection strategies to ensure positive school trajectories. Examples include those who have recently repeated grades, who have high absenteeism, who have repeated more than one grade and are overaged, or who are male migrants who have not started their educational cycle in Chile.

Likewise, the results show that these efforts should be more substantial in public high schools having a lower socioeconomic student population.

In summary, school dropout behaves as described, and its prediction is feasible and socially and economically profitable. Through techniques to make transparent predictions, it is possible to build a robust and stable predictive model that enables informed decision-making specific to the needs of the students.

Acknowledgements We are grateful for the financing granted by the ANID/PIA/Basal Funds for Centers of Excellence FB0003 and ANID-FONDEF IT17I0006 projects.

The authors acknowledge the technical support of Writing Lab, Institute for the Future of Education, Tecnologico de Monterrey, Mexico, in the production of this work.

References

Adelman M, Székely M (2017) An overview of school dropout in Central America: unresolved issues and new challenges for education progress. Eur J Educ Res 6(3, Art no 3). https://doi.org/10.12973/eu-jer.6.3.235

Agencia de la Calidad de la Educación (2021) Indicadores de Desarrollo Personal y Social (IDPS) medidos a través de cuestionarios. Informe Técnico. Accessed: ago. 10, 2021. [Online]. Available: http://bibliotecadigital.mineduc.cl//handle/20.500.12365/4564

Bentéjac C, Csörgő A, Martínez-Muñoz G (2021) A comparative analysis of gradient boosting algorithms. Artif Intell Rev 54(3):1937–1967. https://doi.org/10.1007/s10462-020-09896-5

Bornsheuer JN, Polonyi MA, Andrews M, Fore B, Onwuegbuzie AJ (2011) The relationship between ninth-grade retention and on-time graduation in a Southeast Texas High School 16(2, Art no 2)

Bellei C, Contreras D (2003) Deserción escolar en Chile: contexto y resultados de investigaciones. en 12 años de Escolaridad Oblitatoria, LOM ediciones

Christenson SL, Thurlow ML (2004) School dropouts: prevention considerations, interventions, and challenges. Curr Dir Psychol Sci 13(1 Art no 1). https://doi.org/10.1111/j.0963-7214.2004.01301010.x

Doll JJ, Eslami Z, Walters L (2013) Understanding why students drop out of high school, according to their own reports: are they pushed or pulled, or do they fall out? A comparative analysis of seven nationally representative studies. SAGE Open 3(4, Art no 4). https://doi.org/10.1177/2158244013503834

Dussaillant F (2017) Deserción escolar en Chile. Propuestas para la investigación y la política pública. Doc 18:1–18

Ecker-Lyster M, Niileksela C (2016) Keeping students on track to graduate: a synthesis of school dropout trends, prevention, and intervention initiatives. J-Risk Issues 19(2, Art no 2)

Fortin L, Marcotte D, Diallo T, Potvin P, Royer É (2013) A multidimensional model of school dropout from an 8-year longitudinal study in a general high school population. Eur J Psychol Educ 28(2, Art no 2)

Gasper J, Deluca S, Estacion A (2012) Switching schools: revisiting the relationship between school mobility and high school dropout. Am Educ Res J 49(3, Art no 3) https://doi.org/10.3102/0002831211415250

Gonzalez L, Cramer E (2013) Class placement and academic and behavioral variables as predictors of graduation for students with disabilities. Florida International University

Herbers JE, Reynolds AJ, Chen C (2013) School mobility and developmental outcomes in young adulthood. Dev Psychopathol 25:501–515. https://doi.org/10.1017/S0954579412001204

Jena M, Dehuri S (2020) Decision tree for classification and regression: a state-of-the-art review. Informatica 44(4). https://doi.org/10.31449/inf.v44i4.3023

Kattan RB, Székely M (2017) Analyzing upper secondary education dropout in Latin America through a cohort approach. J Educ Learn 6(4, Art no 4). https://doi.org/10.5539/jel.v6n4p12

Kokkidou E, Rodríguez P, Mondaca J, Matas M (unpublished) El impacto económico de la deserción escolar en Chile

Lundberg SM, Erion GG, Lee S-I (2021) Consistent individualized feature attribution for tree ensembles. ArXiv180203888 Cs Stat, mar. 2019, Accedido: ago. 10, 2021. [Online]. Available http://arxiv.org/abs/1802.03888

Márquez-Vera C, Cano A, Romero C, Noaman AYM, Fardoun HM, Ventura S (2016) Early dropout prediction using data mining: a case study with high school students. Expert Syst 33(1):107–124. https://doi.org/10.1111/exsy.12135

Mduma N, Kalegele K, Machuve D (2019) A survey of machine learning approaches and techniques for student dropout prediction. Data Sci J 18:14. https://doi.org/10.5334/dsj-2019-014

OECD (2010) Overcoming school failure: policies that work. OECD project description

Román M (2013) Factores asociados al abandono y la deserción escolar en américa latina: una mirada en conjunto. REICE Rev Iberoam Sobre Calid Efic Cambio En Educ 11(2, Art no 2)

Rumberger RW (1995) Dropping out of middle school: a multilevel analysis of students and schools. Am Educ Res Assoc 32(3, Art no 3)

Strom RE, Boster FJ (2007) Dropping out of high school: a meta-analysis assessing the effect of messages in the home and in school. Commun Educ October 2014(October 2014). https://doi.org/10.1080/03634520701413804

Stearns E, Glennie E (2006) When and why dropouts leave school: lessons from North Carolina. Youth Soc 38(1, Art no 1)

Şahin Ş, Arseven Z, Kılıç A (2016) Causes of student absenteeism and school dropouts. Int J Instr 6(2, Art no 2). https://doi.org/10.12973/iji.2016.9115a

Sorensen LC (2019) Big Data in educational administration: an application for predicting school dropout risk. Educ Adm Q 55(3):404–446. https://doi.org/10.1177/0013161X18799439

Torres JD, Acevedo D, Gallo LA (2015) Causas y consecuencias de la deserción y repitencia escolar: Una visión general en el contexto latinoamericano. Cult Educ Soc 6(2 Art no 2)

Valenzuela JP, Ruiz C, Contreras M (2021) Revisión de antecedentes sobre exclusión educativa: Una mirada a la deserción y repitencia escolar. Proyecto FONDEF IT17I1006 "Un sistema nacional de protección de trayectorias educativas: disminuyendo la exclusión educativa en la enseñanza escolar y previniendo la deserción en educación superior", ene. 2019. Accessed: ago. 10, 2021. [Online]. Available http://www.ciae.uchile.cl/download.php?file=noticias/00_1619125708.pdf

Weybright EH, Caldwell LL, Wegner L, Smith EA (2017) Predicting secondary school dropout among South African adolescents: a survival analysis approach. South Afr J Educ 37(2, Art no 2). https://doi.org/10.15700/saje.v37n2a1353

Winding TN, Andersen JH (2015) Socioeconomic differences in school dropout among young adults: the role of social relations. BMC Public Health 1–12. https://doi.org/10.1186/s12889-015-2391-0

Witte K, Cabus S, Thyssen G, Groot W, Brink HM (2013) A critical review of the literature on school dropout. Educ Res Rev 10:13–28. https://doi.org/10.1016/j.edurev.2013.05.002

Witte K, Rogge N (2013) Dropout from secondary education: all's well that begins well. Eur J Educ II

Zaff JF, Donlan A, Gunning A, Anderson SE, Mcdermott E, Sedaca M (2017) Factors that promote high school graduation: a review of the literature. Educ Psychol Rev 447–476. https://doi.org/10.1007/s10648-016-9363-5

Chapter 41
Government's COVID-19 Immunization Drive Through National Immunization Management System (NIMS) in Pakistan

Asad Abbas, Liya Wang, and Abdul Mannan

41.1 Background

In December 2019, the world was shaken when the first coronavirus (COVID-19) case was detected in Wuhan, China (Zeng et al. 2020). After that, it was witnessed that the coronavirus became unstoppable and spread globally within a matter of days. In February 2020, the World Health Organization (WHO) several times issued an advisory about deadly viruses and reiterated its consequences. However, notable governmental ignorance worldwide (World Health Organization 2020) was evidenced when almost 200 countries went into lockdown (Roche et al. 2020). In the lockdowns, governments partially or fully halted all socio-economic activities and asked all citizens to immediately observe isolation at home. The cause of the lockdowns was a lack of information about the initial symptoms of the deadly virus.

After immense efforts by medical scientists and paramedic staff, this unknown deadly virus became recognized as Severe Acute Respiratory Syndrome (SARS), belonging to the coronavirus family. Initially declared as the SARS coronavirus, the

A. Abbas (✉)
Writing Lab, Institute for the Future of Education, Tecnologico de Monterrey, Monterrey, NL 64849, Mexico
e-mail: asad.abbas@tec.mx

L. Wang
Center of Microbes, Development and Health, Institut Pasteur of Shanghai Chinese Academy of Sciences, Shanghai, China

A. Mannan
Faculty of Health and Medicine, School of Biomedical Sciences and Pharmacy, University of Newcastle, Callaghan, NSW, Australia

A. Abbas
School of Government and Public Transformation, Tecnologico de Monterrey, San Pedro Garza García, Mexico

© The Author(s), under exclusive license to Springer Nature Singapore Pte Ltd. 2022   507
S. Hosseini et al. (eds.), *Technology-Enabled Innovations in Education*,
Transactions on Computer Systems and Networks,
https://doi.org/10.1007/978-981-19-3383-7_41

WHO later announced it as SARS-Coronavirus (SARS-CoV-2 or COVID-19). The initial symptoms of the COVID-19 pandemic manifested as dry cough, high fever, and loss of taste. After acquiring basic information about COVID-19 symptoms, the WHO issued protection guidelines to avoid transmission of the virus, including social distancing, using face masks, and hand sanitizing (World Health Organization 2021).

41.1.1 Discussion Questions

COVID-19 immunization vaccination drive during the pandemic crisis:

1. What are the strategies of the Pakistani Government to fight the COVID-19 pandemic?
2. How is the government aligning and executing its established policies?
3. What are the guidelines for obtaining COVID-19 vaccination under National Immunization Management System (NIMS) program?

41.2 Pakistani Government Initiatives During COVID-19

During the crisis, each government worldwide planned and executed its national policies to protect its citizens and fight against the COVID-19 outbreak. To combat COVID-19, the government of Pakistan undertook a series of initiatives to battle the virus. It used ICT to effectively implement electronic government (e-government) initiatives (see Table 41.1). The first step was to establish a portal for awareness of the harmful effects of COVID-19 in society. Later, Pakistan's federal government

Table 41.1 Government of Pakistan initiatives to combat the covid-19 pandemic

	Initiatives	Description	URL
1	COVID-19 official website	Detailed information about COVID-19 cases in Pakistan (by province) and around the globe	https://covid.gov.pk
2	Smart lockdown policy	To reduce pressure on hospitals with effective tract, trace, and quarantine strategy	https://ncoc.gov.pk
3	Ehsaas Emergency Cash Program	Financial support to low-income families	https://ehsaas.nadra.gov.pk
4	Pass track	Guidelines for international travels to Pakistan	https://passtrack.nitb.gov.pk
5	National immunization management system (NIMS)	Online registration of COVID-19 vaccination	https://www.nims.nadra.gov.pk

collaborated on new "Smart Lockdown" strategies through stakeholder agreements with provincial governments and local businesses. The reason for enforcing the Smart lockdown policy was the shortage of healthcare capacity, including medical facilities, ventilators, and even Real-Time Polymerase Chain Reaction (RT-PCR) for blood samples and swabbing to confirm COVID-19.

The "Smart Lockdown" strategy helped decrease the chances of further pandemic spread through the trace and quarantine method to lessen the burden on the existing healthcare system. Due to timely coordination and effective implementation of these policies, cases of COVID-19 pandemic rapidly decreased within several weeks. However, this policy impacted low-income class families very harshly, where most people are engaged in labor and daily wage occupations. To tackle the resulting unemployment, the government developed new financial support strategies with the help of a public–private partnership (PPP). The PPP strategies engage the National Database and Registration Authority (NADRA), State Bank of Pakistan (SBP), local commercial banks, and the telecom sector to register and transfer funds through mobile payments (Ar and Abbas 2020). The PPP introduced a financial support program called *"Ehsaas Emergency Cash,"* and the Pakistani government allocated 144 million PKR to support eight million families (Khan et al. 2020). The gradual drop in COVID-19 enabled the federal government, in coordination with the provincial governments, to begin reopening different socio-economic sectors step by step (such as construction, industry, and transportation). The government of Pakistan also allowed international tourists and expatriates who had lost their jobs overseas and urgently wished to return home because of the virus. To maintain the travel history of passengers, the government introduced the *"Pass Track"* mobile application and a website, where passengers were required to enter their personal information and upload a valid COVID-19 certificate before international arrival and departure.

In the third and fourth quarters of 2020, through international efforts of medical scientists, some countries like the USA, UK, Russia, China, and India declared breakthroughs on COVID-19 vaccinations. Some of the vaccinations in advanced-stage development achieved more than 90% efficacy and were in second and third trials (see Table 41.2). Some pharmaceutical companies early attained approval from national health drug authorities and agencies based on their trial results. Pfizer + BioNTech was the first manufacturer to gain approval for the COVID-19 vaccine from WHO due to its efficacy. Based on the trial and efficacy of some vaccinations, most countries worldwide requested pre-bookings. Some countries received the first batch of vaccinations (donations or purchases) and started the vaccination process in December 2020 (SAMAA 2021).

After the announcement of China to donate 5,000,000 coronavirus vaccine doses to Pakistan, National Command and Operation Centre (NCOC) took the initiative to form an effective and transparent strategy to provide vaccinations. The first vaccination dose would be given to frontline/ healthcare workers all across Pakistan. To start the immunization drive, the government established an online registration platform, i.e., the NIMS, to kick-start the COVID-19 vaccinations in January 2021. To continue the immunization drive, the Drug Regulatory Authority of Pakistan

Table 41.2 COVID-19 vaccination manufacturers, name of authorized company, status, and efficacy (SAMAA 2021)

Vaccine manufacturer and product name	Authorized in countries	Vaccinations begin	Status	Efficacy
Pfizer + BioNTech BNT161B2	Belgium, Canada, Chile, Costa Rica, Ecuador, Israel, Jordan, Kuwait, Mexico, Philippines, Qatar, Saudi Arabia, Serbia, Singapore, UK, US, WHO	December 8th, 2020	Trial phases 2/3	95%
Moderna MRNA1273	US, Canada, Mexico, EU, Israel	December 2020	Trial phase 3	94.5%
Gamaleya SPUTNIK V	Russia, Belarus, Argentina, Algeria	December 15th, 2020	Trial phase 3	91.4%
Sinovac Biotech CORONAVAC	China, Turkey	October 2020	Trial phase 3	50%
Bharat Biotech COVAXIN	India	January 16th, 2020	Trial phase 3	Results not released
Sinopharm Beijing BBIBP-CORV	China, UAE, Bahrain, Seychelles, Jordan	July 2020	Trial phase 3	79.3%
Oxford University + AstraZeneca CHADOX1/AZD1222	India, UK	January 2021	Trial phase 3	70.4%
CanSino Biologics + The Military Institute of Biology AD5-NCOV	China	June 2020	Trial phase 3	Results not released

(DRAP) is closely working with the government and vaccine manufacturing companies. DRAP approved two COVID-19 vaccine manufacturers for emergency use authorization in Pakistan: Sinopharm's and AstraZeneca (Drug Regulatory Authority of Pakistan 2021).

41.3 Guidelines For COVID-19 Vaccination Under National Immunization Management System

The COVID-19 vaccination process is operational under the National Command and Operation Center (NCOC 2021), Government of Pakistan. NCOC holds the duty to establish, implement, and execute strategies using set guidelines for immunization throughout Pakistan. From the lockdown strategy to the distribution of vaccines, NCOC has approved several departments to work together during the crucial time. For the immunization drive throughout Pakistan, NCOC introduced a web-and-mobile application platform, the National Immunization Management System (NIMS). NIMS is linked directly with the National Database and Registration Authority (NADRA) and the telecom sector. The telecom companies send SMS messages with basic information about vaccination delivery procedures to citizens registered with mobile numbers. The NIMS online platform directly links to NADRA for registration, appointment, and verification of applicant records.

The NCOC has already enforced an eight-step guideline to register online to receive the coronavirus vaccine dose. The eight steps consist of eligibility, confirmation message, appointment, physical visit to the vaccination center, verification counter, vaccination counter, confirmation SMS, and monitoring (NCOC 2021) (see Fig. 41.1).

As per the NCOC established policy, in the first stage of immunizing, the frontline/healthcare workers (HCW) can receive vaccination by verifying their records via SMS to number 1166 or the NIMS portal (https://rms.nitb.gov.pk/portal2/hcw/register). The applicant receives the registration status message of NIMS within 24 hours. After successfully verifying credentials, the applicant must be registered and enters the requested information in the NIMS system using an Android mobile application (Vaccinator App) or website (https://rms.nitb.gov.pk/portal2/hcw/register). After completing the registration process, the applicant obtains information regarding the nearest vaccination center and the date/time and code. Vaccination centers are linked with NADRA to verify online records (i.e., code), and the health safety vaccination is monitored under NCOC health policies.

Fig. 41.1 National command and operation center—guidelines for vaccination in Pakistan (NCOC 2021)

The government of Pakistan has already announced that in the second stage, the COVID-19 vaccination will become available to citizens over 60. The eligible applicant first verifies their record via SMS; successful verification enables them to register in the NIMS portal to acquire doses from the nearest vaccination center. In the third stage, citizens under 60 years old can register and take the vaccine. The vaccination registration mechanism is the same for all other age categories.

In the future, the government is interested in promoting joint ventures through the public–private partnership program, where the government and its collaborators would engage approved third-party or private laboratories to import approved COVID-19 vaccines to patients under the Drug Regulatory Authority of Pakistan (DRAP).

41.4 Concluding Remarks

During the crisis, the Pakistani government initiated its new public policies against the pandemic at the right time, helping federal and provincial agencies to overcome constraints and limited resources like lack of healthcare facilities and finances. Its visible success was achieved through the COVID-19 awareness initiative and different digital platforms for the immunization drive following national policies complying with WHO pandemic guidelines. Digital governance with a public–private partnership can be a turning point in implementing effective and transparent immunizations throughout a country. In Pakistan, the NIMS, as a digital immunization platform of the government, connects to NADRA to verify individual records while ensuring security and the privacy of personal data. The implementation of NIMS under NCOC guidelines provides transparency, and it also ensures the successful execution of the distribution of vaccinations.

Acknowledgements The authors acknowledge the financial support of Writing Lab, Institute for the Future of Education, Tecnologico de Monterrey, Mexico, in the production of this work.

References

Ar AY, Abbas A (2020) Government ICT-based cross-sectoral collaboration strategy for financial support of low-income families during the COVID-19 pandemic. In: Proceeding 13th international conference on theory and practice of electronic governance (ICEGOV), pp 560–563
Drug Regulatory Authority of Pakistan (2021) Press note—drug regulatory authority of Pakistan. Available https://www.dra.gov.pk/docs/Pressnote_covid_vaccine_drap-edited%20tracked%20(1).pdf. Accessed 11 March 2021
Khan N, Naushad M, Akbar A, Faisal S, Fahad S (2020) Critical review of COVID-2019 in Pakistan and Its impact on Pakistan economy. SSRN Electron J
NCOC (2021) COVID Vaccination. Available https://ncoc.gov.pk/covid-vaccinatino-en.php. Accessed 23 March 2021

Roche B, Garchitorena A, Roiz D (2020) The impact of lockdown strategies targeting age groups on the burden of COVID-19 in France. Epidemics 33:100424

SAMAA (2021) COVID-19 vaccine updates in Pakistan and around the world. Available https://www.samaa.tv/news/2021/02/covid-19-vaccine-updates-in-pakistan-and-around-the-world. Accessed 9 July 2021

World Health Organization (2020) Timeline: WHO's COVID-19 response. Available https://www.who.int/emergencies/diseases/novel-coronavirus-2019/interactive-timeline#event-12. Accessed 29 Dec 2020

World Health Organization (2021) Coronavirus. Available https://www.who.int/health-topics/coronavirus#tab=tab_3

Zeng J-H, Liu Y-X, Yuan J, Wang F-X, Wu W-B, Li J-X, Wang L-F, Gao H, Wang Y, Dong C-F, Li Y-J, Xie X-J, Feng C, Liu L (2020) First case of COVID-19 complicated with fulminant myocarditis: a case report and insights. Infection 48(5):773–777

Chapter 42
Technological Infrastructure and ICT Use by Elementary School Teachers in San José Chiltepec, Oaxaca

Mireya López Luna, Eduardo Cruz-Cruz, and Jimena López Morales

42.1 Introduction

Technological infrastructure is a catalyst for societal progress because advances in science and technology influence all social sectors. Education is enriched by innovations in academic processes, methods, and practices. Nowadays, incorporating Information and Communication Technologies (ICTs) is essential in teaching because it enables students to take the initiative to improve autonomous learning (Sanz 2017). In schoolwork, using ICTs requires migrating from a traditional educational model to one that benefits from using the internet (Andión 2010) and emerging technologies to build new environments for transmitting knowledge (Cabero 2010). Thanks to ICTs, meaningful, high-quality, universal learning for students and better educational management for institutions are possible (Osorio 2016).

This study addresses the use of ICTs in three rural primary schools in San José Chiltepec, a highly marginalized population in Oaxaca, Mexico, that, as of 2015, had 11,019 inhabitants (SEDESOL 2021). The study's objective was to diagnose the technological infrastructure and use of ICTs in the educational processes led by Oaxacan teaching staff.

M. López Luna · J. López Morales
Universidad de la Sierra Juárez, Ixtlán de Juárez, México
e-mail: mireya@unsij.edu.mx

J. López Morales
e-mail: mireya@unsij.edu.mx

E. Cruz-Cruz (✉)
Instituto Tecnológico del Valle de Etla, Santiago Suchilquitongo, Etla, Mexico
e-mail: eduardo.cruz@vetla.tecnm.mx

42.2 Development

42.2.1 Theoretical Framework

The search for educational quality has been enriched by efforts focused on improving educational management, teaching and learning processes, study materials, teacher profiles, and, ultimately, educational infrastructure (Bautista 2019). A pillar of the infrastructure is the belief that technology strongly influences academia and impacts teacher transformation (Salinas 2004). The technology in the classroom to facilitate the transmission of knowledge has been realigned with technological innovations. In its time, television, audio, and videocassettes reigned (Castañeda et al. 2013), replaced today by computer equipment, smart devices, and virtual applications.

ICTs are valued as tools capable of improving school performance through more complete learning where new alternatives open, externally, to decentralize teaching and, internally, improve learning environments with more efficient management tools and information. In primary education, ICTs enable changes and the application of booming educational trends. In this scenario, the students combine their resources and abilities and assume a more active role in the educational process (Meza and Cantarell 2002); they are engaged and motivated, thanks to the innovative use of technology. For their part, the teachers as "senders and transmitters of information" (Castro et al. 2007) must enrich their professional profiles, applying technology to knowledge (Aguiar and Cuesta 2009). They must acknowledge the need to develop digital and technological skills to create didactic materials that attract students and encourage their learning (Toribio 2019). Thus, teachers contribute to improving educational quality (Gómez and Macedo 2010). Currently, education for indigenous populations is not accessible, acceptable, or adaptable. Although these points are crucial to ensuring the excellence of the educational service, we must also recognize that many of the teachers participating in the Mexican educational system in indigenous populations have lower salaries, less academic preparation, and less infrastructure (Köster 2016).

42.2.2 Problem Statement

In primary education, the integration of ICTs has presented two challenges: acquiring technological tools and using them. The state of Oaxaca occupied the last place in the well-being of its population due to marginalization, poverty, and social backwardness of its populations (Bautista and Briseño 2014). In 2010, San José Chiltepec was identified as a municipality having moderate and extreme poverty with an educational lag of 32.7% (higher than the state and national educational lags of 30% and 20.7%, respectively). In addition, 54.5% of the population 15 years and older had incomplete primary education (CONEVAL n.d.).

Table 42.1 Schools and teachers participating in the study

School	Teachers
José Vasconcelos Bilingual Primary	4
Vicente Guerrero Bilingual Primary	6
Martyrs of the Revolución Formal Primary	13

Source Own elaboration from the data collection

The social and economic conditions of the population constitute a mixture of factors that affect the education provided by primary schools and mold the response of students to the teaching and learning process led by the teaching staff. We posed the following research question to diagnose the educational and human resources and understand the technological infrastructure and its possible benefit in educational quality: What advances in technological infrastructure and training courses do teachers bring to the elementary schools in San José Chiltepec, Oaxaca?

42.2.3 Method

The research concluded in the first quarter of 2020 was exploratory and based on the following steps: (1) Choice of schools, which consisted of a non-probabilistic convenience sampling of three primary schools in the locality (Table 42.1), selected for ease-of-access and availability of teachers to participate; (2) Data collection, carried out by applying questionnaire surveys and, (3) Data interpretation using descriptive analysis.

42.2.3.1 Design and Implementation of the Data Collection Instrument

The instrument was designed to understand the technological infrastructure supporting teachers and identify their level of technological training (Annex 1). The questionnaire was applied through a face-to-face survey with the prior authorization of the elementary school management staff.

42.2.4 Results

The study results were derived from descriptive analysis with tables and graphs used to show trends in the data. The information obtained was structured as follows: teachers surveyed, technological tools available and used, software for academic and administrative activities, use of the internet, and refresher courses for technological tools.

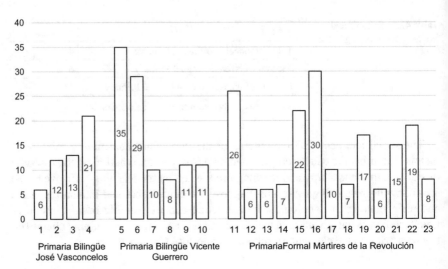

Fig. 42.1 Seniority of teaching staff (years of experience teaching in the three elementary schools). *Source* Own elaboration from the data collection

42.2.4.1 Teachers Surveyed (years of Service)

Of the participants, 15 were women, and eight were men. Figure 42.1 shows the teaching staff's years of experience in the profession. It stands out that teachers with 20–35 years of experience do not consider it essential to include technological tools in the training activities of their students.

42.2.4.2 Available Technological Tools and Their Use

Table 42.2 presents an integral part of this analysis, which identifies the technological tools available in the schools or those available to teachers.

Table 42.2 Technological tools in the primary schools

	Computer	Projector	Digital whiteboard	Tablets	Others
José Vasconcelos Bilingual Primary	1	1	1	0	–
Vicente Guerrero Bilingual Primary	1	1	0	0	–
Martyrs of the Revolución Formal Primary	1	1	1	0	Audiovisual Room, Enciclomedia

Source Own elaboration from the data collection

Table 42.3 Software employed for academic and administrative activities

	Platforms	Websites and webpages	Tutorials
José Vasconcelos Bilingual Primary	0	1	0
Vicente Guerrero Bilingual Primary	0	0	0
Martyrs of the Revolución Formal Primary	0	1	0

Source Own elaboration from the data collection

The José Vasconcelos Bilingual Primary School has a computer, a projector, and an electronic whiteboard. They use the computer and projector sporadically to display videos, PowerPoint presentations, and sometimes certain classes. They use the computer to perform basic jobs solicited; however, they explain that the electronic whiteboard is not used due to lack of training. The Vicente Guerrero Bilingual Primary School has a computer and a projector, but the teachers very rarely use them due to the lack of adequate facilities for their use. The teachers have the training but not the necessary environments, which causes these teams to abandon the equipment. The Martyrs of the Revolution Primary School has a computer, projector, an audiovisual room with a digital whiteboard, and the installation of the Enciclomedia equipment. However, the classrooms have electrical installations in poor condition; any failure in the equipment would be their responsibility. Therefore, they prefer to use personal equipment such as cell phones, speakers, tablets, or laptops.

42.2.4.3 Software for Academic and Administrative Activities

The teachers of the three institutions agree that using ICTs is increasingly essential in their educational tasks to support their classes and fulfill their administrative responsibilities, such as managing the requests for economic resources from various support programs to education.

Only two schools use websites and web pages for administrative procedures and didactic video games to enrich their classes. Table 42.3 details the information about the software used.

42.2.4.4 Use of the Internet and Refresher Courses

Figure 42.2 shows the use of the internet in teaching activities. It can be seen that 20 teachers answered that they use the internet, and three teachers do not use it. It stands out that the three teachers who responded that they do not use the internet have 26, 30, and 35 years of service; they argue that they did not learn with technological tools.

Figure 42.3 shows that 43% of teachers use the internet to download files related

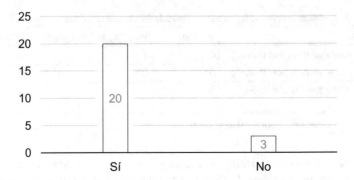

Fig. 42.2 Use of the internet by teaching staff. *Source* Own elaboration from the data collection

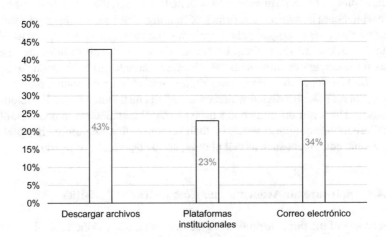

Fig. 42.3 Purpose of the internet use. *Source* Own elaboration from the data collection

to school activities, such as exercises to reinforce topics covered in class and administrative files. Thirty-four percent use personal email to send support files and information about students to supervisors or school zone managers, while 23% consult institutional platforms to manage other educational supports. However, only teachers who are directors or members of certain committees have access to the institutional platforms.

Refresher Courses

The 23 teachers surveyed affirm receiving courses to implement and use technology in their teaching–learning activities. Figure 42.4 reveals that 56% have taken basic courses, and 44% have received mandatory refresher courses at the same institution

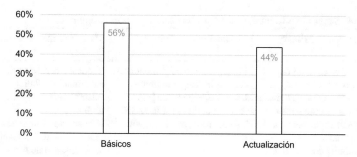

Fig. 42.4 Technology training courses for teaching activities. *Source* Own elaboration from the data collection

free of cost. An important fact is that these courses offer the teachers curricular or continuing education credits, so they are important to them.

In general, teachers responded that they have not taken ICT courses in education on their own due to (a) their high costs and (b) the lack of infrastructure in the schools where they teach. The teachers do not see it viable to prepare much in technology because most learned to use technology during school years. Moreover, additional preparation is not helpful if they have this knowledge because they cannot apply it in the schools due to infrastructure conditions.

42.2.5   Discussion

According to Dix (2017), ICTs encompass computers, projectors, smartphones, and internet broadband, among others, designed to facilitate many learning activities, new ways of learning, and skills for teachers and students. According to Johnson et al. (2013), all teaching practice difficulties in the classroom should be considered, as they can be attitudinal, organizational, and technological in nature. One example is the inequality of infrastructures due to financing, geographical location, school organization, lack of training, rejection of ICTs, and educational policies.

This study identified a lack of adequate primary education infrastructure for ICTs in the schools studied. In some cases, there is a computer, projector, digital whiteboard, audiovisual room, and enciclomedia. However, their use is sporadic and risky in one school due to poor electrical installations, causing teachers not to use the equipment. The other two institutions have limited technological infrastructure.

Another factor interfering with these teachers using ICT in academic and administrative activities is their inadequate training. Some lack interest in updating knowledge in ICTs because they are of little use to them, arguing that they do not have the technological tools in the classrooms. This lack of interest in the subject and seeing this type of knowledge as unnecessary can be considered an attitude of apathy toward ICTs to improve educational processes, aligning with the work of Johnson et al. (2013).

Table 42.4 Suggestions to improve the teaching/learning process using ICTs

José Vasconcelos Primary	Vicente Guerreo Primary	Martyrs of the Revolution Primary
Hire the services of an expert to review the equipment; also, solicit training courses to use it Program a schedule so that all teachers and students can use the equipment Solicit training courses at the beginning of the school year	Educational management must request lacking equipment Likewise, request ongoing training courses for the staff. Use the equipment that you have	Request a review of the electrical installation (identified as a significant problem) Hire an expert to review the status of the unused equipment Make a schedule for the use of the audiovisual rooms by all teachers and students

Design an educational intervention plan that sensitizes the teachers about the benefits of using and exploiting the technological infrastructure

Source Own elaboration

In another order of ideas, Table 42.4 presents some proposals and recommendations to improve the teaching–learning process of primary schools in San José Chiltepec.

Finally, the main limitation identified in the present study corresponded to the collection of data because, due to the work dynamics of the teaching staff, coordinating the times to agree on the space and time to apply the survey was complex.

42.3 Conclusions

Education in marginalized communities presents significant challenges to the educational system, institutions, teachers, and students; therefore, leveraging and using available resources well is essential to compensate for the already critical socioeconomic difficulties.

This exploratory study diagnosed that none of the three schools has enough infrastructure to strengthen traditional education with new technological tools. Therefore, there is no requirement for teachers to innovate the teaching–learning process using these tools. This research shows that the level of technological and pedagogical competencies of the teachers is deficient.

En competencia pedagógica se observa una resistencia al cambio muy alta, donde la justificación es la falta de herramientas tecnológicas en las escuelas. Es importante señalar que los docentes requieren del desarrollo de nuevas estrategias de aprendizaje para innovar en materia pedagógica, las cuales son el comienzo del cambio para la actualización y mejora educativa teniendo presente la gestión de las herramientas tecnológicas para cada escuela.

In the teachers' pedagogical competency, there is a very high resistance to change. The justification is the lack of technological tools in the schools. It is important to note that teachers require the development of new learning strategies to innovate their pedagogy. This is the starting point for change to update and improve education, considering the management of technological tools in each school.

It is hoped that with the information obtained from this study, the rural primary schools in Oaxaca will be able to enrich their educational processes with information and communication technologies for the benefit of Oaxacan children and assurance of their universal right to education in Mexico.

Acknowledgements The authors acknowledge the technical support of Writing Lab, Institute for the Future of Education, Tecnologico de Monterrey, Mexico, in the production of this work.

Annexes

Annex 1

Data collection instrument

General Data					
Name of the school:			Date:		
Profession:		Sex: M F	Years of service:		
Technological Infrastructure and Use of ICTs					
Do you use any technological tools to develop your classes?				Yes	No
Indicate your school's technology equipment:					
Computer	Projector	Tablet	Digital whiteboard	Others:	
Do you have software support at school?				Yes	No
If your previous answer was yes, indicate your software:					
Platforms	Websites and pages	Tutorials	Didactic videogames		
Do you use the internet for teaching activities?				Yes	No
If your previous answer was yes, indicate below which you use on the internet:					
email	Institutional platforms	File Downloads			
Have you taken courses to implement technology in your teaching activities?			Yes		No
If your previous answer was yes, mention what courses you have taken:					
Have you taken technology training courses on your own?			Yes		No
If your previous answer was yes, indicate the type of courses you have taken:					
Basic	Updating				
If you desire, add general comments about the questions:					

Source Own elaboration

References

Aguiar MV, Cuesta H (2009) *Importancia de trabajar las TIC en educación infantil a través de métodos como la webquest*. Revista de Medios y Educación. España. Accessed from: https://www.redalyc.org/pdf/368/36812036006.pdf

Andión M (2010) *Equidad tecnológica en la educación básica: criterios y recomendaciones para la apropiación de las TIC en las escuelas públicas*. Revista Reencuentro. México. Accessed from: https://www.redalyc.org/pdf/340/34015675004.pdf

Bautista E, Briseño M (2014) *El derecho a la educación ante la desigualdad y la pobreza: el caso de Oaxaca, México*. Revista El Cotidiano. México. Accessed from: https://www.redalyc.org/pdf/325/32529943011.pdf

Bautista E (2019) *Condiciones de la educación rural en México. Hallazgos a partir de una escuela multigrado*. Revista Chakiñan de Ciencias Sociales y Humanidades. Ecuador. Accessed from: https://www.redalyc.org/jatsRepo/5717/571763394003/html/index.html

Cabero J (2010) *Los retos de la integración de las TICs en los procesos educativos. Límites y posibilidades*. Revista Perspectiva Educacional. Chile. Accessed from: https://dialnet.unirioja.es/descarga/articulo/3579891.pdf

Castañeda A, Carrillo J, Quintero Z (2013) *El uso de las Tic en educación primaria: la experiencia Enciclomedia*. México: Red de Investigadores Educativos, A. C. Editores

Castro S, Guzmán B, Casado D (2007) *Las Tic en los procesos de enseñanza y aprendizaje*. Revista de Educación Laurus. Venezuela. Accessed from: https://www.redalyc.org/pdf/761/76102311.pdf

CONEVAL (s.f.) *Informe anual sobre la situación de pobreza y rezago social. San José Chiltepec, Oaxaca*. Accessed from: https://www.gob.mx/cms/uploads/attachment/file/34502/Oaxaca_166.pdf

Dix A (2017) Interacción hombre-ordenador, fundamentos y nuevos paradigmas. J Visual Lang Comput. https://doi.org/10.1016/j.jvlc.2016.04.001

Gómez L, Macedo J (2010) *Importancia de las Tic en la educación básica regular*. Revista Investigación Educativa. Perú. Accessed from: https://revistasinvestigacion.unmsm.edu.pe/index.php/educa/article/download/4776/3850/

Johnson D, Johnson R, Holubec E (2013) *El aprendizaje Cooperativo en el Aula*. Buenos Aires: Editorial Paidós

Köster A (2016) *Educación asequible, accesible, aceptable y adaptable para los pueblos indígenasen México: Una revisión estadística*. Revista Alteridad. Ecuardo. Accessed from: https://www.redalyc.org/journal/4677/467746763003/html/

Meza A, Canterrell L (2002) *Importancia del Manejo de Estrategias de Aprendizaje para el uso Educativo de las Nuevas Tecnologías de Información y Comunicación en Educación*. Accessed from: http://funredes.org/mistica/castellano/ciberoteca/participantes/docuparti/esp_doc_71.html

Osorio M (2016) *Alternativas para nuevas prácticas Educativas 3. Las tecnologías de la información y la comunicación (TIC): Avances, retos y desafíos en la transformación educativa*. México: Amapsi Editorial. Accessed from: http://www.educapanama.edu.pa/?q=articulos-educativos/articulos/las-tecnologias-de-la-informacion-y-la-comunicacion-tic-avances-retos

Salinas (2004) *Innovación docente y uso de las TIC en la enseñanza universitaria*. Revista Universidad y Sociedad del Conocimiento. España. Accessed from: https://www.redalyc.org/pdf/780/78011256001.pdf

Sanz G (2017) *Una aproximación a la modalidad de flipped classroom en la asignatura de Bioquímica*. Revista Didáctica, Innovación y Multimedia. Accessed from: https://dialnet.unirioja.es/servlet/articulo?codigo=6062599

SEDESOL (2021) *Datos Generales: San José Chiltepec*. Accessed from: http://www.microrregiones.gob.mx/zap/datGenerales.aspx?entra=nacion&ent=20&mun=166

Toribio M (2019) *Importancia del uso de las TIC en educación primaria*. Revista Atlante: Cuadernos de Educación y Desarrollo. Accessed from: https://www.eumed.net/rev/atlante/2019/02/uso-tic-primaria.html

Chapter 43
Cognitive Performance Identification with BCI Technology

Arturo Corona Ferreira and Erika Yunuen Morales Mateo

43.1 Introduction

Current technological advances allow education stakeholders to explore new alternatives in educational technologies beyond creating content, to understand how learning occurs in students and how to recognize the best teaching practices using neuroscientific methods. Goswami argues that current developments allow neurosciences to advance rapidly in relevant and compatible areas such as education (Goswami 2006).

This report presents the results of measuring undergraduate students' cognitive performance at a public university in Tabasco, Mexico, where the participating students come from rural communities. As Goswami puts it, in educational institutions (EI), teachers are eager to know how the human brain functions for the benefit of their students. Thus, our research work is relevant, carried out in a real context with students in rural communities. We propose using portable BCI devices to read physiological activity in students. Our project produced the resulting data in a public EI in southern Mexico (Goswami 2006) through a methodological infrastructure using BCI devices. Aligning with Fischer, Goswami, and Geake, we seek to promote research on learning and teaching to produce new scientific understandings for education (Fischer et al. 2010).

Since the '90s, advances in the knowledge of the human brain have given way to a new body of knowledge known as educational neurosciences that address teaching and learning processes from pedagogical, psychological, and neuroscientific (Sousa 2010) approaches.

A. . Corona Ferreira (✉) · E. Y. . Morales Mateo
Universidad Juárez Autónoma de Tabasco, Cunduacán Tabasco, Mexico
e-mail: arturo.corona@ujat.mx

E. Y. . Morales Mateo
e-mail: erika.morales@ujat.mx

Neurosciences and information technologies have evolved to such a degree that they support each other to identify the physiological signals generated by motivational stimuli and emotions in the classroom. This fusion allows devices to record a subject's physiological reactions through heart rate measurements, electroencephalography (EEG), image ontology, or facial recognition, to name a few examples. These recordings are converted into data sets, better known as multimodal data.

Immordino-Yang and Faeth (2010) sustain that a wide range of recent neuroscientific research has shown the interrelation of emotions and cognition in learning and memory processes. For this reason, BCI devices, with their virtues of portability and connectivity, have aroused interest as complementary resources to carry out educational research. Table 43.1 reveals a broad interest in the literature in conducting studies of learning processes by analyzing attention levels, meditation, and the influence of emotions on memory and learning.

This article aims to address the gap in understanding the functioning of the human brain in authentic learning contexts, precisely, student learning situations. To understand learning processes, we collected physiological data using EEG techniques from students attending a traditional class while experiencing a written evaluation.

Table 43.1 Research publications considering the use of BCI devices in learning situations

Year	Authors	Publications identified
2017	Xu and Zhong (2017)	Analysis of 22 research papers regarding BCI devices, of which more than 80% considered using BCI
2017	Ko et al. (2017)	Study with EEG inside the classroom where they measure the level of alertness per specific stimuli
2017	Poulsen et al. (2017)	Recording of brain activity of multiple students within a classroom to identify the correlation between subjects from activity evoked by a common video stimulus
2018	Xu et al. (2018)	Review of techniques used to detect emotions in learning contexts
2018	Babiker et al. (2018)	Research report from the Technological University of Petrona, where learning situations of 43 students using BCI devices were analyzed
2020	Srimaharaj et al. (2020a)	Method to accurately identify the level of cognitive performance in students
2020	He et al. (2020)	A review of research on BCI-based multimodal emotion recognition
2021	Davidesco et al. (2021)	Opportunities and limitations of portable brain technologies to complement educational research processes
2021	Open BCI documentation (2021)	Report on its website presenting 220 articles on using BCI devices, of which more than 7% are from learning situations with students

The technological synergy of Big Data makes possible multimodal data sets, which support the frameworks to replicate and study what happens in the learning processes. Tamoliūnė and others state that learning analytics, through their frameworks, help to understand and optimize learning processes in environments where it occurs. They suggest study materials and resources based on test results, personalizing the learning experiences, and strengthening professors' metacognition in their teaching practices (Tamoliūnė et al. 2019).

43.2 Theoretical Framework

Educational neurosciences emerge as a field of research that brings together biology, cognitive science, and pedagogy to lay the foundations for investigating how learning processes and teaching happen from a brain perspective; all to overcome perceptions and myths of brain functioning and learning through that bridges cognitive science and neuroscience, and cognitive science and education (Fischer et al. 2010).

From the above, we can conclude that educational neurosciences provide resources that facilitate research to build deep knowledge about the processes of encoding and transmitting neural information to better understand how the human senses build the fundamental systems for cognitive processes.

Bastiaansen et al. (2019) state that EEG techniques, the basis of BCI devices, operate on the principle that brain activity occurs through changes in the electrical power that travel networks of brain cells. EEG signals are not very informative regarding cognitive processes or emotional processes in the brain. However, after applying well-established signal processing techniques, the recorded signals can be reliably and validly correlated to emotional responses by studying EEG oscillations.

A BCI device has one or more EEG sensors and a data conversion and transmission resource linked to computer equipment and data reading and storage software. The NeuroSky hardware offers advantages over traditional EEGs because it has a headband, is light-weight, comfortable, and does not require a prior procedure to use it. The Neuroexperimenter free-use software was used for this research, exclusively linked to the BCI NeuroSky device by a single EEG sensor.

BCI devices read alpha, beta, gamma, delta, and theta and delta brain signals through EEG sensors. The signals are the product of the physiological activity, which is stimulated by emotions. Xu and Zhong present the analysis of 22 research papers that considered the use of BCI devices. They identified a shortage of studies about collecting data from students' brain waves within their classrooms, so there is a need to conduct studies in this area. On the other hand (Xu and Zhong 2017) (BCI documentation 2021), the manufacturer, OpenBCI, identifies 220 scientific articles on its website. Only ten refer to educational research; this shows an area of opportunity to build proposals for multimodal data analytics through BCI devices.

Besides the hardware, current BCI device manufacturers offer libraries for software development. We used the BCI NeuroSky MindWave device for this research, which works with a sensor placed on the frontal lobe. Additionally, the manufacturer includes software resources with metrics for measuring states of attention and meditation on a scale of 1–100.

He et al. (2020) suggest that multimodal data from discrete emotions can be constructed using facial recognition, while Tyng et al. (2017) argues that BCI devices construct observations from the dimension of valence and arousal. Valence allows the cataloguing of negative and positive emotions. Emotional arousal generates cognitive and affective processes, which are perceived emotionally through self-assessment and the labeling process. These activate psychological and physiological changes generalized to the conditions of excitement, which motivates a subject to behavior that often, although not always, is expressive, objective-oriented, and adaptive. Therefore, emotions have a substantial influence on the cognitive processes of human beings and can provide a frame of reference for perception, attention, learning, memory, reasoning, and problem-solving (He et al. 2020; Tyng et al. 2017).

In Venkatraman, Edlow, and Immordino-Yang, Damasio proposes that emotions are mental and bodily responses that unfold automatically when an organism recognizes that a situation justifies such a reaction. It can be provoked by physical and social circumstances or by inferences, memories, beliefs, or imaginings. Recent technological advances allow access to technological resources to measure emotions; therefore, emotions are a reference to address the study of learning (Venkatraman et al. 2017).

43.2.1   Problem Statement

In current educational contexts, there is subjectivity about the cognitive state that a student maintains. Interviews are usually conducted, and the results are constructed from interpretations of what the interviewer observed and identified. Therefore, this research aimed to construct an evaluative proposal to know and identify the students' cognitive load capacity through attention and meditation metrics from the analysis of three written instruments. Our study presents the case results of 10 students in higher education: five men and five women. We built multimodal data sets for each student and used the E-sense metrics of the NeuroSky device to build a cognitive effort contrast scale. The intent is to replicate these measurements in other academic contexts and, from those analyses, identify good teaching practices.

43.3   Methodology

43.3.1   Research Design

The descriptive method research design analyzed the characteristics of the students while taking an evaluation. The students come from other subjects in the social context and are concentrated in another space with classroom characteristics. We applied evaluation instruments because we wanted to describe the student as he or she faced the situation. The evaluation results were not considered in the study. The research exercise considered the collection of physiological information through the NeuroSky EEG sensor.

The EEG device was used as a systemic instrument for collecting direct observations over an average period of time to obtain the cognitive information of each student through their brain activity in the frontal lobe. Each student was considered as an individual case because they all come from one classroom and were summoned to a specific space in the same institution

Because the research is based on multimodal data, we considered learning analytics as a frame of reference to conduct the qualitative study. According to SoLAR in Corona et al., learning analytics is defined as the collection, measurement, analysis, and reporting of data about students and their contexts to understand and optimize learning and the environments in which it occurs. Specifically, the analysis was performed through a visual analysis of the representing data and compared with the physiological data obtained (Corona et al. 2019).

To provoke similar data among the students, we used three instruments. The first was the Raven progressive matrix test (only the first section was considered). The second was the d2 Test of Attention, and finally, a mathematical operations test was applied, which involved testing the memory. All the participants in the study received a monetary payment to motivate them to participate. All the students were in the final semester of the Bachelor in Computer Systems degree. The duration of the test in each subject averaged 40 min.

We employed EEG sensors using BCI devices for this research, which allowed gathering physiological data from ten voluntary students from the Chontalpa region of the State of Tabasco. According to (He et al. 2020) others, a BCI device has non-invasive sensor technology, which converts physiological signals into signals that can be recognized by a computer for storage in the form of multimodal data.

The data generated by the BCI sensor readings were a product of physiological signals. By employing algorithms of the NeuroExperimentor software, we measured attention and meditation, which served as input to calculate cognitive performance using Eq. 43.1 proposed by Srimaharaj (2020b):

$$\text{Cognitive Performance} = (\text{Attention} + \text{Meditation})/2 \qquad (43.1)$$

43.3.2 Results

The manufacturer's E-sense metrics state that ranges of values above 60 are considered values to highlight; values between 40 and 60 are neutral, and values from 0 to 40 are considered low. When interpreting the graphed results, we expected the last evaluation to be the simplest, so we anticipated a cognitive performance in low values because it did not involve great effort. However, with the d2 Test and the Raven Matrice Test, a greater effort was expected.

Figures 43.1, 43.2, and 43.3 show the testing results, where it can be observed that only two students reached the level of 60. Generally, no outstanding efforts were identified; most student test results fell in the average values for neutral according to the E-sense metric.

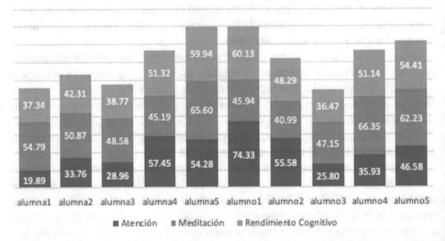

Fig. 43.1 Attention, meditation, and cognitive performance results taken from the Raven Matrix-Test

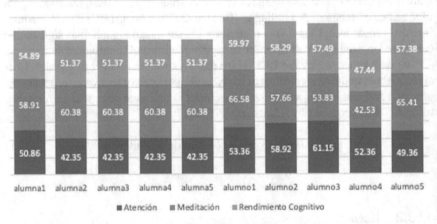

Fig. 43.2 Attention, meditation, and cognitive performance results taken from the d2 Test

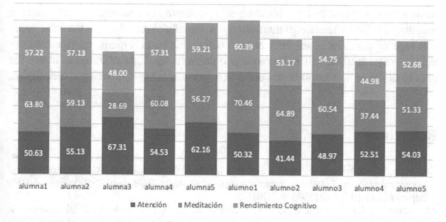

Fig. 43.3 Attention, meditation, and cognitive performance results taken from the Test of memory

43.4   Discussion

The three written evaluations were applied within a classroom, and the results are similar to those presented by Corona et al., where students were in a face-to-face class. The average results of eight participating students gave very similar results. The research requires larger population samples to identify whether the combination of the instruments helps interpret the levels of effort. As a first approach, comparing the results shown in Figs. 43.1, 43.2, and 43.3 indicates that using BCI devices to gather data from active students is a low-cost, simple way to analyze students and their learning situations from new perspectives through educational neuroscience methods. The aim would be to improve teaching activities, learning conditions, and student motivations (Corona et al. 2021).

43.5   Conclusions

Current technological advances allow versatile educational neurosciences research. With practical and easy-to-use hardware and software solutions, learning strategies can be created from different perspectives. As a frame of reference, learning analytics formulate bridges to integrate multimodal data from educational neurosciences to support results and interpretations.

This research aimed to achieve a better understanding of students' cognitive performance. The visualized results identified predominantly low and neutral levels of performance in each case. This is similar to Corona's findings (Corona et al. 2019) in a traditional class, which opens the opportunity for initiatives to replicate the methodology among larger sample populations to compare students' learning situations and cognitive performance in the Chontalpa region of the State of Tabasco. Also, these results suggest that the research infrastructure is sufficient, and the research instruments allow discerning situations not externally observable. On the other hand, this type of research is scarcely carried out within rural regions, so replicating it among larger numbers of indigenous people from the State of Tabasco clears the path to discover new opportunity areas in education using neuroscience techniques.

References

Babiker A, Faye I, Mumtaz W, Malik AS, Sato H (2018) EEG in classroom: EMD features to detect situational interest of students during learning. Multimedia Tools Appl 78(12):16261–16281. https://doi.org/10.1007/s11042-018-7016-z

Bastiaansen M, Lub X, Mitas O, Jung T, Ascenção M, Han I, Strijbosch W (2019) Emotions as core building blocks of an experience. Int J Contemp Hospitality Manag. https://doi.org/10.1108/IJCHM-11-2017-0761

BCI documentation, Open BCI Citation List. 31 Oct 2021. Available: https://docs.openbci.com/citations/

Corona A, Altamirano M, Ortega M, González O (2019) Analítica del aprendizaje y las neurociencias educativas: nuevos retos en la integración tecnológica. Revista Iberoamericana De Educación 80(1):31–54. https://doi.org/10.35362/rie8013428

Corona A, Altamirano M, Ortega M (2021) Empleo de dispositivos BCI en alumnos para la evaluación docente. RIED. Revista Iberoamericana de Educación a Distancia, vol. 24, no.1, pp. 315–328. https://doi.org/10.5944/ried.24.1.27502

Davidesco I, Matuk C, Bevilacqua D, Poeppel D, Dikker S (2021) Neuroscience research in the classroom: portable brain technologies in education research. Educ Res. https://doi.org/10.3102/0013189X211031563

Fischer K, Goswami U, Geake J, Task force on the future of educational neuroscience (2010) The future of educational neuroscience. Mind, Brain, Educ 4(2):68–80

Goswami U (2006) Neuroscience and education: from research to practice? Nat Rev Neurosci 7(5):406–413. https://doi.org/10.1038/nrn1907

He Z, Li Z, Yang F, Wang L, Li J, Zhou C, Pan J (2020) Advances in multimodal emotion recognition based on brain-computer interfaces. Brain Sci 10(10):1–29. https://doi.org/10.3390/brainsci10100687

Immordino-Yang MH, Faeth M (2010) The role of emotion and skilled intuition in learning. In: Mind, brain, and education: neuroscience implications for the classroom, pp 69–83

Ko L, Komarov O, Hairston W, Jung T, Lin C (2017) Sustained attention in real classroom settings: An EEG study. Front Human Neurosci 11

Poulsen A, Kamronn S, Dmochowski J, Parra L, Hansen L (2017) EEG in the classroom: synchronized neural recordings during video presentation. Sci Rep 7(1). https://doi.org/10.1038/srep43916

Sousa D (2010) How science met pedagogy. In: Mind, brain, and education: neuroscience implications for the classroom, pp 9–24. Available: https://readpbn.com/pdf/Mind-Brain-and-Education-Neuroscience-Implications-for-The-Classroom-Sample-Pages.pdf

Srimaharaj W, Chaising S, Sittiprapaporn P, Temdee P, Chaisricharoen R (2020a) Effective method for identifying student learning ability during classroom focused on cognitive performance. Wireless Personal Commun 1–18. https://doi.org/10.1007/s11277-020-07197-2

Srimaharaj W, Chaising S, Sittiprapaporn P, Temdee P, Chaisricharoen R (2020b) Effective method for identifying student learning ability during classroom focused on cognitive performance. Wireless Pers Commun 115(4):2933–2950. https://doi.org/10.1007/s11277-020-07197-2

Tamoliūnė G, Tereseviẻienė M, Duart J, Naujokaitienė J (2019) Disclosing learners' behaviour and engagement in online and blended courses: case study of Vytautas Magnus University.

In: Connecting through educational technology, proceedings European distance and E-learning network, 16–19 June 2019. https://doi.org/10.38069/edenconf-2019-ac-0030

Tyng C, Amin H, Saad M, Malik A (2017) The influences of emotion on learning and memory. Front Psychol 8. https://doi.org/10.3389/fpsyg.2017.01454

Venkatraman A, Edlow B, Immordino-Yang M (2017) The brainstem in emotion: a review. Front Neuroanat 11–15. https://doi.org/10.3389/fnana.2017.00015

Xu J, Zhong B (2017) Review on portable EEG technology in educational research. Comput Hum Behav 81:340–349

Xu T, Zhou Y, Wang Z, Peng Y (2018) Learning emotions EEG-based recognition and brain activity: a survey study on BCI for intelligent tutoring system. Procedia Computer Science 130:376–382

Chapter 44
Using Bots to Conduct Interviews in Journalism and Research Courses

María Leticia Flores-Palacios, Claudia Alicia Lerma-Noriega, and Genaro Rebolledo-Méndez

44.1 Introduction

In university courses where communication management is paramount, students commonly collect data from primary sources to write articles or develop qualitative research. This can be challenging since people are not always interested nor willing to provide information.

To practice their interviewing technique, we developed an artificial intelligence chatbot to conduct interviews in both research and journalism courses to improve the quality and quantity of their questions. Additionally, this mechanism helps students understand the value of information sources such as first-hand data for journalistic and investigative work, essential for keeping up with new professional environments (Marinho and Sánchez-García 2020).

This research explores using chatbots in university courses to strengthen students' skills during the interview process in realistic simulations. Several studies have developed IA-based bots to practice skills in schools. The results show the students feel more confident in their ability and attribute more reliability to the information collected in the second interaction.

The article is divided into six sections. The Theoretical Framework section presents the findings from similar studies. Methodology describes the chatbot's characteristics and exploratory research. The Results section provides positive data about

M. L. Flores-Palacios (✉) · C. A. Lerma-Noriega
Media and Digital Culture, Tecnologico de Monterrey, Monterrey, Mexico
e-mail: lflores@tec.mx

C. A. Lerma-Noriega
e-mail: clerma@tec.mx

G. Rebolledo-Méndez
Writing Lab, Institute for the Future of Education, Tecnologico de Monterrey, Monterrey, Mexico
e-mail: g.rebolledo@tec.mx

© The Author(s), under exclusive license to Springer Nature Singapore Pte Ltd. 2022   535
S. Hosseini et al. (eds.), *Technology-Enabled Innovations in Education*,
Transactions on Computer Systems and Networks,
https://doi.org/10.1007/978-981-19-3383-7_44

the tool's usability, students' confidence in the information collected, and improvements in the second interaction with the bot. The Discussion section presents the study's limitations and some of the students' reactions to interactions with the bot. Finally, the Conclusions section presents the relationship between the results and the heutagogical posture, confirming the need to use technological tools to develop disciplinary competencies, especially during the COVID-19 pandemic, when face-to-face interactions are limited.

44.2 Theoretical Framework

Technology in university courses allows students to work on class content outside the classroom, generating a commitment to master various techniques (e.g., technology skills) that they will undoubtedly use in their professional life (Schena et al. 2018). Twenty-first-century technology implies learning digital culture (Albertos et al. 2016) and developing communicative competency that emphasizes the need to discern, join in, and question what we observe. In this context, future communications professionals must find the most appropriate way to gather information through interviews, such as oral communication activities.

Artificial intelligence in teaching can be beneficial. For example, chatbot contains programmed responses that simulate human conversation and can be leveraged in class (Hernandez de la Rosa 2020), which is excellent because new technologies foster individualized learning and digital skills development (Ocaña-Fernández et al. 2019). The use of automated journalism is relatively new and has focused predominantly on sports and financial news. However, automated journalism is becoming increasingly common and can result in ethical and transparency issues (Schapals 2020).

University students must manage their time and resources effectively to achieve successful results in their studies; technological tools to support their learning can help. College students learn intuitively and use mobile devices and technology tools daily, so encouraging students to improve their skills connects them to a practical need in their professional life (Ramos-Elizondo et al. 2010). Journalism and communications graduates must possess the skills to adapt to contexts and situations in a professional setting where emotional intelligence is key (LaGree et al. 2021).

The need for more autonomous learning lies in the heutagogical perspective (Hase 2000). This method focuses on students who set their own goals, review their learning, and apply their skills in new contexts instead of a traditional pedagogical stance where the teacher determines learning objectives, content, and evaluation.

Some educators have analyzed heutagogical stances in university courses. For example, medical students at Manipal University in India generated learning products from academic work on social networks. They found that heutology, coupled with technology, allowed students greater autonomy, and promoted critical thinking (Abraham et al. 2017). Critical thinking, self-determined learning, and reflection are at the heart of the process of developing skills to face new challenges (Bhoyrub et al.

2010). Artificial intelligence in teaching–learning is gaining ground as schools seek to incorporate technology and achieve personalized learning experiences (Jaiswal and Arun 2021).

Some valuable technological methodologies include recording conversations, transcribing and sharing them with other professionals, capturing photos from a cell phone, and organizing email correspondence (Shaw 2017). Journalists must create multimedia stories using mobile applications (Sutcliffe and Albeanu 2016). Artificial intelligence in journalism facilitates content production in larger quantities than agencies because data and numbers can be described by texts and then inserted into videos (Saad and Issa 2020).

Research carried out in schools of journalism and communications in public universities in Spain found that automation and robot competencies in student courses foster skills such as cooperation and teamwork used in professional environments (Ruiz et al. 2020).

Digital competency is necessary for students and must be present in their curricula independent of the subject area (Sánchez-Caballé et al. 2021). It is crucial to include digital development content in journalism courses (Gómez de Sibandze 2019).

Engineers must go through interview processes but have little training in this skill, so the authors developed an AI-based interview simulator for practice interviews. The simulator can answer questions and summarize the conversations. It is ready to be tested (Laiq et al. 2020).

The technological knowledge that students already have allows them to work from their cell phones and other devices; adding chatbot capabilities promotes communication skills, indispensable in multimedia and a pluri-informed world.

Students taking journalism and research courses must conduct interviews in various class exercises and produce articles and reports with their collected data.

In these courses, teachers traditionally present rudimentary interview elements. Thus, when students go into different professional settings, they often ask cliché, unstructured, or technical questions; as interviewees, they do not devote enough time and attention, resulting in confusion and misunderstanding. This situation reinforces the need to establish best practices and provide continuous feedback during interviewing. In this sense, a chatbot is an educational innovation project because it creates various conversational situations that prepare students for a real-life context in a controlled environment. The process involves capturing the interviewee's attention, establishing rapport, requesting appropriate information, asking relevant questions, changing the pace when an interviewee deviates from the subject, taking control when the interviewee dominates the situation, and ending the conversation achieving the interview's purpose, all with the possibility of interviewing the participant again in the future.

Automated applications shape our lives as traditional media once did, affecting our perception of reality and influencing our behaviors (Isaza-Restrepo et al. 2018). This automation presents academicians the possibilities of an infinity of topics and content, leveraging intelligent agents to advantage (Hípola and Vargas-Quesada 1999).

An AI tool such as a chatbot can respond to different levels of complexity and candor, take note of respondents' moods, and question accuracy, among other skills. The students can practice at their own pace.

Conversational agents (CAs) are software systems designed to interact with humans using natural language (Feine et al. 2019). The authors identified the social factors present in CAs and constructed a taxonomy with four categories: verbal (content and style), visual (kinesic and proxemic), auditory (speech qualities), and invisible (time and touch). The proposed taxonomy provides a guide for classifying and testing social factors in CAs. The authors noted that conversational agents based on text or chatbots were becoming more common and came from the first CA, Eliza, developed by Weizenbaum with a computer program in 1966. Other terms used are chatbot, dialog systems, companions, virtual assistants, and digital assistants.

There are some examples like "Sam," a CA capable of telling stories to 5-year-old children and giving them turns to narrate their versions of the story. The authors noted that new technologies have improved reading and other language skills. The results showed a significant correlation between the chronology of the stories and the occurrences of spatial expression ($r = 0.35, p < 0.05$) and textual discourse ($r = 0.27, p < 0.06$) (Ryokai et al. 2003). Using a CA in university teaching allows one to employ machine learning by feeding experiences to the machine (from big data) to learn independently (Ávila-Tomás 2019). As independent answers and questions are generated, the robot learns and becomes more expansive and profound in the interview. Despite chatbot improvements, one must still measure the software's usability. To do this, one can use various available questionnaires, such as the Software Usability System (SUS) designed by Brooke in 1996 to collect a user's subjective rating of a product's utility. The questionnaire is generally used after testing a system. The main advantage of questionnaires is that they can provide concrete answers with data visualized statistically (Sobron et al. 2010). The information collected improves the user experience (Sánchez Álvarez 2015).

This study reports several findings. First, the exit interview responses at the end of the bot interaction provide information on the application's usability. The students' grades are then presented on a specific class activity after the interview. The SUS results concerning tool learning (factor 1) and the tool's usability (factor 2) are also displayed. Finally, an analysis is shown relating the gender of the students and the bot's gender.

44.3 Methodology

This exploratory study developed a bot with the IBM-Watson system using resources to generate a hybrid application for IBM's mobile and cloud-connected devices, subsequently published on Android and iOS portals. AI modules were used to structure a conversation between the student and the bot (interviewer and interviewee), simulating a real conversation in work environments.

The technical capabilities of IBM-Watson matched the academic needs of investigative and journalism courses that conduct interviews to collect data. From this, the teachers determined the themes and the characters (bots). Each bot acquired a name, photo, occupation, and opinions to have specific characteristics of identity. (The chatbot is available at chatcontext.com).

Beginning the interview, the student considers the topic and the bot's photo to determine its sex and age. The students will have to collect additional information. They ask the bot questions and confront various personalities that force them, in some instances, to rephrase the question to obtain the information. The teachers chose four topical subjects making headlines and eight characters (bots) who could be interviewed. Four bots were males and four females; four were between 18 and 30 years old, and the other four were between 50 and 70. In addition, each bot was associated with ideas that were part of its identity and expressed opinions during the interviews.

In the convenience sample of 112 students, 74 students took a course on qualitative research methodology, and 28 students attended journalism courses. There were 23 men and 89 women aged 20–23 participating. The students were in their fourth semester (February–June 2020) and enrolled in six different programs (Communication, Journalism, Marketing, International Relations, Psychology, and Law) at a private Mexican university.

The students downloaded the Chatcontext application to interview the robot, completed an activity for each course, and answered an electronic questionnaire. Developing the bot allowed practicing various interview exercises using male and female characters of different ages and occupations linked to four specific topics: migration, race representation in the Oscar Awards, new formats for listening to music, and the gender pay gap in sports. The bot used Watson's AI module, which was provided with different questions and answers, training the CA to answer autonomously.

To test the chatbot's effectiveness, we applied an electronic questionnaire with the positive version of the System Usability Scale (SUS), developed and verified in Spanish (Hedlefs Aguilar et al. 2015). This scale measures the ease of learning and usability through ten items.

The SUS is a validated Likert scale with five positive items and five negative items. Hedfels Aguilar et al. (2015) applied a positive version of this scale and validated it with a reliability of 0.96, analyzing two factors: ease of learning (items 1, 2, 3, 5, 6, 7, 8 and 9) and usability (items 4 and 10) (Hedlefs Aguilar et al. 2015).

The study followed a quasi-experimental methodology of repeated measures to analyze the CA's impact on the participants. The students used the bot at two points in the course. In the first exercise, two topics were provided: racial diversity at the Oscar Awards and new formats for listening to music. Four bots were created for these two tracks: a critic, a film director, a digital-music production graduate, and a housewife. In the first measurement, we defined the bot's gender, and in the second measurement, the students could select the CA (and gender) of their choice. In both measurements, the students could choose the topic. The purpose was to evaluate whether the bot's gender influenced learning outcomes. Students then performed an activity solving an exercise related to the class topic.

In the second exercise, four more robots were developed for the two additional topics. These bots represented a priest and a senator in the migration topic, and a sports technical director and a footballer discussing the gender pay gap in sports. These themes were selected because they were relevant topics in the country at the time. Also, men and women of different ages (all legal age) were chosen as bots for each of the themes to provide the interviewer with different situations. At the end of the second interview, the students performed a written activity that posed a more profound challenge in the quantity and complexity of its points. Once the students completed the interview and the practical activity, they again answered the electronic SUS questionnaire.

44.4 Procedure

Students were randomly assigned the bot's gender in the first interview exercise. Fifty percent of male students interviewed a male bot, and the other fifty percent interviewed a female bot. A similar distribution was used for female students. The intention was to identify whether students felt more proficient in the interview if they identified with the bot's gender. With the information gathered, the journalism students produced a news story. The qualitative research students drafted a project proposal with a research question, two specific objectives, and a justification of the relevance of investigating the interview topic. In the second exercise, the students collected the interviewees' opinions, the importance and implications of the topic, and how they visualized the problem in the future. The students freely chose the robot's gender and performed an exercise with the information collected. The journalism students wrote a basic news story. The research students were asked to consider a potential research problem, including fundamental observation techniques (place, people, and categories). They were also asked to consider using a focus group, write trigger questions, and produce a title for their qualitative research. After the interview, the bot asked students two questions. It first asked whether they considered the information collected reliable and then whether they believed they had improved their ability to conduct an interview. Both questions were asked on a 5-point Likert scale, where 1 was "Not at all reliable" and 5 was "Completely Reliable." In the last step, they took a Qualtrics software survey to answer the items corresponding to the SUS. The students were duly informed of the research objectives and the use of this data for academic purposes. They also received help installing the application on their devices. The SUS questionnaire was anonymous and posed no threat to students' safety and integrity.

44.5 Results

The data made it possible to evaluate several aspects. The first results related to the bot's questions at the end of the interview: whether the students considered the information obtained reliable and whether they believed they had improved their skills as an interviewer.

The results showed that both journalism and research students considered the interview information reliable, with a 2.96 mean on the five-point Likert scale in the first exercise. In the second exercise, students averaged 3.58 on the same scale. Both students perceived the information to be more reliable in the second exercise, although there was no added element in the design of the bot's responses.

The bot's second exit question asked whether this exercise improved students' ability to ask questions in an interview. On the same scale from 1 to 5, the means were 3.08 in the first exercise and 3.42 in the second.

Regardless of their study, students perceived improving their ability to conduct interviews, implying a greater sense of confidence, possibly from practicing with the bot.

To analyze the differences in the means in the pre-and post-tests, we used a t-test on different aspects. It was identified that there was no significant difference between the exercise ratings and the bot's gender, indicating that the bot improved students' skills regardless of gender.

After the interview, the students performed a classroom activity. The journalism students wrote a news story, and the research students proposed elements for a research project. The difference between the first activity and the second was the number of written elements and topics aligned with the course program content in the semester. It was imperative to do different exercises that related the practice to the theoretical topics of class subjects.

The teachers evaluated this post-interview activity with a rating from 1 to 3, with 3 representing the highest-quality exercise. Research students averaged 2.61 in the first exercise and 2.66 in the second; journalism students averaged 2.72 in the first and 2.64 in the second. The differences were not significant.

After completing the class activity, students were asked to complete the electronic questionnaire to evaluate factor 1 related to ease of learning and factor 2 on usability.

Factor 1, ease of learning, included eight items: I think I would like to use this website frequently; I found the website to be simple; I think the website is easy to use; I found that several of the features on the website were well integrated; I thought there was much consistency on the website; I imagine that most people could learn to use this website very quickly; I found the website very intuitive, and I felt very confident using the website.

Factor 2, on usability, included two items: I think I will be able to use this website without the support of a technical person, and I was able to use the website without having to learn anything new.

Table 44.1 shows that 55 students participated in the first exercise, and 57 participated in the second a week later. In the second exercise, the students achieved a higher

Table 44.1 Results of applying the chatbot use measurements

Factor	Time of measurement	n	Median
1 Usability	1	55	3.1818
	2	57	3.6776
2 Ease of learning	1	55	3.2818
	2	57	3.8596

Source authors

average in factors 1, ease of learning, and 2, usability. The descriptive statistics in Table 44.1 indicate the statistical significance of the improvement in both factors.

In the second interaction with the bot, students improved in both items related to ease of learning (items 1, 2, 3, 5, 6, 7, 8, and 9) referred to as factor 1, and items related to the tool's usability (items 4 and 10) referred to as factor 2. If we analyze the mean with a t-test, there is a significant difference ($t = -2.7, p = 0.007$) for both factor 1 and factor 2 ($t = -3.47, p = 0.001$).

In the first interview exercise measured using SUS, each student was assigned to a particular gender to have a balanced approach to the different bots. In the second exercise a week later, both the topic and the gender of the bot were freely chosen. There was no significant difference between the student's gender and the bot's gender.

Students' improvement in ease of learning and usability was also analyzed by student career (academic discipline). While all the students were currently coursing journalism or research, those whose professional studies were in communications, marketing, journalism, clinical psychology, and law improved both factors in the second exercise. The international relations students decreased in factor 2, which is understandable given that in the first exercise, they had a mean of 3.87 and 3.6 in the second exercise.

Table 44.2 (Gender) shows that both women and men had a better average in both factors of the SUS scale in the second measurement.

In the second exercise, students demonstrated improvements with the bot in several ways: confidence in improving their skills as interviewers, ease of learning with the tool, and facility using it.

It is noteworthy that in the first interaction, the difference between the student's gender and the bot's gender assigned by the professors was minimal and not significant; in the second exercise, each student was free to choose the gender.

Table 44.2 Student's gender

Student's gender	Factor 1 Measure 1	Factor 1 Measure 2	Factor 2 Measure 1	Factor 2 Measure 2
Male ($n = 11$ and $n = 12$)	3.67	3.36	3.81	3.70
Female ($n = 44$ and $n = 45$)	3.05	3.76	3.46	3.9

Source authors

The difference in the means was also not significant among those who changed the bot's gender between the first and second exercises. This infers that the tool provides learning regardless of the gender of the bot and the topic.

44.6 Discussion

Problems included downloading the application from iOS devices in the first application, so instructions and practice times were adjusted accordingly.

Several students noted that they were unfamiliar with chatbot functioning. This was interesting because university students typically are more familiar with robotic systems due to their technology access and continuous participation in social networks. After analyzing the exercises and the bot's conversation logs, we found that the students had trouble understanding what to do and the type of questions to ask to complete the task. Likewise, the teachers detected that several journalism students failed to ask the bot's full name (to claim it as a genuine and trustworthy source); others only identified its first name. Some research students forgot they were interacting with a bot and acted as if it were a real person.

We observed that these themes and characters were adequate for the first interactions, but updating the themes and generating new personalities is necessary to expand the practice options.

These aspects are relevant because the chatbot is linked to academic exercises and activities. The instructions must be clear enough for students to conduct as many exercises as they want autonomously and independently.

44.7 Conclusions

Artificial intelligence can promote usability, impact learning, and make conversations more natural when students seek to extract more information for academic work or practice. According to heutagogical theory (Hase 2000), students can set their learning goals and apply their experiences to new contexts. This theory suggests that the bot is developed to provide a conversational tool to practice the interview at any time and place, react to questions in different ways, and even reject the interview or control the conversation.

It is a challenge for students to improve their interactive skills, obtain the best quantity and quality of information, and then organize it for writing. For the teacher, this is a new pedagogical strategy (Kuz et al. 2015).

The results indicated that the students performed the task when the bot's gender was either assigned or freely chosen. The objectives were also achieved by determining the degree of learning with this tool and its utility as an educational innovation. Interacting with Chatcontext improved students' confidence and ability to conduct interviews by structuring more precise questions to achieve higher quality information. These aspects will be explored in future work, as such analyses already exist in other countries (García-Avilés 2021).

Education has recently experienced one of its most significant technological transformations (Raposo-Rivas and Martínez-Figueira 2019). Higher education requires innovation because students must integrate into a changing labor force that demands autonomy and collaboration (Nuñez 2017). This goes hand-in-hand with one of the objectives of university studies to acquire better employment skills and perspectives that can be applied to real life (García-Aracil et al. 2021).

The results of this work provide a first approach to using this tool in courses. It shows that it is possible to improve the SUS-measured factors when the bot is used at least a second time, after the AI is learning has improved, and it is a quality model (Pollán 2020). Leveraging young people's interest in mobile technology and devices leads to implementing instruments like the chatbot, which is natural in the educational context (Ramos-Elizondo et al. 2010). It is a new way to energize the rhythm of class dynamics. Above all, it develops students' confidence in oral communication skills in a controlled and safe environment (Campaña-Jiménez et al. 2019).

One element that students value in virtuality is the opportunity to work autonomously and at their own pace (Tejedor et al. 2020). Both students and teachers must have technological skills, particularly considering the impossibility of attending face-to-face classes. The teacher must also tackle the challenge of modifying classes with technology (Opportunity or Educational Crisis 2020). It is imperative to achieve continuity in education with distance learning resources that can be used with a telephone, especially during the COVID-19 pandemic (Tajik and Vahedi 2021). It is also essential to prepare for a professional environment where artificial intelligence is present in various tasks (Túñez-López et al. 2021), such as data collection, editorial automation (Mullin 2016), and information distribution.

Artificial intelligence presents many opportunities to develop educational research. In this case, the bot developed communicative competency in a university to adapt to society's needs (Cuberes and Ventura 2017). Its versatility makes it an option that can impact other academic levels and purposes.

Acknowledgements This work was produced thanks to the Novus Project 2018 awarded by Tecnologico de Monterrey for developing educational innovation.

The authors appreciate the financial support and collaboration of Writing Lab, Institute for the Future of Education, Tecnologico de Monterrey for the facilities provided in mentoring and methodological development, and we acknowledge its technical support.

References

Abraham RR, Komattil R (2017) Heutagogic approach to developing capable learners. Med Teach 39(3). https://doi.org/10.1080/0142159X.2017.1270433

Albertos A, Domingo À, Albertos JE (2016) Estrategia Docente Para El Desarrollo de La Competencia Digital En El Aula Universitaria: Del Uso Recreativo Al Uso Formativo. Educar 52(2):243–261

Ávila-Tomás JF, Olano-Espinosa E, Minué-Lorenzo C, Martínez-Suberbiola FJ, Matilla-Pardo B, Serrano-Serrano E, Dejal G (2019) Nuevas Herramientas de Comunicación Digitales Entre Profesionales de La Salud y Pacientes. A Propósito Del Proyecto Dejal@ Bot. *Rev. Comun. y Salud* **2019**, *9* (2), 55–70

Bhoyrub J, Hurley J, Neilson GR, Ramsay M, Smith M (2010) Heutagogy: an alternative practice-based learning approach. Nurse Educ Pract 10(6):322–326

Campaña-Jiménez RL, Gallego-Arrufat MJ, Muñoz-Leiva F (2019) Estrategias de Enseñanza Para La Adquisición de Competencias En Formación Profesional: Perfiles de Estudiantes. Educar 55(1):203–229

Cuberes CR, Ventura R (2017) Nuevos Planteamientos de Formación Universitaria En Comunicación En España: Análisis de Las Competencias Asociadas al Ámbito de Los Estudios de Comunicación Global. Rev Lat Comun Soc 72:1554–1565

Feine J, Gnewuch U, Morana S, Maedche A (2019) A taxonomy of social cues for conversational agents. Int J Hum Comput Stud 132:138–161

García-Aracil A, Monteiro S, Almeida LS (2021) Students' perceptions of their preparedness for transition to work after graduation. Act Learn High Educ 22(1):49–62

García-Avilés J-A (2021) Journalism innovation research, a diverse and flourishing field (2000–2020). Prof la Inf 30(1)

Gómez de Sibandze E (2019) Artificial intelligence for journalism and media students. In: Kariithi N (ed) How African economies work: a guide to business and economics reporting. Konrad-Adenauer-Stiftung

Hase S, Kenyon C (2000) From Andragogy to Heutagogy. *ultiBASE In-Site*

Hedlefs Aguilar MI, de la Garza González A, Miranda MPS, Villegas AAG (2015) Adaptación Al Español Del Cuestionario de Usabilidad de Sistemas Informáticos CSUQ Spanish Adaptation of Computer System Usability Questionnaire CSUQ

Hernandez de la Rosa E (2020) ¿Cómo aplicar Inteligencia Artificial en educación?

Hípola P, Vargas-Quesada B (1999) Agentes inteligentes: Definición y Tipologia. Los Agentes de Información

Isaza-Restrepo A, Gómez MT, Cifuentes G, Argüello A (2018) The virtual patient as a learning tool: a mixed quantitative qualitative study. BMC Med Educ 18(1). https://doi.org/10.1186/s12 909-018-1395-8

Jaiswal A, Arun CJ (2021) Potential of artificial intelligence for transformation of the education system in India. Int J Educ Dev Inf Commun Technol 17(1):142–158

Kuz A, Falco M, Giandini R, Nahuel L (2015) Integrando Redes Sociales y Técnicas de Inteligencia Artificial En Entornos Educativos

LaGree D, Tefertiller A, Olsen K (2021) Preparing mass communications students for an evolving industry: the influence of emotional intelligence and extracurricular involvement on career adaptability. J Mass Commun Educ 76(1):65–77

Laiq M, Dieste O (2020) Chatbot-based interview simulator: a feasible approach to train novice requirements engineers. In: 2020 10th International workshop on requirements engineering education and training (REET), pp 1–8. https://doi.ieeecomputersociety.org/https://doi.org/10.1109/REET51203.2020.00007

Marinho S, Sánchez-García P (2020) Historia de La Enseñanza del Periodismo En España y Portugal: Una Línea de Tiempo Con Paralelismos y Contrastes. Cuad. Info 47:138–161

Mullin B (2016) Bloomberg EIC: Automation Is 'crucial to the future of journalism. Poynter, 27 Ap. https//www.poynter.org/news/bloomberg-eic-automation-crucial-future-journalism

Nuñez ME (2017) Aprendizaje instantáneo. *Observatorio de innovación educativa*

Ocaña-Fernández Y, Valenzuela-Fernández LA, Garro-Aburto LL (2019) Inteligencia Artificial y Sus Implicaciones En La Educación Superior. Propósitos y Represent. 7(2):536–568

Opportunity or Educational Crisis (2020) Reflections from psychology to face the teaching-learning processes in times of Covid-19. *Revista Internacional De Educación Para La Justicia Social.* 9(3)

Pollán RR (2020) Perspectivas y Retos de Las Técnicas de Inteligencia Artificial En El Ámbito de Las Ciencias Sociales y de La Comunicación. *Anu. Electrónico Estud. en Comun. Soc. Disert.* **2020,** *13* (1), 21–34

Ramos-Elizondo A-I, Herrera-Bernal J-A, Ramírez-Montoya M-S (2010) Developing cognitive skills with mobile learning: a case study. Comun Rev Científica Comun y Educ 17(34):201–209

Raposo-Rivas M, Martínez-Figueira E (2019) ¿ Tecnologías Emergentes o Tecnologías Emergiendo?: Un Estudio Contextualizado En La Práctica Preprofesional. Educar 55(2):499–518

Ruiz MJU, Fieiras-Ceide C, Túñez-López M (2020) L'ensenyament-Aprenentatge Del Periodisme Automatitzat En Institucions Públiques: Estudis, Propostes de Viabilitat i Perspectives d'impacte de La IA. Anàlisi Quad. Comun. i Cult. 62:131–146

Ryokai K, Vaucelle C, Cassell J (2003) Virtual peers as partners in storytelling and literacy learning. J Comput Assist Learn 19(2):195–208

Saad S, Issa T (2020) Integration or replacement: journalism in the era of artificial intelligence and robot journalism. Int J Media J Mass Commun 6(3)

Sánchez Álvarez JF (2015) Método de Evaluación de Usabilidad Aplicada a Productos de Software Que Facilitan El Acceso a Herramientas Informáticas de Personas Con Enfermedades Que Afectan La Motricidad. *Esc. Sist.*

Sánchez-Caballé A, Gisbert-Cervera M, Esteve-Món F (2021) Integrating digital competence in higher education curricula: an institutional analysis. Educar 57(1)

Schapals AK (2020) Automated journalism: expendable or supplementary for the future of journalistic work? Edward Elgar Publishing, In The Future of Creative Work

Schena J, Casademont RB, Singla C (2018) Valoraciones Actualizadas de Las Competencias Profesionales En La Práctica Laboral de Los Periodistas Españoles. Rev Lat Comun Soc 73:531–555

Shaw R (2017) 5 Innovative apps for journalists from 2017

Sobron I, Mendicute M, Altuna J (2010) Full-rate full-diversity space-frequency block coding for digital TV broadcasting. In: 2010 18th European signal processing conference. IEEE, pp 1514–1518

Sutcliffe C, Albeanu C (2016) 12 Essential self-taught journalism skills. https://www.journalism. co.uk/news/ten-essential-self-taught-journalism-skills/s2/a557267/

Tajik F, Vahedi M (2021) Quarantine and education: an assessment of Iranian formal education during the COVID-19 outbreak and school closures. Int J Educ Dev Inf Commun Technol 17(1):159–175

Tejedor S, Cervi L, Tusa F, Parola A (2020) Educación En Tiempos de Pandemia: Reflexiones de Alumnos y Profesores Sobre La Enseñanza Virtual Universitaria En España, Italia y Ecuador. Rev Lat Comun Soc 78:1–21

Túñez-López JM, Fieiras Ceide C, Vaz-Álvarez M (2021) Impacto de La Inteligencia Artificial En El Periodismo: Transformaciones En La Empresa, Los Productos, Los Contenidos y El Perfil Profesional (Impact of Artificial Intelligence on Journalism: Transformations in the Company, Products. Contents and Professi. Commun. Soc 34(1):177–193

Chapter 45
The Dissemination of Children's and Adolescents' Rights in the Design of an Application. The Case of LUDIRECHO

Alma Alejandra Soberano Serrano, Oliva Denisse Mejía Victoria, José Manuel Valencia Moreno, and Rodolfo Alan Martínez Rodríguez

45.1 Introduction

Since the reform of the Political Constitution of the Mexican United States (CPEUM), which took place in 2011, the participation of the Mexican Government in the promotion, respect, and dissemination of Human Rights has become mandatory. For children and adolescents, this reform has meant the participation of both national and international entities in issues concerning children and the integration of laws and legal recommendations toward recognizing their Human Rights. In addition, the collaboration of families, schools, and society should also be expected.Please confirm if the inserted city name is correct. Amend if necessary.Done

In addition, the United Nations (UN), through its specialized agency for Educational, Scientific and Cultural Organization (UNESCO), has reinforced SDG Goal #4 through the 2030 Agenda for Sustainable Development to "Ensure inclusive and equitable quality education and promote lifelong learning opportunities for all." The Incheon Declaration (2015) was also adopted, which sets the corresponding Framework for Action.

A. A. Soberano Serrano (✉) · O. D. Mejía Victoria · J. M. Valencia Moreno ·
R. A. Martínez Rodríguez
School of Administrative and Social Sciences of the Autonomous University of Baja California,
Tijuana, Mexico
e-mail: alma.soberano@uabc.edu.mx

O. D. Mejía Victoria
e-mail: dmejia@uabc.edu.mx

J. M. Valencia Moreno
e-mail: jova@uabc.edu.mx

R. A. Martínez Rodríguez
e-mail: rodolfo.alan.martinez.rodriguez@uabc.edu.mx

S. Hosseini et al. (eds.), *Technology-Enabled Innovations in Education*,
Transactions on Computer Systems and Networks,
https://doi.org/10.1007/978-981-19-3383-7_45

According to data from the National Institute of Geography and Statistics (INEGI 2020), there are currently 126,014,024 people in Mexico. Of these, 21,750,020.54 people (17.26% of the total population) are between 5 and 14 years old, the defined population of children and adolescents. On the other hand, the percentage of households with Internet access in our country is 52.9% and computer users six years of age or older are 65.8% of Mexicans.

It is also necessary to consider that due to the SARS COV 2 virus contingency, there was a transition from face-to-face activities to online activities. Therefore, there is a need to promote Children's and Adolescents' Rights through digital media and be consistent with the contents of the "Key Learning Objectives for Comprehensive Education" issued by the Ministry of Public Education (SEP) in 2017.

Recognizing the Rights of Children and Adolescents goes beyond the legal aspects. These include social psychology, human development, social representations, and the socio-economic, technological, and cultural aspects that affect the upbringing of children and adolescents. All these aspects play a fundamental role in conceptualizing, promoting, and communicating these rights (López Galicia 2016). It is necessary to support the empowerment of minors in Mexico. In other words, the idea that they have rights must start from accepting that they are human beings, and elders who take care of them must understand and reinforce these rights in a scenario of mutual respect and care.

In this regard, López Galicia (2016) writes:

> The idea of establishing children's rights must be reinforced based on their entitlement, based on their human rights, on their basic needs, and on the full respect for their person. This will allow us to deconstruct and redefine the new relationship between adults and children. It will allow us to stop considering them as objects and look at them as holders and subjects of rights, without limitations created by our own cultural, social, and cognitive conceptualizations.

Children's and Adolescents' Rights are included in the CPEUM and international treaties, such as in the Convention on the Rights of the Child in the optional protocols and in the General Law on the Rights of Children and Adolescents (2014) (Ley General de los Derechos, 2014). Minors and their guardians must be informed about and enforce these legal documents.

The Ministry of Public Education (SEP) is responsible for developing the Educational Model for Primary Education. This model specifies the planning, evaluation, and feedback necessary to implement the Human Right to Education established in Article 3 of the CPEUM. In this Model, there is a set of documents called "Aprendizaje Clave para la Educación Integral" (Key Learning Objectives for Integral Education). These documents include the subject "Ethical and Civic Education" at the secondary level. This subject contains the content for the Children's and Adolescents' Rights for Secondary Education.

The curricular content of secondary education in Mexico uses international benchmarks such as the Program for International Student Assessment (PISA) and UNESCO's Agenda 2030. These are used to "guarantee inclusive and quality education to promote learning opportunities for all" (SEP 2017).

The objective of this project is directly related to one of the graduation profile traits of secondary school students, specifically, "Coexistence and citizenship: The student identifies himself/herself as Mexican. Recognizes the country's individual, social, cultural, ethnic, and linguistic diversity and is aware of Mexico's role in the world. Acts with social responsibility, adhering to human rights and respecting the law" (SEP 2017).

Information and Communication Technologies (ICTs) play an essential role in disseminating and exercising Children's and Adolescents' Rights (DNNA). Through ICTs, it is possible to develop innovative applications in the teaching–learning process, primarily due to the interactive processes they offer and the dissemination they allow. For its part, gamification motivates the audience, allows decision-making, and inspires game mechanics (Zichermann 2011). The use of games as a learning tool can lead to gamification in constructing citizenship or implementing public services (Romero-Rodríguez et al. 2017). This is multiplied if the games are online or through virtual applications. These experiences are positive by reinforcing user interaction, facilitating role changes, or achieving common goals. Glover (2013) highlights the goal orientation, recognition, and progress found within video games.

This research project is developed within the scope of the Academic Group (AG) "UABC-321- Innovation, strategic management, and sustainable regional development." This Academic Group is part of the Autonomous University of Baja California. One of the objectives of the Group is to develop research projects that offer practical results and bring users closer to citizen commitment with social responsibility. The LUDIRECHO research project seeks to promote Children's and Adolescents' Rights among this population, their tutors, and the educational system. The project has resources granted by the Teacher Professional Development Program (TPDP) and initiates interdisciplinary attention to problems.

This paper presents some preliminary results, including the contents, which offer clues to help the users advance in the game's missions and simultaneously learn their rights. For this purpose, we conducted documentary research in the categories "Expected learning," "General principles," and "Content of Children's and Adolescents' Rights." A data collection instrument was prepared from the information gathered. The instrument consisted of 180 items submitted for evaluation by external experts and teachers of the Ethics and Civic Education subject in secondary schools. On the other hand, the fundamental concepts of appropriation were created through in-depth interviews held with a group of high school adolescents who had already taken the subject. Based on this information, digital infographics and short videos were created to include the necessary content for the design and development of the proposed application.

Digital infographics were used in this project to convey information iconographically. "Infographics have their own rules, tools, and structure because they use a specific methodology that includes data collection, prioritization, and distribution" (Cortés and Sánchez 2008, p. 3). In addition, infographics are a voice used in the modern era.

Infographics are tools that synthesize information and present it attractively to the viewer, mainly through images and text. Images are ideal for conveying information to children and adolescents, representing the video game's target audience. A better understanding of Children's and Adolescents' Rights through visual media simplifies the content, explains, and attracts attention.

As another preliminary result, this paper describes the type of video game being developed. Since the video game has a formative purpose, learning Children's and Adolescents' Rights, it is considered a *serious* video game. This project aims to use tools such as infographics and a serious video game to support the teaching of Children's and Adolescents' Rights in the secondary education system and disseminate among children and adolescents the rights they have and, above all, that they deserve respect.

This article is structured by sections that include related work, methodology, preliminary results, discussion, and conclusions. In the related work section, publications that disseminate Children's and Adolescents' Rights are presented. Subsequently, the methodology used in this project is described. In the Preliminary Results section, the results achieved so far in the project are reported. This is followed by a discussion of these results. In the last section, the conclusions are presented.

45.2 Related Work

Today, users can own technology because it is part of their learning (Baloco Navarro 2017). Technology can be used to push the human rights agenda forward. Mathiyazhagan (2021) proposes that technology could educate young people about human rights and social justice through virtual reality and facial and image recognition with artificial intelligence (AI).

One of the most widely used technologies today is the smartphone, and with it, a wide variety of applications and uses to support learning. Video games were designed for entertainment, but they have been adapted for learning little by little. When video games are created for learning and not as mere entertainment, they are known as *serious.*

Abt (1970) introduced the term "serious game." The researcher states that games can be included in the teaching–learning process without sacrificing fun. Cheng (2015) (Michael & Chen, 2005) define serious games as the combination of video games and education. In this case, the main objective is learning in any of its forms and not just entertainment. These games interact with the user to promote learning or the exchange of information through entertainment, amusement, and playing (Ulicsak 2010).

In recent years, serious games to raise awareness of Children's and Adolescents' Rights have increased. Table 45.1 displays some examples.

These games are fun and teach Children's and Adolescents' Rights. They were created with different tools from professional developments for fundamental and simple games (like the ones above). Some games require Adobe Flash Player, an application to play multimedia content. This application is now obsolete, so games that use it can no longer be played online. The last one is a set of board games targeted at children.

Table 45.1 Serious games to teach and promote human rights, especially among children and adolescents

Serious game	Description
Right runner	A 5-level game launched by the United Nations Children's Fund (UNICEF). This game teaches about children's rights (the term "child" includes boys and girls) and is set in Latin America and the Caribbean https://www.unicef.org/lac/en/right-runner
Ayiti: The cost of life	This serious game, supported by UNICEF, is designed to demonstrate how poverty could become an obstacle for education. It is no longer in use because it uses the Adobe Flash Player component, which is no longer available https://ayiti.globalkids.org/game/
Blind	This game is about a blind teenager who has to go to school alone. He has to overcome different obstacles on the street and in public transportation, among others. It requires Adobe Flash Player http://youth-egames.org/games/blind/blind.html
Fighters for rights	This game provides information about famous people who have fought for human rights in different countries http://youth-egames.org/games/ffr/ffr.html
The human rights game	Provided by Amnesty International. The objective of this game is to promote reflection on the difference between two situations. One is to be free and have rights, and the other is to not be free and be deprived of the exercise of these rights http://www.amnistiacatalunya.org/edu/4p/es/e-4p-juego.html
CNDH #Entera2	The National Human Rights Commission of Mexico (CNDH) launched an app using the concept "play and learn". This is a playful mechanism for children between 6 and 12 years of age. It allows them to learn the fundamental concepts of Human Rights https://apps.apple.com/mx/app/cndh-entera2/id1553529924
HURI—Human Rights	This game uses digital pedagogies to address issues of diversity, social participation, environment, and peace. The story is to help some YouTubers because their channel has been hacked https://www.apple.com/mx/app-store/
Children's rights—games (Los derechos de las niñas y los niños—Juegos)	It is a collection of serious board games for children. The National Human Rights Commission of Mexico developed them https://www.cndh.org.mx/ni%C3%B1as-ni%C3%B1os/juegos
Roulette, Quiz, Hangman, Word Search, Airplane pairs, Guess the image, True or False	There are online tools that allow the creation of classic games, such as Wordwall. Different types of games have been created to raise awareness of Children's and Adolescents' Rights with this tool. Among them: https://wordwall.net/es/resource/4588985/ruleta-de-los-derechos-del-ni%C3%B1o-ni%C3%B1as-y-adolescentes https://wordwall.net/resource/5923980/derechos-del-ni%C3%B1o https://wordwall.net/es/resource/22506331/derechos-de-los-ni%C3%B1os

Source Elaborated by the authors

There are online tools to develop games such as the classic Word Search, Roulette, Quiz, and Airplane. These tools have also been used to create simple games to teach Children's and Adolescents' Rights, such as "Roulette of Children's and Adolescents' Rights," "Children's Rights," and "Rights or Duties," among others. All these simple games were developed with Wordwall, an online tool.

This project aimed to create a serious game that helps teach and promote Children's and Adolescents' Rights in the public education system in Mexico, especially at the secondary school level. Thus, it aimed not only to create a serious video game but also to be aligned with the thematic content of the public education system. Thus, it supports secondary education teachers in reinforcing content with students and providing the parents with a fun tool to teach their children.

45.3 Methodology

This research design was qualitative and descriptive, using focus groups as an instrument for data collection and measurement. Preliminary results are shown, referring to the development stage of the contents corresponding to the Children's and Adolescents' Rights; also, it defines the use of infographics, videos, and a Nano Massive Open Online Course (MOOC) that will be posted on the application's page for reference.

A selected-topics-and-contents guide was designed based on the expected learning of the Ethics and Civic Education subject. It was also complemented with a subdivision of the Children's and Adolescents' Rights, considering the guiding principles and the content of these Rights. This resulted in three categories of classification that guided the design of multiple-choice questions, the infographics, and the videos produced up to this moment.

The contents designed were based on the requirements of the Convention on the Rights of the Child, the General Law on the Rights of Children and Adolescents in Mexico (LGDNNA). Dissemination documents were also reviewed, including videos, manuals, and infographics from the National Human Rights Commission (Comisión Nacional de los Derechos Humanos 2021), UNICEF Mexico, the National System for the Protection of Children and Adolescents (SIPINNA), and the Supreme Court of Justice of the Nation (SCJN).

Once the categories were defined, a questionnaire of 180 items was developed and submitted for clarity, coherence, and relevance validation. The content and language used in these items were validated according to the methodology of Escobar et al. (2017). Six external experts, teachers of Ethical and Civic Education in secondary schools in Baja California, were selected after using the snowball technique (See Table 45.2).

These teachers were invited to participate and accepted by e-mail. After this, we held a Zoom session in which we explained the procedure and gave them the validation instrument. The validation instrument was based on the Escobar and Cuervo

Table 45.2 Data collection tool validation instrument

Category	Grade	Indicator
Clarity		
The question is easily understood, i.e., its syntax and semantics are appropriate	1. Does not meet the criterion	The question is not straightforward
	2. Low level	The question requires several modifications or a relevant modification in the use of the words according to their meaning or word order
	3. Moderate level	A particular modification of some of the question terms is required
	4. High level	The question is straightforward, having adequate syntax and semantics
Coherence		
The question is logically related to the subject being assessed	1. Does not meet the criterion	The question has no logical connection to the topic
	2. Low level	The question is minimally connected to the topic
	3. Moderate level	The question is somewhat connected to the topic
	4. High level	The question is wholly connected to the topic to be assessed
Relevance		
The question is essential and relevant, i.e., it must be included	1. Does not meet the criterion	The question can be eliminated without affecting the impact of the topic
	2. Low level	The question has some relevance but can be replaced by some other question
	3. Moderate level	The question is moderately relevant
	4. High level	The question is relevant and should be included

Source Escobar-Pérez and Cuervo Martínez (2008). "Content validity and expert judgment: an approach to their use." Advances in Measurement 6 (1). 27–36 methodology, in which clarity, coherence, and relevance indicators are taken into account (Table 45.2).

Once the information on the items had been validated, we considered optimal the questions that attained a score of 12 (i.e., with a score of four or "high level" in each indicator). 110 items were selected as a result. Subsequently, the infographics were created using Canva. Canva is free software that offers pre-designed templates for the adjustment and design of content to be distributed through these visual representations of information and data.

Once the outstanding themes were reviewed (considering that the video game would be hosted on the same platform containing the infographics and videos), we selected the Children's and Adolescents' Rights included in the Convention on the Rights of the Child. Based on these criteria, we created the first 20 infographics that explain and situate these rights within the international legal framework. Subsequently, we made six infographics related to the history and institutions protecting and accompanying children and adolescents to defend these rights. This exercise allowed us to decide that we would make three-minute videos for the most complex concepts, the fundamental principles. These videos would reinforce topics reviewed in class to understand dignity, non-discrimination, equality, and gender equity.

These designed infographics were presented to an informal focus group of eight teenagers from Baja California and Veracruz who had previously studied Ethics and Civic Education. They validated both the content and the visual impact, as indicated in the LEAN UX methodology (2014) (Liikanen et al2014), observing all the requirements foreseen for the users in the design of the products, thus seeking a minimum risk of implementation.

This first focus group was in charge of reviewing the contents of the infographics and their wording. Subsequently, they participated in the presentation of the App prototypes. Eight students were chosen to cover the private, public, and tele-secondary education schemes. This was a controllable and planned number of students for organizing focus groups according to the methodology of Saldanha da Silveira et al. (2015).

45.4 Preliminary Results

As established throughout this document, this project corresponds to the first of three stages in the planned application. The developed contents were suitable to create missions and clues that the adolescents would follow during the video game to be designed. It would also allow them to gradually increase the levels of complexity so that when they reached the goal, they would have advanced in the comprehension of Children's and Adolescents' Rights.

The first result was identifying which Children's and Adolescents' Rights students should know, according to the topics covered in "Ethics and Civic Education" at the secondary level. (See Table 45.3).

Table 45.3 List of thematic contents of Ethics and Civic Education and Children's and Adolescents' Rights

Learning objectives	Children's and Adolescents' Rights
Participate in actions that contribute to strengthening their dignity and developing their potential and capabilities	Right to life, right to live in a family, right to identity, right to substantive equality, right to education
Collective identity, sense of belonging and social cohesion	Right to identity, right to live in a family, right not to be discriminated, right to inclusion, right to association, right to education
Gender equality and perspective	Right to identity, right not to be discriminated, right to inclusion, right to freedom of belief, right to freedom of expression, right to education
The subject of law and human dignity	Right to life, right to identity, right to substantive equality, right not to be discriminated, right to freedom from violence, right to freedom of belief, right to education
Freedom as a value and fundamental human right	Right not to be discriminated, right to inclusion, right to freedom of belief, right to freedom of expression, right to participation, right to association, right to education, right not to be discriminated, right to freedom of expression, right to participation, right to association
Criteria for the responsible practice of freedom: dignity, rights and the common good	Right to education, right to non-discrimination, right to inclusion, right to identity, right to substantive equality, right to a life free of violence

Created according to the categorization designed following the LGNNA and "Key Objectives for the Integral Education of the Ethics and Civic Education subject."

   Twelve of the 20 Children's and Adolescent Rights established by the CNDH were identified; that is, 60% of the Children's and Adolescents' Rights in Ethics and Civic Education were identified. This result was achieved with the collaboration of eight external experts. Six of the experts were Ethics and Civic Education teachers, and the other two were students of the master's degree in Education. Five of the teachers were from local secondary schools, and the other one was a teacher assigned to a secondary school in another state of the Mexican Republic. The two students of the master's degree in education were from different states. They collaborated on a data collection instrument initially consisting of 180 items, which finally comprised 110 items after validation by the eight experts.

   The identified Children's and Adolescents' Rights and the instrument validated by the experts were the sources for designing the infographics and videos. This was the relevant information selected, forming one of the four pillars proposed by the Drummond et al. (2017) framework. This information was also used to construct the questions forming part of the missions to solve the serious video game.

Fig. 45.1 Infographic
"Right to live in a family."
Prepared by the authors
based on information from
the National System for the
Comprehensive Protection of
Children and Adolescents
(SIPINNA 2021)

So far, 20 infographics have been designed and will be placed in a specific section of the project's website. The infographics will be available for reference and for downloading. An example of infographics is shown in Fig. 45.1.

The thematic content of the MOOC and the videos corresponding to the general principles are currently being designed in collaboration with researchers from the Universidad Veracruzana and the Laboratorio Nacional en Informática Avanzada (LANIA). The video game and the corresponding platform are also being designed.

45.5 Discussion

In the educational sciences, there has been a strong interest in using serious games. Building knowledge is the primary learning objective of this type of game (Cheng et al. 2015). For this reason, serious video games are considered for disseminating Children's and Adolescents' Rights in applications oriented to teach particular topics. This type of game involves at least the technology or application development area and the content creation area. However, the purpose of this work was not only to create a serious game but also to incorporate its contents and its use in the Mexican educational system and cover topics taught in secondary education.

To incorporate the application of the teaching of Children's and Adolescents' Rights in the National Education System, we chose the subject of Civic and Ethical Education to analyze its thematic content and the Children's and Adolescents' Rights addresses. This subject is taught at the secondary education level, and through it, the fundamental principles of human rights, especially Children's and Adolescents' Rights, are presented to students. This subject was analyzed by six professors who teach Ethics and Civic Education in two different states of the Mexican Republic and by two students of a postgraduate program in Education in another state. The participation of specialists from three different states of Mexico reduced the bias that could occur due to how the subject is taught locally. However, more participation of professors from other states will be considered later to reduce bias possibility as much as possible.

The Ethics and Civic Education subject analysis was carried out through a data collection tool made up of 180 items. When validated by the six professors and two master's degree students, this tool was reduced to 110 items. The main reason for the reduction of items is that the items were poorly formulated, i.e., they were not well interpreted by the evaluators of the instrument.

Because of the reduction of the items, the identified Children's and Adolescents' Rights were also reduced. Initially, all 100% of the Children's and Adolescents' Rights defined by the CNDH and contained in the General Law of Children's and Adolescents' Rights (LGDNNA) were included. However, now they only represent 60% (see Table 45.3). Sixty percent of Children's and Adolescents' Rights were identified within the Ethics and Civic Education subject. This implies the consensus of the authors of this work, teachers who are teaching this subject daily. This consensus was the starting point for building the different media contents (infographics, videos) and the serious video game.

45.6   Conclusions

Citizen participation, cohesion, and social responsibility are a consequence of education based on the respect and appropriation of human rights. The result of the sum of individual actions aimed at the common welfare is a task of the classroom and the joint work of social actors, including the family and applied research. Through games, we learn and socialize. Information technologies allow the dissemination of serious games with cognitive content that supports the integral formation of the individual and society. Projects such as LUDIRECHO, with the participation of professionals from different disciplines and users in direct contact with the child population daily and who collaborate to develop content, present options for disseminating Children's and Adolescents' Rights. This, in turn, will allow children and adolescents to live a more dignified, free, and democratic life, aligned with UNESCO guidelines and the SDGs.

So far, we have achieved developing support material in the form of infographics and videos that complement the contents of Ethics and Civic Education that are reviewed at the secondary level in secondary education institutions. These will allow the serious video game users to solve the missions and progress in the different game levels. We are moving in the right direction thanks to the validations and feedback received by the focus group with the adolescents and the review of the six external experts, teachers of " Ethics and Civic Education " in secondary schools in Baja, California.

However, the validation of the instrument, carried out by eight experts from three different states, is a current limitation of the research. This situation could be a reason for a bias problem since we do not have a representative population of teachers who teach the Ethics and Civic Education subject.

Subsequently, the support of more teachers will be sought to have sufficient representation. In addition, the creation of more content and the design and development of the serious video game and the project's website will continue.

References

Abt C (1970) Serious games. The Viking Press

Baloco Navarro CP (2017) *En la Frontera del Entretenimiento y la Educación : Juegos Serios.* 2(2), 30–46. http://investigaciones.uniatlantico.edu.co/revistas/index.php/CEDOTIC/art icle/view/1869

Cheng M-T, Chen J-H, Chu S-J, Chen S-Y (2015) The use of serious games in science education: a review of selected empirical research from 2002 to 2013. J Comput Educ 2(3):353–375. https://doi.org/10.1007/s40692-015-0039-9

Comisión Nacional de Derechos Humanos. (2021). *Derecho de las niñas, niños y adolescentes.* https://www.cndh.org.mx/derechos-humanos/derechos-de-las-ninas-ninos-y-adolescentes

Cortés R, Sánchez I (2008) La infografía en los medios impresos, estudio descriptivo de la infografía en el diario La Nación. *Anuario Electónico de Estudios En Comunicación Social "Disertaciones,"* *1*(1). https://www.redalyc.org/articulo.oa?id=511555566005

Drummond D, Hadchouel A, Tesnière A (2017) Serious games for health: three steps forwards. Adv Simul 2(1):1–8. https://doi.org/10.1186/s41077-017-0036-3

Escobar Pérez J, Cuervo Martínez Á (2008) Validez de contenido y juicio de expertos. Una aproximación a su utilización. *Avances En Medición, 6*(1), 27–36. https://dialnet.unirioja.es/servlet/art iculo?codigo=2981181

Glover I (2013) Play as you learn: gamification as a technique for motivating learners. In: Proceedings of EdMedia 2013-world conference on educational media and technology, 1999–2008. Proceedings of world conference on educational multimedia, hypermedia and telecommunications, Oct 1999–2008. http://shura.shu.ac.uk/7172/

Instituto Nacional de Estadística y Geografía (2020) *Datos de población.* Censo de Población y Vivienda 2020. https://www.inegi.org.mx/temas/estructura/

Ley General de los Derechos de las niñas, niños y adolescentes, 1 (2014) (testimony of Congreso de la Unión). http://www.diputados.gob.mx/LeyesBiblio/pdf/LGDNNA_110121.pdf

Liikkanen L, Kilpiö H, Svan L. y Hiltunen M (2014) Lean UX: the next generation of user-centered agile development? In: NordiCHI '14: Proceedings of the 8th Nordic conference on human-computer interaction: fun, fast, foundational, pp 1095–1100. https://doi.org/10.1145/2639189. 2670285

López MA (2016) Una mirada a los Derechos de las niñas y niños: su resignificación. Comisión Nacional de los Derechos Humanos de México. http://appweb.cndh.org.mx/biblioteca/archivos/pdfs/fas-CTDH-Derechos-Ninas-Ninos_1.pdf

Mathiyazhagan S (2021) Field practice, emerging technologies, and human rights: the emergence of tech social workers. J Hum Rights Soc Work. https://doi.org/10.1007/s41134-021-00190-0

Michael D, y Chen S (2005) Serious games: games that educate, train, and inform. Muska & Lipman/Premier-Trade. https://dl.acm.org/doi/book/https://doi.org/10.5555/1051239

Romero-Rodríguez LM, Torres-Toukoumidis A, y Aguaded I (2017) Ludificación y educación para la ciudadanía. Revisión de las experiencias significativas. Educar, 53(1). https://redined.mecd.gob.es/xmlui/bitstream/handle/11162/148208/846-3100-2-PB.pdf

Saldanha da Silveira D, Colomé C, Heck T, Nunes da Silva M, y Viero V (2015) Grupo focal y análisis de contenido en investigación cualitativa. Index de Enfermería, 24(1). https://doi.org/10.4321/S1132-12962015000100016

Secretaría de Educación Pública (2017) Aprendizajes Clave para la educación integral. Formación cívica y ética, educación secundaria. SEP. https://www.planyprogramasdestudio.sep.gob.mx/descargables/biblioteca/secundaria/fcye/1-LpM-sec-Formacion-Civica-y-etica.pdf

Sistema Nacional de Protección de Niñas, Niños y Adolescentes (SIPINNA) (2021) ¿Qué es el SIPINNA? - Dossier informativo. https://www.gob.mx/sipinna/es/articulos/que-es-el-sipinna-dossier-informativo-269151

Ulicsak M (2010) Games in education: serious games. Review for futurelab. Bristol, United Kingdom. Futurelab Innovation in Education. https://www.nfer.ac.uk/games-in-education-serious-games

Zichermann G, y Cunningham C (2011) Gamification by Design: Implementing Game Mechanics in Web and Mobile Apps. O'Reilly Media; 1er edición (22 Agosto 2011)

Chapter 46
School Homework or Assignments and Technological Intervention. A Challenge that Heralds a Paradigm Shift

Martha Guadalupe Escoto Villaseñor, Rosa María Navarrete Hernández, and Rosa Estela Russi García

46.1 Introduction

Homework and academic assignments are complementary activities of specific classes to achieve particular objectives. Their intention is to reinforce the knowledge acquired in the classroom, develop new skills, and pursue established objectives to achieve skills and competencies. Performing the homework and assignments, the students apply the previous knowledge and new knowledge acquired in some subject. In evaluating the tasks, the teacher can identify the student's difficulties and the unclear processes to reinforce and provide methods that help the student achieve the desired goals.

For Stein and Smith (1998), a task is defined as "a segment of class activity dedicated to developing a particular mathematical idea." For this, it is necessary to understand, interpret, identify, analyze, perform elementary operations, use basic formulas, and solve equations and problems relevant to their environment. Students must perform elementary mathematical operations using simple formulas and understand mathematical language to translate and interpret the handled information. This promotes the autonomy of thought to make decisions and channel and interpret the information received.

Incorporating new technologies in schools promotes change in educational methods. Education now confronts new tools that call into question the old methods to perform an activity. The new technological environment transmits and shares information at high speed; thus, it is essential to surf the net and know its multitudinous resources. More importantly, it is vital to understand and manipulate the different

M. G. Escoto Villaseñor (✉) · R. M. Navarrete Hernández · R. E. Russi García
Center of Scientific and Technological Studies No 1, Instituto Politécnico Nacional, Mexico City, Mexico
e-mail: mgesoto@ipn.mx

tools students have to do the homework and school assignments. This way, one can visualize their scope, enabling the planning of new topics that allow a change.

46.2 Development

It must be comprehended that the homework and assignments from the teachers in the mathematics learning unit have ceased to be in tune with current times because the information on any subject and the solution to various problems assigned by the teacher can be solved on the Web. Thus, changes are necessary to train our students to be citizens prepared to live in today's society.

This research project investigates different existing tools on the web and uses them. The tasks or assignments granted by the teacher are not in tune with the current times because the solutions can be found on the Web quickly, easily, and simply. The student problems and activities in mathematics need to be changed, and the teacher must determine what necessary changes will fulfill their training role to prepare citizens for today and the future.

It is relevant to visualize the acceleration and increase of information and the changes that challenge the most recognized traditional educational practices, which have become obsolete.

One must question the problem, know it, analyze it, and decide the most appropriate tools. Does their use achieve the didactic objectives of the homework tasks and school assignments? Review the topic, put it into practice, and consolidate student knowledge, research, and creativity. Consider the practice values and their link to commitment, responsibility, honesty, and punctuality. We want to understand the impact that technology has on students' task performance, how they should adapt to technologies, and thereby make necessary changes so that they can manage the challenges of today's reality.

In the environment of technological change, education faces the need to innovate pedagogical methods to convene and be inspiring for the new generations. In this work, only exploratory research is carried out regarding the resolution of homework tasks and school assignments. We consider it vitally important to analyze different technological tools to mediate tasks. The purpose is to verify if their use meets the objectives established for their utilization.

46.2.1 Theoretical Framework

School tasks comprise a set of practices that affirm and legitimize operating with the traditional knowledge covered in the school. Without ignoring the criticisms of consuming non-school time and its repetitive nature, we want to postulate that tasks are "ways of doing," relevant devices to investigate the transformations of school practices by using digital media in the classroom (Trujillo 2016).

Serrano et al. (2016) affirm that educational technology constitutes a discipline responsible for the study of the media, materials, web portals, and technological platforms to service-learning processes; It includes the resources for training and instructional purposes, designed initially to respond to the needs and concerns of users.

Hoyos (2009) alludes to the instructor examining how students use technology and what they learn from it.

Open the school to reality and take advantage of the possibilities that the environment and context offer to develop a meaningful education in the age of communication. It is not possible, nor should it be, to separate education and the integration of new technologies when talking about "school" (Pérez 2010). As Katherine Neville mentions (1992), those who cannot keep pace with the technological revolution will find themselves obsolete.

The philosopher (Kuhn2000) considers that when the general basic assumptions, theories, laws, and technology adopted by members of the scientific community cannot explain certain phenomena, anomalies, and questions related to the natural sciences, there will be a change of scientific paradigm.

46.2.2 Problem Statement

As teachers, we assign our students homework or assignments to develop outside the classroom as a teaching/learning methodology that usually focuses on a subject or topic reviewed in class. Regarding the mathematics learning units, the study is fundamental for intellectual development. It helps to be logical, reason orderly, and have a mind prepared for thought, criticism, and abstraction. The study of math promotes the construction of language and thought necessary to know the meaning of the symbols and operations used to approach and resolve problems.

Given the availability and accessibility of resources and the response speed of the Web to support students in the homework or assignments from the teacher, education must confront the need to innovate. More, it is necessary to know the tools and resources that students have at their disposal, know their context, navigate, discover, experiment, and analyze this new environment. But what does the Web offer to solve the various homework tasks or assignments that the teachers grant to their students in the mathematics learning units in the upper level of middle school?

46.2.3 Method

Confronted with profound, accelerating technological changes, educators must inno-vate their pedagogical methods. This research work is exploratory, examining math-ematical tasks assigned by the teacher and the use of existing applications on the web. Through this exploration, we sought to show that educational institutions have ceased to be in tune with current times because information on any subject and the solution to various assignments or school tasks can be found on the internet. Hence, changes are necessary for teachers to fulfill their role of training citizens prepared to live in today's society.

In this project, we present some of the objectives related to some of the most common tasks that mathematics teachers in the upper middle-school level usually assign students and some of the existing tools on the web to solve these tasks. This research design is flexible because the primary function is not to prove mathematical solutions but to be the point of debate for a more profound development of the topic.

46.2.4 Results

The tour of the web turned up fascinating links. We took the opportunity to test their resolutions of some tasks or assignments teachers typically give students and examined how the web tools resolved the tasks.

Task solving mathematical problems.

A mathematical problem involves an unknown of a particular mathematical entity, which must be resolved by another entity of the same type that one has to discover. For the resolution, specific steps must be followed to obtain the answer and demonstrate the reasoning.

To resolve mathematical problems on the Web, we have:

Symbolab: equation search and mathematical solver—this software solves algebra, trigonometry, and calculation problems step by step.

- Photomath: solves arithmetic, algebra, and integral calculus problems just by taking a picture.
- Mathematical calculators: provide step-by-step solutions for mathematical prob-lems.
- Socratic: a mobile app to help students with their assignments by providing educational resources such as videos, definitions, questions, answers, links, and more.
- Wolfram Alpha: is an online search engine that answers questions and performs calculations immediately with detailed answers.

This only mentions a few applications. Many more web pages and software apps support the solution of mathematical problems assigned by teachers to their students.

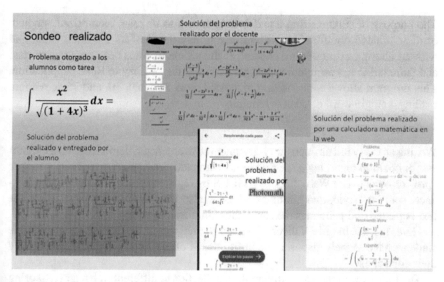

Fig. 46.1 Integral problem. *Source* Own elaboration

In this teaching activity, we gave the task to solve four integral equations reviewed in class to 95 upper middle-level students studying the integral calculus learning unit. They were divided into two groups of 45 and 50 members.

The result was that 20% of these students delivered the task on time but only copied the answers provided by the Photomath app. Five percent used another application to solve the exercises. This is where the question arises: Does the deliverable meet the teacher's objectives when assigning the task? Figure 46.1 shows one of the exercises assigned to the students, the answer provided by the teachers, the answer given by the student, the solution of the problem by Photomath, and the solution of the exercise by a mathematical calculator existing on the web.

Faced with the crisis of the classical paradigm, where immediate alternative answers are not seen, change looks slow, and the use of technology without guidance causes misuse of resources, one must specify and clarify the objective of the task assigned. This is where it is necessary to reinforce the values of honesty and trust upon carrying out school activities and that one should use the various resources skillfully and critically. Emphasize technological resources like computer programs and applications as instruments to support learning and applying mathematics. Every support tool is useful when the students are guided about their appropriate uses. This approach facilitates the changes that are required in this new educational context.

When browsing the Web, we identified this problem of the student not fulfilling the desired objective of the mathematics learning unit; they can complete an assignment on time and in the required format but not achieve the learning.

Task: to make a summary

The purpose of summarizing a text is to reduce it to be read, memorized, studied, or disseminated comfortably, without losing any detail of its Essential Data, and without altering or modifying content. If the article that has been assigned to read and summarize has an internet link, you can use the "I Lazy to Read" application. This program allows summarizing requested work in 5, 20, 30, and 75%, without reading a single word of what is required.

Task: to write an essay

Writing an essay has an expository-argumentative character, demonstrating a hypothesis or position regarding a specific topic, using an argumentative sequence to argue "pro" or object. The Web offers us STILUS by registering; it checks writing, coherence, spelling, style, and grammar. There is also the Pre Post Seo page where the text is pasted and generates the same but with different words.

Here, the teaching task diversifies, and the teacher must know the tools that the students have at their disposal, the utility that it offers, and the benefit provided by their correct use.

The following table is a small sample, a collection of different web pages exploring resources and their use. The invitation is to browse and form criteria for each application as a tool in the educational field.

The purpose is to verify if performing a task using technology meets the objectives or purpose that the teacher has in mind or if it implies a change of conceptualization or method. The invitation is to browse and use the technology available on the web. Here are some pages that may be of interest (Table 46.1).

There is no doubt that the educational paradigm is changing. The old methodologies used for decades require analyses, study, and innovation. From every angle, education must be reinvented without forgetting its bases.

46.2.5   Discussion

The present accumulation of technology provides the ideal environment to investigate, analyze, transform, create, share, venture, and implement…in short, to transmute the educational processes.

The era of connectivism radically invites change in the entire educational context. The evolution integrates education with society's needs without forgetting history and the roots that characterize it. Now, the decisions made derive from the perspective of entrenched education; very little is projected for future education.

Faced with the crisis of the classical paradigm, where immediate alternative responses are not visible, and change is slow, we are at a turning point where education must be renewed and restructured.

Exploratory research in the use of technology in education is vital; analyzing how different tools are used is essential for mediation between education and technology.

In such variable circumstances, uncertain conditions, and trends with no apparent limitations (given the progress and influence of the dissemination of knowledge and

Table 46.1   A sample of different web pages exploring resources and their use

Task assigned by the teacher	Web page	Internet response
Conclusions	Draw.io	Develop the conclusions of your essays
Questionnaires	Braily	Answer all the questions on it
Essays	Quillbot	Paraphrase any text
Generate mental maps	Free online conclusion generator	Generate mind maps, diagrams, etc
Mental Maps	Mind meister	Quick and easy mental maps
Presentation	Beautiful.ai	Presentations that are designed with artificial intelligence
Presentation or summary of a topic	Essaytyper	Write without knowing or writing anything about the subject. Performs immediate tests with artificial intelligence
Problems or questions of Algebra, Geometry, Trigonometry, Biology, Chemistry, Physics, History, and Literature	Socratic by Google	Use your voice or camera to solve Algebra, Geometry, Trigonometry, Biology, Chemistry, Physics, History, and Literature questions
Problems or questions of Algebra, Geometry, Trigonometry, Biology, Chemistry, Physics, History, and Literature	Wólfram Alpha	Answers questions about math, finance, chemistry, physics, music, nutrition, history
Perform textbook page activities	Slader	Textbook Responses
Make a summary	Resoomer	Summarizes texts
References or sources used	Scribbr	Generate references in APA format
References or sources used	Google Scholar	Generate references in APA format
Solve mathematical problems in any subject	Google lens apps	Cell phone app that allows taking a photo of any text and linking it to information on the internet
Summarize	Prepostseo	Paste text and generate the same but with different words
Summarize	I lazy to read	Summarize long texts from any page
Summarize	Tldrthis.com	Reduce any internet article to a few sentences
Summary or presentation of a topic	Smodin.me	Change the summary with other words, paraphrasing
Summary or presentation of a topic	Linguakit	Summarize texts at 5%, 10%, 20%, 30%, and 50% levels

(continued)

Table 46.1 (continued)

Task assigned by the teacher	Web page	Internet response
Texts in English	Hemingwayapp.com	Corrects English texts

Source Own Elaboration

its generalization in digital media), the new era's demands require the development of new skills.

46.3 Conclusions

As mentioned above, a task is a tool within the teaching–learning process, focusing on specific content and pursuing objectives.

All technology creates a new environment, which is not introduced as a passive entity. Instead, it creates a new social and cultural form that shapes the representation of the human being and gives rise to the generation of new technology. It is generating a fundamental change, while education acts as if not affected. The pandemic forced us to use some technological resources. We do not know how these changes will land, evolving educationally at such an accelerated pace.

We must pay attention to every one of the methods employed within education. Change comes slowly in the face of the complexity and evolutionary speed of the context, the linear hierarchy that governs the educational system; it does not transcend a discourse. It is not a process that allows an easy transition in the confusion and uncertainty it causes. In the end, all responsibility reverts to the teacher to make the imminent paradigm shift.

This requires a restructuring in every aspect involved in education, which still has not yet come to the idea of rethinking how to organize all its dimensions to complete the paradigm shift with a prospective look.

Decisions are still made from the retrospective looks toward the future. Before the crisis of the classical paradigm, no alternative answers are glimpsed.

Acknowledgements We thank the National Polytechnic Institute for the support provided for the production of this work.

The authors acknowledge the technical support of Writing Lab, Institute for the Future of Education, Tecnologico de Monterrey, Mexico, in the production of this work.

References

Hoyos V (2009) Recursos tecnológicos en las Escuela y la Enseñanza de las Matemáticas. Tecnologías de la Información y Comunicación Horizontales Interdisciplinario y temas de Investigación. México. Universidad Pedagógica Nacional

Kuhn (2000) Naturalism and the social study of science. Accessed at: https://seis.bristol.ac.uk/
~plajb/research/papers/Kuhn_Naturalism_Social_Study_of_Science.pdfLuján

Neville K (1992) Riesgo calculado. Accessed at: https://www.tagusbooks.com/leer?isbn=978849
9894577&li=1&idsource=3001

Pérez M (2010) Las escuelas y la enseñanza en la sociedad de la información.
Accessed at: https://es.scribd.com/document/273076472/J-PEREZ-TORNERO-Las-Escuelas-y-
La-Ensenanza-en-La-Sociedad-de-La-Infomacion

Serrano J, Gutiérrez I, Prendes M (2016) Internet como recurso para enseñar y aprender. Una
aproximación práctica a la tecnología educativa. Accessed at: https://relatec.unex.es/article/view/
2711

Stein MK, Smith MS (1998) Mathematical tasks as a framework for reflection: from research to
practice. Math Teach Middle Sch, Reston, VA, EUA 3(4):268–275

Trujillo B (2016) La distribución de la atención en el aula en tiempos de la cultura digital: reflexiones
de investigación en un bachillerato público de la ciudad de México. Accessed at: https://www.
periodicos.udesc.br/index.php/percursos/article/view/1984724617342016024

Chapter 47
Digital Tools for Developing Oral English Competency in Trainee Teachers

Fabiola Flora Rodríguez and Gabriela María Farías Martínez

47.1 Introduction

Due to the COVID-19 situation worldwide, the use of technology in the educational field has increased (Monasterio and Briceño 2020), which has allowed us to recognize that more than a distraction, technology is an ally in teaching language when the digital tools are adequate. This makes it possible to identify strengths and areas of opportunity in the teaching of English, specifically in the development of oral competency. According to Larsen-Freeman and Anderson (2011), there are two main ways of thinking about technology in language teaching: technology provides teaching resources, and technology provides learning experiences. This work focuses on the first, that is, on digital tools as teaching resources in the English language. The influence of two digital tools (English Speaking Practice and ELSA Speak) to develop criteria that comprise oral competency in the English language was analyzed, such as fluency, content and vocabulary, pronunciation, and communication skills.

47.2 Development

Within the framework of digital education in the field of education, "the need arises to reorganize new forms and styles of teaching" (Martínez-Pérez 2020, p. 29). New

---

F. Flora Rodríguez · G. M. Farías Martínez
Tecnologico de Monterrey, Monterrey, Mexico
e-mail: gabriela.farias@tec.mx

F. Flora Rodríguez (✉)
CESER, Centro de Estudios Superiores de Educación Rural "Luis Hidalgo Monroy", Tantoyuca, Mexico
e-mail: fabiolafr@ceserluishidalgomonroy.edu.mx

S. Hosseini et al. (eds.), *Technology-Enabled Innovations in Education*,
Transactions on Computer Systems and Networks,
https://doi.org/10.1007/978-981-19-3383-7_47

571

technologies allow us to do things differently from the traditional method of teaching the English language. Nevertheless, this does not mean that the tasks are carried out more quickly, automatically, and reliably, but rather that the technologies become support resources in new scenarios of learning (González Vega 2020). Consequently, developing oral communication skills using technological tools provides teachers and students with an inclusive educational environment for content comprehension supported by the technological avant-garde (Cevallos Vélez et al. 2020).

47.2.1 Theoretical Framework

47.2.1.1 Acquisition of a Second Language

A second language is learned through various exposures to authentic communication situations (Krashen 1982 cited in Raju and Joshith 2018). According to this author, a second language is learned the same way as the mother tongue, i.e., through continuous exposure. To master a language, one must master four skills: writing, reading, listening, and speaking. The latter is one of the most difficult to develop in the classroom because it is developed systematically by listening and speaking regularly with other people (Chamorro-Ortega et al. 2020).

In the 70s, the communicative approach became popular in teaching English as a foreign language. It consists of acquiring the language through its meaningful use. Activities should be included that allow the student to expose themselves to the language in various authentic ways. According to Vigotsky (1978 cited in Ur 2012), learning is acquired through social interactions, so learning activities focused on exchanging ideas, opinions, and facts are essential. They allow the opportunity to get their message across without hindrance.

Different methodologies have been defined, such as the Total Physical Response, the Grammar Translation Method, and the Direct Method (Larsen-Freeman and Anderson 2011). However, it is necessary to analyze how English language teaching has been conducted in *virtual* teaching–learning environments. These environments must facilitate using didactic resources that enhance and balance the four English language communication skills (Ibáñez and Batista 2019). Of these four, oral competency is the one that presents the most significant challenges to students (Cevallos Vélez et al. 2020).

47.2.2 Problem Statement

According to Gudiño et al. (2014), emerging technologies facilitate and develop communication skills in English. However, each emerging technology focuses on a different competency, so it is necessary to use the most relevant to the competency to be developed. Therefore, this study sought to know the relationship of the use of digital tools with the development of oral competency in the English language among trainee teachers at a normal school. The English Speaking Practice and ELSA Speak apps were used in their free versions to conduct daily activities. These focused on meeting four of the five criteria established in the evaluation rubric to measure oral competency at the beginning and end of the study. The criteria are fluency, content, vocabulary, pronunciation, and communication skills.

Regarding the fifth criterion, grammar in communication skills was not addressed during the study. Although the grammatical component is essential for oral communication, a specific grammatical structure was not reviewed with the apps in this study. In this sense, we considered that the participants would express the language with the grammatical structures they already knew. Also, it was sought to analyze how trainee teachers perceive the use of digital tools and their impact on developing oral communication.

47.2.3   Method

The type of qualitative research used was the case study. For Escudero et al. (2008), the case study allows obtaining a holistic result of a situation under study, which provides a wide range of possibilities to address a research problem. This study was carried out in five weeks between March and April 2021, asynchronously due to the COVID-19 contingency, so having connectivity and computer equipment with audio and microphone was essential. A non-probabilistic sampling was carried out. The study group comprised fourteen (14) trainee teachers from the Bachelor's Degree in Primary Education in the Center for Higher Studies in Rural Education "Luis Hidalgo Monroy", a Normal School in Tantoyuca, Veracruz, Mexico. The participants voluntarily agreed to collaborate and had connectivity, computer equipment, and available time.

Two rubrics were used, one to measure the language level according to the Common European Framework of Reference. The second rubric was intended to measure the level of oral competency in the initial and final evaluations. In the latter, the criteria considered were fluency, content and vocabulary, pronunciation, and communication skills. Finally, to obtain data on participants' perception, a self-administered questionnaire with 23 multiple-choice questions was designed as a "selection on a continuum" (Valenzuela and Flores 2013). Also, a partially structured and flexible interview was conducted to gain a broader perspective on how the trainee teachers perceived the use of the apps autonomously to develop their oral competency in the English language.

The data collected were qualitative and quantitative. The quantitative data were collected through the rubrics and the two questions with demographics and the seventeen multiple-choice questions as a "selection on a continuum". The qualitative data were collected through six open-ended questions. Data analysis was done through descriptive statistics techniques based on the dependent and independent variables. The first refers to using the digital tools identified to develop oral competency in the

English language. The second refers to the student's progress in their oral competency using digital tools.

For the qualitative data, interpretive analysis followed the four points described by Miles and Huberman (1994 cited by Valenzuela and Flores 2013): *Data collection*, the instruments were applied to obtain data that may be useful for the investigation; *data reduction*, all data was reorganized into small codes that serve as units of analysis; *data display*, reduced categories were analyzed; and *obtaining and verifying conclusions* where the findings can be observed.

47.2.4 Results

47.2.4.1 Results of Trainee Teachers Using Digital Tools to Develop Oral English Language Competency

To determine the correlations between the English Speaking Practice and ELSA Speak apps with developing oral English language competency among trainee teachers, daily activities were conducted to focus on four criteria established in the rubric: fluency, content and vocabulary, pronunciation, and communication skills. Although the grammatical component is essential for oral communication, we did not review specific grammatical structures using digital tools. Participants used the grammatical structures they already knew.

To visualize the relationship of the digital tools to develop oral competency in the English language, Figs. 47.1 and 47.2 compare the results by evaluation criteria. A significant change in the level of oral competency can be seen in the four categories analyzed: fluency, content and vocabulary, pronunciation, and communication skills.

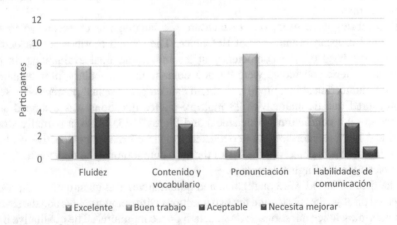

Fig. 47.1 Results of the initial evaluation by criterion (data collected by the authors)

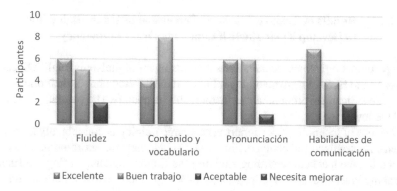

Fig. 47.2   Results of the final evaluation by criterion (data collected by the authors)

The criterion in which the greatest number of participants improved in their scores was pronunciation. Progress was observed in just over 50% of them, and there is an increase in the value range of one point, from "good job" (value 3 points) to "excellent" (value 4 points), as shown in Fig. 47.3.

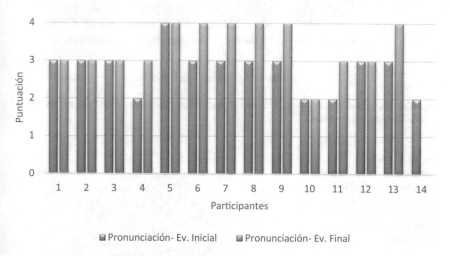

Fig. 47.3   Scores obtained in the pronunciation criterion during the study assessments (data collected by the authors)

47.2.4.2 Results of Trainee Teachers' Perception of Using Digital Tools to Develop Their English Language Oral Competency

The participating trainee teachers agreed that using the digital tools English Speaking Practice and ELSA Speak favorably influenced the development of their oral competency, specifically in pronunciation, fluency, and vocabulary. The vocabulary criterion had the lowest score (Fig. 47.4).

The use of technology as support in academic training is undoubtedly innovative when it is organized and planned. Figure 47.5 shows the different emotions expressed by the trainee teachers regarding studying the English language using the English Speaking Practice and ELSA Speak apps. 84% expressed positive emotions and 16% contrary emotions.

Fig. 47.4 Participants' perception of the use of apps to develop their oral competency by criteria (data collected by the authors)

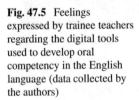
Fig. 47.5 Feelings expressed by trainee teachers regarding the digital tools used to develop oral competency in the English language (data collected by the authors)

47.2.5   *Qualitative Results*

47.2.5.1   On the Evaluation Criteria of Oral Competency

The analysis of Figs. 47.1 and 47.2 shows that the pronunciation criterion was the most improved criterion since 50% of the participants increased their score in the final evaluation of oral competency compared to the initial scores. The scores align with participant comments: "*... there are words that I can now identify their sound and how to pronounce them, and they have already stuck in my mind...,*" "*... it has enriched my knowledge; I was able to practice and know the classification of the sounds,*" and "*I liked the way the activities were carried out; the times were adequate, the activities were exact and appropriate because they allowed me to practice each phrase or word and correct my mispronunciations.*"

Regarding fluency, which refers to the participant's way of expressing themselves correctly with clarity and spontaneity, it was found that 38% of the them improved their score in the final evaluation. Also, all those trainee teachers who were surveyed stated that they fully agreed that English Speaking Practice and ELSA Speak allowed them to be more aware of their fluency when speaking.

Regarding the proper use of vocabulary and the ability to talk about a specific topic, 91% indicated they fully agreed that the apps allowed them to be more aware of their vocabulary. Finally, regarding the fourth analysis criterion referring to awareness about the natural use of the language through digital tools, 100% showed that they were more aware of the natural use of the language since apps showed "*the importance of how to place the lips or the tongue so that it is a more natural pronunciation.*"

47.2.5.2   The Perception of Trainee Teachers of Digital Tools to Develop Their English Language Oral Competency

Participants expressed their feelings regarding using digital tools to learn English during their academic training. The results highlight that apps facilitate motivation and generate feelings of achievement by identifying activities carried out correctly. This was observable in the comments such as "*I felt super good, and it motivated me to continue practicing ENGLISH since I still have much to learn and I was happy to see that I can do it;*" "*I liked working on this platform because it was easy to use... everything is thoroughly explained, and all the activities were related to the topic and were very entertaining,*" and "*I am very satisfied because I was able to practice my English and thus improve my pronunciation.*"

However, one participant commented, "*I felt stressed and in a hurry to try to finish but also because I could not get the correct pronunciations. Although after many attempts, I was able to pronounce it better, and that made me feel good.*" This shows that digital tools can produce a variety of reactions and that, despite being satisfied with the course, feelings of stress and frustration also arise during the process.

47.2.6 Discussion

47.2.6.1 Digital Tools as Promoters of Oral English Language Competency

In virtual environments, digital tools are helpful for innovative teachers who view technology as a support in teaching (Ibáñez and Batista 2019). English Speaking Practice and ELSA Speak facilitate a detailed practice of different criteria: fluency, pronunciation, and communication skills. Therefore, they were the most appropriate for this study. It was found that indeed, they positively promote the development of oral competency through asynchronous activities that can be carried out in different spaces at different times. This creates optimization of class hours for specific exercises such as more meaningful conversations where the language is varied and authentic, as proposed in the communicative approach (Larsen-Freeman and Anderson 2011).

Also, practicing the four criteria mentioned previously makes possible the generalized use of these tools in the six English courses in the Bachelor of Primary Education curriculum. This curriculum proposes assessments with the same criteria. This benefits the trainee teachers from first to sixth semester.

The participating trainee teachers showed authentic development of oral English language competency by continuously using these tools. Those who did not do it continuously at least maintained their level. This suggests including technological tools to support English teachers because six hours a week is not enough for students to exercise the four skills, certainly not the oral skill which presents the biggest challenge (Cevallos Vélez et al. 2020). Therefore, using digital tools that offer students fun and dynamic ways to continue practicing the language outside of class is worthwhile.

Technology will be an ally in the educational field as long as students' digital literacy is continuously practiced (García 2017). Casillas and Ramírez (2018), using the term "digital habitus," agree that digital literacy goes beyond informational knowledge. ICTs advance and change constantly. What today is considered innovative, current, and modern, in a short time, can be considered the opposite.

47.2.6.2 Technological Tools as a Motivating Element in the Self-regulation of English Language Learning

Knowing the perception of trainee teachers regarding the digital tools they use in their educational process is essential. One of the main factors for success in digital education is that they can self-regulate their knowledge and maintain enough motivation to complete the academic assignments. They must organize their times and work the activities without the synchronous guidance of the teacher, who becomes a guide in the steps to follow.

The immediate feedback provided by digital tools reveals the areas of strength and opportunity, making it possible to personally attend them at the most convenient pace. ELSA Speak, for example, provides a percentage according to the number of words or phrases pronounced correctly. The higher the percentage, the better the pronunciation has been. The desire to reach 100% and repeat the exercise as many times as necessary motivates students similar to a video game.

Although less than half of the trainee teachers pointed out motivation as an emotion while using digital tools to learn English, using the tools must be designed, planned, and executed with delicacy, or there can be negative consequences. It was found that stress and frustration arose when the students did not achieve the expected results in the exercises, which shows that the ability to self-regulate one's learning also includes the ability to self-regulate emotions.

47.3   Conclusions

The use of Information and Communication Technologies (ICT) are increasing in the teaching–learning processes, so the institution, teachers, and students must be open to digital tools. They can help strengthen innovation and excellence in education. Innovative teachers always seek to provide the best academic experiences for their students, modeling excellent behavior for trainee teachers who will transfer their learning experiences to their teaching practices.

These digital tools made it possible to practice fluency, content and vocabulary, pronunciation, and communication skills outside the classroom, also to optimize class-hour for specific language production activities. A language program can be implemented to achieve better results specially if it includes financing for the paid versions, and an English laboratory that provides connectivity to students for practice with these digital tools.

47.3.1   Limitations and Future Research

English Speaking Practice and ELSA Speak have been shown to help improve the development of oral competency in trainee teachers. However, it is pertinent to make a wise selection of digital tools since most contain two versions. The first is a free version, and the second is a paid one. In this study, limited work was done with ELSA Speak, which only allowed two exercises per level to be carried out in its free version. Thus, there is a possibility that using the full versions would have more impact because the practice would be more constant. This is an alternative for educational institutions to support the best versions of digital tools. As for English Speaking Practice, it only contains a free version that allows unlimited use. However, it requires excellent connectivity for long audio and voice recordings.

It is essential to propose digital tools to develop English oral competency in both virtual and face-to-face teaching environments. Their ubiquity and easy use result in a high level of motivation that influences self-directed learning.

This study can lead to new research that expands the knowledge generated. Therefore, we propose the following:

- Oral proficiency in a language is not a skill that shows significant progress in just over a month. The study should analyze results for an entire school year or a semester. Thus, more stable results could be obtained to know if self-esteem in long-term activities remains intact.
- The evaluation criteria in this study contemplated four aspects of verbal ability. However, grammar was a missing element. Incorporating these five criteria would be a better reference per the English language proficiency levels in the Common European Framework of Reference. Based on this, a question in proposed: Do digital tools influence the development of English language proficiency among Trainee teachers?

References

Casillas M, Ramírez A (2018) El habitus digital: una propuesta para su observación. En R. Castro y H. J. Suárez (Coords.), *Pierre Bourdieu en la sociología latinoamericana: el uso de campo y habitus en la investigación* (pp. 317–341). Cuernavaca, Morelos: Universidad Nacional Autónoma de México, Centro Regional de Investigaciones Multidisciplinarias. Accessed at https://www.uv.mx/personal/mcasillas/category/menu-general/tipo/cap-libro/

Cevallos Vélez K, Palma Cedeño M, Cevallos Vélez K, Baquezea Ponce G (2020) Enseñanza de inglés como lengua extranjera (efl) en el desarrollo de la destreza speaking a través de clases virtuales en la educación superior. *Revista Cognosis, revista de filosofía, letras y ciencias de la educación, 5.* Accessed at https://revistas.utm.edu.ec/index.php/Cognosis/article/view/2785

Chamorro-Ortega C, Bejarano-Criollo S, Guano-Merino D (2020) ¿Qué habilidad lingüística se hace más compleja enseñar en el aula de inglés como Lengua Extranjera? *Revista científica dominio de las ciencias*, 6(2), 302–318. Accessed at https://dialnet.unirioja.es/servlet/articulo?codigo=7491394

Escudero J, Delfín L, Gutiérrez L (2008) El estudio de caso como estrategia de investigación en las ciencias sociales. *Ciencia Administrativa.* (1), 7–10. Accessed at https://www.uv.mx/iiesca/files/2012/12/estudio2008-1.pdf

García S (2017) Alfabetización digital. *Razón and palabra.* 1(98). 1605–4806. Accessed at http://revistarazonypalabra.org/index.php/ryp/article/view/1043

González Vega K (2020) Influencia de los recursos digitales en la enseñanzaandel aprendizaje del idioma inglés en las escuelas normales de Oaxaca, México. *Revista boletín REDIPE, 9*(7), 150–164. Accessed at https://revista.redipe.org/index.php/1/article/view/1027

Gudiño S, Lozano F, Fernández J (2014) Uso de Facebook para la socialización del aprendizaje de una segunda lengua en nivel medio superior. Sinéctica, *Revista Electrónica de Educación,* (42), 1–16. Accessed at: https://www.redalyc.org/articulo.oa?id=99829581004

Ibáñez R, Batista M (2019) Los Entornos Virtuales de Enseñanza-Aprendizaje en el desarrollo de la competencia comunicativa en idioma inglés. *Referencia pedagógica, 7*(2), 231–245. Accessed at https://rrp.cujae.edu.cu/index.php/rrp/article/view/187

Larsen-Freeman D, Anderson M (2011) Techniques and principles in Language teaching. Oxford University Press, United Kingdom

Martínez-Pérez M (2020) Herramientas digitales para la enseñanza del idioma inglés. *Con-Ciencia boletín científico de la Escuela preparatoria No. 3, 7*(14), p. 28–32. Accessed at https://repository.uaeh.edu.mx/revistas/index.php/prepa3/article/view/6112

Monasterio D, Briceño M (2020) Educación mediada por las tecnologías: un desafío ante la coyuntura del Covid-19. *Observador Del Conocimiento, 5*(1), 100–108. Accessed at http://www.oncti. gob.ve/ojs/index.php/rev_ODC/article/view/132

Raju N, Joshith V (2018) Krashen's theory of second language acquisition: a practical approach for English language classrooms. Int J Innov Knowl Concepts 6(12):179–184. Accessed at https:// www.researchgate.net/profile/Paramita_Roy4/publication/334732910_International_Journal_ of_Innovative_Knowledge_Concepts/links/5d3dfef94585153e592a9f3e/International-Journal- of-Innovative-Knowledge-Concepts.pdf#page=186

Ur P (2012) A course in English language teaching. Cambridge University Press, Cambridge, United Kingdom

Valenzuela JR, Flores M (2013) *Fundamentos de investigación educativa, volumen 2*. Editorial digital. México

Chapter 48
Investigating the Well-Being of Adolescents in Virtual Education: Methodological and Ethical Challenges of Photoprovocation

Denise Oyarzún Gómez

48.1 Introduction

The educational systems during the COVID-19 pandemic have transformed and migrated their processes to virtuality, encountering new challenges to the formative trajectories of the students. Mental health has become more relevant throughout this process because its stability is an essential condition for learning and strengthening the wellbeing of those in each educational community.

Worldwide, during the confinements of COVID-19, institutions turned to greater use of educational platforms, digital tools, data analytics, and the privatization and commercialization of educational technologies (Sepúlveda-Escobar and Morrison 2020; United Nations Educational, Scientific and Cultural Organization [UNESCO] 2020a) to give continuity to educational continuity. The socio-health crisis quickly made evident the unequal social, economic, and technological situations schools faced while continuing young people's studies (Osorio et al. 2021).

Research in educational communities has also become virtual. Photo-provocation is a technique that uses photos to facilitate conversations on specific topics among participants (Banks 2001; Harper 2002; Hurworth et al. 2005). There are multiple ways to use this technique in research (Shaw 2020). However, the conditions for applying it virtually with adolescents have not been sufficiently described because face-to-face methodology dominated for decades.

Thus, this article aims to describe the conditions of applying photo-provocation with secondary students in the Metropolitan Region of Chile. The technique requires the researcher to take photographs and use them to stimulate dialogue about the wellbeing of students in eight schools that have operated virtually in 2020 and 2021.

D. Oyarzún Gómez (✉)
Universidad Central de Chile, Santiago, Chile
e-mail: denise.oyarzun@ucentral.cl

48.2 Context

In Chile and the world, the COVID-19 pandemic socio-health crises generated drastic changes in people's daily lives. Educational systems were not excepted; the face-to-face training that characterized them had to be discontinued. In Chile, as of March 16, 2020, the suspension of face-to-face classes was decreed nationally in all educational institutions (Ministry of Education [MINEDUC] 2020a).

Distance and hybrid education for continuity of studies required virtual platforms. The Ministry of Education of Chile (MINEDUC) and the educational institutions themselves became responsible for strengthening the educational system in Chile. However, the magnitudes of the educational gaps detected in Chile in 2020 due to previously existing inequalities became especially significant (MINEDUC 2020b). In this sense, it is crucial to understand that educational losses occur not only at the level of learning but also at the socio-emotional level.

48.2.1 State of the Art

Oyarzún et al. (2021a, 2021b) propose that conceptualizing wellbeing implies identifying a theoretical perspective (psychological, subjective, social, or other) on which a proposal or interventional research project with secondary students is based. Subjective wellbeing refers to a person's cognitive and affective assessments of their life, including satisfaction (global and by area) with life and positive and negative affects (Diener et al. 1999).

Maintaining wellbeing is a challenge for all members of educational communities. Those working in education need to develop adaptive skills and resilience. In this framework, social-emotional learning is a valuable tool to mitigate the harmful effects of the socio-health crisis and a condition for learning (Economic Commission for Latin America and the Caribbean [ECLAC] 2020). In Chile, MINEDUC (2020a) has developed a series of resources on social-emotional support aimed at the educational community. However, its self-application format reduces the chances of improving the mental health of students and teachers.

48.2.2 Problem Statement

In the framework of research and the era of information technologies and communications (ICT), young people feel at ease, comfortable, and secure making visual productions instead of working only with the verbal language predominant in adult life (Prosser and Burke 2008). Visual language allows us to further incorporate other dimensions of human experience and encourage divergent thinking (Bagnoli 2009).

Photo-provocation is a technique in the research process, dynamizing the social practice that is the interview (Corredor-Álvarez and Íñiguez-Rueda 2016) beyond conventional interview methods (Banks 2001). When photo-provocation is used, the photographs themselves are the center of attention, not the people in the group (Hall et al. 2007). This helps avoid some of the stresses that interviewees may experience in one-on-one interviews. In addition, the technique facilitates participation by young people with verbal communication problems, shyness, and insecurity (Banks 2007).

This research is a way to critically examine wellbeing and encourage students to be more aware of institutional practices and move closer to a more socially just conception of education. The use of photos raises questions that help perturb and interrupt young people's conventional knowledge or opinions, in this case about wellbeing, life satisfaction, and affections or emotions. The photo method reveals some of the school practices before and during the coronavirus pandemic in Chile.

48.3 Method

The participants of the CIP2019013 Project formed a non-probabilistic, convenience sample (Flick 2018). The inclusion criteria were young people 14–18 years old in secondary education (high school) in one of the participating schools in the project. The exclusion criteria were students who had a psychological or psychiatric problem or diagnosis that hindered their participation in the project.

The sample comprised 180 students (100 women and 80 men) from eight Chilean schools in the 1st to 4th years of high school. The administrative dependency of the educational centers was three public, four subsidized, and one private school in the Metropolitan Region of Chile. Five students dropped out during this qualitative technique due to lack of access or poor internet connectivity. These students were not included in the sample.

Photo-provocation (or photo-elicitation) is a qualitative technique based on visual and verbal languages that uses photos to provoke or elicit opinions and discussions among participants (Banks 2001) during individual or group interviews (Harper 2002; Hurworth et al. 2005). Operationally, once the topics have been defined for the intervention, the first step is to select the source of the photographs, i.e., directly from a camera or indirectly from the web. During photo-provocation, people are stimulated by photos during the interview to help them remember, reconstruct, analyze, or narrate various situations, usually the defined topics (Corredor-Álvarez and Íñiguez-Rueda 2016). Photo-provocation is a strategy for collecting subjective information from the perspective of the people directly involved in the process (from Cook and Hess 2007).

As for this research's production **procedure**, we downloaded 16 photos from each school's official page, social networks, and website. The photos depicted male and female students, faculty, and managers. The general-themed photographs illustrated places of school activity such as the façade/entrance, the courtyard, the corridors, and external shots of the school campus and its location. Photographs with specific themes included the face-to-face classrooms, the virtual classrooms, and the group and individual activities of students and teachers, always related to the research purpose. The research team was trained in photo-provocation with an application protocol that integrated a script of questions related to the research topics. The photos were linked to the presented questions to facilitate the ethically responsible use of the technique.

Photo-provocation was applied synchronously for 45–60 min during class hours on the Meet platform. A researcher in charge of the application worked with student teams of four or six students in each educational level (first through fourth years) per high school. It began with the presentation of the participants and the technique, followed by sharing the screen to show the photos. The photo was displayed for a minute, and the initial question was presented: What is your school life like? This was followed by students' responses. Then the screen was shared with additional photos and the questions included, What does wellbeing mean to you? How satisfied are you with your life in general or any particular environment (school, family, neighborhood)? How have you felt lately? In addition, in the group interviews, the students were explicitly asked if they recognized the situations depicted in the photos and if there were less familiar photos.

The CIP2019013 Project was approved by the Scientific Ethics Committee of the Central University of Chile. **Ethical considerations** also meant that the directors of the eight participating schools agreed to participate in the project. Informed consent was sent to the parents by email, and the informed assent was accepted virtually and recorded to the students. All information was kept confidential; the students were not identified by their real or full names, and a pseudonym was used when making the transcript to maintain anonymity.

Thematic analysis (Braun and Clarke 2006) was used since it pointed to both the photos and the words generated in the photo-provocation with the students. Additionally, the analysis of photographic material was explored from two perspectives: thematic or internal narrative (description of each element of the photograph) and thematic or external narrative (interpretive analysis of the relationship and coherence of the description, symbolism, and text accompanying the photo and between the photo and what was communicated) (Banks 2007).

48.4 Results

The project's preliminary results indicate that most of the students confirmed that the photos represented everyday situations in their school context. Photo-provocation applied in a virtual group played a vital role in both descriptive and argumentative situations, providing a friendly environment and atmosphere, which improved students' knowledge of each other. The students also expressed that the photos depicted their school life, mainly before and during the coronavirus pandemic. Table 48.1 synthesizes the preliminary findings of the photo-provocation. All the

Table 48.1 Principal findings of photo-provocation

Photo	Question	Student response
	Who can describe what is seen in the photograph? How is your school life?	The photo looks to me like a central courtyard where recess is held and shared by the students Eh, the truth is that I like the school because all the teachers are comprehensible. I also like it because I have been in it all my life, and I feel that, yes, it will change me, I will not be the same (Student, female, 15 years old, subsidized school)
	What do you see in the photograph? What does wellness mean to you as a student?	They are schoolchildren. I just don't know a picture of them Wellbeing is being well with oneself in the environment you are in. And if, for example, you feel bad in the environment, you look for another (Student, male, 16 years old, subsidized school)
	Do you know who is in the photograph? How satisfied are you with your life in general or some realm in particular? (school, family, neighborhood)?	Yes, they are students in the school Satisfaction, fine, because when I need help with a task, they help me here in the house, but, more or less like that, because maybe being locked up without being able to do anything eh... You get bored and stressed faster... being in the house all day too, the brothers argue (Student, female, 16 years old, public school)

(continued)

Table 48.1 (continued)

Photo	Question	Student response
	What do you see in the photograph? How have you felt lately?	Hybrid classes with students online and face-to-face I've felt more or less ok. Yesterday I lost a relative, but I have been able to face it, uh, And I have also had several problems, as well as with people in the school, and that has also affected me a little, but I have tried to be as positive as possible (Student, male, 18 years old, private school)

photographs were captured from each school's website. (Note: this educational institution has forms or letters that refer to the author's permissions to publish according to Intellectual Property Law N17.336, Chile Ministry of Education.)

The analysis of the photo-provocation from the thematic or external narration resulted in a series of elements in the photograph. In most of the photos, people could be seen in open and closed places of the school. The thematic or internal narrative showed the multiple meanings of wellbeing, global and environmental satisfaction, and the affects of the students. The most prevalent barriers were (a) feeling uncomfortable in the family environment and (b) missing the face-to-face school activities carried out with classmates, teachers, and other members of the educational community.

The project's preliminary results suggest that wellbeing is built from a multidimensional perspective integrating individual, social, and community components. This interesting finding aligns with what Rivera-Vargas et al. (2021) proposed, i.e., the pandemic has shown how the search for community wellbeing has resulted in values to get out of the global health crisis. For the authors, both in the present and future, these are values that should underpin the configuration of educational systems. Additionally, UNESCO (2020b) recommends promoting communication and networking among teachers to fortify students' continued wellbeing, mutual support, and pedagogical learning.

Other interesting results were that in the photo-provocation, the focus was on the photos presented and not on the context surrounding the application of the technique. Therefore, the use of this technique has produced optimal results because it facilitates the positive development of the verbal language of the students. Simultaneously, the imbalances between interviewers and students were reduced because the technique provided them with a better ability to apply various meanings to their school experiences.

48.5 Discussion

In this research, photo-provocation turned out to be a visual and verbal technique recommended for research with adolescents because it encouraged their virtual participation. The use of photos opened access to the perspectives of the high school students. It also promoted dialogue by challenging the social hierarchies frequently imposed by the adult world, offering reflection, analysis, and an approach to past and present perspectives of secondary school students about wellbeing.

The preliminary results of the research show, like Pachmayer and Andereck (2017), that in photo-provocation, the attention focused on the photos and not the technique facilitating the conversation among the students. This, in line with what Arias (2011) proposed regarding the participation of informants, is part of the analysis of the images themselves, both the connection to the photographs and their connection to broader practices and events.

The visual and verbal data analysis was explored from two perspectives: thematic or internal and external narrative (Banks 2007). The former identified that photo-provocation centered on students' need to dialogue about school experiences associated with their wellbeing before and during the pandemic, expressed by the participants while talking about the contextual photos of their school. The use of the technique was relevant to the group to which this research was directed: public, subsidized, and private schools, finding differences in the perceptions of wellbeing among the students, which will be explored more profoundly in a future publication.

It is pointed out that the technique has limitations in the virtual context. In most of the applications, there was no face-to-face contact with the students, who did not turn on their cameras for various reasons, including difficulties in internet connectivity or their decision not to show their personal images.

48.6 Conclusions

The preliminary results of the virtual application of photo-provocation indicate that this technique must be carefully planned to ensure that research receives adequate technical, financial support and technologies. The visual process can offer a unique perspective on students' lives that permits the research team to delve deeper into understanding wellness experiences in the school context.

When using photos like these, it is essential to "break the frame" (Harper 2002) in the sense of leading discussions about the topics that interest the research team. The photos used in this research reflected situations that are common in a face-to-face and virtual school context. In addition, the research team was attentive to preserving the participants' ethical rights based on what was proposed by Hill (2005).

The article included the theoretical-methodological considerations of photo-provocation applied virtually in eight high schools in Chile. Preliminary research findings may guide those working in teacher training to consider foto-provocation methods pedagogically and methodologically to hear adolescent voices.

Acknowledgements Appreciation is expressed to the Research and Postgraduate Directorate of the Central University of Chile that sponsored the Research and Development Project CIP2019013 *"School-Neighborhood and its Influences on the Well-being of Adolescents: Research and Applied Intervention"* and the alliance with the Cooperative University of Colombia and the Scientific University of the South-Peru.

The author acknowledges the technical support of the Writing Lab, Institute for the Future of Education, Tecnologico de Monterrey, Mexico, in the production of this work.

References

Arias D (2011) El co-relato de la imagen fotografica: la arqueologica visual como metodologica en la exploración de la memoria etnohistorica. Quaderns de l'Institut Catala d'Antropologia 16(1–2):173–188

Bagnoli A (2009) Beyond the standard interview: the use of graphic elicitation and arts-based methods. Qual Res 9(5):547–570. https://doi.org/10.1177/1468794109343625

Banks M (2001) Visual methods in social research. SAGE Publications

Banks M (2007) Using visual data in qualitative research. SAGE Publications

Braun V, Clarke V (2006) Using thematic analysis in psychology. Qual Res Psychol 3(2):77–101. https://doi.org/10.1191/1478088706qp063oa

Comisión Económica para América Latina y el Caribe [CEPAL] (2020) La educación en tiempos de la pandemia de COVID-19. https://repositorio.cepal.org/handle/11362/45904

Corredor-Álvarez F, Íñiguez-Rueda L (2016) La fotoprovocación como método. Su aplicación en un estudio de la autonomía en personas con diagnóstico de Trastorno Mental Severo. Empiria 35:175–204. https://doi.org/10.5944/empiria.35.2016.17173

Cook T, Hess E (2007) What the camera sees and from whose perspective: fun methodologies for engaging children in enlightening adults. Childhood 14(1):29–45. https://doi.org/10.1177/0907568207068562

Diener E, Suh EM, Lucas RE, Smith HL (1999) Subjective wellbeing: three decades of progress. Psychol Bull 125(2):276

Flick U (2018) An introduction to qualitative fourth edition. SAGE Publications

Hall L, Jones S, Hall M, Richardson J, Hodgson J (2007) Inspiring design: the use of photo-elicitation and lomography in gaining the child's perspective. In: Proceedings of HCI 2007 The 21st British HCI Group Annual Conference University of Lancaster, UK 21, Sept 2007, pp 1–10. https://doi.org/10.14236/ewic/HCI2007.23

Harper D (2002) Talking about pictures: a case for photo elicitation. Vis Stud 17(1):13–26. https://doi.org/10.1080/14725860220137345

Hill M (2005) Ethical considerations in researching children's experiences. In: Greene S, Hogan D (eds) Researching children's experience: approaches and methods. SAGE Publications, pp 61–86

Hurworth R, Clark E, Martin J, Thomsen S (2005) The use of photo-interviewing: three examples from health evaluation and research. Eval J Australas 4(1–2):52–62. https://doi.org/10.1177/1035719X05004001-208

Ministerio de Educación [MINEDUC] (2020a) Educación en Pandemia. Principales medidas del Ministerio de Educación en 2020a. https://www.mineduc.cl/wp-content/uploads/sites/19/2021/01/BalanceMineduc2020a.pdf

Ministerio de Educación [MINEDUC] (2020b) Impacto del COVID-19 en los resultados de aprendizaje y escolaridad en Chile. Análisis con base en herramienta de simulación proporcionada por el Banco Mundial. https://www.mineduc.cl/wp-content/uploads/sites/19/2020b/08/EstudioMineduc_bancomundial.pdf

Osorio-Saez E, Eryilmaz N, Sandoval-Hernandez A, Lau Y, Barahona E, Bhatti A, Caesar Ofoe G, Castro Ordóñez L, Cortez Ochoa A, Espinoza Pizarro R, Fonseca Aguilar E, Isac M, Dhanapala K, Kumar Kameshwara K, Martínez Contreras Y, Mekonnen G, Mejía J, Miranda C, Moh'd S, Morales Ulloa R, Morgan K K., ... & Zionts A (2021) Survey data on the impact of COVID-19 on parental engagement across 23 countries. Data Brief 35:106813. https://doi.org/10.17632/kvv dgvs8zs.2

Oyarzún D, Salinas M, Marticorena M (2021a) Investigar el Bienestar en Comunidades Educativas. Reporte Proyecto I+D CIP2019013, vol 1. Universidad Central de Chile. https://ucdc.ent.sirsid ynix.net/client/es_CL/search/asset/1047324/0

Oyarzún D, Pezoa C, Soto G (2021b) Teorizar el Bienestar en Comunidades Educativas. Reporte Proyecto I+D CIP2019013, vol 2. Universidad Central de Chile. https://ucdc.ent.sirsidynix.net/client/es_CL/search/asset/1047323/0

Pachmayer A, Andereck KL (2017) Photo elicitation in tourism research: investigating the travel experiences of study abroad participants. https://scholarworks.umass.edu/cgi/viewcontent.cgi?article=2057&context=ttra

Prosser J, Burke C (2008) Image-based educational research. In: Knowles J, Cole A (eds) Handbook of the arts in qualitative research: perspectives, methodologies, examples and issues. SAGE Publications, pp 407–419

Rivera-Vargas P, Miño-Puigcercós R, Passerón E, Herrera Urízar G (2021) ¿Hacia dónde va la escuela? Resignificar su sentido en la era del COVID-19. Psicoperspectivas 20(3):1–13. https://doi.org/10.5027/psicoperspectivas-vol20-issue1-fulltext-2401

Sepúlveda-Escobar P, Morrison A (2020) Online teaching placement during the COVID-19 pandemic in Chile: challenges and opportunities. Eur J Teach Educ 43(4):587–607. https://doi.org/10.1080/02619768.2020.1820981

Shaw PA (2020) Photo-elicitation and photo-voice: using visual methodological tools to engage with younger children's voices about inclusion in education. Int J Res Method Educ 1-15. https://doi.org/10.1080/1743727X.2020.1755248

United Nations Educational, Scientific and Cultural Organization [UNESCO] (2020a) Education in a post-covid world: Nine ideas for public action. UNESCO Futures of Education Series. https://en.unesco.org/news/education-post-covid-world-nine-ideas-public-action

United Nations Educational, Scientific and Cultural Organization [UNESCO] (2020b) Respuesta del ámbito educativo de la UNESCO al COVID 19. Notas temáticas del Sector de Educación. https://unesdoc.unesco.org/ark:/48223/pf0000373271_spa

Chapter 49
Impact of Sars-Cov-2, COVID-19 on the Digital Competencies of Professionals in Training Processes in Latin America

Vicente Román Acosta, Patricia Sofía Madrazo Gómez, and Rebeca Román Julián

49.1 Introduction

In early 2020, the Sars-Cov-2, COVID-19 health crisis generated a differentiated work environment forcing everyone to adapt, collaborate, and learn virtually at all educational levels of any latitude. The far-ranging impact of the health confinements and the untimely need for isolation caused the cessation of face-to-face classroom activities. The sudden migration to virtual, distant teaching/learning modalities exacerbated the demand for broadband services and technological devices. For teachers, who had scarce familiarization with Information and Communication Technologies (ICT) and Learning and Knowledge Technologies, there was little training for professional digital skills.

In this regard, the NU.CEPAL report mentions the relevance of the skills necessary for the correct use of ICT, identified in the pandemic context as critical competencies (NU.CEPAL 2020). From this perspective, this research aimed to analyze the preferences of professionals in the teaching and learning processes, the perception of their digital competencies, their environments, platforms and transmission channels, their training processes, and the primary components that describe their work. We intended to offer a before-and-after-pandemic educational panorama of Latin America.

To this end, we used the Latin American adaptation of the European Framework for Digital Competency (Cabero-Almenara and Palacios-Rodríguez 2020) as a tool to arrive at a better understanding of what it means to be digitally competent so that teachers could develop and evaluate their own digital competency. We

V. Román Acosta · P. S. Madrazo Gómez · R. Román Julián (✉)
Brain Training Institute, Mexico, Mexico
e-mail: educacion@integrandoequipos.com

© The Author(s), under exclusive license to Springer Nature Singapore Pte Ltd. 2022   593
S. Hosseini et al. (eds.), *Technology-Enabled Innovations in Education*,
Transactions on Computer Systems and Networks,
https://doi.org/10.1007/978-981-19-3383-7_49

aimed at educators in all spaces (community, recreation, technical, corporate, or organizational): teachers and academicians to address the identified challenges.

The World Health Organization's (WHO) declaration of Sars-Cov-2, COVID-19 as a pandemic in March 2020 thrust educational systems into an abrupt change for which they were unprepared. Some remained in denial of the situation, professionals who waited for the pandemic to pass, doing everything the same. Some incorporated improvements in form and substance, some expressed resistance to change, and others are still adapting to overcome technological gaps. School closures to contain the pandemic have accelerated the deployment of distance education solutions to ensure pedagogical continuity (UN 2020).

In this scenario, there are challenges for students of any educational level to perform their tasks effectively. Some show interest in education in the home, but connectivity makes it infeasible due to price and quality. In Mexico, less than 9% of cities have good enough connectivity to sustain training processes remotely. Other students lack technological resources. All agree that they were not prepared to cohabit with all family members in the same space and take on the home, education, and work tasks.

With these problems identified, we determined the following research objectives: (a) To know the perception of professionals in training processes regarding their mastery of technologies, (b) To describe the preferred digital tools of the professionals in training processes, and (c) To analyze the virtual work environment of the professionals in training processes. The results from achieving the research objectives answer the research question: What is the perception of professionals in training processes regarding their digital skills?

49.2 Theoretical Framework

For the study's purposes, we describe the professional trainers who impart teaching and learning processes. They include teachers, academicians, recreational teachers, executive coaches, ontologists, health coaches, facilitators, psychologists, therapists, competency trainers, experiential facilitators, field guides (*wilderness/outdoor*), extreme activity guides, and andragogical specialists or pedagogues.

According to Silva-Quiroz et al. (2018), there is a need to continuously train digital technologies in professional practice. ICTs are increasingly essential tools in people's lives, allowing paradigms to be questioned regarding the form and depth of contextual relating and generating deeper interactions, contributing to collective knowledge. These tools allow incorporating those who are far away, promote interculturality, and improve the educational experience based on learning and knowledge technologies (TAC) (Moya 2013).

Similarly, Naresh (2020) shares that ICTs are the key elements contributing to universal access to education, educational equity, learning outcomes, teaching quality, professional development of training teachers, and educational management, among others. Within this order of ideas, digital culture has transformed how people perceive their lives, education, work, recreation, and connectivity. Adopted technologies in the immediate and daily environments of most human beings have led to the necessary digital literacy.

Being digitally competent means generating educational innovations and developing creative processes through methodologies, strategies, and learning tools supported by digital technologies. According to Lázaro et al. (2015), these are essential to developing communicative, social, and civic skills, acquiring digital competency as a transversal benefit, understanding it as that which "involves the safe and critical use of information society technologies for work, leisure and communication" (CUE 2018, p. 9).

The adoption and integration of ICT in the teaching and learning environment offer more opportunities for teachers and students to work in a globalized digital era (Lawrence and Tar 2018). Thus, digital competency is vital for citizens to learn permanently and to develop in the educational field. Silva-Quiroz et al. (2018) propose four dimensions:

1. Didactic, curricular, and methodological.
2. Planning, organization, and management of digital spaces and technological resources.
3. Ethical, legal, and security aspects.
4. Personal and professional development.

For professionals who have been obligated to perform their training processes using ICT, their academic thinking has transformed to regard them as an efficient way to improve their resources in the classroom, learning activities, evaluations, interactivity, individualized and group instruction, and communication with students and other academicians in other latitudes and institutions, using different digital means. According to Usmani et al. (2021), using ICT in the educational system benefits the teacher and the student with an education of real value. These various tools contribute to improving skills. Combining traditional teaching methods with learning management systems now occurs in both developed and developing countries; thus, the world understands that education is no longer confined to physical spaces.

In this regard, Torres et al. (2021) raise the need for a change in the profile of the teacher at all levels, proposing a methodological renovation in which the teacher assumes the role of facilitator in the teaching–learning process focusing on students, to encourage their participation and collaborative work, promote their learning autonomy and the acquisition of competencies, so they can develop themselves to face of the demands of the century XXI.

Based on the references described above and the review of existing instruments to analyze the digital competency of educators, we defined an implementation model for the Latin American context, which helps those who guide educational processes to evaluate them comprehensively.

49.3 Methodology

The exploratory, descriptive, and quantitative research were conducted by applying a diagnostic questionnaire proposed by the European Framework of Digital Competence (Cabero-Almenara and Palacios-Rodríguez 2020) to measure the digital competencies of the mediators or facilitators preparing for the future. We adapted the instrument to the Latin American context (pre-trans) Sars-Cov-2, COVID-19, and validated it through expert judgment. The instrument's reliability was analyzed using Cronbach's alpha coefficient as a measure of internal consistency, obtaining a value of 0.96. The non-probabilistic convenience sample comprised 272 professionals in training processes from 16 countries, with the professional profile including experienced educators, facilitators, teachers, and process mediators in community, recreational, technical, corporate, organizational, or teaching or academic contexts.

For the data collection, we applied a self-administered survey on the *Survey-Monkey* platform, and we used the SPSS statistical package (version 21.0) for the data analysis. The construct of interest was defined operationally conformed by the following dimensions: (1) professional commitment, (2) digital resources, (3) teaching and learning, (4) evaluation, (5) empowering students, (6) facilitating digital competencies, (7) digitally linked platforms and (8) demographics.

49.4 Results and Discussion

According to the **Demographics of the research sample,** 40% of the participants were men and 60% women; their predominant age range was from 30 to 50 years. Their years of experience as a training facilitator broke down as follows: 20 or more years (29.8%), 15–19 years (18%), 10–14 years (21.7%), and 10 years or less (30.5%). Among the teaching areas, the education sector and the corporate-executive sector stood out. 69% indicated that they had a maximum of 7.5 years of experience using digital technology.

Table 49.1 presents the **Professional Commitment** to both asynchronous and synchronous training, which the respondents indicated they accessed.

Table 49.1 Professional commitment

Participation in online training	Persons: number of responses	Percentage: relative frequency (%)
Frequently	116	42.6
Sometimes	103	37.9
Almost never	42	15.4
Never	11	4.1
Total	272	100.00

Table 49.2 Digital resources

Search for digital resources	Persons: number of responses	Percentage: relative frequency (%)
New digital resources	95	34.9
Compile information to generate their own hybrid	82	30.1
Sometimes have generated their own digital resources	47	17.3
Compiles existing resources	29	10.7
Has not needed to do it	19	7
Total	272	100.00

One of the critical competencies that any educator needs are knowing the various Digital Resources available and identifying effectively which ones they require to attain their teaching and learning objectives (see Table 49.2).

The **Teaching and Learning** dimension refers to the design, planning, and implementation of digital technologies in the different stages of the learning process (see Table 49.3).

As an essential part of educational processes, **the evaluation** makes possible the opportunity to provide effective feedback (see Table 49.4 results).

Digital technologies can facilitate participation, which **Empowers the Students** (see Table 49.5).

To **facilitate students' digital competence,** the configuration of tasks that require them to use digital media to communicate and collaborate with each other after the training process shows in Table 49.6 that they are rarely used.

The dimension that alludes to the remote linking software and platforms and interventions that the training facilitators have used are ranked by stability in Fig. 49.1. Zoom, Google Meet, and Teams are the most used platforms.

Table 49.3 Teaching and learning

Use of digital tools	Persons: number of responses	Percentage: relative frequency (%)
To improve teaching	82	30.1
To implement innovative pedagogical and andrological strategies	73	26.8
Uses primary functions of the digital assets available	66	24.3
Uses a great variety of digital resources	47	17.3
Does not use digital tools	4	1.5
Total	272	100.00

Table 49.4 Evaluation

Use of digital tools for feedback	Persons: number of responses	Percentage: relative frequency (%)
Sometimes used digital formats	109	40.2
Uses a variety of digital resources	92	33.9
Not in digital format for feedback	64	23.4
Responds that feedback is not necessary	7	2.5
Total	272	100.00

Table 49.5 Empowering the students

Use of digital tools to facilitate student participation	Persons: number of responses	Percentage: relative frequency (%)
Yes, uses digital motivators and stimuli	107	39.3
Involves some digital media	76	27.9
Uses digital technologies systematically	59	21.7
Does not use the alluded technologies	20	7.4
It is not possible to use them	10	3.7
Total	272	100.00

Table 49.6 Facilitates digital competency

Use of digital tools to communicate and collaborate	Persons: number of responses	Percentage: relative frequency (%)
Uses ICT frequently	110	40.4
Rarely or occasionally uses ICT	134	49.4
It is not possible to do it	28	10.2
Total	272	100.00

On the other hand, Fig. 49.2 presents the platforms most used depending on their relevance, ease of handling, and internal features, highlighting *Whatsapp, Google Drive, and Mentimeter.*

Figure 49.3 shows the preference order of the training processes dictated by the corporate or academic organizations.

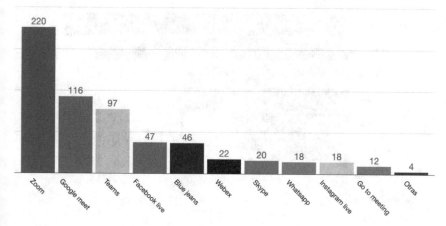

Fig. 49.1 Remote digital transmission platforms ranked by stability

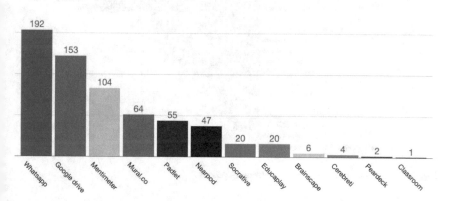

Fig. 49.2 Platforms most used according to relevance

Figure 49.4 presents in order of preference the roles that most describe the training process in environments with digital technology, the most prominent being the facilitator or mediator of training processes.

Figure 49.5 shows the behavior of professionals' use of digital technologies in training processes before and during the pandemic.

Based on the above, 89% of respondents who apply digital skills agree or strongly agree with knowing how to use the Internet competently. In comparison, 10.6% show neutrality or disagree with the statement, and only 0.4% strongly disagree.

Concerning the work environment, the training facilitators reported their affirmations or denials that the organization for which they work supports personal skills development through continuous personal development activities. 68% agreed or

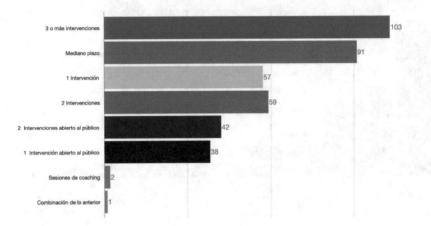

Fig. 49.3 Training processes of the organization

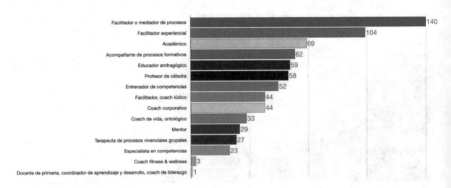

Fig. 49.4 Roles that most describe the training process

strongly agreed, while 24.6% responded in some situations, and 7.4% disagreed or strongly disagreed.

Figure 49.6 shows the before-and-after pandemic personal assessments by the training facilitators of their competency classifications.

The results presented a significant growth in ICT use among the professionals in training processes, directly related to the global conditions caused by the Sars-Cov-2, COVID-19 pandemic. This data aligns with Naresh (2020) about the importance of technologies to facilitate greater access to education, quality teaching–learning processes, advancement of the facilitators in digital competencies, and optimizing management activities.

This research shows that regardless of their pre-pandemic competencies, workplaces, specialties, gender, ages, or previous experiences, the professionals in training processes demonstrated interest in improving their competencies and adaptation skills. An example is that 83.8% of the sample had to implement, improve, or develop their technological tools, digital platforms, or software skills, especially during the

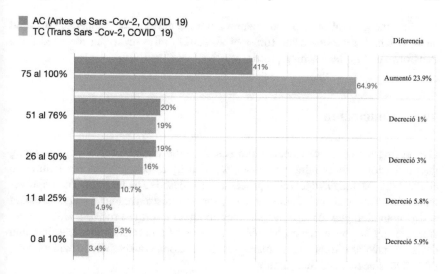

Fig. 49.5 Delivery of online (streaming) training processes using remote digital platforms

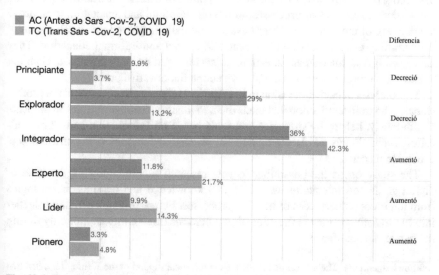

Fig. 49.6 Personal assessments of the level of digital competency by the teachers

first eight months of the pandemic. The data relating to digital competence through educational innovations and creative processes supported by ICT, as Lázaro et al. (2015) emphasize.

In addition to the above, respondents were also curious about new applications, programs, and digital resources that they did not use before the pandemic, such as membership in specific social networks to expand their skills and better connect with the users of their training processes. This can be considered clear evidence of reducing the generation gap and openness toward developing competencies based on ICT, which refers to what Torres et al. (2021) raise regarding the need for a transformation in the teaching profile.

49.5 Conclusion

Concerning the scope of research and based on the digital transformation among the professionals in training processes, we identify as changes that the latitude to connect the teaching and learning processes has ceased to be relevant. The improvement of professionals in training, students, and administrative management; adopted active methodologies in real university classrooms or informal processes are required. Adaptability has been made possible by the sum of communication, learning, and decision-making efforts among managers, facilitators, connectivity providers, and, of course, students and their families.

According to the research carried out, specifically in Latin America, professionals in training processes have gone through the phases of denial, uncertainty concerning the academic and student processes, joint collaboration, and adaptation to improve the delivery of their training. They have substantially improved the development of their training programs, which has benefited formal and informal education. They have used ICT as the primary axis in their teaching and learning processes, enabling students to improve their skills, and have adopted innovative practices.

The analysis of each dimension is an empirical reference to generate in the professionals who train a reflection that leads them to identify the opportunities to innovate continuously, helped by strategies and tools based on Information and Communication Technologies and Learning and Knowledge Technologies, to construct new educational scenarios.

The study opens the possibility to new research such as knowing the state of digital skills and interaction with ICT and knowledge and learning technologies from the users' experiences of training processes. Future research can delve deeper into the transformations in the educational field making an impact, not only during the pandemic but after it.

Acknowledgements The authors acknowledge the technical support of the Writing Lab, Institute for the Future of Education, Tecnologico de Monterrey, Mexico, in the production of this work.

References

Cabero-Almenara J, Palacios-Rodríguez A (2020) Marco Europeo de Competencia Digital Docente «DigCompEdu». Traducción y adaptación del cuestionario «DigCompEdu Check-In». Edmetic 9(1):213–234

Consejo de la Unión Europea (2018) Recomendación del Consejo, de 22 de mayo de 2018, relativa a las competencias clave para el aprendizaje permanente. Bruselas: Diario Oficial de la Unión Europea

Lázaro JL, Estebanell M, Tedesco JC (2015) Inclusion and social cohesion in a digital society. Univ Knowl Soc J 12(2). Accessed at https://rusc.uoc.edu/rusc/es/index.php/rusc/article/view/v12n2-lazaro-estebanell-tedesco/2610.html

Lawrence J, Tar U (2018) Factors that influence teachers' adoption and integration of ICT in teaching/learning process. Educ Media Int 55(4). https://doi.org/10.1080/09523987.2018.143 9712

Moya M (2013) De las TICs a las TACs: la importancia de crear contenidos educativos digitales. DIM: Didáctica Innovación y Multimedia 27:1–15

Naresh R (2020) Education after COVID-19 crisis based on ICT tools. Purakala 31:464–468

NU.CEPAL (2020) The COVID-19 pandemic is exacerbating the care crisis in Latin America and the Caribbean. Accessed at https://repositorio.cepal.org/bitstream/handle/11362/45352/4/S2000260_en.pdf

Organización de las Naciones Unidas (2020) La educación durante la Covid-19. Accessed at: https://www.un.org/sites/un2.un.org/files/policy_brief_-_education_during_covid-19_and_bey ond_spanish.pdf

Silva-Quiroz J, Lazaro JL, Miranda-Arredondo P, Canales-Reyes R (2018) El desarrollo de la competencia digital docente durante la formación del profesorado. Opción 34(86):423–449. Accessed at https://produccioncientificaluz.org/index.php/opcion/article/view/23850

Torres C, Acal C, El Honrani M, Mingorance ÁC (2021) Impacto en el entorno de aprendizaje virtual debido a COVID-19. Sostenibilidad 13(2):582

Usmani RSA, Saeed A, Tayyab M (2021) Papel de las TIC para la comunidad en la educación durante COVID-19. ICT Solutions for Improving Smart Communities in Asia, pp 125–150. IGI Global

Chapter 50
Latent Variables Associated with Teachers' Views About ICT and Integrating Them in Classroom Processes

Valentina Canese, Roberto Paez, Jessica Amarilla, and Pamela Rodriguez

50.1 Introduction

ICT implementation has gained more traction in education in recent years; however, it is not an immediate solution to educational problems because it is a complex process that does not imply a single solution. Its implementation must be integrated with new teaching–learning pedagogies (Venkatesh et al. 2016; Firmin and Genesi 2013). Therefore, it is crucial to rethink the role of technology, those who use it in the classroom, and how they use it because adding technological tools does not necessarily improve education (Hennessy et al. 2005); they must be integrated efficiently to benefit learning (Dwyer 2015).

The multitudinous factors to ponder include the knowledge of technological pedagogical content, teaching experience, and teacher and student training (Mishra and Koehler 2006; 2013; Li et al. 2018; Ahmadi 2018). Also, it is necessary to anticipate the difficulties that can arise, such as the lack of access to technological tools (especially in rural areas), the lack of relevance to the teachers, the number of students in the classroom, and the administrative support in the implementation processes (Francom 2016).

V. Canese (✉) · R. Paez · J. Amarilla · P. Rodriguez
Universidad Nacional de Asunción, San Lorenzo, Paraguay
e-mail: vcanese@facen.una.py

R. Paez
e-mail: robertopaez@facen.una.py

J. Amarilla
e-mail: isl-jamarilla@fil.una.py

P. Rodriguez
e-mail: prodriguez@facen.una.py

S. Hosseini et al. (eds.), *Technology-Enabled Innovations in Education*,
Transactions on Computer Systems and Networks,
https://doi.org/10.1007/978-981-19-3383-7_50

50.2 Development

50.2.1 Theoretical Framework

Analyses of technology adoptions have resulted in ICT implementation models that consider aspects such as their valuation in the educational process (Wozney et al. 2006), the pedagogy underpinning their use, the strategies and types of activities (Graves and Bowers 2018; Redecker 2017; Castañeda et al. 2018), and the barriers that affect teachers' attitudes (for example, institutional support, internet access, and ICT training) (Lawrence and Tar 2018). Barriers to the use of ICT in the classroom have been classified as internal and external (Ertmer et al. 2015; Lawrence and Tar 2018) and range from access to devices and technological infrastructure to teachers' attitudes about their use (Ertmer 2015; Lawrence and Tar 2018).

Teacher training is vital to adopt new ICT strategies in the classroom. Training must consider disciplinary, pedagogical, and technological aspects (TPACK model) to achieve proper integration and the individual circumstances of each teacher (Morales-Soza 2020). A recurring theme in ICT teacher training models is technology access and familiarizing the teachers as the foremost step in training and subsequently developing more complex skills. They infer a system of cumulative knowledge building on the basic skills that the teacher must have to develop more complex ICT skills (Almenara and Gimeno 2019). Finally, it should be noted that other technology use-and-implementation models in the classroom contemplate their responsible use from a perspective of social commitment, going beyond teacher training for purely academic purposes (Castañeda et al. 2018).

50.2.2 Problem Statement

In Paraguay, educational projects have been implemented that encompass integrating ICT to develop classes through regional and national initiatives. For example, Misiego and Demelenne (2015) highlight the pedagogical changes, socialization process, teacher digital competencies, and the students' cognitive processes in the "One Computer per Child" program. Likewise, the Ministry of Education and Sciences (MEC) launched the project "Improving learning conditions through ICT incorporation in educational establishments and management units in Paraguay." Aquino et al. (2018) report on teacher training in ICT use, available resources, difficulties encountered, and the frequency of use of ICT and areas for improvement. However, it is necessary to have more information complementing the literature on ICT implementation in the education system in Paraguay. Thus, this work aims to provide information on the use and scope of ICT in medium-level educational institutions in Paraguay through an exploratory study on the teaching experience, examining the factors affecting their use.

50.2.3 Method

This work is part of a more extensive study with an exploratory, qualitative, and quantitative design. The exploratory phase included data collected through six focus groups with secondary (high school) teachers in Paraguay selected by intentional sampling considering urban, semi-urban, and rural areas. Quantitative data were collected using an online questionnaire adapted from the study by Wozney et al. (2006) that includes 30 questions regarding access to and use of technology, teacher skills and training, and level of institutional support. One hundred and seventeen secondary school teachers from all over the country participated. A qualitative content analysis was carried out first, resulting in the following categories: virtual platforms, teaching materials, technological resources and infrastructure, and teacher training. Next, a univariate and multivariate descriptive analysis was performed using an Excel electronic spreadsheet and the IBM SPSS 21 statistical software. In addition, the Student's T-test, Chi-square (95% confidence) tests, and Exploratory Factor Analysis technique were performed.

50.3 Results

50.3.1 Qualitative Analysis

Table 50.1 presents the highlights of the qualitative analysis carried out with the data obtained from the focus groups on their experiences with ICT in official secondary institutions (high schools).

Based on these results, the questionnaire applied to teachers in its validation stage was adapted, of which the following points stand out:

- The majority of respondents indicated having at least average competency in using ICT (77%), with 31% identifying themselves as advanced and 9% expert.
- The main difficulty mentioned by the actors was access to computer tools in the educational institution where they provide services.

50.3.2 Exploratory Factor Analysis on Teachers' Professional Opinions on ICT

As a multivariate analysis technique, Exploratory Factor Analysis is used to reduce the spectrum of variables in the applied questionnaire and associate them with common characteristics in a lower and sufficient number of components that appropriately explain in an acceptable percentage the total variability of the analyzed set. Regarding Factor Analysis, Díaz and Morales (2012) indicate:

Table 50.1 Aspects of virtual teaching—focus groups

Categories	Principal results
Virtual Platforms	Most of the teachers were trained on at least one platform (TEAMS by the MEC) Many teachers tried to use synchronous classes, then gave up because of difficulties in accessing the internet
Didactic Materials for E-learning	Approve the materials developed and proposed by the Ministry of Education and Sciences In rural areas, materials in the Guarani language were needed Many used self-elaborated materials
Resources and Technological Infrastructure	Institutions have computer labs, but they are not enough for the number of students, and internet access is insufficient or non-existent They highlighted the acquisition of equipment such as notebooks, computers, tablets, and high-end cell phones to develop classes and adequate internet service
Teacher Training	Little training before the pandemic, but faced with it, the MEC began virtual ICT training. Teachers had to learn in record time about virtual platforms and adapting distance education. They sometimes accessed training by self-management or collaboration among colleagues

> A procedure to achieve this objective is to try to include the maximum information contained in the original variables in a smaller number of derived variables, maintaining as far as possible a solution easily interpreted. (p. 351)

In addition, the principal components method was used for the extraction of factors, as indicated by Malhotra (2008):

> In principal component analysis, the total variance of the data is considered. This type of analysis is recommended when the main interest of the researcher is to determine the minimum number of factors that explain the maximum variance of the data for use in subsequent multivariate analysis. (p.630)

Exploratory Factor Analysis was used with the 30 variables in the applied Questionnaire that refer to the teachers' professional opinions on ICT. We sought to evidence latent variables. The Kaiser-Meyer-Olkin (KMO) sample adequacy measure gave a result of 0.938, indicating that the multivariate method of factor analysis was appropriate for the data. In addition, Bartlett's sphericity test yielded a p-value lower than the standard level of 5%, which indicated the significant correlation between the variables for the effective search for new variables that arise from the associations among the given ones (Table 50.2).

The method of obtaining the factors was through the Principal Components Method using IBM SPSS 21 software. The following inclusion criteria were considered: self-values greater than one, which ensures a more significant proportion of

Table 50.2 Statistical measures to confirm the adequacy of Factor Analysis for the teaching opinion data on ICT

KMO and Bartlett test		
Kaiser-Meyer-Olkin measure of sampling adequacy		0.938
Bartlett sphericity test	Approximated chi-square	4253.686
	gl	435
	p-value	0.000

Table 50.3 Selected factors and proportion of variance explained—teachers' opinions about ICT

Factor	Initial self-values		
	Total	% of the variance explained	% accumulated
1	17.118	57.059	57.059
2	4.302	14.341	71.400
3	1.163	3.878	**75.278**
4	0.883	2.942	78.220
5	0.731	2.437	80.657
…			
…			
…			
28	0.047	0.156	99.725
29	0.044	0.146	99.871
30	0.039	0.129	100.000

variance explained by the selected factors and the proportion accumulated by the selected factors (Table 50.3).

The rotation of factors through the Varimax method was used with the factorial loads to identify to what factors the variables were associated with greater weight, helping to identify the new variables obtained. The factorial loads of the 30 associated variables were attributed to one of the factors having a reference value greater than 0.500. Below are the variables with the greatest explanatory weight in each of the components (Table 50.4).

In summary, from the teachers' professional opinions on ICT, it was possible to identify three factors that explain 75% of the underlying total variability and present sample adequacy and homogeneity per the validation of the multivariate model. The factors were named according to the nature of the variables whose factorial loads were greater toward that factor. See Table 50.5 summary.

Table 50.4 Factor loadings of the variables with the obtained factors—professional opinion on ICT

Matrix of rotated components[a]

	Component		
	1	2	3
V1	0.838	0.25	0.044
V2	0.331	0.68	0.179
V3	0.801	0.25	0.271
V4	0.866	0.21	0.159
V5	−0.02	0.78	0.052
V6	0.897	0.11	0.012
V7	0.8	0.21	0.458
V8	0.196	0.63	0.561
V9	0.362	0.53	0.589
V10	0.758	0.2	0.452
V11	0.649	0.415	0.557
V12	0.741	0.275	0.533
V13	0.428	0.584	0.45
V14	0.22	0.826	0.214
V15	0.844	0.244	0.23
V16	0.197	0.764	0.003
V17	0.786	0.232	0.41
V18	0.763	0.205	−0.002
V19	0.515	0.456	0.453
V20	0.895	0.14	0.258
V21	0.919	0.134	0.214
V22	0.395	0.593	−0.079
V23	0.28	0.695	−0.119
V24	0.155	0.833	0.209
V25	0.789	0.361	0.083
V26	0.187	0.742	0.31
V27	0.254	0.77	0.363
V28	0.111	0.8	0.182
V29	0.272	0.746	0.247
V30	0.856	0.262	−0.077

Extraction Method: Principal Component Analysis
Rotation method: Varimax normalization with Kaiser

Table 50.5 Factors associated with the teachers' opinions on ICT

Factor	Context	Variation explained (%)
Motivation and possible performance of students	The highest rate of joint variation explained refers to the efforts made during the migration to the virtual modality, focusing on achieving student motivation and evidencing their highest potential outcomes	57
Technical and pedagogical difficulties of technology-mediated education	Difficulties associated with the evaluation related to the pedagogical aspect, difficulties of internet access, and use of the platforms were the most cited	14
Teachers' professional development	Aspects of teacher education and professional training	4

50.3.3 Exploratory Factor Analysis on the Degree of ICT Integration in Teaching Processes by the Teachers Surveyed

The exploratory factor analysis was repeated to reduce the explanatory dimension of 34 variables of the questionnaire regarding the degree to which teachers integrated ICT into the development of their classes.

We also proceeded to the calculation of the KMO global sample adequacy measure (0.872) and the Bartlett test (p-value < 0.05). As Table 50.6 shows, the results indicated that the selected multivariate analysis was adequate to the data.

The factors were obtained By the Principal Components Method using the IBM SPSS 21 software. To select the most relevant ones, we used the criteria specified by Pérez (2004), Malhotra (2008), Garza et al. (2013), and other authors: self-values greater than one, which ensures a more significant proportion of variance explained by the selected factors and the proportion accumulated by the selected factors (Table 50.7).

With the rotation of factors by the Varimax method, we could identify with the help of the factorial loads to which factor the variables were associated with greater weight. This helped to identify the new variables obtained for the degree of ICT

Table 50.6 Statistical measures to confirm the adequacy of Factorial Analysis to the data on the degree of ICT integration in the classroom

KMO and Bartlett test		
Kaiser-Meyer-Olkin measure of sample adequacy		0.872
Bartlett sphericity test	Approximated chi-square	2783.135
	gl	561
	p-value	0.000

Table 50.7 Factors selected and proportion of variance explained—degree of integration of ICT in the classroom

Factor	Initial self-values		
	Total	% of the variance explained	% accumulated
1	12.481	36.710	36.710
2	3.589	10.555	47.265
3	2.154	6.335	53.599
4	1.656	4.871	58.470
5	1.444	4.246	62.716
6	1.315	3.868	66.584
7	1.172	3.448	**70.032**
8	0.974	2.866	72.897
…			
…			
…			
33	0.101	0.296	99.769
34	0.079	0.231	100.000

integration. The factorial loads of the 34 variables studied were attributed to one of the factors per a reference value greater than 0.500. Below are the variables with the greatest explanatory weight in each of the components (Table 50.8).

With the 34 variables referring to the degree of ICT integration in the teaching processes, we could identify seven factors that explain 70% of the joint variability, with sample adequacy measures that verify the procedure's usefulness. According to the factorial loads of each variable with the factors mentioned above, they were (Table 50.9).

From the comparative analysis of the results obtained by the focus groups and the Technology Implementation Questionnaire, the following is summarized (Table 50.10).

Finally, the teachers assessed on a scale of 1–6 the aspects related to incorporating ICT in the classroom, their perceptions of virtual education didactics, and the support they received from the educational institutions:

The ICT integration process mean was 4.9 with a standard deviation of 1.3, indicating a positive bias. The interpretation is that the pandemic contributed to the acceleration of technology in the class processes.

The degree-of-knowledge mean about the didactics of virtual education was 2.8 before the pandemic, which rose to 4.0 after the forced migration to virtual teaching.

The support received from their institutions had a 3.2 point mean with a standard deviation of 1.3. Here, the perceptions were dispersed; there were very satisfied teachers and others very dissatisfied.

Table 50.8 Factorial loads of the variables with the factors obtained—degree of integration of ICT in the classroom

Matrix of rotated components[a]

	Component						
	1	2	3	4	5	6	7
V1	0.110	0.092	0.044	0.196	0.034	0.309	0.691
V2	0.291	0.156	0.076	0.231	0.247	0.085	0.687
V3	0.167	−0.056	0.149	0.433	0.501	0.048	0.301
V4	0.306	0.103	0.173	0.156	0.745	0.229	0.027
V5	0.143	0.081	0.074	0.294	0.780	0.278	−0.024
V6	−0.039	0.214	0.110	0.139	0.737	0.058	0.114
V7	0.211	0.501	0.014	0.004	0.473	0.252	0.183
V8	0.843	0.244	0.110	−0.009	0.053	0.060	0.182
V9	0.764	0.324	0.189	−0.044	0.103	0.077	0.124
V10	0.796	0.235	0.310	0.013	0.162	0.015	0.055
V11	0.577	0.297	0.047	0.279	0.086	0.429	0.043
V12	0.161	0.252	−0.001	0.046	0.370	0.588	0.250
V13	0.561	−0.029	0.199	0.269	0.255	0.567	−0.008
V14	0.403	0.057	0.191	0.286	0.185	0.686	0.040
V15	0.233	0.231	0.257	0.514	−0.040	0.149	−0.069
V16	0.008	−0.109	0.290	0.588	0.035	0.420	−0.020
V17	0.056	0.086	0.110	0.756	0.236	0.216	0.196
V18	−0.105	0.142	0.096	0.699	0.352	0.129	0.263
V19	−0.165	0.170	0.008	0.687	0.227	0.105	0.344
V20	0.137	0.408	0.071	0.633	0.090	0.002	−0.010
V21	0.125	0.699	−0.053	0.403	0.195	0.118	0.030
V22	0.222	0.721	0.217	0.187	0.156	0.092	0.052
V23	−0.091	0.283	0.084	0.191	0.263	0.642	0.190
V24	0.326	0.653	0.218	0.225	−0.020	0.352	0.046
V25	0.095	0.494	0.126	0.243	0.044	0.519	0.248
V26	0.374	0.594	0.385	0.074	0.021	0.148	0.201
V27	−0.223	0.135	0.522	0.144	0.235	0.440	0.272
V28	0.099	0.023	0.713	0.138	0.167	0.204	0.048
V29	0.447	0.558	0.433	−0.036	0.141	0.032	0.155
V30	0.170	−0.026	0.683	0.129	−0.021	−0.220	0.372
V31	0.382	0.537	0.359	−0.008	0.245	−0.002	0.012
V32	0.374	0.399	0.649	0.081	0.202	0.078	−0.015
V33	0.170	0.362	0.725	0.155	0.083	0.097	−0.069

(continued)

Table 50.8 (continued)

Matrix of rotated components[a]

	Component						
	1	2	3	4	5	6	7
V34	0.196	0.150	0.843	0.099	0.023	0.137	−0.067

Extraction Method: Principal Component Analysis
Rotation method: Varimax normalization with Kaiser
[a]Rotation has converged in 23 iterations

Table 50.9 Factors associated with the incorporation of ICT in classes

Factor	Context	Variability explained (%)
Planning requirements and formal presentation of documents associated with the development of classes	Incorporate ICT according to the formalisms of the subjects and especially the requirements to transmit knowledge to students through virtual means	37
Development of classes by virtual platforms and their implications for technical-pedagogical training	Incorporate ICT to the extent they are trained and informed about their technical and pedagogical usefulness	11
Development of own didactic materials, audiovisuals	Incorporate audios, videos, PowerPoint presentations mainly in the development of their classes	6
Requirements of the study program for the subject being taught	Incorporate programs, software, simulators per the program requirements	5
Communication media with colleagues and students	Incorporate ICT to establish formal means of communication and meetings with colleagues and students (TEAMS, Google Meet, WhatsApp, etc.)	4
Curricular adjustments to satisfy the current context	Incorporate ICT only as a means of adapting to the Pandemic	4
Promotion of research and innovation in the classroom	Incorporate ICT as a facilitator for research and innovation in the classroom (WebQuests, online forums, YouTube, etc.)	4

50.4   Discussion

Considering the qualitative and quantitative results, we observed that two of the study participants' main difficulties were access to technological tools and internet connection. In both analyses, it was possible to see that the circumstances unleashed

Table 50.10 Results comparison of focus groups and teacher questionnaire

	Focus groups	Teacher questionnaire
The student is the focus of the efforts	Teachers develop their own teaching materials that involve the language and context of the student	The motivation for the student to reach their full potential is the central axis of the responses
Access to technological resources	Infrastructure in institutions is present but insufficient Self-management for the acquisition of resources	Infrastructure in institutions is present but insufficient Teleworking forced the teachers to acquire their own resources
Difficulties	Access to resources by the students Limited internet access Management of the platforms by the students	Access to resources by the students Limited internet access Management of the platforms by the students

due to the pandemic revealed the insufficient infrastructure in educational institutions, which presents an obstacle to the teaching–learning process. For this reason, the teachers participating in the study expressed the need to acquire equipment and internet connectivity with their own resources. Likewise, teachers pointed out that the lack of access and connectivity is especially noticeable among the students. The gaps between educational actors with access and those without access negatively affect the students' educational quality (Giovannella et al. 2020). This lack of infrastructure and access to resources and the internet constitute a problem not only in Paraguay. Other studies have evidenced this problem before and during the COVID-19 pandemic (Francom 2016; Wright and Wilson 2011; Fernández et al. 2020; Jain et al. 2021).

Thus, without access to a good quality internet signal, teachers see the use of certain tools as unlikely due to the required technological demand. Although teachers have benefited from training in tools such as Microsoft Teams by the MEC, this does not guarantee their efficient use. Notably, the literature indicates that the availability of resources alone does not lead to the meaningful implementation of ICTs. Access to and using technological tools is a more complex process that addresses attitudes, expectations, and appropriation of technology for its constant and varied use (Van Dijk 2017; Calderón 2020; Bhaumik and Priyadarshini 2020).

Another point of convergence between the qualitative and quantitative phases of the study was the teaching approach to the students. The pandemic forced the teachers to look for ways to reach them through ICT; they had to adapt and train. Therefore, the pandemic's acceleration of the learning and use of ICTs by the teaching community-generated training spaces through governmental provision or self-management; i.e., the pandemic created the opportunity to adopt ICTs (Jagannathan 2021). In addition, the provision of supporting teaching materials by the relevant authorities was highlighted. Therefore, while the crisis brings to light the lack of resources, it also highlights the opportunity to learn, re-imagine education, and promote collaborative work within the educational community (Harris 2020; Hargreaves and O'Connor 2018; Azorín 2020).

Thus, the support of educational institutions is crucial. Because teachers' perceptions about institutional support are disparate, an action plan by educational leaders would ensure the continuity of the teaching and learning process (Hernández 2020). It would focus efforts not only on the teaching of content but on affective learning environments that benefit the students (Cáceres-Piñaloza 2020).

50.5 Conclusions

The exploratory study results from the focus groups and the validation of the applied Teacher Questionnaire allowed identifying problems and potentialities of incorporating ICT in the teaching processes in secondary education in Paraguay. In a high percentage, teachers consider the students' learning requirements and motivation when selecting and applying technological resources. At the same time, they insist on the need for educational institutions to provide sufficient technological infrastructure for all actors. The problem of access to high-quality and low-cost internet must be addressed to successfully implement virtual education. The multivariate analysis identified three main factors in teachers' opinions on ICT and seven factors related to incorporating ICT in the classroom; there was an explanatory rate of more than 70% in both cases. From this exploratory study, a probabilistic sample of all secondary education teachers in Paraguay will be obtained to analyze the use and appropriation of ICTs to reemphasize the results obtained in this preliminary study and discover other associated elements.

Acknowledgements This study was conducted with support from CONACYT, Paraguay (PINV18-121). The content is the sole responsibility of the authors, and in no case should it be considered to reflect the opinion of CONACYT. We thank all the participants in this study.

The authors acknowledge the technical support of the Writing Lab, Institute for the Future of Education, Tecnologico de Monterrey, Mexico, in the production of this work.

References

Ahmadi D, Reza M (2018) The use of technology in English language learning: a literature review. Int J Res Engl Educ 3(2):115–125. https://doi.org/10.29252ijree.3.2.115
Almenara JC, Gimeno AM (2019) Las TIC y la formación inicial de los docentes. Modelos y competencias digitales. Profesorado, Revista de Currículum y Formación del Profesorado 23(3):247–268
Aquino JR, Aranda Z, Centurión B, Fabio de Garay LM, Melgarejo M, Ocampos BM, Orúe G, Orrego A, Rojas CME (2018) Informe Final de resultados de la Encuesta a Docentes y Directores Institucionales Beneficiadas con Laboratorios Móviles. Ministerio de Educación y Ciencias. Accessed at https://nube.stp.gov.py/s/aCy9NBWoSigBmaG#pdfviewer

Azorín C (2020) Beyond COVID-19 supernova. Is another education coming? J Prof Capital Community 5(3/4):381–390. https://doi.org/10.1108/JPCC-05-2020-0019

Bhaumik R, Priyadarshini A (2020) E-readiness of senior secondary school learners to online learning transition amid COVID-19 lockdown. Asian J Distance Educ 15(1):244–256. https://asi anjde.org/ojs/index.php/AsianJDE/article/view/456

Cáceres-Piñaloza KF (2020) Educación virtual: Creando espacios afectivos, de convivencia y aprendizaje en tiempos de COVID-19. CienciAmerica 9(2):38–44. https://doi.org/10.33210/ca.v9i 2.284

Calderón D (2020) Jóvenes y desigualdad digital: Las brechas de acceso, competencias y uso. Centro Reina Sofía sobre Adolescencia y Juventud. https://www.adolescenciayjuventud.org/blog/ analisis-y-debate/jovenes-y-desigualdad-digital-las-brechas-de-acceso-competencias-y-uso/

Castañeda L, Esteve F, Adell J (2018) ¿Por qué es necesario repensar la competencia docente para el mundo digital? RED. Revista de Educación a Distancia (56). https://doi.org/10.6018/red/56/6

Díaz L, Morales M (2012) Análisis estadístico de datos multivariados. Editorial de la Universidad Nacional de Colombia, Bogotá, p 665

Dwyer B (2015) Engaging all students in internet research and inquiry. The reading teacher, 69(4):383–389. https://doi.org/10.1002/trtr.1435

Ertmer PA, Ottenbreit-Leftwich A, Tondeur J (2015) Teacher beliefs and uses of technology to support 21st-century teaching and learning. In: Fives HR, Gill M (eds) International handbook of research on teacher beliefs. Routledge, Taylor & Francis, New York, pp 403–418

Fernández J, Domínguez J, Martínez P (2020) De la educación presencial a la educación a distancia en época de pandemia por Covid 19. Experiencias de los docentes. Revista Electrónica Sobre Cuerpos Académicos y Grupos de Investigación 7(14):87–110

Firmin MW, Genesi DJ (2013) History and implementation of classroom technology. Procedia Soc Behav Sci 93:1603–1617. https://doi.org/10.1016/j.sbspro.2013.10.089

Francom GM (2016) Barriers to technology use in large and small school districts. J Inf Technol Educ: Res 15:577–591. Retrieved from http://www.informingscience.org/Publications/3596

Garza J, Morales B, González B (2013) Análisis Estadístico Multivariante—Un enfoque teórico y práctico. Mc Graw Hill Interamericana Editores, México, p 712

Giovannella C, Marcello P, Donatella P (2020) The effects of the Covid-19 pandemic on Italian learning ecosystems: the school teachers' perspective at the steady-state. ID&A Interact Des Architect(s) 45:264–286

Graves KE, Bowers AJ (2018) Toward a typology of technology-using teachers in the "New Digital Divide": a latent class analysis (LCA) of the NCES fast response survey system teachers' use of educational technology in U.S. Public Schools, 2009 (FRSS 95). Teach Coll Rec 120(8):1–42

Hargreaves A, O'Connor MT (2018) Collaborative professionalism: when teaching together means learning for all. Corwin Press, Thousand Oaks, CA

Harris A (2020) COVID-19—school leadership in crisis? J Prof Capital Community, ahead-of-print (ahead-of-print). https://doi.org/10.1108/jpcc-06-2020-0045

Hennessy S, Ruthven K, Brindley S (2005) Teacher perspectives on integrating ICT into subject teaching: commitment, constraints, caution, and change. J Curriculum Stud 37(2):155–192. https://doi.org/10.1080/0022027032000276961

Hernández A (2020) COVID-19: el efecto en la gestión educativa. Revista Latinoamericana De Investigación Social 3(1):37–41. https://bit.ly/3lrCb3f

Li Y, Garza V, Keicher A, Popov V (2018) Predicting high school teacher use of technology: pedagogical beliefs, technological beliefs and attitudes, and teacher training. Technol Knowl learn. https://doi.org/10.1007/s10758-018-9355-2

Jagannathan S (2021) The digital learning opportunity. Learning in the 21st century. In: S. J. (ed), Reimagining digital learning for sustainable development: how upskilling, data analytics, and educational technologies close the skills gap. Routledge, New York, Taylor & Francis, pp 17–35

Jain S, Lall M, Singh A (2021) Teachers' voices on the impact of covid-19 on school education: are ed-tech companies really the panacea? Contemp Educ Dialogue 18(1):58–89. https://doi.org/10. 1177/0973184920976433

Misiego P, Demelenne D (2015) Las prácticas pedagógicas y la incorporación de la computadora en el aula: una experiencia desde el programa "Una computadora por niño" (Paraguay). Perspectiva Educacional 54(1):131–148. https://doi.org/10.4151/07189729-Vol.54-Iss.1-Art.169

Lawrence JE, Tar UA (2018) Factors that influence teachers' adoption and integration of ICT in the teaching/learning process. Educ Media Int 55(1):79–105. https://doi.org/10.1080/09523987.2018.1439712

Malhotra K (2008) Investigación de Mercado. Pearson Educación S.A. México. 920 p

Mishra P, Koehler MJ (2006) Technological pedagogical content knowledge: a framework for teacher knowledge. Teach Coll Rec 108(6):1017–1054

Morales-Soza M (2020) TPACK para integrar efectivamente las TIC en educación: Un modelo teórico para la formación docente. Revista Electrónica De Conocimientos Saberes y Prácticas 3(1):133–148. https://doi.org/10.5377/recsp.v3i1.9796

Pérez C (2004) Técnicas de Análisis Multivariante de Datos—Aplicaciones con SPSS. Pearson Educación S.A, Madrid, p 646

Redecker C (2017) European framework for the digital competence of educators: DigCompEdu (No. JRC107466). Joint Research Centre (Seville site)

Van Dijk J (2017) Digital divide: impact of access. In: The international encyclopedia of media effects, pp 1–11. https://doi.org/10.1002/9781118783764.wbieme0043

Venkatesh V, Rabah J, Fusaro M, Couture A, Varela W, Alexander K (2016) Factors impacting university instructors' and students' perceptions of course effectiveness and technology integration in the age of web 2. 0. McGill J Educ 51(1):533–561. https://doi.org/0.7202/103 7358ar

Wozney L, Venkatesh V, Abrami P (2006) Implementing computer technologies: teachers' perceptions and practices. J Technol Teach Educ 14(1):173–207

Wright VH, Wilson EK (2011) Teachers' use of technology: lessons learned from the teacher education program to the classroom. SRATE Journal 20(2):48–60. Retrieved from https://files.eric.ed.gov/fulltext/EJ959529.pdf

Chapter 51
Analysis of Indicators for the Proper Development of Virtual Courses on the Moodle Platform

Yamile Peña Cruz and Geilert De la Peña Consuegra

51.1 Introduction

Current higher education, both in Cuba and worldwide, requires the proper use of virtualization in the formative educational environment in all substantive processes developed for this modality. The various devices available to teachers and students, the technological development achieved, and the speed with which these technologies are replaced and perfected obviously mark an intrinsic trajectory in which it is necessary to incorporate all the required contextual elements for their development and educational improvement.

The implementation and development of Information and Communication Technologies (ICT) in the current educational space has established an excellent opportunity to develop new, necessary skills in the professional who must perform in today's social contexts.

Thus, new variants and alternative teaching–learning models have emerged and built that leverage the strengths and potential of ICTs to improve the educational training processes.

It is counterproductive that, in these times, professionals and researchers in the various fields and branches of knowledge do not possess the basic knowledge that guarantees their incursion into ICT in their respective fields. These technologies are dispersed and inserted in multiple social fabrics and among all age groups. Therefore, the significance of their use in all current processes is substantially established, as Margalef (2008) affirms. Aligning with the criteria expressed by Área and Pessoa

Y. Peña Cruz (✉)
University of Havana, Havana, Cuba
e-mail: gmilenium2017@gmail.com; ypcruz.1987@gmail.com

G. De la Peña Consuegra
Technical University of Manabí, Portoviejo, Ecuador
e-mail: geilet.delapena@utm.edu.ec

© The Author(s), under exclusive license to Springer Nature Singapore Pte Ltd. 2022   619
S. Hosseini et al. (eds.), *Technology-Enabled Innovations in Education*,
Transactions on Computer Systems and Networks,
https://doi.org/10.1007/978-981-19-3383-7_51

(2012), in the Web 2.0 environment, the mere simple and effective use of ICT is not sufficient or acceptable. ICTs must guarantee transcendence to other planes of effectiveness in alliance with cultured and autonomous knowledge, even to attain the requirements of Web 3.0 (Caro and Valverde 2014).

Cuban society is undergoing a significant change in using ICTs. However, it is also true that in education, these steps are being taken for various reasons at still slow speeds because traditionalism, to a large extent, is still present. The resources are tailored to correspond with the school contents. This is carried out little by little and supported by regulations that proscribe their selection and construction.

From this perspective, some years ago, the concept of PLE (Personal Learning Environment) was born, a revolution in education in favor of student-centered learning. It gave rise to greater individualization and personalization in the essentials and procedures of the teaching and learning process, overcoming the limitations of Virtual Learning Environments based on LMS (Learning Management System) Torres Kompenm et al. (2008).

By carrying out a simple exercise of reviewing and verifying various web pages or university web portals, one can have much certainty that this open, flexible, and "remote" way of teaching and learning becomes stronger with each adjustment. It is pertinent to recognize that more spaces previously attended by traditional education are occupied every day by virtual modalities. This perspective of carrying out educational processes openly, remotely, and collaboratively has awakened and consolidated expectations and feasibility, demonstrating a significant capacity to guarantee the democratization of education and continuous vocational training (Murga 2012), among other possibilities.

It is necessary to attend and pay attention to the fact that education offered through a distance modality is still young and developed, perfected, and consolidated more every day for various training processes. It is constantly updated to incorporate the latest technological advances and results achieved in this field. Therefore, preparing the faculty and ensuring educational technology accessibility and management are crucially required. Being demanding about training professionals and continuous postgraduate training in ICTs makes them deeply aware of their potential. It results in their self-learning based on profound competencies, skills, procedures, knowledge, and mastery.

Academic training platforms or e-learning platforms are computer programs installed on a server machine that customers access, usually as registered (Arias 2008) users. It is a widespread concept that has acquired incredible value, about which more than one researcher and expert offer significantly varied considerations. This type of knowledge transmission is effective because of its advantages. However, many agree on its limitations, for example, when printed contents are entirely replaced, or because the visual contact with other students and the teacher-tutor in physical spaces where effective interactions occur do not exist. However, the use of the Internet is indisputably necessary, enabling various variants of knowledge transmission.

Multiple advantages include active learning with exhaustive monitoring of the training process, flexibility, capacity, full access at all times, no required displacements, and no geographical barriers. The virtual online modalities guarantee adequate adaptation with individualized learning rhythm; the course begins when the student wishes and has unlimited virtual resources, among other advantages.

Moodle, for example, is an open-source e-learning platform with the largest number of users worldwide. As of February 2019, the registered user base included more than 148,638,403 users, spread across 92,970 sites in 229 countries, with more than 17,983,626 courses and translated into approximately 91 languages (Accessed February 18, 2019. https://moodle.org/).

It is a virtual teaching platform made with free software designed to help educators create high-quality online courses and virtual learning environments. It supports teachers in creating online learning communities and offers different activities for existing courses within the (Dougiamas 2008) platform. It has become one of the most used platforms by the educational community to teach various courses in different (Cole and Foster 2007) languages.

However, it is very known that the use of this platform is hardly guaranteed by the various faculties and disciplinary programs at the University of Havana. Also, despite a central technology department in the institution, they do not share or work with quality indicators to develop and implement the courses uploaded in Moodle.

Specifically, in the University of Havana environment, faculty use of this platform in the various courses is very meager and limited due to the lack of knowledge about how to employ it and the limitations of connectivity and the internet in general.

51.2 Development

The main objective of this work is to propose indicators for evaluating the quality of the virtual courses offered in the Virtual Teaching–Learning Environment (Entorno Virtual de Enseñanza Aprendizaje) (EVEA) of the University of Havana.

Likewise, we suggest that the results achieved by the authors reveal the reality and relevance to an existing need, and the indicators enable the systematic improvement in developing virtual courses on the Virtual Teaching–Learning Environment platform of this institution.

51.2.1 Theoretical Discussion

Although it is not easy to find a consensus in defining the term e-learning (also known as tele-training, network learning, online training, etc.), perhaps the best known and adopted is the definition by Rosenberg (2002), who defines this concept as a teaching system that uses internet technologies to provide multiple solutions that improve knowledge and performance.

The most used computer systems for this purpose, according to (Muñoz 2009) are the so-called intelligent tutoring systems (ITS) and learning management systems (LMS).

B-learning (blended learning) is also present as a design to respond to the inadequacies and weaknesses of the latter learning modality. This concept has been born in the bosom of the purest tradition by experts in educational technology. They have always preferred a certain eclecticism, confronted with the evidence that all theories work in part.

Blended learning represents a new learning model that effectively combines face-to-face education supported by material and online resources to develop and strengthen students' knowledge. It promotes developing a multitude of learning skills using information and communication technologies (ICT).

In recent years, m-learning has also been consolidated as another learning modality carried out through mobile terminals. This is still in development, considering that it has weaknesses such as little or no connection, the short duration of battery life in these terminals, and the lack of investment. However, mobile learning offers innovative tools such as an integrated camera, front and back, that facilitate many uses such as "augmented reality," GPS for content geolocation, and internet connection with servers (LMS, web tools, etc.). Even portable Moodle can be used easily.

These modalities are developed primarily using various educational platforms, proprietary code (such as Blackboard, WebCT, E-learning, eCollege, FirstClass), and open source (ATutor, Sakai, Moodle, among others). Due to its specific characteristics and requirements, the latter guarantees the development of several virtual courses and enhances learning from the network.

In the case of the University of Havana, the EVEA site (http://evea.uh.cu) offers 116 virtual courses on the Moodle platform (Annex 1). A distribution by undergraduate and postgraduate is not defined at first glance, information is required by the users who enter the site. However, a significant variety is shown in the virtual ecosystem of courses by faculties, study centers, and web addresses, although it is still considered poor and innocuous.

At present, standards, procedures, and strategies are established that do not obey a systematic quality measurement process, as (Dusen and Gerald 2009) point out. Some requirements or guidelines have been established to ensure that teachers when structuring their courses, comply to achieve optimal server capacities; that is, the requirements are technological. So, it is also necessary to establish quality pedagogical-didactic indicators or requirements for performance.

Monti and San Vicente (2006) suggest three categories to evaluate different platforms: didactic-functional, technological, and financial. They also present the experiences of guiding a language learning course in an e-learning modality.

On the other hand, Gallego et al. (2007) carry out an evaluation to determine the advantages and disadvantages of the Moodle platform and propose new functionalities to improve its limitations. However, this work does not evaluate the proposed improvements.

Kakasevski et al. (2008) evaluated the standard Moodle modules. From the results, they presented a series of recommendations for the users of the platform. Also, Al-Ajlan and Zedan (2008) described the strengths and limitations of the Moodle platform compared to other platforms.

Arias (2008) evaluated the Moodle platform to validate an evaluation questionnaire for e-learning platforms. Other studies by authors such as Ardila-Rodríguez (2011), Rubio et al. (2009), Berrocal (2013), and Romero and Vera (2014) have ventured into this subject, offering significant contributions. In Cuba, mention can be made of particular studies in university institutions, among which the University of Computer Sciences stands (Donatien Goliath 2016) out.

Although these various studies have been carried out, evidence provided by works related to evaluating the Moodle platform is scarce.

Quality indicators can be designed based on experience or knowledge about the area or field in which you work. These concerning the training processes in virtual environments are constituted, fundamentally, by specific characteristics that translate into variables susceptible to measurement, grouped by processes and fundamental axes of analysis, from statistical and multivariable examinations in a representative sample of the existing courses.

To establish the quality of a course or set of courses offered in virtual environments, one must know the definition developed by Ruiz De Miguel (2002, p. 37) that:

> "(...) training in virtual environments is of quality when it enhances in the student the development of their maximum capacities to interact and interrelate with teachers and peers, and learn in an educational environment mediated by information and communication (Ruiz De Miguel 2002) technologies."

The quality indicators have to provide all the tools and procedures to establish whether the training design corresponds to the general theoretical conception of training in a virtual environment. Then an evaluation system must be applied that assesses whether or not the design complies to standardize and synthesize quality.

51.2.2 Problem Statement

In the Virtual Teaching–Learning Environment (EVEA) of the University of Havana, a series of virtual courses have been set up on the Moodle platform, ensuring undergraduate and postgraduate professionals' training from various perspectives and needs of the faculties, departments, and study centers.

At the University of Havana, design aspects for virtual courses and their evaluation have been identified as follows:

- The materials for the different online courses were not made for online training, and there is no diversity of formats, evidencing a significant amount of flat materials.
- The instrumentation and assembly of the virtual courses in the Moodle platform of the University of Havana to date lack profound evaluation because no instruments are applied to evaluate their integral quality.
- For the design of the virtual courses, there is no multidisciplinary team of graphic designers, pedagogues, specialists in the subjects to be taught, and computer

scientists, who enrich and construct these courses homogeneously, tending to aspects of structure and functional quality.

- Many teachers do not have the necessary skills, competencies, or knowledge to design virtual courses. They do not have experience in virtual training, so they are largely unaware of the virtual inadequacies of the students and the elements required to elaborate the courses.
- There are only minimal structuring requirements for the resources used to develop virtual courses, mainly concerning the weight or volume of information, so their number and size have been restricted. Moreover, the mechanisms of systematic improvement for the virtual courses are still considered insufficient.
- There is no accurate definition of quality indicators to orient or guide the work, which would systematize the necessary elements to ensure quality in structuring the virtual courses uploaded in the virtual platforms.

At the beginning of 2018, the team of professors in the Technology and Educational Innovation group of the Center for Studies for the Improvement of Higher Education (CEPES) met and put together a set of aspects to consider for determining the resources and content regulations (referring to volume), motivated by the capacity of the assigned servers and their availability.

Therefore, it was necessary to develop a series of indicators to guarantee improvements in the utilization process and that the courses be designed and instrumented to guarantee better teaching–learning processes in the various subjects or teaching activities, including the use of the Moodle platform.

51.2.3   Methodology

The research conducted is considered descriptive and experimental. It describes the analysis and deduction carried out pertinent to the functioning of the existing virtual courses and the aspects related to the need to elaborate and apply quality indicators to them.

Information was obtained based on applying methods such as participant scientific observation, interviewing users, technicians, professors who developed and coordinated the administration of the virtual course, and specialists in educational technology at the university. The objective was to gather information about the virtual courses' operation, potentialities, weaknesses, and limitations.

The experimental character was expressed mainly in obtaining information in the fieldwork, the primary application of the proposed indicators, and the proposal of systematic use to improve these after the first experience.

51.2.4 Results

Regarding the operation of the course and the platform, we organized the information related to the correct use of technological, academic, and administrative devices to analyze if there is quality in the training processes in virtual environments, as proposed by Cabero (2005) and Aguilar (2008).

It was also required to consider a series of elements to develop virtual courses and quality assurances, which must at least attend to:

Pedagogical Quality: Determine everything related to the structure of the contents, the activities, the evaluation system, the modular learning, the approaches of present learning, communicative and language elements, etc.

Didactic quality: The versatility of the course to teach in different ways, the architecture of the contents, the elements of resources and multimedia used, etc.

Usability: Attend to the ease and relevance of navigation, interaction with the user, aesthetic quality, motivational aspects, etc.

Technological quality: Guarantee connectivity, use of technological terminals, structuring and linking in educational platforms or institutional portals where the courses could be accessed, aesthetics of the public interface, etc.

The quality indicators must be considered before executing and implementing the virtual course; this allows standardizing and homogenizing crucial aspects of the courses' structure and content in the various university applications. Although it is possible to consider the quality indicators from the results achieved retrospectively, that is, once the course is over, this would have another intention, objective, and execution.

The proposed quality indicators are as follows:

Pedagogical and Didactic Quality

- Level of consistency, updating, and content and activities consistency in the learning and thematic units and coding with the maximum linguistic richness through the insertion of visual, written, sound, and audiovisual texts (multimedia and hypermedia).
- The presentation and description of the course program with all its sections and essential elements.
- Orientation and explanation of the evaluative activities and how to conduct them at each assessment moment in the course.
- Level of use of structured spaces for synchronous and asynchronous communications.
- Use of graphics, images, locutions, musical fragments, and video micro-recordings by students and teachers.
- Promote research and inquiry activities based on problem-solving, properly elaborated and proposed by the student, or oriented or suggested by the teacher.

- Use of open didactic formulations through easy access to information sources (virtual libraries, FTP sites, among others).
- Planning surveys before, during, and after developing the course; using inquiry instruments (virtual surveys) to improve all the course elements (contents, tasks and activities, the form of evaluation, etc.).
- For specific contents with relevant activities, the institutional assurance level that the performance and monitoring of virtual laboratory practices or simulations will promote the construction of individual and shared knowledge.
- Level of use of previous learning organizers (concept maps).
- Presentation of glossaries of rich and updated terms.
- Level of orientation and use of primary and complementary bibliographies.
- The insertion of links to stable sources of additional documentation (links to articles, news, videoconferences, etc.)
- Integration and adequate structuring of exercises and activities considering the previous orientation and the corresponding specific objectives.
- Use of the various evaluation modalities (self-evaluation, co-evaluation, inter-evaluation, and hetero-evaluation) as required by the process relating to the teaching–learning products.

Technical and Technological Quality

- The necessary technological infrastructure, accessibility, and complexity sufficient for the advances happening.
- Level of security in the course registration, evaluations, forum contents, and other spaces of exchange.
- The feasibility of the course navigation, demonstrated by simple, intuitive, pleasant, and safe user interactions.
- Guarantee of security control and access to the processes; the integrity, availability, and confidentiality of the resources, data, courses, etc.
- The versatility to monitor the students' performance and the status of their ups and downs.

Organizational and Creative Quality

- Level of versatility when designing and implementing the system; the amount of help for the students, considering their different learning and curricular rhythms.
- Level of organized content and activities through indexes and concept maps.
- Level of multimedia integration (video streaming and video conferencing).
- Quality of the generation and use of evaluation tools.
- Presence of content creation and implementation activities.
- Availability and monitoring of the program, maintenance, and updating of the program, creation of shared knowledge, and dissemination of grades.

Communication Quality

- Creation of forums or discussion groups with the proper guidance of teachers and the presence of all students.
- Use of e-mail systems (internal and external).

- Level of use and updating of the bulletin board.
- The efficiency of the calendar and its personalization.
- Organization and integration of chat sessions among teachers, tutors, and students and the archiving of their contents.
- Level of planning and establishing audio conferencing and archiving content in compressed format.
- Orientation and planning of student and teacher presentations to humanize the initial moments and help establish affective cyber-relationships.

We consider that the systematization and improvement of these indicators favor the necessary rigor required for the structuring, conception, development, and execution of the virtual courses conceived.

On more than one occasion, it has been stressed and emphasized that the natural emergence of teaching and learning initiatives mediated by telematic technologies in the last decade of the twentieth century and beginning of the twenty-first have generated dissimilar points of view and favorable and unfavorable opinions about these processes, even feeding controversies and theoretical debates on the usefulness of contributions in this regard.

We consider that, if appropriately used, with the required quality and appropriate pedagogical, didactic, technical, and technological elements, the teaching–learning processes and their socio-cultural consequences can be perfected.

51.3 Conclusions

The Moodle platform's main advantages to develop both undergraduate and post-graduate virtual courses are consistent with the demands and objectives of distance and blended education at the University of Havana.

Its utilization must begin with the necessary quality evaluation of the structuring and construction of the courses on the Moodle platform. Thus, quality will be reflected in their execution and yield positive results.

There are different international and national solutions to evaluate the quality of virtual courses and the various educational platforms. All are diverse in nature and emphasize, at least, the technological and pedagogical aspects. The most evaluated are technology, evaluation, content, objectives, and general orientation.

The criteria expressed in our study of the Moodle platform's functionality at the University of Havana are primarily guided by the need to consolidate the indicators that facilitate and guide the proper construction of these courses. The indicators are organized per Pedagogical and Didactic Quality, Technical and Technological Quality, Organizational and Creative Quality, and Communication Quality. This is a necessity due to the commonplace use of this technological tool in dissimilar educational environments. It is obviously necessary to continue delving into all possible alternatives and variants on this subject.

Acknowledgements The authors acknowledge the technical support of the Writing Lab, Institute for the Future of Education, Tecnologico de Monterrey, Mexico, in the production of this work.

Appendix 1

Faculty	Virtual courses on platform
Psychology	22
Spanish for non-Spanish speakers	1
Physics	6
Law	32
Biology	20
Mathematics-Computing	2
Arts and letters	5
Chemistry	7
Philosophy	1
Geography	1
Accounting	6
Centers of studies	
Center for the Improvement of Higher Education (CEPES)	5
Language Center	2
CEPES	2
CEDEM	1
Directorates	
Directorate of Scientific and Technical Information	1
Teaching Directorate for Computer Sciences	2
Total	116

Source Elaboration of the authors. Accessed March 15, 2019, at http://evea.uh.cu

References

Aguilar M (1 de mayo de 2008) El uso de las webquest, los wiki y los blogs en la docencia universitaria (experiencia en la formación de maestros). Accessed at http://www.utn.edu.ar
Al-Ajlan A, Zedan H (2008) Why Moodle. In: 12th IEEE international workshop on future trends of distributed computing systems, pp 58–64
Ardila-Rodríguez M (2011) Indicadores de calidad de las plataformas educativas digitales
Área M, Pessoa T (2012) De lo sólido a lo líquido: las nuevas alfabetizaciones ante los cambios culturales de la Web 2.0. Comunicar. Revista Científica de Educomunicación 38:13–23

Arias MJ (2008) Evaluación de la calidad de Cursos Virtuales: Indicadores de calidad y construcción de un cuestionario de medida. Aplicación al ámbito de asignaturas de Ingeniería Telemática. Universidad de Extremadura, Tesis Doctoral, Departamento de ciencias de la educación, Mérida, España

Berrocal E (2013) Evaluación de las plataformas de enseñanza virtual de las universidades públicas andaluzas para la mejora del proceso de enseñanza-aprendizaje orientado al EEES basado en Blended-Learning. Proyecto de Investigación, Universidad de Granada, Granada

Cabero J (2005) La evaluación de medios audiovisuales y materiales de enseñanza. En: Cabero J (ed) Tecnología educativa. Editorial Síntesis, Madrid, España, pp 87–106

Caro M, Valverde M (2014) Aprendizaje bimodal de las competencias comunicativa y digital en contextos formales de Educación Superior: la realización procesual de Trabajos Fin de Grado en Moodle. Revista Internacional de Aprendizaje y Cibersociedad 18(1):43–55. Accessed 2003 at http://www.col.org/resources/publications/consultancies/Pages/2003-06-OpenSrc.aspx

Cole J, Foster H (2007) Using Moodle: teaching with the popular open source course management system. O'Reilly Media, Inc.

Donatien Goliath K (2016) Indicadores para evaluar la calidad de los cursos virtuales para la formación postgraduada en la Universidad de las Ciencias Informáticas. La Habana

Dougiamas M (2008) Accessed 2 Sept 2009 from http://www.moodle.org

Dusen V, Gerald C (2009) The virtual campus: technology and reform in higher education. ERIC Digest. Accessed at http://www.eric.ed.gov/PDFS/ED412816.pdf

Gallego A, Requena J, Pujol M, Montoyo J (2007) Mejora del sistema Moodle mediante personalización de contenido y generación evolutiva de actividades aleatorias. XIII Jornadas de Enseñanza Universitaria de la Informática (Jenui 2007), ISBN 978-84

Kakasevski G, Mihajlov M, Arsenovski S, Chungurski S (June 2008) Evaluating usability in learning management system Moodle. En: ITI 2008—30th international conference on information technology interfaces. IEEE, pp 613–618

Margalef JM (2008) Retos y perspectivas de la alfabetización mediática en España. Ministerio de Educación, Madrid

Monti S, San Vicente F (2006) Evaluación de plataformas y experimentación en Moodle de objetos didácticos (nivel A1/A2) para el aprendizaje E/LE en e-learning. RedELE, Revista electrónica de didáctica/español lengua extranjera, 8.moodle. (s.f.). Accessed 18 Feb 2019 at https://moodle.org

Muñoz P (2009) Teoría del modelado del E-learning y aplicación a un sistema de pistas adaptativo en tutoría inteligente utilizando técnicas de web semántica. Tesis doctoral, Universidad Carlos III de Madrid, Madrid

Murga M (2012) Escenarios de innovación e investigación educativa. What is e-Learning 2.0. The eLearning Guilds' Learning Solutions. E-Magazine pp 1–9. Madrid: Universitas. Schlenker B. Recuperado el 25 de agosto de 2008. http://www.learningsolutionsmag.com/articles/83/what-is-e-learning-20

Romero L, Vera M (2014) Generación de Indicadores de calidad específicos para aulas virtuales de apoyo al dictado presencial en carreras de grado universitarias

Rosenberg M (2002) E-learning: Estrategias para transmitir conocimiento. McGrawHill SIGOSSEE/JOIN-Open Source for Education in Europe, Bogotá, Colombia. Accessed 20 Apr 2010 at http://www.guidance-research.org/sigossee/join/sp/lms/catalog.htm/view

Rubio M, Morocho M, Torres J, Maldonado J, Alejandro J, Ramírez I (2009) Guía de evaluación para cursos virtuales de formación contínua. Instituto Latinoamericano y del Caribe de Calidad en Educación Superior a Distancia. UTPL, Loja-Ecuador

Ruiz De Miguel C (2002) Validación y propuesta de modelo de calidad de la educación infantil. Tesis doctoral, Universidad Complutense de Madrid, Madrid

Torres Kompenm R, Eddirisngha P, Mobbs R (2008) Building web 2.0-base personal learning environments-a conceptual framework-Fifth EDEN Research Workshop. Accessed at http://www. eden-online.org/online/book/papers/124.pdf

Printed in the United States
by Baker & Taylor Publisher Services